Lecture Notes in Computer Science 14055

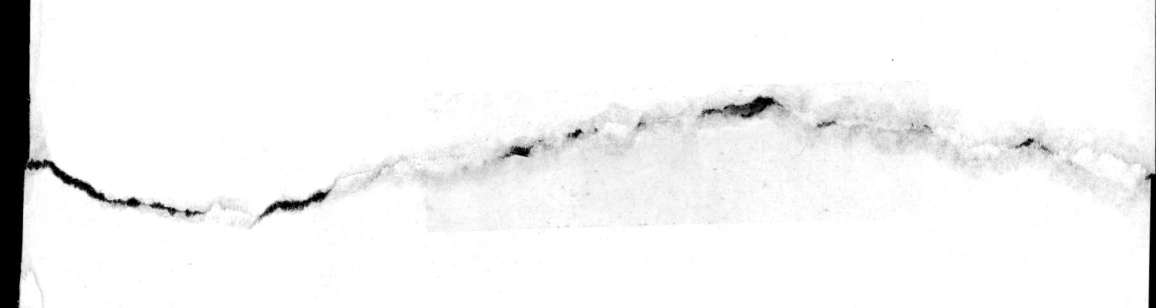

The series Lecture Notes in Computer Science (LNCS), including its subseries Lecture Notes in Artificial Intelligence (LNAI) and Lecture Notes in Bioinformatics (LNBI), has established itself as a medium for the publication of new developments in computer science and information technology research, teaching, and education.

LNCS enjoys close cooperation with the computer science R & D community, the series counts many renowned academics among its volume editors and paper authors, and collaborates with prestigious societies. Its mission is to serve this international community by providing an invaluable service, mainly focused on the publication of conference and workshop proceedings and postproceedings. LNCS commenced publication in 1973.

Qin Gao · Jia Zhou · Vincent G. Duffy ·
Margherita Antona · Constantine Stephanidis
Editors

HCI International 2023 – Late Breaking Papers

25th International Conference on Human-Computer Interaction
HCII 2023, Copenhagen, Denmark, July 23–28, 2023
Proceedings, Part II

Editors
Qin Gao
Tsinghua University
Beijing, China

Jia Zhou
Chongqing University
Chongqing, China

Vincent G. Duffy
Purdue University
West Lafayette, IN, USA

Margherita Antona
Foundation for Research and Technology - Hellas (FORTH)
Heraklion, Crete, Greece

Constantine Stephanidis
University of Crete and Foundation for Research and Technology - Hellas (FORTH)
Heraklion, Crete, Greece

ISSN 0302-9743 ISSN 1611-3349 (electronic)
Lecture Notes in Computer Science
ISBN 978-3-031-48040-9 ISBN 978-3-031-48041-6 (eBook)
https://doi.org/10.1007/978-3-031-48041-6

This Springer imprint is published by the registered company Springer Nature Switzerland AG
The registered company address is: Gewerbestrasse 11, 6330 Cham, Switzerland

Foreword

Human-computer interaction (HCI) is acquiring an ever-increasing scientific and industrial importance, as well as having more impact on people's everyday lives, as an ever-growing number of human activities are progressively moving from the physical to the digital world. This process, which has been ongoing for some time now, was further accelerated during the acute period of the COVID-19 pandemic. The HCI International (HCII) conference series, held annually, aims to respond to the compelling need to advance the exchange of knowledge and research and development efforts on the human aspects of design and use of computing systems.

The 25th International Conference on Human-Computer Interaction, HCI International 2023 (HCII 2023), was held in the emerging post-pandemic era as a 'hybrid' event at the AC Bella Sky Hotel and Bella Center, Copenhagen, Denmark, during July 23–28, 2023. It incorporated the 21 thematic areas and affiliated conferences listed below.

A total of 7472 individuals from academia, research institutes, industry, and government agencies from 85 countries submitted contributions, and 1578 papers and 396 posters were included in the volumes of the proceedings that were published just before the start of the conference. Additionally, 267 papers and 133 posters were included in the volumes of the proceedings published after the conference, as "Late Breaking Work". The contributions thoroughly cover the entire field of human-computer interaction, addressing major advances in knowledge and effective use of computers in a variety of application areas. These papers provide academics, researchers, engineers, scientists, practitioners and students with state-of-the-art information on the most recent advances in HCI. The volumes constituting the full set of the HCII 2023 conference proceedings are listed on the following pages.

I would like to thank the Program Board Chairs and the members of the Program Boards of all thematic areas and affiliated conferences for their contribution towards the high scientific quality and overall success of the HCI International 2023 conference. Their manifold support in terms of paper reviewing (single-blind review process, with a minimum of two reviews per submission), session organization and their willingness to act as goodwill ambassadors for the conference is most highly appreciated.

This conference would not have been possible without the continuous and unwavering support and advice of Gavriel Salvendy, founder, General Chair Emeritus, and Scientific Advisor. For his outstanding efforts, I would like to express my sincere appreciation to Abbas Moallem, Communications Chair and Editor of HCI International News.

July 2023 Constantine Stephanidis

HCI International 2023 Thematic Areas and Affiliated Conferences

Thematic Areas

- HCI: Human-Computer Interaction
- HIMI: Human Interface and the Management of Information

Affiliated Conferences

- EPCE: 20th International Conference on Engineering Psychology and Cognitive Ergonomics
- AC: 17th International Conference on Augmented Cognition
- UAHCI: 17th International Conference on Universal Access in Human-Computer Interaction
- CCD: 15th International Conference on Cross-Cultural Design
- SCSM: 15th International Conference on Social Computing and Social Media
- VAMR: 15th International Conference on Virtual, Augmented and Mixed Reality
- DHM: 14th International Conference on Digital Human Modeling and Applications in Health, Safety, Ergonomics and Risk Management
- DUXU: 12th International Conference on Design, User Experience and Usability
- C&C: 11th International Conference on Culture and Computing
- DAPI: 11th International Conference on Distributed, Ambient and Pervasive Interactions
- HCIBGO: 10th International Conference on HCI in Business, Government and Organizations
- LCT: 10th International Conference on Learning and Collaboration Technologies
- ITAP: 9th International Conference on Human Aspects of IT for the Aged Population
- AIS: 5th International Conference on Adaptive Instructional Systems
- HCI-CPT: 5th International Conference on HCI for Cybersecurity, Privacy and Trust
- HCI-Games: 5th International Conference on HCI in Games
- MobiTAS: 5th International Conference on HCI in Mobility, Transport and Automotive Systems
- AI-HCI: 4th International Conference on Artificial Intelligence in HCI
- MOBILE: 4th International Conference on Design, Operation and Evaluation of Mobile Communications

Conference Proceedings – Full List of Volumes

1. LNCS 14011, Human-Computer Interaction: Part I, edited by Masaaki Kurosu and Ayako Hashizume
2. LNCS 14012, Human-Computer Interaction: Part II, edited by Masaaki Kurosu and Ayako Hashizume
3. LNCS 14013, Human-Computer Interaction: Part III, edited by Masaaki Kurosu and Ayako Hashizume
4. LNCS 14014, Human-Computer Interaction: Part IV, edited by Masaaki Kurosu and Ayako Hashizume
5. LNCS 14015, Human Interface and the Management of Information: Part I, edited by Hirohiko Mori and Yumi Asahi
6. LNCS 14016, Human Interface and the Management of Information: Part II, edited by Hirohiko Mori and Yumi Asahi
7. LNAI 14017, Engineering Psychology and Cognitive Ergonomics: Part I, edited by Don Harris and Wen-Chin Li
8. LNAI 14018, Engineering Psychology and Cognitive Ergonomics: Part II, edited by Don Harris and Wen-Chin Li
9. LNAI 14019, Augmented Cognition, edited by Dylan D. Schmorrow and Cali M. Fidopiastis
10. LNCS 14020, Universal Access in Human-Computer Interaction: Part I, edited by Margherita Antona and Constantine Stephanidis
11. LNCS 14021, Universal Access in Human-Computer Interaction: Part II, edited by Margherita Antona and Constantine Stephanidis
12. LNCS 14022, Cross-Cultural Design: Part I, edited by Pei-Luen Patrick Rau
13. LNCS 14023, Cross-Cultural Design: Part II, edited by Pei-Luen Patrick Rau
14. LNCS 14024, Cross-Cultural Design: Part III, edited by Pei-Luen Patrick Rau
15. LNCS 14025, Social Computing and Social Media: Part I, edited by Adela Coman and Simona Vasilache
16. LNCS 14026, Social Computing and Social Media: Part II, edited by Adela Coman and Simona Vasilache
17. LNCS 14027, Virtual, Augmented and Mixed Reality, edited by Jessie Y.C. Chen and Gino Fragomeni
18. LNCS 14028, Digital Human Modeling and Applications in Health, Safety, Ergonomics and Risk Management: Part I, edited by Vincent G. Duffy
19. LNCS 14029, Digital Human Modeling and Applications in Health, Safety, Ergonomics and Risk Management: Part II, edited by Vincent G. Duffy
20. LNCS 14030, Design, User Experience, and Usability: Part I, edited by Aaron Marcus, Elizabeth Rosenzweig and Marcelo Soares
21. LNCS 14031, Design, User Experience, and Usability: Part II, edited by Aaron Marcus, Elizabeth Rosenzweig and Marcelo Soares
22. LNCS 14032, Design, User Experience, and Usability: Part III, edited by Aaron Marcus, Elizabeth Rosenzweig and Marcelo Soares

23. LNCS 14033, Design, User Experience, and Usability: Part IV, edited by Aaron Marcus, Elizabeth Rosenzweig and Marcelo Soares
24. LNCS 14034, Design, User Experience, and Usability: Part V, edited by Aaron Marcus, Elizabeth Rosenzweig and Marcelo Soares
25. LNCS 14035, Culture and Computing, edited by Matthias Rauterberg
26. LNCS 14036, Distributed, Ambient and Pervasive Interactions: Part I, edited by Norbert Streitz and Shin'ichi Konomi
27. LNCS 14037, Distributed, Ambient and Pervasive Interactions: Part II, edited by Norbert Streitz and Shin'ichi Konomi
28. LNCS 14038, HCI in Business, Government and Organizations: Part I, edited by Fiona Fui-Hoon Nah and Keng Siau
29. LNCS 14039, HCI in Business, Government and Organizations: Part II, edited by Fiona Fui-Hoon Nah and Keng Siau
30. LNCS 14040, Learning and Collaboration Technologies: Part I, edited by Panayiotis Zaphiris and Andri Ioannou
31. LNCS 14041, Learning and Collaboration Technologies: Part II, edited by Panayiotis Zaphiris and Andri Ioannou
32. LNCS 14042, Human Aspects of IT for the Aged Population: Part I, edited by Qin Gao and Jia Zhou
33. LNCS 14043, Human Aspects of IT for the Aged Population: Part II, edited by Qin Gao and Jia Zhou
34. LNCS 14044, Adaptive Instructional Systems, edited by Robert A. Sottilare and Jessica Schwarz
35. LNCS 14045, HCI for Cybersecurity, Privacy and Trust, edited by Abbas Moallem
36. LNCS 14046, HCI in Games: Part I, edited by Xiaowen Fang
37. LNCS 14047, HCI in Games: Part II, edited by Xiaowen Fang
38. LNCS 14048, HCI in Mobility, Transport and Automotive Systems: Part I, edited by Heidi Krömker
39. LNCS 14049, HCI in Mobility, Transport and Automotive Systems: Part II, edited by Heidi Krömker
40. LNAI 14050, Artificial Intelligence in HCI: Part I, edited by Helmut Degen and Stavroula Ntoa
41. LNAI 14051, Artificial Intelligence in HCI: Part II, edited by Helmut Degen and Stavroula Ntoa
42. LNCS 14052, Design, Operation and Evaluation of Mobile Communications, edited by Gavriel Salvendy and June Wei
43. CCIS 1832, HCI International 2023 Posters: Part I, edited by Constantine Stephanidis, Margherita Antona, Stavroula Ntoa and Gavriel Salvendy
44. CCIS 1833, HCI International 2023 Posters: Part II, edited by Constantine Stephanidis, Margherita Antona, Stavroula Ntoa and Gavriel Salvendy
45. CCIS 1834, HCI International 2023 Posters: Part III, edited by Constantine Stephanidis, Margherita Antona, Stavroula Ntoa and Gavriel Salvendy
46. CCIS 1835, HCI International 2023 Posters: Part IV, edited by Constantine Stephanidis, Margherita Antona, Stavroula Ntoa and Gavriel Salvendy
47. CCIS 1836, HCI International 2023 Posters: Part V, edited by Constantine Stephanidis, Margherita Antona, Stavroula Ntoa and Gavriel Salvendy

48. LNCS 14054, HCI International 2023 - Late Breaking Papers: Part I, edited by Masaaki Kurosu, Ayako Hashizume, Aaron Marcus, Elizabeth Rosenzweig, Marcelo Soares, Don Harris, Wen-Chin Li, Dylan D. Schmorrow, Cali M. Fidopiastis, and Pei-Luen Patrick Rau
49. LNCS 14055, HCI International 2023 - Late Breaking Papers: Part II, edited by Qin Gao, Jia Zhou, Vincent G. Duffy, Margherita Antona, and Constantine Stephanidis
50. LNCS 14056, HCI International 2023 - Late Breaking Papers: Part III, edited by Hirohiko Mori, Yumi Asahi, Adela Coman, Simona Vasilache, and Matthias Rauterberg
51. LNCS 14057, HCI International 2023 - Late Breaking Papers: Part IV, edited by Vincent G. Duffy, Heidi Krömker, Norbert A. Streitz, and Shin'ichi Konomi
52. LNCS 14058, HCI International 2023 - Late Breaking Papers: Part V, edited by Jessie Y. C. Chen, Gino Fragomeni, and Xiaowen Fang
53. LNCS 14059, HCI International 2023 - Late Breaking Papers: Part VI, edited by Helmut Degen, Stavroula Ntoa, and Abbas Moallem
54. LNCS 14060, HCI International 2023 - Late Breaking Papers: Part VII, edited by Panayiotis Zaphiris, Andri Ioannou, Robert A. Sottilare, Jessica Schwarz, Fiona Fui-Hoon Nah, Keng Siau, June Wei, and Gavriel Salvendy
55. CCIS 1957, HCI International 2023 - Late Breaking Posters: Part I, edited by Constantine Stephanidis, Margherita Antona, Stavroula Ntoa, and Gavriel Salvendy
56. CCIS 1958, HCI International 2023 - Late Breaking Posters: Part II, edited by Constantine Stephanidis, Margherita Antona, Stavroula Ntoa, and Gavriel Salvendy

https://2023.hci.international/proceedings

https://2023.hci.international/proceedings

25th International Conference on Human-Computer Interaction (HCII 2023)

The full list with the Program Board Chairs and the members of the Program Boards of all thematic areas and affiliated conferences of HCII2023 is available online at:

http://www.hci.international/board-members-2023.php

HCI International 2024 Conference

The 26th International Conference on Human-Computer Interaction, HCI International 2024, will be held jointly with the affiliated conferences at the Washington Hilton Hotel, Washington, DC, USA, June 29 – July 4, 2024. It will cover a broad spectrum of themes related to Human-Computer Interaction, including theoretical issues, methods, tools, processes, and case studies in HCI design, as well as novel interaction techniques, interfaces, and applications. The proceedings will be published by Springer. More information will be made available on the conference website: http://2024.hci.international/.

General Chair
Prof. Constantine Stephanidis
University of Crete and ICS-FORTH
Heraklion, Crete, Greece
Email: general_chair@2024.hci.international

https://2024.hci.international/

Contents – Part II

Technologies for the Aging Population

Using Artificial Intelligence and Companion Robots to Improve Home Healthcare for the Elderly

Pietro Battistoni[1], Andrea Antonio Cantone[1], Mariarosaria Esposito[1], Rita Francese[1], Francesca Pia Perillo[1], Marco Romano[2](✉), Monica Sebillo[1], and Giuliana Vitiello[1]

[1] Department of Computer Science, University of Salerno, 84084 Fisciano, SA, Italy
{pbattistoni,acantone,francese,fperillo,msebillo,gvitiello}@unisa.it, m.esposito281@studenti.unisa.it

[2] Faculty of Political Science and Psychosocial Studies, Università degli Studi Internazionali di Roma–UNINT, 00147 Roma, Italy
marco.romano@unint.eu

Abstract. Several statistical reports have addressed the problem of increasing old age and the related increase in emergency room requests in hospital centers. In this paper, interviews were conducted with specialists in the field of geriatrics, a branch of medicine that deals with disorders and diseases related to aging, with the aim of understanding the main health and cognitive problems of an elderly person. From the data that emerged from the interviews conducted, it was realized that the elderly tend to alarm physicians about any alterations, whether serious or not. This behavior causes an increase in healthcare costs associated with keeping more individuals in the emergency room. According to experts, one of the useful practices to keep cognitive impairment under control is mental training. In this context, the constant intervention of a caregiver, whether a family member or a person from outside the family, is helpful, so strategies to cope with the stress involved in managing a patient with dementia need to be improved. Therefore, the emotional state of the caregiver should be a factor that should not be underestimated. Based on these aspects, the goal is to reinvent caregiving so that it is automated and effective. In this article, we focus on the use of robots, with the integration of artificial intelligence, to monitor the health and cognitive status of an elderly person at home. We present the design of a system involving four actors and show a usage scenario.

Keywords: Companion Robot · Artificial Intelligence · Healthcare

Q. Gao et al. (Eds.): HCII 2023, LNCS 14055, pp. 3–17, 2023.
https://doi.org/10.1007/978-3-031-48041-6_1

1 Introduction

In recent years, the increase in the elderly population has been growing rapidly. According to the National Institute of Statistics (ISTAT)[1], the population of the European Union (EU) is aging. Among EU member states, the highest average age in 2020 was observed in Italy (47), followed by Germany and Portugal (both 46), Bulgaria and Greece (both 45), and the lowest in Cyprus and Ireland (both 38) and Luxembourg and Malta (both 40). New forecasts of the EU's demographic future confirm the presence of a potential crisis picture. Indeed, it is estimated that in 2050 the proportion of people over 65 will be 35.9 percent of the total population (up from 23.5 percent today), with an average life expectancy of 82.5 years. The social impact will be significant, having to meet the needs of an increasing proportion of the elderly [17]. This increase also causes healthcare demands to be higher than in previous years, which have already worsened to date as a result of the Covid-19 pandemic.

Cognitive decline contributes to the worsening situation. Cognitive decline is an impairment of cognitive function that is natural as a consequence of advancing age, aggravated especially in the elderly by social isolation due to the pandemic period [30]. In this article, we present interviews conducted with specialists in the field of geriatrics, a branch of medicine that deals with disorders and diseases related to aging. According to experts, one of the useful practices for keeping cognitive impairment under control is mental training. It should be noted that the constant intervention of a caregiver, whether a family member or a person from outside the family, is useful in this context, so it is necessary to improve strategies for dealing with the stress involved in managing a patient with dementia. Therefore, according to the studies and interviews conducted, the emotional state of the caregiver should be a factor that should not be underestimated. Based on these aspects, we formulated the following Research Question:

RQ: *How a technological contribution can help improve the lives of older people?*

From the results of the interviews, the main objective of the work is to analyze how we can automate and make health care more effective, from a technological point of view.

To date, we do not have a causal treatment for severe cognitive impairment, only drugs aimed at mitigating its clinical manifestations. In other words, the increase in old age also leads to an increase in the number of emergency room requests, and the pandemic period, a consequence of social isolation involving the entire world population, has increased cognitive impairment in the elderly.

Just as the integration of various sensors, tools, and assistive technologies provides support to disabled users, such as blind people [27], deaf people [5,6], dyslexics [11], these technologies combined with robotics and artificial intelligence help mitigate cognitive decline or simply keep the elderly person company by guiding them in their daily activities. The technological system must pose as an able companion, gaining a great degree of trust.

[1] https://www.istat.it/, last access 15 May 2023.

In particular, areas of interest focus on monitoring:

- **Physical health.** Monitor the state of health to ensure a preventive diagnosis of any abnormal health conditions. With the cooperation of the system with medical personnel and caregivers, greater safety is also guaranteed.
- **Mental health.** Monitor the state of mental health, so as to allow the elderly person's parents, caregivers, and medical personnel to be aware of the mental health of the elderly person.
- **Emotional state.** Monitoring the emotional state of the elderly person allows you to intervene if, for example, the sense of loneliness is high.
- **Medical prescription.** Monitoring the prescription allows medical personnel to know if the elderly person is following the therapy regulations.

The paper is structured as follows: Sect. 2 presents some robot categories. Section 3 examines some related works and Sect. 4 describes the requirements analysis. Section 5 describes the project design and Sect. 6 shows a usage scenario. Finally, Sect. 7 draws conclusions and future work.

2 Robot's Category

The origin of the term *Robot* is linked to the Czech writer Karel Čapek, who coined the word in the year 1920 in the Utopian Drama entitled RUR (Rossumovi Univerzální Roboti - Universal Robots of Rossum). It was there that an imaginary humanoid appeared for the first time, identified as a robot to recall the Czech word "robota", a term that literally means "slave labor". Nowadays, the use of robots is finding wide use in different sectors: industry [13,16], healthcare [3,4,10], education [7,29] and others.

In general, the classification of robots is a complex thing, as there are various aspects to take into account. We can classify robots following various macro-categories [12] that can be defined according to various factors, such as:

- positioning: there are in fact stationary robots that are not capable of moving, and mobile robots, equipped with legs or wheels that make the robot capable of moving through space;
- application: there are basically two types of robotic applications depending on whether these are less used in industry. For example, among the robots in the industrial sector, we find robots that help in warehouse management to stack pallets. Otherwise, we talk about non-industrial robots, such as those used in personal care.
- to architecture: we refer here to robots that have a different hardware and/or software architecture

Another classification is possible according to the main functionalities that they perform. For example, Autonomous Mobile Robot (AMR) is a robot that uses sensors and cameras to move around. AMR robots are very flexible platforms and guarantee a high degree of customization to be integrated into various application areas [2]. Unlike AMRs, Automated Guided Vehicles (AGVs) need physical guidance to move [21]. There are also robots that are based on a structure very similar to the human one, called Humanoid Robots (HR) that are able to move in a very similar humans way. These can be useful for exploring areas that are unsafe or inaccessible to humans [25].

In this work, we focus on a type of robot categorized as Healthcare Robots (HcR), which have the main goal of assisting people [19]. In this specific case, we refer to an elderly population.

2.1 Robots in Older Adults' Heathcare

The use of robots in elderly care is an evolving field of research and development aimed at meeting the growing health and home care needs of the elderly worldwide. Thanks to technological innovation, sophisticated and intelligent robots have been created that can perform a wide range of tasks, from helping with daily activities such as washing and preparing meals to medication management, health monitoring, and disease prevention. Elderly care robots must be able to interact with people naturally, using natural language and intuitive gestures. They must also be able to sense their surroundings through sensors and adapt to the specific needs of each patient.

The ultimate goal is to create robots, which, thanks to Artificial Intelligence, are able to provide high-quality, personalized care to the elderly, improving their quality of life and reducing the workload of caregivers. It could also reduce the cost of home and hospital care, providing an affordable and sustainable solution for families or communities wishing to care for the elderly.

Home care is one of the areas of greatest interest for the use of robots, as it allows for personalized and continuous care, without necessarily having to resort to being housed in specialized facilities.

However, the use of robots in care requires a number of assessments and precautions in order to ensure the safety and quality of care provided. Therefore, the investigation of issues related to the use of robots in patient care represents an important challenge for modern-day scientific and technological research to find innovative and sustainable solutions that meet the needs of contemporary society.

3 State of the Art

Research highlights the importance of developing robots for the care of the elderly that are able to provide emotional and social support, monitor the state of health, provide assistance in the daily management of activities, and be accessible and safe. In addition, it is important to consider the use of Machine Learning (ML) algorithms and the inclusion of creative and artistic activities to improve the cognitive and psychological well-being of the elderly. These aspects can contribute to improving the quality of life of the elderly and ensuring their adequate and sustainable care.

Broadbent et al. highlighted the need to provide greater security for the elderly, following a survey carried out in a non-profit retirement village [8]. According to the study participants, the essential features of a robot are the ability to detect falls or the removal of a person from the area of the village, as well as assistance in the administration of drugs and measuring vital signs. Other valued tasks include physical assistance, such as lifting heavy objects, cleaning, and turning on/off appliances and lights. Based on the results obtained, the study mainly focuses on cognitive assistance, such as vital data collection, entertainment, and mental training. However, an analysis of the collected data is lacking.

Gross et al. conducted a study on the home health of the elderly with the goal of enabling them to live in their own homes as long as possible [14]. They showed how the robot used has several features, such as face recognition [32,33], the detection of falls and obstacles [31]. They do not focus on the cognitive state of the elderly.

According to a study by Schaeffer et al., it is important for a home care robot to be able to entertain and provide active support in an emergency. The study focuses on the goal of improving the assisted person's independence and quality of life [28]. Technological support will provide security and be able to reduce medical expenses. The study provides a comprehensive overview of all the fundamental aspects that a companion robot should have to address the issues of the elderly. Again, no mention is made of data analysis.

Regarding the integration of ML algorithms in a healthcare robot, the study conducted by Alaskaret et al. shows that the increasing age of the population contributes to a growing and increasing demand for healthcare and that the best solution at the moment is to use ML algorithms to address some of the problems faced by healthcare organizations [1]. The study also provides an overview of some examples of ML algorithms used in various states and countries to support healthcare.

A study conducted by Lukasik et al. on 178 students at the Poznan University of Medical Science identified the main characteristics that a medical nurse robot should possess in order to perform its work under optimal conditions [23]. These include the ability to remember medicines, assist in people's safety, monitor health status, prevent cognitive decline, and encourage physical activity.

Other research has confirmed the importance of these functions, but none seems to dwell on analyzing the data collected and constantly sending data to doctors or family members of the elderly.

In [22] Leonardsen et al. analyzed the effectiveness of using creative and artistic activities in the mental training of the old people. Their study of 453 elderly people aged 65 to 108 showed that such activities can have a positive impact on the cognitive well-being and psychological well-being of the elderly.

After focusing on how technology support can help, we focus on understanding which data is useful to monitor and how these should be monitored. It is therefore useful to understand what a possible assessment scale might be useful to consider for monitoring the health of the elderly person. In this regard, in [15]

Hammond et al. highlight how the increase in the value of the Modified Early Warning Score (MEWS) scale is directly proportional to the frequency of a new hospitalization in intensive care. This scale is also used on discharge from intensive care units. In [20] Koksal et al. also highlight the effectiveness of the MEWS table, which is used for the monitoring of patients in the emergency room; while the Rocha et al. [26] study highlights the effectiveness of the MEWS table on patients, showing how increasing the value of the scale also increases the clinical instability of the patient.

In addition, it is critical to focus on the usability and User eXperience of social robots to ensure that they are accepted and used effectively by the elderly. This requires the adoption of a clear and intuitive user interface that enables the elderly to easily understand the robot's functionality and interact with it without difficulty. Voice commands and intuitive gestures can be implemented to further simplify the use of social robots [9,18,24].

4 Requirements Analysis

To make the analysis of the requirements, some interviews were conducted with geriatricians, who are involved in the prevention, diagnosis, and treatment of diseases typical of old age. Ten experts were contacted using the "*MioDottore*" application. This app allows users to search for doctors and health facilities within their area or in different cities. Users can make appointments for medical examinations, book visits or consultations online, receive appointment reminders, access their medical records, and manage their bookings.

The purpose of the interviews was to understand what are the significant aspects to carry out a clinical evaluation of older people. This assessment includes:

- aspects related to the *physical state* and *health* of the older people;
- aspects related to *cognitive decay.*

For an effective analysis, geriatricians were subjected to a series of questions with the aim of understanding the most common problems that doctors have when they treat older people, such as:

1. the parameters to be monitored;
2. methods used to monitor the parameters;
3. the most frequent signs of concern;
4. how much they accept the idea of a product that uses artificial intelligence in the medical field;
5. functional requirements, in order to understand the main functionalities useful to ensure a better quality of life for elderly people in their home.

All the points described earlier are analyzed in the following paragraphs.

4.1 Parameters to be Monitored

Regarding the parameters to be monitored, physicians consider vital signs monitoring to be relevant to detect early signs of health concerns for the elderly. Vital signs measure basic body functions; in effect, they provide a snapshot of what is happening inside the body, providing important information about the status of organs. For this reason, vital signs monitoring is critical, allowing physicians to assess a patient's physical well-being. Based on the results of vital signs monitoring, the physician can perform additional tests, diagnose a problem, or suggest lifestyle changes.

4.2 Methods Used to Monitor the Parameters

Vital parameters are also used as input into a specific scoring table, called the Modified Early Warning Score (MEWS), shown in Fig. 1.

	3	**2**	**1**	**0**	**1**	**2**	**3**
Systolic blood pressure	≤70	71-80	81-100	101-199		≥200	
Heart rate		≤ 40	41/50	51/100	101-110	111-129	≥ 130
Respiratory rate		≤ 9		9/14	15/20	21/29	≥30
Temperature		≤35		36-38.4		≥38.5	
Conscious level				A	B	C	D

Fig. 1. Table representing the values and corresponding weights of the MEWS table.

The conscious level, unlike the others, is measured without numerical but textual values. The table shows the letters *A,B,C,D* representing the following states:

A: indicates a "patient awake" state of consciousness;
B: indicates a "responds to verbal stimulus" state of consciousness;
C: indicates a "responds to painful stimulus" state of consciousness;
D: indicates a "does not respond to painful stimulus" state of consciousness.

The MEWS table is useful in identifying health problems. The score ranges from a minimum of 0 to a maximum of 14. The purpose of using this tool is to be able to predict the instability of the patient, and try to prevent a worsening or irreversible condition, signaling to the caregiver the need to implement and intensify care.

4.3 Most Common Signs of Concern

In general, according to interviews with doctors, the most frequent signs of concern are atypical changes in vital parameter values. These may be due to causes of concern, so careful monitoring must be done to ensure that vital parameters do not drop or rise rapidly over time. In addition to this, the MEWS chart helps to understand the occurrence of clinical deterioration. Indeed, the purpose of using this tool lies in its ability to predict patient instability based on the MEWS score value: patients with *low MEWS* can continue receiving their usual care and observation; patients with *high MEWS* should be watched more attentively and considered for transfer to a higher care unit.

4.4 Acceptability of a Product that Uses AI in the Medical Field

The greatest concerns of the doctors interviewed relate to fears that artificial intelligence will replace the doctor; in particular, the adoption of such technologies could lead to the replacement of their role in diagnosing and treating patients, resulting in job reductions and the loss of traditional medical skills. Others have raised concerns about legal liability in the event of errors caused by AI algorithms.

In response to these problems and concerns, the data to be sent to physicians after analysis was structured with a Machine Learning model. In particular, it was considered of paramount importance to send all measured vital parameters in addition to the AI analysis. In this way, the medical prognosis would always be the result of the physician's knowledge and studies. In this way, the physician would be able to establish an increasing degree of confidence in the new technology through its daily use.

Despite these concerns, the majority of respondents believe that the use of AI in medicine is seen as a promising solution, but the resulting concerns and challenges need to be addressed, including ethical issues related to transparency in the use of these systems.

4.5 Functional Requirements

From the analysis of the interviews, the most important functional requirements (FR) concern two macro areas: *monitoring* and *communication.*

Monitoring. To ensure constant monitoring of the health of the elderly through the acquisition of their vital parameters, as well as their emotional state. It is also essential to monitor the correct intake of drug therapy, in order to avoid possible complications. In more detail:

FR_1 the robot must measure the vital parameters of the elderly person automatically, by taking advantage of the potential of medical wrist sensors;

FR_2 the ability to have easy access to measured vital signs, with a historian allowing the doctor and caregiver to understand if there are problems in the elderly person;

FR_3 the possibility of having a categorization of the health status of the elderly person, so as to understand how serious the situation is;

FR_4 the robot must measure the state of mental health of the elderly person, through special tests;

FR_5 the system must give doctors and family members the opportunity to view the elderly person's therapy. It is very important to know if the elderly person is following medical therapy or not, in order to exclude this as the cause of the elderly person's disease.

Communication. The aim of the proposed system is to provide precise information about the health status of the patient, by detecting vital signs and generating an alarm in the event of any problems, with the additional sending of vital signs that led to the distress call. In more detail:

FR_6 ability to communicate with the robot with the use of voice, supporting voice help requests;

FR_7 ability to communicate with the robot using a tablet connected to the robot itself;

FR_8 ability to communicate with the robot thanks to facial recognition, able to understand the emotions of the elderly person;

FR_9 the system must provide cognitive testing to prevent cognitive decay;

FR_10 the robot must be able to send the emergency signal to the doctors in case of unstable vital parameters, with relative state of severity.

5 Project Design

The idea of the work is to monitor the elderly in their daily routine through technological support. To do this, it is very important a good integration of various sensors. It will be possible to use both sanitary sensors and non-sanitary sensors. The first one could be integrated into a bracelet for the measurement of vital signs. The second one, such as air quality measurement or GPS sensors could be useful to keep track of the position of the elderly person.

5.1 Planned Project Model

The planned project model involves four actors. The first one is (1) a robot that interacts with several sensors and allows it to monitor (2) the elderly person. It is also able to help (3) doctors and (4) relatives of the person involved or caregivers to monitor vital signs and the state of the physical and emotional health of the elderly person (Fig. 2).

In more detail, the main idea of the project is to integrate robots, sensors, and artificial intelligence to improve the life and safety of the elderly person. The robot must be able to receive data from appropriate sensors capable of collecting the vital signs of the elderly person. These sensors can be integrated into a specific bracelet, worn by the elderly person and with which he does not have to interact directly. The vital parameters of the elderly person, in fact, will be measured automatically and the data related to the vital parameters will be

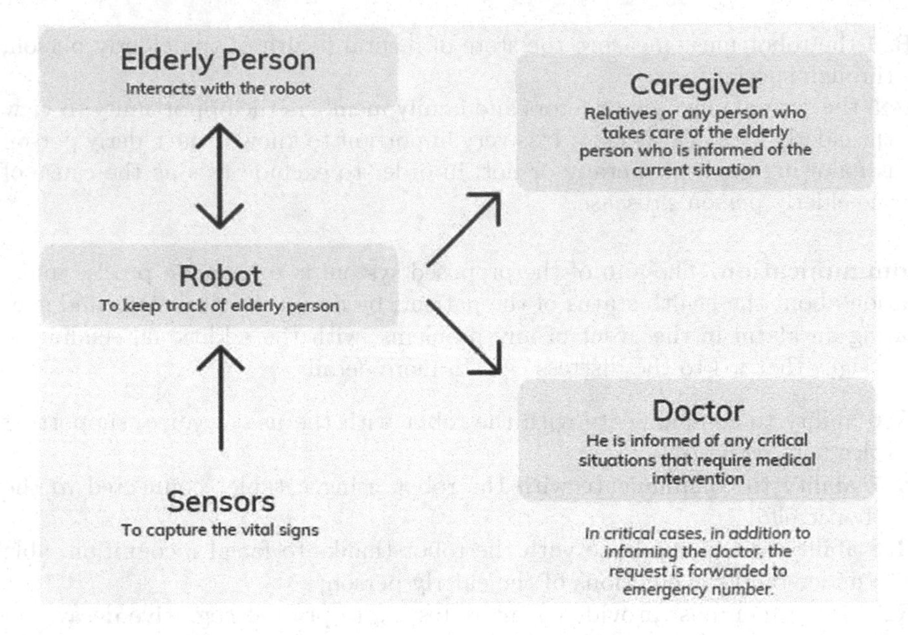

Fig. 2. Scheme of communication between the actors of the system

sent to the Machine Learning model that will make the prediction, telling if the elderly person is sick or not.

In this way, the doctor and family members of the elderly person are alerted to any unstable clinical situations. When the doctor receives the alert of the robot he can understand the severity of the alarm and in this way, he has the opportunity to intervene quickly according to the specific situation. In the event that the robot claims that the health situation is not good, the doctor can go to the elderly person's house and notify the robot of his arrival. In addition, if the elderly person's vital signs are too worrying, the robot may decide to send a request for help to the hospitals, in order to operate promptly.

The robot must be able to communicate not only with the doctor but also with the elderly person. To do this you can use both a spoken mode and a dedicated tablet, with which the elderly person can enter useful information to understand his state of health. With the tablet, the elderly person can select the medicines he has taken, so the robot collects the data and manages to keep his medical routine updated. In addition, the elderly person can also make specific games to train his mind to improve the situation of cognitive decay. The robot must also send the health situation to the medical staff in order to keep the doctor updated on the health status of the elderly person. The doctor and caregiver should be able to request a history of the clinical situation of the elderly person. In addition, another specific tablet will be provided to caregivers, who can integrate activities for the elderly person. Through this tablet, it is also possible to track the daily life of the elderly person, in order to understand if he has eaten, if he has taken his medicines, or the level of his cognitive state. In addition, the robot could be integrated with an emotional recognition mechanism to understand the emotional state of the elderly person. This is very useful in case older people live alone in their own home.

6 Usage Scenarios

To better understand the functional requirements and how the actors interact with each other with our project idea, the following is a scenario that helps to understand how the collaborative approach takes place. There are four actors in the scenario:

- the robot;
- Anthony, the elderly person;
- the doctor Joseph;
- Lisa and Romolo, the family members of the elderly person.

Here is a scenario with some illustrations to help you understand the situation. In addition, in the scenario, the identifiers of the specific reference requirements are given between the square brackets.

Anthony Castelnovo is an elderly person who is going through a phase where he is having difficulty taking care of himself independently. Lisa and Romolo, his children, are very busy because of their work and cannot personally care for their father, but they feel safe in entrusting him to the services of a special robot that cooperates with sensors and an artificial intelligence model to help the elderly person live in his home safely for as long as possible.

The robot, at regular intervals, monitors Anthony's vital parameters through the use of a bracelet that the elderly person wears [**FR_1**] and, thanks to a built-in machine learning model, classifies the collected parameters and saves them to allow them to be accessed at a later time [**FR_3**].

Recently, Dr. Joseph, the Castelnovo family doctor, prescribed Joseph a specific therapy consisting of regular medication to keep his heart rhythm under control. Recently, however, it happens that Anthony forgets to take the medication to follow the therapy. Very often it is the robot that reminds him to take his medication. Considering only last week, Antony was about to forget to take his medication six times out of fifteen, a very high number given the importance of medication.

However, it happens that Antony decides he does not want to take them, so the robot alerts both the doctors and family members [**FR_5**], who call Antony to find out why he does not want to follow the medication. After the robot's warning about not taking her medication, Lisa went to her father's house and alerted the robot to her arrival. Since Lisa has more free time after work and goes to her dad's house every week, Anthony has not stopped taking his medication.

Anthony does not usually contact his doctor, even when he does not feel well; the robot helps him communicate indirectly with Dr. Joseph. In fact, the doctor is informed by the robot about any abnormalities in automatically detected vital parameters [**FR_10**], and is able to request the history of parameter measurements from the robot remotely [**FR_2**].

Using emotion recognition, the robot is also able to understand Antony's mental and emotional state. In the event that he feels sad or lonely, the robot suggests that Anthony contact a friend or entertain himself with specific games that not only keep him company but also help prevent cognitive impairment [**FR_4, FR_8, FR_9**]. Interactions between Antony and the robot are through voice recognition [**FR_6**], however, sometimes questions arise that are preferably answered by Antony through a tablet with a user-friendly interface. The tablet was also provided to Anthony's family, allowing them to monitor their father's well-being even from a distance [**FR_7**].

7 Conclusions and Future Work

In this article, we focused on the use of robots for elderly care. After an overview of the main categories of robots and a review of existing literature from interviews with ten geriatricians, we defined the functional requirements of the system and the design of the system.

In addition, we presented a usage scenario to better understand the functional requirements and how the actors involved in the system interact with each other.

In the future, we plan to implement the system and run an experiment involving all the defined actors.

Acknowledgement. We acknowledge financial support from the project PNRR MUR project PE0000013-FAIR.

References

1. Alaskar, K.M., et al.: Artificial intelligence (AI) in healthcare management. J. Pharm. Negat. Results 1011–1020 (2022)
2. Alatise, M.B., Hancke, G.P.: A review on challenges of autonomous mobile robot and sensor fusion methods. IEEE Access **8**, 39830–39846 (2020). https://doi.org/10.1109/ACCESS.2020.2975643
3. Amato, F., Di Gregorio, M., Monaco, C., Sebillo, M., Tortora, G., Vitiello, G.: The therapeutic use of humanoid robots for behavioral disorders. In: Proceedings of the International Conference on Advanced Visual Interfaces. AVI 2020. Association for Computing Machinery, New York (2020). https://doi.org/10.1145/3399715.3399960
4. Amato, F., Di Gregorio, M., Monaco, C., Sebillo, M., Tortora, G., Vitiello, G.: Socially assistive robotics combined with artificial intelligence for ADHD. In: 2021 IEEE 18th Annual Consumer Communications & Networking Conference (CCNC), pp. 1–6 (2021). https://doi.org/10.1109/CCNC49032.2021.9369633
5. Battistoni, P., Di Gregorio, M., Romano, M., Sebillo, M., Vitiello, G., Solimando, G.: Sign language interactive learning - measuring the user engagement. In: Zaphiris, P., Ioannou, A. (eds.) HCII 2020. LNCS, vol. 12206, pp. 3–12. Springer, Cham (2020). https://doi.org/10.1007/978-3-030-50506-6_1

6. Battistoni, P., Sebillo, M., Di Gregorio, M., Vitiello, G., Romano, M.: Prosign+ a cloud-based platform supporting inclusiveness in public communication. In: 2020 IEEE 17th Annual Consumer Communications & Networking Conference (CCNC), pp. 1–5 (2020). https://doi.org/10.1109/CCNC46108.2020.9045191
7. Belpaeme, T., Kennedy, J., Ramachandran, A., Scassellati, B., Tanaka, F.: Social robots for education: a review. Sci. Robot. **3**(21), eaat5954 (2018)
8. Broadbent, E., Jayawardena, C., Kerse, N., Stafford, R., MacDonald, B.A.: Human-robot interaction research to improve quality of life in elder care-an approach and issues (2011)
9. Cantone, A.A., Mortezapour, A., Sebillo, M., Tortora, G., Vitiello, G.: Personalized IoT's service providers: a neurocognitive approach to assess their usability (2023)
10. Cifuentes, C.A., Pinto, M.J., Céspedes, N., Múnera, M.C.: Social robots in therapy and care. Curr. Robot. Rep. **1**, 59–74 (2020)
11. Di Gregorio, M., Romano, M., Sebillo, M., Vitiello, G.: Dyslexeasy-app to improve readability through the extracted summary for dyslexic users, pp. 1–6 (2022). https://doi.org/10.1109/CCNC49033.2022.9700618
12. Dobra, A.: General classification of robots. size criteria. In: 2014 23rd International Conference on Robotics in Alpe-Adria-Danube Region (RAAD), pp. 1–6 (2014). https://doi.org/10.1109/RAAD.2014.7002249
13. Golnazarian, W., Hall, E.: Intelligent industrial robots (2002). https://doi.org/10.1201/9780203908587.ch6.5
14. Gross, H.M., et al.: Robot companion for domestic health assistance: implementation, test and case study under everyday conditions in private apartments. In: 2015 IEEE/RSJ International Conference on Intelligent Robots and Systems (IROS), pp. 5992–5999. IEEE (2015)
15. Hammond, N.E., Spooner, A.J., Barnett, A.G., Corley, A., Brown, P., Fraser, J.F.: The effect of implementing a modified early warning scoring (MEWS) system on the adequacy of vital sign documentation. Aust. Crit. Care **26**(1), 18–22 (2013)
16. Çiğdem, S., Meidute-Kavaliauskiene, I., Yıldız, B.: Industry 4.0 and industrial robots: a study from the perspective of manufacturing company employees. Logistics **7**(1), 17 (2023). https://doi.org/10.3390/logistics7010017
17. Ismail, Z., Wan Ahmad, W.I., Hanin Hamjah, S., Astina, I.K.: The impact of population ageing: a review. Iran. J. Public Health **50**(12), 2451–2460 (2021). https://doi.org/10.18502/ijph.v50i12.7927
18. Jung, M., Lazaro, M.J.S., Yun, M.H.: Evaluation of methodologies and measures on the usability of social robots: a systematic review. Appl. Sci. **11**(4), 1388 (2021). https://doi.org/10.3390/app11041388
19. Kar, S.: Robotics in healthcare. In: 2019 2nd International Conference on Power Energy, Environment and Intelligent Control (PEEIC), pp. 78–83 (2019). https://doi.org/10.1109/PEEIC47157.2019.8976668
20. Köksal, Ö., Torun, G., Ahun, E., Sığırlı, D., Güney, S., Aydın, M.: The comparison of modified early warning score and glasgow coma scale-age-systolic blood pressure scores in the assessment of nontraumatic critical patients in emergency department. Niger. J. Clin. Pract. **19**(6), 761–765 (2016)
21. Le-Anh, T., De Koster, R.: A review of design and control of automated guided vehicle systems. Eur. J. Oper. Res. **171**, 1–23 (2004). https://doi.org/10.1016/j.ejor.2005.01.036
22. Leonardsen, A.C.L., Hardeland, C., Helgesen, A.K., Bååth, C., Del Busso, L., Grøndahl, V.A.: The use of robotic technology in the healthcare of people above the age of 65-a systematic review. In: Healthcare, vol. 11, p. 904. MDPI (2023)

23. Łukasik, S., Tobis, S., Kropińska, S., Suwalska, A.: Role of assistive robots in the care of older people: survey study among medical and nursing students. J. Med. Internet Res. **22**(8), e18003 (2020)
24. Mahmoudi Asl, A., Molinari Ulate, M., Franco Martin, M., van der Roest, H.: Methodologies used to study the feasibility, usability, efficacy, and effectiveness of social robots for elderly adults: scoping review. J. Med. Internet Res. **24**(8), e37434 (2022). https://doi.org/10.2196/37434
25. Mahum, R., Shafique Butt, F., Ayyub, K., Islam, S., Nawaz, M., Abdullah, D.: A review on humanoid robots. Int. J. Adv. Appl. Sci. **4**, 83–90 (2017). https://doi.org/10.21833/ijaas.2017.02.015
26. Rocha, T.F.D., Neves, J.G., Viegas, K.: Modified early warning score: evaluation of trauma patients. Revista brasileira de enfermagem **69**, 906–911 (2016)
27. Romano, M., Bellucci, A., Aedo, I.: Understanding touch and motion gestures for blind people on mobile devices. In: Abascal, J., Barbosa, S., Fetter, M., Gross, T., Palanque, P., Winckler, M. (eds.) INTERACT 2015. LNCS, vol. 9296, pp. 38–46. Springer, Cham (2015). https://doi.org/10.1007/978-3-319-22701-6_3
28. Schaeffer, C., May, T.: Care-o-bot-a system for assisting elderly or disabled persons in home environments. In: Assistive Technology on the Threshold of the New Millenium, vol. 3 (1999)
29. Sánchez, H., Martínez, L.S., González, J.D.: Educational robotics as a teaching tool in higher education institutions: a bibliographical analysis. J. Phys. Conf. Ser. **1391**(1), 012128 (2019). https://doi.org/10.1088/1742-6596/1391/1/012128
30. Stuart, A., et al.: Loneliness in older people and COVID-19: applying the social identity approach to digital intervention design. Comput. Hum. Behav. Rep. **6**, 100179 (2022). https://doi.org/10.1016/j.chbr.2022.100179
31. Volkhardt, M., Schneemann, F., Gross, H.M.: Fallen person detection for mobile robots using 3D depth data. In: 2013 IEEE International Conference on Systems, Man, and Cybernetics, pp. 3573–3578. IEEE (2013)
32. Weinrich, C., Vollmer, C., Gross, H.M.: Estimation of human upper body orientation for mobile robotics using an SVM decision tree on monocular images. In: 2012 IEEE/RSJ International Conference on Intelligent Robots and Systems, pp. 2147–2152. IEEE (2012)
33. Weinrich, C., Wengefeld, T., Schroeter, C., Gross, H.M.: People detection and distinction of their walking aids in 2D laser range data based on generic distance-invariant features. In: The 23rd IEEE International Symposium on Robot and Human Interactive Communication, pp. 767–773. IEEE (2014)

Developing an Online Learning Tool to Improve Financial Literacy in Older Adults: An Intergenerational Co-design Case Study

Ke Chen[1] (✉) and Vivian Weiqun Lou[2]

[1] Department of Psychology and Behavioral Sciences, Zhejiang University, Hangzhou, China
kechen@zju.edu.cn

[2] Social Work and Social Administration, Sau Po Centre on AgeCing, The University of Hong Kong, Pokfulam, Hong Kong, China

Abstract. With aging, individuals are responsible for managing and spending their retirement assets, along with making complicated decisions on medical care, aged care, and estate planning, all while facing a decline in their cognitive performance and financial literacy. Older people are the most vulnerable groups in financial literacy and financial management. Providing older people with financial inclusion and financial literacy programs is essential. This article described an intergenerational, co-design process of developing an online interactive learning tool that could enhance financial literacy for older people and their families. Seven older adults and four law students were recruited and trained as co-designers. They interviewed 60 older individuals in Hong Kong to identify misconceptions, knowledge gaps, and suboptimal financial decisions made by them. These qualitative data were analyzed and utilized to create an online learning tool to address the greatest common misconceptions. The online learning tool consists of a self-assessment quiz and instructive animations, which are shared on a website that was open to the public. We discussed the benefits and difficulties of involving co-designers of different ages in the research and design process. This study contributes to a better understanding of how to carry out intergenerational co-design activities in the context of social and healthcare research.

Keywords: Co-design · Older People · Financial Literacy · Online Learning

1 Background

Population aging is one of the greatest social transformations, which will have an impact on all facets of society, including the labor market, economic performance, and financial sustainability of public health care, pensions, and social protection systems [1]. As the population ages and becomes more apparent, financial planning and asset management throughout retirement are issues of growing public policy importance. The lack of financial literacy, accessibility to financial services in an increasingly digital world, and the absence of financial products that meet their needs are all obstacles to older people's financial well-being [2–4]. The quality of financial decisions is significantly influenced

Q. Gao et al. (Eds.): HCII 2023, LNCS 14055, pp. 18–27, 2023.
https://doi.org/10.1007/978-3-031-48041-6_2

by financial literacy. Financial literacy entails being aware of a particular financial product's functions, features, similarities and differences with other potential products, as well as any potential limitations of the product and the operational procedures for using the product, all of which are necessary to carry out a particular financial plan. Older people are the most vulnerable groups in financial literacy and financial management [5]. It is critical to offer financial inclusion and financial literacy initiatives to older persons.

Older people frequently encounter circumstances that necessitate important financial decisions. Older individuals are responsible for managing their retirement assets and distributions, making complicated decisions on medical care and estate planning, they are also facing a decline in their cognitive performance and financial literacy [2, 6]. Issues with retirement financial management, such as wills, powers of attorney, guardianship, life insurance, bank loans, reverse mortgages, and other financial issues, affect the daily lives and well-being of older people. People above the age of 50 have been shown in surveys to lack a financial understanding of and interest in retirement products like public annuities and reserve mortgages [7–9]. Additionally, they lacked an understanding of estate planning and the products that were available, such as wills and the enduring power of attorneys (EPAs). Previous research has demonstrated that older persons encounter particularly significant obstacles to obtaining legal assistance when making financial decisions that are at odds with their values, wishes, and preferences [10, 11]. Lack of knowledge or confusion about the products available for financial planning, uncertainty about where one can seek help and the costs involved, and reluctance to consider death and disease are some of the obstacles to financial planning. Because of this, older persons are more prone to suffer from poor quality of life and financial exploitation/abuse [3, 12]. To close the knowledge gap and increase their financial literacy and well-being, it is crucial to understand the current status quo of financial products.

In the present study, the financial and legal knowledge pertaining to six retirement products—joint accounts, reverse mortgages, annuities, enduring power of attorneys (EPAs), guardianship orders, and wills—was examined. This study concentrated on these six retirement-related products because they are readily available in Hong Kong's retirement market but are relatively complex, necessitating that people put off immediate gratification in favor of future gain, switch from asset accumulation to decumulation, and take precautionary decisions. The six products cover money management, estate planning, preparation for mental incapacity and death, and wealth transfer. Older people's knowledge and decisions on these available products are not well understood. Understanding older people's financial decisions in preparation for retirement protection and health challenges would have important social policy implications.

The level of financial literacy among older people has only been partially studied using large-scale surveys [5, 13]. Surveys can be useful when a researcher wants to identify statistical relationships among variables. However, surveys fail to provide a deep understanding of underlying reasons and motivations contributing to financial knowledge and literacy, a topic that might involve myth and/or diversified interpretations. Recent health and social research is seeing an increase in the use of older persons as co-researchers or co-designers [14, 15]. This co-design method is promising since it may facilitate an enhanced understanding of the subject due to the co-designers' insider knowledge experience and expertise in framing research questions and interpretation data [16]. The co-designers in older age are themselves older and aging, thus they may contribute significant viewpoints, abilities, expertise, and personal aging experiences to the current research. They are able to build a stronger emotional connection and understanding with the target community to which they belong, thus enhancing the quality of research data obtained [14, 17]. They are also strongly committed to aging research, especially if it will help them connect with others and bring about real social change [18].

Nevertheless, despite this rise in co-design, significant participation of older individuals as engaged stakeholders in retirement planning is still uncommon. Ageism and other forms of social exclusion are accountable for the marginalization of older people's voices. The stratified life course results in the geographical, institutional, and cultural separation of persons of different ages, and modern age-segregated society employs chronological age to assign roles and rights to individuals as well as to define entry into and exit from expected activities [19]. This social separation leads to ageism, stereotyping, prejudice, and discrimination against people based on their age. The intergroup theory proposed that prejudice can be lessened by contact, in which intergenerational groups are united within contexts that allow both parties equal status, where they cooperate on tasks with common goals, and have the support of relevant institutions and authorities that create norms of acceptance [20, 21]. Therefore, the intergenerational co-design method can be used to challenge traditional societal and personal ageist assumptions, practices, attitudes, and capabilities. However, research involving older adults alongside younger adults in the format of intergenerational co-design remains rare.

The goal of this study is to better understand the financial literacy and knowledge gaps among older persons in Hong Kong as well as to create a knowledge translation tool for improving financial literacy. We describe and reflected on the intergenerational, co-design process of creating an online interactive learning tool.

2 Methods

This research adopted a novel three-stage, co-design method [22, 23], in which older people partnered with law students and academic staff as co-designers during the research process. Figure 1 presents the co-design research process. The study was approved by the Human Research Ethics Committee of the University (EA1907015). All co-designers provided their written consent, which covered the roles and responsibilities for training, participant recruitment, data collection, analysis, and dissemination, as well as other activities.

2.1 Co-designer Recruitment and Capacity Building

Stage 1 of the co-design process comprised recruiting and training co-designers. We recruited co-designers using a criterion sampling strategy. To be eligible criteria for co-designers had to be over 50 years of age and Cantonese speaking, or had to be enrolled in the Faculty of Law at the time of application. Potential co-designers were expected to have an enthusiasm for research, be skilled at communicating and listening, be motivated to complete research tasks that would enhance older adults' financial literacy, and be

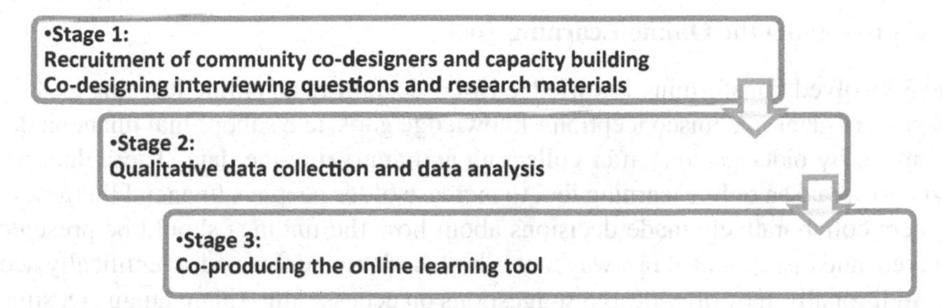

Fig. 1. Co-design research process

willing to participate in research training sessions provided by the project. To recruit co-designers, the university's campus was covered in recruitment advertisements, and targeted emails were sent to students in the Faculty of Law. Seven older individuals (mean age = 63, standard deviation = 6.08, four women) and four law students enrolled in either the Bachelor or Master of Law program (mean age = 26, standard deviation = 10.8, three women) were recruited and trained.

The four capacity-building training sessions were attended by all the co-designers. During these sessions, they gained background knowledge about the objectives and context of the research, were given a basic understanding of financial products, agreed upon their respective roles, responsibilities, and levels of participation, improved their research knowledge and skills, created interviewing guidelines and questionnaires, and developed relationships and peer support.

2.2 Qualitative Data Collection and Data Analysis

Stage 2 was data collection. Data collection was done using a qualitative approach that combined focus groups with semi-structured individual interviews. To delve deeper into people's personal experiences with financial planning, individual interviews were held. The focus group technique was employed to record a wide range of individual attitudes, thoughts, and justifications for decision-making with regard to financial products.

After taking part in the training sessions, the co-designers subsequently recruited and interviewed older people. One student and one older person were matched during the data-collecting period based on their mutual availability. The research staff served as facilitators and simply offered technical support while the co-designers conducted all of the interviews using the interview guide that was jointly established during training sessions. All co-designers conducted 31 individual interviews with adults aged 50 to 70, and five co-designers facilitated four focus groups with a sample of 29 older adults. A total of 60 people participated in the study (63.3% were female). The majority had obtained an upper secondary education or above (76.6%), were retired (63.3%), were married (71.6%), lived in private permanent housing (78.3%), had children (60%), and lived with family members (85%).

The qualitative information was audio recorded, then it was transcribed. Two academic staff members iteratively analyzed the data using the QSR NVivo 11 software package. In two meetings, the results and findings were discussed and confirmed by co-researchers.

2.3 Co-designing the Online Learning Tool

Stage 3 involved transforming knowledge by co-designing an online learning tool. The co-designers identified misconceptions, knowledge gaps, and suboptimal financial decisions made by older persons after collecting and analyzing the data. These data were utilized to create an online learning tool to increase older people's financial literacy. Co-designers collaboratively made decisions about how the findings should be presented, displayed, and disseminated in a way that is both understandable and scientifically accurate. Additionally, they offer design suggestions on accessibility (plain language, simple layout, text with visual and audio representation) and usability (sound effects, text size, automation speed).

3 Results

3.1 Misconceptions About Financial Products

Joint accounts (69.6%) and wills (32.6%) were the six financial products that the participants presently use most frequently, followed by private annuity plans (30.4%), public annuities (8.7%), and guardianships (6.5%). Participants also had other types of investment products (10.9%) including stocks, bonds, insurance products, and bank deposits. None of the participants had prepared an enduring power of attorney or reverse mortgage.

The many financial products available for retirement are understood at varying degrees by the participants. Large numbers of participants were familiar with wills and joint accounts. They were aware of but lacked an understanding of annuities and reverse mortgages. The majority of our participants were not familiar with the enduring power of attorneys and guardianship orders and had a poor level of knowledge to distinguish carefully among the many alternatives.

During the interviews, participants exhibited some misconceptions and knowledge gaps about existing financial products. Some of them might not have the required knowledge to make informed decisions. These misconceptions may explain why older people make suboptimal financial decisions for their legal and financial interests. Insufficient knowledge may also increase exposure of financial abuse, misuse, and misconduct. In addition, older people may not have access to the information or do not know exactly where to obtain information to carry out financial decisions. Even if participants are given the information about the products, the choice environment may be too complex for them (e.g., many potential or alternative choices) to evaluate the options appropriately and choose the one most meets their needs. Previous studies have identified that individuals often fail to plan for retirement due to a lack of sufficient domain-specific knowledge [24–26]. Listed below are key biases and misconceptions found in the interviews.

Actions that had been taken by participants to prepare for contingencies include setting up a joint bank account, auto-pay, third-party mandate, and wills; or granting informal access to family members to a bank account via sharing card number, pin, and ATM password. Joint accounts were used by 69.6% of participants. Interestingly, the joint account was frequently used as a substitute for the enduring power of attorneys and wills. Participants saw a spouse- or parent-child joint bank account as a cheap and easy way to plan for health challenges or to avoid probate. Many participants took it for granted that joint assets will automatically belong to the survivor upon the death of one account holder, without knowing whether the "survivorship clause" (a survivorship clause operates to transfer the beneficial interest in the asset to the survivor) applies to their joint accounts.

Adding an authorized person to an account was also used to plan for emergencies or health challenges. Some participants would assign someone they trust to help make decisions on their behalf through sharing delegation or general power of attorney. However, very few participants know that the delegation and general powers of attorney are limited to only dealing with financial affairs and will cease to be legally effective upon the donor (or account holder) becoming mentally incapacitated. The enduring power of attorneys and guardianship orders was not well-known by the public. Many participants were not aware of the different options available (letters of delegation, general power of attorneys, enduring power of attorneys, guardianship orders, written wills), and they cannot tell what options are suitable in the circumstances when someone has lost mental capacity or is deceased.

The decision of taking part in the annuities was perceived as a capital lockage and liquidity constraint that limits urgent funding. Medical expenses can be huge in old age and older people usually need to prepare extra money available for illness or other unexpected needs. The life annuity plan in Hong Kong has introduced special withdrawals to meet medical and dental expenses in the guaranteed income period. The withdrawal can be used for surgery, medical treatment, or examination considered necessary by doctors. Depending on the policy provisions, some private annuity products may also offer advance income withdrawal for critical illnesses. Annuitants need to be aware that after the advance withdrawal, the subsequent annuity income, the death benefit (if applicable), and the total amount of benefits paid will be reduced accordingly.

Mortgaging a household to pay for retirement income was considered as lost ownership of the property by participants. Participants heard of a reverse mortgage but lacked an understanding of the product. Most participants thought that if they take out a mortgage loan, the lender owns the property, and they cannot retain the ownership of the home. Participants asked how the property value would be determined, how housing price fluctuations influence payout arrangements, who would provide the reverse mortgages schemes, whether the government would provide a guarantee in the event of provider default, how product payments would be affected by the tax, how much are the administration and interests fees, whether the property could be rented out after signing the contract, and the arrangement of moving out or rent out for long-term aged care. Leaving an inheritance for heirs was identified as the biggest reason for the resistance to reverse mortgages.

3.2 Creating an Online Learning Tool

After identifying the knowledge gaps via qualitative interviews, the team created an online learning tool to address the greatest common misconceptions held by most participants. The online learning tool consists of an online self-assessment quiz and six instructive animations (Fig. 2). To accommodate the varied learning preferences of older adults, these forms were developed based on qualitative data and suggestions from co-designers. Only one issue was focused on each of the six topics of our interest, i.e., joint accounts, reverse mortgages, annuities, enduring power of attorneys, guardianship orders, and wills. The online learning tool is interactive in terms of its Q&A feature. The descriptions of the tool were based on real-life scenarios using characters presenting various roles. Personal relative scenarios enable learners to apply knowledge easily and directly in their daily roles and tasks. Using examples from real-world situations can make online learning more engaging, relatable, understandable, and remembered. The online form can be either a self-learning tool or an additional educational resource to enhance knowledge of long-term financial planning. We developed a publicly available website (https://www.ageing.hku.hk/besmart) intending to communicate the research findings to older people, their families, and relevant professional groups.

Six "true or false" questions made up the online self-assessment quiz. It takes ten minutes for self-administration. After responding to all questions, responders can view the right and wrong answers, along with a brief explanation. As a result, the quiz can be used for self-learning. The quiz can also be used by instructors as a test material to assess the baseline financial knowledge of the audience or to evaluate their understanding of a certain topic and their capability to apply it to practical situations.

Additionally, six educational animations have been produced. The average runtime of each animation is one minute. Those animations can be easily integrated into social media platforms such as YouTube and Facebook for public education. Each animation can also be included in other learning exercises like public lectures, seminars, and workshops or used as a case study for group work.

Fig. 2. The online learning tool (quiz on the left and animations on the right)

4 Discussion

Older people might not have the necessary financial and legal knowledge to make an informed financial decision. Empowering older people by addressing the knowledge gaps and misconceptions will improve their financial literacy and assist their decision-making. Using a co-design method, this study developed an online learning tool consisting of an online self-assessment quiz and six animations, which served as a case study to improve financial literacy in the older population.

The current study makes the following contributions. First, the study adds to a growing body of research that seeks to place older people's voices to centre stage and provides insights into the process of planning, recruiting, training, reflecting, transforming, and working with co-designers in a meaningful manner. Many of the benefits raised by this study are in line with past participatory research in general, including collaborating, empowerment, co-learning, reflexive, capacity building, and action [18, 27–29]. The co-design approach enables older people to develop digital solutions for themselves. Using the co-design methodology, older adults can create digital solutions on their own. The research team, the participants, and the findings all benefited from the active participation of older individuals.

Second, the project adds an intergenerational angle to the existing literature by involving university law students to work in pairs with older adults, providing a direct response to the WHO's call for combating ageism via intergeneration contact [30]. As this article demonstrated, law students used their legal knowledge and skills in research design and conduct, whereas older researchers were involved in recruiting target participants, establishing rapport with the participants, and contributing their lay knowledge, expertise, and personal experiences to data collection, analysis, and dissemination. Both older and younger co-designers were greatly encouraging each other's contributions under these cooperative conditions. Through positive interpersonal contact and the participatory nature of the research process, the method demonstrates the potential to reduce ageist attitudes and stereotypes for participants and academics.

Third, while the co-design approach offers advantages, it also presents relational and operational difficulties. For academic researchers, this method is time-consuming and labor-intensive because it takes a lot of work to establish equal relationships and competencies. For instance, finding a mutually convenient time to pair with older persons who might have other obligations and students who need to be in class requires more work. In practice, not every co-designer who is older is prepared to put in a lot of effort throughout the entire research process [14, 27]. Doyle and Timonen [31] argued that sharing knowledge rather than research tasks, through entire phases of the research is more appealing to older people. In this project, we focused on the adaptability of participation at various research stages based on ongoing discussions with co-designers. This adaptability entails matching people's skills and expectations to appropriate roles within a project [14, 27].

There are several suggestions made that might enhance the intergenerational co-design method. The process can be facilitated by ongoing discussions about how the research process will be governed and who will participate in which stages of the research. Different ages and statuses present an unavoidable power imbalance. The Confucian virtue of filial piety and hierarchical rank between generations are highly valued in Hong Kong's sociocultural setting, therefore normative power relationships based on age are regularly reported and equal group status in intergenerational programs is challenging to attain. This necessitates that academic scholars designate spaces for favorable group dynamics and a non-hierarchical structure for communications and reflections.

The study has a number of limitations. First, six questions in the online learning tool are not enough to address all of the misconceptions found in the qualitative interview. This tool can be further expanded based on the knowledge gaps and suboptimal choices made by participants. Second, older individuals who are not familiar with digital and online technology may not be able to use the online learning tool. Therefore, the materials have been disseminated to social workers in local community centers, the Elder Academy, and the Investment and Financial Education Council to urge them to incorporate them into offline educational activities including public lectures, seminars, and workshops. Third, additional research is needed to examine the tool's usability and user experience among older persons and to confirm its efficacy in boosting financial literacy.

Funding. This work was supported by the Humanity and Social Science Youth Foundation of the Ministry of Education of China (22YJC840004) and the Investor and Financial Education Council (RS190211).

References

1. Chen, X., et al.: The path to healthy ageing in China: a Peking university-lancet commission. Lancet **400**, 1967–2006 (2022)
2. Gamble, K.J., Boyle, P.A., Yu, L., Bennett, D.A.: Aging and financial decision making. Manage. Sci. **61**, 2603–2610 (2015)
3. DeLiema, M., Deevy, M., Lusardi, A., Mitchell, O.S.: Financial fraud among older Americans: evidence and implications. J. Gerontol. B Psychol. Sci. Soc. Sci. **75**, 861–868 (2020)
4. Kiso, H., Hershey, D.A.: Working adults' metacognitions regarding financial planning for retirement. Work Aging Retirement **3**(1), 77–88 (2017). https://doi.org/10.1093/workar/waw021
5. Fong, J.H., Koh, B.S.K., Mitchell, O.S., Rohwedder, S.: Financial literacy and financial decision-making at older ages. Pac. Basin Financ. J. **65**, 101481 (2021)
6. Cao, T.: Financial preparation and needs of older people. Asia Pac. Inst. Ageing Stud. Newsl. **6**, 18 (2015)
7. Lee, S.Y., Chou, K.L., Chan, W.S., van Kippersluis, H.: Consumer preferences and demand for annuities: evidence from Hong Kong. J. Aging Soc. Policy **31**, 170–188 (2019)
8. Chou, K.L., Chow, N.W.S., Chi, I.: Willingness to consider applying for reverse mortgage in Hong Kong Chinese middle-aged homeowners. Habitat Int. **30**, 716–727 (2006)
9. He, A.J., Qian, J., Chan, W.-S., Chou, K.-L.: Willingness to purchase hypothetical private long-term care insurance plans in a super-ageing society: evidence from Hong Kong. J. Aging Soc. Policy **35**, 1–26 (2023)
10. Ries, N.M., Johnston, B., McCarthy, S.: Legal education and the ageing population: building student knowledge and skills through experiential learning in collaboration with community organisations. Adel. L. Rev. **37**, 495–522 (2016)
11. Samsi, K., Manthorpe, J.: I live for today: a qualitative study investigating older people's attitudes to advance planning. Health Soc. Care Community **19**, 52–59 (2011)
12. Wood, S., Lichtenberg, P.A.: Financial capacity and financial exploitation of older adults: research findings, policy recommendations and clinical implications. Clin. Gerontol. **40**, 3–13 (2017)
13. Tilse, C., Setterlund, D., Wilson, J., Rosenman, L.: Minding the money: a growing responsibility for informal carers. Ageing Soc. **25**, 215–227 (2005)
14. Baldwin, J.N., Napier, S., Neville, S., Wright-St Clair, V.A.: Impacts of older people's patient and public involvement in health and social care research: a systematic review. Age Ageing **47**, 801–809 (2018)
15. Corrado, A.M., Benjamin-Thomas, T.E., McGrath, C., Hand, C., Laliberte Rudman, D.: Participatory action research with older adults: a critical interpretive synthesis. Gerontologist **60**, e413–e427 (2020)

16. Lushey, C.J., Munro, E.R.: Participatory peer research methodology: an effective method for obtaining young people's perspectives on transitions from care to adulthood? Qual. Soc. Work. **14**, 522–537 (2014)
17. Littlechild, R., Tanner, D., Hall, K.: Co-research with older people: perspectives on impact. Qual. Soc. Work. **14**, 18–35 (2015)
18. Buffel, T.: Older coresearchers exploring age-friendly communities: an insider perspective on the benefits and challenges of peer-research. Gerontologist **59**, 538–548 (2019)
19. Morrow-Howell, N., Lawlor, E.F., Macias, E.S., Swinford, E., Brandt, J.: Making the case for age-diverse universities. Gerontologist **60**, 1187–1193 (2020)
20. Pettigrew, T.F., Tropp, L.R., Wagner, U., Christ, O.: Recent advances in intergroup contact theory. Int. J. Intercult. Rel. **35**, 271–280 (2011)
21. Vrkljan, B., et al.: Creating an intergenerational university hub: engaging older and younger users in the shaping of space and place. Gerontol. Geriatr. Educ. **40**, 244–260 (2019)
22. Grigorovich, A., Kontos, P., Jenkins, A., Kirkland, S.: Moving toward the promise of participatory engagement of older adults in gerotechnology. Gerontologist **62**, 324–331 (2022)
23. Righi, V., Sayago, S., Blat, J.: When we talk about older people in HCI, who are we talking about? Towards a turn to community in the design of technologies for a growing ageing population. Int. J. Hum. Comput. Stud. **108**, 15–31 (2017)
24. Dickinson, C., Bamford, C., Exley, C., Emmett, C., Hughes, J., Robinson, L.: Planning for tomorrow whilst living for today: the views of people with dementia and their families on advance care planning. Int. Psychogeriatr. **25**, 2011–2021 (2013)
25. Hershey, D.A., Jacobs-Lawson, J.M., McArdle, J.J., Hamagami, F.: Psychological foundations of financial planning for retirement. J. Adult Dev. **14**, 26–36 (2008). https://doi.org/10.1007/s10804-007-9028-1
26. Ries, N.M.: Enduring powers of attorney and financial exploitation of older people: a conceptual analysis and strategies for prevention. J. Aging Soc. Policy **34**, 357–374 (2022)
27. Mey, E., van Hoven, B.: Managing expectations in participatory research involving older people: what's in it for whom? Int. J. Soc. Res. Methodol. **22**, 323–334 (2019)
28. Kong, T.S.K.: Gay and grey: participatory action research in Hong Kong. Qual. Res. **18**, 257–272 (2018)
29. Bombard, Y., et al.: Engaging patients to improve quality of care: a systematic review. Implement. Sci. **13**, 98 (2018). https://doi.org/10.1186/s13012-018-0784-z
30. World Health Organization: Global report on ageism. World Health Organization, Geneva (2021)
31. Doyle, M., Timonen, V.: Lessons from a community-based participatory research project: older people's and researchers' reflections. Res. Aging **32**, 244–263 (2010)

A Study on the Continuous Usage Factors of Perceived Ease of Use, Social Influence, and Performance Expectancy for Elderly People

Peicheng Guo[1], Pei-Luen Patrick Rau[1(✉)], Dian Yu[1], Yuan Gao[1], Ca Ryn Ng[1], Xuemeng Yu[2], Xiaolie Lin[2], and Kinoshita Masafumi[2]

[1] Department of Industrial Engineering, Tsinghua University, Beijing, China
rpl@mail.tsinghua.edu.cn

[2] Department of Digital Solution, Hitachi (China) Ltd., Beijing, China

Abstract. This research focused on the continuous usage of gerontechnology products by discussing the impact of three factors - perceived ease of use, social influence, and performance expectancy. Through experimental research, this article explored 1) what frequency of task splitting can enhance the continuous usage willingness; 2) what frequency of organizing participation in social activities can improve the continuous usage willingness; and 3) what frequency of organizing self-reevaluation can ensure effective usage willingness. Through experiments and data analysis of a 14-day health care knowledge learning for the elderly, we found that splitting the task of learning health care knowledge into completing the learning task every two days or more frequently, within 10–15 min each time, can ensure the user stickiness of the elderly and increase their willingness to continue using the product. Elderly people who participate in social activities more frequently and those who have a higher frequency of self-reevaluation are more willing to continue using the technology and recommend the product to others.

Keywords: Gerontechnology · Continuous usage · Perceived ease of use · Social impact · Performance expectation · Elderly people

1 Introduction

1.1 Continuous Usage of Gerontechnology Products

In recent years, with the increasing trend of aging population, the number of elderly people has been growing year on year. Ensuring their health and quality of life has become an urgent problem for the whole society to solve. At the same time, with the continuous advancement and application of technology, the development of the smart elderly care industry has brought about the flourishing rise of intelligent health products, providing new solutions for the health of the elderly. The inconvenient usage of gerontechnology products made it impossible for people to ignore the issue of continued use of these products. Merely having these technological products is not enough; we also need to think about how to ensure their continuous usage in order to achieve the maximum health benefits.

Q. Gao et al. (Eds.): HCII 2023, LNCS 14055, pp. 28–38, 2023.
https://doi.org/10.1007/978-3-031-48041-6_3

With the continuous development of technology, elderly people are gradually starting to become more exposed to technological products. To better understand the acceptance and usage behavior of elderly people, researchers have proposed a series of technology acceptance models. These models include the Theory of Reasoned Action (TRA), Technology Acceptance Model (TAM), Unified Theory of Acceptance and Use of Technology (UTAUT), and Senior Technology Acceptance Model (STAM).

The Theory of Reasoned Action (TRA), proposed in 1975 by Fishbein and Ajzen [1], stated that a person's behavior is driven by their intentions, which are determined by their attitudes and subjective norms towards the behavior. The Technology Acceptance Model (TAM), proposed by Davis in 1985 [2], is used to predict information technology acceptance and usage behavior. The model suggested that Perceived Usefulness (PU) and Perceived Ease Of Use (PEOU) are important attitude factors for information system acceptance and usage. The Unified Theory of Acceptance and Use of Technology (UTAUT) [3] is based on eight user acceptance models and has stronger predictive power. The model suggested that direct determinants of usage intention include performance expectancy, effort expectancy, and social influence. The model also pointed out that the direct determinants of user usage behavior include behavioral intention and facilitating conditions. The Senior Technology Acceptance Model (STAM), proposed in 2014 by Chen and Chan [4], is based on the above models and took into account the special needs, characteristics, abilities, and limitations of elderly people. The model suggested that elderly people's technology acceptance is closely related to cognitive and emotional factors.

Particularly, the continuous usage of technology by people is determined by their continuance intention and their habits [5]. Continuance intention is influenced by satisfaction with past experiences, which are shaped by cognitive and affective beliefs. Habit, which is also influenced by satisfaction, affects continuous usage behavior. Besides, the continuous usage can be evaluated from both the users' willingness to continue own usage of the product, as well as the intention to recommend the product to others [6].

Multiple factors influence the continuous usage behavior of technology products by elderly people, including cognitive and affective factors, gender, age, perceived ease of use, social influence, performance expectancy, and more. Among them, perceived ease of use, social influence, and performance expectancy have been widely mentioned in several technology acceptance models, including the Theory of Reasoned Action (TRA), the Technology Acceptance Model (TAM), the Unified Theory of Acceptance and Use of Technology (UTAUT), and the Senior Technology Acceptance Model (STAM). In addition, these three factors played different roles in the measuring of acceptance and continued use of technology products for older adults, covering different stages of product usage.

Research targeting these three factors can help to comprehensively understand the impact of different use stages of technology products among older adults and reveal the influence on their behavior of continuous usage. Therefore, this paper will focus on the discussion and research of perceived ease of use, social influence, and performance expectancy.

1.2 Perceived Ease of Use, Social Influence and Performance Expectancy

Perceived ease of use affects the user's experience and ease of operation when using the product. For elderly people, the simplicity and usability of interface design, interaction mode and operation process of technology products will have a huge impact on their experience. Social influence plays a key role during and after using the products. Older adults' technology use behaviors are continuously influenced by their social environment and others. Attitudes, support, and encouragement from family, friends, and social circles can positively influence older adults' technology product use, making them more willing to try and continue using them. Performance expectancy influences users' expectations before using a product. When deciding whether to use a certain technology product, users will have certain expectations about the performance, functions and effects of the product. This section will elaborate on each factor in detail.

Perceived ease of use refers to *"the degree to which a person believes that using a particular system would be free of effort"* [7]. It is strongly related to the difficulty and learnability of the product system. Whiteside's research summarized that ease of use and learnability are closely related and concluded that they are consistent [8]. Improving users' perceived learnability can reduce their anxiety towards using technology products, increase their acceptance, and improve the likelihood of continuous use. To improve users' perceived learnability, the total task load can be divided into short chapters to reduce the task difficulty that the user needs to complete each time, thus improving the product's ease of use and learnability. For example, for elderly users taking healthcare knowledge courses, the total learning task can be divided into short chapters to reduce the amount of information that the elderly need to comprehend each time, thereby reducing the difficulty of learning. This raises a new question: at what frequency should the chapters be learned to improve learnability while maintaining users' willingness to continue using the product? With a given number of tasks, the higher the learning frequency, the less content is learned each time and the easier it is to be understood. Conversely, when the learning frequency is low, the amount of content learned each time will increase, and the difficulty of learning will also increase. In this case, will elderly users' willingness to continue using the product be affected by the increased difficulty? This article will conduct experimental research on this issue.

Social influence refers to *"the degree to which an individual perceives that important others believe he or she should use the new system"* [3]. The UTAUT model pointed out that social influence is one of the key factors determining users' intention to use. Product systems can increase users' social influence when using the product through organizing community services and activities. For example, in learning healthcare knowledge, regular community activities can be organized during the learning process to promote a sense of belonging among elderly users, thereby increasing the stickiness of the product system services. However, there is still limited research on the frequency to organize social activities to improve the willingness of elderly users to continue using the product system.

Performance expectancy refers to *"the degree to which an individual believes that using a system will help him or her to attain gains in job performance"* [3]. It is a key factor in determining the acceptance and eventual use of a technology product, and can be seen as the expected benefits of using the product system. For example, in the context of learning about healthcare knowledge, performance expectancy can be defined as the extent to which elderly people believe that learning about healthcare knowledge will help them perform better in terms of their physical and mental health, as well as their diet. Improving performance expectancy can be achieved through self-reevaluation [9], which encourages users to compare their situation before and after using the product. The question arose as to how often self-reevaluation should be implemented during the learning process to ensure the continuous usage of the product.

In summary, this article conducted experimental research on the following objectives:

- Objective 1: To study what frequency should tasks be split at to better improve user's intention to continue using the technology.
- Objective 2: To investigate at what frequency organizing social activities can better enhance the intention to continue using the technology.
- Objective 3: To examine at what frequency organizing self-reevaluation can ensure effective intention to continue using the technology.

2 Methodology

2.1 Materials

In this study, we selected 24 one-minute health and wellness knowledge videos and two articles on the debunking of healthy food myths, with a total learning and reading time of about 80 min, in the context of China. The themes include pain relief therapy for neck, shoulder and back, Tai Chi therapy exercises, health education and anti-rumor promotion. The experimental content was divided into a 14-day health and wellness knowledge learning task according to the experimental group. During the experiment, the researchers distributed the above content to the participants through online WeChat groups at scheduled times based on the experimental grouping.

2.2 Study Design and Procedure

All participants were invited to participate in a 14-day online health and wellness knowledge learning and discussion, with a total learning time of approximately 80 min. The experimenters published the learning content in the online WeChat group according to the arranged learning content of each group. To ensure the effectiveness of learning, participants were required to go through the course content on the day it was published and had to complete a quiz after each learning session to verify their sufficient engagement. In addition, after the 14-day learning period, the experiment was concluded with a questionnaire survey to measure the participants' willingness to continue learning in the future.

Participants under the experimental theme on enhancing the learnability of skills through task decomposition were divided into three groups. As shown in Table 1, the frequency of tasks completion was divided into daily (D1), every two days (D2), and every week (D3), with each group's task completion time being 4–5 min, 10–15 min, and 26–39 min, respectively.

Participants under the experimental theme on testing the frequency of social influence were also divided into three groups. In addition to learning health and wellness knowledge every day, the three groups also participated in community discussions organized by the researchers every day (S1), every two days (S2), and every week (S3), respectively, including online discussions of experiences, sharing of experiences, and commenting, etc. Community discussions were conducted in the form of online small group discussions.

Participants under the experimental theme on measuring self-reevaluation were divided into two groups. On top of learning health and wellness knowledge every day, the two groups also conducted self-feedback evaluations every two days and every week, respectively. For the group that conducted self-reevaluation every two days (E1), each participant was asked to summarize and evaluate their own physical condition and learning outcomes after the first use and every two days after that. The researchers provided feedback on the comparison of each participant's answer score and the overall score. For the group that conducted self-reevaluation every week (E2), each participant was asked to conduct self-feedback evaluation after the first use and one week after use, and in the final week. The evaluation content was the same as that of group E1.

Table 1. Experiment groupings and respective tasks

Experimental Themes	Groups	Tasks
Perceived Ease of Use: Decomposing task difficulty	D1	Task completion every day, 4–5 min each time, 14 days to complete 80 min of total learning time
	D2	Task completion every two days, 10–15 min each time, 14 days to complete 80 min of total learning time
	D3	Task completion every week, 26–39 min each time, 14 days to complete 80 min of total learning time
Social Influence	S1	Organize community discussion every day
	S2	Organize community discussion every two days
	S3	Organize community discussion every week
Performance Expectancy: Self-reevaluation	E1	Self-reevaluation every two days
	E2	Self-reevaluation every week

2.3 Participants

As middle-aged people will soon enter old age, their behavior towards product use is also crucial, so we also included middle-aged people around 40 years old in our study. A total of 82 Chinese middle-aged and older adults (24 men, 58 women, mean age 55.98, SD = 10.48) were invited to participate in the online healthcare learning and discussion in the experiment. All participants were healthy without physical or mental disabilities, and had experience in using mobile phones. Before the start of the experiment, each participant signed an informed consent form.

2.4 Measures and Questionnaire Design

Participants were asked to fill out a questionnaire after the 14-day online health knowledge learning to measure their willingness to continue using similar products or services. The questionnaire was divided into two parts. The first part recorded background information such as the participant's name, age, and group. The second part measured their continued usage willingness. Participants were asked to rate the items on a 5-point Likert scale based on their participation experience and intentions during the experiment. The specific items are as follows:

If there is a future product or service that provides you with a series of tutorials on what you have experienced, how much do you agree with the following statements (Table 2):

Table 2. The questionnaire items

Number	Questionnaire Items
Q1	I predict that I will continue to use this product that provides tutorials in the future
Q2	I would recommend this product to my friends and family
Q3	I will continue to use this product for future exercise and share the experience with friends and family

3 Results

According to the reliability analysis results, the Cronbach's α coefficient was 0.881, which indicated a good internal consistency and scale reliability of all the questionnaire items. The mean scores of overall willingness to continue usage and each questionnaire item for each experimental group are shown in Table 3, and the statistical graph is shown in Fig. 1. The data collected from the questionnaire was analyzed using independent sample t-tests to compare the differences between the groups in each experimental theme. Table 4 shows the results of the data with significant differences. The overall willingness to continue using the product was compared by taking the average of the total scores of each questionnaire respondent. In addition, by comparing the differences between each group for each item, we found that there were significant differences in item Q2: "I would recommend this product to my friends and family" in some groups, while other individual items did not show significant differences and were therefore not shown in the table below.

During the 14-day healthcare knowledge learning process, we split the learning tasks into three groups of equal weightages, based on different learning frequencies (learning every day D1, learning every two days D2, and learning every week D3). According to the data, we found that the group with higher frequency of participation did not necessarily have a higher willingness to continue using the product. The group receiving learning content every two days (D2) had a higher overall intention to continue using the product,

Table 3. Mean score values for each question item of the continuous use questionnaire

Themes	Group	n	Overall willingness to continue usage		Q1		Q2		Q3	
			M	SD	M	SD	M	SD	M	SD
Perceived Ease of Use: Decomposing task difficulty	D1	12	4.56	0.50	4.58	0.51	4.58	0.69	4.50	0.52
	D2	12	4.72	0.42	4.75	0.45	4.67	0.49	4.75	0.45
	D3	11	4.12	1.01	4.27	0.90	3.81	1.08	4.27	1.19
Social Influence	S1	8	4.96	0.12	4.88	0.35	5.00	0.00	5.00	0.00
	S2	8	4.83	0.25	4.88	0.35	4.75	0.46	4.88	0.35
	S3	7	4.43	0.71	4.29	0.95	4.29	0.95	4.71	0.48
Performance Expectancy: Self-reevaluation	E1	12	4.89	0.22	4.83	0.39	4.92	0.29	4.92	0.29
	E2	12	4.61	0.62	4.83	0.39	4.42	0.90	4.58	0.67

Table 4. T-test results for comparisons between groups in each experimental theme

Groups		Overall willingness to continue usage		Q2: Willingness to recommend the product to family and friends	
		Sig.	t	Sig.	t
D1	D2	0.503	– 0.883	0.310	– 0.348
	D3	0.074	1.321	**0.040***	**2.065***
D2	D1	0.503	0.883	0.310	0.348
	D3	**0.036***	**1.885***	**0.003****	**2.463****
D3	D1	0.074	– 1.321	**0.040***	**– 2.065***
	D2	**0.036***	**– 1.885***	**0.003****	**– 2.463****
S1	S2	**0.021***	**1.271***	**0.000*****	**1.528*****
	S3	**0.000*****	**2.081*****	**0.000*****	**2.136*****
S2	S1	**0.021***	**– 1.271***	**0.000*****	**– 1.528*****
	S3	**0.000*****	**1.509*****	**0.013***	**1.229***
S3	S1	**0.000*****	**– 2.081*****	**0.000*****	**– 2.136*****
	S2	**0.000*****	**– 1.509*****	**0.013***	**– 1.229***
E1	E2	**0.019***	**1.472***	**0.006****	**1.832****

*: significant at $p < 0.05$, **: significant at $p < 0.01$, ***: significant at $p < 0.001$

as well as a higher average score for each question item in the questionnaire than the other two groups. Independent sample T-tests showed that the group receiving learning

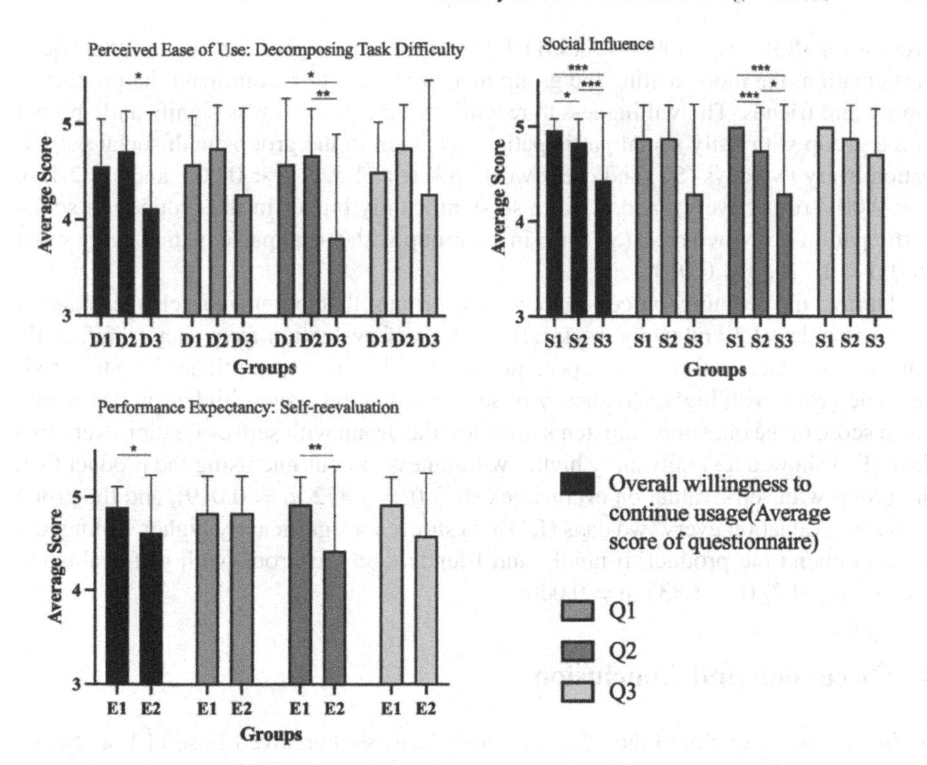

Fig. 1. Graphical representation of mean scores of the continuous use questionnaire based on experimental themes

content every two days (D2) had significantly higher overall willingness to continue using the product ($t = 1.885$, $p = 0.036$) compared to the group receiving learning content every week (D3), while there were no significant differences between the other groups ($p > 0.05$). In addition, the group receiving learning content every day (D1) had a significantly higher willingness to recommend the product to friends and family ($t = 2.065$, $p = 0.040$) compared to the group receiving learning content every week (D3). The group receiving learning content every two days (D2) had a significantly higher willingness to recommend the product to friends and family ($t = 2.463$, $p = 0.003$) compared to the group receiving learning content every week (D3).

During the learning process, among the groups that organized community discussions (every day S1, every two days S2, and every week S3), the higher the frequency of social participation, the higher the willingness to continue using the product. This was demonstrated by the fact that the group with higher frequency of social participation had a higher overall mean score on the questionnaire items. Besides, the overall willingness to continue using the product was significantly higher in the group with daily social participation (S1) than in the groups with social participation every two days (S2) and every week (S3) ($t = 1.271$, $p = 0.021$, and $t = 2.081$, $p < 0.001$, respectively). In addition, the overall willingness to continue using the product was significantly higher in the group with social participation every two days (S2) than in the group with social participation every week (S3) ($t = 1.509$, $p < 0.001$). Furthermore, the higher the frequency of social participation, the more willing the group members were to recommend the product to family and friends. The willingness to recommend the product was significantly higher in the group with daily social participation (S1) than in the groups with social participation every two days (S2) and every week (S3) ($t = 1.528$, $p < 0.001$, and $t = 2.136$, $p < 0.001$, respectively), and it was also significantly higher in the group with social participation every two days (S2) than in the group with social participation every week (S3) ($t = 1.229$, $p = 0.013$).

During the learning process, among the groups that organized self-reevaluation (every two days E1 and every week E2), higher self-evaluation frequency significantly improved product performance expectations and willingness to continue using the product. The group with higher frequency of self-reevaluation scored higher on the overall mean score of the questionnaire items. Besides, the group with self-evaluation every two days (E1) showed a significantly higher willingness to continue using the product than the group with self-evaluation every week (E2) ($t = 1.472$, $p = 0.019$), and the group with self-evaluation every two days (E1) also showed a significantly higher willingness to recommend the product to family and friends than the group with self-evaluation every week (E2) ($t = 1.832$, $p = 0.006$).

4 Discussion and Conclusion

In this study, we explored the effects of three factors - Perceived Ease of Use, Social Influence, and Performance Expectancy - on the intention to consistently use health care products or services related to learning health knowledge by comparing experimental groups with different learning frequencies split by total task volume, social engagement frequency, and self-reevaluation frequency, respectively. Through data analysis, we found that in the group that split the amount of tasks by time frequency, it was not the group that engaged in learning more frequently that had the higher intention of continued use among older users. From the average scores, the group that participated in learning every 2 days (D2) had higher scores than the other two groups. The possible reason for this is that the more frequent the learning, the less content is learned each time and the easier it is to understand. However, the frequency of learning and the time constraint of tightly scheduled courses caused the older users to have a lower intention to continue using the program, as evidenced by the fact that the D1 group, which learned every day, scored lower than the D2 group which learned every two days. On the other hand, the lower the frequency of learning, the more the content of each learning session increases, and the difficulty of each learning session also increases. In this case, older users' willingness to continue using the program will be affected by the increased difficulty. The data showed that the D3 group, which participated in learning every week, had the lowest average score for each item, and the group that completed every 2 days (D2) had a significantly higher overall willingness to continue using than the group that completed every other week (D3). In addition, users in the remaining two groups were also more willing to recommend the product to others than the group that completed it every other week (D3). Therefore, when designing a product for older adults, if considering splitting the amount of tasks to improve the ease of use, a balance between the frequency of engagement and the amount of tasks per session should be considered to ensure the users' willingness to continue using the product.

Additionally, for groups that included social influence factors in the learning process, members who had a higher social participation frequency had a higher willingness to continue using and recommending the product. In the groups that required participants to periodically complete self-reevaluation, members with a higher self-reevaluation frequency had a higher willingness to continue using and recommending the product.

Several conclusions can be drawn based on these findings. First, designers in charge of similar technology products or services, should pay close attention to the frequency of content distribution for middle-aged and elderly people with certain reading abilities, for them to be independently engaged in healthcare learning. The amount of task content that need to be completed by users can be split and released to users on a regular basis to improve the ease of learning. However, there is a need to balance the frequency of participation and the amount of task content in order to improve the product's ease of use and users' willingness to continue using it. According to the experimental results, an engagement frequency too high may cause users to feel overwhelmed with pressure, while extremely low engagement frequency may increase the difficulty of learning content, where both affect users' willingness to keep using the product. Therefore, designers should reasonably arrange the learning frequency and task volume according to the characteristics and needs of target users in order to provide a better experience and increase the willingness to use continuously. Secondly, the more socially involved group members showed higher willingness to continue using and recommending, therefore designers should focus on how to promote social participation, such as providing social features or creating community platforms to increase social engagement. Finally, for product performance expectancy, a higher frequency of self-reevaluation can significantly increase product performance expectations and continued use intention. Providing a mechanism for self-evaluation and feedback to elderly people can help them continuously adjust and improve their expectations of the product, thus enhancing continued use intention.

These findings have practical implications for designers of gerontechnology products, provided useful references and guidance. However, this study has some limitations. We only explored the impact of three variables on the willingness to continue using the product. Future research can consider exploring the impact of other variables such as product characteristics, gender, age, perceived usefulness, effort expectation, etc. In addition, we only explored the frequency of these three variables, while future research can explore more dimensions, such as form and content, to obtain more comprehensive and accurate conclusions.

References

1. Fishbein, M., Ajzen, I.: Belief, Attitude, Intention and Behavior: An Introduction to Theory and Research. J. Bus. Ventur. **5**, 177–189 (1975)
2. Davis, F.D.: A technology acceptance model for empirically testing new end-user in-formation systems : theory and results. Ph. D. Dissertation, Massachusetts Institute of Technology (1985)
3. Venkatesh, V., Morris, M.A., Davis, G.B., Davis, F.D.: User acceptance of information technology: toward a unified view. Manage. Inf. Syst. Q. **27**(3), 425 (2003). https://doi.org/10.2307/30036540

4. Chen, K., Chan, A.H.: Gerontechnology acceptance by elderly Hong Kong Chinese: a senior technology acceptance model (STAM). Ergonomics **57**(5), 635–652 (2014). https://doi.org/10.1080/00140139.2014.895855
5. Kim, Y., Zhang, P.: Continued use of technology: combining controlled and automatic processes. In: International Conference on Information Systems, pp. 214 (2010). http://aisel.aisnet.org/icis2010_submissions/214/
6. Farris, P.: Marketing Metrics: 50+ Metrics Every Executive Should Master. Wharton. Pearson Education, Incorporated (2006)
7. Davis, F.D.: Perceived usefulness, perceived ease of use, and user acceptance of information technology. MIS Q. **13**(3), 319 (1989). https://doi.org/10.2307/249008
8. Whiteside, J., Jones, S.C., Levy, P.S., Wixon, D.: User performance with command, menu, and iconic interfaces. SIGCHI Bulletin **16**(4), 185–191 (1985). https://doi.org/10.1145/1165385.317490
9. Prochaska, J.O., Redding, C.A., Evers, K.E.: The Transtheoretical Model and stages of change. In: Glanz, K., Rimer, B.K., Viswanath, K. (eds.) Health behavior: Theory, research, and practice, pp. 125–148. Jossey-Bass, San Francisco (2015)

Predicting and Understanding Care Levels of Elderly People with Machine Learning

A Random Forest Classifier Integrated with E-Health App and FHIR-Based Data Modeling

Naguib Heiba(✉), Yehya Mohamad, Carlos A. Velasco, Henrike Gappa, Thomas Berlage, and Sandra Geisler

Fraunhofer Institute for Applied Information Technology FIT Schloss Birlinghoven, Sankt Augustin, Germany
{naguib.heiba,yehya.mohamad,carlos.velasco.nunez,henrike.gappa, thomas.berlage,sandra.geisler}@fit.fraunhofer.de

Abstract. Home care is a particularly important service for elderly people who need assistance with their management of everyday life from both formal and informal caregivers. In Europe 80% of care is provided by family and friends. Therefore, strengthening the home care by informal caregivers is a crucial task and requires smart solutions to stabilize the current situation. INGE smart solution addresses the challenge of determining and predicting accurate and appropriate care levels for the growing population of elderly individuals in need of care. To be able to achieve this goal, information and structured data are needed to support the smart approach of service development effectively. The proposed approach in INGE utilizes assessment ratings from consultancy visits as features to train and test the developed machine learning model. The performance of the developed random forest-based machine learning model is evaluated using various metrics such as accuracy, precision, recall, F1-score, and confusion matrix and compared with real data collected during the INGE project using the INGE app. The proposed approach achieves an 80% accuracy rate in predicting the care level of care dependents based on category ratings. The used dataset for training the model consists of 454 consultancy visits. The trained model shows that ratings of category self-care have the highest impact on care dependent's care level sorting as it contributes by 27.1%. This study shows the potential of the INGE smart solution in optimizing both home care situation and care level classification.

Keywords: Human computer interaction · E-Health · Home care consultancy · Machine learning · HL7/FHIR

1 Introduction

The significance of home care services has been increasingly recognized, particularly in Europe, over the past few years, mainly driven by the ongoing demographic changes. Home care services provided for elderly in need of care are offered by formal caregivers,

Q. Gao et al. (Eds.): HCII 2023, LNCS 14055, pp. 39–54, 2023.
https://doi.org/10.1007/978-3-031-48041-6_4

and informal caregivers such as, family members, close friends, and trusted individuals within the social network of the care dependent [1]. As of the end of 2019, almost 5 million care dependents were counted in Germany only [5], and more than half of all people in need of long-term care are cared for by informal caregivers alone at their homes [4, 5]. The disappearance of this critical caregiving support would require building up to 30,000 new nursing homes and three million new nursing staff would have to be employed [9]. The escalating number of care dependents particularly in long-term care has greatly expanded the challenges faced by informal caregivers, involving physical, mental, and emotional stresses [6, 7]. Therefore, an in-home care consultancy visit was implemented in Germany, aiming to support the care dependent and their informal caregivers.

In Germany, care dependents are categorized into 5 different groups of care levels [12]. Each care level represents the stage of dependency of the care dependent when it comes to managing their everyday life. A care dependent's skills to live independently is assessed as well on a smaller scale during in-home care consultancy visits and reassessed in follow-up visits, which is usually scheduled every 6 months for care dependents in care levels 2 and 3, and every 3 months for care dependents in care level 4 and 5. These visits are obligatory for informal caregivers who receive care allowance, as stated in paragraph 37.3 SGB XI[1] of the German law. These visits primarily aim to support home care by providing advice, and suggesting services and aids that are financially covered by the statuary health insurance.

The consultancy visits are conducted in the care dependent's home and are carried out by a professional nurse typically employed at a mobile nursing service. However, the restricted visit time (ca. 35 min) puts high demands on the consulting nurses' knowledge about home care and suitable support measures which influence the service quality. Moreover, the lack of standardized documentation of the visit outcomes causes broad and inconsistent output. Therefore, the nationally funded research project INGE integrate4care[2] offers smart solution utilizes digitized approaches by providing an app for nurses to assess the home care situation, document the visit outcomes, and suggest procedures, services, and aids. For this purpose, it utilizes a comprehensive catalogue of over 200 predefined measures fully or partially financed by the German statutory health insurance. The app contains different assessment category items to be completed by the nurses during the in-home consultancy visit. Furthermore, the app provides rules and utilizes machine learning components [14] for generating early warnings in case a care dependent or their informal caregivers provide information indicating a decline in the home care situation. Additionally, by utilizing the recorded ratings of the category items stored in the INGE app, a machine learning model can predict the appropriate care level for the care dependent, compared to the ratings of the other care dependents stored in the associated database.

[1] https://www.gesetze-im-internet.de/sgb_11/__37.html.

[2] digitale INtegrierte GEsundheits- und Pflegeversorgung mit IT-gestütztem Pflegeberatungsbesuch nach §37.3 SGB XI/ Digital integrated health and home care with IT-supported in-home care consultancy in conformance to §37.3 social security statute book XI - https://www.gewi-institut.de/projekte/inge/.

2 Development of the INGE Application

For handling the constantly increasing need for care by elderly people, informal care plays a crucial role particularly when considering the escalating staff shortage of nursing professionals. However, informal caregivers, who are often elderly themselves, often have additional obligations such employment or childcare, increasing the likelihood of overburdening. This can result in health risks for the informal caregiver or an institutional placement of the care dependent. Therefore, informal caregivers need suitable help to maintain a home care setting that is satisfactory for both the informal caregivers and their care dependent relative also long-term.

To effectively support home care, an in-home care consultancy visit was implemented in Germany. These visits aim to assess the individual care situation and identify useful support measures (i.e., interventions) involving the care dependents and their informal caregivers. However, so far, no clear standards exist for this consultancy visit, so the quality depends heavily on the knowledge and experience of the nurse conducting the visit and the result of the assessment, i.e., the information gained about the home care situation, is not documented in a digitized way that can be accessed by other nurses when carrying out a follow-up visit. As a result, achieving continuous care planning and acquiring knowledge about the progression of home care situations, such as conducting a risk assessment for proactive measures to maintain a home care setting or potentially improve it through the utilization of machine learning algorithms, becomes significantly challenging.

To improve this situation, the INGE app was developed during the INGE project. The INGE app provides a tool for conducting a quality assured in-home care consultancy visit and document results to allow for analysis by machine learning. For this purpose, an assessment was developed with 44 items based on the NBA[3] [10] and the BICS-D[4] [13] which is a validated inventory that allows to investigate psychosocial impairments and the caregiver burden caused by caregiving. Items from both assessments were selected according to their relevance for home care. Response scales were taken over from the originals, being in most cases a 4 or 5-point Likert scale rating how independent a care dependent can achieve a certain task, e.g., groom themselves or carry out household activities. A detailed description of the assessment can be found in [2].

Unfortunately, the INGE app is so far only available in German. As it can be seen in the screenshot of the INGE-app in Fig. 1, all categories to be assessed are listed on the top level: "Kognition & Kommunikation/Cognition & Communication", "Mobilität/Mobility", "Selbstversorgung/Self-care" and "Verhalten/Behaviour". In addition to this the "Gesundheitsstatus/Health Status" of the care dependent with among others diagnoses, medication intake, wound care and how independently this can be managed by the care dependent is investigated and the "Angehörigenbelastung/Burden on Informal Caregivers". Nurses are expected to rate for instance the care dependent's skill level regarding a certain assessment item on the provided Likert scales. In case

[3] Neues Begutachtungsassessment zur Feststellung der Pflegebed¨urftigkeit/New Assessment Tool for determining dependency on care.

[4] Berliner Inventar zur Angehörigenbelastung-Demenz/Berlin Inventory of Caregiver Stress - Dementia.

a predefined cut-off value is achieved, e.g., nurses observed that the required skill is not fully available anymore only partially, three measures are presented to nurses that they may suggest to prevent worsening the situation. In Fig. 1, item "Erkennen von Risiken und Gefahren/recognizing risks and hazardous situations" the cut-off value was reached and, therefore, "Hausnotruf/ installing an emergency call service", "Ortungssystem (GPS Sender)/GPS tracking system" and/or "Herdsensor/ stove guard" is suggested by the INGE-app as possibly suitable measures to counteract consequences of this loss of skills. The preselected measures are taken from the Remedies and Aid Registry for Care in Germany which is a catalogue with over 200 measures recommended for home care and will be financially supported by the statuary health insurances. The registry includes aids such as walkers, sensor technologies like stove guards, and services to manage everyday life better in home care like housekeeping or day care. The preselection of measures was achieved by nurses in the INGE project who are highly experienced with home care. It is always the decision of the consulting nurses though, whether they want to propose a measure at all, any of the preselected measures or another one. During the project, the machine learning component constantly analyzed item ratings and decisions of nurses and the result was used for discussion with the nurses in the project to update preselected measures according to their recommendations [9].

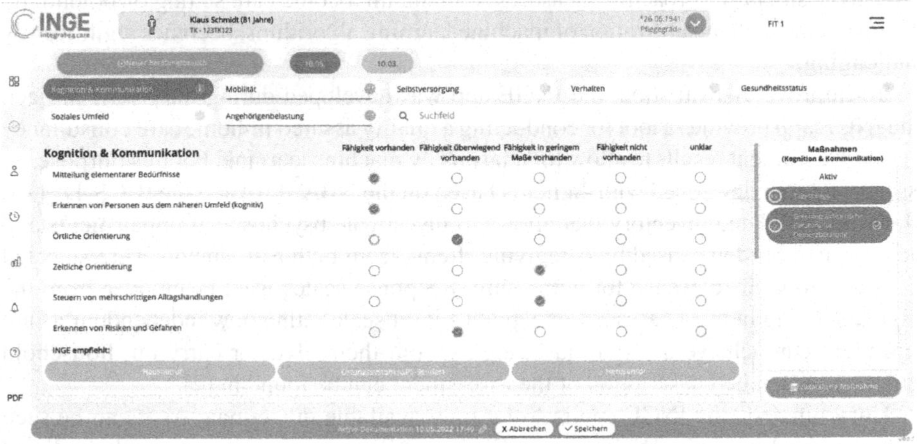

Fig. 1. Screenshot of cognition and communication category assessment items in the INGE app.

As displayed in Fig. 1, a red circle surrounds a rating to indicate the rating of the previous consulting visit, so nurses are aware of what was the status until the ongoing visit and whether a deterioration in care dependents' skills or the burden on informal caregivers happened. For instance, item "Örtliche Orientierung/orientation in regard to location" in Fig. 1 was rated in the previous visit with rating "Fähigkeit vorhanden/capability present" while in the ongoing visit the rating has changed to "Fähigkeit überwiegend vohanden/Capability predominantly present" which means the situation of the care dependent has worsened since the last visit.

3 INGE Data Model Using FHIR Resources

The INGE data model (see Fig. 2) conforms to the HL7 FHIR[5] resources [11] and guidelines, where all objects are defined based on user requirements. Within this data model, information regarding care dependents is stored in the *Patient* resource, and each care dependent is associated with a particular nursing center, which is stored in the *Organization* resource. The nurses conducting the home care consultancy visits are stored within the Practitioner resource and linked to the corresponding *Organization* through the *PractitionerRole* resource. The predefined catalog of aids and services in the INGE app, developed by experts, is stored in the Measure resource, and does not have a direct association with a specific care dependent. When a nurse suggests a measure to a care dependent, the suggestion is then stored in Procedure resource and references both the Measure and the *Patient*. The interaction between the care dependent and nurses during the visit is stored in Encounter resource, which is primarily used to record details and information about the actual activities that occurred. The care level of each care dependent is stored in the Observation resource. With each new visit, a new object is created in the Observation resource to record the current actual care level of the care dependent. The PlanDefinition resource consists of a group of pre-defined actions. These actions are stored in the Action resource, and each object in the Action resource includes a reference for a Questionnaire object [2]. Finally, a ServiceRequest resource is used to record requests for services by referencing objects from *Patient* resource and from PlanDefinition resource with the state of the request such as active, on-hold, revoked, etc.

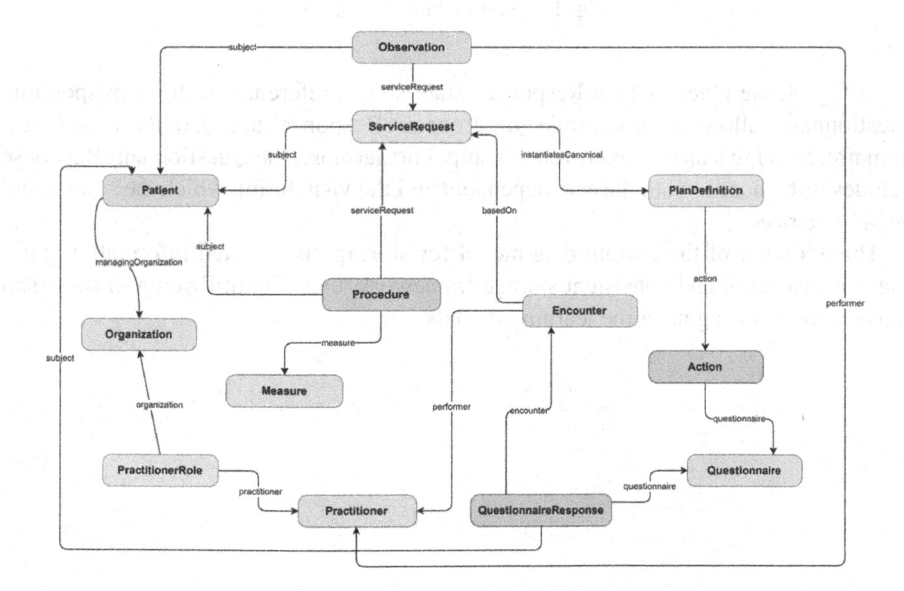

Fig. 2. INGE data model based on FHIR resources.

[5] Fast Healthcare Interoperability Resources.

Figure 3 shows two items from the "Cognition and communication" questionnaire [12], which is stored in FHIR Questionnaire resource. Each item includes a "LinkId" parameter which is used when storing the associated rating of the item in the QuestionnaireResponse resource. The rating for each item is stored as a valueCoding which is usually a number between 0 and 3 or 4, depending on the assessment item.

```
{
  "resourceType": "Questionnaire",
  "id": "7223",
  "title": "Cognition & communication",
  "subjectType": [
    "Patient"
  ],
  "item": [
    {
      "linkId": "KK1",
      "text": "Communication of basic needs",
      "type": "choice",
      "answerValueSet": "http://inge.smart-q.de/ValueSet/value-set-
kk"
    }
    ],
      "linkId": "KK2",
      "text": "Recognising people from the immediate environment",
      "type": "choice",
      "answerValueSet": "http://inge.smart-q.de/ValueSet/value-set-
kk"
    }
  ]
}
```

Fig. 3. Questionnaire instance

In Fig. 4, the QuestionnaireResponse establishes a reference to the corresponding Questionnaire, allowing for multiple QuestionnaireResponses to link to the same Questionnaire, forming a one-to-many relationship. Furthermore, the QuestionnaireResponse includes references to both the care dependent and the visit during which the assessment items were rated.

The adoption of the current data model for storing visit-related information guarantees a structured and consistent storage framework, enabling utilization in statistical analysis and building machine learning models.

```
{
  "resourceType": "QuestionnaireResponse",
  "id": "7426",
  "partOf": [
    {
      "reference": "Encounter/7419",
      "type": "Encounter"
    }
  ],
  "questionnaire": "https://inge-database-url/Questionnaire/7223",
  "subject": {
    "reference": "Patient/3665",
    "type": "Patient"
  },
  "item": [
    {
      "linkId": "KK1",
      "text": "Communication of basic needs",
      "answer": [
        {
          "valueCoding": {
            "code": "3"
          }
        }
      ]
    },
    {
      "linkId": "KK2",
      "text": "Recognising people from the immediate environment",
      "answer": [
        {
          "valueCoding": {
            "code": "2"
          }
        }
      ]
    }
  ]
}
```


Fig. 4. QuestionnaireResponse instance

4 Data Preparation and Preprocessing

Data preparation and preprocessing pipeline involves several essential steps to transform raw data, stored in FHIR resources, into structured and informative tables. These steps include handling missing values [15], extracting relevant features [16], and combining data from different resources into unified tables. Additionally, calculating category ratings based in assessment item ratings and scaling all category ratings to ensure the validity for training and testing in machine learning algorithms.

To enhance the scaling process [17] and facilitate their utilization in machine learning models, all category ratings derived from all care levels are transformed into percentage values. The assessment categories consist of different number of items, each utilizing a Likert scale with values ranging from 0 to 3 or 4, depending on the specific item. The higher the ratings on these items, the poorer the state of the care dependent regarding that assessment item.

4.1 Data Retrieval from FHIR Repository

The initial step in data preparation and preprocessing is retrieving the required resources data from the FHIR repository. The key resources required include *Patient*, Encounter, Observation, *Organization*, Questionnaire, QuestionnaireResponse, Measure, and Procedure. There are various methods and tools available for fetching and retrieving the required data from the FHIR repository. Some of these methods are: FHIR GraphQL API[6], fhircrackr[7], Bunsen[8], and FhirExtinguisher[9]. Throughout the INGE project, different methods and tools were tested and FhirExtinguisher was chosen due to its user-friendly nature. FhirExtinguisher requires Java 8[10] and a modern browser to interact with the tool's graphical user interface. After successfully fetching the required resources, the tool offers the option to save the retrieved data in CSV (Comma-Separated Values) file format for local download and further analysis.

The subsequent step after downloading the required CSV files, involves data preprocessing, which is executed in Python[11] using various libraries within Jupyter Notebook[12]. This stage incorporates several techniques to enhance data quality, including addressing missing values, performing grouping and combination operations, and managing categorical variables. Specifically, categorical variables, such as "yes" or "no" responses from QuestionnaireResponse items, are converted into numerical representations using label encoding. Additionally, diverse methodologies are applied to handle text, numeric, and temporal data. Furthermore, average ratings for each category are calculated, and these ratings are appropriately scaled. Through the data preprocessing phase, valuable insights regarding significant numerical values and figures are obtained. For instance, the distribution of care dependents across different care levels, the number of visits conducted for each care level (as displayed in Table 1), and the average ratings for each category across all care levels can be examined.

Table 1. Care dependents distribution over all care levels.

Care level	Number of care dependents	Number of total visits
1	5	5
2	209	346
3	71	106
4	53	116
5	12	34

[6] https://hl7.org/fhir/graphql.html.
[7] https://cran.r-project.org/web/packages/fhircrackr/index.html.
[8] https://engineering.cerner.com/bunsen/0.5.10-SNAPSHOT/.
[9] https://github.com/JohannesOehm/FhirExtinguisher.
[10] https://www.java.com/en/.
[11] https://www.python.org/.
[12] https://jupyter.org/.

As previously mentioned, each assessment category contains a varying number of items, with each item utilizing a Likert scale ranging from 0 to 3 or 4, depending on its specific nature. To mitigate the impact of this variation, the decision was made to calculate the overall rating for each assessment category as a percentage. The outcomes of these calculations are visually represented in Fig. 5. Deliberately, the assessment category ratings for care dependents in care level 1 were excluded from the analysis due to an insufficient number of care dependents and consultancy visits within this care level.

Within Fig. 5, the assessment category "Social Environments" (SU) demonstrates the highest ratings for care levels 2, 3, and 4, indicating that care dependents in these levels encounter significant challenges when interacting with both familiar and unfamiliar individuals. Additionally, they face difficulties in managing social events within their environment, such as household tasks and maintaining daily activities. The "Self-care" assessment category follows closely, positioning the second-highest ratings in care levels 2, 3, and 4, while presenting it as the category with the most asserted issues for care dependents in care level 5. The "Self-care" category involves various aspects, including a care dependent's ability to maintain personal hygiene, independently utilize bathroom facilities, manage the consequences of incontinence, dress/undress, and eat and drink independently [9].

Except for care level 2, which has the lowest ratings in the "Cognition and Communication" assessment category, the "Behavior" category records the lowest ratings across the other three care levels.

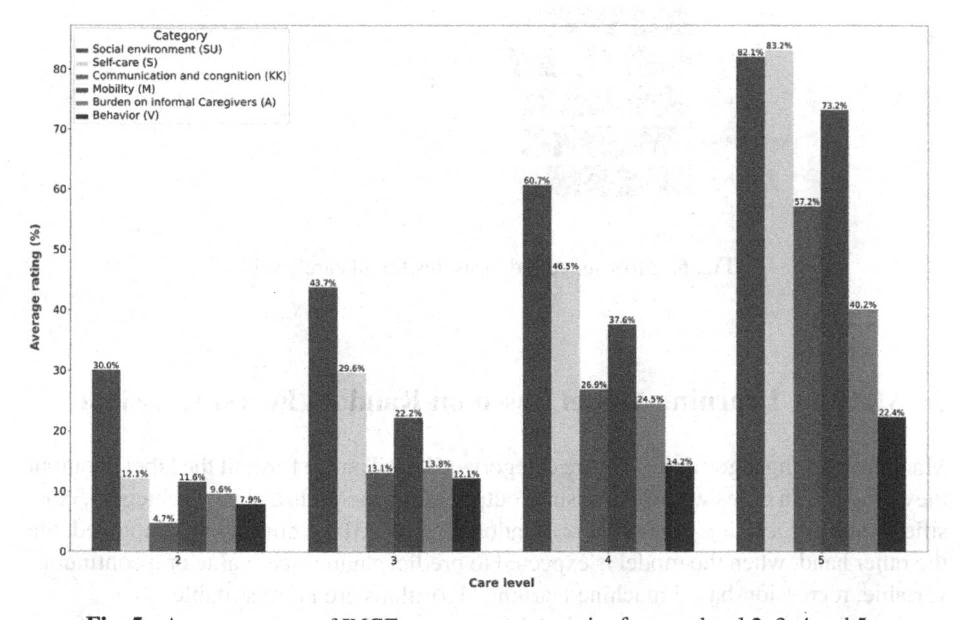

Fig. 5. Average scores of INGE assessment categories for care level 2, 3, 4 and 5.

Additionally, the data preprocessing stage also reveals the ranking of the suggested measures. As previously mentioned, the INGE app incorporates a comprehensive catalogue of preselected measures, comprising more than 200 services and aids carefully added by domain experts based on previous consultancy visits for care dependents across all care levels.

During these visits, nurses have the right to decide either proposing one or multiple measures from the catalogue, or alternatively, suggesting alternative options.

Figure 6 provides an overview of the top 10 most frequently suggested measures across all care levels. The analysis highlights that "Assistance services: assistance with housekeeping" appears as the most frequently recommended measure, with a total count of 102 occurrences. This measure involves providing support for the care dependents and their informal caregivers in performing household tasks such as cleaning, meal preparation, simple maintenance tasks, etc. However, some of these suggested measures may be rejected either by the care dependent and their informal caregiver or by the payer, indicating the need for further consultation and status evaluation.

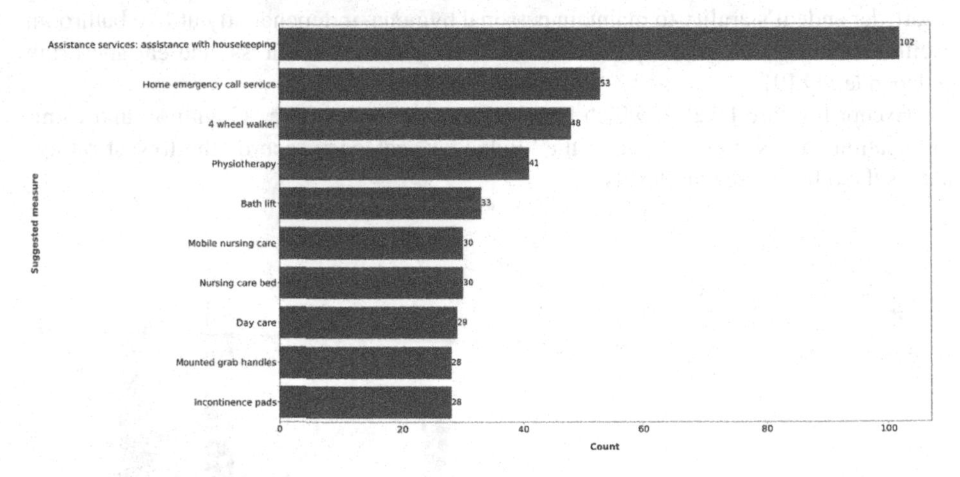

Fig. 6. Most suggested measures for all care levels

5 Machine Learning Model Based on Random Forest Classifier

Machine learning algorithms [18] are categorized based on the form of the label or output they produce. In cases where the desired output of the model is a class or category, classifiers such as Decision Trees [23] or Random Forests [3] are commonly employed. On the other hand, when the model is expected to predict a numerical value or a continuous variable, regression-based machine learning algorithms are more suitable.

To train and test a model to predict the care level of a care dependent, a classifier is to be chosen as the appropriate machine learning algorithm for this task. The engineered features [19] used were the category percentage ratings. These scores were found to have the most significant impact on determining the care level for each care dependent.

Care dependents with missing category scores were excluded from the model building process. Only care dependents with complete information, comprising all six category percentage ratings, were included in the training and testing datasets. This approach ensured that the model was trained and evaluated using a consistent set of data points, enabling reliable predictions based on the available information for each care dependent.

5.1 Methodology of the INGE Model

To improve the performance and interpretability of the INGE model, additional mechanisms and components have been incorporated. The two essential components were feature importance analysis [20] and hyperparameter tuning [21].

Feature importance analysis is utilized during the model training process to identify the most effective features in predicting the care level. By determining the relative importance of each feature, patterns among the category ratings can be identified.

Hyperparameter tuning promotes diversity within the Random Forest algorithm. Random Forest algorithm consists of ensemble of decision trees. Each decision tree can be advanced to utilize different subsets of features and instances, therefore, reducing the possibility of biased results which in return optimize the model's predictions.

In order to apply the two mentioned mechanisms efficiently, a GridSearchCV[13] technique was applied, considering different hyperparameters added altogether in a parameter grid. The parameter grid hyperparameters can be described as follows:

- n_estimators: This parameter determines the number of decision trees within the ensemble. The values added to this parameter to be explored for the optimum prediction accuracy were 64, 100, 128, and 200.
- max_features: the maximum features parameter represents the maximum number of features considered for each data split during the implementation of each decision tree. The values investigated were between 2 to 6. The goal of testing different number of features is to obtain the widest range of feature interactions.
- bootstrap: The bootstrap parameter defines whether bootstrap samples[14] should be used to train individual decision trees or not. The only options in this parameter are True or False. Both values were evaluated and used for examining the impact of bootstrap sampling on the overall INGE model performance.
- oob_score: The out-of-bag (OOB) score estimates the model's performance using the samples that were not included in the bootstrap samples.

The applied GridSeachCV technique on the model created by the Random Forest classifier using the provided parameter grid identified the best parameters to use for training the INGE model (see Table 2).

[13] Exhaustive search over specified parameter values for an estimator.

[14] Randomly selecting rows from the dataset allows the selection of some samples multiple times, while excluding some of the samples unselected.

Table 2. INGE Model hyperparameters values

Hyperparameter	Best value
bootstrap	False
max_features	2
n_estimators	128
oob_score	False

5.2 INGE Machine Learning Model Results

The INGE machine learning model has demonstrated promising outcomes, as proven by the generated classification report and feature importance ranking. These evaluation metrics provide insights into the model's performance and the significance of the input features in determining the care level of each care dependent.

Classification Report

The classification report (see Table 3) offers a comprehensive summary of the model's performance by providing key metrics such as precision, recall, F1-score, and support for each care level. These metrics assess the model's ability to accurately classify care dependents into their respective care levels. The different metrics can be described as follows:

- Precision: precision refers to a measure of how many correctly predicted care levels for care dependents by the model are actually correct. It represents the percentage of true positives (correctly identified care levels) among all care levels predicted as positive. Precision is computed individually for each care level.
- Recall: recall represents the sensitivity or true positive rate. It quantifies the ability of the INGE model to accurately identify care dependents and assign them to their appropriate care levels. Specifically, recall measures the proportion of actual positive care dependents that are correctly classified into their respective care levels. The calculation of recall is performed individually for each care level, providing insights into the model's capability to predict the correct care level for each care dependent. It reflects the model's effectiveness in correctly identifying care dependents and assigning them to their appropriate care levels. The higher the recall value is, the more successful the model is when making predictions. The main difference between precision and recall is precision focuses on the accuracy of positive predictions and minimizing false positives, while recall focuses on the ability to capture all positive instances and minimize false negatives.
- F1-Score: f1-score is a metric that combines precision and recall into a single value to provide an overall measure of a model's performance. It is the harmonic mean of precision and recall. A higher F1-score indicates better overall performance in achieving a balance between precision and recall.
- Support: support refers to the number of care dependents belonging to each care level in the test dataset. It gives insights in case of imbalances inside the dataset.

- Accuracy: accuracy is the overall percentage of correct predictions made by the model. This serves as an indicator of the overall performance of the model. The INGE model has successfully been capable of predicting the care level of a care dependent with accuracy of 80% based on the six category ratings.
- Macro avg: macro average calculates the average of precision, recall, and F1-score across all care levels. It deals with each care level equally, regardless of the number of care dependent in each of the care levels.
- Weighted avg: while weighted average is like the Macro average, it considers the support values (or number of care dependents in each care level) when calculating the average of precision, recall, and f1-score.

Table 3. INGE model classification report

	precision	Recall	F1-score	support
1	0.00	0.00	0.00	2
2	0.84	0.89	0.87	40
3	0.75	0.69	0.72	17
4	0.61	0.61	0.61	26
5	1.00	0.80	0.89	6
Accuracy			0.80	91
Macro avg	0.64	0.60	0.62	91
Weighted avg	0.78	0.80	0.79	91

Due to the lack of sufficient visit numbers for care level 1, precision, recall, and f1-score are being set to 0.0.

Feature Importance

The inclusion of six different categories as features in the development of the INGE machine learning model has played a significant role in predicting the appropriate care level for individual care dependents. Among these categories, the "Self-Care" category has demonstrated the highest contribution of 27.1% in assigning care levels (as shown in Table 4), which aligns with findings from the German Medical Service of Health Insurance (Medizinischer Dienst)[15] indicating the importance of the "Self-Care" category in care level assignments. According to the feature importance report of the INGE model, the "Mobility" category holds the second highest importance, contributing 20.9%. Additionally, the "Cognition and Communication" category ranks lowest in terms of importance, contributing 11.9% in assigning care levels.

[15] https://www.md-nordrhein.de/fileadmin/MD-zentraler-Ordner/Downloads/01_Pflegebegutachtung/230123_Pflegeflyer_ENG_01_BF.pdf.

Table 4. INGE model Feature Importance based on contribution in care level selection.

Rank	Category	Contribution
1	Self-Care	27.1%
2	Mobility	20.9%
3	Social Environment	14.7%
4	Burden on Informal Care Givers	12.8%
5	Behavior	12.4%
6	Cognition and Communication	11.9%

5.3 Limitations, Challenges, and Potential Enhancements

While the model has shown promising results, it is essential to acknowledge the impediments and constraints and identify areas for further improvements.

One of the primary challenges encountered during developing the INGE model was the limited number of visits and the quality of the recorded ratings. The accuracy of the predictions relies on the data quality and representation. However, only 454 visits with complete ratings were available for developing the model. The relatively low number of available visits may have affected the performance and the accuracy of the model. To improve the performance of the model, it is essential to record more high-quality data for training and testing purposes.

Another challenge faced was the class imbalance [22] in the dataset, which refers to the inconsistent distribution of care dependents over care level. Such imbalance can result in biased predictions and affect the overall accuracy of the model. Although techniques such as oversampling and under-sampling were tested, they did not significantly improve the model's accuracy. Among the considered algorithms, Random Forest presented the highest potential.

Furthermore, the validation of the model performance requires new, unseen data. Therefore, it is important to continue recording high-quality data, including category ratings, during home care consultancy visits to optimize the created model and enhance the overall performance and accuracy. While adding more features does not necessarily guarantee improved accuracy and performance, careful selection and engineering of relevant features when predicting the care level can lead to improved accuracy without overfitting the model.

6 Conclusion

Home care by informal caregivers necessitates more effort to decrease the burden and challenges faced by both care dependents and their families. The consistent and structured documentation for each consultancy visits or advisory service is crucial to improve the quality of predictions when utilizing machine learning components or building rule-based systems. Utilizing HL7 FHIR resources for implementing the INGE data model has facilitated consistency and smoothed the process of data preparation and preprocessing. The clear structure and robust interoperability offered by HL7 FHIR resources have proven helpful in ensuring the reliability and efficiency of data handling [8].

A crucial component of the INGE smart solution for supporting home care effectively is the utilization of machine learning, specifically through the analysis of assessment item ratings. The INGE machine learning model has demonstrated promising results in predicting care levels for care dependents. However, the limitations arise from the lack of recorded visits, particularly for care dependents in care level 1. Addressing this issue by increasing the number of recorded visits would improve the accuracy and reliability of care level predictions.

While the INGE app was initially designed to address in-home care consultancy visits in Germany, it can be efficiently adapted to meet the healthcare requirements of other EU-countries. Through standardized assessment category items and following a standardized data model similar to the employed data model in INGE, a broader range of consistent data can be stored, facilitating further technological analysis and the development of additional machine learning components.

The Random Forest based machine learning model developed within the INGE project has shown 80% accuracy in care level predictions based on 454 consultancy visits, utilizing assessment category ratings as features. As the number of high-quality recorded visits increases, the accuracy and overall performance of care level predictions for care dependents in INGE model will improve. Moreover, it will enable the detection of patterns based on assessment item ratings and their specific combinations, highlighting how these patterns affect the care dependents' ability to manage their daily lives efficiently.

References

1. European commission: communication on the European care strategy (2022). https://www.epsu.org/sites/default/files/event/files/9%20Sept_European%20care%20strategy_EASPD%20webinar.pdf. Accessed 22 June 2023
2. Mohamed, Y., et al.: How to overcome lack of health record data and privacy obstacles in initial phases of medical data analysis projects. Comput. Inform. **41**(1), 233–252 (2022). https://doi.org/10.31577/cai_2022_1_233
3. Breiman, L.: Random forests. Mach. Learn. **45**, 5–32 (2001). https://doi.org/10.1023/A:1010933404324
4. Statistische bundesamt: long-term care (2023). https://www.destatis.de/EN/Themes/Society-Environment/Health/Long-Term-Care/_node.html. Accessed 22 June 2023
5. Statistische bundesamt: people in need of long-term care (2019). https://www.destatis.de/EN/Themes/Society-Environment/Health/Long-Term-Care/Tables/people-long-term-care.html#fussnote-1-50564. Accessed 22 June 2023
6. Thomas, P., et al.: Complaints of informal caregivers providing home care for dementia patients: the Pixel study. Int. J. Geriatr. Psychiatry **17**(11), 1034–1047 (2002). https://doi.org/10.1002/gps.746
7. Plöthner, M., et al.: Needs and preferences of informal caregivers regarding outpatient care for the elderly: a systematic literature review. BMC Geriatr. **19**(1), 82 (2019). https://doi.org/10.1186/s12877-019-1068-4

8. Saripalle, R., Runyan, C., Russell, M.: Using HL7 FHIR to achieve interoperability in patient health record. J. Biomed. Inform. **94**, 103188 (2019). https://doi.org/10.1016/j.jbi.2019.103188
9. Gappa, H., et al.: A step forward in supporting home care more effectively. In: DSAI 2022: Proceedings of the 10th International Conference on Software Development and Technologies for Enhancing Accessibility and Fighting Info-exclusion, pp. 31–36 (2022). https://doi.org/10.1145/3563137.3563159
10. Wingenfeld, K., Büscher, A., Gansweid, B.: Das neue begutachtungsassessment zur feststellung von pflegebedürftigkeit. Abschlussbericht zur Hauptphase **1**, 1–128 (2008)
11. HL7. (n.d.). HL7 FHIR: fast healthcare interoperability resources. http://hl7.org/fhir/. Accessed 22 June 2023
12. Schwinger, A., Tsiasioti, C.: Pflegebedürftigkeit in Deutschland. In: Jacobs, K., Kuhlmey, A., Greß, S., Klauber, J., Schwinger, A. (eds.) Pflege-Report 2018, pp. 173–204. Springer, Heidelberg (2018). https://doi.org/10.1007/978-3-662-56822-4_16
13. Schlomann, A., et al.: Berlin inventory of caregiver stress - dementia (BICS-D). Gerontologist **61**(5), 173–184 (2021)
14. Dong, X.L., Rekatsinas, T.: Data Integration and machine learning. In: Proceedings of the 2018 International Conference on Management of Data, pp.1645–1650 (2018). https://doi.org/10.1145/3183713.3197387
15. Heymans, M.W., Twisk, J.W.R.: Handling missing data in clinical research. J. Clin. Epidemiol. **151**, 185–188 (2022)
16. Verdonck, T., Baesens, B., Óskarsdóttir, M., vanden Broucke, S.: Special issue on feature engineering editorial. Mach. Learn. (2021).https://doi.org/10.1007/s10994-021-06042-2
17. Ahsan, M., Mahmud, M., Saha, P., Gupta, K., Siddique, Z.: Effect of data scaling methods on machine learning algorithms and model performance. Technologies **9**, 52 (2021). https://doi.org/10.3390/technologies9030052
18. Ray, S.: A quick review of machine learning algorithms. In: 2019 International Conference on Machine Learning, Big Data, Cloud and Parallel Computing (COMITCon), pp. 35–39 (2019). https://doi.org/10.1109/COMITCon.2019.8862451
19. Xu, Y., Hong, K., Tsujii, J., Chang, E.I.-C.: Feature engineering combined with machine learning and rule-based methods for structured information extraction from narrative clinical discharge summaries. J. Am. Med. Inform. Assoc. **19**, 824–832 (2012). https://doi.org/10.1136/amiajnl-2011-000776
20. Rogers, J., Gunn, S.: Identifying feature relevance using a random forest. In: Saunders, C., Grobelnik, M., Gunn, S., Shawe-Taylor, J. (eds.) SLSFS 2005. LNCS, vol. 3940, pp. 173–184. Springer, Heidelberg (2006). https://doi.org/10.1007/11752790_12
21. Regis, R.G.: Hyperparameter tuning of random forests using radial basis function models. In: Nicosia, G., et al. Machine Learning, Optimization, and Data Science. LOD 2022. LNCS, vol. 13810, pp. 309–324 .Springer, Cham (2023). https://doi.org/10.1007/978-3-031-25599-1_23
22. Krawczyk, B.: Learning from imbalanced data: open challenges and future directions. Prog. Artif. Intell. **5**(4), 221–232 (2016). https://doi.org/10.1007/s13748-016-0094-0
23. Myles, A.J., Feudale, R.N., Liu, Y., Woody, N.A., Brown, S.D.: An introduction to decision tree modeling. J. Chemom.Chemom. **18**, 275–285 (2004). https://doi.org/10.1002/cem.873

The Effect of Fashion Model Walking Program Using Kinect on the Movement Activity of the Elderly

SungHee Hong[1,2](✉), SunHee Park[2], and SunOk Jung[2]

[1] Human Movement Technology Lab, 102-Dong, 903-Ho, World Meridian Apt, 74 Olympic-Ro, Songpa-Gu, Seoul, South Korea
hongsungh22@hanmail.net

[2] Dongduk Women's University, Performing Arts Center, Road Name Address: 126 Dongsung-Gil, Jongno-Gu, Seoul, South Korea

Abstract. The purpose of this study is to implement a walking program for the elderly by applying fashion model walking using Kinect. The skeleton through the avatar of the model walking that appears on the screen is given as feedback to the participant. The given information is implemented using Kinect, and the game proceeds with accurate gait balance control and the angle of the spine, which is the center of the body, in the walking program according to the body balance. Joint Value Using Unity 3D's human pose library, Kinect modeling where 21 values out of a total of 95 joint values are presented. It is a game-type program in which the score of the spine angle and joint value is also lowered if the center of gravity of the body is not accurately displayed in the gait motion. Walking (right, left), turn (half, full turn, right, left respectively), pose (right center pose, left center pose) motion animations were filmed in real time. The walking motion appeared at normal speed only up to the step divided into two steps. When working with turns, full turns tended to be much more difficult than half turns. However, as the number of exercises increased, the degree of agreement between the angle of the spinal axis and the angle of the joints improved. In other words, the higher score that appears through the game format improves the control of walking balance and body balance, and the lower the accuracy of the body balance, the lower the score. This research program can be used as rehabilitation exercise for people with developmental disabilities, elderly people with dementia, and patients with Alzheimer's disease.

Keywords: Fashion model walking · Elderly movement activity · Azure Kinect Introduction

1 Introduction

Currently, the problem of the elderly due to aging is being solved by developing and implementing national care programs not only in Korea but also in major countries abroad [1]. Interventions to solve problems of physical function and cognitive function of the

Q. Gao et al. (Eds.): HCII 2023, LNCS 14055, pp. 55–67, 2023.
https://doi.org/10.1007/978-3-031-48041-6_5

elderly using Information & Communication Technology (ICT) are being studied. ICT, a compound word of Information Technology (IT) and Communication Technology (CT), collects, produces, processes, and preserves information by using the hardware of information devices and the software technology necessary for the operation, management, delivery, and management [2]. These ICTs are key to constructing stability for managing and accessing the health of older adults during activities of daily living [3]. Given that ICT provides cognitive and challenging activities [4], that is, the innovativeness and high prevalence of ICT-based interventions are thought to be a new way to solve the daily life problems and depression of the elderly due to aging. Therefore, it is important to apply ICT-based interventions to the elderly and study their effects before entering a super-aged society. Likewise, studies on ICT-based interventions for the elderly are being actively conducted in Korea, such as overseas studies to manage and evaluate the health of the elderly using ICT and to improve the welfare and quality of life of the elderly. However, research on working with the case of fashion models is insufficient. Today, with the development of IT technology, the population using computers and smart devices is increasing, and a world without computers and smart phones has become an unimaginable everyday life. As of 2020, Japan's population over the age of 65 was 36.19 million, accounting for 28.8%. One of the various measures for the elderly that the Japanese government, which predicts that the elderly population will reach 30% in 2025, is a game. Japan's Yomiuri Shimbun reported that views on games are changing in terms of improving the health and social activities of the elderly. Gschwind et al. (2015) used Kinect with a tablet for 16 weeks. Kinect is a low-cost depth measurement camera released by Microsoft, which provides RGB images and joint tracking information along with real-time depth information [5]. Through the intervention, the risk of falling decreased and there was a significant improvement in quality of life [6]. To solve the problems of the elderly due to aging, various studies are being conducted. The problems of the elderly due to aging can be largely divided into problems caused by deterioration of physical function and cognitive function [7]. To solve the problem of body function, there are preceding studies on upper extremity function, gait, and interventions centered on activities of daily living. Rikli and Jones (2013) suggested the definition of functional fitness of the elderly as an important factor, 'the ability to perform activities of daily living independently without feeling fatigued'. In addition, the aging of the elderly experiences a decrease in coping ability in unexpected situations due to a decrease in not only physical strength, but also overall body functions and body balance ability from body control [8–10]. In the aging process, the elderly are accompanied by confusion in various bodily functions, decreased motor sensation, decreased muscle mass, increased vibration sensory threshold, and decreased cognitive abilities such as memory process and attention span [11]. Such changes in physical function, such as the back, often lead to gait instability and a decrease in balance ability, limiting the elderly's social autonomy and in some cases causing falls [12]. It was reported that falls ranked first. As the cause of falls, as age increases, the decrease in balance and muscle endurance, especially the decrease in physical function due to the decrease in lower extremity muscle endurance, is also an important cause of falls [13, 14]. According to a study by Maki [15], walking speed, stride length, and step distance were reported to be closely related to falls, and Morse (1993) reported that 10–25% of elderly people who fall due to lack of balance and abnormal gait. I am reporting that Judge [16], reported that muscle weakness in the elderly affects balance and that muscle strength is needed to overcome postural instability. As such, balance and gait of the elderly have a direct relationship with muscle strength, and a study by Brown (1995) found that the strength of the lower extremities of the elderly has a high correlation with walking and balance abilities [17].

Looking at the exercise effects of the elderly, it has been reported that regular exercise, lower extremity muscle strength training, and balance training are effective in preventing falls in the elderly and enhance various sensory and motor functions necessary for the body to maintain stability [18]. Elderly gait can be safely walked by the elderly when the center of gravity of the body is well established. Elderly gait and body alignment are both important issues for the health and safety of older people. Elderly walking can cause problems with gait due to reduced flexibility and weakened muscle strength due to age. Accordingly, it is necessary to practice walking for the elderly to walk safely in various places through the elderly walking program. Body alignment necessary for walking is a way to maintain the posture and balance of the elderly. Older adults may lose their posture as muscle strength and flexibility decrease due to aging. To prevent this, it is necessary to maintain balance and correct posture through body alignment exercises. In the virtual reality system created based on the balance maintenance learning presented in the study of body balance, the user appeared on the monitor using the avatar and copied the movement of the balance maintenance to provide visual and auditory feedback. Various contents such as ski turning, ski jumping, soccer heading, and sliding were continued for more than 6 weeks, and the results of evaluation with the bug balance scale and TUG (Timed Up and Go test) showed that the ability to maintain static balance was like that of people who learned at general rehabilitation centers. Although improvements were made, the ability to maintain dynamic balance showed that virtual reality-based learning provided more improvements. And satisfaction was high because virtual reality-based learning was convenient and fun without visiting a rehabilitation center [19].

For the elderly who watch the fashion modeling activities of senior models, the energetic walking on stage is expressed as an object of envy to the viewer. Confidence expressed by their walking and walking step movements expressing well-controlled body balance are studied as development of body balance.

In this study, a fashion model walking program developed using Kinect is applied to the elderly. This is recognized as the body balance gait posture in the unbalanced body posture gait. It is to implement a learning program in the form of a game that affects the body balance effect according to the elderly walking learning progressed with feedback. Practice on the real fashion show stage and runway space is a part that requires a leader in terms of cost and manpower. On a virtual stage, the elderly can direct and practice the model's walking as it is, and the game-type walking program models the walking of a fashion model that measures correct posture and balanced movements and provides feedback to each user. In addition, various contents can be presented through research conducted through a virtual fashion show stage. Through this study, we propose a Kinect-based walking program that aims to be active as a rehabilitation exercise for people with developmental disabilities, elderly people with dementia, and patients with Alzheimer's disease.

2 Methods

2.1 Fashion Model Walking Posture Program Production

Walking posture recognition is extracted after comparing the specific color area of the skeleton of the input image generated through the Kinect motion camera with the color information. Calculate the angle and slope between the extracted areas to determine whether to walk. This is a character created with the Unity 3D program. The movement of the character along the angle and slope calculated through the character makes it easier to understand the content. This process was expressed more realistically by using the humanoid control function tool. Following Kinect, the official name of the program used for production is 'Unity'. Among them, we are creating in the 'Unity URP 3D' environment. The Universal Render Pipeline (URP) is a pre-built scriptable render pipeline created by Unity. URP helps you quickly and easily implement optimized graphics on various platforms such as mobile, high-end consoles, and PC through an artist-friendly workflow. Issuetracker.unity3d.com Unity was used. Unity is a program used when developing games, and it has good interoperability with the current program, C#. The animation function of was used. In the currently produced program, a program was developed that detects human motion and displays motions that humans can imitate in front of their eyes so that users can follow them while watching them on the screen.

2.2 Research Design

The progress of the program design was determined as the concept of the game. One doctor of dance (movement analysis), two doctors of model studies (Kinect walking video demonstrators are two PhDs majoring in modeling and have worked as domestic and foreign models for many years. Fashion Show has had experiences such as Louis Vuitton, Celine, YSL, Valentino, Gucci, Prada, Fendi 2002 Bazaar of the Year Award, 2002 Modeling in Paris Fashion Shows – CHANEL, HERMES fashion show, and one dance movement analyst participated.), and Kinect program technicians participated in setting up the fashion model walking motion. Participants were asked to follow the movements of their avatars on the game screen. At the same time as the walking action avatar appears, the participant's appearance is also projected on the screen as an avatar. When adjusted to a certain level of motion, the score of the motion ratio increases, and a 'ding-dong' sound is heard and the next walking motion proceeds. This was set for the adaptability and motivation of the game, and the values of the skeleton's joints and axes were assigned to each action according to the recognition of the walking action. (See Fig. 1).

2.3 Azure Kinect

Azure Kinect is a developer with advanced AI sensors that provide visual and audio models with sophisticated computer vision, with more sophisticated sensor functionality than the existing Kinect1 and Kinect360 (see Fig. 2). Azure Kinect includes a depth sensor, an array of spatial microphones with video cameras, and a direction sensor, an all-in-one compact device with multiple modes, options, and SDK (Software Development Kinect).

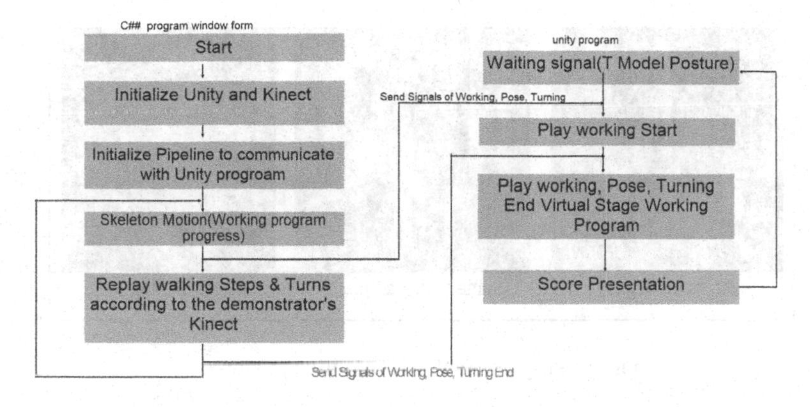

Fig. 1. Research design model

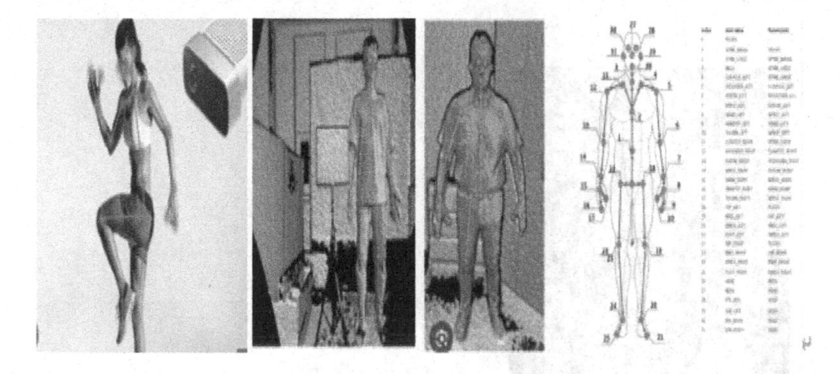

Fig. 2. Main components of the frame (https: azure.microsoft.com)

2.4 Motion Recognition Program Progress

The first scene of the walking motion calculates the spinal axis and joint values for by recording the individual's brief name, gender, and date of birth (see Fig. 3).

The humanoid is manipulated using a humanoid control function called Human Pose within the Unity3D program (name of model and each joint). Just as a real person makes a specific motion by contracting and relaxing muscles, posture is controlled by bending and extending muscles related to each joint. The amount of error is calculated by comparing the triaxial contraction values of each muscle. Spine error. Thigh error, knee error, and ankle error are added and averaged. The match rate is indicated as a minimum of 0% and a maximum of 100%. In case of mismatch, it is displayed in red, and in case of agreement, it is displayed in green. When the match rate is 60% or higher, glitter is displayed to indicate match. Calculate the relative position of the pelvis based on the position of the two legs of the model. The position of the pelvis of the user's two legs reference model is display ed as a blue cylinder and a red line to visually indicate

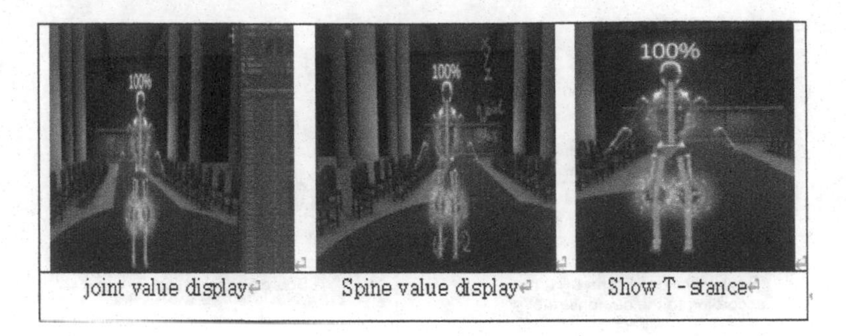

Fig. 3. Program motion recognition progress.

how distorted the position of the user's pelvis is. 4 Fashion model walking posture measurement (see Fig. 4).

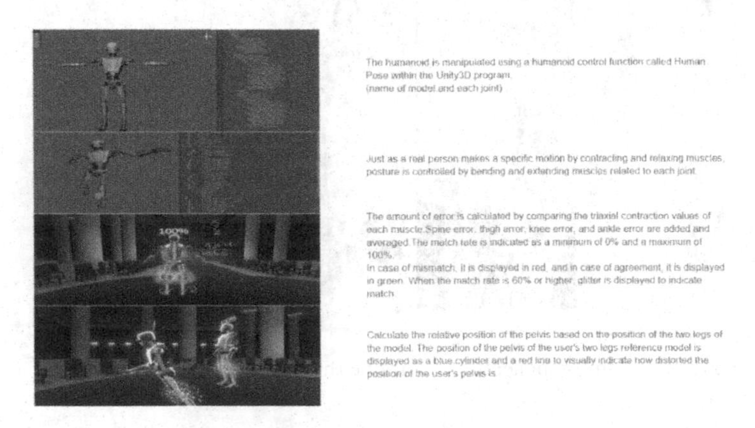

Fig. 4. Humanoid model and names of each joint and axis

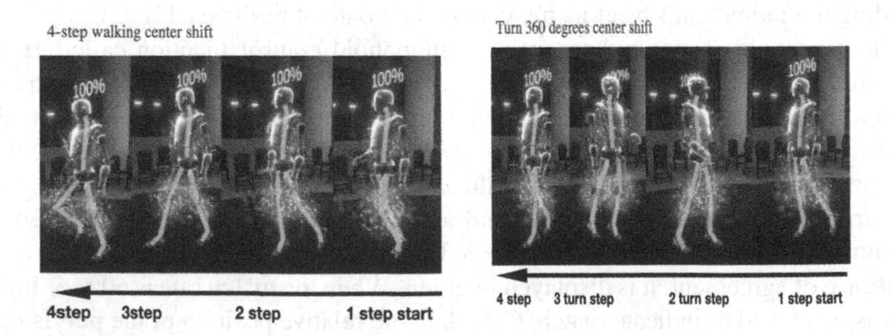

Fig. 5. Walking 4-step centering process, 360-degree full turn step process.

The standing pose, walking pose, and turn pose were photographed as separate motions. Walking and turn animations were filmed in real time. This data is utilized for comparison with the user's working data is. Model walking was divided into 4 steps. (See Fig. 5).

3 Result

Motions are scored as a percentage of the skeleton based on the player's ability to perform the motion. A bell and a percentage score were added if the movement exactly matched the picture of the Kinect skeleton displayed on the screen. Data on motion performance ability at the time of participation in the motion game and after participation were evaluated. 3 axes for a total of 7 joints using Unity 3D's Human Pose library for each motion calculation: pose data (see Fig. 6), model pose skeleton (see Fig. 7), walking, half-turn, full-turn (see Fig. 8) values and 21 values for a total of 95 joint values were recorded.

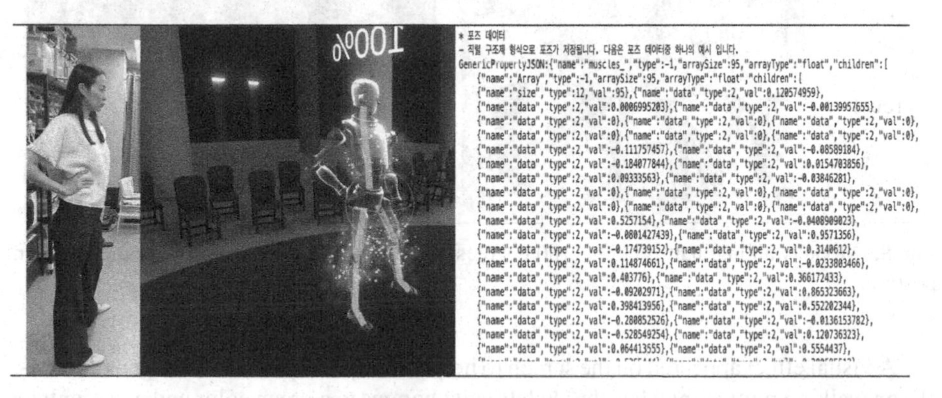

Fig. 6. Pose data processing.

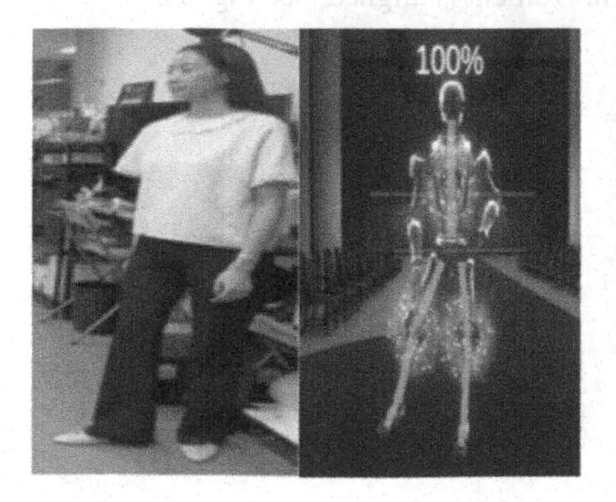

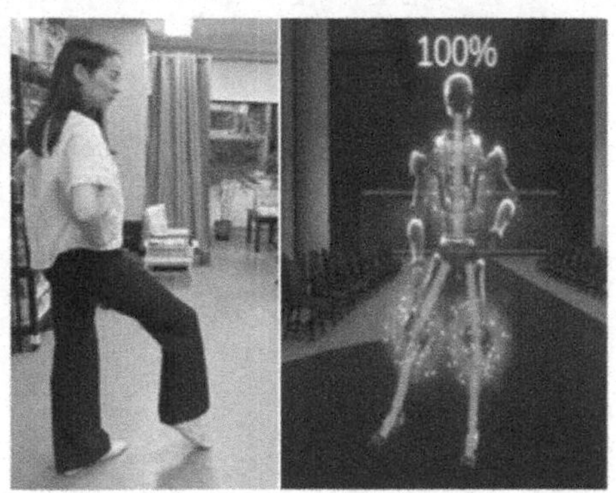

Fig. 7. Model poses and skeleton movements.

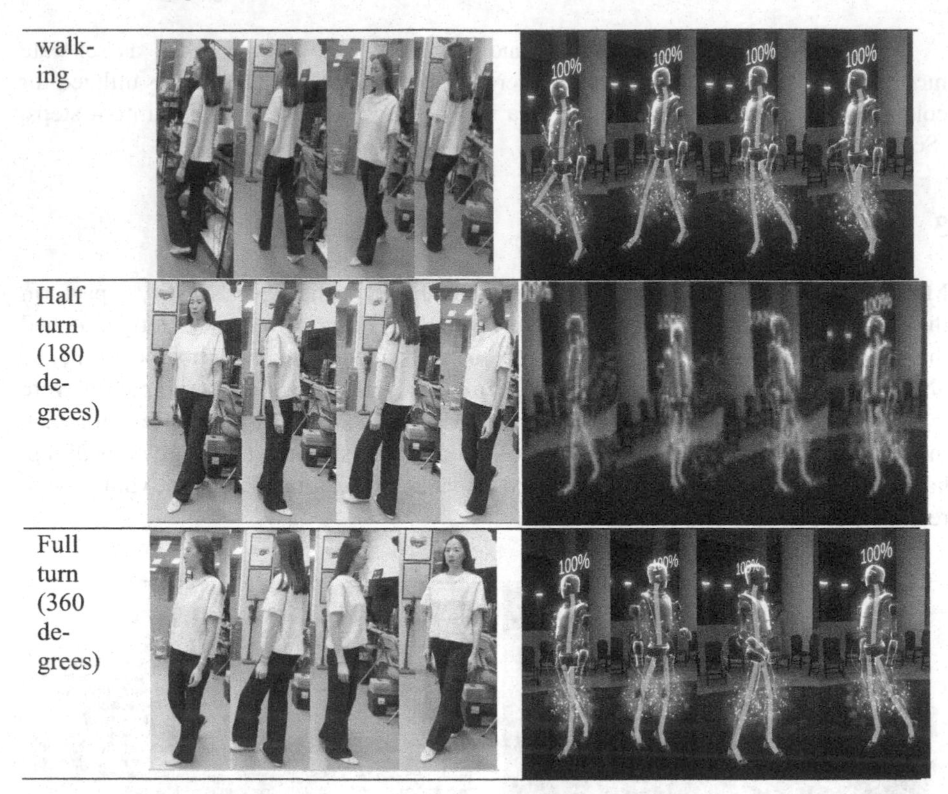

Fig. 8. Model walking, half rotation (180 degrees), full turn (360 degrees) posture and skeleton posture.

A visual effect appeared on the screen to help participants perceive changes in scores. When walking motion matches the skeleton, it changes to a green color and a percentage number appears. If the skeletons do not match, a red color appears, and the colors change in order of red-yellow-green until the center movement is aligned (see Fig. 9).

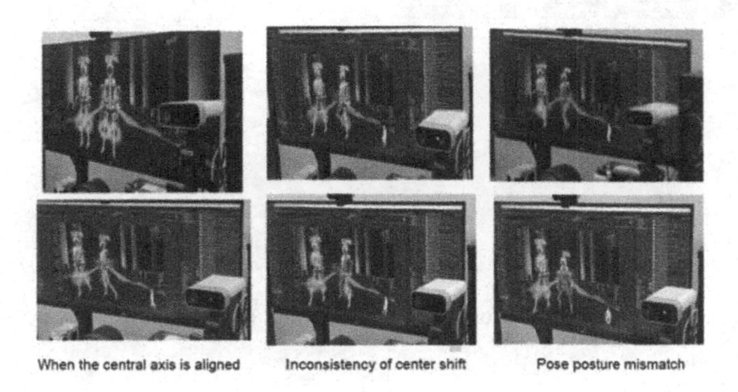

Fig. 9. Skeleton central axis, walking joint position, appearance in case of congruence and mismatch of posture. (Color figure online)

4 Conclusion

The purpose of this study is to implement a walking program for the elderly by applying fashion model walking using Kinect and apply it to the elderly to be a game-type learning program that proceeds to recognize walking balance control and body balance. The given information is implemented using Kinect, and the game proceeds with accurate gait balance control and the angle of the spine, which is the center of the body, in the walking program according to the body balance. Joint Value Using Unity 3D's human pose library, Kinect modeling where 21 values out of a total of 95 joint values are presented. It is a game-type program in which the score of the spine angle and joint value is also lowered if the center of gravity of the body is not accurately displayed in the gait motion.. As a result of implementing the program of this study, the participants showed that the balance of the center of gravity of the body was good in pose motion 1, 2, and position at first, and the matching rate increased as the participation in Kinect practice increased. The walking motion appeared at normal speed only up to the step divided into two steps. When working with turns, full turns tended to be much more difficult than half turns. However, as the number of exercises increased, the degree of agreement between the angle of the spinal axis and the angle of the joints improved.

Motions are scored as a percentage of the skeleton based on the player's ability to perform the motion. A bell and a percentage score were added if the movement exactly matched the picture of the Kinect skeleton displayed on the screen. At the time of Record the measured data Excel value (see Fig. 10).

Record the measured data in Excel so that you can check the value (see Fig. 10).

Calculation is performed using the 3-axis values for a total of 7 joints (21 values in total).

Using Unity 3D's human pose library, 21 values out of a total of 95 joint values are used.

Due to the nature of the working data, values such as arm position were excluded.

Calculation method

Absolute value (user axis value - model axis value).

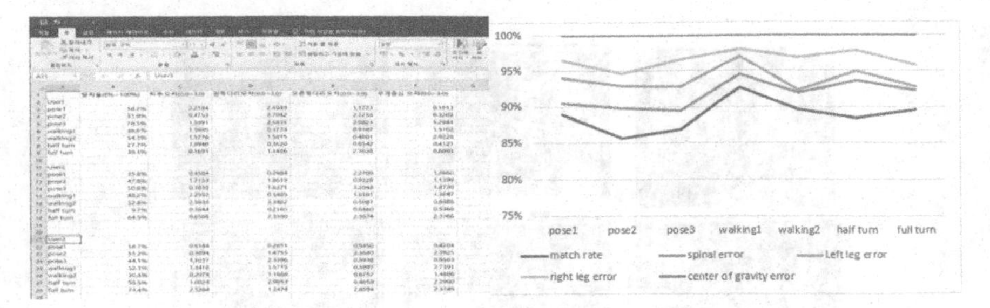

Fig. 10. Record the measured data Excel value.

spine gap = Mathf. Abs (me_muscle1 - you_muscle1) + Mathf.Abs(me_muscle2 - you_muscle2) + Mathf.Abs(m _muscle3 - you_muscle3);

After calculating the absolute difference, the difference is displayed as 0 to 100%.

float sum = spine gap + left gap + right gap.

float percent_ = remap float (sum, 2.5f, 0f, 0, 100);

Pose. (See Fig. 11).

- Standing pose, walking pose, and turn pose were filmed separately.

  Walking and turn animations were filmed in real time.

  This data is utilized for comparison with the user's walking data.

  Pose data

- Pose is saved in serial structure format. The following is an example of one of the pose data.

  Generic Property JSON:{"name": "muscles", "type":-1.

1,"arraySize":95,"arrayType":"float","children":[
{"name":"Array","type":-1,"arraySize":95,"arrayType":"float","children":[
{"name":"size","type":12,"val":95},{"name":"data","type":2,"val":0.120574959},
{"name":"data","type":2,"val":0.0006995203},{"name":"data","type":2,"val":-0.00139957655},
{"name":"data","type":2,"val":0},{"name":"data","type":2,"val":0},{"name":"data","type":2,"val":0},
{"name":"data","type":2,"val":0},{"name":"data","type":2,"val":0},{"name":"data","type":2,"val":0},
{"name":"data","type":2,"val":-0.111757457},{"name":"data","type":2,"val":-0.08589184},
{"name":"data","type":2,"val":-0.184077844},{"name":"data","type":2,"val":0.0154703856},
{"name":"data","type":2,"val":0.09333563},{"name":"data","type":2,"val":-0.03846281},

Fig. 11. Example of one of the pose data.

5 Suggestions

As a result of implementing the program of this study, the participants showed that the balance of the center of gravity of the body was good in pose motion 1, 2, and position at first, and the matching rate increased as the participation in Kinect practice increased.

The walking motion appeared at normal speed only up to the step divided into two steps (see Fig. 12). When working with turns, full turns tended to be much more difficult than half turns. However, as the number of exercises increased, the degree of agreement between the angle of the spinal axis and the angle of the joints improved.

The given time to appear on the screen is not set. It made me have a part that needed time for posture correction. In this study, the ratio was measured by selecting 4 walking and poses as case studies. In order to organize the data, data were collected through postures of motions according to game motions, and when the motions matched the motion program, a ding-dong sound feedback was given to increase the score. On the other hand, the ratio is lowered for scenes in which the participant's posture expresses inconsistent motion. He rendered his own image on the screen and confirmed his movement through it. The tester was given a visual effect of sparkling when the skeletons matched).

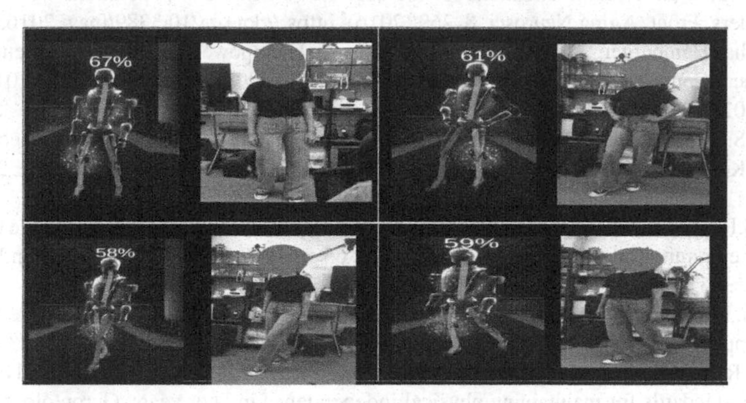

Fig. 12. Working program implementation.

In this study, a walking program is implemented to utilize the walking of the most representative fashion model of walking as the content of this study. We present a gesture recognition application based on the Kinect sensor using the Unity3D engine. In fact, by recognizing the movement of various gestures, interaction with the object was implemented. In addition to the previously provided gestures, additional user-defined gestures are also easily supported. The fashion model walking program promoted the improvement of the user's exercise performance by delivering the user's posture accuracy during walking and posing as feedback. The image of the user exercising with the camera and the standard walking posture are displayed on the screen at the same time, and real-time feedback is given to the accuracy of the walking, turn, and pose postures, and the program is implemented so that the correct posture can be gradually made. The posture correction system that recognizes the movement of the body center through walking movement is a program that can suggest a walking posture by using an avatar that matches the axis of the spine to the user. It has the advantage of not having the burden of expensive personal training and time management. It has the advantage of being able to exercise easily at home for the elderly who have difficulty walking. It is efficient in terms of space as it does not require a lot of space. Since users and trainers are provided as avatars, users can exercise interestingly. In the future research direction, it is necessary to implement more accurate angles and improve the AR avatar part, and if each other's coordinates can be transmitted through the existing exercise platform as an additional function, it will be able to contribute to rehabilitation exercise research. The use of fashion model avatars increases the need and efforts to preoccupy the development of work programs using VR (virtual reality) and AR (augmented reality), which can change the existing research flow into the future research direction.

References

1. Kang, J.K., Lee, J.Y.: Status and Tasks of ICT-based Welfare services for the elderly living alone. J. Digit. Convergence **13**(1), 67–76 (2015). https://doi.org/10.14400/JDC.2015.13.1.67
2. Lee, G.W., Son, H.W.: Geospatial Information Systems Thesaurus. Seoul: Gamebook (2016)
3. Gros, A., et al.: Recommendations for the use of ICT in elderly populations with affective disorders. Front. Aging Neurosci. **8**, 269 (2016). https://doi.org/10.3389/fnagi.2016.00269
4. Amichai-Hamburger, Y., McKenna, K.Y., Tal, S.: E-empowerment: empowerment by the internet. Comput. Hum. Behave. **24**(5), 1776–1789 (2008). https://doi.org/10.1016/j.chb.2008.02.002
5. Cho, S.Y., Byun, H.R., Lee, H.K., Cha, J.H.: Hand gesture recognition from kinect sensor data. Korean Soc. Broad Eng. **17**(3), 447–458 (2012). https://doi.org/10.5909/JBE.2012.17.3.447
6. Ma, S.R.: The effects of exertainment task oriented upper limb motor task on muscle tone and upper extremity function in stroke patients over 65 years. J. Korea Entertainment Ind. Assoc. **11**(7), 335–345 (2017). https://doi.org/10.21184/jkeia.2017.10.11.7.335
7. Moon, M.S., Jung, M.Y.: A systematic review on the association between cognitive function and upper extremity function in the elderly. Ther. Sci. Neurorehabilitation **5**, 23–33 (2016)
8. Rikli, R.E., Jones, C.J.: Development and validation of criterion-referenced clinically relevant fitness standards for maintaining physical independence in later years. Gerontologist **53**(2), 255–267 (2013)
9. Daubney, M.E., Culham, E.G.: Lower-extremity muscle force and balance performance in adults aged 65 years and older. Phys. Ther. **79**(12), 1177–1185 (1999)
10. Gauchard, G.C., Gangloff, P., Jeandel, C., Perrin, P.P.: Physical activity improves gaze and posture control in the elderly. Neurosci. Res. **45**(4), 409–417 (2003)
11. Lach, H.W., Reed, A.T., Arfken, Cl.: Falls in the elderly: reliability of a classification system. J. Am. Geriatr. Soc. **39**, 197–202 (1991)
12. Kollegger, H., Baumgartner, C., Wober, C., Oder, W., Deecke, L.: Spontaneous body sway as a function of sex, age, and vision: posturographic study in 30 healthy adults. Eur. Neurol. **32**, 253–259 (1992)
13. Tinetti, M.E., Speechley, M., Ginter, S.F.: Risk factor falls among elderly persons living in the community. N. Engl. J. Med. **319**, 1701–1707 (1988)
14. Tinetti, M., Willams, T.F., Mauewski, K.: Fall risk index for elderly patients based on number of chronic disabilities. Am. J. Med. **80**, 429–434 (1986)
15. Maki, B.E.: Gait changes in older adult: Predictors of falls or indicators of fear? J. Am. Geriatr. Soc. **45**(3), 313–319 (1997)
16. Judge, J.O., Lindsey, C., Underwood, M., Winsemius, D.: Balance improvement in older women: effect of exercise training. Phys. Ther. **73**(4), 253–262 (1993)
17. Brown, M., Sinacore, D.R., Host, H.: The relationship of power to function in the older adult. J. Gerontd. **50**, 55–59 (1995)
18. Campbell, A.J., Barrie, M.J., Spears, G.F.: Risk factors for fall in a community based prospective study of people 70 years and older. J. Gerontol. **44**, 112–117 (1989)

19. Lupu, R.G., Ungureanu, F., Botezatu, N., Ignat, D., Moldoveanu, A.: Virtual reality-based stroke recovery for upper limbs using leap motion. In: 2016 20th International Conference on System Theory, Control and Computing (ICSTCC), Sinaia, pp. 295-299 (2016)

Cute Signs or Aposematic Signs? An ERP Study on Older Adults' Perception of Fall Prevention Signs

Yunshan Jiang[1], Shunji Wu[2], and Jia Zhou[1](✉)

[1] School of Management Science and Real Estate, Chongqing University, Chongqing, People's Republic of China
jiazhou@cqu.edu.cn
[2] Huawei Digital Technologies (Cheng Du) Co., Limited, Chengdu, People's Republic of China

Abstract. Falls are a significant cause of injury for older adults. Although fall prevention signs are everywhere, their effects on older adults' risk perception are not clear. Inspired by hedgehogs and bees, this study proposed aposematic signs to warn older adults of possible fall risks and comparatively tested cute signs. Three types of warning signs (Apo, Cute-K, and Cute-W) and two perceptual sensitivities (high vs. low) of older adults were investigated. Apo, Cute-W, and Cute-K evoke risk perception of older adults through eye-catching images, kid injury images, and funny images, respectively. 26 subjects aged between 56 and 79 were recruited to measure their average amplitude of N300 and subjective risk perception by a virtual reality experiment. The results showed that the type of warning signs had a significant effect on objective emotional arousal. High perceptual sensitivity had a significant effect on subjective risk perception (perceived likelihood of fall, fall anticipation emotion, and fall anticipation worries). The results suggest that Apo warning signs could be given primary consideration when designing warning signs for older adults in fall-prone areas. More fall intervention approaches should focus more on older adults with low perceptual sensitivity.

Keywords: Older adults · Risk perception · Fall prevention signs · Perceptual sensitivity · EEG

1 Introduction

Aging has become a global population trend, and falls are a serious impediment to healthy aging [1]. The global incidence of falls among people over 70 years old is 32%–42% according to the report of WHO [2]. Furthermore, according to the forecast of the United Nations, the proportion of people over 65 years old will reach one-sixth of the global population by 2050 [3].

The causes of falls in the elderly are varied and mainly related to the deterioration of physiological and cognitive functions, policy interventions, and environmental factors. However, research found that as many as one-third of falls in older adults are related to environmental hazards [4]. More specifically, according to the latest Chinese Cause of

Q. Gao et al. (Eds.): HCII 2023, LNCS 14055, pp. 68–84, 2023.
https://doi.org/10.1007/978-3-031-48041-6_6

Death Detection Dataset (2021), almost half of the deaths caused by falls occur in the home [5].

Although modifications to the home environment are effective in preventing falls [6], older adults' low risk perception can still cause falls. Studies of brain mechanisms have found that the insula is less activated in response to risk information in older adults than in younger adults, making it difficult for older adults to perceive risk information in their surroundings [7]. A review of older adults' attitudes, beliefs, and behaviors regarding fall prevention showed that some older adults do not believe they are at risk for falls because they feel healthy and confident [8]. Consequently, the level of risk perception sensitivity is the unmissable factor of whether older adults can perceive the risk information and make the right behavior.

Risk perception is an important ability for older adults to identify information about hazards in their environment. Research on risk perception has been conducted in three main areas: risk characteristics, risk perception type, and ways of informing risk [9]. Risk perception is often understood as the perceived likelihood of a potential outcome or exposure to a threat. However, decades of research have shown that risk perception is largely a construct of intuition and emotion, rather than an assessment of the probability of risk occurrence and consequences [10]. Numerous studies have classified risk perception measurement dimensions such as probability, consequence, and emotion into cognitive components and affective components [11]. A meta-analysis of health behaviors demonstrated that combining cognitive and emotional components increases behavioral intention and health-related behavior execution [12].

Warning signs are a typical method of alerting people to hazards by conveying attention signals. Warning signs' design related to important factors includes text, size, graphics, format, and color [13]. Although warning signs are everywhere, the signs which combined emotional and cognitive components are less designed. Moreover, most of the current research on warning signs is based on behavioral experiments by subjective measurements. Objective responses, such as objective neurophysiological responses, are less investigated. Despite Zhu et al. [14] analyzed the text and shape of warning signs for risk perception and their neural mechanisms by recording participants' subjective and objective reactions. But the design of warning signs in [14] did not combine the emotional and cognitive factors.

Therefore, this study mainly explores two questions: (1) What are the differences in risk perception and related neurophysiological responses of different types of warning signs for older adults? (2) How do older adults' characteristics affect risk perception and related neurophysiological responses?

2 Literature Review

2.1 Fall Risk Perception Theory

The most commonly reported theories related to fall risk perception are the Health Belief Model (HBM) [15], Protection Motivation Theory (PMT) [16], and Protective Action Decision Mode (PADM) [17]. In contrast to HBM and PMT, PADM focuses more on the risk perception process itself and integrates people's reactions to impending hazards into a multi-stage model that includes a pre-decision process, a perception process, a decision process, and risk response behavior. In studies of older adults fall risk perceptions, most studies would combine the above theories for semi-structured interviews [18], questionnaires for structured research [19], and structural equation modeling to analyze the effects of relevant factors on fall risk perceptions [20].

2.2 Factors in Fall Risk Perception

Through the literature review, the main factors influencing the fall risk perception in older adults include fall experience, age, gender, and environment.

Fall Experience: Fall experience can significantly affect fall risk perception [20]. Both fall frequency and fall injury were associated with confidence in fall prevention [21].

Age: Fall risk perception is related to age, but there is no uniform conclusion as to whether the ability to perceive risk increases or decreases with age. Some studies suggest that the subjective risk perception of falls increases with age [22]. And other studies have shown that older adults believe they are at a lower risk of falling compared to younger adults [23].

Gender: Although most studies have shown that men have lower perceptions of fall risk [22], there are still some studies that have concluded that there is no significant difference in the effect of gender on fall perception [24].

Environment: The main external factors for falls in the elderly are environmental factors. However, current research on fall factors has focused on the residential environment of older adults, and there is a lack of research on the influence of the environment on the subjective risk perception of falls [25].

2.3 Warning Sign

Warning signs are an important means of alerting people to perceived dangers. The design elements of a warning sign include text, size, graphics, format, and color [13]. The three most commonly used warning words recommended by the American National Standards Institute are DANGER, WARNING, and CAUTION. Most guidelines and standards also recommend the appropriate use of the shape of the environment in warning signs as an indication of the type of hazard. Some studies have shown that the shape of the environment on warning signs can elicit emotional responses and induce different levels of hazard perception [26]. Specifically, inverted triangles induce higher hazard perceptions compared to right triangles, diamonds, circles, and rectangles [27]. Fall warning signs are currently used more often in hospitals, such as hanging yellow warning signs at the head of patients' beds to reduce the risk of falls for patients or their families.

Kindchenschema cute, Whimsical cute, and Aposematism are three typical warning signs currently in use. Kindchenschema cute mainly summarizes the features of young kids' appearance and behavior [28]. Thus, it induces psychological representations of vulnerability and enhances risk perception [29]. Whimsical cute adds a humorous design feature that will attract attention and elicit pleasant mental representations [30]. The design feature of Aposematism triggers avoidance behavior, and some studies have shown that Aposematism causes drivers to engage in more avoidance behavior [31].

3 Materials and Methods

3.1 Participants

This experiment used convenience sampling and recruited subjects by posting information to the elderly community. Subjects were required to be 55 years of age or older and capable of voluntary movement, excluding conditions that would make EEG inappropriate, such as recent sedation, sleeping agents, or the use of pacemakers. After the pre-experiment, 27 elderly subjects (Ages: 56–79, M = 68.4, SD = 4.931; 9 males, 18 females) from the community surrounding Chongqing University were recruited. The experimental design and protocol of the study took full account of the principles of safety and fairness, and its study content posed no harm or risk to the subjects. Subjects will be recruited based on the principle of voluntary and informed consent, and the rights and privacy of the subjects will be protected to the maximum extent possible, and there will be no conflict of interest between the study content and the study results.

3.2 Experiment Design

A mixed within-group and between-group design of 4 (warning sign type) × 2 (perceived sensitivity) was conducted. The type of warning signs was the within-group variable and the perceived sensitivity was the between-group variable.

The types of warning signs are Kindchenschema cute (Cute-K), Whimsical cute (Cute-W), Aposematism (Apo), and Non-cue. Fall perception sensitivity is measured by the Activities-Specific Balance Confidence scale (ABC). It has been shown to have strong test-retest reliability (r = 0.92) [32].

The five dependent variables included both subjective risk perception and objective emotional arousal. The subjective risk perception includes four variables: the perceived likelihood of falling, perceived severity of falling, anticipatory emotions of falling, and anticipated worry of falling. All were assessed by Likert scales (1–5) except for the perceived likelihood of falling which was assessed by a visual analog scale (0%–100%). The objective emotional arousal measure is N300. Higher negative N300 has been shown in previous studies to represent emotional arousal to a combination of markers at higher risk levels [14].

3.3 Stimuli

Prototyping of Warning Signs: The warning signs for the experiments were designed by the authors who summarized the design essential points through literature reading and were created by art and design professional students. The final design of the three types of warning signs is shown in Fig. 1(a)–(c). The basic layout of the warning signs is based on the ISO standard, which adopts the basic layout reference standard (ISO 3864–1:2011) for the top and bottom arrangement of the graphic basic information and supplementary text, as shown in Fig. 1(d). The environment in which the warning signs are used is taken from the 9 environmental scenarios at the intermediate scale (HSSAT) [33]. By combining the warning signs with the environment, a total of 4 × 9 = 36 stimulus images were obtained as the standard stimuli for the EEG experiments, and the actual stimulus images are shown in Fig. 1(e).

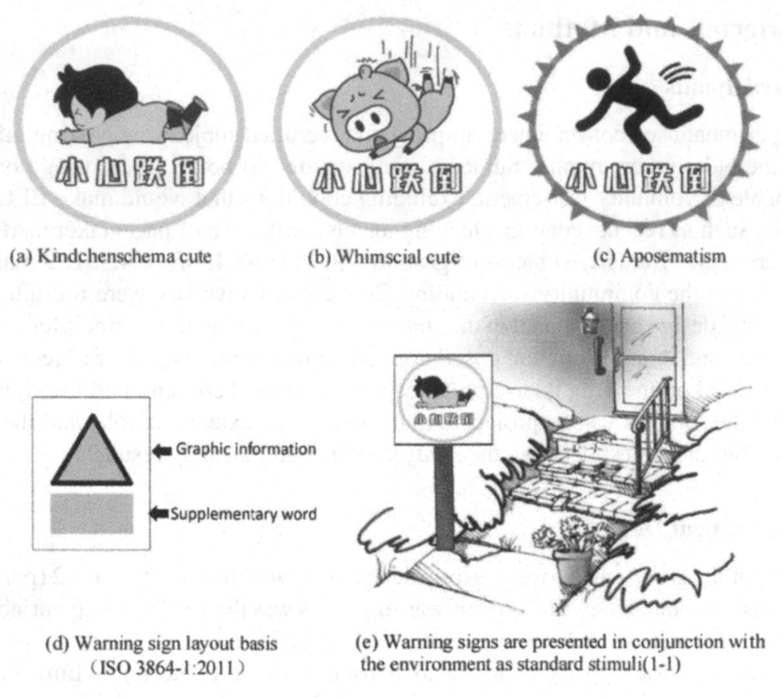

Fig. 1. Naturalistic warning logo design materials and examples

EEG Prototype Design: To avoid the Relevance-for-task effect, we used neutral cell phone images obtained from the internet with copyright permission as the target stimuli. Since different ratios of the target stimulus to the standard stimulus can affect the experimental results [34], the ratio of the probability of occurrence of the target and standard stimuli was set to 1:4. The final number of target stimuli was 9, the standard stimulus pictures were 36, and the total number of stimulus pictures was 45.

The experiments were conducted using Brain product (18 vmp) EEG equipment, psychological experiment design software E-prime3.0, and a specialized scripting language E-Basic for EEG prototyping.

3.4 Procedure

The experiment was completed in 401, Human-Computer Interaction Laboratory, Process Building, Area A, Chongqing University, and the site picture is shown in Fig. 2. The whole experimental process includes four phases.

Experimental Introduction, Basic Information, and Perceptual Sensitivity Measurement: Experimental purpose and precautions were presented. Questionnaires for basic personal information and perceived sensitivity were completed.

EEG Experimental Training: Subjects were trained before the EEG experiment. The training materials were abstract black and white pictures that were completely different from the formal experiment to reduce interference with the formal experiment.

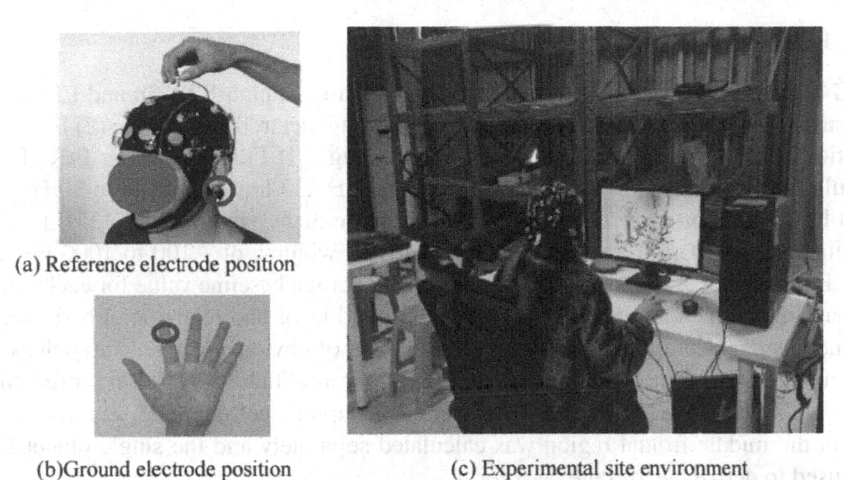

(a) Reference electrode position

(b)Ground electrode position

(c) Experimental site environment

Fig. 2. Equipment and experimental environment

Formal EEG Experiments: The order of stimulus presentation was designed using a Latin square to balance the learning effects. Subjects could choose to take a break at any time during the experiment to relieve visual fatigue. Each subject completed 225 trials (45 stimuli × 5 groups). The stimulation flow for each trial is shown in Fig. 3.

Risk Perception Questionnaire: Subjects rated supervisor risk perception on 36 standard stimuli with the assistance of the experimenter. A total of 216 evaluation items (36 × 6 subitems) were included for each subject.

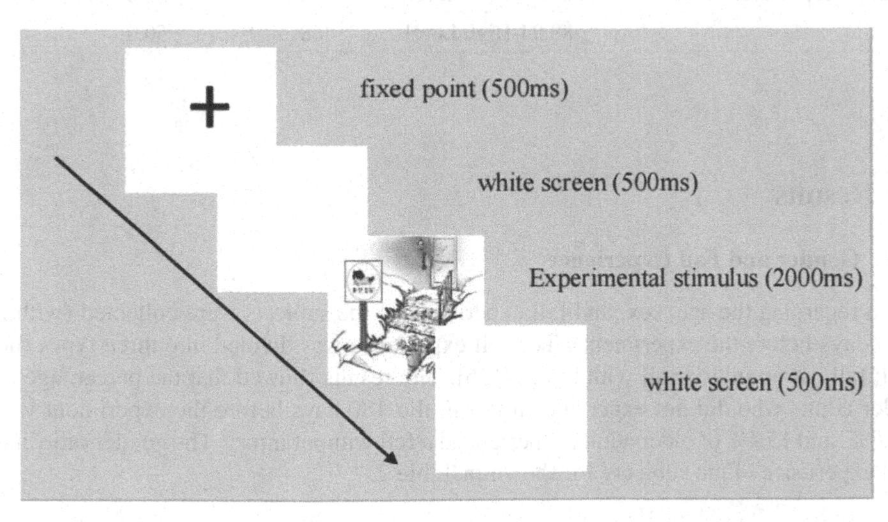

Fig. 3. Sequence of stimuli in a single EEG experiment trail

3.5 EEG and Statistical Analysis

EEG Data Analysis: EEG data were analyzed using Matlab R2013b and EEGLAB. The analysis process includes (1) Input of positioning electrodes and data; (2) Electrode positioning; (3) Down sampling and re-referencing; (4) Filtering: using FIR (Finite Impulse Response) filter with high pass set to 0. 1 Hz,33 low passes set to 30 Hz, and a 50 Hz depression filter to eliminate industrial frequency interference [35]; (5) The continuous EEG data were segmented with a time window of −100 to 1000 ms, and the EEG signal of −100 to 0 ms was used as the average baseline value for each period for baseline correction [35]; (6) Interpolation of bad leads and rejection of bad epochs; (7) Independent Component Analysis; (8) Removal of obvious interference such as eye movement components; (9) The average vibration amplitude of N300 in a predefined event window (275–325 ms) [14] for a specific group of electrodes (F3, Z, F4, C3, CZ, C4) in the middle frontal region was calculated separately and the single object ERP was used to derive the average waveform.

Data from subject #2 in this experiment were not included in the analysis (due to the effective epoch rate of 24.5% after excluding bad segments).

Personal Trait Level Pre-processing: Since refinement of high score levels can lead to interference with the results [36], the perceptual sensitivity characteristics were divided into high and low levels. The fall perceptual sensitivity stratification is shown in Table 1.

Table 1. Stratification of Fall perception sensitivity

		Frequency	Percent (%)
Fall perception sensitivity	< 89.94-Low Level	468	50.0
	≥ 89.94-High Level	468	50.0

4 Results

4.1 Gender and Fall Experience

Data regarding the age, sex, and fall experience of the subjects were collected (within 180 days before the experiment). The fall experience was divided into three types (no fall; fall but no injury; fall with injury) [36]. The results showed that the percentage of older adults who did not experience a fall in the 180 days before the experiment was 84.6%, and 15.4% of older adults experienced a fall without injury. The gender ratio and fall experience of the subjects are shown in Table 2.

4.2 Subjective Risk Perception

The subjective risk perception included four independent variables (perceived likelihood of fall, perceived severity of fall, expected emotion of fall, and expected worry of fall).

Table 2. Description of background information of subjects

Variables	Type	Number of Subjects	Percent (%)
Gender	Male	8	30.8
	Female	18	69.2
Fall experience	No fall	22	84.6
	Fall with no injury	4	15.4

A total of 936 (36 standard stimuli × 26 number of subjects) valid subjective data were collected for these four variables. The results showed no interaction effect between the four independent variables.

Perceived Likelihood of Falling: The results showed no significant difference in the perceived likelihood of falling among the different warning sign types. Older adults with high levels of perceptual sensitivity had significantly higher scores than those with low perceptual sensitivity ($F_{(1,928)} = 6.876, p < 0.01$). The score of fall perception likelihood for different warning sign types and perceived sensitivity levels is shown in Fig. 4. For the different types of warning signs, subjects had the highest perceived likelihood of falling for Cute-K and the lowest perceived likelihood of falling for Non-cue, but there was no statistically significant difference. For different levels of perceptual sensitivity, low perceptual sensitivity subjects (Mean = 49.4, SD = 25.69) had significantly lower perceptual likelihood scores than high perceptual sensitivity subjects (Mean = 53.4, SD = 27.95).

The Mann-Whitney U test was used to analyze the relationship between the perceived likelihood of falling with gender and fall experience, respectively. The relationship between environment and perceived likelihood of falling was examined by the Friedman test. The results showed that gender ($Z = -0.574, p = 0.566$) did not have a significant effect on the perceived likelihood of falling, while both fall experience ($Z = -4.042, p < 0.001$) and environment ($\chi^2 = 140.8, p < 0.001$) influenced the perceived likelihood of falling.

Perceived Severity of Falling: The results showed that different types of warning signs ($F_{(3,928)} = 0.021, p = 0.996$) and levels of perceived sensitivity ($F_{(1,928)} = 0.885, p = 0.347$) did not have a significant effect on the perceived severity of falls. The scores of fall perceived severity for different warning sign types and perceived sensitivity levels are shown in Fig. 5. Subjects had the highest perceived fall severity score in the Non-cue condition (Mean = 3.56, SD = 1.284), followed by the Cute-K condition (Mean = 3.55, SD = 1.290), the Apo condition (Mean = 3.53, SD = 1.362), and the Cute-W condition (Mean = 3.53, SD = 1.311). Subjects with high levels of perceived sensitivity scored higher in the perceived severity of falls (Mean = 3.49, SD = 1.343; Mean = 3.59, SD = 1.275).

The effects of gender ($Z = -0.887, p = 0.375$) and fall experience ($Z = -1.834, p = 0.067$) on the perceived severity of falls were not significant, and environmental changes ($\chi^2 = 375.1, p < 0.001$) significantly affected perceived severity of falls.

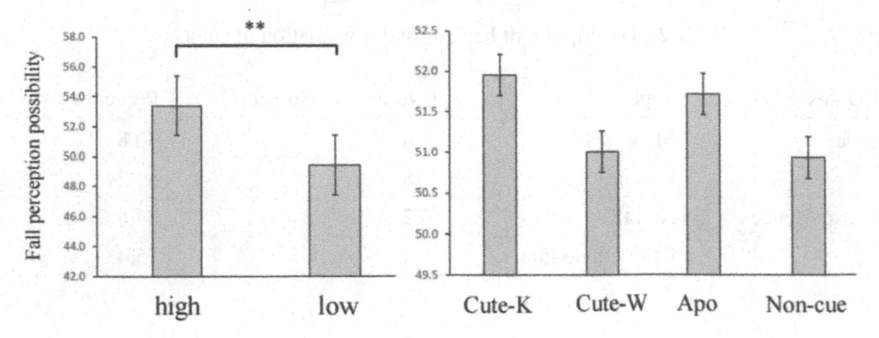

Note: ①Error bar =±1SE; ②**p < .01,two-tailed

Fig. 4. Score of perceived likelihood of falling under different warning sign types and perceived susceptibility

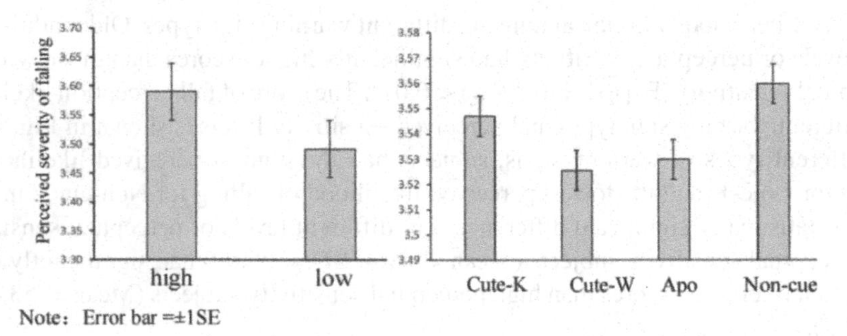

Fig. 5. Score of perceived severity of falling under different warning sign types and perceived susceptibility

Anticipatory Emotions of Falling: The results showed that different types of warning signs did not have a significant effect on fall anticipation emotion, while high perceptual sensitivity subjects had significantly higher fall anticipation emotion scores than low perceptual sensitivity subjects ($F_{(1,928)} = 13.831$, $p < 0.001$). The scores of fall anticipation emotions for different warning sign types and perceived sensitivity levels are shown in Fig. 6. Subjects had the highest fall anticipation emotion score in the Cute-K condition (Mean = 2.58, SD = 1.087), which was higher than the Cute-W condition (Mean = 2.57, SD = 1.106), Apo condition (Mean = 2.58, SD = 1.127), and Non-cue condition (Mean = 2.54, SD = 1. 109). Low perceptually sensitive subjects (Mean = 2.42, SD = 0.966) had significantly lower scores for fall anticipation emotions than high perceptually sensitive subjects (Mean = 2.72, SD = 1.211).

The effect of gender ($Z = -0.824$, $p = 0.410$) on fall expectancy emotion was not significant, while fall experience ($Z = -3.264$, $p = 0.001$) and environmental changes ($\chi^2 = 147.3$, $p < 0.001$) significantly affected fall expectancy emotion.

Anticipatory Worries of Falling: The results showed no significant effect on fall anticipation apprehension by different types of warning signs, while high perceptually sensitive subjects scored significantly higher than low perceptually sensitive subjects ($F_{(1,928)}$

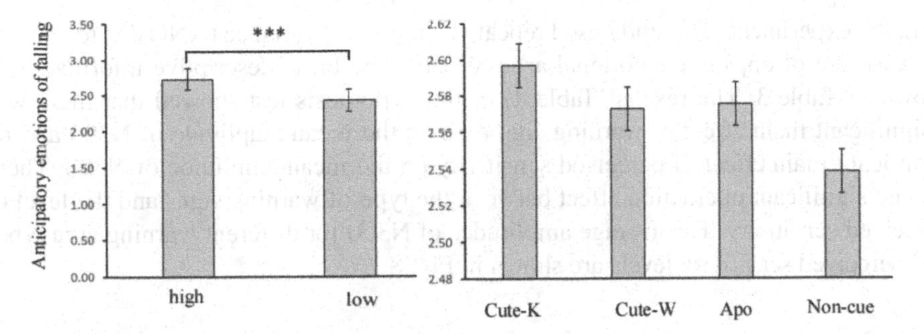

Note: ①Error bar =±1SE; ②***p < .01,two-tailed

Fig. 6. Score of anticipatory emotions of falling under different warning sign types and perceived susceptibility

= 7.472, p < 0.01). Subjects had the highest fall anticipation worries scores in the Cute-K condition (Mean = 2.79, SD = 1.190), followed by Cute-W (Mean = 2.77, SD = 1.252), Apo (Mean = 2.73, SD = 1.129), Non-cue (Mean = 2.73, SD = 1.234). The scores of fall anticipation worries were (Mean = 2.67, SD = 1. 126) for subjects with low perceptual sensitivity level and (Mean = 2.84, SD = 1.308) for subjects with high perceptual sensitivity level. The scores of fall anticipation worries for different warning sign types and perceived sensitivity levels are shown in Fig. 7.

The results showed that gender (Z = −1.781, p = 0.75)and fall experience (Z = −1.951, p = 0.051)did not have a significant effect on fall anticipation apprehension. Environmental changes ($\chi^2 = 129.8$, $p < 0.001$) significantly affected fall anticipation apprehension.

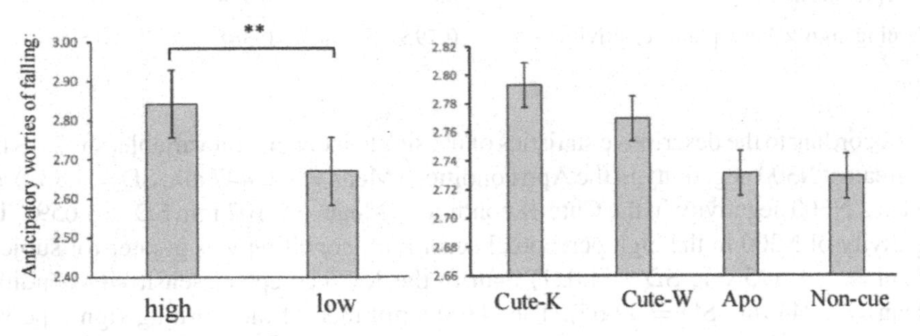

Note: ①Error bar =±1SE; ②**p < .01,two-tailed

Fig. 7. Score of anticipatory worry of falling under different warning sign types and perceived susceptibility

4.3 Objective Emotional Arousal

The specific metric of objective emotional arousal is the average amplitude of N300. A total of 5850 (26 Subject × 45 Stimulation × 5 trial) valid value segments were received from the experiment. The study used repeated analysis of variance (ANOVA) to analyze the variance of objective emotional arousal data. The basic descriptive information is shown in Table 3. The results (Table 4) of the hypothesis test showed that there was a significant main effect of warning sign type on the mean amplitude of N300 and no significant main effect of perceived sensitivity on the mean amplitude of N300. There was no significant interaction effect between the type of warning signs and the level of perceived sensitivity. The average amplitudes of N300 for different warning sign types and perceived sensitivity levels are shown in Fig. 8.

Table 3. Mean(M) and standard deviation (SD) of the amplitude 300 by the subjects

Warning sign	High level		Low level	
	M	SD	M	SD
Cute-K	0.89	3.946	1.31	3.498
Cute-M	0.16	3.845	1.75	2.549
Apo	−1.81	4.731	0.92	4.926
Non-cue	0.30	3.392	0.20	3.560

Table 4. N300 mean amplitude of the repeated measure ANOVA results

	F (1,24)	p	η^2
Warning sign	5.110	0.033*	30.8
Perceptual sensitivity	0.015	0.904	69.2
Warning sign × Perceptual sensitivity	0.795	0.381	15.4

According to the descriptive statistics of the single independent variable, subjects had the greatest N300 negativity in the Apo condition (Mean = −0.447 mn, SD = 4.932) and the least N300 negativity in the Cute-K condition (Mean = 1.102 mn, SD = 3.659). The negativity of N300 in the high perceptual sensitivity condition was greater for subjects (Mean = −0. 115 mn, SD = 4.021) than in the low perceptual sensitivity condition (Mean = 1.044 mn, SD = 3.665). The N300 amplitude of the warning sign type was further analyzed statistically based on the LSD (Least Significance Difference) method for a two-by-two comparison. The results of the analysis are shown in Table 5. The results showed that both Cute-K and Cute-W were significantly different from the mean amplitude value of N300 of Apo, respectively. The Apo condition induced significantly higher N300 negativity than Cute-K (p = 0.032) and Cute-W(p = 0.044). The ERPs results are shown in Fig. 9.

ERP waveform graph and Grand graph (Fig. 9.) were acquired by EEG data processing. A negative component was found during the 275–325 ms latency in the middle frontal region, which is in agreement with previous ERP studies [14]. The study used a paired-sample T-test to analyze data on gender and fall experience. The results showed

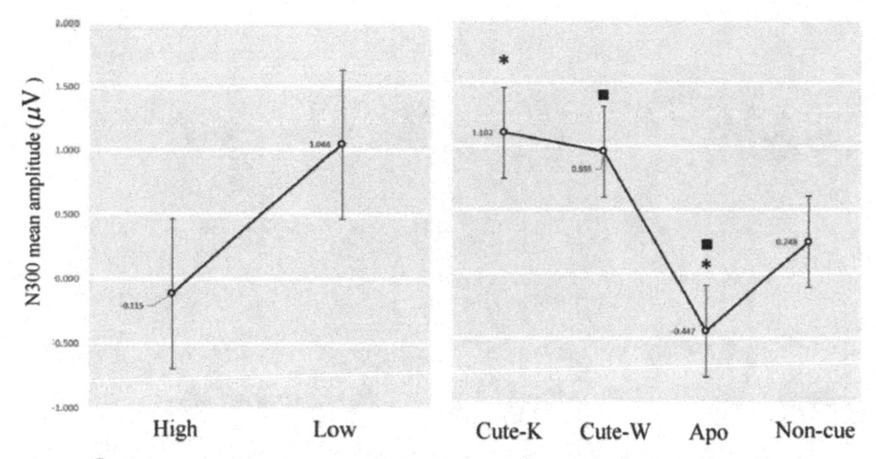

Note: ①Identical markers in the graph indicate a significant difference between the two levels; ②Error bar=±1SE

Fig. 8. Amplitude of N300 of anticipatory worry of falling under different warning sign types and perceived susceptibility

Table 5. Post hoc test for interactive gestures warning signs

two-by-two comparison	Diff	SE	P
1–2	0.147	0.553	0.793
1–3	1.549*	0.679	0.032
1–4	0.854	0.547	0.131
2–3	1.402*	0.659	0.044
2–4	0.708	0.626	0.270
3–4	−0.694	0.751	0.365

Note: 1 for "Cute-K", 2 for "Cute-W", 3 for "Apo", and 4 for "Non-cue" in the contrast column "; *. Indicates the significance level of 0.05 between levels (two-tailed)

that the effect of fall experience ($t = 1.836$, $p = 0.076$) on N300 was not significant; women had a higher negative N300 than men ($t = 2.339$, $p = 0.021$).

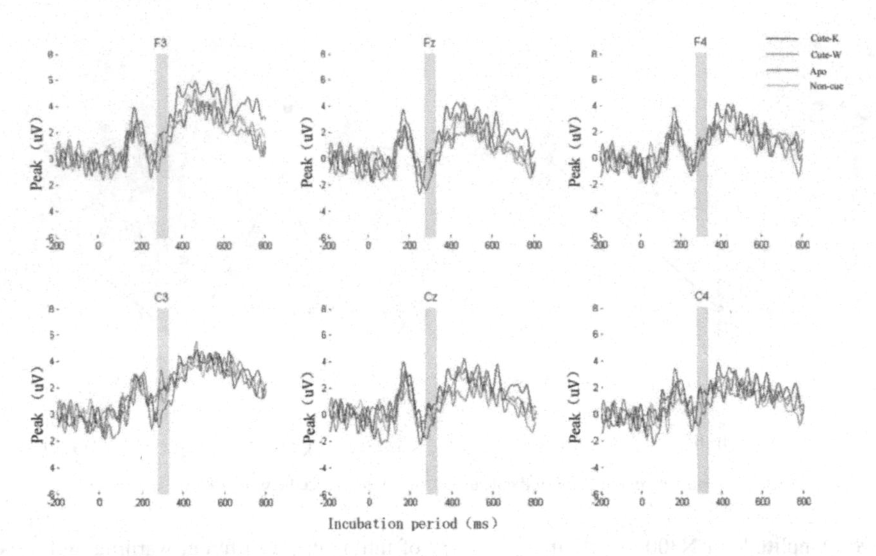

(A) Grand-averaged ERPs evoked by cute-K\cute-W\Apo\Non-cue at six electrodes from the frontal and central regions

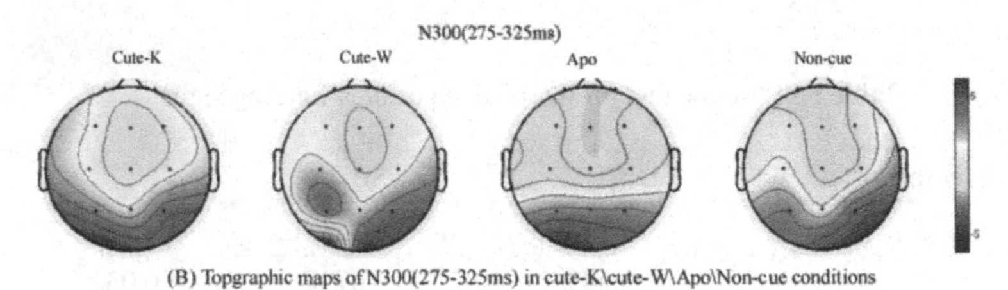

(B) Topgraphic maps of N300(275-325ms) in cute-K\cute-W\Apo\Non-cue conditions

Fig. 9. ERPs results. Grand average ERPs of N300 evoked by the standard stimulus obtained from the frontal and central regions (F3, Fz, F4, C3, Cz, C4)

5 Discussion

Different warning signs evoke different objective emotional arousal in older adults when faced with the risk of falling. Older adults evoked the greatest N300 amplitude negativity in the Apo warning sign condition (Mean = −0.447 mn, SD = 4.932) and were significantly higher than Cute-K(p = 0.032) and Cute-W(p = 0.044). This is similar to the results of experiments conducted by Valner et al. [31]. The findings suggest that different types of warning signs affect the avoidance behavior of older adults in hazardous situations, and that warning signs of Apo enable older adults to make safer decisions than other signs.

Cute-K has been shown to evoke cautious and protective behavior [37]. Cute-W has been shown to induce permissive behavior [30]. However, this study did not find any significant difference in subjective risk perception and objective emotional arousal between the two types of cute warning signs. The results of the study indicate that different cute types of warning signs do not affect older adults' judgment of falls. However, it has been shown that neutral baby faces have a significantly greater effect on motivation to view and attention preference than happy and sad faces when compared to pictures of babies with facial expressions [38]. Since the infant expressions used in this study were all on the negative side, further research is needed to prove whether the effect of different cute types of warning signs on the perception of fall risk in older adults is different.

Compared to the results of objective emotional arousal, none of the subjective risk perception scores of older adults in different warning sign situations were significantly different. This result may be because people's responses to visual cues are momentary and change quickly, and most people are largely unaware of the subjective perception of different visual cues. Although the different warning signs did not fully corroborate in subjective and objective responses, the results of this study demonstrate the possibility of applying N300 component analysis to fall interventions [14].

6 Conclusion

This study investigated the effects of different warning sign types and the level of perceived sensitivity of older adults on objective emotional arousal (ERP) and subjective risk perception in a fall-prone environment based on risk perception, respectively. The results showed that the type of warning signs had a significant effect on objective emotional arousal ($F_{(1,24)} = 5.110$, $p = 0.033$, $\eta^2 = 0.176$). Compared to Cut-K, Cut-W, and Non-cue, Apo elicited the highest negative mean N300 amplitudes (Mean $= -0.447$, SD $= 4.932$). The individual's high level of perceived sensitivity had a significant effect on risk perception (perceived likelihood of fall: $F_{(1,928)} = 6.876$, $p < 0.01$; fall anticipation emotion: $F_{(1,928)} = 13.831$, $p < 0.001$; fall anticipation worries: $F_{(1,928)} = 7.472$, $p < 0.01$).

The results suggest that Apo warning signs could be given primary consideration when designing warning signs for older adults in fall-prone areas. More fall intervention approaches should focus more on older adults with low perceived sensitivity (ABC scale score < 89.94). The findings of this study guide how warning signs should be installed to trigger safe behavior in older adults in hazardous scenarios and situations.

The limitations of this study are that the design of the experimental signs was not standardized in terms of form and color and that the effects of different warning signs on the perceived dangers of the elderly after removing the textual information were not explored.

Acknowledgment. The authors would like to acknowledge the support from the National Natural Science Foundation of China (72171030).

References

1. World report on ageing and health. https://www.who.int/publications-detail-redirect/9789241565042. Last accessed 31 Mar 2023
2. WHO global report on falls prevention in older age: https://www.who.int/publications-detail-redirect/9789241563536. Last accessed 31 Mar 2023
3. United Nations: World Population Prospects 2019: Highlights. https://www.un.org/en/desa/world-population-prospects-2019-highlights. Last accessed 31 Mar 2023

4. Blanchet, R., Edwards, N.: A need to improve the assessment of environmental hazards for falls on stairs and in bathrooms: results of a scoping review. BMC Geriatr. **18**, 272 (2018). https://doi.org/10.1186/s12877-018-0958-1
5. China Cause of Death Detection Dataset (2021). https://ncncd.chinacdc.cn/xzzq_1/202101/t20210111_223706.htm. Last accessed 2023/03/31
6. Slaug, B., Granbom, M., Iwarsson, S.: An aging population and an aging housing stock – housing accessibility problems in typical swedish dwellings. J. Aging Env. **34**, 156–174 (2020). https://doi.org/10.1080/26892618.2020.1743515
7. Moyer, M.W.: Why older adults are too trusting. Sci. Am. Mind **24**, 9 (2013). https://doi.org/10.1038/scientificamericanmind0513-9b
8. Stevens, J.A., Noonan, R.K., Rubenstein, L.Z.: Older adult fall prevention: perceptions, beliefs, and behaviors. Am. J. Lifestyle Med. **4**, 16–20 (2010). https://doi.org/10.1177/1559827609348350
9. Wilson, R.S., Zwickle, A., Walpole, H.: Developing a broadly applicable measure of risk perception. Risk Anal. **39**, 777–791 (2019). https://doi.org/10.1111/risa.13207
10. Siegrist, M., Árvai, J.: Risk perception: reflections on 40 years of research. Risk Anal. **40**, 2191–2206 (2020). https://doi.org/10.1111/risa.13599
11. Rahn, M., Tomczyk, S., Schmidt, S.: Storms, fires, and bombs: analyzing the impact of warning message and receiver characteristics on risk perception in different hazards. Risk Anal. **41**, 1630–1642 (2021). https://doi.org/10.1111/risa.13636
12. Machado Nardi, V.A., Teixeira, R., Ladeira, W.J., de Oliveira Santini, F.: A meta-analytic review of food safety risk perception. Food Control **112**, 107089 (2020). https://doi.org/10.1016/j.foodcont.2020.107089
13. Laughery, K.R., Wogalter, M.S.: A three-stage model summarizes product warning and environmental sign research. Saf. Sci. **61**, 3–10 (2014). https://doi.org/10.1016/j.ssci.2011.02.012
14. Zhu, L., Ma, Q., Bai, X., Hu, L.: Mechanisms behind hazard perception of warning signs: an EEG study. Transport. Res. F: Traffic Psychol. Behav. **69**, 362–374 (2020). https://doi.org/10.1016/j.trf.2020.02.001
15. Ahn, S., Oh, J.: Effects of a health-belief-model-based osteoporosis- and fall-prevention program on women at early old age. Appl. Nurs. Res. **59**, 151430 (2021). https://doi.org/10.1016/j.apnr.2021.151430
16. Preissner, C.E., Kaushal, N., Charles, K., Knäuper, B.: A protection motivation theory approach to understanding how fear of falling affects physical activity determinants in older adults. J. Gerontol.: Ser. B **78**, 30–39 (2023). https://doi.org/10.1093/geronb/gbac105
17. El-Bendary, N., Tan, Q., Pivot, F.C., Lam, A.: Fall detection and prevention for the elderly: a review of trends and challenges. Int. J. Smart Sens. Intell. Syst. **6**, 1230–1266 (2013). https://doi.org/10.21307/ijssis-2017-588
18. Vincenzo, J.L., Patton, S.K., Lefler, L.L., McElfish, P.A., Wei, J., Curran, G.M.: A qualitative study of older adults' facilitators, barriers, and cues to action to engage in falls prevention using health belief model constructs. Arch. Gerontol. Geriatr. **99**, 104610 (2022). https://doi.org/10.1016/j.archger.2021.104610
19. Gravesande, J., Richardson, J., Griffith, L., Scott, F.: Test-retest reliability, internal consistency, construct validity and factor structure of a falls risk perception questionnaire in older adults with type 2 diabetes mellitus: a prospective cohort study. Archiv. Physiother. **9**, 14 (2019). https://doi.org/10.1186/s40945-019-0065-4
20. Kaushal, N., Preissner, C., Charles, K., Knäuper, B.: Differences and similarities of physical activity determinants between older adults who have and have not experienced a fall: testing an extended health belief model. Arch. Gerontol. Geriatr. **92**, 104247 (2021). https://doi.org/10.1016/j.archger.2020.104247

21. Kiyoshi-Teo, H., et al.: Older hospital inpatients' fall risk factors, perceptions, and daily activities to prevent falling. Geriatr. Nurs. **40**, 290–295 (2019). https://doi.org/10.1016/j.gerinurse.2018.11.005
22. Hughes, K., et al.: Older persons' perception of risk of falling: implications for fall-prevention campaigns. Am. J. Public Health **98**, 351–357 (2008). https://doi.org/10.2105/AJPH.2007.115055
23. Morgan, J., Reidy, J., Probst, T.: Age group differences in household accident risk perceptions and intentions to reduce hazards. Int. J. Env. Res. Public Health **16**(12), 2237 (2019). https://doi.org/10.3390/ijerph16122237
24. Twibell, R.S., Siela, D., Sproat, T., Coers, G.: Perceptions related to falls and fall prevention among hospitalized adults. Am. J. Crit. Care **24**, e78–e85 (2015). https://doi.org/10.4037/ajcc2015375
25. Romli, M.H., Mackenzie, L., Lovarini, M., Tan, M.P., Clemson, L.: The clinimetric properties of instruments measuring home hazards for older people at risk of falling: a systematic review. Eval. Health Prof. **41**, 82–128 (2018). https://doi.org/10.1177/0163278716684166
26. Larson, C.L., Aronoff, J., Steuer, E.L.: Simple geometric shapes are implicitly associated with affective value. Motiv. Emot. **36**, 404–413 (2012). https://doi.org/10.1007/s11031-011-9249-2
27. Ma, Q., Bai, X., Pei, G., Xu, Z.: The hazard perception for the surrounding shape of warning signs: evidence from an event-related potentials study. Front. Neurosci. **12**, 824 (2018). https://doi.org/10.3389/fnins.2018.00824
28. Lorenz, Konrad: Die angeborenen Formen möglicher Erfahrung (The innate conditions of the possibility of experience). Zeitschrift für Tierpsychologie **5**(2), 235–409 (2010). https://doi.org/10.1111/j.1439-0310.1943.tb00655.x
29. Ngai, S.: The cuteness of the avant-garde. Crit. Inq. **31**, 811–847 (2005). https://doi.org/10.1086/444516
30. Nenkov, G.Y., Scott, M.L.: "So cute i could eat it up": priming effects of cute products on indulgent consumption. J. Consum. Res. **41**, 326–341 (2014). https://doi.org/10.1086/676581
31. Valner, R., Dydynski, J.M., Cho, S., Kruusamäe, K.: Communication of hazards in mixed-reality telerobotic systems: the usage of naturalistic avoidance cues in driving tasks. Hum. Factors: J. Hum. Factors Ergon. Soc. **63**, 619–634 (2021). https://doi.org/10.1177/0018720820902293
32. Morgan, M.T., Friscia, L.A., Whitney, S.L., Furman, J.M., Sparto, P.J.: Reliability and validity of the falls efficacy scale-international (FES-I) in individuals with dizziness and imbalance. Otol. Neurotol. **34**, 1104–1108 (2013). https://doi.org/10.1097/MAO.0b013e318281df5d
33. Edwards, N., Dulai, J., Rahman, A.: A scoping review of epidemiological, ergonomic, and longitudinal cohort studies examining the links between stair and bathroom falls and the built environment. Int. J. Env. Res. Publ. Health **16**(9), 1598 (2019). https://doi.org/10.3390/ijerph16091598
34. Nieuwenhuis, S., Slagter, H.A., von Geusau, N.J.A., Heslenfeld, D.J., Holroyd, C.B.: Knowing good from bad: differential activation of human cortical areas by positive and negative outcomes. Eur. J. Neurosci. **21**, 3161–3168 (2005). https://doi.org/10.1111/j.1460-9568.2005.04152.x
35. Ni, Z., Wang, L., Meng, J., Qiu, F., Huang, J.: EEG signal processing in anesthesia feature extraction of time and frequency parameters. Procedia Environ. Sci. **8**, 215–220 (2011). https://doi.org/10.1016/j.proenv.2011.10.035
36. Taylor, S.F., Coogle, C.L., Cotter, J.J., Welleford, E.A., Copolillo, A.: Community-dwelling older adults' adherence to environmental fall prevention recommendations. J. Appl. Gerontol. **38**, 755–774 (2019). https://doi.org/10.1177/0733464817723087

37. Jia, H.M., Park, C.W., Pol, G.: Cuteness, nurturance, and implications for visual product design (2015)
38. Jia, Y.C., et al.: Adults' responses to infant faces: Neutral infant facial expressions elicit the strongest baby schema effect. Q. J. Exp. Psychol. **74**(5), 853–871 (2021). https://doi.org/10.1177/1747021820981862

Older Adults' Engagement with Short Video Applications During the COVID-19 Pandemic: Perceived Affordances and Constraints

Jingwen Lian[1](✉), Xinyue Li[1], Mengyuan Zhao[2], Yuxiang (Chris) Zhao[3], and Qinghua Zhu[1]

[1] School of Information Management, Nanjing University, Nanjing 210023, China
jwlian@smail.nju.edu.cn
[2] Fudan University Library, Shanghai 200433, China
[3] School of Economics and Management, Nanjing University of Science and Technology, Nanjing 210094, China

Abstract. The spread and proliferation of short video applications (like TikTok) equip older adults more opportunities to obtain information and pleasure, especially in the COVID-19 pandemic. However, research on the use of TikTok among older adults is limited. In this exploratory study, we conducted interviews and on-site observations with 11 older adults aged 50 years or older who had experience using TikTok. This study explored the experience of TikTok's specific features for older adults from a need-affordance-features perspective, including the needs met and challenges encountered by older users. The findings show that older users' perceptions of the affordances provided by TikTok can be divided into two categories of egocentric affordance and allocentric affordance, totaling nine. We also identified three perceived constraints, including user interface design, privacy and security, and operability. The study extends the understanding of social media affordances from the perspective of older adults and also provides practical insights for the design and service improvement of short video applications.

Keywords: COVID-19 · Older Adults · Perceived Affordances · Perceived Constraints · Short Video Applications

1 Introduction

In recent years, short video applications have gained rapid tractions among public due to the proliferation of mobile devices and advancement of 5G technology. In their nascent stage, short videos applications took identity and emotion sharing as the underlying logic, with the characteristics of low content production thresholds and fast dissemination [1]. They conquered user-generated-content (UGC) users with their instrumentality, sociality, and fragmentation, erasing the lines between content providers and consumers. While there are multiple short video applications in the market, TikTok has emerged as the leading short video application globally. It is available in 155 countries, with over 800 million monthly active users worldwide and 2 billion downloads [2]. During the

Q. Gao et al. (Eds.): HCII 2023, LNCS 14055, pp. 85–99, 2023.
https://doi.org/10.1007/978-3-031-48041-6_7

COVID-19 pandemic, people spent increasingly more time on short video applications, looking for new means for entertainment and staying connected. This increase in demand further boosted the download volume of TikTok [3].

Previous studies or surveys have generally indicated that TikTok is a social media platform mainly targeted at young people [4]. However, this latest social media behemoth has now penetrated the older population, especially during the COVID-19 pandemic [5]. Compared to other groups, older adults are more susceptible to experiencing isolations and encountering difficulties in accessing information and maintaining social connections [6]. Short video applications offer a novel way to enhance the digital lives of older adults, particularly during the pandemic. However, older adults usually have low digital literacy [7] and may be faced with many challenges in the use of short videos. Existing literature has paid little attention to the use of TikTok among older adults, especially lacking an understanding of their overall perception of TikTok use. Previous research focusing on older adults has predominantly centered on their content generation and self-representation on TikTok [8, 9], but has not explored the interaction between older adults and the platform's technology especially in the pandemic.

To better understand older adults' utilizations of TikTok, this study conducted interviews and on-site observations of 11 older adults who had experiences in TikTok during the COVID-19 pandemic. This study adopted a Need-affordance-features (NAF) perspective [10] to investigate how older adults interact with various features of TikTok, particularly focusing on how well these features satisfy their needs and causing limitations. Unlike technological determinism, the idea of affordance acknowledges and priorities the role of humans in the use of technology [11]. The NAF perspective, based on self-determination theory and psychological ownership theory, is often used to understand the interaction between users and specific features of social media, which helps researchers to identify relevant needs and affordances, as well as motivations for use [12, 13].

We found that older adults' perceived affordance of TikTok were richer than anticipated, which meets different psychological needs of older adults. However, these affordances also presented some constraints for older adults. This study extends the disclosure on social media affordance [10], by adopting the perspective of older adults and with a focus on the unique context of the COVID-19 pandemic. This study also contributes practical insights for short video platforms to improve their services and designs. Finally, the findings from the context of COVID-19 pandemic can enhance the understanding and comprehensions of older adults' use of digital technologies in health crises and provide references to improve their digital literacy.

2 Related work

2.1 Affordance Theory And Need-Affordance-Features Perspective

The concept of affordance, originated from Gibson [14] in ecological psychology, refers to the interaction between an actor with the environment. Norman [11] applied this concept to the field of design and offered a different insight. He argued that affordance depends on the individual's subjective perception and understanding of external features. Hutchby [15] was the first to apply affordance to technologies, understanding it as an IT artifact. According to him, affordance can explain how technology enables or constrains specific human action, yet technology does not necessarily lead to human action. With the prevalence and development of social media platforms, affordance theory has been applied broadly in related domains. In recent years, some scholars developed and employed different typologies to conceptualize affordances within social media contexts. Treem and Leonardi [16] proposed four dimensions of social media affordances (i.e., visibility, associating, editability, and persistence). Majchrzak and Faraj [17] put forward four categories of affordances for knowledge sharing: meta voicing, trigger attending, network-informed associating and generative role-taking. In addition, other scholars successively proposed functional media affordance [18], communication affordance [19], and social business technology affordance [20]. Karahanan et al. [10] proposed the Needs-Affordances-Features (NAF) perspective for social media, which identified the most integrated social media affordance through a comprehensive literature review and analysis of social media applications. This provides a systematic framework for understanding the affordances of social media and the users' psychological needs.

While many theories of technology use emphasize situational motivation, the NAF theory focuses on general life needs that go beyond specific contexts [10]. The field of psychology believes that every person has innate psychological needs and is driven to engage in activities that satisfy their needs [21, 22]. Therefore, the NAF perspective suggests that users' intrinsic psychological needs serve as a motivating factor for their utilization of social media, and that the affordances offered by social media can satisfy these needs [10]. Nowadays, the NAF perspective has been applied widely in social media studies to identify relevant needs, affordance, and motivations for use based on specific features of social media, providing insights into the design of social media features. For example, Wei [12] drew on the NAF perspective to investigate the impact of three psychological needs (i.e., need for competence, autonomy and relatedness) on both work-related and social-related social media use. Abhari's study applied the NAF perspective to figure out psychological motivation of the use of Business Intelligence tools [13].

2.2 Social Media Use

Social media is defined as a new type of online media that provides users with a great venue for engagement. Participation, openness, dialogue, community and connectivity are its main features [23]. In the last decade, social media research has been booming. Previous studies on social media use have primarily investigated usage motivation [24–26], usage intensity [27, 28], usage behavior [29, 30], problematic use (e.g., addiction) [31–33] etc. The main theories used in this field are Technological Acceptance Model (TAM), affordance theory, the Uses and Gratification theory (UGT), Theory of Planned Behavior (TPB), Unified Theory of Acceptance and Use of Technology (UTAUT), and Diffusion of Innovation Theory (DIT). In particular, social media research around affordance theory has become increasingly numerous. Although most of the current literature focuses on ubiquitous platforms like Facebook, Twitter and enterprise social media, the exploration of affordances present in short video platforms is relatively limited [34]. Considering the increasing popularity of short video platforms, it is particularly important to investigate its affordances and need met.

Empirical studies on social media use have been conducted on a wide variety of populations, such as adolescents, corporate employees, and nurses. The aging trend of society has brought more attention to older adults. Extant literature has focused more on the accessibility [35, 36], acceptance [37, 38], adoption [31, 39], and age-appropriate design [40, 41]of technologies. This was based on the hypothesis that older adults do not use new technologies and that there is a digital divide with younger people. In fact, an increasing number of studies have yielded results that are completely opposite to this hypothesis [42]. Recently, researchers have focused on the experience and impact of social media use among older adults. For example, Kusumota et al. [43] found that the use of social media had positive results (63.6%) in minimizing loneliness and/or social isolation in older adults compared to various other technologies. Milovich et al. [44] investigated whether interventions using free social networking platforms could improve the cognitive speed of older adults. Han et al. [45] explored the factors of social media use among older adults and the role of social media in promoting their health. Some studies adopted affordance theory to understand older adults' social media use, including their need satisfaction [46], motivations [47], and effects on intergenerational segregation [48], more often in the context of Facebook, ignoring the specific features of short video applications.

3 Method

Semi-structured interviews were conducted to understand the experiences of a small group (N = 11) of older adults who were engaging with TikTok during COVID-19 pandemic. Purposive and snowball sampling methods were employed to recruit participants. The eligibility criteria are as follows: (1) aged 50 or older, based on Zulman et al.'s [49] definition; (2) had used TikTok at least once during the COVID-19 pandemic.

3.1 Participants

A county in eastern China was the initial recruitment site, where the researchers identified several participants and used a snowball sampling technique to find additional participants. According to eligibility criteria, a total of 11 older adults were recruited to participate in the interview. The participants were individually contacted by the investigators and they provided informed consent prior to their participation in this study. The demographic details are shown in Table 1. The sample included 7 females and 4 males, ranging in age from 50 to 78 with 55 being the average. In terms of educational background, four participants have completed primary education, six have completed secondary education, while only one has completed higher education. It is worth noting that the majority of participants in the study chose to continue working even after reaching retirement age.

3.2 Data Collection

Data collection was conducted in November and December 2022. Each interview was conducted face-to-face in participant's home, lasting approximately 60 min. Each participant was provided with a 100 CNY honorarium for their participation. We have

Table 1. Demographic details of the participants.

Participants ID	Gender	Age	Educational Background	Household members	TikTok Usage (approximate time)	Working status
1	Male	50	Secondary	Partner, children	5 years	still working
2	Female	62	Secondary	Children	10 months	retired at home
3	Female	56	Primary	Living alone	5 years	still working
4	Female	53	Primary	Partner	2 years	still working
5	Male	54	Tertiary	Partner	3 years	still working
6	Female	50	Primary	Partner, children	4 years	still working
7	Male	50	Secondary	Living alone	4 years	still working
8	Female	52	Secondary	Children	2 years	retired at home
9	Male	51	Secondary	Partner	5 years	still working
10	Female	51	Secondary	Partner	1 year	still working
11	Female	78	Primary	Children	5 years	retired at home

designed an interview protocol that aims to gain insights into participants' understanding and utilization of specific features on TikTok, as well as their experiences with these features, both positive and negative. The protocol also delves into the challenges that users encounter when using TikTok in their daily lives. Through this protocol, we hope to gather comprehensive and valuable data that can shed light on how people interact with the platform and the impact it has on their lives. The interviews were audio-recorded with the consent of the participants. The participants were informed that the content of their narratives would be used strictly for research purposes. To maintain the anonymity of the data, participants were asked to avoid mentioning their names in the interviews. We also encouraged participants to use TikTok after the formal interview. We conducted on-site observations and interacted with participants as necessary. The field notes obtained from observation are used as supplementary material for later coding analysis to provide additional details that participants may have overlooked during the interview process.

3.3 Data Analysis

All interviews were voice recorded and transcribed for data analysis. Then the interview transcripts were analyzed using an open coding method [50]. We conducted a bottom-up thematic analysis with the interview data to identify key themes related to our research questions. To enhance the reliability of the coding scheme, process, and outcomes [51], two native Mandarin-speaking researchers were involved in the coding work. We first coded a transcribed interview independently. Then we compared their coding results to identify differences in their codes through a face-to-face meeting. After two rounds of discussion, we resolved such discrepancies and reached a consensus on our codes (an acceptable inter-coder reliability score of $K = 0.92$). Throughout the coding process, we compared new codes with existing ones, and adjusted the coding scheme as necessary by reorganizing or combining codes to ensure accuracy [52]. This iterative process improved the coding scheme over time, helping us identify important themes in the data. Further, all the codes were translated into affordances and constraints related to the use of TikTok in older adults' daily life.

4 Results

This study identified 9 major affordances and constraints related to use TikTok as summarized in Fig. 1. Referring to the social media affordance framework proposed by Karahanna et al. [10], perceived affordances were categorized into Egocentric and Allocentric affordances. Here, we define each affordance and illustrate how different features shape the affordances of TikTok. Table 2 shows the mapping between perceived affordances and the specific features of TikTok.

4.1 Perceived Egocentric Affordance

Self-presentation. Self-presentation affordance refers to how users utilize social media to express their values, preferences, expertise, and other aspects of their personality through sharing information about themselves [10]. On TikTok, users have the opportunity to showcase themselves to others through the "creating a profile" or "uploading videos" functions. Self-presentation help users fulfill their autonomy need and expressing self-identify need [10], enabling them to freely choose what to share and how to present themselves. All interviewees have set their avatars with their own photos or things they like. For example, *"My TikTok avatar is an orchid, because I really like plants, especially orchid"* (P4). More than half of the interviewees' posted video content is related to selfies, group shots, hobbies, work and family life (P1, P3, P6, P7). By uploading videos, users can satisfy their needs of having a place and maintaining continuity of self-identity [10]. As P6 reported, *"TikTok gives me a special place to post videos related to myself... I post videos every day, some of my current life and some of my youthful photos"* (P6).

Content Sharing. Content sharing allows users to distribute content to others that may not necessarily be related to themselves [10]. In addition to uploading self-related content, many interviewees also upload content related to their observations, funny videos,

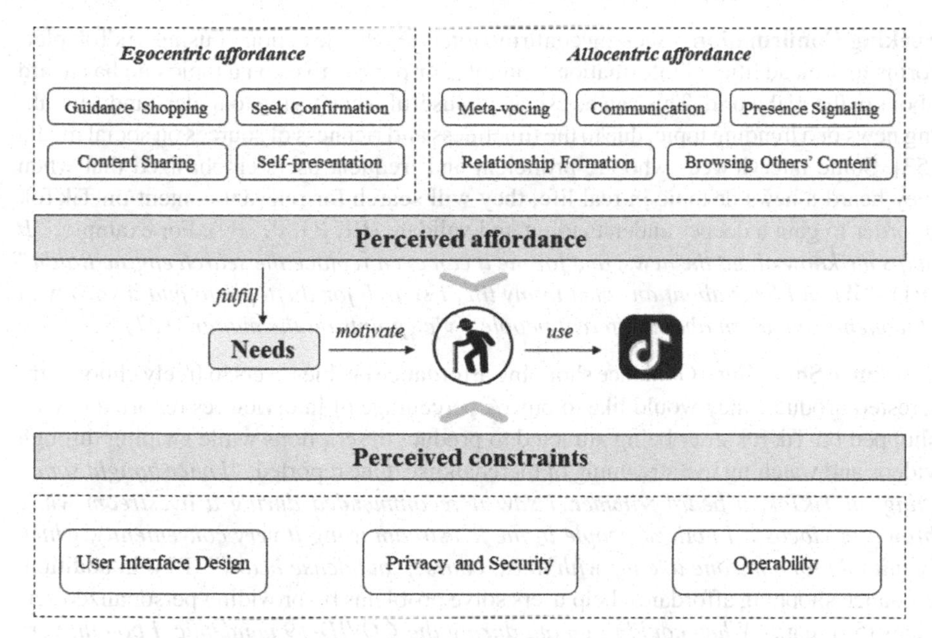

Fig. 1. Perceived affordances and constraints when older adults engage with TikTok

Table 2. Mapping of TikTok features to perceived affordances

	Perceived affordances	Features
Egocentric affordance	Self-presentation	creating a profile, uploading videos
	Content sharing	uploading videos
	Seek confirmation	searching
	Guidance shopping	watching videos, live streaming
Allocentric affordance	Presence signaling	online reminder, watching videos
	Relationship formation	following
	Browsing others' content	watching videos, following
	Meta-voicing	liking, commenting, favoring, forwarding
	Communication	direct messaging

and so on. For instance, *"I will share some beautiful sceneries when I see it, which will make people feel enjoyable"* (P1, P6). Some interviewees also use the forwarding and sharing function, forwarding to their personal homepage, sharing with specific individuals, and even across platforms such as WeChat. Content sharing is motivated by many reasons, such as spreading positive energy (P6, P7), alerting their children about scams (P4, P8), educating their family on COVID-19 preventions (P1, P3), and amplifying the reach of missing persons' announcements (P7). This affordance helps users fulfill the need for autonomy and expressing self-identify [10].

Seeking Confirmation. Seeking confirmation refers to the action of using TikTok platforms to seek additional information, opinions, or perspectives on a topic one has heard about in the real world. This can be especially useful when trying to understand a breaking news or a trending topic, due to the timeliness and richness of sources on social media [53]. Some interviewees who are proficient and frequent users emphasized that when they heard a news or topic in real life, they will search for relevant content on TikTok in order to gain a deeper understanding and validate (P1, P5, P7, P9). For example, *"It helps me know about the news, and for me it can even replace the search engine Baidu"* (P1). *"When I hear about an event in my life, I search for the topic to find a variety of statements and learn about different people's viewpoints on the matter"* (P7).

Guidance Shopping. Guidance shopping affordance enables users to freely choose "interested product" they would like to buy. A percentage of interviewees reported having shopped on TikTok after being attracted to product descriptions while swiping through videos and watching live streaming of merchandise. One reported, *"I once bought something on TikTok, a beard trimmer. I saw it recommended during a livestream while browsing videos... I noticed people in the livestream using it very conveniently, which is suitable for someone like me with thick, coarse, and dense beard"* (P7). In addition, guidance shopping affordance help users solve problems by providing personalized services [54], e.g., *"When couldn't go out during the COVID-19 pandemic, I bought very much on it. I think it's just like Taobao. I asked for information about the products during the live streaming, such as the size of the clothes to see if they fit me. The people on the live streaming did answer my questions, which felt good"* (P1).

4.2 Perceived Allocentric Affordance

Presence Signaling. Presence signaling affordance allows users to show whether they are online and available, or to check if other users are currently available [10]. Many participants mentioned their desire to see which of their friends are currently online and available for interaction. As one stated, *"I want to know if friends are online, especially family members who are not around, so that I can know if they are free right now"* (P8). Based on our data, we found that participants were able to determine if their friends were online by observing whether there was a green dot on their friends' avatars or if they had posted a video. One participant stated that *"Sometimes I stay up late and then when I see my friend still online, which is a green dot on his avatar, I would send a message asking him why he is still up so late"* (P6). And another commented *"Sometimes when I brush the videos of people I followed, I suddenly see a video my friend just posted, I instantly know that he is also on TikTok"* (P5).

Relationship Formation. Relationship formation refers to the affordance to enable users to build a relationship with someone in social media [10]. During the pandemic, many participants turned to TikTok to connect with others while in isolations. All respondents mentioned that they use the "following" feature to build social connections, which includes following people they don't know and people they do know, resulting in friends and follow-only relationships. For example, *"Besides my family and friends, I also follow some of my peers at work, mainly because I want to know what they are doing and* *learn from them"* (P1). Besides, TikTok provides users with the ability to freely choose whom to follow through its relationship formation affordance. As a participant said, *"I only follow people I know well, while sometimes unknown people follow me"* (P5), while another one said, *"I also follow people I don't know if I think they are interesting or I am lonely in physical isolations"* (P4). The latter way helped to form a new relationship with people all over the country, and this was particularly important during the pandemic as traditional forms of socializations were limited.

Browsing Others' Content. Browsing videos is the most commonly used feature of TikTok. The participants reported that they frequently browse videos on TikTok, as they can freely explore content that they are interested in. For example, one participant with a chronic disease of hyperglycemia stated, *"My blood sugar is high, so I have to exercise every day. When I can't go out during the COVID-19 pandemic, I want to learn how to exercise at home by watching videos on TikTok"* (P11). The participants also browse through other users' content by "following" users who share content they are interested in and visiting their profiles. One said, *"I like to watch videos about family routines and children's education-related content because I am not well-educated and can't understand anything else. For instance, I have watched the videos of '吉家女' from beginning to end, and sometimes I would click into her avatar to see if she had posted any updates"* (P6). In addition, some interviewees expressed that they become interested in other people's content when they receive notifications about videos posted by those they follow. As described in P10, *"I only watch the videos of people I follow. When I open TikTok and see a red number on 'Follow' or 'Friends', I will click on it and watch it"*. Browsing other people's content helped participants know what others were doing, increased their sense of connection with others, and helped them learn more about themselves, e.g., *"Sometimes when I see how difficult some people's lives are, I realize that my own problems are nothing in comparison"* (P4).

Meta-voicing. Meta-voicing affordance enables individuals have an opportunity to engage in online conversation by reacting to content shared by others [15]. According to interviewees, they provided feedback by liking, commenting, forwarding or favoriting others' posts. Some interviewees reported that they express their approval and enjoyment of certain themed videos, such as acts of kindness, talent show, and humor actions, by "liking" and "forwarding" videos (P2, P5, P6, P7, P8, P9). Some interviewees mentioned that they would "favorite" or "forward" some videos about knowledge and life experience sharing, e.g., *"I previously favorited a video that talks about how to use empty bottles. I thought the content it presented was very useful"* (P8). Also, interviews can observe how others react to their own posts and experience peer acceptance, e.g. *"I posted some videos of me singing and received some 'liking' from others...and someone complimented me in the comments...I feel that means I am not bad at singing ha-ha"* (P7). This may enhance the feeling of connection with "peers" [10]. Unlike the act of presenting oneself and sharing content, in meta-voice, the user contributes additional knowledge to pre-existing online content rather than solely expressing their own viewpoint [17].

Communication. Communication affordance refers to the possibility for individuals to communicate directly on TikTok. Interviewees can exchange personal messages or instant messages with others on TikTok, which help them build relationships with others. One mentioned, *"I met an old hometown friend on TikTok, and then chatted with him through 'direct messaging'. We didn't have any other ways to contact each other before, and it feels good to be able to connect now"* (P6). Further, communication affordance can satisfy someone's need of expressing themselves, e.g., *"I chat every day on TikTok, ... I often forward some videos to my family and then attach my opinions"* (P7).

4.3 Perceived Constraints

While the older adults in our casc all reported positive comments on the use of TikTok, they also mentioned some problems and challenges they encountered in engaging with TikTok. Three perceived constraints emerged from the analysis.

User Interface Design. As older adults grow older, their actions and cognition begin to slow down, so they may encounter some problems when interacting with the interface of short video platforms. Based on our interviews and on-site observation, we found that many participants were vulnerable to mis-touch when interacting with the interface. Some interviewees mentioned that they often accidentally click on links within the videos while watching, and are involuntarily redirected to other pages such as live streaming rooms, external platforms, or the page of topics, and find it difficult to return back. As one interviewee put it: *"...My fingers are not very flexible... I can easily click on the live streaming or the ad link. The ad link would jump to another platform and at first, I didn't know what was happening..."* (P11). In addition, some respondents indicated that there are too many pages that can be switched currently, but they do not understand the functions of each page, which can lead to confusions (P4, P8, P11), e.g., *"There are too many pages for me...and I can only brush the video simply, as well as like, comment, favorite and forward...and sometimes can't remember"* (P8). It's worth noting that although TikTok offers an option to turn on an "elderly mode" in the settings, which includes larger fonts and simplified functions, interviewees were unaware of its existence and none of them had enabled it.

Privacy and Security. Privacy and security is an another recurrent theme of older adults' concerns in the interviews. In our study, some of the interviewees expressed concern that the commenting and online status features on TikTok could potentially compromise their personal privacy and even lead them to avoid using these features. For example, P4 said, *"I generally don't comment, as it leaves my trace behind. If strangers see it, they can view my homepage by clicking my avatar or id"*, while P7 stated, *"I don't like the online status notification. I feel like it exposes my personal information"* (P7). In addition, some interviewees stopped using certain functions that require authorized information due to concerns about security risks, such as *"I haven't bought anything on it. When you're ready to purchase, a window pops up asking you to agree to authorize personal information. I think it's unreliable"* (P2).

Operability. Previous studies suggest that the ease of use and perceived usefulness of the technology significantly influence elderly's continued adoption of technology [55, 56]. In this interview, older adults are still faced with some technological challenges.

Some interviewees mentioned that the process of cross-platform forwarding is complicated (P2, P10, P11), e.g., *"...I saw a video about how to wear a mask correctly during the COVID-19 pandemic, and I wanted to forward it to my family group on WeChat. However, it cannot be forwarded with one click, and I don't know how to operate it"* (P2). It was also suggested that the steps for making videos were also complicated and difficult to learn, e.g., *"I have no problem watching videos, but when it comes to uploading videos, especially those with music and subtitles, I feel it's very difficult. There are too many steps involved and I also need to type..."* (P3). In addition, some interviewees reported problems and bad experiences about purchasing goods on TikTok. An interviewee said: *"Sometimes I also watch product live streaming and then want to buy things...I need to provide my address, but I don't know how to type and can't fill it out..."* (P11).

5 Discussion and Conclusions

This paper investigates the perceived affordances and constraints of older adults' use of TikTok during the COVID-19 pandemic. The study found that elderly individuals could effectively utilize the various functional features of TikTok to satisfy their psychological requirements. We have sorted out a list of perceived affordances of older adults' engagement with TikTok, including self-expression, content sharing, seeking confirmation, shopping, presence signaling, relationship formation, browsing others' content, meta-voicing, and communication. Despite older adults being more proficient in using TikTok than anticipated, they still face some challenges, primarily related to user interface design, privacy and security, and operability.

The study's findings indicate that certain affordances were emphasized during the COVID-19 pandemic, including guidance shopping, relationship formation, browsing other users' content, and content sharing. Due to mobility restrictions during the lockdown, older adults, who were more susceptible to the virus, were encouraged to stay at home. As a result, they turned to TikTok more frequently as a means of coping with the pandemic's effects, utilizing different perceived affordances. For example, browsing others' content enabled them to follow exercise videos and workout at home when they were unable to engage in outdoor activities like walking or square dancing. Browsing others' content also provided an access to a wide range of information, including pandemic-related content. Moreover, the guidance shopping affordance has allowed some older adults to meet their daily shopping needs without leaving home. Furthermore, relationship formation and content sharing affordances enabled older adults to socialize with others through the internet, which helped them combat loneliness and social isolation during the pandemic.

This study helps to improve the age-appropriate design of TikTok. In spite of its simple and easy gesture interactions, older adults who lack finger dexterity may still encounter difficulties while using short video applications. While TikTok has developed an elder mode for the elderly population with larger fonts, icons, and simplified functional modules, older users still reported difficulty perceiving the presence of this version and finding a way to activate it. This finding highlights the importance of ensuring that age-appropriate versions are easily accessible and enabled by older people. This has broader implications for short-video apps like TikTok and other social media platforms.

This study also contributes to breaking stereotypes about older adults and their technological competence. Digital technology developers are often misled by such stereotypes [57]. However, the findings indicate that older adults perceive a richer affordance of TikTok than what researchers predicted. Although older adults face barriers to using TikTok due to cognitive decline and slower mobility, they still perceive diverse social media affordances. Additionally, previous studies have shown that older adults lack knowledge of potential online risks [58]. In contrast, this study found that older adults have a certain level of privacy and security awareness when using TikTok. They are aware that online status and comments could compromise their privacy and are concerned about the security risks of providing information required for authorization and purchases.

This study was limited by its small sample size, which constrains its generalizability. However, the study provided valuable data that enhances our understanding of older adults' engagement with TikTok. The findings shed light on the design of short video technology to better meet the needs of older adults. Moreover, this study was conducted during the COVID-19 pandemic, which can raise awareness and understanding of older adults' use of digital technologies during health crises and also provide insights into how to improve older adults' digital literacy.

Acknowledgments. This work was funded by the Key Projects of the National Social Science Foundation of China under Grant (No. 22&ZD327).

References

1. Yu, X., Zhang, Y., Zhang, X.: The short video usage motivation and behavior of middle-aged and old users. Library Hi Tech (2022). https://doi.org/10.1108/LHT-09-2021-0318
2. Mhalla, M., Yun, J., Nasiri, A.: Video-sharing apps business models: TikTok case study. Int. J. Innov. Technol. Manag. **17**(07), 2050050 (2020)
3. Li, Y., Guan, M., Hammond, P., Berrey, L.E.: Communicating COVID-19 information on TikTok: a content analysis of TikTok videos from official accounts featured in the COVID-19 information hub. Health Educ. Res. **36**(3), 261–271 (2021)
4. Vaterlaus, J.M., Winter, M.: TikTok: an exploratory study of young adults' uses and gratifications. Soc. Sci. J. 1–20 (2021)
5. Ng, R., Indran, N.: Not too old for TikTok: how older adults are reframing aging. Gerontologist **62**(8), 1207–1216 (2022)
6. Xie, B., Charness, N., Fingerman, K., Kaye, J., Kim, M.T., Khurshid, A.: When going digital becomes a necessity: ensuring older adults' needs for information, services, and social inclusion during COVID-19. J. Aging Soc. Policy **32**(4–5), 460–470 (2020)
7. Castilla, D., et al.: Teaching digital literacy skills to the elderly using a social network with linear navigation: a case study in a rural area. Int. J. Hum Comput Stud. **118**, 24–37 (2018)
8. Ng, R., Indran, N.: Granfluencers on TikTok: factors linked to positive self-portrayals of older adults on social media. PLoS ONE **18**(2), e0280281 (2023)
9. Bibeva, I.: An exploration of older adults' motivations for creating content on TikTok and the role this plays for fostering new social connections (Dissertation). http://urn.kb.se/resolve?urn=urn:nbn:se:mau:diva-46219. Last accessed 4 Mar 2023
10. Karahanna, E., Xu, S.X., Xu, Y., Zhang, N.A.: The needs–affordances–features perspective for the use of social media. MIS Q. **42**(3), 737–756 (2018)

11. Norman, D.A.: The Psychology of Everyday Things. Basic Books, New York (1988)
12. Wei, S., Chen, X., Liu, C.: What motivates employees to use social media at work? A perspective of self-determination theory. Ind. Manag. Data Syst. **122**(1), 55–77 (2022)
13. Abhari K, Vomero A, Davidson E.: Psychology of business intelligence tools: needs-affordances-features perspective. In: Hawaii International Conference on System Sciences 2020 (HICSS-53) (2020)
14. Gibson, J.J.: The concept of affordances. In: Shaw, R., Bransford, J. (eds.) Perceiving, Acting, and Knowing: Toward an Ecological Psychology, pp. 67–81. John Wiley & Sons, New York (1997)
15. Hutchby, I.: Technologies, texts and affordances. Sociology **35**(2), 441–456 (2001)
16. Treem, J.W., Leonardi, P.M.: Social media use in organizations: exploring the affordances of visibility, editability, persistence, and association. Ann. Int. Commun. Assoc. **36**(1), 143–189 (2013)
17. Majchrzak, A., Faraj, S., Kane, G.C., Azad, B.: The contradictory influence of social media affordances on online communal knowledge sharing. J. Comput.-Mediat. Commun. **19**(1), 38–55 (2013)
18. Rice, R.E., Evans, S.K., Pearce, K.E., Sivunen, A., Vitak, J., Treem, J.W.: Organizational media affordances: operationalization and associations with media use. J. Commun. **67**(1), 106–130 (2017)
19. Fox, J., McEwan, B.: Distinguishing technologies for social interaction: the perceived social affordances of communication channels scale. Commun. Monogr. **84**(3), 298–318 (2017)
20. Wang, P., Li, H., Suomi, R.: Value co-creation in business via social media: a technology affordance approach. In: Pacific Asia Conference on Information System 2016 proceedings, p. 355 (2016)
21. Deci, E.L., Ryan, R.M.: Intrinsic Motivation and Self-determination in Human Behavior. Springer Science & Business Media, Berlin (2013)
22. Deci, E.L., Ryan, R.M.: The" what" and" why" of goal pursuits: human needs and the self-determination of behavior. Psychol. Inq. **11**(4), 227–268 (2000)
23. Enginkaya, E., Yılmaz, H.: What drives consumers to interact with brands through social media? A motivation scale development study. Procedia Soc. Behav. Sci. **148**, 219–226 (2014)
24. Cheung, M.L., Ting, H., Cheah, J.H., Sharipudin, M.N.S.: Examining the role of social media-based destination brand community in evoking tourists' emotions and intention to co-create and visit. J. Prod. Brand Manag. **30**(1), 28–43 (2021)
25. Alhabash, S., Ma, M.: A Tale of Four Platforms: Motivations and Uses of Facebook, Twitter, Instagram, and Snapchat Among College Students? Soc. Media + Soc. **3**(1) (2017)
26. Hilvert-Bruce, Z., Neill, J.T., Sjöblom, M., Hamari, J.: Social motivations of live-streaming viewer engagement on Twitch. Comput. Hum. Behav. **84**, 58–67 (2018)
27. Roberts, J.A., David, M.E.: On the outside looking in: Social media intensity, social connection, and user well-being: the moderating role of passive social media use. Canadian J. Behav. Sci. **55**(3), 240–252 (2023)
28. Jung, J., Barron, D., Lee, Y.A., Swami, V.: Social media usage and body image: Examining the mediating roles of internalization of appearance ideals and social comparisons in young women. Comput. Hum. Behav. **135**, 107357 (2022)
29. Cao, D., Meadows, M., Wong, D., Xia, S.: Understanding consumers' social media engagement behaviour: An examination of the moderation effect of social media context. J. Bus. Res. **122**, 835–846 (2021)
30. Shahbaznezhad, H., Dolan, R., Rashidirad, M.: The role of social media content format and platform in users' engagement behavior. J. Interact. Mark. **53**(1), 47–65 (2021)
31. Chen, A.: From attachment to addiction: the mediating role of need satisfaction on social networking sites. Comput. Hum. Behav. **98**, 80–92 (2019)

32. Wang, C., Lee, M.K.O., Hua, Z.: A theory of social media dependence: evidence from microblog users. Decis. Support Syst. **69**, 40–49 (2015)
33. Vannucci, A., Simpson, E.G., Gagnon, S., Ohannessian, C.M.: Social media use and risky behaviors in adolescents: a meta-analysis. J. Adolesc. **79**, 258–274 (2020)
34. Ronzhyn, A., Cardenal, A.S., Batlle Rubio, A.: Defining affordances in social media research: a literature review. New Med. Soc. **25**(11), 3165–3188 (2022)
35. Yu, R.P., Ellison, N.B., McCammon, R.J., Langa, K.M.: Mapping the two levels of digital divide: Internet access and social network site adoption among older adults in the USA. Inf. Commun. Soc. **19**(10), 1445–1464 (2016)
36. Reneland-Forsman, L.: 'Borrowed access'–the struggle of older persons for digital participation. Int. J. Lifelong Educ. **37**(3), 333–344 (2018)
37. Ramírez-Correa, P.E., Rondán-Cataluña, F.J., Arenas-Gaitán, J., Grandón, E.E., Alfaro-Pérez, J.L., Ramírez-Santana, M.: Corrigendum: segmentation of older adults in the acceptance of social networking sites using machine learning. Front. Psychol. **12**, 765840 (2021). https://doi.org/10.3389/fpsyg.2021.765840
38. Ramírez-Correa, P., Grandón, E., Arenas-Gaitán, J., Rondán-Cataluña, J., Ramírez-Santana, M.: Acceptance of social networking sites by older people before and after COVID-19 confinement: a repeated cross-sectional study in Chile, using the theory of planned behaviour (TPB). Int. J. Environ. Res. Public Health **19**(20), 13355 (2022)
39. Yang, Y., Yuan, Y., Archer, N., Ryan, E.: Adoption of social media and the quality of life of older adults. In: 2016 49th Hawaii International Conference on System Sciences (HICSS), pp. 3133–3142. IEEE (2016)
40. Devos, P., Jou, A.M., De Waele, G., Petrovic, M.: Design for personalized mobile health applications for enhanced older people participation. Eur. Geriatr. Med. **6**(6), 593–597 (2015)
41. Frohlich, D.M., Lim, C., Ahmed, A.: Co-designing a diversity of social media products with and for older people. In Proceedings of the 7th international conference on software development and technologies for enhancing accessibility and fighting info-exclusion, pp. 323–330 (2016)
42. Beringer, R.: Busting the myth of older adults and technology: an in-depth examination of three outliers. In: Patrick Rau, P.-L. (ed.) CCD 2017. LNCS, vol. 10281, pp. 605–613. Springer, Cham (2017). https://doi.org/10.1007/978-3-319-57931-3_48
43. Kusumota, L., et al.: Impact of digital social media on the perception of loneliness and social isolation in older adults. Rev. Latino-Am. Enfermagem (2022). https://doi.org/10.1590/1518-8345.5641.3526
44. Milovich, M., Burleson, D.: Connections and cognitive speed of older adults: using a social media intervention to improve cognitive speed. Commun. Assoc. Inf. Syst. **47**(1), 62 (2020)
45. Han, M., Tan, X.Y., Lee, R., Lee, J.K., Mahendran, R.: Impact of social media on health-related outcomes among older adults in Singapore: qualitative study. JMIR Aging **4**(1), e23826 (2021)
46. Jung, E.H., Sundar, S.S.: Status update: gratifications derived from Facebook affordances by older adults. New Media Soc. **20**(11), 4135–4154 (2018)
47. Jung, E.H., Sundar, S.S.: Older adults' activities on Facebook: can affordances predict intrinsic motivation and well-being? Health Commun. **37**(5), 597–607 (2022)
48. Wang, X., Gu, J., Hu, A., Ling, H.: Impact of online social media communication and offline geographical distance on elder users' intergenerational isolation: from technology affordance perspective. In: Zhou, J., Salvendy, G. (eds.) ITAP 2018. LNCS, vol. 10926, pp. 547–559. Springer, Cham (2018). https://doi.org/10.1007/978-3-319-92034-4_41
49. Zulman, D.M., Kirch, M., Zheng, K., An, L.C.: Trust in the internet as a health resource among older adults: analysis of data from a nationally representative survey. J. Med. Internet Res. **13**(1), e1552 (2011)
50. Strauss, A., Corbin, J.M.: Basics of Qualitative Research: Techniques and Procedures for Developing Grounded Theory. Sage Publications, India (1998)

51. Lincoln, Y.S., Guba, E.G.: Naturalistic inquiry. Sage (1985)
52. Charmaz, K.: Constructing Grounded Theory: A Practical Guide Through Qualitative Analysis. Sage (2006)
53. Tyshchuk, Y., Hui, C., Grabowski, M., Wallace, W.A.: Social media and warning response impacts in extreme events: results from a naturally occurring experiment. In: 2012 45th Hawaii International Conference on System Sciences, pp. 818–827. IEEE (2012)
54. Dong, X., Wang, T.: Social tie formation in Chinese online social commerce: the role of IT affordances. Int. J. Inf. Manage. **42**, 49–64 (2018)
55. Braun, M.T.: Obstacles to social networking website use among older adults. Comput. Hum. Behav. **29**(3), 673–680 (2013)
56. Ramírez-Correa, P., Grandón, E.E., Ramírez-Santana, M., Órdenes, L.B.: Explaining the use of social network sites as seen by older adults: the enjoyment component of a hedonic information system. Int. J. Env. Res. Public Health **16**(10), 1673 (2019). https://doi.org/10.3390/ijerph16101673
57. Mannheim, I., et al.: Inclusion of older adults in the research and design of digital technology. Int. J. Environ. Res. Public Health **16**(19), 3718 (2019)
58. Velki, T., Romstein, K.: User risky behavior and security awareness through lifespan. Int. J. Electr. Comput. Eng. Syst. **9**(2), 53–60 (2018)

Usability Evaluation of the Aging Scenario Wiki as a Learning Tool

Zekai Lu[1,2,3], Yaru Li[4,5(✉)], Siwei Wang[6], Aoran Wu[7], Jiaoyun Yang[1,2,3], Honglin Chen[5], and Ning An[1,2,3]

[1] School of Computer Science and Information Engineering, Hefei University of Technology, Hefei, China
[2] Key Laboratory of Knowledge Engineering with Big Data of Ministry of Education, Hefei University of Technology, Hefei, China
[3] National Smart Eldercare International S&T Cooperation Base, Hefei University of Technology, Hefei, China
[4] School of Public Health and Health Management, Anhui Medical College, Hefei, China
[5] Department of Social Sciences, University of Eastern Finland, Kuopio, Finland
liyaru@ahyz.edu.cn
[6] School of Law and Administration, Guangdong Open University, Guangzhou, China
[7] Harvard Graduate School of Education, Harvard University, Cambridge, USA

Abstract. The Chinese government has developed a unique "Smart Eldercare" model that utilizes digital technologies to address the growing needs of its rapidly aging population. To implement this model, the government has initiated policies to accelerate talent cultivation, highlighting the importance of Smart Eldercare education at different levels in universities and vocational schools. This paper presents the design and development of an aging scenario Wiki and conducts a usability evaluation of this Wiki as a collaborative learning tool for nascent Smart Eldercare education. First, during the development phase, we conducted lab-based usability testing using 18 tasks of 3 types with 12 student participants who followed the think-aloud protocol. Our analysis identified seven usability issues, and we subsequently addressed them in the optimization phase. Second, we evaluated the usability of the aging scenario Wiki as a learning tool in actual work teaching activities involving 54 students who collaborated on creating aging scenarios. The evaluation yields a System Usability Scale score of 67.45 and a C usability rating, indicating the areas for further improvement. Overall, the aging scenario Wiki demonstrated the potential to be a practical and effective learning tool for nascent Smart Eldercare education. Our study highlights the importance of user-centered design and usability testing in developing educational resources for emerging fields such as Smart Eldercare.

Keywords: Aging Scenario · Wiki · Usability Testing · Collaborative Learning · Smart Eldercare

Q. Gao et al. (Eds.): HCII 2023, LNCS 14055, pp. 100–116, 2023.
https://doi.org/10.1007/978-3-031-48041-6_8

1 Introduction

1.1 Background and Motivation

With the global population aging, China is exploring a unique "Smart Eldercare" model to respond to the social service needs of older adults [9]. This approach integrates information technology with eldercare services to offer intelligent care solutions for older adults. This model represents a cutting-edge concept in eldercare.

Education is an effective means to disseminate the concept of Smart Eldercare. Smart Eldercare education can help the public form the proper perspective of aging to encourage the integration of eldercare and new technologies. It helps provide intelligent solutions to eldercare services for older adults (Fig. 1).

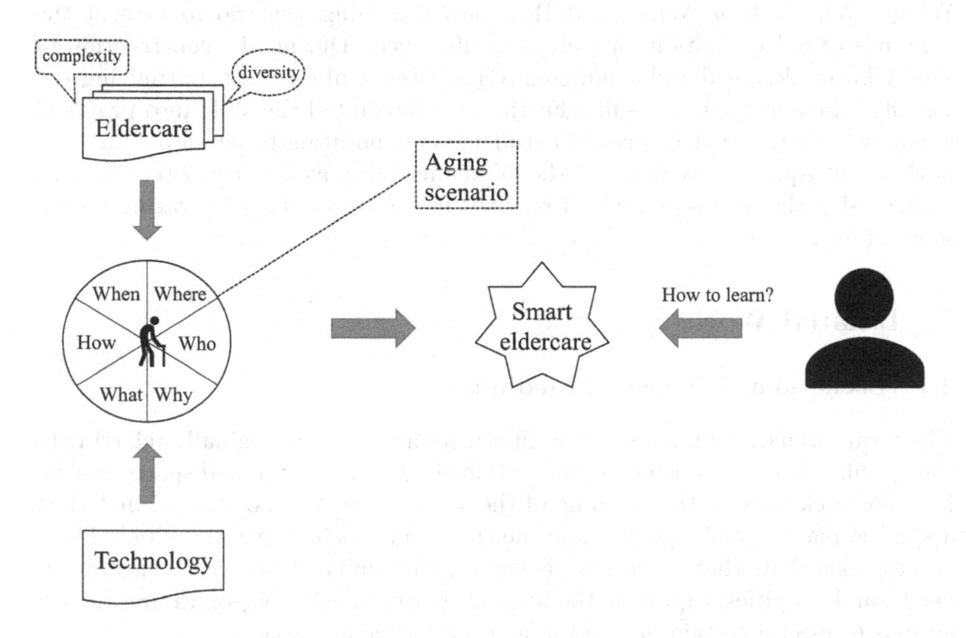

Fig. 1. The challenge of Smart Eldercare education

1.2 Objectives and Research Questions

In recent years, the higher education system has begun to introduce eldercare courses. Some colleges of pharmacy offer geriatrics-focused elective courses to train healthcare professionals [15]. To enhance pharmacotherapy education in geriatrics, Estus et al. have proposed an active-learning course model that involves site visits, interviews, and interactions with older adults, leading to a positive perception of aging among students. Experiential geriatric education has also been integrated into pharmacy curricula in Qatar and Canada, aiding in students' preparation for eldercare [33]. In some universities, geriatric education is included in the health curriculum, requiring students to partner with elderly individuals for people-centered nursing, which has yielded favorable results [31]. However, the majority of the current eldercare education adopts teacher-centered learning which ignores teaching students how to learn and encouraging lifelong learning. How to use student-centered learning to encourage students to learn the knowledge of Smart Eldercare autonomously and develop active methodologies remains a challenge.

1.3 Significance and Contributions

This study developed an aging scenario Wiki as a collaborative learning tool for nascent Smart Eldercare education. We incorporated the elements of When, Where, Who, Which, What, and How into the aging scenario to present the demands of older adults intuitively and effectively. During the construction of the Wiki, we designed and conducted a lab-based usability test, optimizing the website based on the test results. Further, we integrated the Wiki into practical teaching activities that involved 54 students collaborating to develop aging scenarios. Subsequently, we assessed the Wiki's usability as a learning tool for this course using the SUS score, which resulted in a C-grade usability rating with a score of 67.45.

2 Related Works

2.1 Scenario as a Teaching Medium

The term "scenario" finds its root in literature and drama, originally referring to the specific character's behavior and actions in a certain time and space. Joshua Meyrowitz elaborated the meaning of the scenario as: "In most cases, including a specific place, specific people, specific time and specific activities [20]." These descriptions show that "scenario" is the organic unity of people, environment, needs, and activities, capturing the life picture of a specific person taking certain actions to meet a certain demand in a specific time and space.

In recent years, the concept of "Scenario" has been extended beyond its original definition and has become a mode of thinking that connects products and users. Scenarios allow those who need information and those who provide it to gain a shared understanding through interaction [23]. Furthermore, scenarios are useful for describing and evaluating situations, expressing needs, and providing opportunities to understand intentions and information [17]. The application of scenarios in the development of AI applications for nursing care is seen as promising by Seibert et al. [27]. Several governments have begun constructing Smart Eldercare application scenarios, stimulating the development of the Smart Eldercare industry, and improving the acquisition and satisfaction of older adults. The research on different aging scenarios helps to pay attention to the actual needs of older adults and improve the eldercare service [2].

2.2 Collaborative Learning

In the field of education, collaborative learning [29] is an approach that involves learners working together in groups to solve problems, complete tasks, or create products. This method builds around a community of learners and teachers who share experiences and knowledge [32]. Collaborative learning aims to guide participants in building knowledge through exploration, discussion, negotiation, and debate [32]. The core elements of collaborative learning include positive interdependence, individual responsibility, face-to-face and verbal interaction, social skills, and team reflection.

Johnson et al. view collaborative learning as an interactive system designed to foster interaction among team members [13], in which each member is responsible for their own learning as well as that of the group. Salinas posits that group interaction results in acquiring a range of competencies and attitudes [25], while Barros et al. suggest that the process involves students learning by suggesting and sharing ideas to solve a task [5]. An argues that collaborative learning can create a dynamic environment where everyone can contribute to knowledge sharing on digital aging and draw upon each other's expertise to develop innovative solutions and approaches to addressing digital aging challenges [1].

2.3 Usability Testing in Human-Computer Interaction Research

Usability testing is a process that allows actual users to test a product and collect user feedback [24]. The formative and summative conceptions of usability testing serve different purposes. The former aims to identify and address usability issues during the product development process to enhance its usability [24], while the latter focuses on measuring the extent to which users can achieve their goals using the product [12]. Before each test, it is necessary to clarify the specific objectives before formulating the test plan.

Usability testing can be divided into laboratory testing and remote testing according to the different environments of test users. Both types of tests can capture the main usability issues of a website [30]. Laboratory-based usability testing is a traditional way. It is effective in revealing the usability issues of websites and other applications [6,7]. A typical laboratory-based usability test involves relatively few participants [22]. Participants represent real users, come to the laboratory alone, and use the system or website for fundamental tasks. Observers in the same room or adjacent rooms usually record the time required for users to complete each task, the completion of the task, and what participants do and say while performing the task. At the end of the task, there are two broad classes of usability test results: problem reports and quantitative measurements. Problem reports mean describing usability problems that prevent a target user from achieving a target task with reasonable effort and within a reasonable time [19]. The quantitative measurements use standardized usability questionnaires. The most widely used standardized usability questionnaires are Questionnaire for User Interaction Satisfaction [10], the Software Usability Measurement Inventory [14], the Post-Study System Usability Questionnaire [16], and the System Usability Scale [8].

3 Design and Development of Aging Scenario Wiki

In this section, we developed an Aging Scenario Wiki for Smart Eldercare education. Figure 2 shows the architecture.

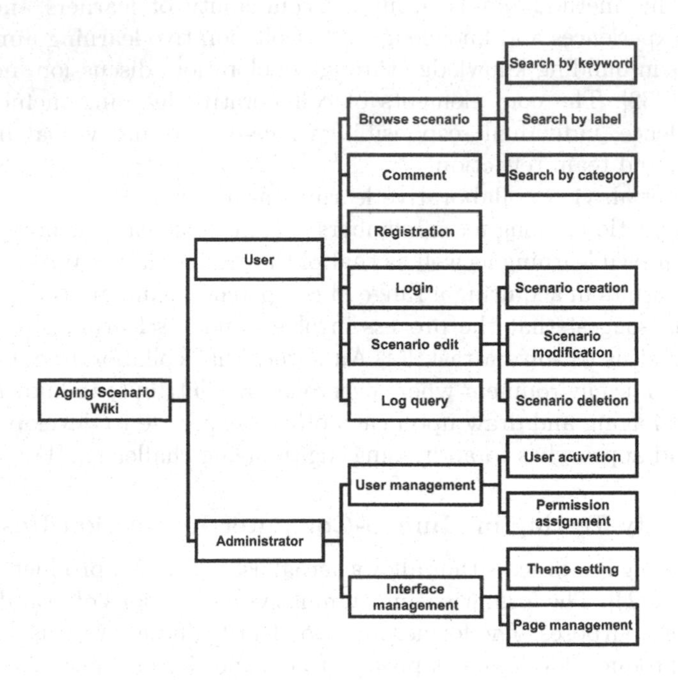

Fig. 2. The architecture of Aging Scenario Wiki

3.1 Scenario-Based Approach to Smart Eldercare Education

We present a teaching approach for incorporating aging scenarios into Smart Eldercare education. We use the aging scenario to present the demands of older adults. Each aging scenario includes a set of nine entries [2]. They are background, scenario elements(including main users, main places, main people, occurrence frequency, impact depth, impact breadth, and urgency), scenario cases, scenario requirements, existing schemes, emerging schemes, associated scenarios, scenario labels, and references.

We engaged two undergraduate students and seven postgraduate students from Hefei University of Technology to manually create 140 aging scenarios over a period of 15 days. From the perspective of older adults, based on Maslow's hierarchy of needs, we divided five hierarchies of needs for physiology, safety, belongingness and love, esteem, self -actualization. We have also considered caregivers, communities, eldercare institutes, government, and society to include more perspectives. Under each hierarchy of needs, we set up different categories. See Table 1 and Table 2 for the specific number of scenarios in each category. These scenarios will become the first batch of knowledge in the aging scenario Wiki.

Table 1. The perspective of the older adults

Maslow's hierarchy of needs	Frequency	Categories	Frequency
Physiological needs	17	Air	1
		Water	1
		Food	2
		Sleep	3
		Transportation	7
		Excretion	1
		Sex	2
Safety needs	61	Safety	25
		Safety	21
		Employment	3
		Property	8
		Resource	4
Belongingness and love needs	18	Friendship	1
		Family	2
		Affiliation	1
		Emotion	14
Esteem needs	8	Self-esteem	6
		Confidence	2
Self-actualization needs	10	Creativity	1
		Release potential abilities	4
		Accept the fact	1
		Spontaneity	4

3.2 Wiki as a Collaborative Learning Tool for Smart Eldercare Education

Wiki is a tool based on Web 2.0 technology. Web 2.0 is a user-centered Internet application model that promotes collaboration and communication between people by allowing users to create, share, and interact with content. Wiki allows users to create and edit content and constantly improve and update it through collaboration. It can enable users to focus on information exchange and collaboration tasks, and they will not be disturbed by the complex technical environment [3,18]. Users can use the Wiki to document work and continuously record iterations when developing projects. In particular, wiki users can collaborate to develop topics jointly. Also, the wiki environment can record the individual changes in the system at each time to restore the page to its previous state at any time. As a tool for group authoring, wikis can pull team members into a group, allowing them to jointly edit and build documents on one interface [11]. At the same time, by continuously acquiring new knowledge and the mainte-

Table 2. Hierarchy of needs under multiple perspectives

Hierarchy of needs	Frequency	Categories	Frequency
Caregiver needs	5	Caregiver	5
Community needs	6	Community infrastructure	1
		Community management and construction	5
Eldercare institute needs	9	Management of eldercare institutes	6
		Cognitive disorder management in eldercare institutes	2
		Operation in eldercare institutes	1
Government needs	1	Government regulation	5
Society needs	1	Society	5

nance of administrators, the Wiki can become a knowledge base focusing on a certain kind of knowledge. In a broad sense, a wiki can be considered a learning object if it contains an educational purpose [21].

3.3 Development of Aging Scenario Wiki

We deploy the aging scenario Wiki on wiki.js (version No. 2.5.219). The operating system is a Linux system based on a docker container, with a 4-core CPU and 15.67 GB memory allocated. The database uses PostgreSQL (version No. 13.3), and the running environment is based on node.js (version 14.17.6). The Wiki is an open platform, and the URL is https://stgawiki.dataee.net.

As shown in Fig. 2, system functionalities can be categorized into user functionalities and administrator functionalities. Here are some common features of each:

Adminstrator. The administrator is a built-in user and can manage users, including user verification and permission assignment. After user verification, the administrator can assign users to groups with different levels of permissions. Additionally, administrators have interface management capabilities and can change the website's theme style. As a superuser, the administrator has the ability to view and modify all pages within the wiki.

User. There are three types of users: guest, student, and instructor.

Any visitor can visit the website as a guest. The aging scenario Wiki is designed to be open to the public, allowing visitors to browse and comment on aging scenarios without the need for registration or login. The website provides a search function to facilitate users in finding and locating aging scenarios. The search function can search based on keywords, tags, or categories provided by the user, and display results that match the search criteria on the website.

The instructor needs to register and wait for the administrator's verification to get an account with the instructor's permission. The instructor can create a Smart Eldercare class wiki and invite students to join the course. In the class wiki, the instructor has the permission of an administrator.

Upon registering and logging in to the website, a student is invited by the instructor to the Smart Eldercare class. The class features an operation guide for students to reference, followed by the ability to create and edit pages within the class wiki. Notably, each page has a page creator, and two other features: visibility and modifiability. The visibility and modifiability of a page can only be authorized by the page creator.

In the course, both the instructor and students have the opportunity to fully leverage the wiki's functionality to facilitate course-related activities. The instructor can generate a page containing course materials, announcements, and other relevant information. Students are able to edit their own notes, class discussions, and assignments on their respective pages. When working in groups, students can create a discussion page to exchange ideas and collaborate on developing projects.

After the course, the instructor is able to utilize the log function to evaluate the usage of the Wiki by students. The log tracks various activities, such as visits to others' wikis, comments, collaborative editing, and discussions. They can be used for the evaluation of course grades. The final submitted assignment can also be used as a scoring item. If it is a personal assignment, the instructor can score it directly. If it is a collaborative writing task, the instructor can view their specific contribution through the log and avoid laziness in the group.

4 Usability Testing of Aging Scenario Wiki

In this section, we designed a usability test and optimized the wiki site.

4.1 Lab-Based Usability Testing Methodology

Setting the Goals. The goal of the usability test was to confirm how the aging scenario Wiki works when used by users. To further solve this problem, the research process was divided into three tasks. The three tasks were the guest task, the student task, and the instructor task.

Designing the Test. With the clear test goal, we formulated specific test questions representing the above roles. According to the different roles of users, we developed three different types of tasks. The questions under each type of task were to test the design of the website, not the skills of users.

We first conducted a pilot test with a novice student. Based on the results of the pilot test, we identified a need to slightly modify the wording of several questions to eliminate ambiguity and facilitate users' understanding. We also eliminated two redundant questions and rearranged the sequence of the questions in the test questionnaire. As a result of these modifications, the final version of the usability test questionnaire consisted of 18 task-oriented questions.

Guest Task

1. Click on a scenario of interest on the home page and read it.
2. Write comments under the article for the first task.
3. Does the website have the scenario of older adults falling in the bathroom?
4. Is the scenario of kinship maintenance under the Family Category?
5. Find some safety-related scenarios of older adults through label search.
6. How do you find a scenario similar to one of the older adults falling in the bathroom?

Student Task

1. Is there an operation guide on the website?
2. Create a scenario of emergency rescue for the older adult (XX) in the class wiki, XX is your test ID, and the template is the scenario of emergency rescue for the older adult.
3. Add the picture_ (33).png under the photo file for case one of the scenario of emergency rescue for the older adult.
4. Change the scenario demand of the emergency rescue for the older adult to "if the elderly have abnormal physical conditions when they are alone at home..."
5. Add the scenario of prevention of getting lost for the older adult with home cognitive impairment in the associated scenario and add hyperlinks.
6. Delete the fourth reference of the scenario of emergency rescue for the older adult.

Instructor Task

1. Create a course (XX) wiki, XX is your test ID.
2. Check the scenario of sleep health of the older adult (XX). Whether there is any unreasonable place in the scenario. If so, inform the contributor to modify it. If not, skip the task.
3. Query the log of the above scenario.
4. Move the location of the scenario of sleep health of the older adult (XX) to the course (XX) wiki.
5. Delete the scenario of the safety of caregivers (XX).
6. Contact the administrator.

After the final confirmation of the test questions, we selected problem reports to present the test results. The test results focused on identifying usability issues with the Wiki site rather than providing a detailed analysis of its performance. We considered complex data collection techniques unnecessary. Instead, We use the think-aloud method [28], which involved the participants explaining their thought processes and opinions and interacting with a tester to complete tasks. This allowed us to gain direct insight into which parts of the interface caused the most problems.

Finally, we outlined the details of our usability test design, including the duration, required equipment, and testing environment. We planned to conduct tests at regular intervals of every half hour and complete all tests within two days. Participants were required to have a standard personal computer with internet access and a web browser. To provide a relaxed and realistic testing environment, we allowed participants to use their own computers. The only limitation was that the test environment should be quiet and private enough. Therefore, we prepared a dedicated room that was soundproof and comfortable for participants to use, which did not interfere with their testing experience.

4.2 Participants and Tasks

We recruited 3 female graduate students and 9 male graduate students from the Hefei University of Technology to participate in the usability test of the website.

In the study, we performed 12 rounds of testing, each with one participant and one tester. Each participant would be informed to complete 18 task-oriented questions. The tester was responsible for interacting with participants and recording what happened during the test. Before the task, participants received a questionnaire containing 18 questions and a test ID that logs in to the system. Each participant was asked to read the question aloud and describes their thoughts using the think-aloud method when completing the task and browsing the website.

Each usability test lasted approximately 40 to 60 min. The tester encouraged participants to attempt as many questions as possible. We redirected the user's initial access interface to the home page, allowing participants to directly perform the first task after logging into their account. They were asked to complete the tasks in order. But if they failed to find an answer to a question, they could choose to skip the question or ask the tester for help. Before the test ends, the tester would ask the participant if they were ready to end the test. After receiving an affirmative answer, the tester announced the end of the test.

After the usability test, participants were asked to provide feedback, including their opinions on the website. The tester then reviewed the recorded observations and comments to identify issues with the website and functions that worked well.

4.3 Results Analysis and Optimization

The results of the usability test showed that the participants were able to complete all the tasks, indicating that the website's predefined functions were realized. Meanwhile, we identified a total of 7 usability issues from the 12 observer records. In response, we made some changes to the aging scenario Wiki.

During the test, participants used their commonly used screen resolutions, with most using 1366 * 768 or 1600 * 900 pixels. However, due to the home page layout being designed for a 1920 * 1080 pixel screen, most participants experienced incomplete page content display. To address this issue, we reconfigured the CSS of the web page and set different page layouts for users with different computer resolutions.

When reading the aging scenario, some participants raised doubts about the three elements of users, places, and people in the scenario. They could not understand the meaning of ticking the options before them. Participants thought that only the relevant options should be added and unsuitable options could be removed. We considered this suggestion reasonable and adopted it.

During testing, the participants found the guidance on the home page to be unclear. Specifically, when searching for the operation guide, 50% of participants initially overlooked the "operation guide" link on the home page. Instead, they looked for the operation guide through the navigation bar or search box. It took them longer. Participants noted that the font size was too small and the font color was too similar to the background, making it difficult to notice. Some participants suggested changing the font color to white, which we implemented to improve visibility.

Participants faced difficulties when using the navigation bar, stating that it was cluttered and lacked hierarchy, making it inconvenient to locate scenarios by category. To address this issue, we streamlined the navigation bar, reducing it to five options: home page, label, user center, operation guide, and contact administrator. Additionally, the categories are now located in the root directory, enhancing the user experience.

Searching by labels is an important method for finding information. But during our usability testing, 75% of the participants could not locate the label search function on their first attempt. They felt that the button for label search was not prominent and the location was too remote. Once finding the label button, the participants found that the distribution of labels was disorganized and difficult to navigate, with redundant and unnecessary labels. To address these issues, we streamlined the scenario labels and redesigned the label search button to make it more prominent and accessible.

When performing the scenario construction task, the customize "template" option did not meet the usability standard. Participants did not realize that the "template" can help them quickly build a scenario architecture. Instead, they chose to create a new blank interface and built the scenario from scratch. Only a few participants used this option. As a result, most participants spent a lot of time completing this task, and the results were not satisfactory. Therefore, we described the role of "template" in detail in the "operation guide" so that the users could understand the function of the "template" button.

Participants tended to ignore the administrator's contact information at the bottom of the home page when finding the administrator's contact information. Instead, they relied on their previous experience to locate the answer in the settings. To make it easier for users to provide feedback and suggestions, the administrator's contact information has been moved to a more prominent location.

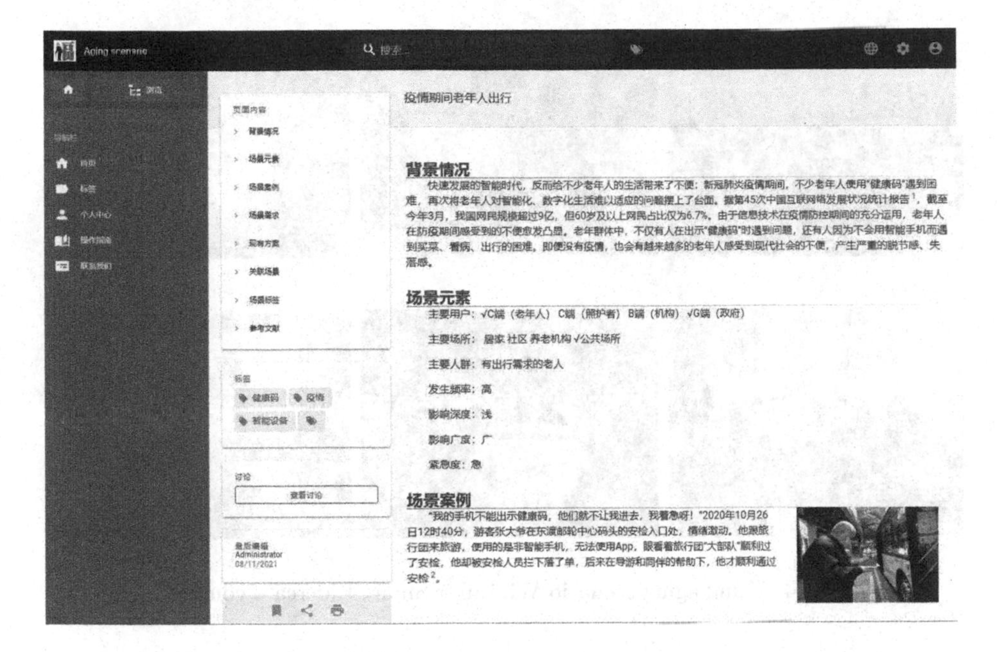

Fig. 3. The interface of an aging scenario

In summary, the observation of testers and the feedback of students participating in the test are valuable in revealing the causes of site failure and helping find the usability issues. Figure 3 shows an aging scenario interface after iteration.

5 Evaluation of Aging Scenario Wiki as a Learning Tool

In this section, we used the Wiki in actual teaching activities and evaluated its usability as a learning tool.

5.1 Use of Aging Scenario Wiki in Actual Teaching Activities

Figure 4 shows a group of teachers and students carrying out a Smart Eldercare course, by using a wiki, https://stgawiki.dataee.net/. The program was intended to deepen students' understanding of aging scenarios through collaborative learning. The course restricted only students could publish aging scenarios on the platform, while it was a public wiki that could be freely accessed by the public.

Participants. 54 s-year students majoring in geriatric health care and management from Anhui Medical College participated in the teaching activities, comprising 24 male and 30 female students.

Fig. 4. Using aging scenario Wiki in a Smart Eldercare course

Procedure. Before the commencement of the course, we invited a teacher and assigned her instructor permission to utilize our Wiki and negotiated this teaching activity.

During the teaching activity, the teacher first explained the activity. The students were told that their task would be to work in a team to develop wiki entries to elaborate on the concepts or descriptions of aging scenarios. They were assigned this task and provided a 120-min deadline to complete it. At the same time, the teacher informed the students that the platform kept a history of the aging scenarios development process so that teachers could evaluate each student's contribution. The feature helped the teacher to evaluate the work of each group member. In addition, the teacher was responsible for clarifying any concerns with the project and the use of the wiki platform. The teacher guided the students to ensure their work would achieve the requisite quality.

Then, the students started the development of the aging scenarios. They were divided into 9 groups. After familiar with the operation of the Wiki through the operation guidelines we provided them, they logged in to the Wiki and uploaded aging scenarios about the digital divide designed before the class. The teacher showed some existing problems with the uploaded aging scenarios and instructed students to use several search tools which could help them during the development of the project. From that point on, the groups collaborated to iterator the aging scenarios with the team. The creator of the aging scenario allowed the rest of the group to read the page and contribute as necessary. The group members searched for information about the aging scenario they collaborated on editing to help the creator iterate the aging scenario. When encountering difficulties, the team members sought solutions through active dialogue and communication.

At the end of the course, we invited students to take a questionnaire about our aging scenario wiki site. The online questionnaire aimed to evaluate the usability of using our Wiki as a learning tool for Smart Eldercare teaching.

5.2 Student Feedback and Evaluation

During the course, 54 students majoring in geriatric health care and management developed and contributed 150 aging scenarios related to the digital divide to the wiki platform used in the teaching activities. These scenarios covered a wide range of issues, such as social isolation among older adults, access to healthcare services, digital literacy, and technology acceptance.

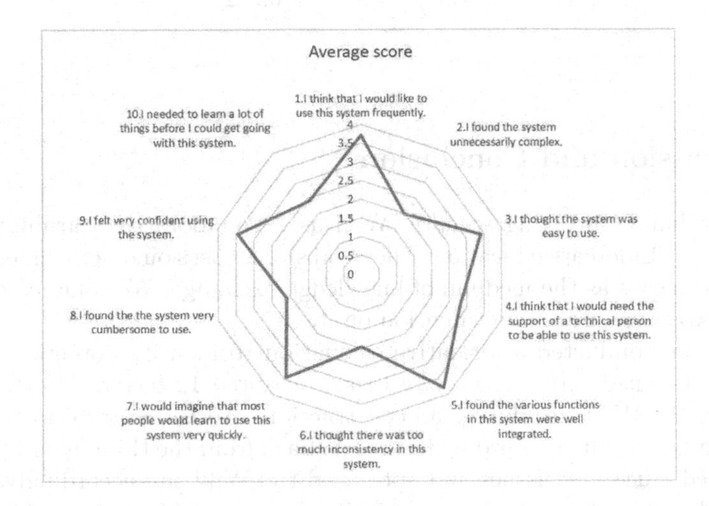

Fig. 5. The questionnaire score

We evaluated the students' perceptions and satisfaction through System Usability Scale [8]. It consists of 10 items, odd-numbered items are positive statements, and even-numbered items are negative statements. It is divided into completely disagree, disagree, unsure, agree, and strongly agree according to the perceived intensity of the audience, corresponding to a score of 1–5, respectively. SUS scores reflect overall satisfaction, while questions 4 and 10 measure learnability and the other 8 questions measure usability [4]. We collected survey data through 53 questionnaires.

Figure 5 and Table 3 show the results. From Table 3, the SUS score is 67.45. According to the SUS database [26], it can be converted to a percentile rank which means that the Wiki's usability is higher than about 50% of other websites. According to the SUS grading range of the fractional curve [4], the usability rating of this system is C and the adjective rating is "OK". Questions 1, 6, and 9 show high user satisfaction and students are more inclined to use the Wiki as a tool for lifelong learning.

According to Fig. 5, we find that the learnability score is only 60.38, indicating that our Wiki requires a certain learning cost or time for first-time users. Based on feedback from students, we learn that most of the difficulties occur when creating pages. They need guidance from professional technical personnel or a detailed operation manual to help use the Wiki for the first time. On the other side, the usability score is 69.22 which shows the usability of the Wiki is acceptable.

Table 3. SUS score

SUS score	Learnability score	Usability score
67.45	60.38	69.22

6 Discussion and Conclusion

This study builds an aging scenario Wiki as a collaborative learning tool for nascent Smart Eldercare education. The Wiki site focuses on older Chinese adults and uses scenarios as the medium of knowledge exchange. We conducted a user-centered two-stage usability evaluation on it.

Firstly, we conducted a formative evaluation to identify potential usability issues. We designed three types of 18 tasks, recruited 12 testers, and tested the usability of the Wiki site during its construction. We chose problem reports to present the test results. According to the feedback from the think-aloud protocol, we identified 7 usability issues and optimized the Wiki site accordingly.

Secondly, we performed user testing with a group of 54 participants to assess the system's usability in a more realistic setting. We incorporated it into our teaching activities, and 54 students actively engaged in developing 150 aging scenarios about the digital divide. The development of these aging scenarios was a collaborative effort among the students, who worked in groups to identify and analyze the challenges faced by older adults in using digital technologies. They then used this analysis to develop scenarios that highlighted the potential risks and benefits of technology use in the context of aging. After the course, we evaluated the usability of Wiki as a learning tool through quantitative measurements using SUS. The SUS score was 67.45 and the usability rating of the Wiki was C.

Overall, this Wiki provided the students with a practical and meaningful learning experience that allowed them to apply their knowledge and skills to real-world problems in the field of Smart Eldercare. Our study emphasizes the significance of adopting a user-centered design in developing educational resources for emerging fields such as Smart Eldercare.

One limitation of this study is the C-grade usability rating of the Wiki indicated by the SUS score. It indicates the Wiki has the area for further iterative improvement. Future research will focus on improving the usability of the Wiki platform. This could involve conducting additional user testing and collecting feedback from users to identify specific areas for improvement. The iterative design process can then be used to implement changes and improvements to the platform.

Acknowledgements. This work was partially supported by Anhui Province Higher Education Institution Quality Project "Smart Eldercare" (2019kfkc010) and Hefei University of Technology Teaching Reform Demonstration Course Project "Smart Eldercare" (KCSZ2020038).

References

1. An, N.: Toward learning societies for digital aging. arXiv preprint arXiv:2305.01137 (2023)
2. An, N., Xu, Y., Gao, Q., Zhu, W., Wu, A., Chen, H.: Automatically labeling aging scenarios with a machine learning approach. In: Duffy, V.G., Gao, Q., Zhou, J., Antona, M., Stephanidis, C. (eds.) HCII 2022. LNCS, vol. 13521, pp. 242–260. Springer, Cham (2022). https://doi.org/10.1007/978-3-031-17902-0_18
3. Archambault, P.M., et al.: Wikis and collaborative writing applications in health care: a scoping review. J. Med. Internet Res. **15**(10), e2787 (2013)
4. Bangor, A., Kortum, P., Miller, J.: Determining what individual SUS scores mean: adding an adjective rating scale. J. Usability Stud. **4**(3), 114–123 (2009)
5. Barros, B., Verdejo, M.: Entornos para la realización de actividades de aprendizaje colaborativo a distancia. Inteligencia Artificial. Revista Iberoamericana de Inteligencia Artificial **5**(12), 39–49 (2001)
6. Battleson, B., Booth, A., Weintrop, J.: Usability testing of an academic library web site: a case study. J. Acad. Librariansh. **27**(3), 188–198 (2001)
7. Becker, D.A., Yannotta, L.: Modeling a library web site redesign process: developing a user-centered web site through usability testing. Inf. Technol. Libr. **32**(1), 6–22 (2013)
8. Brooke, J., et al.: SUS-a quick and dirty usability scale. Usability Eval. Ind. **189**(194), 4–7 (1996)
9. Chen, H., Hagedorn, A., An, N.: The development of smart eldercare in China. The Lancet Regional Health-Western Pacific (2022)
10. Chin, J.P., Diehl, V.A., Norman, K.L.: Development of an instrument measuring user satisfaction of the human-computer interface. In: Proceedings of the SIGCHI Conference on Human Factors in Computing Systems, pp. 213–218 (1988)
11. Duffy, P., Bruns, A.: The use of blogs, wikis and RSS in education: a conversation of possibilities. In: Learning on the Move: Proceedings of the Online Learning and Teaching Conference 2006, pp. 31–38. Queensland University of Technology (2006)
12. Dumas, J.S., Dumas, J.S., Redish, J.: A practical guide to usability testing. Intellect books (1999)
13. Johnson, D.W., Johnson, R.T., Smith, K.A.: Cooperative learning returns to college what evidence is there that it works? Change Mag. High. Learn. **30**(4), 26–35 (1998)
14. Kirakowski, J.: The software usability measurement inventory: background and usage. In: Usability Evaluation in Industry, pp. 169–178 (1996)
15. Lee, J.K., Tomasa, L., Evans, P., Pho, V.B., Bear, M., Vo, A.: Impact of geriatrics elective courses at three colleges of pharmacy: attitudes toward aging and eldercare. Curr. Pharm. Teach. Learn. **11**(12), 1239–1247 (2019)

16. Lewis, J.R.: Psychometric evaluation of the post-study system usability questionnaire: the PSSUQ. In: Proceedings of the Human Factors Society Annual Meeting, vol. 36, pp. 1259–1260. Sage Publications, Los Angeles (1992)
17. Lin, C.-Y., Okamoto, M.: The method of user's requirement analysis by participation of the user: constructing an information system for travelers. In: Kurosu, M. (ed.) HCD 2009. LNCS, vol. 5619, pp. 862–868. Springer, Heidelberg (2009). https://doi.org/10.1007/978-3-642-02806-9_99
18. Majchrzak, A., Wagner, C., Yates, D.: The impact of shaping on knowledge reuse for organizational improvement with wikis. MIS Q. 455–469 (2013)
19. Marshall, C., Mcmanus, B., Prail, A.: Usability of product X-lessons from a real product. Behav. Inf. Technol. **9**(3), 243–253 (1990)
20. Meyrowitz, J.: The impact of electronic media on social behavior (1985)
21. Nash, S.: Learning objects, learning object repositories, and learning theory: preliminary best practices for online courses. Interdisc. J. E-Learn. Learn. Objects **1**(1), 217–228 (2005)
22. Nielsen, J., Landauer, T.K.: A mathematical model of the finding of usability problems. In: Proceedings of the INTERACT'93 and CHI'93 Conference on Human Factors in Computing Systems, pp. 206–213 (1993)
23. Ohnishi, J., Go, K.: Requirement engineering. Kyoritsu Shuppan (2002)
24. Rubin, J., Chisnell, D.: Handbook of Usability Testing: How to Plan, Design and Conduct Effective Tests. Wiley, Hoboken (2008)
25. Salinas Ibáñez, J.M., et al.: Enseñanza flexible, aprendizaje abierto: las redes como herramientas para la formación. Revista electronica de tecnologia educativa, Edutec (1999)
26. Sauro, J.: Measuring usability with the system usability scale (SUS) (2011)
27. Seibert, K., et al.: Application scenarios for artificial intelligence in nursing care: rapid review. J. Med. Internet Res. **23**(11), e26522 (2021)
28. Simon, K.E.H.: Protocol Analysis: Verbal Reports as Data. MIT Press, Cambridge (1984)
29. Smith, B.L., MacGregor, J.T.: What is collaborative learning (1992)
30. Tullis, T., Fleischman, S., McNulty, M., Cianchette, C., Bergel, M.: An empirical comparison of lab and remote usability testing of web sites. In: Usability Professionals Association Conference (2002)
31. Willis, J.L., et al.: Impact of interprofessional geriatric teamwork on students' perceptions of older persons and collaborative practice. Gerontol. Geriatr. Educ. **44**(1), 118–130 (2023)
32. Zhu, C.: Student satisfaction, performance, and knowledge construction in online collaborative learning. J. Educ. Technol. Soc. **15**(1), 127–136 (2012)
33. Zolezzi, M., Sadowski, C.A., Al-Hasan, N., Alla, O.G.: Geriatric education in schools of pharmacy: students' and educators' perspectives in Qatar and Canada. Curr. Pharm. Teach. Learn. **10**(9), 1184–1196 (2018)

Augmented Reality (AR) Application Superimposing the Falling Risks of Older Adults in Residential Settings and Coping Strategies: Building an Image-Based Scene Detection Model

Takahiro Miura[1(✉)], Emiko Uchiyama[2], Shujirou Imaeda[3], Wataru Takano[4], Yuka Sumikawa[5], Toshiaki Tanaka[6], and Toshio Otsuki[6]

[1] National Institute of Advanced Industrial Science and Technology (AIST), 6-2-3 Kashiwanoha, Kashiwa, Chiba 277-0882, Japan
miura-t@aist.go.jp
[2] Graduate School of Information Science and Technology, The University of Tokyo, 7-3-1, Hongo, Bunkyo-ku, Tokyo 113-8656, Japan
[3] Nikken Sekkei Ltd., 2-18-3 Iidabashi, Chiyoda, Tokyo 102-8117, Japan
[4] Center for Mathematical Modeling and Data Science (MMDS), Osaka University, 1-3 Machikaneyama, Toyonaka, Osaka 560-8531, Japan
[5] Graduate School of Medicine, The University of Tokyo, 7-3-1, Hongo, Bunkyo-ku, Tokyo 113-0033, Japan
[6] Institute of Gerontology (IOG), The University of Tokyo, 7-3-1, Hongo, Bunkyo-ku, Tokyo 113-8656, Japan

Abstract. Falls often cause bone fractures and are a typical risk factor for older people to become hospitalized or bedridden and require nursing care. Since the risk of falls increases due to a complex combination of physical and environmental factors, it is essential to examine the physical characteristics of the individuals and the characteristics of the environment in which they interact with. However, the risk of falls has not been quantified in environments where falls frequently occur, and moreover, the association of fall risk with physical factors remains unclear. Meanwhile, handrails and other devices are sometimes installed in buildings to prevent falls, but it is not easy for older adults and their caregivers to grasp the necessity and criteria for installing such devices. In this paper, our goal is to develop a smartphone application for augmented reality (AR) superimposition of fall prevention measures within the real-life environment of a house. This article reports on the current development progress of a prototype for the application.

Keywords: Augmented reality (AR) · smartphone · scene detection · house · older adults · falling risks

Q. Gao et al. (Eds.): HCII 2023, LNCS 14055, pp. 117–124, 2023.
https://doi.org/10.1007/978-3-031-48041-6_9

1 Introduction

Aging is accompanied by a decline in physical function, making it easier for people to fall [3,6,8,9]. Falls often cause bone fractures and are a typical risk factor for older people to become hospitalized or bedridden and require nursing care. Tokuda et al. reported that 25% and 9% of older adults whose age ranged 85–99 and 65–84 experienced ambulance transport because of the emergency medical care [15]. Also, fall is one of the critical factors that cause such transport: 51% and 34% of older adults whose age were 85–99 and 65–84 were transported for their falls [15]. Since older adults spend more time in their homes than other generations, it is necessary to reduce the risk of falls in the moving spaces of residences in a hyper-aged society.

The risk of falls increases due to a complex combination of physical and environmental factors [1,2,13,14]. As such, it is essential to examine the physical characteristics of the individuals and the characteristics of the environment in which they interact with. However, the prior studies on falls have mostly been conducted in the laboratory or in the hospital settings, with limited research on falls within the home. Various studies investigated older adults who had experienced indoor falls, and classified falls among older adults in their homes [4,11,12]. They found that most of the falls leading to serious injuries, such as bone fractures, occurred during nighttime transfers between the bedroom and toilet. However, the risk of falls has not been quantified in environments where falls frequently occur, and moreover, the association of fall risk with physical factors remains unclear. Meanwhile, handrails and other devices are sometimes installed in buildings to prevent falls, but it is not easy for older adults and their caregivers to grasp the necessity and criteria for installing such devices.

Therefore, the final goal of our study is to develop an application that provides feedback on fall prevention measures based on a fall risk assessment that incorporates the physical characteristics of older adults and the characteristics of their living environment. Specifically, this article aims to develop a smartphone application for augmented reality (AR) superimposition of fall prevention measures within the real-life environment of a house.

In addition to recognizing the current location (scene detection) and the presence of objects (object detection), we have developed an AR function that superimposes information on necessary objects. We mainly report on the former function, which recognizes the current location within the scene.

2 Overview of Our Application

We developed a prototype application that employs the camera of a smartphone to recognize indoor locations where falls are likely to occur, and presents an appropriate home repair guide through the implementation of an AR function. Figure 1 shows the screenshots of the developed application. To achieve this, we developed: a) a recognition model for the current location (room) using images, and b) an interface for a smartphone application capable of AR superimposition.

Fig. 1. The screenshots of the prototype smartphone application with AR superimposed guide. In each figure, the app performed scene detection to recognize the location and displayed the result at the bottom of the screen. Additionally, the app also superimpose environmental information to be checked for the recognized objects (a toilet seat and a bathtub in the middle and right figures, respectively).

2.1 Building a Recognition Model for Current Location (Room) Using Images

Method. We trained a convolutional network (CNN) using TensorFlow (Keras) on 10 distinct categories of images of places such as bathrooms, stairs, and bedrooms (Programming language: Python 3.8.11, Operating System: macOS 11.1.5). The images used were 7,808 images extracted from the MIT Place365 dataset, MyNursingHome dataset, and the Staircase Image dataset [5,7,16]. Table 1 shows a breakdown of the images used for training and validation. The number of images used for training and validation was equal. The quantity of images is not balanced, but this is because we tried to increase the number of images wherever possible. For training, we not only used these images, but also randomly generated images that were flipped left and right, rotated, and enlarged using data augmentation techniques [10].

The CNN used in this study had 11 layers, including input and output layers. The input images were passed through a 3×3 filter in the convolution layer, resulting in 64 feature maps. In the subsequent pooling layer, the image size was reduced by max pooling, which selects the maximum value within a small region. The output image from this process, which was repeated twice, enters the fully-connected layer, was transformed by the ReLU function, and then identified in

Table 1. Breakdown of the images used for training and validation. The number of images used for training and validation was equal.

Type	#	Type	#
Bathroom	197	Dining room	274
Bedroom	662	Kitchen	734
Children room	112	Living room	706
Closet	135	Staircase	1488
Corridor	346	Toilet	1500

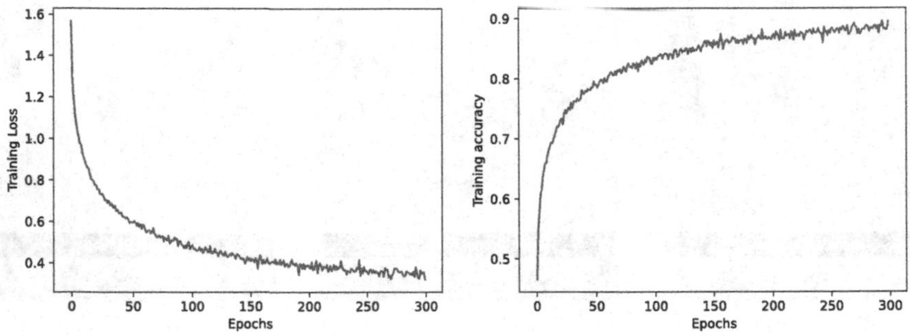

Fig. 2. Training loss (left) and accuracy (right) as a function of number of epochs.

the output layer. A softmax function was employed as the activation function in the output layer. The maximum number of training cycles was set to 300 epochs, however, to prevent the possibility of over-training, the number was set to 192 epochs based on the loss of validation data. At that time, the steps per epochs were 631 epochs.

In evaluating the model's performance, we report on accuracy, precision, recall, and F-measure. Then, we analyze the built model by creating a confusion matrix using the images for validation, as shown in Table 1.

Results. Figure 2 shows the training loss and accuracy as a function of number of epochs. As a result of the CNN training, the performance of our model were as follows: accuracy: 0.882, precision: 0.914, recall: 0.857, and F-measure: 0.885.

Figure 3 shows the confusion matrix between the actual and predicted image types. Our classifier relatively well identified the images of the toilet, bedroom, closet, and dining room, while the predictions of the kitchen, children's room, and bathroom were not reasonably as well identified. This result may be because many images of the successfully identified areas, especially the closet, contained unique objects to other spaces. The image classification of the toilet may have also performed well because of its distinctive toilet seat. However, approximately 20% of the images were misidentified as a bathroom because the bathroom also had a toilet seat.

Kitchen images were often misidentified as bedroom, dining rooms, and living rooms. Since the images of kitchens varied from wood-grained to marble-toned

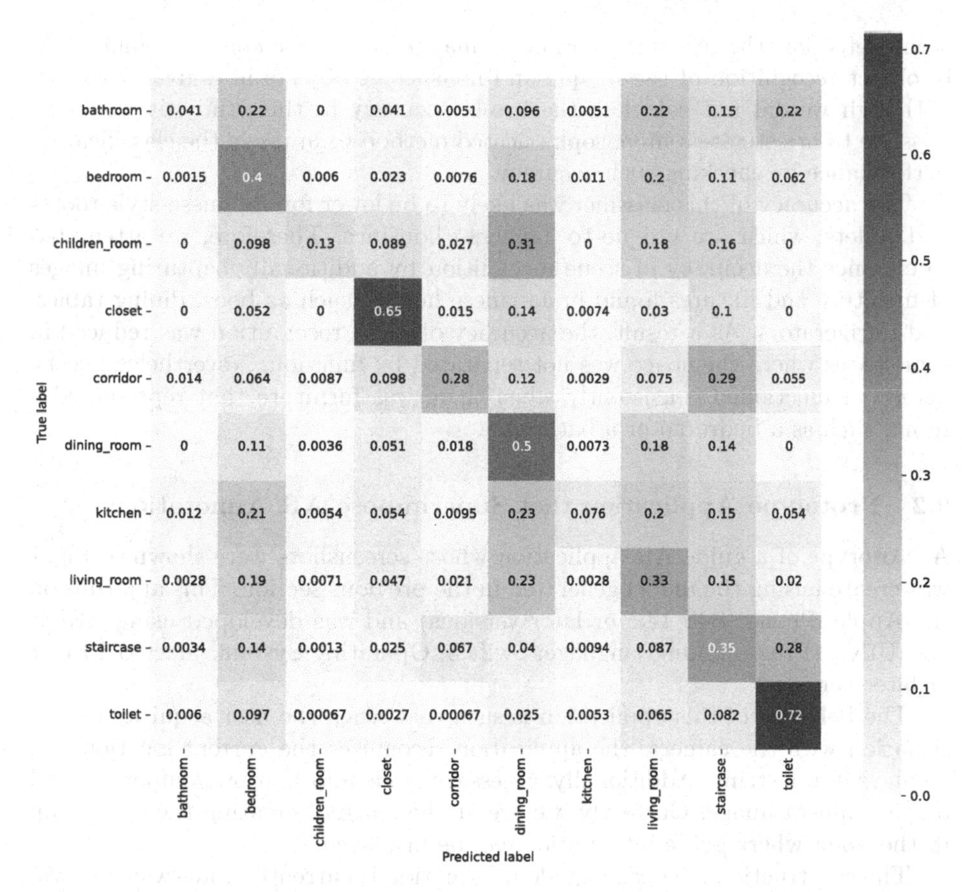

Fig. 3. Confusion matrix of our classifier. The numerical values in the cells indicate the predicted probabilities.

and included tables covered with tablecloths of various patterns, it is possible that the wood-grained kitchens induced the misidentification as a dining room or a living room, while marble-toned images with table with tablecloths resulted in occasional misidentification as a bedroom. Images of children's rooms were generally misrecognized as dining rooms, bedrooms, or living rooms. The authors checked these images and found that there were desks usually in the dining room, beds usually in the bedroom, and sofas usually in the living room. Thus, it may be necessary to use a multi-label recognition method in addition to the revisions of labels. The bathroom images were often misrecognized as a toilet, living room, or bedroom. This misrecognition may be caused by the presence of a toilet seat and a washbasin in the bathroom images or the inclusion of a bathtub images that looks like a bed at first glance to a human.

Therefore, the recognition rate of scene detection tends to increase when there are unique objects in the scene, while it decreases when objects in the scene are supposed to exist in multiple locations. To improve the efficiency of scene detection, the recognition accuracy may increase based on the combination of object recognition of the unique and nonspecific objects in a given location. Although we did not calculate the top-N accuracy in this study, it would be possible to investigate a more sophisticated method to improve the classification performance by checking such accuracy.

The accuracy of this classifier was likely to be lower for Japanese-style rooms and toilets, which are unique to Japanese housings. Therefore, we attempted to enhance the accuracy of scene recognition by additionally capturing images of furniture and fixtures found in Japanese homes, such as beds, dining tables, and refrigerators. As a result, the accuracy of scene recognition was reduced in some cases where the space was not separated by function. Nevertheless, scene detection functioned consistently when there was furniture that represented a room, such as a bedroom or a bathroom.

2.2 Prototype Application that Superimpose AR Annotations

A prototype of a guide AR application whose screenshots were shown in Fig. 1 was created using the model generated in the previous section. This app runs on the Apple iPhone (iOS 14.5 or later versions) and was developed using ARKit and UIKit (Programming language: Swift 5, Operating System: macOS 10.15.7 or later versions).

The behavior of this application is such that when the user acquires a room situation with the camera, the application recognizes the current location and displays it as a string. Additionally, necessary guide information is superimposed on the camera image. Currently, we are at the stage of creating the system up to the point where guide information can be displayed.

The construction of specific guide information is currently underway and will be reported in a subsequent study.

3 Summary and Future Work

To develop an application that provides feedback on fall prevention measures based on a fall risk assessment that incorporates the physical characteristics of older adults and the characteristics of their living environment, we developed a prototype application that employs the camera of a smartphone to recognize indoor locations where falls are likely to occur, and presents an appropriate home repair guide through the implementation of an AR function. Particularly in this article, we mainly stated the scene detection function that recognizes the current location within the scene.

Our study yielded the following results:

- To build an image-based scene detector, we employed a convolutional network (CNN) with data augmentation on images of 10 different locations, including bathroom, stairs, and bedroom, etc. The training results of the CNN showed that our model performed as follows: accuracy: 0.882, precision: 0.914, recall: 0.857, and F-measure: 0.885.

- Our scene detector identified images of bedroom, closets, dining rooms, and toilet relatively well, but did not predict kitchens, children's rooms, and bathrooms as well.
- We developed a prototype of a guide AR application whose behavior is that when the user acquires a room situation with the camera, the application recognizes the current location and displays it as a string. Then, necessary guide information is superimposed on the camera image.

In the future, we plan to work on the development of object recognition in conjunction with room recognition to generate detailed context-sensitive guides. Furthermore, we will develop a method to evaluate the risk of falling, taking into account the physical condition of older adults living in the house where the application will be used. In parallel with these efforts, we will attempt to improve the interface based on interviews with caregivers and nurses.

Acknowledgment. This work was supported by SECOM Foundation and JSPS KAKENHI Grant Numbers JP20K20494, JP21H04580, and JP21H00915.

References

1. Ambrose, A.F., Paul, G., Hausdorff, J.M.: Risk factors for falls among older adults: a review of the literature. Maturitas **75**(1), 51–61 (2013)
2. Campbell, A.J., Borrie, M.J., Spears, G.F.: Risk factors for falls in a community-based prospective study of people 70 years and older. J. Gerontol. **44**(4), M112–M117 (1989)
3. Chang, J.T., et al.: Interventions for the prevention of falls in older adults: systematic review and meta-analysis of randomised clinical trials. BMJ **328**(7441), 680 (2004)
4. Imaeda, S., et al.: The measures against fall prevention at home by multidisciplinary specialists for elderly people who experienced fall and femoral fractures based on their environmental changes Part 1 - to clarify the architectural factors on reasons of falls at home. J. Architect. Plann. (Trans. AIJ) **85**(773), 1387–1395 (2020)
5. Ismail, A., Ahmad, S.A., Soh, A.C., Hassan, M.K., Harith, H.H.: MYNursingHome: a fully-labelled image dataset for indoor object classification. Data Brief **32**, 106268 (2020)
6. Lord, S.R., Menz, H.B., Tiedemann, A.: A physiological profile approach to falls risk assessment and prevention. Phys. Ther. **83**(3), 237–252 (2003)
7. Patil, U., et al.: Deep learning based stair detection and statistical image filtering for autonomous stair climbing. In: 2019 Third IEEE International Conference on Robotic Computing (IRC), pp. 159–166. IEEE (2019)
8. Rubenstein, L.Z.: Falls in older people: epidemiology, risk factors and strategies for prevention. Age Ageing **35**(suppl_2), ii37–ii41 (2006)
9. Scheffer, A.C., Schuurmans, M.J., Van Dijk, N., Van Der Hooft, T., De Rooij, S.E.: Fear of falling: measurement strategy, prevalence, risk factors and consequences among older persons. Age Ageing **37**(1), 19–24 (2008)
10. Shorten, C., Khoshgoftaar, T.M.: A survey on image data augmentation for deep learning. J. Big Data **6**(1), 1–48 (2019)

11. Son, B.K., et al.: Multiple turns: potential risk factor for falls on the way to the toilet. Geriatr. Gerontol. Int. **19**(12), 1293–1295 (2019)
12. Tanaka, T., et al.: Environmental and physical factors predisposing middle-aged and older Japanese adults to falls and fall-related fractures in the home. Geriatr. Gerontol. Int. **18**(9), 1372–1377 (2018)
13. Tinetti, M.E.: Preventing falls in elderly persons. N. Engl. J. Med. **348**(1), 42–49 (2003)
14. Tinetti, M.E., Speechley, M., Ginter, S.F.: Risk factors for falls among elderly persons living in the community. N. Engl. J. Med. **319**(26), 1701–1707 (1988)
15. Tokuda, Y., Abe, T., Ishimatsu, S., Hinohara, S.: Ambulance transport of the oldest old in Tokyo: a population-based study. J. Epidemiol. **20**(6), 468–472 (2010)
16. Zhou, B., Lapedriza, A., Xiao, J., Torralba, A., Oliva, A.: Learning deep features for scene recognition using places database. In: Advances in Neural Information Processing Systems, vol. 27 (2014)

Learning Processes of Touchscreen Gesture Interaction in Older Adults and Children

Takahiro Miura[1(✉)], Ken-ichiro Yabu[2], Masatomo Kobayashi[3], Atsushi Hiyama[4], Michitaka Hirose[5], and Tohru Ifukube[2]

[1] National Institute of Advanced Industrial Science and Technology (AIST), 6-2-3 Kashiwanoha, Kashiwa, Chiba 277-0882, Japan
miura-t@aist.go.jp
[2] Research Center for Advanced Science and Technology, The University of Tokyo, 4-6-1, Komaba, Meguro-ku, Tokyo 153-8904, Japan
[3] IBM Research—Tokyo, 19-21 Hakozaki, Nihonbashi, Chuo, Tokyo 103-8510, Japan
[4] Hitotsubashi University, 2-1 Naka, Kunitachi, Tokyo 186-8601, Japan
[5] Graduate School of Information Science and Technology, The University of Tokyo, 7-3-1, Hongo, Bunkyo-ku, Tokyo 113-8656, Japan

Abstract. Touchscreen mobile computers, including smartphones, are widely used today by people of all ages across the globe, from children to senior citizens. In Japan, significant numbers of seniors, such as active ones, have begun to learn how to use computers, including smartphones and other touchscreen devices. The Global and Innovation Gateway for All School Program has allowed children to own and use such devices. Despite the availability of scientific knowledge on how children and seniors interact with smartphone applications, not all of them find it easy to manipulate mobile touchscreens. In this article, we establish brief best practices for designing touchscreen interfaces. First, we summarize the existing literature on touchscreen interaction with children and seniors and then measure their performance of gesture interaction. The tasks included basic gestures, such as taps, swipes, and pinching motions. The results showed that the older adults became significantly faster in tapping and swiping with repetition of the gesture interactions, while no such learning effect was observed in children. We also observed differences between the strategies of older adults and children in tapping and pinching in/out.

Keywords: Smartphones · older adults · children · gesture interactions · tapping · swiping · pinching in/out

1 Introduction

Globally, particularly in the US, the EU, and East Asia, one of the most critical contemporary issues is the need to develop countermeasures to the declining birth rate, also population aging [4]. In Japan, in 2021, the population ratios

Q. Gao et al. (Eds.): HCII 2023, LNCS 14055, pp. 125–139, 2023.
https://doi.org/10.1007/978-3-031-48041-6_10

of under 15 and over 65 years old were 28.9% and 11.8%, respectively [1,2,6]. These rates are expected to increase to as much as 40.5% and 8.4% by 2055 [11]. As such, it is necessary to present and implement a social model that can ensure the sustainable development of society, even in a hyper-aging society with a decreasing birth rate.

In hyper-aged society with a low birthrate, it is necessary for people in other age groups to participate in various fields of society because the productive age population is small. Meanwhile, touchscreen computers, including smartphones and tablet computers, have gained popularity worldwide, and even seniors and children are using them more frequently. The Ministry of Internal Affairs and Communications in Japan published a white paper on telecommunications, indicating that the rates of older touchscreen computer owners are increasing [3]. With such spread of smartphones and similar information and communications technologies (ICTs), the introduction of ICTs is progressing in various social activities. In the field of citizen science, for example, the data collected is becoming increasingly refined and massive with the spread of smartphones equipped with built-in advanced sensors [5,19,22]. Similarly, given the current status of digital transformation [25] in the field of employment [16,24], it is desirable for information and communications technologies (ICTs), especially touchscreen computers, which are becoming increasingly popular, to be usable to all regardless of age, gender, disabilities, and other individual characteristics.

To better accommodate seniors, we should address usability issues with touchscreen interfaces. However, there have been various hurdles in the use of ICT among older adults. In addition to personal computer interfaces such as mouse and keyboard, some researchers have reported experimental studies on touchscreen terminals [9,10,12]. The hurdles to ICT use among older adults are also affected by social influence and context of use, as well as individual characteristics such as self-efficacy, anxiety, health conditions, cognitive ability, attitude to life and satisfaction, and physical functioning. Moreover, the influence of relationships with others, such as facilitating conditions and social relationships, also affect the hurdles to use [8,18,21,26,27].

Meanwhile, hurdles in the use of ICTs exist even for children. The initial study using touchscreen devices [20] reported five major issues such as relating to developmental issues, input device preference, technical issues, individual differences in children's use of the touchscreen and issues of collaboration. Later, various studies proposed evidence-based design recommendations for children's touchscreen interfaces based on developmental appropriateness [15,23].

However, there have been few quantitative studies on the process of touchscreen terminal habituation and its variation among older adults and children. In particular, the results of analysis of in-the-wild results on the process of gestures, which is the basis of operation, would be academically useful.

Therefore, our ultimate goal is to establish design applications for touchscreen interfaces that can cater to both novices and well-experienced older adults. Specifically, this paper compares the performance of seniors' and children's gestures on touchscreen devices as their interactions experience increases. To achieve this, we developed a gesture checking application and evaluated it during ICT seminars for senior and child beginners.

The following are our research questions:

Q1. How about the learning effects of tapping on novices and trained older adults and children?
Q2. Are there any learning effects of swiping between these older adults and children?
Q3. Does repeated pinch-in/out improve performance in older adults and children?

2 Method

2.1 Participants

We evaluated 23 Japanese seniors between the age of 63 to 81 years old (mean age: 72.5 ± 6.1) who were novice users of touchscreen computers and had participated in our ICT seminars designed for senior beginners.

In addition, we evaluated 74 third-grade elementary school students with ages ranges from 8 to 9 years old.

2.2 Outline of Gesture Checking Application

An experimental application shown in Fig. 1 was developed for iOS devices. The application's behavior was adapted from the research by Kobayashi et al. and Miura et al. [12,17] in their studies on investigating the quantitative gesture accuracy of older adults.

We used an iPhone 5 s with a 4.0-in screen and 640 × 1136-pixel resolution running iOS 9–12 in our experiment to match the condition of previous studies. For the tapping session, each trial began when a white, square button target appeared randomly on the screen, as shown in the left panel of Fig. 1, and it ended when the participant briefly placed and removed their finger from the target. The targets were selected at random from three sizes: 30, 50, and 70 pixels corresponds to 4.8 mm, 8.0 mm, and 11.2 mm, respectively in older adults while 40, 50, and 60 pixels corresponds to 6.4 mm, 8.0 mm, and 9.6 mm, respectively in children.

These sizes represent the optical sizes of mini-sized keyboard buttons (30–40 px, 4.8–6.4 mm), general buttons (50–60 px, 8.0–9.6 mm), home screen icons (75 px, 12.0 mm), respectively. The reason for changing the button size between children and older adults was based on that children do not always have higher levels of finesse. The target turned blue as the participant touched it, and the next target appeared once the previous one was dismissed. Participants completed 10 tapping trials after having some practice trials.

In the swiping (dragging) session using the interface shown in Fig. 1(b), each trials started with the appearance of a 200 × 200-pixels image at a random location on the screen and ended when the image was swiped into a green square target (also 200 × 200 pixels) with 20-pixel-wide borders, always displayed at the center of the screen. The width of the borders of the target rectangle represented the tolerance, so errors up to 10 pixels in any direction were allowed

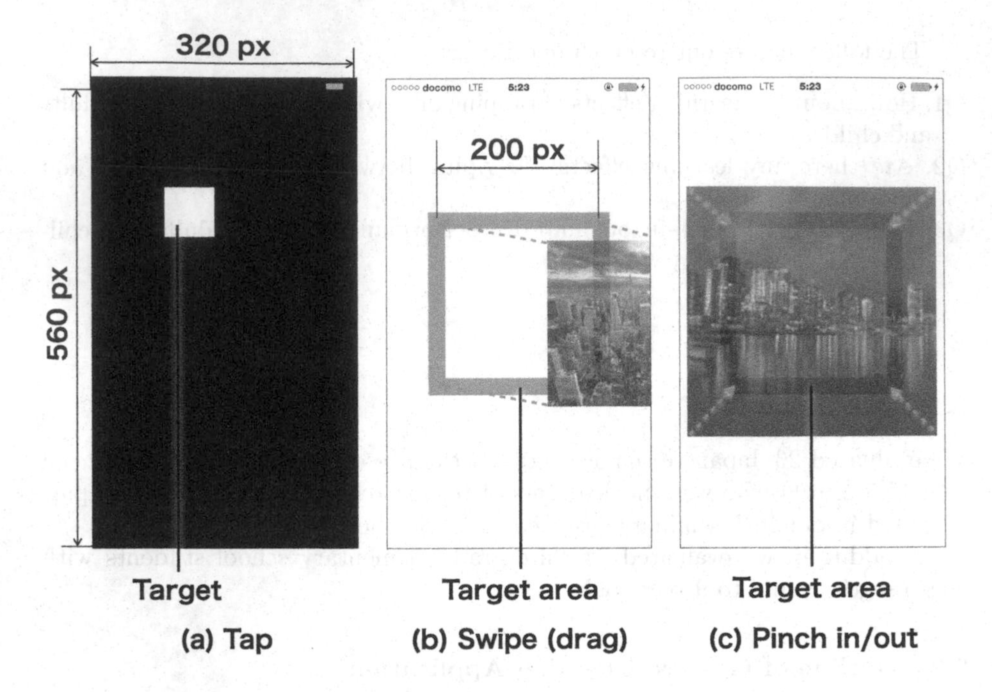

Fig. 1. Experimental application to practice and assess three standard touchscreen operations: tapping, swiping (dragging), and pinching. The text, lines, and arrows shown in are annotations not displayed during the experiments.

for the final image location when the trial ended. Participants completed some practice trials and 10 timed trials, just as in the tapping trials.

During the pinching in/out session whose experimental interface was Fig. 1(c), each trial started with the appearance of a square image with a variable size at the center of the screen and concluded once the image was adjusted to match the target size using two-finger pinching or spreading motions. The initial image size varied between 50, 100, 300, or 400 pixels, whereas the target remained the same at 200 pixels, which was consistent with the target size used in the swiping trials. The participants conducted pinch-out interaction in the size conditions of 50 and 100 pixels, and pinch-in in those of 50 and 100 pixels. The final image size was allowed to range from 190 to 210 pixels. Similar to the swiping trials, the participants were given a few practice trials, but only 10 timed trials were conducted in a session.

2.3 Procedure

The gesture evaluation using the app shown in Fig. 1 was conducted in ICT seminars for older adults and children taken place by us from 2015 to 2017. The contents of the seminars were as follows:

1. Explanation of interface elements of a smartphone: buttons, switches, and screens.
2. Practice of gestures by using the application whose interfaces.
3. How to use various applications like camera, map, alarm, and other frequently-used applications.

We first instructed the participants to hold the smartphone with their non-dominant hand and manipulate it with their dominant hand. Then, they completed a series of gesture tasks. For seniors, one session included tapping 10 times, swiping 5 times, and pinching in/out 5 times. After finishing one session of gestures, we asked the participants to continue conducting these gestures at their own pace as they liked. If they wished to continue, we provided them with a smartphone pre-installed with our application. In older adult groups, if they wanted to borrow the smartphone, we lent it to the participants and asked them to launch and play our application.

2.4 Data Analysis

We first aggregated the participants' data on task completion time by session for the older adults and children groups. In the tapping condition, we calculated the correct rates, centroid coordinates of a tapped finger for different button sizes in each session. For the swipe and pinch gestures, we checked the finger speed changes [px/s] and speed changes [px/s] of pinching, respectively, in session times.

Subsequently, we conducted an analysis of variance (ANOVA) or regression analysis to identify significant differences among performance metrics mentioned before and to examine the main effects of groups (older adults or children), repeat counts of sessions, and task conditions for these performance metrics. Before the ANOVA was performed, the aligned rank transform (ART) [7,28] was conducted on the scales, as the responses were non-normally distributed. Then, the significance of the main effects was determined using post hoc multiple comparison methods based on the least-square means and Turkey's multiplicity adjustment [13,14].

3 Results and Discussion

3.1 Tapping

Figure 2 (a) and (b) display the change in task completion time per repetition of sessions for tapping at different button sizes in older adults and children, respectively. A regression analysis assuming a gamma distribution performed on task completion time confirmed a significant main effect for age group ($p < 0.001$) and a significant interaction between age group and button size ($p = 0.046 < 0.05$). Taks completion time decreased significantly with the number of repetitions in older adults ($p < 0.01$). In contrast, children generally showed no significant the change of task completion time, or if significant, no substantial

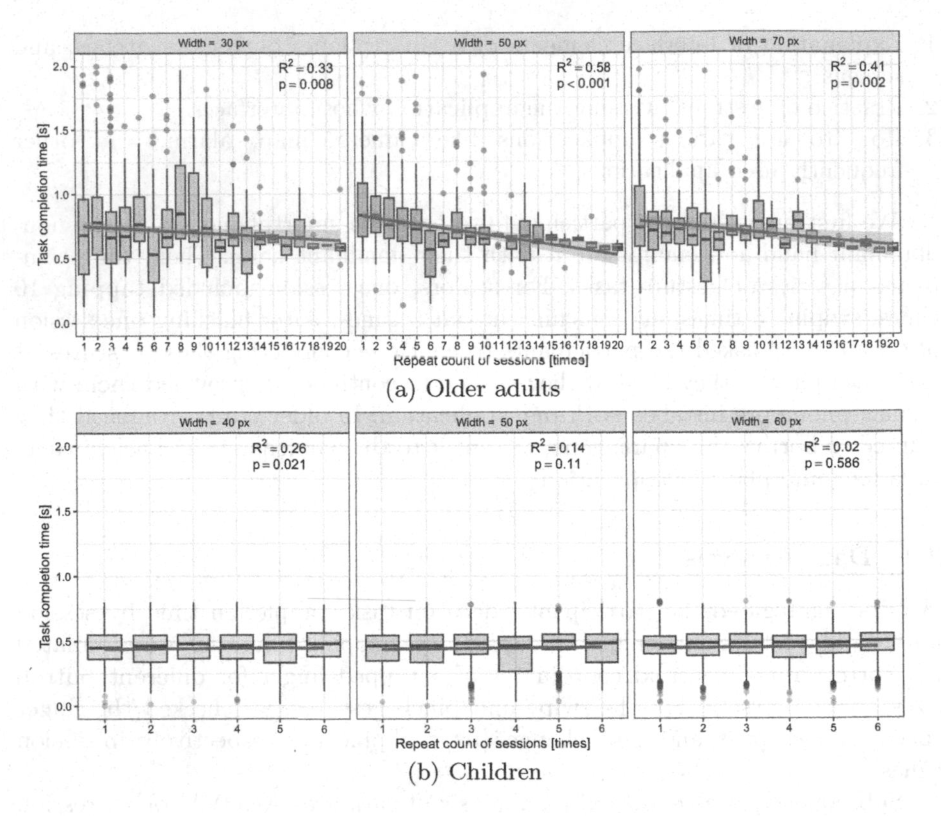

Fig. 2. Task completion time of tapping in different button sizes as a function of repeat count of sessions. The blue line is the regression curve, and the gray area is the 95% confidence interval. The p and R^2 values represent the value in the partial regression coefficient and determination coefficient, respectively. (Color figure online)

change. Among older group, the highest variations in completion time occur in the 30 px width button condition, as shown in the upper left graph of Fig. 2.

Figure 3 (a) and (b) display the change in correct rates per repetition of sessions for tapping at different button sizes in older adults and children, respectively. A logistic regression analysis performed on correct rates confirmed significant main effects for age group ($p < 0.001$) and button size ($p < 0.001$) and a significant interaction between age group and button size ($p < 0.001$). Correct rates generally increased significantly with the number of repetitions in older adults, especially when the button size was 30 or 70 pixels. Likewise for the children, the correct rates generally increased significantly, especially when the button size was 40 or 50 px while there was no increase in the correct rates when the button size was 60px due to repeated practice among the children.

Figure 4 shows the distance between centroids of presented buttons and tapped positions in older adults and children. An ANOVA performed on changes in these distances confirmed significant main effects for age group and whether correct tapping or not ($p < 0.001$) and a significant interaction between these

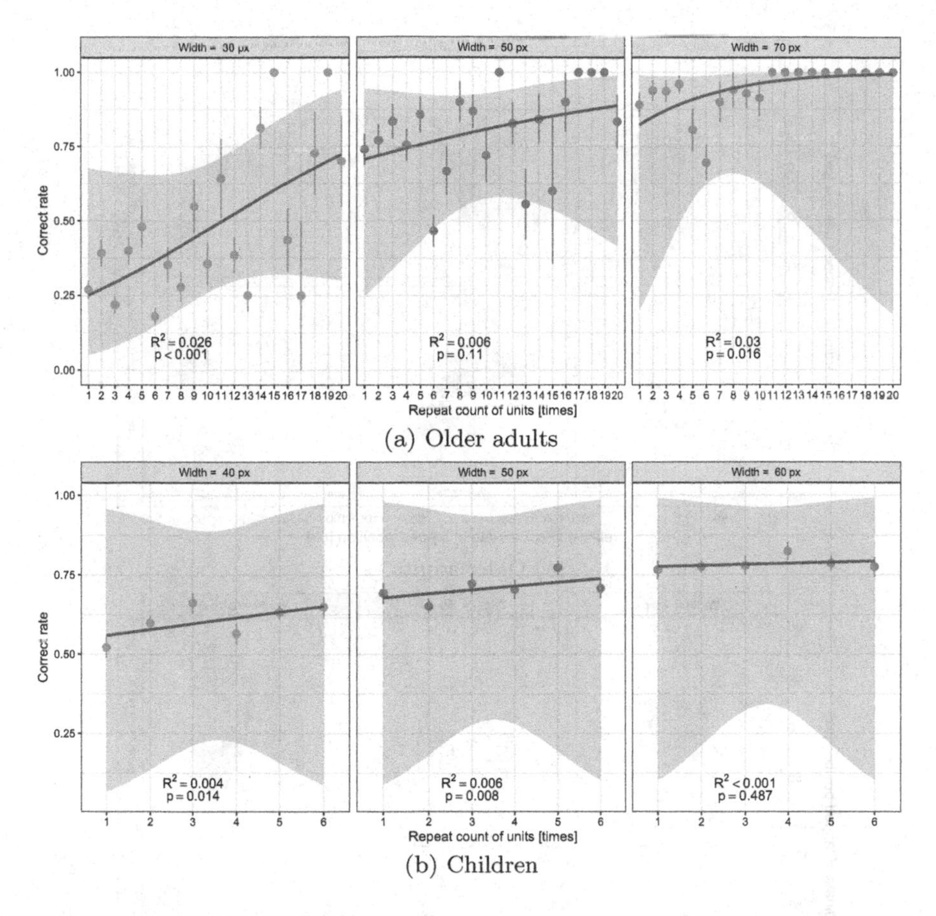

(a) Older adults

(b) Children

Fig. 3. Correct rates of tapping in different button sizes. Each point is the mean value, and error bars indicate standard errors. The blue line is the logistic regression curve, and the gray area is the 95% confidence interval. The p-value represents the value in the partial regression coefficient, and we employed Nagelkerke's pseudo-determination coefficient for the R^2 value. (Color figure online)

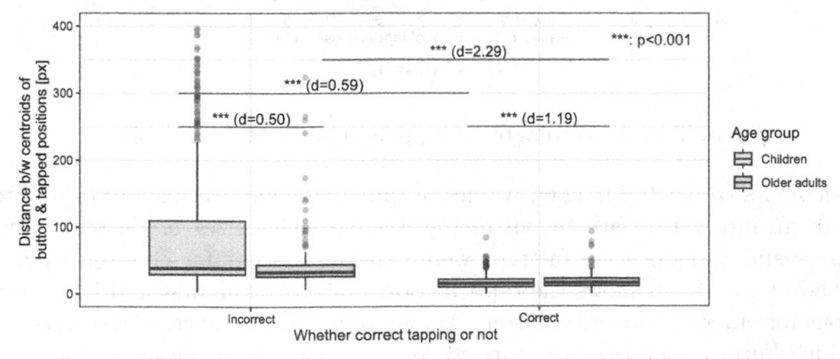

Fig. 4. Distance between centroids of presented buttons and tapped positions in older adults and child

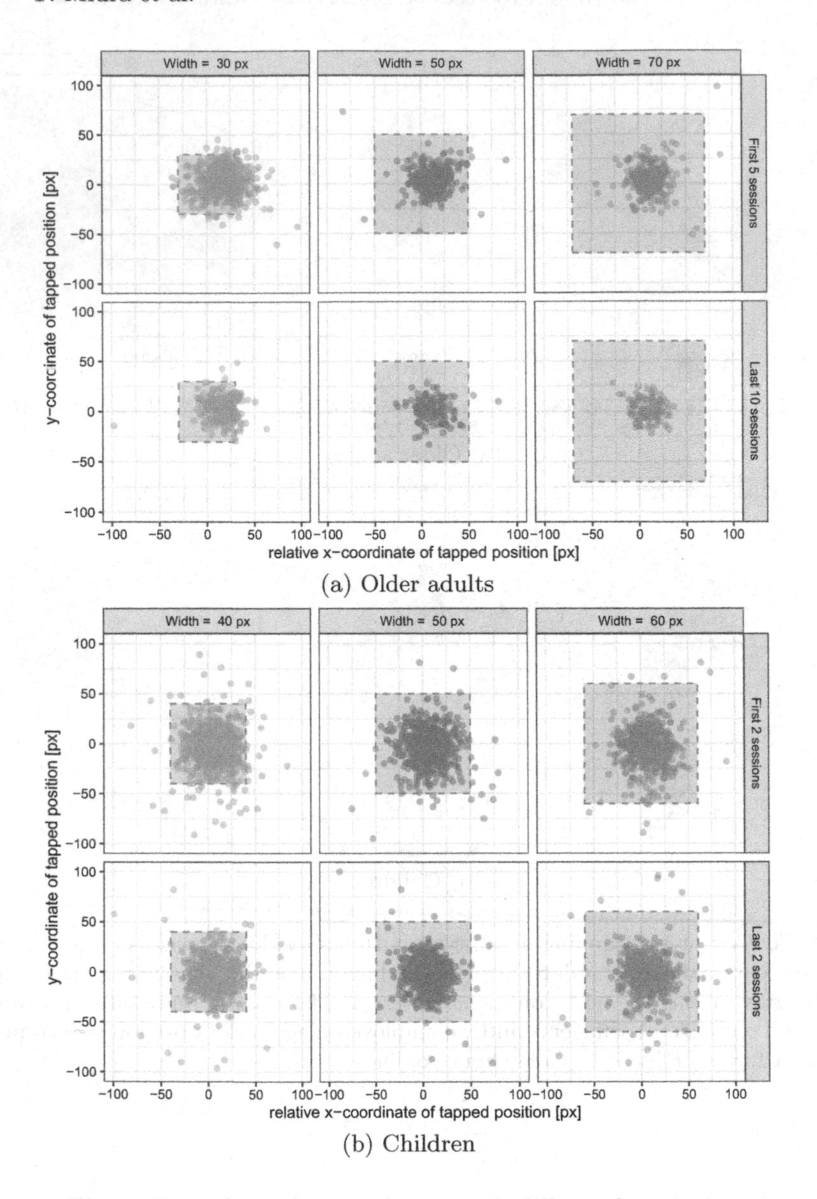

(a) Older adults

(b) Children

Fig. 5. Tapped coordinates of tapping in different button sizes

two elements ($p < 0.001$). The p-values of multiple comparisons and effect sizes of such an interaction are shown in Fig. 4. The effect sizes of these distances on successful and unsuccessful taps were generally larger for children than for older adults. Figure 5 shows the tapped coordinates for the first and last several sessions for older adults and children. Among older adults, particularly in the 30-px width button condition, the tapped coordinates became closer to the center after the 10th sessions. On the other hand, there were fewer changes of tapped positions. According to Kobayashi et al., the distribution of contact points of

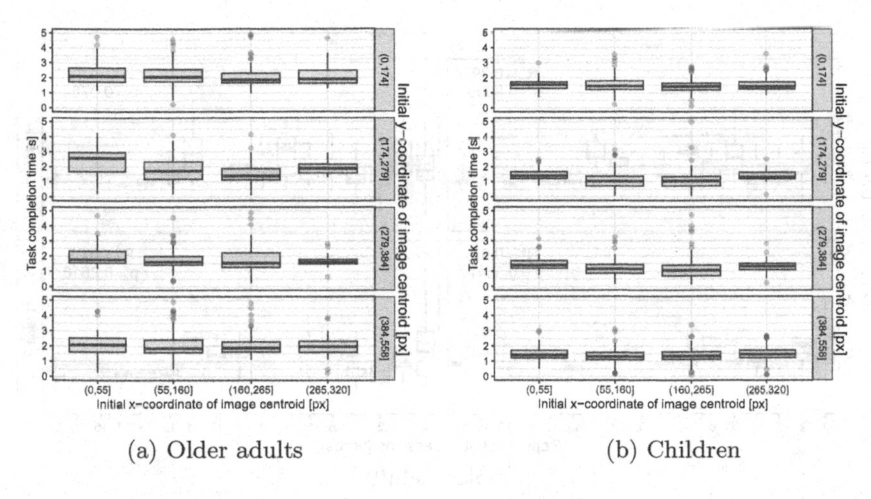

(a) Older adults (b) Children

Fig. 6. Task completion time of swiping for each position when the initial coordinates of the target image on the screen are divided into 4 (vertical) $\times$ 4 (horizontal).

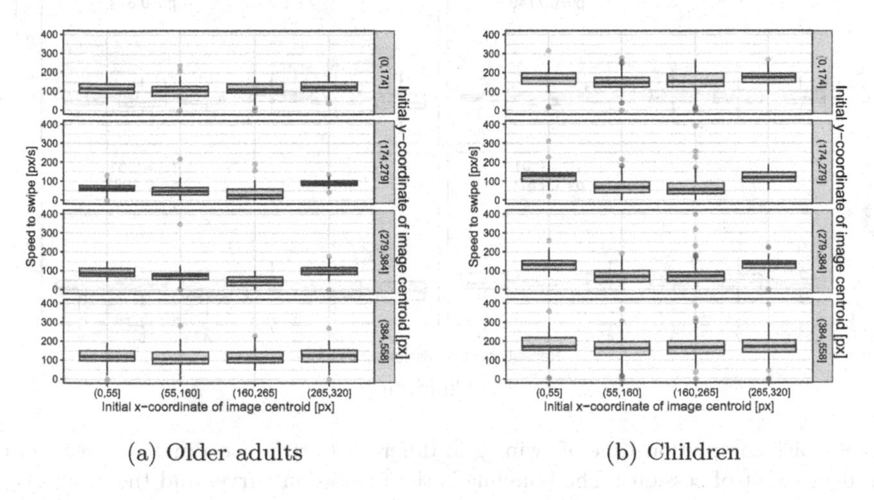

(a) Older adults (b) Children

Fig. 7. Finger speed of swiping for each position when the initial coordinates of the target image on the screen are divided into 4 (vertical) $\times$ 4 (horizontal).

older adults was wider in the 30-px width button condition [12]. The difference between our study and theirs might be due to the computer literacy level of the participants. Since our participants aimed for perfection and feared making mistakes, they were more likely to focus on accuracy, whereas Kobayashi et al.'s computer-literate participants might have been less concerned about making mistakes.

3.2 Swiping

An ANOVA performed on changes in the task completion time and finger speed of swiping confirmed significant main effects for age group ($p < 0.001$), and the

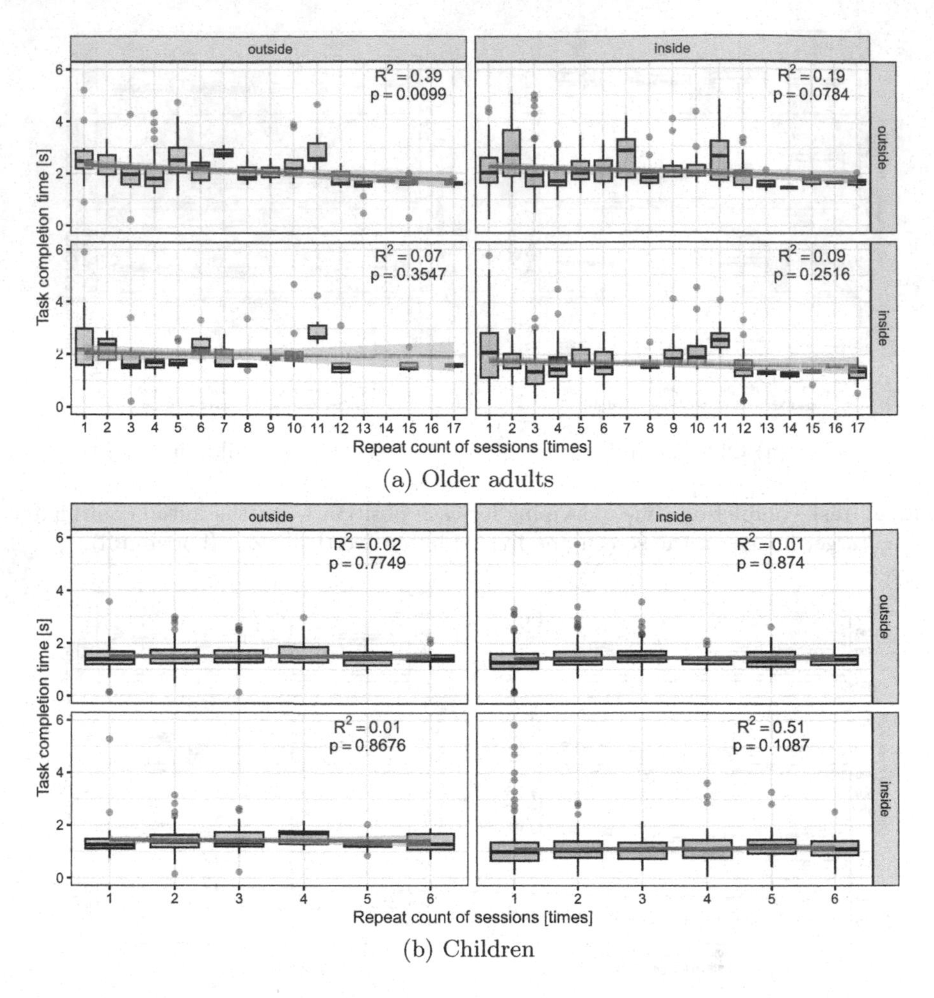

Fig. 8. Task completion time of swiping in different button coordinates as a function of repeat count of sessions. The blue line is the regression curve, and the gray area is the 95% confidence interval. The p and R^2 values represent the value in the partial regression coefficient and determination coefficient, respectively. (Color figure online)

initial x and y coordinates of an image ($p < 0.001$) and a significant interaction between the initial x and y coordinates of an image ($p < 0.001$). As with tapping, children could generally perform swiping significantly faster than older adults in task completion time ($p < 0.001, d = 1.16$ (large)) and finger speed ($p < 0.001, d = 0.84$ (Large)). Regarding initial target positions of a target image, Figs. 6 and 7 show the task completion time and finger speed for positions when the initial coordinates of the target image on the screen are divided into 4 (vertical) × 4 (horizontal), respectively. The initial position of the target tended to be similar for both older adults and children when it took a long time.

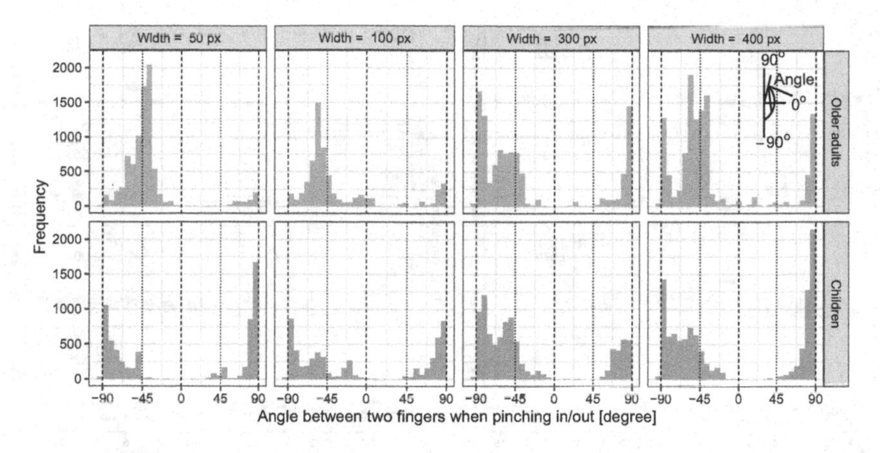

Fig. 9. Angle between two fingers when pinching in/out among age group and initial width of an image

In particular, it took significantly longer and swiped faster when the target was placed on the outside x and/or y coordinates of the screen than the inside of the screen ($p < 0.001, d = 0.53 \sim 0.84$ (middle to large)).

Figure 8 shows the task completion time of a swipe in relation to the number of session iterations. In this figure, the positions on the vertical and horizontal screens in Figs. 6 and 7 are summarized according to whether they are inside or outside relative to the center positions. Similar to the trend observed for tapping in particular, swipe completion times in older adults significantly decreased with an increasing number of sessions ($p < 0.01$), especially for the top and bottom edges of the right and left sides of the screen. Even at the top and bottom edges of the screen center, the task completion time was likely to decrease significantly with an increasing number of sessions ($p = 0.08 < 0.10$). On the other hand, the task completion time of swiping did not change as the number of sessions increased for the children ($p > 0.05$).

A similar trend for swipe completion time was observed for the finger speed of older adults, which tended to be faster as the number of sessions increased with marginal significance, especially at the top and bottom, left and right edges ($p = 0.06 < 0.10$).

3.3 Pinching

Figure 9 shows the angle between the two fingers during pinch-in (width of an initial image: 50 and 100 px) and pinch-out (width of an initial image: 300 and 400 px) for older adults and children. For older adults, the angle between the two fingers during pinch-out was about 45°, while the angle during pinch-in was about 90°. On the other hand, children generally had a pinch-out angle of about 90°, and a pinch-in angle of about 90°, followed by a pinch-in angle of about 45°. The reason for this result might be due to differences in hand size and their flexibility.

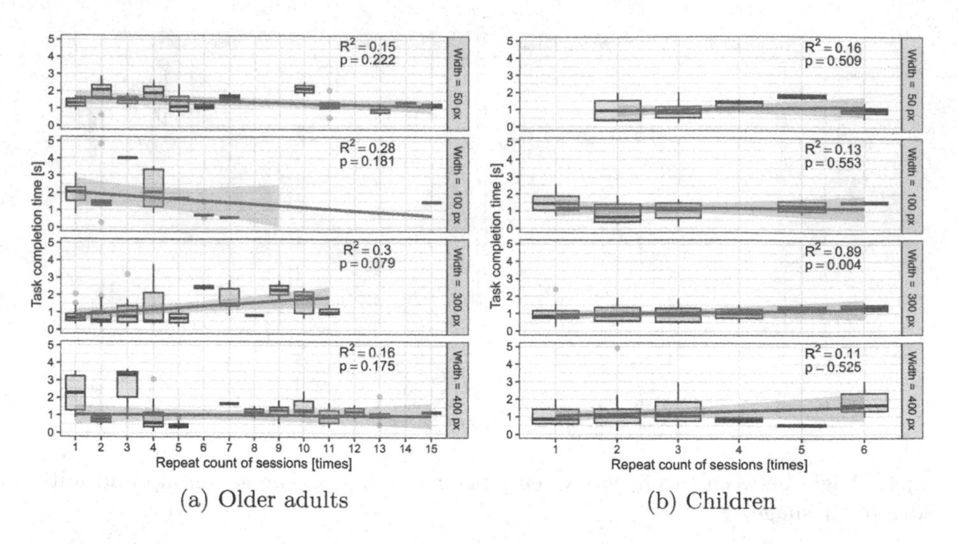

(a) Older adults (b) Children

Fig. 10. Task completion time of pinching in/out in initial image sizes as a function of repeat count of sessions. The blue line is the regression curve, and the gray area is the 95% confidence interval. The p and R^2 values represent the value in the partial regression coefficient and determination coefficient, respectively. (Color figure online)

Figure 10 shows the task completion time and finger speed of the pinching in/out. An ANOVA performed on changes in the task completion time of pinching confirmed significant main effects for initial image size for pinching ($p = 0.003 < 0.01$) and a significant interaction among the age group and the initial image size ($p = 0.011 < 0.05$). As with pinching, there were no significant difference in task completion time between older adults and children ($p = 0.36 > 0.10, d = 0.10$ (Negligible)). Regarding the initial width of an image, pinching out a 100 px image took significantly longer than pinching in 300 or 400 px image ($p < 0.05, d = 0.47 \sim 0.53$ (small to medium)). Multiple comparisons of the interaction among the age groups and the initial image size showed that pinching out at 50 px took significantly longer than pinching in at 400 px among older adults ($p = 0.013 < 0.05, d = 0.65$ (medium)), while this difference was not observed for children ($p = 0.999 > 0.10, d = 0.47$ (medium)). Regarding task completion time with number of repetitions, no significant changes were observed for either older adults or children ($p > 0.10$). However, the time required for 300 px pinch-ins increased as the number of repetitions increased, as shown in Fig. 10. The reason for this is not clearly understood, but it could be fatigue due to repetition of the task.

4 Conclusion and Future Work

To investigate the changes in gesture interaction performance in older adults and children, we developed a gesture checking application and conducted an evaluation involving primarily novice older adults and children. Our study yielded the following results:

A1. In the tapping task, older adults showed a learning effect of completion time and correct rates with repetition, whereas children did not. In addition, the older adults became more accurate with repeated button tapping, while little learning effect was observed for the children. However, the children generally adopted a strategy of rapid and repeated tapping. As a result, the task completion time was shorter for the children.

A2. In swiping, the older adults showed a learning effect in terms of task completion time and finger speed with increasing repetitions, while the children did not. The learning effect was observed for larger movements by swiping, such as moving an object on the edge inward, which were performed faster. The task completion time was shorter for the children.

A3. In pinch-in/out gestures, the learning effect was not generally observed for either older adults or children. As with tapping and swiping, children conducted a pinch-in/out significantly faster. The results showed that older adults tended to pinch out in a 45-degree diagonal direction and pinch with a vertical to 45° diagonal range. In contrast, the children tended to pinch out vertically and pinch in vertically or diagonally.

Acknowledgment. This work was supported by JSPS KAKENHI Grant Numbers JP20H01753, JP21H00915, JP21H04580, and JP21K18483. We would also like to thank all those who cooperated in the experiment.

References

1. A 2016 Declining Birthrate White Paper. http://www8.cao.go.jp/shoushi/shoushika/whitepaper/measures/english/w-2016/
2. Annual Report on the Aging Society 2017 (in Japanese). http://www8.cao.go.jp/kourei/whitepaper/w-2017/zenbun/29pdf_index.html
3. Information and Communications in Japan 2021. https://www.soumu.go.jp/main_sosiki/joho_tsusin/eng/whitepaper/2021/
4. World Population Prospects 2022. https://www.un.org/development/desa/pd/sites/www.un.org.development.desa.pd/files/wpp2022_summary_of_results.pdf
5. Bonney, R., et al.: Next steps for citizen science. Science **343**(6178), 1436–1437 (2014)
6. Cabinet Office, J.: Annual Report on the Ageing Society [Summary] FY2020, July 2020. https://www8.cao.go.jp/kourei/english/annualreport/2020/pdf/2020.pdf
7. Elkin, L.A., Kay, M., Higgins, J.J., Wobbrock, J.O.: An aligned rank transform procedure for multifactor contrast tests. In: The 34th Annual ACM Symposium on User Interface Software and Technology, pp. 754–768 (2021)
8. Guner, H., Acarturk, C.: The use and acceptance of ICT by senior citizens: a comparison of technology acceptance model (TAM) for elderly and young adults. Univ. Access Inf. Soc. **19**, 311–330 (2020)
9. Hanson, V.L.: Web access for elderly citizens. In: Proceedings of the 2001 EC/NSF Workshop on Universal Accessibility of Ubiquitous Computing: Providing for the Elderly, pp. 14–18 (2001)

10. Iwase, H., Murata, A.: Empirical study on the improvement of the usability of a touch panel for the elderly-comparison of usability between a touch panel and a mouse-. IEICE Trans. Inf. Syst. **86**(6), 1134–1138 (2003)
11. Kaneko, R., et al.: Population projections for Japan: 2006–2055 outline of results, methods, and assumptions. Jpn. J. Popul. **6**(1), 76–114 (2008)
12. Kobayashi, M., Hiyama, A., Miura, T., Asakawa, C., Hirose, M., Ifukube, T.: Elderly user evaluation of mobile touchscreen interactions. In: Campos, P., Graham, N., Jorge, J., Nunes, N., Palanque, P., Winckler, M. (eds.) INTERACT 2011. LNCS, vol. 6946, pp. 83–99. Springer, Heidelberg (2011). https://doi.org/10.1007/978-3-642-23774-4_9
13. Lenth, R., Singmann, H., Love, J., Buerkner, P., Herve, M.: Emmeans: Estimated marginal means, aka least-squares means. R package version **1**(1), 3 (2018)
14. Lenth, R.V.: Least-squares means: the R package lsmeans. J. Stat. Softw. **69**(1), 1–33 (2016)
15. McKnight, L., Fitton, D.: Touch-screen technology for children: giving the right instructions and getting the right responses. In: Proceedings of the 9th International Conference on Interaction Design and Children, pp. 238–241 (2010)
16. Meske, C., Junglas, I.: Investigating the elicitation of employees' support towards digital workplace transformation. Behav. Inf. Technol. **40**(11), 1120–1136 (2021)
17. Miura, T., Sakajiri, M., Eljailani, M., Matsuzaka, H., Onishi, J., Ono, T.: Accessible single button characteristics of touchscreen interfaces under screen readers in people with visual impairments. In: Miesenberger, K., Fels, D., Archambault, D., Peňáz, P., Zagler, W. (eds.) ICCHP 2014, Part I. LNCS, vol. 8547, pp. 369–376. Springer, Cham (2014). https://doi.org/10.1007/978-3-319-08596-8_57
18. Miura, T., et al.: Attitude to use information and communication technology in older adults under "stay home" to prevent COVID-19 infection. In: Gao, Q., Zhou, J. (eds.) HCII 2022, Part I. LNCS, vol. 13330, pp. 541–554. Springer, Cham (2022). https://doi.org/10.1007/978-3-031-05581-2_37
19. Preece, J.: Citizen science: new research challenges for human-computer interaction. Int. J. Hum.-Comput. Interact. **32**(8), 585–612 (2016)
20. Romeo, G., Edwards, S., McNamara, S., Walker, I., Ziguras, C.: Touching the screen: issues related to the use of touchscreen technology in early childhood education. Br. J. Edu. Technol. **34**(3), 329–339 (2003)
21. Shore, L., Power, V., De Eyto, A., O'Sullivan, L.W.: Technology acceptance and user-centred design of assistive exoskeletons for older adults: a commentary. Robotics **7**(1), 3 (2018)
22. Silvertown, J.: A new dawn for citizen science. Trends Ecol. Evol. **24**(9), 467–471 (2009)
23. Soni, N., Aloba, A., Morga, K.S., Wisniewski, P.J., Anthony, L.: A framework of touchscreen interaction design recommendations for children (TIDRC) characterizing the gap between research evidence and design practice. In: Proceedings of the 18th ACM International Conference on Interaction Design and Children, pp. 419–431 (2019)
24. Trenerry, B., et al.: Preparing workplaces for digital transformation: an integrative review and framework of multi-level factors. Front. Psychol., 822 (2021)
25. Vial, G.: Understanding digital transformation: a review and a research agenda. J. Strateg. Inf. Syst. **28**(2), 118–144 (2019)
26. Wang, H., Tao, D., Yu, N., Qu, X.: Understanding consumer acceptance of healthcare wearable devices: an integrated model of UTAUT and TTF. Int. J. Med. Informatics **139**, 104156 (2020)

27. Wildenbos, G.A., Peute, L., Jaspers, M.: Aging barriers influencing mobile health usability for older adults: a literature based framework (MOLD-US). Int. J. Med. Informatics **114**, 66–75 (2018)
28. Wobbrock, J.O., Findlater, L., Gergle, D., Higgins, J.J.: The aligned rank transform for nonparametric factorial analyses using only ANOVA procedures. In: Proceedings of the SIGCHI Conference on Human Factors in Computing Systems, pp. 143–146 (2011)

Emotion Estimation for Elderly People with Dementia Using EEG and HRV

Yuri Nakagawa(✉) and Midori Sugaya

Shibaura Institute of Technology, 3-7-5, Toyosu, Koto-Ku, Tokyo 135-8548, Japan
{nb23112,doly}@shibaura-it.ac.jp

Abstract. In recent years, the number of elderly people with dementia has been increasing worldwide, and at the same time, the demand to care for elderly people with dementia has also been increasing. However, there is a chronic shortage of caregivers. Caregivers working in actual nursing homes have difficulty estimating the emotions of elderly people with dementia. Therefore, the purpose of this study is to estimate the emotions of elderly people with dementia using a method called Emotion Map, which estimates emotions from physiological signals. To achieve this, we conducted an investigation of physiological signals suitable for elderly people with dementia with the data collection in actual care facilities. The Emotion Map using pNN20 as an index of heart rate variability (HRV) can evaluate high-valence responses to stimuli that induce pleasant emotions, suggesting its effectiveness in estimating emotions in elderly people with dementia. In the future, it will be necessary to also investigate EEG indexes that estimate emotions with different levels of arousal and to increase the number of experiments.

Keywords: emotion estimation · elderly · dementia

1 Introduction

Recently, the number of dementia patients has been increasing worldwide. Similarly, it is estimated that the percentage of elderly people with dementia will increase to about 20% of the elderly population in Japan by 2025 [1]. Since most elderly dementia patients require care, the demand to care for them is expected to increase. Particularly, the symptoms of dementia patients' care involve various problems such as memory impairment, behavioral disorders, and psychological disorders, many of which do not respond to drug therapy [2]. Therefore, it is necessary to provide a close care by caregivers. As a result, a lot of workload are placed on the caregivers of elderly dementia patients. However, there is a chronic shortage of caregivers, and several other problems such as caregivers are being under significant stress. To improve the quality of life of elderly dementia patients, it is necessary to reduce the workload on caregivers as much as possible.

To investigate the workload felt by caregivers in taking care of the elderly dementia patients, we conducted interviews with caregivers working in actual nursing home. The obtained responses were summarized into two categories:

Q. Gao et al. (Eds.): HCII 2023, LNCS 14055, pp. 140–149, 2023.
https://doi.org/10.1007/978-3-031-48041-6_11

1. The wandering and desire to return home of elderly dementia patients often come from negative emotions such as anxiety, so it is necessary to notice such emotions and work to resolve them through communication. However, due to the amount of work and the number of staff, it is not easy to always pay attention to elderly dementia patients and notice negative emotions. Especially for the elderly with dementia, it is sometimes difficult to express emotions, making it difficult to notice changes in emotions.
2. As caregivers, they want to provide better service to elderly dementia patients, but it is difficult to improve care for dementia patients who have difficulty expressing their own emotions and have no reaction to any care. Therefore, they feel that if they can understand whether dementia patients feel comfortable or not, they can provide better care.

From these responses, we found that caregivers feel that it is not easy to notice the emotions of elderly dementia patients. Even if they cannot always pay attention to elderly dementia patients' emotions or if the patients have difficulty expressing emotions, providing a tool to help estimate elderly dementia patients' emotions can reduce the workload on caregivers and lead to better service, which can improve the QoL of elderly dementia patients and the caretakers.

2 Literature Survey and Issues

Various methods have been proposed to estimate emotions such as self-reports in which people report their emotions by answering questionnaires, facial expression recognition and physiological signal measurement from heart rate, electroencephalogram (EEG), etc. [3]. Self-report is a method of estimating emotions from questionnaires or interviews. However, this method may not be suitable for the elderly people with dementia who may have difficulty understanding their own emotions or reporting them [4]. Facial expression measurement captures emotions by detecting facial feature points from facial images or observing electromyogram activity of facial muscles. In actual nursing homes, installing cameras to capture facial expressions can be costly, and there may be situations where cameras cannot capture faces due to blind spots or the orientation of the elderly people's faces.

In contrast, using physiological sensors for emotion estimation is relatively less affected by cost since wearable sensors can be used. Additionally, since these sensors can be worn on the body, they are less affected by the behavior of the elderly people with dementia. Moreover, by using physiological sensors that are difficult for people to manipulate compared to self-report or facial expressions, more objective results can be obtained. Therefore, using physiological signals is considered to be an effective means of estimating emotions for the elderly people with dementia in care settings.

There have been studies on estimating emotions of elderly people with dementia from their physiological signals [5–7]. Zeng et al. constructed a model to classify changes in emotions from EEG and Heart Rate Variability (HRV) to support communication between elderly people with dementia and caregivers. A maximum accuracy of 93.3% was obtained for the classification of arousal using CNN [5]. However, creating correct labels for changes in emotions is necessary for constructing such a model. This requires answering a 9-point scale questionnaire every 15 s for 6 types of videos, which can be a workload for elderly people with dementia.

On the other hand, Han et al. compared the self-reported emotions of elderly people with dementia with the results of physiological measurements by EEG and HRV to form the background of the difficulty of elderly people with dementia in expressing their emotions appropriately [6]. In the experiment, elderly people with dementia and healthy elderly people watched videos that evoked two emotions, negative emotion (fear) and positive emotion (fun), and compared the results of self-reported emotions to the physiological measurements by EEG and HRV. However, when comparing the results of self-reported emotions between elderly people with dementia and healthy elderly people, opposite results were obtained. On the other hand, similar results were obtained when comparing the results of physiological measurements. This suggests that using physiological measurements to estimate the emotions of elderly people with dementia is effective. However, the comparison between the results of physiological measurements and the emotions they represent is insufficient, and there is a challenge in discussing how to estimate emotions from physiological measurements.

For that matter, an emotion estimation method called Emotion Map has been proposed for healthy adults, which visualizes human emotions from HRV and EEG [8]. Emotion Map uses Russell's circumplex model, a psychological model that represents human emotions on a circular plane with bipolar dimensions: valence and arousal [9] (Fig. 1).

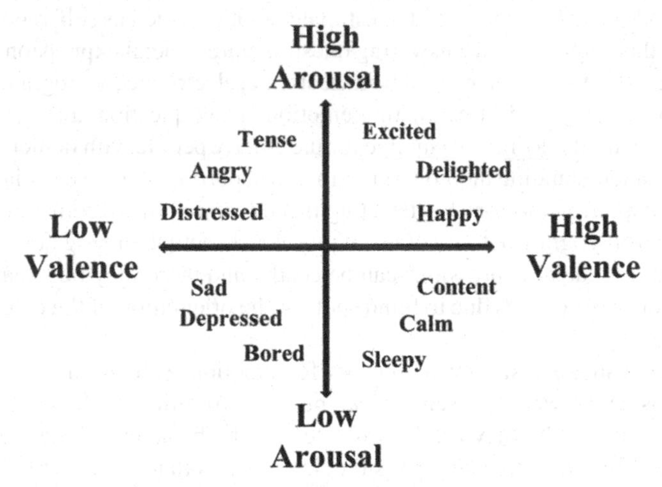

Fig. 1. 2D model of emotion [9].

In Emotion Map, HRV and EEG values are respectively associated with the x-axis (valence) and y-axis (arousal) on a two-dimensional coordinate system. The results are shown as a point on the two-dimensional coordinate system of valence and arousal, and emotions are evaluated based on which quadrant the point is located in. The quadrants are named HVHA (High Valence – High Arousal), LVHA (Low Valence – High Arousal), LVLA (Low Valence – Low Arousal), and HVLA (High Valence – Low Arousal) (Fig. 2).

For example, if the measurement result is plotted in HVHA, it is estimated that the valence and arousal are both high, and the emotion is associated with joy, happy or pleasure. However, HRV and EEG are known to change with age. Therefore, using Emotion Map to estimate emotions does not necessarily require questionnaire results, and it is possible to directly estimate emotions from physiological measurements. Therefore, it is considered to be an effective method for estimating emotions of elderly people with dementia. However, discussions on suitable physiological indexes for elderly people and cases where visualization is difficult are lacking.

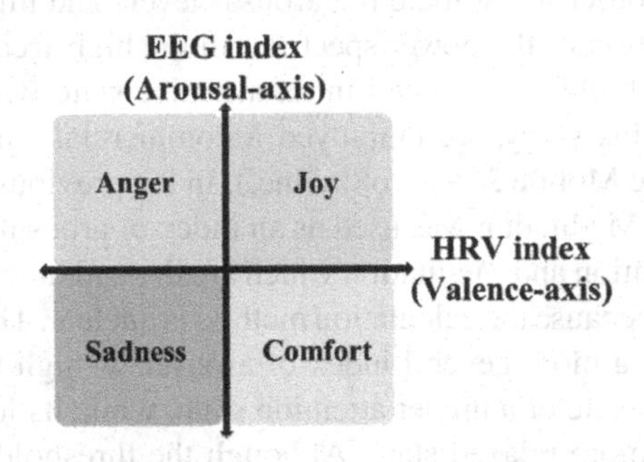

Fig. 2. Emotion Map [8]

3 Purpose and Proposal

In this study, we propose to examine a method for estimating emotions of elderly people with dementia using physiological signals to make it easier to estimate emotions. We also propose to use data from elderly people with dementia who receive care services at actual nursing home for the experiment to clarify appropriate emotion estimation methods for them.

3.1 Consideration of an Emotion Map Suitable for the Elderly

Emotion Map is a method to visualize human emotions from HRV and EEG, as described in Sect. 2. As the Emotion Map is an emotion estimation method for healthy adults, this study examines appropriate physiological indexes for estimating emotions in elderly people with dementia.

HRV index of valence axis. HRV refers to the variation of the R-wave interval (RRI) in the electrocardiogram (ECG) waveform and is expressed as the variability of the RRI [10]. HRV is strongly related to sympathetic and parasympathetic activity and is known to correlate with stress. Several parameters can be calculated based on the RRI [11]. One of them is pNNx, which refers to the ratio of the difference between adjacent RRIs over x as time (ms) and is known to increase when sympathetic activity is activated. In previous studies, pNN50 was proposed as the HRV index for the valence axis. However, HRV is known to change with age. Thus, using pNN50 as the valence axis for elderly people with dementia may not be appropriate [12]. Therefore, in this study, we use the value of pNN20 [13], which is also related to people's stress state, to estimate valence and compare it with pNN50. A large value of pNNx indicates a parasympathetic-dominant state, indicating a high valence level, while a small value indicates an unpleasant state. The threshold for low valence and high valence is set to the resting value measured before the experiment, considering individual differences. In this study, we employed a wireless ECG sensor, Mybeat WHS-1 (Union Tool Co.).

EEG index of Arousal Axis. EEG is a type of physiological signal obtained from brainwave activity. In order to estimate the arousal level. The highly arousing state is indicated by the activation of the power spectrum in the high-frequency band and vice versa. In other words, highβ is activated in an attentive state while lowα is activated in a relaxed state. In this study, we employed a commercial single-channel wireless EEG sensor, MindWave Mobile 2 (NeuroSky Inc.). In the previous study, the difference between Attention and Meditation was used as an index of arousal. However, this index is calculated from Attention and Meditation which are dependent on MindWaveMobile2 and has low versatility because the calculation method is unclear. Therefore, in this study, highβ/highα is used as a more general index of arousal. A high value of highβ/highα indicates a β-dominant state or a higher attention state, while its low value indicates an α-dominant state or a more relaxed state. Although the threshold for low arousal and high arousal could be set to 1 using the ratio of α and β bands for arousal-axis, it was considered to set the threshold for low arousal and high arousal to the resting value measured before the experiment considering the individual differences.

3.2 Data Collection in Nursing Home

In this study, we conduct experiments using elderly people with dementia residing in actual nursing home since we aim to estimate the emotions of elderly people with dementia rather than healthy young adults (Fig. 3). Therefore, we decided on the experimental procedure and sensors to be used through discussions with caregivers to avoid burdening elderly people with dementia with complex tasks as much as possible. Music was used

Fig. 3. Experiment scene

as a stimulus to elicit emotions to avoid demanding complex tasks. In addition, sensors with uncomfortable feelings were avoided, and wireless EEG and ECG sensors were used.

4 Experiment Method

4.1 Participants

We recruited three elderly people with dementia, who are in the age of 90 to 96 years old living in a nursing home. In the experimental results (Sect. 5), they will be named as participants A, B, and C.

4.2 Emotional Stimuli

We employed music adopted from a music database created through discussions with researchers and professional musicians at Jyväskylä University [14]. Two types of emotional stimuli were used in this study. The first one (music1) was used to evoke high pleasantness and low arousal. The other (music2) was used to evoke high pleasantness and high arousal. Before the experiment was conducted, the volume was checked and adjusted so that the music could be heard by the experimenters.

4.3 Experiment Setup and Procedure

In the experiment, we collected EEG and HRV data while the participants were listening to the music to evoke emotions as shown in the experimental setup in Fig. 4.

1. Participant wears EEG and ECG sensors and the data recording is started.
2. Participant rests for 2 min.
3. Participant listens to music1 for 2 min.
4. Participant answers the questionnaire about music1.
5. Participant rests for 2 min.
6. Steps 3 to 5 are repeated for music2.

Note that this paper only presents EEG and HRV results. The questionnaire result will be used for our further analysis.

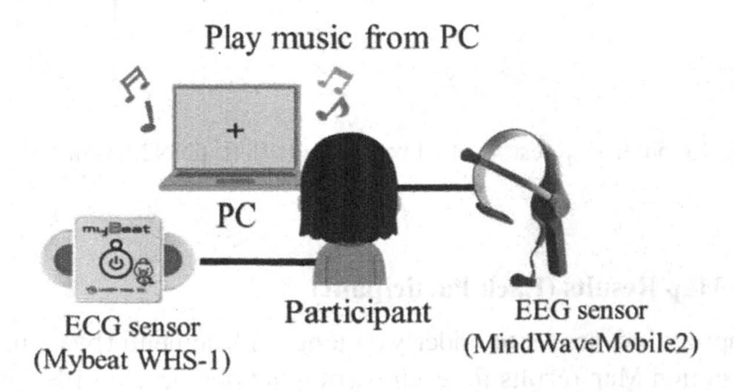

Fig. 4. Experiment setup

5 Experimental Results and Discussion

5.1 Emotion Map Results (All Participants)

We used the experimental results for plotting the emotions on an Emotion Map to evaluate the most appropriate physiological indexes. The origin of the Emotion Map corresponds to the values during rest for the valence and arousal axis. Therefore, the results for music1 and music2 are plotted based on the difference between their mean values and the mean values during rest for each condition. The axis labels for each Emotion Map indicate the differences Δ(pNN50), Δ(pNN20), and Δ(high β/high α).

The Emotion Map created from the average values of all participants is shown in Fig. 5. For the Emotion Map with pNN50 as the valence axis, music1 was plotted in HVHA and music2 was plotted in LVHA. As for valence, music1 tends to induce high valence, but music2 tends to induce low valence. When using pNN50 as the valence axis, it was evaluated that the participant was in a relaxed state while listening to music1 and in a tense state while listening to music2. As for arousal, both music1 and music2 tend to induce high arousal. High arousal means that highβ was dominant compared to highα during rest. As highβ is known to be dominant during attentive states, it is possible that participants were paying attention to the music compared to the resting period.

The results of the Emotion Map with pNN20 as the valence axis showed that both music1 and music2 were plotted in HVHA, in contrary to the hypothesis for music1. As for valence, the higher pNN20 values compared to the resting period indicate that the music stimuli tend to induce a more comfortable state. As for high arousal, as previously mentioned, it is possible that participants were paying attention to the music stimuli compared to the rest period. Thus, it is considered that both music1 and music2 evoked enjoyable or exciting emotions for all participants. However, the number of participants in this study was only three, making the results susceptible to individual differences.

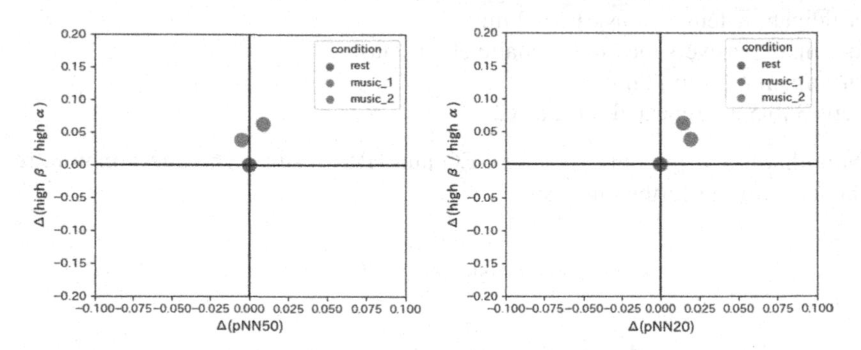

Fig. 5. Emotion Map results of all participants (left: pNN20, right: pNN50)

5.2 Emotion Map Results (Each Participant)

To select appropriate indexes for the elderly patients with dementia by comparing the two indexes, the Emotion Map results for each participant obtained for pNN50 and pNN20 are shown in Figs. 6 and 7, respectively.

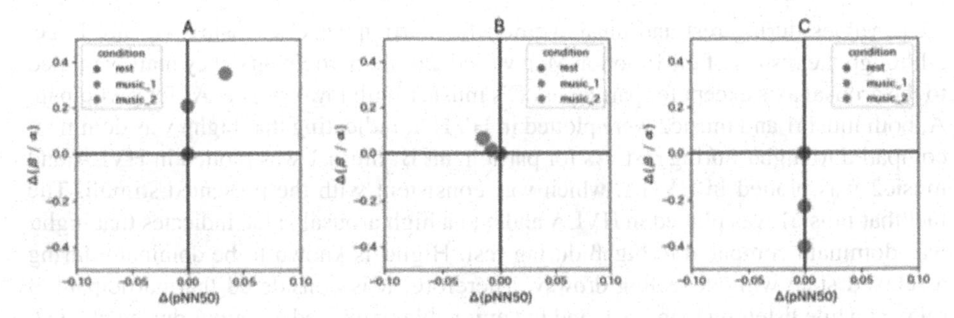

Fig. 6. Emotion Map results of each participant using pNN50 (left: A, center: B, right: C)

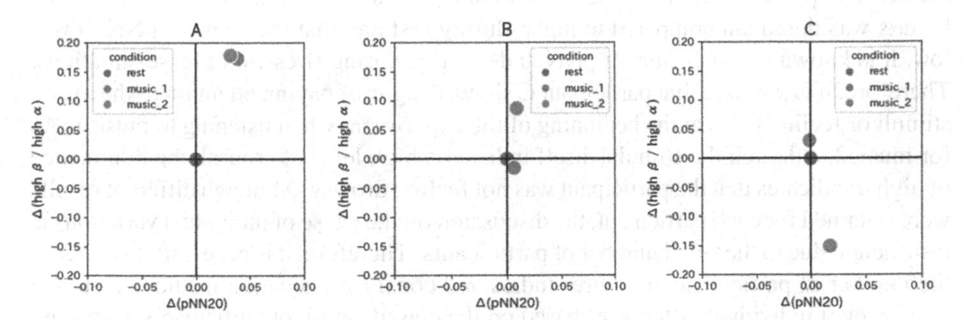

Fig. 7. Emotion Map results of each participant using pNN20 (left: A, center: B, right: C)

For the Emotion Map using pNN50 for each individual, the valence values for music2 of participant A and music1 and music2 of participant C were plotted on the arousal-axis, and no differences were observed compared to the resting period. The possibility of the values being the same between rest and emotional stimuli or being 0 for both cannot be ruled out. Therefore, to confirm this, the values of pNN50 for rest and music were plotted in Fig. 8, which showed that the values of pNN50 were 0. Therefore, it is possible that using pNN50 as an index of heart rate variability for elderly patients with dementia is not appropriate.

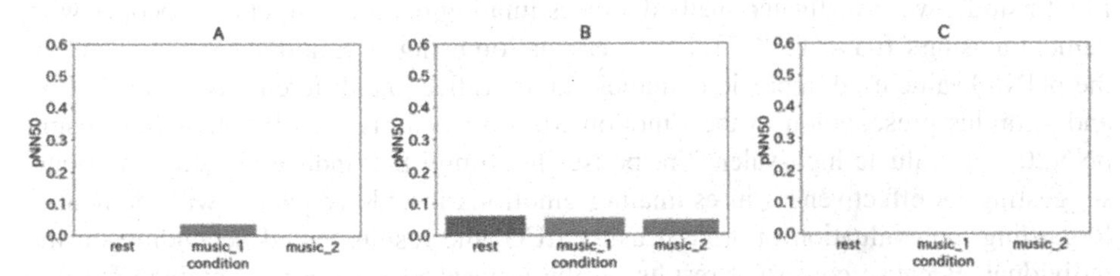

Fig. 8. Comparison of pNN50 for each condition of each participant (left: A, center: B, right: C)

pNN20. For the Emotion Map using pNN20 for each individual, all results except for participant C's music1 were plotted in HVHA or HVLA. The difference between the mean values during rest and music stimuli for participant C's music1 was not large. Although the results of the Emotion Map varied among participants, they mainly related to the arousal axis except for participant C's music1 with low valence. As for participant A, both music1 and music2 were plotted in HVHA, indicating that highβ was dominant compared to highα during rest. As for participant B, music1 was plotted in HVLA and music2 was plotted in HVHA, which was consistent with the presented stimuli. The fact that music1 was plotted in HVLA and had a high arousal value indicates that highα was dominant compared to highβ during rest. Highα is known to be dominant during a relaxed state without feeling drowsy. Therefore, it is considered that participant B relaxed while listening to music1, and felt enjoyable or excited emotions during music2, which induced high arousal. As for participant C, music1 was plotted in LVHA and music2 was plotted in HVLA. The fact that music1 was plotted in LVHA indicates that highαs was dominant compared to highβ during rest and that the value of pNN20 was low. It is known that the value of pNN20 decreases during stressful or tense situations. Therefore, it is possible that participant C showed signs of paying attention to the music stimuli or feeling tense at the beginning of the experiment when listening to music1. As for music2, although the stimulus itself induced a high level of arousal, the dominance of high α indicates that the participant was not feeling drowsy. Although different results were obtained for each participant, the discussion on the cause of individual variations is insufficient due to the small number of participants. Therefore, it is necessary to increase the number of participants in future studies and consider evaluation methods that take into account individual differences based on the classification of participants according to their cognitive levels.

It was shown that it is difficult to capture HRV in elderly patients with dementia using pNN50. In contrast, using pNN20, it was possible to estimate emotions evoked by comfortable music as emotional stimuli as high valence and observe the difference between rest and stimulus presentation. Therefore, the Emotion Map with pNN20 as a HRV index is a potential method for estimating emotions in elderly patients with dementia.

6 Conclusion

In this study, we investigated methods for estimating emotions in elderly people with dementia using EEG and HRV. Emotion estimation using an Emotion Map showed that the pNN50 value used in previous studies cannot reflect the difference between resting and stimulus presentation in the Emotion Map. In contrast, the Emotion Map using pNN20 can evaluate high-valence responses to stimuli that induce pleasant emotions, suggesting its effectiveness in estimating emotions in elderly people with dementia. Regarding the evaluation of arousal using EEG, the results varied depending on the individual. Because consistent results on the arousal axis were not obtained for two different music stimuli that induce arousal, it is necessary to consider using other indexes as the arousal axis. In the future, we will continue to collect data from the elderly people who are the current residents of nursing home, and investigate evaluation methods that consider individual differences based on the classification of participants according to level of cognitive function, with more participants. We will also investigate methods and systems that can be applied in actual caregiving situations.

Acknowledgment. The authors would like to thank the staff members of the "Care Home for the Elderly Sawayaka Kinu no Sato Shinshu Okaya" for their cooperation in this experiment, the participants and their families, Mr. Eiji Otsuka and Mr. Yosuke Uchida of TPR Corporation for their support in conducting this experiment.

References

1. Cabinet Office: 2016, Annual Report on the Aging Society: 2016 (Summary). https://www8.cao.go.jp/kourei/whitepaper/w-2017/zenbun/pdf/1s2s_03.pdf. (in Japanese)
2. Duong, S., Patel, T., Chang, F.: Dementia: what pharmacists need to know. Can. Pharm. J. **150**, 118–129 (2017)
3. Bradley, M.M., Lang, P.J.: Measuring emotion: the Self-Assessment Manikin and the Semantic Differential. J. Behav. Ther. Exp. Psychiatry **25**, 49–59 (1994)
4. World Health Organization: Dementia. https://www.who.int/news-room/fact-sheets/detail/dementia. Last accessed 1 Feb 2023
5. Fangmeng, Z., Peijia, L., Iwamoto, M., Kuwahara, N.: Emotional changes detection for dementia people with spectrograms from physiological signals. Int. J. Adv. Comput. Sci. Appl. (2018). https://doi.org/10.14569/IJACSA.2018.091006
6. Han, D.H., et al.: Biosignals to detect the imbalance of explicit and implicit affect in dementia: a pilot study. Am. J. Alzheimers Dis. Other Demen. **34**, 457–463 (2019)
7. Seo, J., Laine, T.H., Oh, G., Sohn, K.-A.: EEG-based emotion classification for alzheimer's disease patients using conventional machine learning and recurrent neural network models. Sensors **20**, 7212 (2020)
8. Ueno, S., Zhang, R., Laohakangvalvit, T., Sugaya, M.: Evaluating comfort in fully autonomous vehicle using biological emotion map. In: Stanton, N. (ed.) AHFE 2021. LNNS, vol. 270, pp. 323–330. Springer, Cham (2021). https://doi.org/10.1007/978-3-030-80012-3_38
9. Russell, J.A.: A circumplex model of affect. J. Pers. Soc. Psychol. **39**, 1161 (1980)
10. Shaffer, F., Ginsberg, J.P.: An overview of heart rate variability metrics and norms. Front. Public Health **5**, 258 (2017)
11. Castaldo, R., Melillo, P., Bracale, U., Caserta, M., Triassi, M., Pecchia, L.: Acute mental stress assessment via short term HRV analysis in healthy adults: a systematic review with meta-analysis. Biomed. Signal Process. Control **18**, 370–377 (2015)
12. Umetani, K., Singer, D.H., McCraty, R., Atkinson, M.: Twenty-four hour time domain heart rate variability and heart rate: relations to age and gender over nine decades. J. Am. Coll. Cardiol. **31**, 593–601 (1998)
13. Pereira, T., Almeida, P.R., Cunha, J.P.S., Aguiar, A.: Heart rate variability metrics for fine-grained stress level assessment. Comput. Methods Programs Biomed. **148**, 71–80 (2017)
14. Eerola, T., Vuoskoski, J.K.: A comparison of the discrete and dimensional models of emotion in music. Psychol. Music **39**, 18–49 (2011)

A Study on the Design Strategy of Walking Health APP for the Elderly from the Behavioral Theory Perspective

Xiaoli Niu[1], Honghai Li[1(✉)], and Chen Zhang[2]

[1] Beijing Information Science and Technology University, Beijing 100192, China
Lihonghai@bistu.edu.cn
[2] Tsinghua University, Beijing 100084, China
zhangchen2020@mail.tsinghua.edu.cn

Abstract. Based on the relevant elements of the theory of planned behavior and its practical application, this paper builds a design model of walking health APP for the elderly and performs the design research process according to the design model. Guided by the theory of planned behavior, the non-interventional behavior observation method and semi-structured interviews were used to investigate the elderly groups in five typical communities in Beijing, and the behavioral characteristics of the elderly were recorded and analyzed in the process of walking behavior in different scenarios, to obtain the factors influencing the walking behavior of the elderly group. Through the analysis of laboratory video data and the transformation of influencing factors, four typical walking modes of the elderly were output. At the same time, combined with the travel mode and the aging design method, the design strategy suitable for the APP of walking health of the elderly is proposed, and the analysis and evaluation of the walking behavior and the travel behavior of the elderly are recorded and tracked in the form of an APP. Based on the principle of cognitive walking, the Smart Healthy Walking APP is tested by the 5-level Likert scale to verify the effectiveness of the proposed design strategy. The research in this paper provides a new idea for the user research of health products for the elderly and provides a solution for the analysis, evaluation and transformation of the elderly's travel environment.

Keywords: Theory of Planned Behavior · User Research · Walking Behavior Model · Intelligent Video Analysis · Application Design Strategy

1 Introduction

By the end of 2021, the elderly population aged 60 and over accounted for 18.9% of the total population in China. It is predicted that China will enter the stage of moderate aging during the period of the 14th Five-Year Plan [1]. As the physical condition of the elderly changes, their daily activities are mainly leisure activities, and the frequency of walking behavior increases [2]. At the same time, degradation of physiological functions leads to changes in gait and hidden dangers, such as falls. Falls are the main cause of

Q. Gao et al. (Eds.): HCII 2023, LNCS 14055, pp. 150–170, 2023.
https://doi.org/10.1007/978-3-031-48041-6_12

serious accidental injuries in the elderly. The first step in preventing falls is to assess the risk of falls and identify risk factors [3]. Among them, gait characteristics can be used to distinguish whether there are physical obstacles and as predictors of future risk of falling [4].

The travel behavior of the elderly not only reflects their health status, but also affects their health status. Research on travel health of the elderly has also attracted much attention. In recent years, several studies have used dynamic monitoring and intelligent analysis to achieve physical monitoring and evaluation of the elderly [5–7]. The body recognition and detection system monitor the user's physical state in real time and dynamically through wearable smart products and lacks other influencing factors such as the outdoor environment of walking. In addition, in terms of healthy travel, wearable products will interfere with the elderly to some extent during their travel. Intelligent video analysis can compensate for the lack of wearable products and meet the diverse travel needs of the elderly.

Scholars have done a lot of research on the characteristics of the elderly, walking behavior, and user experience from the perspective of interaction design and medical treatment. As far as interaction design is concerned, Zeyan Chen et al. proposed the APP interaction design method for the elderly based on fault tree analysis (FTA) from the perspective of user satisfaction, and optimized and improved the existing design by qualitatively and quantitatively analyzing the fault tree and sorting the importance of basic events [8]; Zehang Cheng et al. searched the literature on the design of the elderly user interface in Asia, in order to summarize current methods and trends in the design of interfaces for the elderly in Asia. The relevant research was found to mainly help the elderly to improve their ability to live alone, improve their health, and provide social information for the elderly, and most of them were user-centered interface designs. It was noted that the cognitive ability and physical ability of the elderly should be considered when designing interfaces [9]. As far as medical treatment is concerned, David Bastos and others have created a physical activity monitoring system for smart cities based on studying context awareness. During the walking of elderly people, the APP collects data in real time through sensors, and health professionals can use these data to monitor the physical condition of users and provide suggestions on the Web to supervise and motivate the elderly to adopt an active and healthy lifestyle [5]. Yiannis Koumpouros uses a highly user-centered design method to develop mobile health applications for pain management, considering technical decisions, economic issues, user-friendly issues, resource usage, given time frames, etc., and conducts in-depth usability testing and analysis with scales. The final solution supports the monitoring of the management, reporting and effect of the treatment, with the objective of providing services to patients and physicians with chronic diseases or acute pain [10].

However, current research on walking health products is mainly based on user needs, and there are few user studies of the behavior of walking itself. At the same time, most of the current user research on health APPs for the elderly lacks theoretical guidance, resulting in unreasonable program settings and unsatisfactory use effects. Therefore, based on the relevant elements and research status of the planned behavior theory model, this study produces the design model suitable for the elderly walking health APP and conducts user research on the elderly's walking behavior in the Beijing urban area under the guidance of the planned behavior theory, to gain insight into the influencing factors of elderly walking behavior, build a new model suitable for urban elderly walking and the design strategy of the walking health APP, and realize the intelligent terminal of the elderly' urban travel analysis and evaluation platform by combining deep learning and human gait feature extraction technology, to provide a reference for health management and community construction of the elderly.

2 Research on the Theory of Planned Behavior

2.1 Concepts of the Theory of Planned Behavior

The Theory of Planned Behavior (TPB) is developed based on Fishbein's proposed Theory of Multi-attribute Attitude [11] and the Theory of Reasoned Action (TRA) [12]. Because the theory of rational behavior believes that the occurrence of behavior is controlled by the individual's will, but in reality, the individual's control of the will is also affected by other factors. Therefore, the American psychologist Ajzen added perceived behavior control variables to the theory of reasoned action and proposed the Theory of Planned Behavior [13].

The Theory of Planned Behavior consists of five elements: Attitude Toward the Behavior, Subjective Norm, Perceived Behavioral Control, Behavioral Intention, and Behavior. The structural model of the theory is shown in Fig. 1 where

1) Behavior is an explicit and observable response to a specific goal at a specific time and situation, including four elements: Target, Action, Context, and Time, namely TACT [14]. Behavior is determined by behavioral intention and perceived behavioral control in specific situations.
2) Attitude refers to the individual's cognitive and emotional evaluation of certain behavior in a specific situation. If it is a positive evaluation, it will promote the behavior intention to become stronger and then produce behavior; Subjective Norm refers to the social pressure perceived by individuals when performing a certain behavior in a specific situation, including surrounding interpersonal relationships (family, friends, colleagues), policies (national policies, company regulations), etc. When individuals subjectively believe that people around them support them to take this action, the individual's behavioral intention will become stronger; Perceived Behavioral Control refers to the degree of difficulty perceived by individuals when they take a certain behavior in a specific situation, reflecting the individual's cognition of experience or expected results. When individuals think that the more experience they have or the smaller the expected results are hindered, the perceived behavioral control is stronger; Behavior Intention refers to the degree of willingness of an individual to take a certain behavior in a specific situation.
3) The formation of behavior patterns includes three stages. Behavioral intention is the main variable in the theory of planned behavior, which can directly predict decision behavior. Attitude toward the behavior, subjective norm and perceived behavioral control are three variables that determine behavioral intention and are positively correlated with them [15]. Among them, perceived behavioral control can directly predict the possibility of behavior; corresponding beliefs determine the attitude toward the

behavior, subjective norms and perceived behavioral control, while other internal factors (age, experience, emotion, etc.) and external factors (situation, media intervention and cultural background, etc.) indirectly affect attitude toward behavior, subjective norms, and perceived behavioral control by influencing beliefs [16].

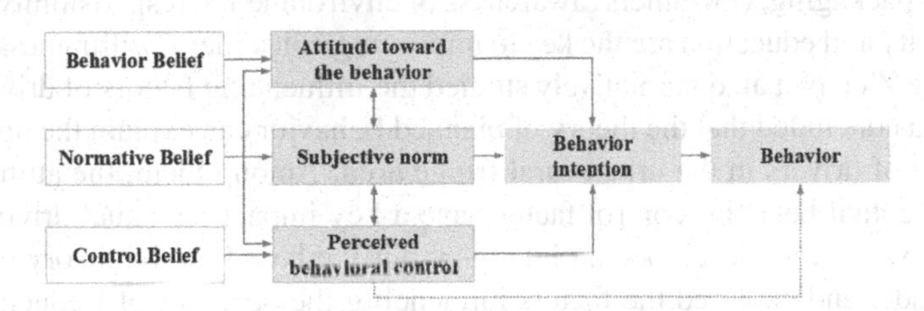

Fig. 1. Structural model of the theory of planned behavior.

The theory of planned behavior could explain the reasons and motivations of people to perform or not to perform a certain behavior in a specific situation, and effectively indicate the main influencing factors of behavior from three aspects: attitude, subjective norm, and perceptual behavior control. The theory of planned behavior has been widely used in various behavior studies and has good explanatory and predictive power [15]. Starting from the individual's characteristics, this theory focuses on the individual's background characteristics, social factors, actual conditions, etc., and deeply discusses the relevant influencing factors and influencing paths in the whole process of behavior change, and then adopts targeted intervention to guide the individual to regulate behavior and promote behavior change. It is an effective framework to predict and guide individual behavior change.

2.2 Research on the Theory of Planned Behavior in the Field of Health and Travel Behavior

The theory of planned behavior is one of the commonly used theories in the field of health behavior. This theory can enhance specific groups' awareness of healthy behaviors by influencing attitudes, subjective norms, and perceived behavioral control, to solve the problem of insufficient attention to health behavior or untimely discovery.

The Theory of Planned Behavior can Analyze the Influencing Factors of Behavior and Predict Behavioral Intention. The theory of planned behavior is widely used in analyzing the factors influencing behavior. Researchers often use the core variables of the theory of planned behavior as the baseline to construct a research framework to explore the influencing factors of user specific behaviors. Since its introduction, the theory of planned behavior has been widely used in the treatment of chronic diseases [17].

Based on the theory of planned behavior, Kai Chen et al. proved the effect of variables such as attitude and social norms on travel intention through two sets of experimental comparisons, and there are differences between the two groups due to different perceptions of green travel [18]. Based on the theory of planned behavior and the theory of normative values, Zhanqiong He extracted the environmental impact factors of urban travel and revealed the factors and the mechanism of urban travel environment on the intention of green travel from the perspective of individual social psychology [19]. Chi Pan et al.' s reference to the theory of planned behavior to construct a model of consumers' willingness to accept green packaging and to explore the impact mechanism of consumers' willingness to accept. The study concluded that the usefulness and ease of use of green packaging, consumers' awareness of environmental responsibility, and adequate publicity and education are the key to improving consumers' willingness to accept [20]. Huiling Zhang et al. quantitatively studied the influencing factors of driver driving behavior and concluded that the theory of planned behavior can explain the unsafe driving behavior of drivers in the urban-rural fringe area. Among them, the attitude factor and the perceptual behavior control factor have a key impact on actual driving behavior [21]. Li Nana et al. developed an interview outline based on the theory of planned behavior model and explored the factors influencing the behavior of frequent visits of the elderly through semi-structured interviews [22].

Theory of Planned Behavior can be Applied to Behavioral Intervention. Research on behavioral intervention with the theory of planned behavior focuses on two types. The first is to take targeted intervention measures based on behavioral influencing factors. By combing the research status of the theory of planned behavior in chronic disease management, Can Zhang et al. have concluded that the intervention mainly adopts a combination of online and offline methods, and presents the intervention content in a variety of forms such as text, pictures, videos, and brochures [17]. Based on the theory of planned behavior, Meixian Yao et al. explored the behavioral intention of the management of the alarm of the ECG monitor of neonatal nurses and proposed the corresponding intervention measures for the behavioral influencing factors explored [23].

The second is to establish an intervention model based on the main variables of the theory of planned behavior and verify the intervention effect through experiments. Through controlled trials, Dou Han et al. concluded that the exercise intervention of the smartphone APP based on the theory of planned behavior is beneficial in improving the glucose metabolism of prediabetics and improving the exercise efficiency of patients [24]. Longju Qi et al. used the theory of planned behavior as a guiding framework to develop a theoretical model of home exercise and the corresponding intervention measures for liver cancer patients during the perioperative period. When comparing exercise compliance before and after the intervention, it was concluded that the theoretical model of planned behavior significantly improved the compliance rate of participants' self-exercise monitoring [25].

In summary, the theory of planned behavior model can accurately explain and predict behavior and is an effective theory to study user behavior. When the theory of planned behavior is applied to the interpretation and prediction of behavior, it should be combined with the characteristics of the research object to perform a personalized analysis. At the same time, it can be combined with specific situations to add new variables to the theoretical model or combine other theoretical methods to improve the accuracy of the theoretical model.

3 User Research on Walking Health of the Elderly from the Perspective of the Theory of Planned Behavior

3.1 Research Model Construction Based on the Theory of Planned Behavior

Yong Huang explored and verified the theory of planned behavior on the factors influencing urban residents' smart travel intentions. The research results confirmed the theoretical effectiveness of the theory of planned behavior. The relationship view is applicable to research on the intention of smart travel; on the other hand, the attitude toward the behavior, the subjective norm, and the perceived behavioral control have a significant positive impact on the intention of smart travel, and the attitude of travel has the most significant impact on the intention of smart travel [26]. Therefore, based on the three-factor framework of attitude toward the behavior, subjective norm, and perceived behavioral control in the theory of planned behavior, this article combines user research methods such as noninterventional behavioral observation and semi-structured interviews to gain insight into the walking behavior of urban elderly people. The main factors influencing them and provide targeted solutions, with the aim of meeting the needs of the aging population and improving the experience of the elderly in using travel tools.

According to the theoretical model of planned behavior, combined with the characteristics of urban elderly walking behavior and the APP design process, a walking health APP design model for the elderly based on the theory of planned behavior was constructed [27], as shown in Fig. 2. The behavioral attitude of the elderly should include positive and negative feelings in walking behavior, subjective norms include family and social factors and perceived behavioral control includes internal control factors (self-condition, etc.) and external control factors (environmental influence, etc.). Attitude toward the behavior, subjective norm, and perceived behavioral control of the elderly jointly affect and determine the behavioral intention of healthy walking and traveling. Behavioral intention determines the occurrence of healthy walking and traveling behavior for the elderly.

Firstly, using the theoretical framework of planned behavior, conduct user research on healthy walking behavior among elderly groups, including lifestyle observation and semi-structured interviews, and summarize and analyze the main influencing factors and core needs of healthy walking behavior according to the user research results; secondly, according to the behavior The influencing factors of attitude, subjective norm and perceived behavior control and the laboratory video data analysis are used to transform the travel influencing factors, output the walking health travel factor indicators of the elderly, and combine the appropriate aging design method and interface design elements to propose the elderly The design strategy of Walking Health APP; based on the design strategy again, the design practice of "Smart Health" APP is carried out; finally, the usability test of the practice plan is carried out to verify the feasibility of the user research output design strategy based on the theory of planned behavior.

3.2 User Research Execution Process

User research on walking and healthy travel among the elderly is divided into two stages: behavior observation and semi-structured interview. Using the noninterventional

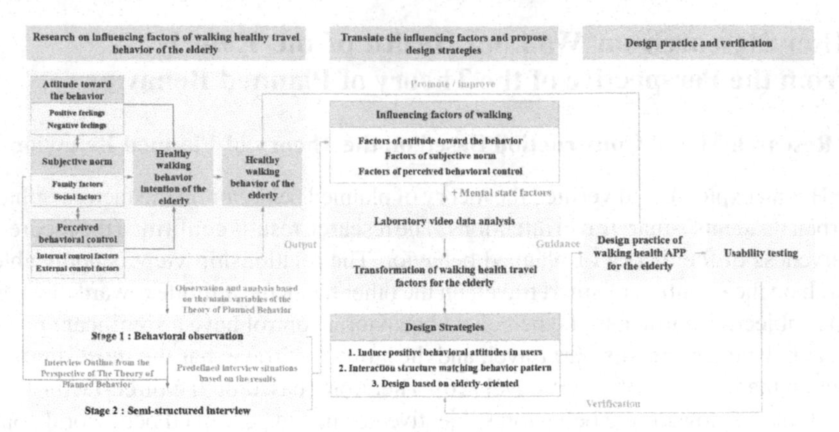

Fig. 2. Model of the walking health APP for the elderly based on the theory of planned behavior.

behavior observation method and semi structured interview method to investigate elderly groups in five communities in Beijing, to study the walking behavior process of elderly in different scenarios, focusing on their travel patterns, behavior processes, and behaviors; combined with The theory of planned behavior, through the analysis of the walking behavior and typical action postures of the elderly group, understands the walking behavior intention of the elderly in different scenarios, to obtain the influencing factors of the healthy walking behavior of the elderly and the APP design requirements.

Behavior Observation. The first stage is behavior observation. Typical communities in downtown Beijing are selected for observation and video recording of the walking behavior of the elderly. Typical communities (community and surrounding facilities are complete) include places where the elderly often move, such as supermarkets/vegetable markets, kindergarten/elementary schools, parks, etc. Guided by the theory of planned behavior, by observing the walking behavior of the elderly in the travel environment, the behavioral characteristics of the behavior of the elderly group are excavated, and the preliminary influencing factors of the healthy walking behavior of the elderly are explored.

(1) *Research Object.* This study chooses the community-led short-distance walking behavior without presets and randomly selects elderly people who walk in different scenes in the community and surrounding areas. The number of observations is more than 30 people. The general health of walking is good and they can independently perform walking behavior.
(2) *Research Methods.* Select the inside and surrounding areas of the community (entertainment places provided by the community, passing places, public places at home and around the community, shops, etc.), the road from departure to destination (public passing places, transportation, etc.), functional places in the residential area (kindergarten, vegetable market interior, shops, etc.) these three observation points. Using the nonintervention follow-up observation method, the walking behavior of the elderly in the travel environment was randomly observed through video acquisition and real-time recording. Since the subjective normative dimension in the theory

of planned behavior is mainly from the perspective of the actors themselves, it is not easy to observe intuitively. This search mainly on the behavioral attitude and perceived behavioral control dimensions in the theory. The main observation records are: walking scene, walking interruption mechanism, walking gestures, carrying items, etc.

(3) *Research Results.* The research team followed and photographed more than 30 elderly people, analyzed the behavior observation results, and concluded that the scenes where the walking behavior of the elderly is relatively concentrated include shopping (mainly grocery shopping), picking up children, and entertainment. The action decomposition analysis and the walking interruption mechanism analysis of the walking behavior are carried out in these three scenarios, respectively. The specific analysis of the grocery shopping scene is shown in Table 1. The walking behavior of the elderly in the grocery shopping scene can be subdivided into carrying heavy objects, dragging a trolley, and pushing a trolley; the walking behavior of the elderly in the pick-up and drop-off scene can be subdivided into carrying a child in a car, carrying a child in a toy, and holding a child; The walking behavior of the elderly in the entertainment scene can be subdivided into sports, playing chess, and walking. There are different degrees of difference in the main force points of the body and the gait of different actions in each scene. At the same time, physical factors, traffic factors, and object factors will all affect the walking behavior of the elderly and cause different degrees of interruption.

Through the above observations and by combing the results, it is found that the walking of the elderly is affected by many factors. First of all, in terms of behavior and attitude, most elderly people ignore the mechanism of walking interruption during walking, and have a poor attitude towards intervention objects; in terms of subjective norms, they will be affected by others in the scene they are in, and the influence is even greater in a crowded environment. In terms of perceived behavior control, the elderly will change their walking behavior due to factors such as their body, travel purpose, task type, carrying items, traffic environment, etc. The results of behavior observation will be further verified in user interviews.

Semi-structured Interview. The second stage is a semi-structured interview, which presets specific categories of people, scenes, influencing factors, and interview routes, and conducts targeted interviews on the walking and travel conditions of the elderly. Based on the above behavioral observations of the elderly, interviews were conducted on the influencing factors of their healthy walking behavior, and the final influencing factors of the elderly's healthy walking behavior were obtained. Due to the complex walking behavior of the elderly in the entertainment scene and too many subjective influencing factors, interview research is only carried out on the scene of shopping for vegetables and picking up and dropping off children.

(1) *Research Object.* Using random sampling and street interview, elderly people with walking behavior was randomly selected near the vegetable market and at the gate of the kindergarten. Inclusion criteria: 1) age ≥ 60 years; 2) ability to walk independently; 3) clear language and voluntary interview. Exclusion criteria: 1) hearing or comprehension impairment; 2) refusal to accept interviews.

Table 1. Analysis of the action and environment of grocery shopping.

Walking in the grocery shopping scene	Task factor 1	Task factor 2	Task factor 3	Traffic factors
	Carrying heavy objects A small number of elderly people do not rely on foreign objects and bring their shopping bags of vegetables.	**Towing trolley** Most people use a trolley that can be towed, which can be operated with one hand. There are empty cars and loads in use.	**Pushing cart** This elderly has obvious inconvenience in legs and feet. They use their hands to assist their movements.	
Action factors	Shoulders; Hands. The main force points are shoulders and hands. Heavy objects will slow down and have a large controllable range when avoiding vehicles and pedestrians.	Shoulders; Hands. The main stress points are the shoulders and hands. The shoulders sink on the side of the cart and the hands push forward while holding the handle tightly.	Shoulders; Waist; Hands. The stress points are the shoulders, waist, and hands. The bending action is obvious and the pressure on the waist is the greatest at this time.	There is quicker foot speed and more observant action when navigating intersections and sidewalks.
Object Factors	Shopping bags, satchels, etc.	Shopping trolley	Shopping cart	1. When passing the intersection, the speed of the cart will be accelerated; 2. When passing obstacles, tools such as trolleys will be lifted or carried.

(2) *Research Methods.* Interview content focused on the walking behavior of the elderly, used interview outline based on the theory of planned behavior and behavior observation results. During the interview process, the elderly was questioned around behavior observation and interview questions. The outline of the interview used in this study is shown in Table 2.

This study adopts a semi-structured interview method. The same researcher conducts one-on-one in-depth interviews with the elderly in the scene of grocery shopping and picking up children. The route is investigated in advance and the most representative node on the route is selected as the interview location.

(3) *Research Results.* The research team obtained a total of 10 groups of effective interview data. Through interview analysis, the influencing factors of elderly walking behavior based on the theory of planned behavior are shown in Fig. 3. In the dimension of attitude toward the behavior, most elderly people think that walking is an

Table 2. Description of the interview.

	Interview dimension	Interview content
1	Basic Information	1) Age? 2) How is your physical condition now? 3) Is there any discomfort? 4) What impact does it have on daily life)?
2	Cognitive measurement	Compared with before, what obvious changes do you feel in your body?
3	Attitude measurement	1) What problems do you encounter in your daily activities and how do you deal with them? 2) What kind of travel do you usually choose? 3) What do you think are the advantages/disadvantages of walking for yourself?
4	Subjective normative measure	1) What activities do you have every day, what problems will you encounter during the activities, and how to deal with them? 2) What individuals or groups are around you that influence your daily walking behavior?
5	Perceived Behavioral Control Measures	1) What tools do you use for your walks or everyday activities? 2) What circumstances (factors) would make you choose to travel by foot? 3) What conditions (factors) affect your walking trips?
6	Demand measurement	In what way do you hope to solve the problems encountered in the activity?

effective way of exercising, and they will deliberately increase their walking behavior in daily life. In the subjective norm dimension, family factors, social factors including hospital recommendations and subjective influence of tasks during the travel process can put pressure on them and cause them to pay deliberate attention to walking behavior. In the dimension of perceived behavioral control, their own health status, as well as the spatial environment and natural environment such as interventions and traffic in the behavior process will affect walking behavior. At the same time, the psychological state during walking will also affect the healthy walking intention of the elderly, and then affect the walking behavior. The psychological state here is affected by external macro factors including interventions, traffic, and other spatial environment and natural environment. Among them, the self-efficacy of perceived behavioral control and external macro factors are the main factors that affect the walking intention of the elderly and even directly affect their walking behavior.

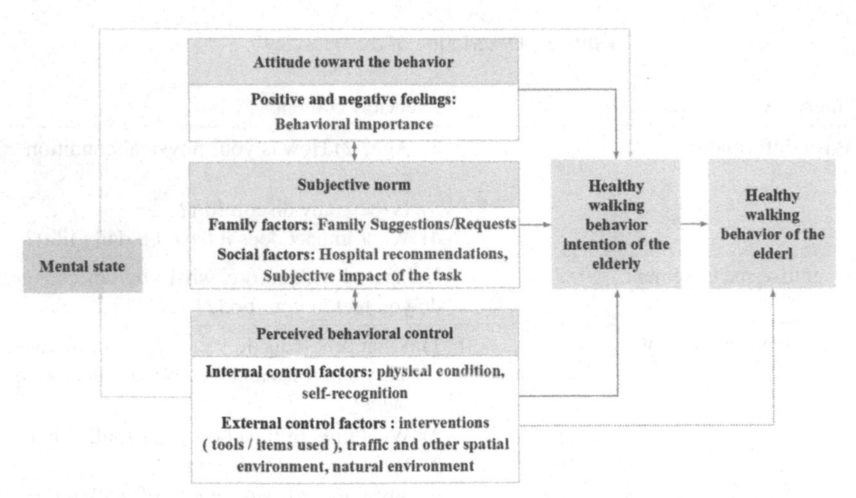

Fig. 3. Influencing factors on the walking behavior of the elderly based on the theory of planned behavior.

4 Transformation of Influencing Factors and Design Strategies of Healthy Walking Behavior of the Elderly

Sampling and analyzing the walking videos of the elderly collected in the early stage and obtaining the gait models of different categories of elderly people through laboratory video analysis. This model can be compared with the standard gait model to output the gait health conclusions of the elderly and suggestions. On this basis, combined with the influencing factors obtained from the above user research, the elderly walking health travel factor indicators are output, which can be used as the basis for the design of the APP, and a design strategy for the elderly walking health APP is proposed based on the theory of planned behavior.

4.1 Laboratory Video Data Analysis

In this study, mobile phone tracking shots were taken of elderly people's walking behavior in different scenarios. A deep learning-based human detection and pose estimation framework was used to extract the key point trajectories of the human body and the temporal sequence of body skeleton for each of the walking videos of the senior person. Spatiotemporal gait and balance related parameters were then estimated, and gait models were established for elderly people in different travel scenarios, to assess and predict their motor functions and travel ability.

The video analysis process is shown in Fig. 4. The input video frames are first processed by a deep learning method based on Convolutional Neural Network (CNN) for target detection and tracking, i.e., detection and tracking of the elder person to be analyzed in the video. The target detection and tracking network could be accomplished with a model pre-trained on public datasets as a generic backbone network for video feature extraction, followed by a task-specific network for predicting human bounding boxes and tracking. Once the target person is acquired, a 2D human key point and pose estimation network is used to extract key points including the face and major joints of the body and to obtain the correct connections between the key points to form a human skeleton model. Generic models for key point detection and pose estimation include OpenPose proposed by Carnegie Mellon University and Google's MediaPipe, the former for multi-person detection and the latter for single person and deployable on mobile devices. Kinematic parameters based on the human skeleton and key points are extracted, including cadence, stride time and length, step width, single and double limb support times, swing to stance ration, joint angles for lower limbs, and bilateral and multiple statistics for each parameter.

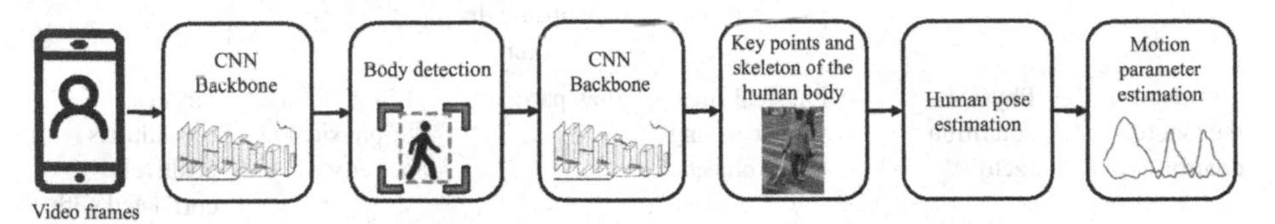

Fig. 4. Video analysis process.

4.2 Transformation of Walking Health Travel Factors for the Elderly

According to the influencing factors obtained from the above user research results, the final index library of walking travel factors for the elderly is output, as shown in Table 3.

This indicator library is divided into two dimensions. The first dimension is objective indicators, including task factors, natural environment factors, and space environment factors for elderly walking. The second dimension is subjective indicators, including cognitive factors, action factors, carrying factors, physical factors, and psychological factors.

Table 3. Indicators of walking health and travel factors for the elderly.

Dimension	Influencing factors	Task factor			Healthy travel intention
		Grocery shopping	Child pick-up and drop-off	Entertainment	
Attitude toward the behavior	Behavioral importance factors	General emphasis on behavior	General emphasis on behavior	Pay attention to behavior	The more you pay attention, the stronger the intention

(*continued*)

Table 3. (*continued*)

Dimension	Influencing factors	Task factor			Healthy travel intention
		Grocery shopping	Child pick-up and drop-off	Entertainment	
Subjective norm	Family factors	Family support	Family support	Family support	Family and social support promote travel intentions
	Social factors	The elderly is the main force of family procurement	The teacher does not recommend that the elderly pick up and drop off children	Encourage the elderly to be more active	
Perceived behavioral control	Physical condition factors	Physical stress when carrying heavy objects	Slow pace	Limited range of physical activity	Physical condition is positively correlated with intention
	Self-cognitive factors	Find the route	Pick-up and drop-off rules	Entertainment rules	Effective cognition promotes travel intention
	Object Factors	Shopping bags, grocery shopping carts	Children's toy cars and trolleys	Sports tools, Entertainment tools	Carrying too much weight will reduce the intention to travel
	Natural environmental factors	Degradation of environment and route perception in the elderly under rain, snow and extreme weather	Outdoor is the same as the first two tasks; indoor is not affected	Good environmental factors promote travel intention	
	Space environment factors	Walk fast and avoid cars when crossing roads and sidewalks	---		

(*continued*)

Table 3. (*continued*)

Dimension	Influencing factors	Task factor			Healthy travel intention
		Grocery shopping	Child pick-up and drop-off	Entertainment	
Psychological factors	Slow down due to safety pressure when crossing the road	Fast travel due to time pressure	Happy mood, more relaxed	Psychological tension produces negative intention; relaxation produces positive intention	

4.3 Design Strategy of Walking Health APP for the Elderly

Based on the analysis of laboratory video data and the transformation of walking travel factors for the elderly, the design strategy of walking health APP for the elderly is proposed to guide the design practice.

Induce Positive Behaviors from Users

(1) Use health questionnaires and scales to assess your health problems and your cognition and attitude toward healthy behaviors, to implement targeted health education for the elderly, help them establish positive behavioral intentions, and promote behavioral changes.

(2) Combining deep learning and human gait feature extraction technology with the walking health APP of the elderly, tracking the walking behavior of the elderly, and realizing the intelligent terminalization of the urban travel analysis and evaluation platform for the elderly. It is mainly used to record, analyze, evaluate, and monitor the mobility of the elderly. Users upload videos related to personal walking behavior through the APP, and the back-end realizes the feature extraction of motion functions through intelligent video recognition technology, synchronously feeds back to the front end in the form of graphics and text, and gives travel improvement suggestions and methods.

(3) Combining intelligent video analysis to provide personalized health knowledge to the elderly, improve awareness of health behaviors, make them aware of their health problems and coping methods, and establish positive behavioral beliefs. Intelligent video analysis includes travel video analysis and motion function analysis. Travel video analysis mainly realizes the recording and tracking of actual travel data through gait extraction; motion function analysis is based on the completion of tasks such as squatting up, turning around, side-shooting walking, and standing up and walking. Realize the initial diagnosis of physical health problems.

Interaction Structure Matching Behavioral Patterns

(1) *Setting of the User Model.* By establishing the gait model for the elderly in different travel scenarios and the transformation of walking travel factors, this paper concludes

that the factors that affect the walking behavior of the elderly and then their gait can be divided into two main dimensions. The first dimension is whether to carry items, such as shopping bags, shopping carts, etc., and the second dimension is the psychological factors of the elderly under the pressure of time, traffic safety, and tasks. Based on these two dimensions, four typical elderly walking patterns are produced as shown in Fig. 5.

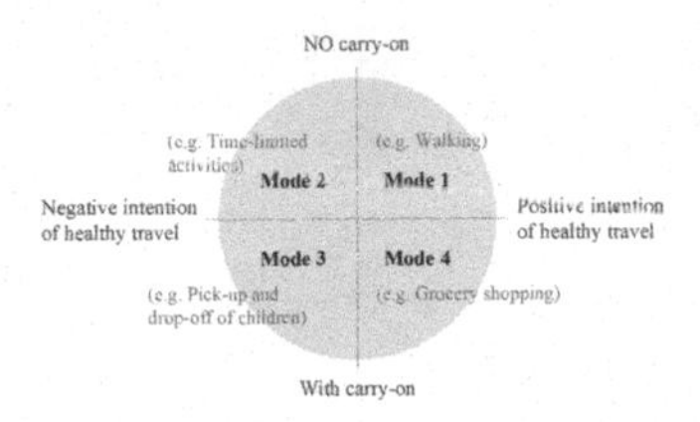

Fig. 5. Elderly walking model.

Mode 1, no items or tools, healthy travel intention is positive (such as walking).
Mode 2, no items or tools, healthy travel intention is negative (such as time-limited activities).
Mode 3, having articles or tools, healthy travel intention is negative (such as pick-up and drop-off of children).
Mode 4, having goods or tools, healthy travel intention is positive (such as grocery shopping).

Under different walking modes, the same elderly person will have different gait characteristics, so the product function should satisfy people with different walking modes. By defining the walking mode, it can better solve the problem of extracting gait features and output of travel suggestions, to improve behavior intention. In the future, the elderly gait health monitoring system should provide a comparison between elderly gait and healthy gait under different modes, to provide a more targeted management during walking.

(2) *Guide Behavioral Decision Making Based on Choice of Travel Mode.* In the Theory of Planned Behavior, behavior refers to the explicit and observable response of an individual to a specific goal at a specific time and environment, so the operational definition of behavior in research should include the four elements of Target, Action, Context, and Time. The behavior pattern can be intuitively defined through the four elements of behavior. In the walking behavior of the elderly, the task type of walking is the target; since the walking behavior of the elderly is complex and the action is difficult to define, the possible carrying objects during the walking process are used to replace the action; the travel route is used to represent the context, and the route is connected to the Tencent map, you can define the destination; the travel times are in the form of time slots, and every three hours is a period, and the basis for defining the period is the travel height and low peak.

Based on the theory of planned behavior, four elements of task type, carry-on, travel route, and time are used to intuitively define the walking travel behavior pattern of the elderly. There are two situations for selection the travel mode. One is to configure the travel mode before uploading/shooting the video. When analyzing the video, the background analyzes the gait according to the selection of tasks, carrying objects, and weather conditions, which can ensure the effect of video analysis. Output more targeted suggestions; the other is to configure the itinerary before traveling to get reliable travel suggestions. The travel suggestions mainly include walking suggestions defined in the background, route display, and other travel mode suggestions provided according to the travel mode. The selection of the travel mode and the output suggestions can guide the user's behavior decision making, enhance the behavioral intention of walking healthy travel, and induce the improvement of the user's walking travel behavior.

Design Based on Elderly-oriented. Adopt the aging-friendly design method and design the travel products for the elderly from the perspective of aging and user experience, to meet the needs of aging and improve the experience of the elderly in using travel tools. Combined with artificial intelligence means, the functions and interface design of the walking health APP for the elderly are carried out.

The APP function design follows the design principles of easy understanding (in line with the minds of elderly users), easy operation (reduced operation, effective interaction, voice), and easy trust (feedback, personalized service). The main functions include completing the travel configuration, travel behavior analysis and evaluation, and health assessment questionnaires through the APP, and finally achieving the recording and tracking of actual travel data and providing suggestions and methods for travel improvement.

The design of the APP interface meets the principles of easy reading (design specification) and easy identification. The interface design is carried out from the logic layer, interaction layer, and information layer, respectively, to improve the operation efficiency and usability of the product.

5 Design Practice and Verification of the Design of the Walking Health APP for the Elderly

Guided by influencing factors based on the theory of planned behavior and the proposed design strategy, the design practice of the walking health APP for the elderly is carried out, and then the user usability test method based on cognitive walkthrough is adopted to verify the effectiveness of the design strategy and prove that the proposed design strategies can better guide design practice.

5.1 Design Practice

The content of this design practice is based on the output of the design strategy above to optimize the process experience. While solving user needs, based on the aging-adaptive design method, the interface design is carried out from the logic layer, interaction layer, and information layer to improve the operation efficiency and usability of the product.

The overall interface adopts a "shallow and narrow" interaction method to reduce the interaction level and user cognitive load.

As travel and health software, it provides users with a safe and reliable visual experience and an operation experience in color matching and layout. Simplify the design layout of the interface, reduce the burden on users, so that users can focus more on the content itself; hierarchical optimization of complex information to improve the efficiency of users in accepting content information and the ease of use of products; in the design process, the barrier-free color design is completed through the strong light test. The page flow and partial interface of the APP are shown in Fig. 6.

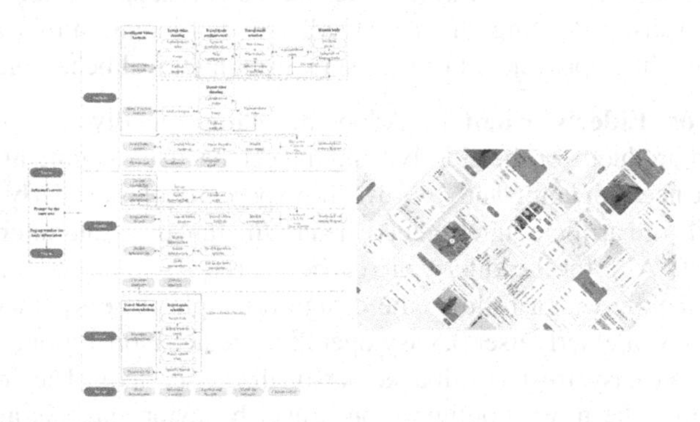

Fig. 6. APP page flow and partial interface display.

5.2 Design Practice Verification

The usability test of the Smart Healthy Walking APP developed in the Android environment is carried out to verify whether the design strategy based on the theory of planned behavior to expand user research output is effective and effective. The testing process is shown in Fig. 7. Set the operation task based on the principle of cognitive walkthrough. After completion, the 5-level Likert scale was used to score the elderly's compliance with APP travel mode, scale/education effect, and APP use satisfaction from 1(strongly opposed) to 5 (strongly agree) points from the three dimensions of effectiveness, efficiency, and user satisfaction. The test content is shown in Table 4.

Fig. 7. Testing process.

Table 4. Test contents.

test type	Specific tasks	Test content
APP travel mode compliance	1.1 Shoot/upload travel videos (complete travel mode configuration) 1.2 Complete a trip configuration (next trip) and view travel suggestions in Travel	1) The mode configuration before shooting/uploading the travel video is in line with my travel habits 2) The travel mode configured in the itinerary during the trip conforms to my travel habits 3) The mode selection of the itinerary configuration during travel can define my travel behavior 4) The travel suggestions after the itinerary configuration can guide my travel process
Scale/Mission Effectiveness	2.1 Complete at least one questionnaire/scale from the health assessment 2.2 Check out the latest health knowledge	5) The health assessment allows me to recognize my health problems 6) Health knowledge can help me understand healthy behaviors 7) Health assessment and health knowledge can arouse my attention to my health
APP usage satisfaction	3.1 Open the APP to complete the login 3.2 Fill in the basic information	8) I can complete the task and remember the general function 9) The APP is easy to operate and will not burden me 10) I am satisfied with the visual design of the APP

A total of 30 valid scales were collected. The Cronbach's alpha reliability coefficient of the overall scale was 0.793. Among them, the Cronbach's alpha reliability coefficient of the APP travel mode compliance dimension was 0.822, the Cronbach's alpha reliability coefficient of the scale/education effect dimension was 0.864, and the Cronbach's alpha reliability coefficient of the APP use satisfaction dimension was 0.815. It shows that the reliability of this test is high, and the data are valuable for further testing.

Further analysis of the data shows that the coefficient of variation of the topic is less than 0.15, and there is no abnormal value in the test data. The average value of the results can be described and analyzed directly. The data analysis of the specific test results is shown in Table 5. It can be seen from the data in the table that the average value of the questions is greater than 4.5 points. The average values of the three content dimensions of the compliance of APP travel mode, scale/education effect, and satisfaction with APP use are 4.8, 4.833, and 4.589, respectively, which are all in the peak range. It shows that the description sentences of the scale are all positive expressions. Therefore, it is concluded that the design strategy based on the theory of planned behavior proposed in this paper to carry out user research output is more feasible, which can induce users' positive behavior attitude, travel mode selection can guide behavior decision making, and the use effect of the design scheme is ideal.

Table 5. Data analysis of test results.

Title	Number of samples	Minimum value	Maximum value	Mean value	Standard deviation
1	30	4	5	4.733	0.45
2	30	4	5	4.833	0.379
3	30	4	5	4.833	0.379
4	30	3	5	4.800	0.484
5	30	4	5	4.833	0.379
6	30	4	5	4.833	0.379
7	30	4	5	4.833	0.568
8	30	3	5	4.633	0.615
9	30	3	5	4.567	0.626
10	30	3	5	4.567	0.568

6 Conclusion

This paper conducts user research under the guidance of the theory of planned behavior, constructs the design strategy for walking for the elderly from the perspective of the theory of planned behavior and verifies the feasibility of the design strategy through practice and testing. It shows that the research on the walking behavior of the elderly is used as a medium of product attributes guide the design direction, which not only helps to explore the influencing factors in the process of user behavior intuitively and effectively, but also helps to design products that conform to the logic of user behavior and conform to the user 's habits from the perspective of aging. This paper not only applies the theory of planned behavior to the field of user research on the walking health of the elderly, but also combines artificial intelligence to realize the intelligent terminalization of the travel analysis and evaluation platform for the elderly and provide more targeted management for walking behavior. It is of great significance for walking health monitoring, gait description, disease prevention, and fall prevention of the elderly.

Acknowledgments. This work was supported by the National Key R&D Program of China (2021YFE0111800).

This work was supported by Humanities and Social Sciences Foundation of Ministry of Education of the people's Republic of China (Grant Number: 18YJC760039).

References

1. Liu, C.R.: 'Healthy aging' is the Lowest Cost and the Best Way to Deal with the Aging Population in China, p. 012. China Youth Daily (2022)
2. Guo, R., He, Y.M.: Research on the optimization of community walking environment based on the behavioral characteristics of the elderly——taking the Haicheng street community in harbin as an example. In: 2020/2021 China Urban Planning Annual Conference and 2021 China Urban Planning Academic Season, p. 11 (2021)
3. Zhang, Y., Wang, L.C., Ye, M.Z., Wu, J.W., W, X.Q., Zheng, G.H.: Effect of cognitive reserve on fall risk among community-dwelling older adults. Chin. Nurs. Res. **37**, 1246–1250 (2023)
4. Zhao, S.Y.: Research on the Relationship between Physical Condition and Gait Characteristics of the Elderly. Soochow University (2021)
5. Bastos, D., et al.: SmartWalk Mobile – A Context-Aware m-Health App for Promoting Physical Activity Among the Elderly. In: Rocha, Á., Adeli, H., Paulo Reis, L., Costanzo, S. (eds.) WorldCIST'19 2019. AISC, vol. 931, pp. 829–838. Springer, Cham (2019). https://doi.org/10.1007/978-3-030-16184-2_79
6. Ureña, R., Gonzalez-Alvarez, A., Chiclana, F., Herrera-Viedma, E., Moral-Munoz, J.A.: Intelligent m-health app to evaluate the elderly physical condition. In: New Trends in Intelligent Software Methodologies, Tools and Techniques: Proceedings of the 17th International Conference SoMeT_18, p. 87. IOS Press (2018)
7. Berrocal, J., Garcia-Alonso, J., Murillo, J.M., Mendes, D., Fonseca, C., Lopes, M.: Context-aware mobile app for the multidimensional assessment of the elderly. In: 2018 13th Iberian Conference on Information Systems and Technologies (CISTI), pp. 1–6. IEEE (2018)
8. Chen, Z.Y., Li, Y.F., Zhu, L.P.: Interaction design of elderly APP based on FTA. Packag. Eng. **40**, 190–197 (2019)
9. Cheng, Z., Sabran, K.: User interface design for the Asia elderly: a systematic literature review (2021)
10. Koumpouros, Y.: A highly user-centered design approach for developing a mobile health app for pain management (PainApp). In: The 14th PErvasive Technologies Related to Assistive Environments Conference, pp. 320–329 (2021)
11. Fishbein, M.: An investigation of the relationships between beliefs about an object and the attitude toward that object. Hum. Relat. **16**, 233–239 (1963)
12. Fishbein, M., Ajzen, I.: Belief, Attitude, Intention, and Behavior: An Introduction to Theory and Research. Addison-Wesley (June 1, 1975) (1977)
13. Ajzen, I.: The theory of planned behavior. Organ. Behav. Hum. Decis. Process. **50**, 179–211 (1991)
14. Ajzen, I.: Constructing a TPB questionnaire: Conceptual and methodological considerations (2002)
15. Duan, W.T., Jiang, G.R.: A Review of Theory of Planned Behavior. Advances in Psychological Science No.102, pp. 315–320 (2008)
16. Yan, Y.: A review on the origins and development of the theory of planned behavior. Chin. J. Journalism Commun. **36**, 113–129 (2014)
17. Zhang, C., Shi, J.H.: Research progress on the application of theory of planned behavior in chronic disease management. Chin. Nurs. Res. **37**, 1208–1212 (2023)

18. Chen, K., Liang, H.K.: Exploring sources and performance of divergences in the context of green commuting-a case of beijing residents. Soft Science **30**, 109–113 (2016)
19. He, Z.Q., Yin, X.: Research on the impact of urban travel environment on green travel behavior. Ecol. Econ. **37**, 88–96 (2021)
20. Pan, C., Guo, Z.D.: Influencing mechanism of public acceptance willingness on green packaging. Packag. Eng. **40**, 136–142 (2019)
21. Zhang, H.L., Wang, Y., Yang, J.Y.: Influence factors analysis on driver's driving behavior on road section at urban-rural fringe based on TPB theory. J. Chongqing Jiaotong Univ. (Nat. Sci.) **37**, 105–110 (2018)
22. Li, N.N., Shou, J.: Influencing factors of frequent visits of the elderly in a community health service center based on the theory of planned behavior: a qualitative study. Chin. Gen. Pract. **24**, 70–74 (2021)
23. Yao, M.X., Wu, G.L., Peng, Z.H., Chen, J.J., Lu, X.X.: Behavioral intention of alarm management in ECG monitor of nurses in neonatology department from the perspective of planned behavior theory: a qualitative study. Chin. Nurs. Manag. **23**, 215–219 (2023)
24. Han, D., Wang, X.Y.: Application of exercise intervention program based on smart phone APP in prediabetic patients. Chin. Nurs. Res. **36**, 128–132 (2022)
25. Qi, L.J., Xu, F.X., Jiang, F.C., Zhou, S.P., Chen, S.Y., Liao, Z.H., et al.: Application of planned behavior theory in home exercise for patients with liver cancer during perioperative period. J. Nantong Univ. (Med. Sci.) **43**, 174–177 (2023)
26. Huang, Y.: Research on the Influencing Factors of Urban Residents' Intelligent Travel Intentions Based on Theory of Planned Behavior. Wuhan University of Technology (2017)
27. He, C.Q., Zhu, M., Zhang, H.X., Hou, G.H.: Handicraft mass innovation platform for the young elderly from the perspective of TPB. Packag. Eng. **43**, 72–83 (2022)

Design and Research of Ageing-Appropriate Social App for Customized Health Tourism

Yadie Rao, Xiaoqing Su, Yuan Feng, and RongRong Fu(✉)

College of Art Design and Media, East China University of Science and Technology, Shanghai, China
1109226815@qq.com

Abstract. At present the elderly kang travel has become a hot spot of elderly economy, but the existing elderly travel mobile applications there are a series of problems, mainly embodied in the lack of attention to kang scene, ignore the elderly users to travel software personality customization, social and other functions, ignore the user for vision, cognition and other physiological and psychological problems caused by the interface layout difference demand. In order to solve the above problems, this paper positions the travel scene as health travel, through the user interview and the questionnaire of the Kano model, and locate the design form of the health travel app that meet the needs of the elderly users, and then assist the subsequent design practice of health travel app. Finally, in the usability scale of the design effectiveness evaluation section, the paper verifies that this method can effectively improve the user satisfaction of the health care travel app design, and provides a method for the travel app design for the elderly group.

Keywords: User experience · Aging design · Interface design · Kano model · Eye movement experiment

1 Introduction

1.1 Research Background

With the deepening of the aging degree of China's population and the promotion of the "Healthy China" strategy, the health care travel industry, involving tourism, pension, medical care, health care, culture, sports and other formats, is booming [1], Has become a new trend in the "silver travel" market [2]. According to the 48th study of the Statistical Report on Internet Development in China, among the online population as of June 2021, there were nearly 300 million people aged 50 and above, accounting for 28% of the total population, and the fastest growth rate [3]; The application and popularization of digital technology is opening a new era of digital health travel for elderly users. The elderly are older and young, so it is more necessary to provide more help and care to this special group. In the case of insufficient cognitive and physical aspects, the physical and mental characteristics and user experience [4]. However, due to the emergence of the industry, the travel app has a single function, fuzzy interface specification and other problems.

Q. Gao et al. (Eds.): HCII 2023, LNCS 14055, pp. 171–190, 2023.
https://doi.org/10.1007/978-3-031-48041-6_13

In order to design the health travel app that meets the emotional needs of the elderly and meets their visual habits, this paper targets the elderly group aged 50 and above, excavates the core function requirements of the app, and obtains the preference of the interface design elements through the eye movement experiment, and meets the needs of the elderly users, thus assisting the subsequent design practice of the health travel app.

1.2 Determine the Target User Groups

The local tourism regulations of Shaoxing city define the elderly tourists as "groups aged 55–75 who are able to take care of themselves, and individuals or groups who can participate in tourism activities". However, the data show that the elderly over 70 years old rarely travel, and the elderly aged 65–70 only account for 7.5% of the total number of elderly tourists, while the elderly aged 55–65 are the group with the highest travel rate [5]. Although the elderly in this age group have a certain degree of aging, they have not completely lost and still have the vitality to travel. Meanwhile, their leisure time and strong economic strength provide material conditions for their willingness to travel, and they are the most potential users in the future travel groups. Therefore, this paper positions the elderly as 55–65 with self-care ability.

2 Research and Analysis of User Group Needs

This paper mainly selects the elderly aged 55–65 who have the ability to take care of themselves as the user group. Firstly, this chapter uses the method of desktop research to consult relevant information, and conducts a preliminary survey on the physical and psychological changes of the elderly at this age stage, as well as the demand for tourism. Secondly, the information obtained from the desktop research is used to form an interview outline for the elderly users and conduct user interviews. At the same time, the user needs are extracted through user interviews, and the questionnaire is set to build kano model to classify and sort user needs, and form design principles according to the results of kano model.

2.1 Literature Research for Users of Target Groups

In the current tourism market, the consumption potential of the elderly group can not be underestimated. Compared with young people, some elderly users with financial strength have more time and are more willing to travel. According to the National Tourism Administration, the number of elderly tourists will reach 226 million by 2020, and the cost of the elderly on tourism will reach 114.26 billion yuan. According to the Report on the Tourism Consumption Behavior of the Elderly People in China, 81.2 percent of the middle-aged and elderly respondents are willing to travel if their physical and economic conditions are allowed. At the same time, compared with the young people, the elderly pay more attention to the health tourism sector. Secondly, with the acceleration of the digital process of various industries, more and more elderly people begin to pay attention to the online travel software.

However, with the growth of age, the physical and psychological conditions of the elderly have changed, and the demand points and adaptation degree of digital and smart products are different from those of the young people. First, the vision of most older people decreases with age, and the current ordinary app interface design does not meet the reading needs of older people. Although many enterprises have realized the needs of the elderly, so that the existing app interface design has been modified for aging, their functions have been reduced, and some apps are very difficult to find, which can not well solve the food problem of the elderly [6]. Secondly, as the physical functions of the elderly are declining with the growth of age, the elderly face many inconveniences during the travel and need the attention of others. However, the current apps on the market only support the search and purchase of travel packages, and cannot help the elderly during the travel.

Through the investigation and analysis of the target user groups and other competitive products in the market, the needs and pain points of the users are preliminarily mastered. Secondly, the interview outline is formed through the information obtained to further obtain the user needs.

2.2 User Interviews for the Target User Groups

In the qualitative analysis of the needs of the elderly users, this paper adopts semi-structured interviews to investigate the needs of the elderly according to the interview outline, and allows the users to play freely during the interview, and record these new demand points. In this interview, 10 elderly users aged between 55 and 65 were interviewed. These users all have the experience of using smart devices or have the tendency to use smart devices. The outline of this interview is shown in Table 1 below.

Through the interview with these 10 users, we found that most of the elderly users tend to go to offline travel agencies or use the form of telephone communication to book trips, but they also said that this way is not convenient, requires a lot of energy and lack of channels to obtain a large number of travel packages for comparison. Therefore, we are still looking forward to the travel app designed for the elderly users. However, some elderly people who have used apps report that the travel app on the market is messy and does not conform to the habits of the elderly users, so it is very difficult to use. Secondly, for travel methods, most elderly users are more inclined to follow group Tours and customized travel. Therefore, we summarized the five main pain points of interface functions, travel package selection, problems during travel, multi-code management and function guidance, as shown in Table 2 below.

Table 1. Interview outline.

Classification	Queation
1. Basic information	1) Gender
	2) Age
	3) Intelligent device usage/internet access
	4) Travel frequency/willingness
	5) Family situation
2.Travel preferences	1) How do you usually obtain travel information?
	2) May I ask which type of travel package do you prefer?(Free travel/group tours/customization)
	3) May I ask your attitude towards health tourism?
	4) May I ask your attitude towards customized travel?
	5) May I ask if you usually travel together or with your family? Which method do you prefer?
3. App usage/preferences	1) Do you usually use the app to book and purchase travel packages? If not, why is it?
	2) What problems have you encountered while using these apps?
	3) What is the biggest problem you are currently facing when using smart products?
	4) If there is a travel app specifically designed for the elderly, what problems do you hope it can solve?
4. Travel challenges	1) What are you most worried about during your trip?
	2) Have you ever experienced any discomfort during your travels?
	3) Do you have any dissatisfaction with your current travel experience? How do you want to improve?

Table 2. Summary of five types pain points.

Classification	Pain point
1. Interface functions	1) At present, the font size of most app interfaces is relatively small, and some small characters cannot be read clearly when wearing reading glasses
	2) The main information on the interface is not prominent, the information is too cluttered, and I don't know what to look at every time

(*continued*)

Table 2. (*continued*)

Classification	Pain point
	3) The function prompts are not clear enough, and some function icons are not easy to understand
2. Travel Package Selection	1) There are too few options available, and customized travel can only choose basic information such as departure time and location
	2) Most group outings involve various age groups, lacking peers and unable to meet social needs
	3) The collection of information lacks specificity and is difficult to meet some of the special needs of the elderly
3. Travel in progress	1) Currently, apps are difficult to cope with and solve problems that occur during travel, and do not have such features
	2) Tour guides or apps on the journey lack care for the elderly
	3) Users lack the ability to independently solve problems during their travels
4. Multi code management	1) The scenic area code and ride code are usually not in the same software, and finding them is very difficult, with multiple levels of interaction, which is very inconvenient
5. Functional guidance	1) At present, the software on the market lacks detailed functional guidance, and it is difficult to find guidance portals
	2) The guidance content is mostly written and complex, which is very unfriendly to the elderly user group

2.3 Kano Model Construction

After the user interview for the target user groups, this paper concludes with five categories of pain points, including the interface function and travel package selection. This chapter focuses on the further analysis of the five types of pain points to derive the design principles of the travel app design for the elderly users.

Therefore, considering the need to classify and sort user needs, this chapter uses the kano model to analyze user needs, so as to derive the design principles more scientifically and accurately. A total of 178 questionnaires were distributed in this kano model construction, of which 176 were valid. The problem is shown in Table 3:

Table 3. Content of KANO questionnaire.

Number	Content
Q1	The interface design is reasonable, and the font size can meet reading needs
Q2	Reasonable information layout, extracting important information, and being able to see important information at a glance
Q3	The information prompt is mainly written, making it easy for users to understand
Q4	Customized travel can also customize other activities during the journey
Q5	The main user group of the app is the elderly, who can travel with their peers
Q6	Pay attention to users' needs during the journey and try to meet their special needs as much as possible
Q7	Provide solutions for unexpected events during the journey, and provide full tracking services on the app throughout the journey
Q8	Centralize the management of scenic area access codes and traffic codes that may be used during travel, and reduce interaction levels for user convenience
Q9	More convenient and efficient guidance method, replacing text guidance
Q10	Reduce the interaction level of the guidance portal and try to provide full guidance throughout the use process
Q11	The interface design style is in line with user aesthetics

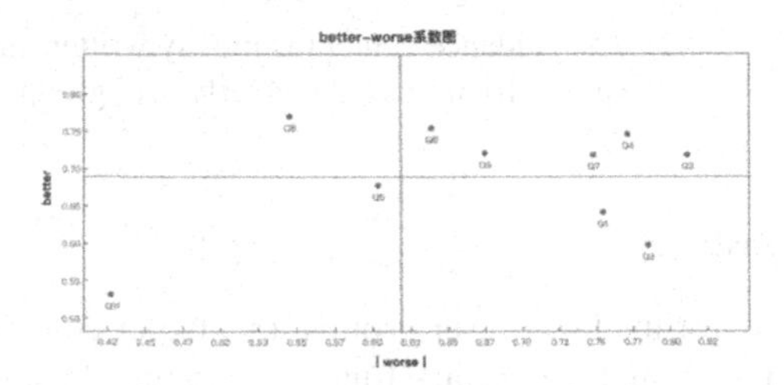

Fig. 1. Better-worse coefficient plot.

According to the survey results of the above 11 questions, determine the priority of the problem, and draw the better-word coefficient diagram (as shown in Fig. 1 above) to determine the demand attributes. As shown in the figure, the requirements in the fourth quadrant (essential requirements), which is Q1-for font size optimization and Q2-for interface information hierarchy optimization. The second is the demand in the first quadrant (expectation demand), that is, Q3-the demand for the optimization of information prompt, Q4-for expanding the scope of travel customization, Q6-for increasing the attention of users during the journey, Q7-for providing full service during the journey and Q9-to change the guidance mode. Finally, the need to fall into the second quadrant should be realized, that is, the charm demand, Q8-add the function of multi-code management. Due to the Q5 requirements in the third quadrant-for peer members and Q11-for interface appearance, it indicates that the user group does not pay much attention to such requirements, and the main focus is still on the experience of interface design, and the ease of use and availability of the software.

3 Research on Interactive Interface Design Principles

In order to analyze the interface interaction design principles that meet user preferences in customized travel applications, this paper collects the main functional interfaces of the three on-market-mainstream software. The design preferences of the target users for the interface samples were analyzed through the eye movement experiment, and a questionnaire survey was conducted after the experiment, thus, to extract the design elements that the users are most concerned about in each sample. In order to obtain user feedback, the application design is conducted on this basis.

3.1 Eye Movement Experiment

Experimental Equipment: The eye movement equipment is SMI EMG eye tracker, laptop computer, Begaze, iView ETG data analysis software, etc.

Experimental Materials: The three application samples in the experiment are all from the mainstream tourism application market. Among them, Ctrip is a middle and high-end business tourism application, Tongcheng travel is a customized travel and group tour application, and rural is a special health tourism application. The home page of the three applications, customized travel page, customized program content page and community page were intercepted as experimental materials.

Participants: Thirty users aged 55–65 years were invited to this experiment. There were 16 female subjects and 14 male subjects. Before the experiment, the subjects were well rested, physically and mentally healthy, with normal vision or normal vision after correction.

Experimental Environment: The experiment is conducted in a sound insulation, light insulation laboratory. During the experiment, there was no interference from anyone except for the tester and the subjects.

Experimental Indicators: The total fixation duration, fixation points, first fixation duration, and heat map in the eye movement data were used as indicators to evaluate user attention.

Experimental Steps: First, three-point calibration, then let the user perform the task of finding the "custom travel" button in the three apps and record the completion time of the task. After completion of the task, three applied stimulus samples were presented, each for 30000ms until the stimulus material was presented.

3.2 Data Analysis

The samples were divided into three groups, Group A: Ctrip, Group B: same trip, Group C: Rural Health Residence. Among the three groups of samples, the intercepted home page samples were named A1, B1 and C1, the customized travel pages were named A2, B2 and C2, the customized scheme content pages were named A3, B3 and C3, and the community pages were named A4, B4 and C4.

The user movement behavior on three sets of samples were processed and analyzed using Begaze analysis software. "Home page" is divided into four areas of interest: search area, King Kong area, content area and navigation bar for total fixation length, fixation points and first gaze duration analysis. By combining Table 4 and Fig. 2 with the important performance indicators of the interest area and Fig. 3 and the heat map of the home page, it can be seen that the part with the highest user attention is the King Kong area, followed by the content area, and then the search area and the navigation bar.

Table 4. Analysis table of eye movement data.

Test material	AOI	Average fixation/ms	Fixation count	First fixation/ms
A1	Search area	205.2	3.0	132.5
	Diamond area	244.8	25.5	248.2
	Content area	281.8	34.5	347.6
	Navigation bar	202.6	17.0	192.4
B1	Search area	76.6	10.0	95.2
	Diamond area	242.1	19.5	140.6
	Content area	78.7	13.0	124.2
	Navigation bar	111.9	5.0	120.6
C1	Search area	239.6	23.0	256.8
	Diamond area	259.0	25.0	232.0
	Content area	244.0	33.0	215.3
	Navigation bar	170.0	16.0	172.5

Fig. 2. Key performance indicators of AOI on the homepage

Fig. 3. Heat map of homepage.

For customized travel apps, the most important function button is "customization". Therefore, this experiment gave the subject to set the task of finding the button on the front page and timed, and the results are Table 5 below. Samples A1 and B1 both put the "custom" button on the second page displayed after sliding, which is not conducive to looking for this function. In particular, there are too multifunctional buttons in the King Kong area of sample A1, which increases the reading burden of users, makes the important functions not prominent, and reduces the ease of application. Sample C1 puts this function button in the most prominent area of the home page, but the definition of the function name is not clear, which increases the learning cost of users.

According to the above analysis of the eye movement track of the home page, four points should be paid when designing the home page: 1. Secondly on the design of the content area; 2. First, the important function button should be placed in a prominent position; 3. The home page of customized tourism application should be as simple as possible; 4. Avoid the name and icon design with vague meaning.

Table 5. Completion time of finding the "Customize" button.

Test material	Average completion time/s
A1	24.40
B1	17.95
C1	28.80

The analysis of customized travel pages, customized scheme content pages and community pages is conducted in the form of heat map, so as to intuitively see the design areas that users are most concerned about in these three types of pages. The results are as shown in Fig. 3. On the far left of Fig. 3 is the heat map analysis results of customized travel pages A2, B2 and C2. It can be seen that the most concerned part is the content area of customized travel below, especially the text part of the content area. The second is the tag bar above the content area, and the information filling area for customized travel. From the thermal map analysis results of A3, B3 and C3 in Fig. 4, it can be seen that the content page of the customized scheme pays the most attention to the content introduction of the customized travel scheme, followed by the graphic introduction of the detailed content of the customized scheme below. The results of A4, B4 and C4 show that in the community page, users are most concerned about the introduction of information containing text information in the picture, followed by the classification column of information in the community, and the text and text posts published by users.

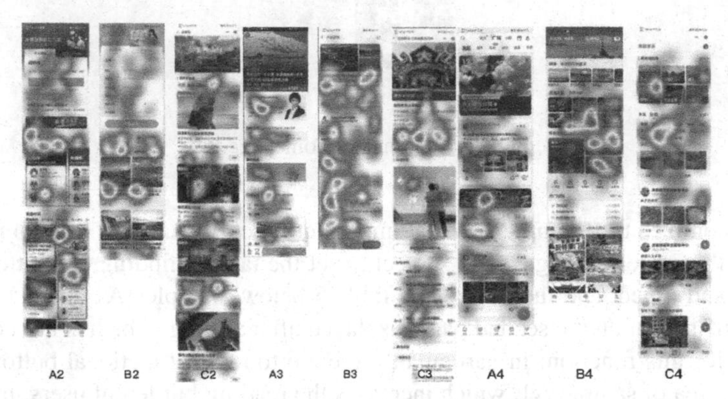

Fig. 4. From left to right are heat maps of customized travel pages, customized plan content pages, and community pages.

3.3 Research on the Interface Interaction Design Paradigm Based on the Nielsen Design Principles

1) Aesthetic principles and simple principles

   The interface does not contain irrelevant information. In the above task for the "custom" button, all three applications took more than 15 s. There is too much redundant information in the page, and the important functions are not emphasized. Therefore, in the customized tourism application suitable for aging, the page information level should be reduced as far as possible, and unnecessary information should be deleted. At the same time, the interface design style should be made in line with the aesthetic preferences and reading habits of elderly users, the font, the design style should be simplified, and the color of important information should be bright, so as to reduce the burden of elderly users visually.

2) Assist with memory principles

   Minimize the memory load of user operations to make the user's actions and options visible [7]. According to the analysis results of the eye movement experiment, it can be seen that the design area should be focused on each main page. During the design, the hierarchy priority of information in the design area should be planned as far as possible, so that the important information of travel can be clearly visible, and there is no need for secondary operation to obtain important information. There are many personal belongings and important events to be remembered during the travel process, but the elderly users have problems of forgetfulness. The application design should also consider how to reduce the cost of memory in terms of item carrying and health management. For example, add a travel assistant function to remind users about important events and items in the form of memos.

3) The principle of error prevention

Carefully design to prevent the occurrence of wrong operations, and remind the user may make mistakes, such as deleting the possible consequences. Because older users operate smartphones far less well than ordinary users, this principle needs to be paid more attention to. In the customized travel function, there is more information that the elderly users need to fill in, which needs to focus on filling in. However, according to the results of the eye movement experiment, the users' attention to it is in the middle, so the design proportion of this part should be increased, so that all kinds of information to be filled in is clearly visible and easy to modify.

4 Design of —— "Luyou" Based on User Experience

4.1 Design Positioning

Summarize the previous interviews, questionnaires, and user visual preferences obtained from the eye movement experiment, and the four design dimensions of the health travel APP for the elderly are concluded: customization, emotional, community, and aging.

Among them, customization, emotion and community are the summary of users' functional needs. Customized emphasizes the combination of travel personalization and cost performance, and simplifies the customization process from the perspective of user experience. At the emotional level, the design of the voice window can be achieved through the use of voice, reducing the panic of the elderly users and more affinity. Community is an insight into the social needs of users, following the differences between the social modes of aging users and ordinary groups, and creating an online travel social mode in line with the elderly group. Suitable aging is the optimization of the priority of interface design elements and the fluency of operation process analyzed in the use process of the eye movement experiment.

4.2 Interface and Visual Design

(1) IP image design

The design inspiration of IP image comes from deer, so the animal image is IP appearance design prototype: firstly, the Chinese pronunciation of deer and "road" expresses the good wishes of the product to users "travel happily and find more beautiful scenery on the way"; secondly, deer is a symbol of auspiciousness and longevity in China, which can meet the expectation of the target group for the good implication. In the design style of IP image, the concrete deer form is simplified and anthropomorphic, so as to increase the recognition and affinity of the product (Fig. 5).

(2) Interface specification

In terms of color specification, the main color adopts the deep sea blue, thus giving people a sense of quiet and distant. This color also makes users have associations about distant mountains and oceans, and also combines the rhythm of Chinese culture, as shown in Fig. 6. The font adopts the PingFang SC commonly used in

Fig. 5. Design of IP image.

the existing APP as the basic font, and Source Han Serif SC is used as the auxiliary font. In order to facilitate the elderly to watch and read the interface, the font size is larger than that of the conventional application, see Fig. 7 for details. In terms of icon design, the tag bar, the diamond area and the linear icon at the bottom and highlight the simple and understandable design concept (Fig. 8).

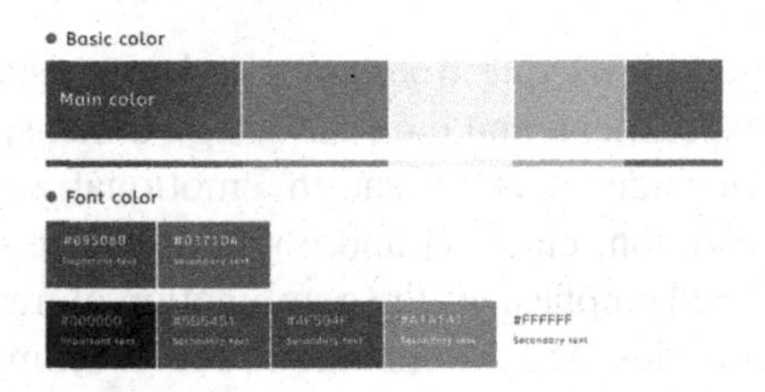

Fig. 6. Color specifications.

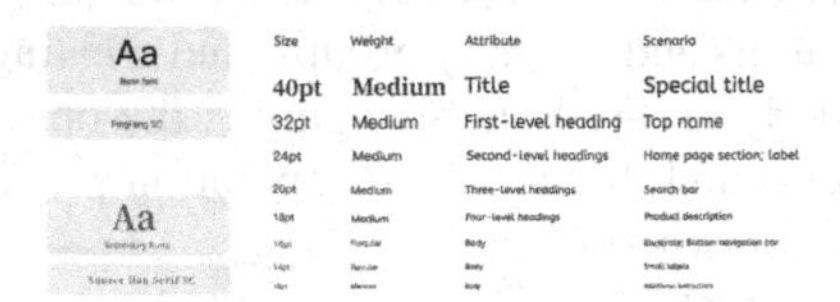

Fig. 7. Font specifications.

Fig. 8. Icon design.

4.3 Interface Function Design

The functional architecture of "Luyou" APP is divided into five modules: home page, community, one card, deer voice window and mine, and these five core functions are taken as the primary navigation system. The information of other levels is expanded under each module of each function, as shown in Fig. 9. Studies show that conform to the interaction of the elderly level from instructions to the results feedback not more than five levels, otherwise thc complexity of the product will greatly reduce the user experience, therefore, deer swim app from the main interface to details interface up to four levels, the greatest extent to avoid the interface logic complex user experience problems.

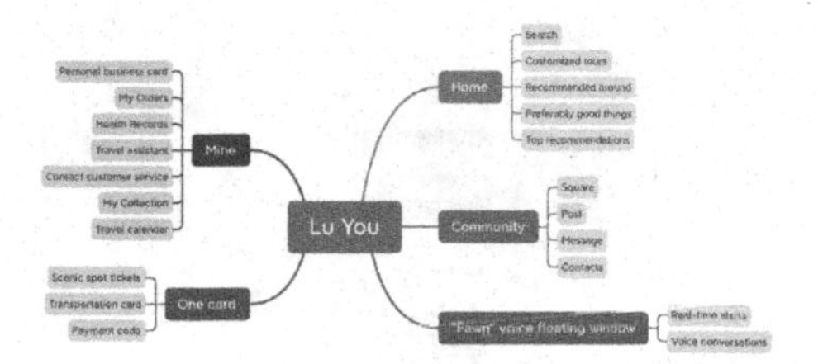

Fig. 9. Functional architecture diagram of the "Luyou" app.

Among them, the "My" module contains personal business card, my order, health records, travel assistant, contact customer service, my collection, travel calendar 7 function columns, health records include the user's basic medical history, medication, heart rate and blood samples, so that the physical condition is one of the limitations of the travel package recommendation; travel assistant is a travel memo for the elderly users' memory decline, will remind the ID card, charge bank, medicine and other necessary items; travel calendar travel time in the "my" interface, in order to remind and record the user's travel time. Related interface is shown in Fig. 10.

Fig. 10. Interfaces of "Mine" and important feature details.

The content contained in the home page is relatively complex. In order to make these information more clear and concise, the home page is mainly divided into five modules from top to bottom: search, Banner, King Kong area, Tab bar and recommended content (Fig. 11). Among them, Banner area, as the focus of users, is used to display the main content recommended by platforms such as discount activities and popular packages. King Kong District only displays three core functions: customized tourism, peripheral recommendation and optimization, So as to strengthen its guidance of users; The operation process interface of customized tourism is shown in Fig. 12, Users need to complete the basic travel information such as travel date, number of people and preference, To customize its own travel plan, The plan is accurate to the daily schedule and can be modified; The unfolding interface of preferred objects and peripheral is recommended as shown in Fig. 13, According to the physical and psychological characteristics of the elderly, the recommendation of health care products in each city, And provide online purchase channels for recommended items, The surrounding recommendation will recommend high rated food, scenic spots and hospitals according to the positioning of users. The Tab column contains recommendations of travel packages with different topics (popular, peripheral tour, natural oxygen bar, etc.). Click the details page after the travel package as shown in Fig. 14.

Fig. 11. Homepage.

Fig. 12. Customized travel function details page.

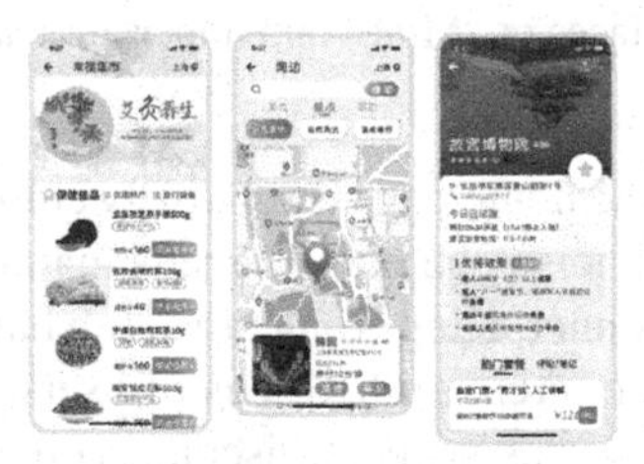

Fig. 13. Detailed page for selecting good products and surrounding recommended functions.

Fig. 14. Recommended Travel Package Details Page.

In the community, users can browse the posts of nearby or friends, post by themselves, and view and reply to friends 'messages, as shown in Fig. 15. The travel posts in the community will recommend different topics (landscape, traditional Chinese medicine health, charming cape) according to users' preferences and past browsing records, and users can freely switch topics for browsing. When users need to post, they will provide a post template to reduce the difficulty of Posting, and provide topic selection and location addition functions, so that users can find the same good circle. In the friend message interface, in order to reduce the difficulty of users to send messages and enhance the travel attributes of the community, the app has added the function of sharing trips and inviting friends to travel together.

Fig. 15. Interfaces of community and its main function pages.

In order to facilitate users to travel in different cities, the one-card is included in one of the four main interfaces, which covers bus and subway cards in different cities, tickets of different scenic spots and payment codes, as shown in Fig. 16.

The purpose of deer voice window setting is to meet the needs of users with poor vision, provide multi-modal interactive content, and provide voice guarantee for the fluency of user operation software. Users can wake them up by calling their names "Deer" and "Deer", or by clicking the deer icon in the navigation bar at the bottom. After wake up, users can realize the functions of voice dialogue, reading this page and emergency call. Then the interface is shown in Fig. 17. At the same time, because the elderly needs special attention, the deer voice window also has the function of real-time reminder of weather changes and abnormal user body data.

Fig. 16. Interface of smart card.

Fig. 17. "Xiaolu" voice window wake-up interface.

5 Design Evaluation

5.1 Evaluation of the Eye Movement Experiment

Experimental Materials: The materials of this experiment are the home page, customized tourism page, customized scheme content page and community page in the design scheme "Luyou" app. The experimental materials were grouped into group D, and were successively named D1, D2, D3, and D4.

Participants: 15 users aged 55–65 years old, including 7 women and 8 men. All the subjects volunteered to participate in the experiment, had good rest, were healthy physically and mentally, and had normal vision.

Experimental environment: The experiment in a sound insulation, light insulated laboratory.

Experimental Indicators: The total fixation duration, fixation points, first fixation duration, and heat map in the eye movement data were taken as indicators.

Experimental Procedures: Three-point calibration, then let the user perform the task of finding the "custom travel" button and record the duration of the task. After the task, other stimuli were presented successively, with each stimulus presented for 30000 ms.

5.2 Data Analysis

After the experiment, the average time of users looking for the "custom" button on the "Luyou" app was compared with the average time of the other three samples, as shown in Table 6 below. The Luyou app significantly makes it easier for users to find the feature and reducing task time. On the interest area of the home page in Table 7, Fig. 18 and the heat map of Fig. 19, we shows that the design of the home page meets the user attention preferences obtained from the three samples of the above eye movement experiment. At the same time, the design of the home page is more concise, emphasizing the main functional areas, and reducing the learning cost of users.

Table 6. Comparation of co mpletion time for f ind ing the 'Customize' button.

Test material	Average completion time/s
A1	24.40
B1	17.95
C1	28.80
D1	3.43

Table 7. Analysis table of eye movement data on homepage of "Luyou ".

Test material	AOI	Average fixation/ms	Fixation count	First fixation/ms
D 1	Search area	126.6	13.5	136.7
	Diamond area	212.3	20.0	148.8
	Content area	272.7	65.5	194.5
	Navigation bar	233.8	9.0	389.0

Fig. 18. Key performance indicators of AOI on the homepage of "Luyou".

D2, D3 and D4 in xxx are the heat maps of customized travel page, customized scheme content page and community page respectively. After increasing the proportion of design, users pay attention more on all kinds of important information to be filled in. In the customized scheme content page, the most concerned point is also in the most important area, the detailed content of the scheme. On the community page, user attention is more average.

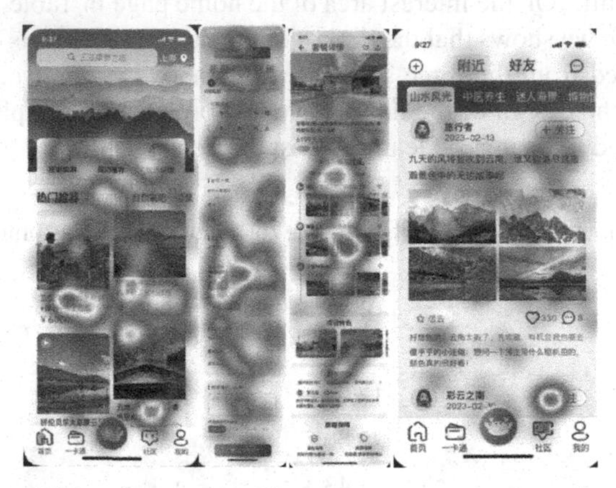

Fig. 19. From left to right are heat maps of homepage, customized travel page, customized plan content page, and community page.

5.3 System Usability Scale Survey

To verify the usability and ease of use of this design scheme, a questionnaire was conducted in the evaluation section combined with eye movement experiments. The questionnaire was designed according to the SUS system usability scale with 10 questions. Among them, questions No. 4, 5 and 10 investigated the accessibility of the design scheme, questions No. 2, 3, 7 and 8, and the satisfaction of questions No. 1, 6 and 9. The content of the questionnaire is shown in the following table [8]. The scale design is shown in Fig. 20 below, with 1 point for strong opposition and 5 points from left to right: 1, 2, 3, 4 and 5 (Table 8).

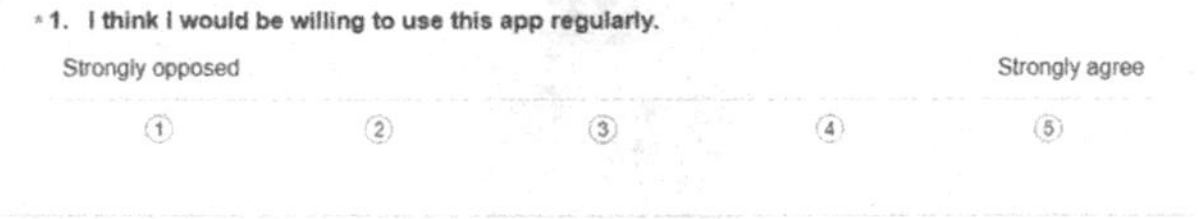

*1. I think I would be willing to use this app regularly.

Strongly opposed　　Strongly agree

① ② ③ ④ ⑤

Fig. 20. Design of System Availability Scale (Partial).

Table 8. Average score of system availability scale.

Number	Content	Average score
Q1	I think I would be willing to use this app regularly	4.75
Q2	I don't think this application needs to be so complex	2.25
Q3	I think this application is easy to use	4.75
Q4	I think I need professional support to use this application	1.25
Q5	I found that the different functions in this application are well integrated together	4.00
Q6	I think there are too many inconsistencies in this application	1.75
Q7	I think most people will quickly learn to use this application	4.50
Q8	I think this application is very cumbersome to use	1.25
Q9	I feel very confident in using this application	4.25
Q10	I need to learn a lot before using this application	1.50

It can be seen from the table above that the application of "Luyou ou" has excellent scores in terms of easy learning, availability and satisfaction. Combined with the results of the eye movement experiment, the availability and user preference of the application are higher than the three competing samples.

6 Conclusion

This study constructed a kano model based on the physiological and psychological characteristics of users aged 55–65 years, using user interviews and questionnaires, to explore the needs of older users for customized health care travel. Through the eye movement experiment, the users' attention to each design area of tourism application is analyzed, and the interaction design principles and priorities of customized health tourism application for aging are summarized in combination with the Nielsen design principles. Finally, the eye movement experiment and the system usability scale are used to verify the accessibility, availability and satisfaction of the design scheme. This study focuses on the elderly users as a marginal group in the digital age, and focuses on how to meet the special needs of the elderly users in the customized health care tourism. At the same time, a set of user experience optimization process for aging tourism applications is formed, and the design principles are derived, which provides certain theoretical support and design reference for the design of aging customized health tourism applications.

References

1. Xi, Y.: Digital enables the integrated development of the cultural and tourism industry. Cult. Ind. (13), 7–9 (2023)
2. Lin J.: Interactive Redesign Study of Aged Tourism Products. Beijing Institute of Technology (2015)

3. Dong, D.: Interface Design and Research of Intelligent Travel APP for the Elderly Based on Service Design. Nanjing University of Posts and Telecommunications (2022)
4. Huixia, Z.: Research on the demand analysis and design of digital communication products for the elderly. Mod. Electron. Technol. **39**(11), 129–132 (2016)
5. Qin, L.: Travel Product Design and Research for the Elderly. North China University of Technology (2020)
6. Zhang, J., Li, Y., Zhu, L.: Optimized design of elderly APP based on Logistic regression. Packag. Eng. **43**(10), 91–98 (2022)
7. She, R., Feng, S.: Evaluation of the usability of mobile long forms based on eye tracking. Des. Art Res. **12**(06), 145–150+160 (2022)
8. Hajesmaeel-Gohari, S., Khordastan, F., Fatehi, F., et al.: The most used questionnaires for evaluating satisfaction, usability, acceptance, and quality outcomes of mobile health. Bmc Med. Inform. Dec. Mak. **22**(1), 22 (2022)

"I Simply Accept the Terms and Conditions so that I Can Use an App at All": Smartphone Use and Privacy Among Older Adults in Switzerland

Sarah Speck[1](✉), Cora Pauli[1], Cornelia Ursprung[1], Miriam Wallimann[1], Robert Huber[2], and Sabina Misoch[1]

[1] Institute for Ageing Research, University of Applied Sciences of Eastern Switzerland, Rosenbergstrasse 59, 9001 St. Gallen, Switzerland
sarah.speck@ost.ch

[2] Pappy GmbH, Flüelastrasse 6, 8048 Zurich, Switzerland

Abstract. Digitalization and ageing population are two of the main trends of the 21st century. Most people, including older adults, are now digitally connected to the world for e.g., managing health and finances and this has become indispensable parts of our lives. A device like a smartphone is easily at hand and ready to use anytime, anywhere. However, this widespread usage produces huge amounts of data, which is not without risks, especially for older users in terms of data protection and privacy. This paper investigates behaviours, attitudes, and experiences regarding privacy settings and take a closer look at the phenomenon of resignation and the privacy paradox within the research project *Easierphone. Easierphone* app *Easierphone* aims to simplify smartphone use for older adults and other vulnerable people by replacing the Android surface with an easier one. For data collection, 30 qualitative interviews and diaries were used during installation and testing of the app. Regarding privacy and data protection, most of our participants stated that they generally do not read the terms of use in the digital world carefully. Nonetheless, they still agree to them, so they can use an app or a digital service which clearly illustrates the privacy paradox.

Keywords: Ageing · Digitalization · Older Adults · Smartphone Use · Privacy · Data Protection · Privacy Paradox · Resignation

1 Introduction

Digitalization and ageing population are two of the main trends of the 21st century. Most people, including older adults (≥60 years), are now digitally connected to the world; online services, i.e., to maintain social connections or for managing health and finances, have become indispensable parts of our lives. A device like a smartphone is easily at hand and ready to use anytime, anywhere. Smartphone ownership per person increased globally to over 83% in emerging economies and over 94% in advanced economies [1]. Older adults in Switzerland also show high use of information communication technology [2], and almost 70% are using smartphones in their daily life [3].

Q. Gao et al. (Eds.): HCII 2023, LNCS 14055, pp. 191–202, 2023.
https://doi.org/10.1007/978-3-031-48041-6_14

However, this widespread usage produces huge amounts of data, which is not without risks, especially for older users in terms of data protection and privacy as they are less experienced [4, 5]. The increase in smartphone ownership, hence use, are not without consequences as every move and action online generates data and leaving data traces [4]. Leaving data traces happens both, conscious and unconscious. Related to older adults this sometimes also means that they pull back from using digital technologies which van Dijk [6] describes as one of the barriers which restrict access to digital technologies. This is because older adults are more cautious and lack knowledge how to protect their online data. However, over and over the experience is made that for instance information overload, such as terms and conditions for a download of an app, leads to paradoxical behaviour which stands in contrast to their attitude concerning privacy and data protection as users just accept settings [7, 8]. Zeissig et al. [4] found in their studies that the older adults tend to protect their online data and maintain online privacy more than younger generations. Despite this result, they also found that attitude towards online privacy differs from actual behaviour and privacy concerns. The issues of older adults' online privacy behaviours, data protection, and their use of digital devices still need further research (e.g., 4, 9–12). Further, older adults are a special group when it comes to usage of digital technologies, they are more cautious and careful in using these technologies and less experienced than their younger counterparts whom we know as digital natives.

This paper gets in at exactly this point: older adults and their attitudes, behaviours made in the field of privacy and data protection using their smartphones. We investigate their views and experiences they made in general with privacy relating to smartphone use and online activities and their experiences during *Easierphone* testing. *Easierphone* is an app developed in collaboration with Pappy GmbH in the context of the AAL-program funded research project. The app *Easierphone* aims to simplify smartphone use for older adults and other vulnerable people. The app is designed for the less tech-savvy in this heterogenous age group and intends to replace the common Android interface with a simplified, more user-friendly one [13]. Furthermore, *Easierphone* app enables remote access for a trusted assistant (e.g., family members, friends) by mirroring the screen on the assistant's device, so they can give virtual assistance when users face usability problems. Additional functionalities, such as a machine learning algorithm to detect changes in usage behaviours (by measuring screen time) or a step counter, are optional functions within the app. Here the potential end user and our participants are confronted with several questions around privacy and data protection concerning certain *Easierphone* features. Who is allowed to see my steps per day? Who will I give permission to remotely adjust settings on my smartphone? Who do I choose as trusted assistant for the remote assistance?

Within the bigger scope of the project, we here explicitly focus on aspects of privacy for this paper – an important current challenge [11]. Particularly we want to investigate this from a viewpoint of older users. We examine their behaviours, attitudes, experiences, and decisions regarding privacy settings and take a closer look at the phenomenon the privacy paradox [8, 14]. The privacy paradox amongst others describes the fact that older adults are more concerned about online privacy risks but at the same time have fewer protective strategies compared to younger generations [4, 5]. In addition, we want to carve out the differences between subjective users' perceptions and smartphone providers' objective framework regarding (online) privacy and data protection. With the focus on simplifying older adults' smartphone use, our research project around the *Easierphone* app needs to adhere to Android system requirements for the installation, while still trying to make this process as simple as possible. Users are still required to give several permissions from download to setup of the app, e.g., allowing automatic import of contacts into *Easierphone*'s contact function, or allowing remote access which is required for the assistant functionality. This raises additional questions of privacy and data protection: What data can be accessed by the assistant, e.g., tracking of routes walked, step counter and screen usage data. If enabled, these can be remotely observed by the assistant in their *Easierphone* app. It is a balancing act between the privacy of *Easierphone*'s main user and what data their assistants, or third parties are able or allowed to see, and track. While older adults as main users of the app may think they are being watched and patronized, assistants might have the best intentions. The boundary between useful remote access and someone's privacy being violated can vary strongly between different users' subjective point of view and need to be further investigated to enable improvement for further development [13].

2 Privacy among Older Adults in the Digital World

2.1 Privacy Attitudes and Behaviors

Privacy research is a large field, rooted in diverse disciplines. "Privacy can and does mean different things to different people" [15] (p. 642 9). In general, there is still lack of an agreed upon definition since privacy appears in many fields of life. However, key of privacy research and definition determination were made by Altman [16] and Westin [17]. Whereas Altman's definition includes limiting social interaction and focuses more on physical space of privacy and territoriality, Westin's definition focuses more on how information about or from persons are dealt with [7].

Hitherto, scholars working on privacy within the context of the digital world and digital technologies mainly align with the information and location sharing preferences [7, 18, 19]. Privacy perceptions and behaviours related to digital technologies have been widely studied in the last decade (see e.g., 20–22) also the question of privacy in the public referring to developments in information and digital technology has been in-depth researched [23].

However, the topic has been less researched with reference to the social group of older adults increasingly using digital technologies, for surfing the web, health services, services for financial issues, and smartphone use for example in daily life. Elueze and Quan-Haase [12] explored attitudes and concerns of older adults' in their digital lives. Based on Westin's typology of privacy types they carved out a total of five privacy types among older adults and found that attitudes and behaviours among older adults are highly diverse ranging from fundamentalists (being suspicious about everything) to marginally concerned ones (see also Courtney [24]). In general, using digital technologies, increases concerns regarding privacy [25]. Among older adults where studies found that most of them are less experienced in the digital world which in return plays out on low digital literacy. Hence, older adults feel less secure to use digital technology and assess risks with disclosing personal information higher than their younger counterparts. Van Dijk's

[6] research showed that questions about privacy and security even are main reasons for drawbacks and not using digital technology and among older people as the main barrier for not using digital technologies. Also, Kwasny et al. [26] noted that older adults tend to protect their personal data more than their younger counterparts and that privacy attitude, behaviour and concerns differ among young and old. Interestingly, they found, emerging from data of their studies, that Westin's definition on privacy accords more to younger people, and Altman's definition suits more for older adults in the context of digital technologies.

Generally, older adults have also less experience or understanding of online privacy, strategies of protecting personal data than people who grew up in the digital age. For the present research paper and study, we refer on the concept of privacy paradox and by examining attitudes, behaviours and experiences concerning online privacy in this light we will carve out the most striking topics older persons mention.

2.2 The Privacy Paradox

Talking about privacy, the concerns and behaviour referring to the protection of personal data, privacy paradox is not far off. People trade personal information for benefits; however, their attitude, concern and behaviour vary highly when it comes to disclosure of personal information. For instance, Sayre and Horne [27] found that people freely share information for free benefits (here groceries) in return. Also, certain areas of life are more private than others [28]. Several research on attitude and behaviour related to privacy showed that often attitudes of persons to disclose their personal information (= intention to disclose) are more cautiously made than actual behaviour in this context. Actual disclosure differs significantly from a person's intention or attitude [8, 27]. Norberg et al. [8] for example found in their study about personal information disclosure that intentions of people differ a lot from their actual behaviours, although they seem to be concerned about their personal information and privacy which is known as the privacy paradox. The privacy paradox describes the fact that people are more concerned about their personal information, e.g. in online privacy risks but in parallel have few protective strategies to withhold personal information, or rather are actually more open to share their personal information and disclose when it comes to usage of certain services or benefits (cf. e.g., [4, 5, 29].

Privacy is closely connected to trust and risk. Studies have found that in general a higher risk which is connected to negative outcomes influences the individual's concerns relating to privacy (see e.g., [30]). Trust on the other hand also plays a significant role when it comes to disclosure of personal information. In general, the more known or established a company or institution is, the higher the trust or willingness to disclose information [31]. Notwithstanding, trust depends on the context as it works differently in online or offline contexts [8]. In addition, in the context of privacy, the privacy calculus is a model that explains the paradoxical behaviour: Users weigh up the expected benefits of online transactions against feared privacy risks. If the expected benefits outweigh the risks, users disclose content despite their fears [32, 33].If the expected benefits outweigh the risks, users disclose content despite their fears [32].

For the present study, we are interested how the privacy paradox appears in attitude and actual behaviour of our older participants in the context of the Easierphone field tests and what older adults' opinions are regarding use of the *Easierphone* app and their smartphones, and further their concerns regarding online privacy in general. Some test persons explicitly mentioned they have no concerns regarding online privacy. For this publication focus on the ones that were expressing concerns.

3 Research Design and Applied Methods

3.1 Easierphone: A Multi-National Project

Easierphone is a multinational European research project funded under the EU Active Assisted Living Programme. The aim of this programme is to promote cooperation between end-users, industry, and research. The project consists of six project partners from Switzerland, the Netherlands, and Poland and has a duration of 30 months (April 2021-September 2023).

The focus of the project is not only to develop an app for older people, but to follow this path in a participatory manner and with participative methods together with the target age group. During the entire project duration, the app is being tested in three successive project phases (pilot 1, 2 and 3) in a real live setting with potential end users (seniors, relatives, caregivers) and continuously developed further based on their feedback. Each participating country is responsible for the national data collection but works with the same survey tools. In pp2, questions of privacy and data protection from the user's point of view are very much in the foreground: On the one hand, specifically related to the use of *Easierphone*, but we also wanted to deepen the perspective of older users on the topic of online privacy in general. During the tests, we meticulously explain to the participants what the app tracks, how tracking can be disabled and how the participants themselves have control over various functions. Also, with respect to the remote access of their assistants.

In each pilot, the IAF team conducts interviews with three single testers and seven tandems (main user plus assistant), resulting in a total of 30 tests in Switzerland. Both, the single testers, and the main users of the tandem must be at least 65 years old. Another inclusion criterion is that the main users own a smartphone but do not feel confident in using it. The living situations of the participating seniors were very diverse, with married, single, and widowed persons participating, some with kids some without. It was important to recruit a diverse sample because the population group "older adults" is very heterogeneous, and this is also reflected in the use of technologies or needs regarding the use of technology. The age and other sociodemographic characteristics of the tandem assistants are not relevant. However, they should feel confident enough in using the smartphone to be able to support the main user.

3.2 Applied Methods

The project's approach is based on a user-centred design [34], where the app is being tested in a real-life setting over several weeks to allow the participants the opportunity to get to know the app and to assess it comprehensively in an everyday setting. Each wave of field testing (pilot 1–3) comprises three dates with face-to-face interviews [35] with the test persons. In addition to the interviews, the study is methodologically based on the think-aloud method [36, 37] and a diary study (paper and pen).

Each of the three face-to-face interviews focuses on different topics: In the first interview, the app is downloaded and installed. One focus here is on questions and problems that arise in this context. The topics of privacy and data protection play a major role here, as the users must give various consents. In addition, the use of the app is explained. Furthermore, it is stated how the test persons generally use their smartphone to understand barriers and needs. The test persons are given the task of trying out the individual functions of the app until the next interview (time span are about 2–3 weeks). The second interview is mainly about usability problems, needs that are not covered by the app and suggestions for improvement. In the third and last interview includes questions about usability again and questions about how the test persons generally obtain information about new apps or digital services.

The interviews are based on semi-structured guidelines and during the interviews the test persons carry out all operating steps as independently as possible and are asked to say out loud everything they do, see, and think. Using the think aloud method, the researchers can understand live which problems and questions are relevant right in the moment of the app use.

Furthermore, the participants are asked to keep a diary (paper & pen method) during the testing period. As soon as they notice something, have problems, ideas for solving problems, questions, and suggestions, they write them down in short form. These notes are always discussed at the beginning of the interviews and flow into the protocols as well. The purpose of the long-term test is for the test persons to get to know the app comprehensively and to try it out. This enables the researchers to develop a deeper understanding of usability issues and user needs. Furthermore, this form of testing can also be used to explore contexts of use and the conditions of acceptance (which framework conditions are central to this).

In addition to usability issues, the focus of Pilot Programme 2 and 3 is strongly on privacy. This applies to the tandem function as well as to online privacy in general. Part of the questionnaire focuses on understanding what concerns the test persons have in this regard and what protection strategies they pursue. All interviews are audio-recorded and selectively transcribed in anonymised form. The selective transcriptions are analysed using qualitative content analysis [38] after each survey wave. Based on this we formed categories relating to privacy issues.

4 Experiences on Online Privacy Behaviours and Needs from a Participants' Perspective

Test participants showed great heterogeneity regarding the extent and content of concerns they uttered. While most participants stated that they were generally not concerned about data privacy, some participants stated that this topic was very important to them. In the following, we present the most striking topics extracted from the interview data relating to online privacy in the context of the *Easierphone* app use, and online privacy in general. The ad-hoc reactions to installation and agreements to terms and conditions and privacy settings can be subsumed under the following categories: Cost-benefit trade-off/privacy calculus, the necessity of trust, coercion and resignation.

Basically, for the installation process of the *Easierphone* app it can be said that the process is largely determined by the Android system requirements. Here, *Easierphone* attempts to make the process as simple as possible while complying to Android guidelines (e.g., asking for various permissions directly on the device). In all real-life interview settings, the test persons and assistants were accompanied or advised by an IAF staff.

4.1 Privacy Calculus and the Privacy Paradox

Most of the test persons in our sample would in fact like to read the general terms and conditions in more detail before they agree, to know more precisely what they are agreeing to. Or in any case, they take the position that they should actually read them. However, they are not prepared to invest the necessary time or are too impatient for a detailed discussion of the general terms and conditions. One of them stated: "I was going to read it first, but it takes too long, so I think, just agree and skip it" (interview LB12). Also, the phrase, "I don't feel like it" (RD07), was often mentioned. They feel the effort is too great for something that, from their point of view, cannot be avoided anyway. However, a feeling of ambivalence and resignation remains: if you want to use the app, you simply have to accept the terms and conditions. This behaviour relates to the privacy calculus which explains the paradoxical behaviour of the persons as they evaluate potential risks of disclosing private data or agreement against benefit, i.e., here use of the app [32, 33].This behaviour relates to the privacy calculus which explains the paradoxical behaviour of the persons as they evaluate potential risks of disclosing private data or agreement against benefit, i.e., here use of the app [32]. In the explicit context of *Easierphone* testing, the participants also mainly skipped the terms and conditions as they were working or accompanied by IAF staff walking them through the installation process. However, the notification of the *Easierphone* app that the app or data downloaded could be "harmful" irritated a few participants. However, as a cognitive strategy to put aside concerns in the concrete context of testing, test persons often told, "I trust the research project" and it was accepted without deeper scrutiny. One test person even mentioned that they trust the project and, "that everything relating to it [the project] is legally okay" (interview RB05). This relates to findings of Earp, Baumer [31] who examined the effect of a brand name status and found that in general, people are more open to share or agree to disclose when the company is more well-known. Since the testing was conducted by members of the IAF that is affiliated to the University of applied Sciences Eastern Switzerland, this could have a similar effect in trustworthiness. The statements found in the testing inevitably lead to the next topic of trust in the field of privacy.

The concept of privacy paradox describes the feelings and behaviour of many test persons very well. They describe a contradiction between what they actually do and what they think they should do. The paradoxical behaviour is explained by various factors: there is a lack of willingness to invest the necessary time to read the relevant GTCs or to familiarise themselves with this topic at all. In addition, it is often described that the topic of online privacy is very complex and that the respondents feel overwhelmed by it. This felt lack of knowledge to a feeling of resignation, which in this case does not lead to not using something but to using something despite reservations and question marks. The sometimes-paradoxical behaviours regarding privacy can be understand as resignation to the demands of online privacy but also as cost-benefit trade-off. Some subjects use cognitive and practical strategies to overcome this contradictory situation and feel more secure. For example, they say "I have nothing to hide" (GH07) or "I am not important enough, so no one is interested in my online data" (DG07). Others consistently avoid doing online banking with their mobile phones.

4.2 Necessity of Trust

The reactions to the possibility of tandem are often pragmatic. Some already know the principle of "remote access" from the use of the PC (e.g., via TeamViewer) and find it a very practical solution to avoid travel times and regard it is a good thing to transfer this method to the *Easierphone* tandem function. The fact that the main user has control over the access options of the assistant is perceived positively and strengthens the test persons' sense of control over their privacy and make them feel secure when using the tandem functionality. The test persons also see the fact that a tandem partner does not have access to content (chats, emails) but only to interfaces as positive. The ability to view content, however, would be an absolute no-go.

Very few of the test persons see the tandem function as a possibility to provide remote help as critical or a threat to their privacy. The general thrust is that there should be trust in the assisting person, if this trust exists, one has no concerns, if the trust does not exist, one simply does not want to have the person in question as an assistant. Some respondents think that the tandem function is practical but find the asymmetry between the main user and the assisting person problematic: they think that both parties should have equal access to the other person's smartphone.

Regarding the function of AI module within *Easierphone* app, such as activity tracking, the test persons are more critical about the access possibilities of third parties. Several test persons emphasise that they do not want their location to be visible or third parties to see how much they have moved or travelled. A test person here mentioned, "It is nobody's business if I sit on the sofa for a whole day" (EL01). They would feel controlled, their autonomy restricted, and their dignity violated because they no longer have control over their own privacy. Self-tracking per se is not interesting for many of the test persons. Some use a smartwatch (not connected to the smartphone) and have no need for another tool or emphasise that they don't have their smartphone on them at home and that measured values are therefore not correct anyway. Considering these findings and seeing trust as heuristic in giving agreement to access to another person, or disclose personal information, Scholz and Lubell (1998) [39] this could shorten decision-making procedure.

The view of the assistants (relatives) is clearly differing here: especially if they perceive a relative/partner as fragile (e.g., at risk of falling), the possibility of tracking provides security to them. However, the situation is somewhat different with the emergency call function: here, everyone agrees that location sharing is essential and attractive. Hence, sensitivity to tracking is strongly situational. In general, test persons mentioned during the interviews that active agreement on permissions are necessary as they want to know what the other person, the assistant, knows and has access to.

4.3 Coercion and Resignation

The reflections on concerns, and strategies regarding online privacy in general coincide with those we have in the *Easierphone* app. Some respondents feel safe online because they have "nothing to hide" from a subjective point of view. What is sensitive or could be compromising is highly subjective and can also be interpreted as a mental strategy to mitigate concerns about online privacy by downplaying the importance of their own personal data and disclosure of it. Others think they should protect themselves or read terms and conditions but feel overwhelmed to understand the detailed content and do not want to invest the necessary time. They are of the opinion that the topic of online privacy is too complex and untransparent for laypeople and that they lack the necessary basic knowledge. They feel overwhelmed by the topic, but the benefits of various information, services and apps outweigh their concerns, and they accept everything, but also in the sense of resignation.

Here the privacy paradox appears clearly: Test persons accept terms and conditions although they know they should read the small print including terms and conditions. This behaviour stands in contradiction with their attitude to preferably protect their personal data and not to disclose too much to the public (see also [8]). Nonetheless, a few test persons strictly follow certain strategies to protect their privacy, e.g., in the case of smartphone use: they do not have any bank data stored on their smartphone. The answer to cost-benefit considerations in the context of online privacy is often very pragmatic as one of the citations shows: "I pay the price of getting advertising so that I can use certain apps for free" (interview WG09), or: "I simply accept the terms and conditions so that I can use an app at all" (interview LB12).

In summary, it can be said that privacy concerns are often pushed into the background in favour of simplicity, timesaving, and pragmatism, or are overcome by downplaying them. However, a certain unease or contradictory feelings about online privacy remain. The respondents ultimately feel helpless and impotent when asked how they could overcome these contradictions. The sometimes-paradoxical behaviours relating to privacy can be understand as resignation to the demands of online privacy.

5 Conclusion and Outlook

Easierphone app aims at simplifying smartphone use for older adults and other vulnerable persons. However, usage is not without risk, i.e., disclosure of personal information and acceptance of terms and conditions. Many test persons perceived the basic idea of Easierphone, especially to make the home screen clearer, very positively. However, several participants did mention that it took and still takes time to become familiar with the new layout and functionality of the *Easierphone* app, which also led some participants to preferably use the familiar home screen of their smartphone despite the perceived advantages of *Easierphone.*

We were interested in the behaviours, attitudes, experiences regarding privacy settings and take a closer look at the phenomenon of resignation and the privacy paradox within the research project. The reactions to the topic of online privacy were very heterogeneous. For some, it was generally not a worrying issue, but others expressed reservations but showed resignation and/or paradoxical behaviour. As far as the tandem function was concerned, the conviction of control was greater and the necessary actions to maintain the desired level of privacy towards the assistant were understandable and convertible.

In contrast, it is interesting that what is required by law to protect online privacy (that T&Cs must be shown, and users must give their consent before taking an action) is of little use on a subjective level of being in control over one's privacy in our cases. Test persons were more concerned about what their app assistant or third parties could know about them rather than giving consent for any terms and conditions. It was striking that for example permission granting to access or track routes walked to a known person are more sensitive than maybe also disclosing personal information to a company, here the research institute. This could also be the case because there is a lack of knowledge or willingness, or also lack of experience to deal in detail with the complex issues of online privacy. From a subjective point of view, feelings of coercion, powerlessness and ambivalence are therefore prevalent among the people who have concerns.

This case study shows that experiences and opinions are quite diverse despite a relatively small sample, however, representation was not an aim in the study but to collect and grasp what older adults think about this topic and how behaviour and attitude appear in real life. Privacy and ethical concerns were addressed at several points throughout the pilot testing by the interviewers (e.g., during the installation process of different Easierphone features. While most participants stated that they were generally not concerned about data privacy, some participants stated that this topic was very important to them and that they e.g., try to be vigilant and critical before accepting terms. However, when agreeing to terms of use or grant permission for a function most of the test persons reported to adopt a rather pragmatic approach which can be stated as privacy paradox (i.e., accepting without reading terms (thoroughly). Interesting here is, that test persons distinguished between data that is sensitive (e.g., bank details) and data that they personally perceived as non-confidential (e.g., content of text messages).

To conclude it can be said that the experiences and opinions, attitudes and behaviour of individuals are highly heterogenous. Are there any ways to resolve the privacy paradox and enable older people to have a better sense of control over their online privacy and thus lower the barrier to digitalisation for older adults? Due to the relatively small sample size (it is part of a larger research project), it is difficult to generalize or even to find similarities among the different test persons. However, the privacy paradox appears frequently appears among them, be it conscious or not. The bridge between real-world privacy strategies and online privacy strategies could ease online privacy strategies, for instance like the assistant app (clear and comprehensible, to what functions the assistant has access and possibility to say yes or no: like closing a door or closing a curtain). Here, further research on what cognitive strategies individual people use to overcome ambivalence, paradoxical feelings, respectively to endure the paradoxical feelings with reference to online privacy is needed.

Acknowledgements. We thank all older participants and their tandem partners without whom we could not have undertaken this research, we would like to extend our sincere thanks for their openness, interest, and valuable time in all interviews in pilot 1 and 2. Further, we thank the European AAL Programme (EU Active Assisted Living Programme) for funding this research project.

References

1. Pew Research Center: Smartphone Ownership Is Growing Rapidly Around the World, but Not Always Equally (2019). https://www.pewglobal.org/wp-content/uploads/sites/2/2019/02/Pew-Research-Center_Global-Technology-Use-2018_2019-02-05.pdf
2. Seifert, A., Martin, M., Perrig-Chiello, P.: Bildungs- und Lernbedürfnisse im Alter: Bericht zur nationalen Befragungsstudie in der Schweiz (2021)
3. Seifert, A., Ackermann, T.P., Schelling, H.R.: Digitale Senioren 2020: Nutzung von Informations- und Kommunikationstechnologien durch Personen ab 65 Jahren in der Schweiz (2020)
4. Zeissig, E.-M., Lidynia, C., Vervier, L., et al.: Online privacy perceptions of older adults. In: Zhou, J., Salvendy, G. (eds.) ITAP 2017. LNCS, vol. 10298, pp. 181–200. Springer, Cham (2017). https://doi.org/10.1007/978-3-319-58536-9_16
5. Bartol, J., Prevodnik, K., Vehovar, V., et al.: The roles of perceived privacy control, Internet privacy concerns and Internet skills in the direct and indirect Internet uses of older adults: conceptual integration and empirical testing of a theoretical model. New Med. Soc. 146144482211227 (2022). https://doi.org/10.1177/14614448221122734
6. van Dijk, J.: The one-dimensional network society of manuel castells. New Media Soc. **1**, 127–138 (1999). https://doi.org/10.1177/1461444899001001015
7. Kwasny, M.N., Caine, K.E., Rogers, W.A., et al.: Privacy and technology: folk definitions and perspectives. In: CHI 2008 ACM, pp. 3290–3296 (2008)
8. Norberg, P.A., Horne, D.R., Horne, D.A.: The privacy paradox: personal information disclosure intentions versus behaviors. J. Consum. Aff. **41**, 100–126 (2007). https://doi.org/10.1111/j.1745-6606.2006.00070.x
9. Rauschnabel, P.A., He, J., Ro, Y.K.: Antecedents to the adoption of augmented reality smart glasses: a closer look at privacy risks. J. Bus. Res. **92**, 374–384 (2018). https://doi.org/10.1016/j.jbusres.2018.08.008
10. Ghaiumy Anaraky, R., Byrne, K.A., Wisniewski, P.J., et al.: To disclose or not to disclose: examining the privacy decision-making processes of older vs. younger adults. In: Kitamura, Y., Quigley, A., Isbister, K. et al. (eds.) Proceedings of the 2021 CHI Conference on Human Factors in Computing Systems. ACM, New York, NY, USA, pp. 1–14 (2021)
11. Stephanidis, C., Salvendy, G., Antona, M., et al.: Seven HCI grand challenges. Int. J. Hum.-Comput. Interact. **35**, 1229–1269 (2019). https://doi.org/10.1080/10447318.2019.1619259
12. Elueze, I., Quan-Haase, A.: Privacy attitudes and concerns in the digital lives of older adults: Westin's privacy attitude typology revisited. Am. Behav. Sci. **62**(10), 1372–1391 (2018). https://doi.org/10.1177/0002764218787026
13. Speck, S., Pauli, C., Ursprung, C., et al.: Easierphone: participative development of a senior-friendly smartphone application. In: Proceedings of the 9th International Conference on Information and Communication Technologies for Ageing Well and e-Health, pp. 199–207 (2023)
14. Colnago, J., Cranor, L., Acquisti, A.: Is there a reverse privacy paradox? An exploratory analysis of gaps between privacy perspectives and privacy-seeking behaviors. Proc. Priv. Enhancing Technol. **2023**(1), 455–476 (2023). https://doi.org/10.56553/popets-2023-0027
15. Karat, C.-M., Brodie, C., Karat, J.: Human-computer interaction viewed from the intersection of privacy, security, and trust. In: Sears, A., Jacko, J. (eds.) The Human-Computer Interaction Handbook, vol. 20071544, pp. 639–658. CRC Press (2007)
16. Altman, I.: The Environment and Social Behavior: Privacy, Personal Space, Territory. Brooks/Cole Publishing Company, Monterey, California, Crowding (1975)
17. Westin, A.F.: Privacy and Freedom. Atheneum, New York (1967)

18. Olson, J.S., Grudin, J., Horbitz, E.: A study on preferences on sharing and privacy. In: Proceedings of the SIGCHI Conference on Human factors in Computing Systems, San Jose, California, USA (2005)
19. Ludford, R.J., Priedhorsky, R., Reily, K., et al.: Capturing, sharing, and using local place information. In: Proceedings of the SIGCHI Conference, San Jose, California, USA (2007)
20. Bélanger, C.: Privacy in the digital age: a review of information privacy research in information systems. MIS Q. **35**, 1017 (2011). https://doi.org/10.2307/41409971
21. Li, Y.: Empirical studies on online information privacy concerns: literature review and an integrative framework. Commun. Assoc. Inform. Syst. (2011). https://doi.org/10.17705/1CAIS.02828
22. Jeff Smith, H., Dinev, T., Xu, H.: Information privacy research: an interdisciplinary review. MIS Q. **35**(4), 989 (2011). https://doi.org/10.2307/41409970
23. Nissenbaum, H.: Protecting privacy in an information age: the problem of privacy in public. Law Philos. **17**, 559–596 (1998). https://doi.org/10.1023/A:1006184504201
24. Courtney, K.L.: Privacy and senior willingness to adopt smart home information technology in residential care facilities. Methods Inf. Med. **47**, 76–81 (2008). https://doi.org/10.3414/me9104
25. Tsai, H.-Y.S., Shillair, R., Cotten, S.R.: Social support and "playing around": an examination of how older adults acquire digital literacy with tablet computers. J. Appl. Gerontol. **36**, 29–55 (2017). https://doi.org/10.1177/0733464815609440
26. Kwasny, M.N., Caine, K.E., Rogers, W.A., et al.: Privacy and Technology: Folk Definitions and Perspectives. In: Proceedings of teh SIGCHI Conference Human Factor Computer System, pp. 3291–3296 (2008). https://doi.org/10.1145/1358628.1358846
27. Sayre, S., Horne, D.A.: Trading secrets for savings: how concerned are consumers about club cards as a privacy threat? In: ACR North American Advances (2000)
28. Phelps, J., Nowak, G., Ferrell, E.: Privacy concerns and consumer willingness to provide personal information. J. Public Policy Mark. **19**, 27–41 (2000). https://doi.org/10.1509/jppm.19.1.27.16941
29. Kokolakis, S.: Privacy attitudes and privacy behaviour: a review of current research on the privacy paradox phenomenon. Comput. Secur. **64**, 122–134 (2017). https://doi.org/10.1016/j.cose.2015.07.002
30. White, T.B.: Consumer disclosure and disclosure avoidance: a motivational. Framework **14**, 41–51 (2004)
31. Earp, J.B., Baumer, D.: Innovative web use to learn about consumer behavior and online privacy. Commun. ACM **46**, 81–83 (2003). https://doi.org/10.1145/641205.641209
32. Schomakers, E.-M., Lidynia, C., Ziefle, M.: A typology of online privacy personalities. J. Grid Comput. **17**, 727–747 (2019). https://doi.org/10.1007/s10723-019-09500-3
33. Lutz, C., Hoffmann, C.P., Ranzini, G.: Data capitalism and the user: an exploration of privacy cynicism in Germany. New Media Soc. **22**, 1168–1187 (2020). https://doi.org/10.1177/1461444820912544
34. Tullis, T., Albert, B.: Measuring the user experience: Collecting, analyzing, and presenting usability metrics, 2nd edn. Elsevier/Morgan Kaufmann, Amsterdam, Boston (2013)
35. Misoch, S.: Qualitative Interviews. De Gruyter (2019)
36. Nørgaard, M., Hornbæk. K.: What do usability evaluators do in practice? In: Carroll, J.M., Bødker. S., Coughlin, J. (eds.) Proceedings of the 6th conference on Designing Interactive systems. ACM, New York, NY, USA, pp. 209–218 (2006)
37. Ericsson, K.A., Simon, H.A.: Protocol Analysis. The MIT Press (1993)
38. Mayring, P.: Qualitative Content Analysis [28 paragraphs]. Forum Qualitative Sozialforschung/Forum: Qualitative Social Research (2000)
39. Scholz, J.T., Lubell, M.: Trust and taxpaying: testing the heuristic approach to collective action. Am. J. Political Sci. **42**, 398 (1998). https://doi.org/10.2307/2991764

Too Smart to Make a Phone Call: A Focus Group Study on the Use of Smartphones Among Older Adults

Guolong Sun, Honglian Xiang, Susu Zhang, Jia Zhou(✉), and Yunshan Jiang

School of Management Science and Real Estate, Chongqing University, Chongqing, China
jiazhou@cqu.edu.cn

Abstract. Making a phone call through smartphones seems to be quite simple, but it is not necessarily true for older adults. With the rapid iteration of mobile operating systems, older adults need to keep up with updates in a timely manner. In this case, it is still not clear how well older adults deal with updated interface of smartphones. Therefore, this study explored this question and chose basic functions as a starting point. A focus group study was conducted to identify usability problems and to propose design solutions. It comprised four stages: introduction, review, discussion, and design & presentation. Through this process, new usability issues were identified, and multiple design ideas were proposed, including interface design, operational design, and functional design, which were further categorized into fonts and icons, color and contrast, text and images, layout design, feedback function, and auxiliary function design. These ideas aim to address accidental touch issues, cognitive issues, and design flaws, thereby improving the user experience for older individuals. These design ideas might enhance the usability of smart phones for older adults.

Keywords: Focus Group · Calling App · Older Adults · Mobile Phone

1 Introduction

1.1 Calling App and Aging Population

Due to the global trend of population aging, users of smartphones are gradually aging [1, 2]. For older adults, one of the important functions of smartphones is the calling app, which can increase social support, especially for those who live alone. Many older adults are living alone around the world [3, 4]. Lonely people may rely more on their smartphones to connect with relatives, alleviate negative emotions, and gain social support [5–8].

However, older adults may face several usability issues when using mobile phones due to the decline in visual, auditory, and cognitive abilities. Visual acuity decreases sharply after the age of 50 [9, 10], and 60-year-olds require three times as much light as the average 20-year-old to see the same level of detail [9]. Similarly, changes or gradual loss of hearing are often related to aging, which is influenced by many factors such as

Q. Gao et al. (Eds.): HCII 2023, LNCS 14055, pp. 203–216, 2023.
https://doi.org/10.1007/978-3-031-48041-6_15

work exposure, diet, and genetics, but noticeable hearing damage often occurs at around 50 years of age [11]. The same changes occur with cognitive abilities as well. Schaie [12] showed that cognitive function is relatively stable before the fifth decade of life, after which decline becomes evident and the incidence of cognitive impairments increases sharply with age. And skills that depend on fast processing, accurate logical thinking, and spatial abilities are significantly affected as people age [9]. Additionally, there is evidence to support the theory that older adults have difficulty coping with tasks that require divided attention, and while problem-solving skills increase before the age of 40–50, there is a decline related to experience after this period [13]. As the decline in visual, auditory, and cognitive abilities among older adults, many usability issues arise when they use calling applications.

1.2 Related Research

Many studies have shown that older adults encounter a range of problems with the design of mobile applications, such as buttons, menus, functions, display, size, and color [14, 15]. Older adults often need to devote a significant amount of time and effort to learning and understanding complex interface layouts, leading to a decrease in their willingness to use mobile applications [16]. Some studies have found that older adults have difficulty using touch screens due to their large fingers [17], so increasing the size of buttons can help with touch operations [18]. However, simply adjusting the size of buttons has limited effects, and older adults need to understand the interaction logic of the application. Using tutorials and training can improve the performance and attitudes of older adults towards smartphones [19], but this incurs significant costs. Although there is a substantial amount of research on smartphone use among older adults and proposed solutions, few studies have focused specifically on calling applications for seniors. And related studies also need to incorporate the interaction habits of older adults. To design a calling app suitable for older adults, in-depth research on this software is needed.

Therefore, this study organized a focus group aimed at improving the interface, operation, and function design of the pre-installed calling app. The goal was to address usability issues that older adults encountered when using calling apps, as identified in our previous research, and to provide design ideas for future software development.

2 Methods

2.1 Participants

A total of 6 participants were initially recruited to participate in the focus group, but due to an unexpected issue during the experiment, one participant had to withdraw early, leaving 5 participants (4 females and 1 male) between the ages of 20 and 24 who completed the entire focus group. Participants were recruited by filling out an online questionnaire and screened by the experimenter. All participants were undergraduate or graduate students majoring in Art Design at Chongqing University and claimed to have had contact with older adults who experienced difficulties using mobile phones, particularly when using calling apps. This experience enabled them to apply their expertise in designing user interfaces that cater to the habits of older adults and address the usability issues collected. All participants signed an informed consent form before the beginning of the study. As an incentive and thanks for their participation, we provided each participant with a 90 yuan reward.

2.2 Moderator and Assistant Moderator

The moderator and the assistant moderator are a PH.D. and an assistant researcher, respectively. They specialize in older adults and have a clear understanding of the usability issues that arise for older adults when using the calling app. Furthermore, the moderator has adequate hosting skills, including being mentally prepared, controlling reactions to participants, using appropriate conclusions, etc. [20]. The assistant moderator is responsible for recording including video, audio, and text, assisting the moderator, and controlling the progress of the experiment.

2.3 Procedure

The focus group was conducted at Chongqing University for a total of 3 h, with a 20-min break provided, which ensured that each participant was able to fully engage in the discussion. To ensure the data can be fully collected, the whole process of the experiment was recorded with an iPhone camera for video and a Huawei tablet audio for audio, with the consent of all participants. The experiment is divided into four phases: introduction, review, discussion, and design & presentation.

In the introduction phase, the Moderator first introduced the purpose of this study, which was to design a calling app that meets the habits of older adults, and described the rules and considerations of the focus group. Then, each participant signed an informed consent form and filled out a questionnaire about their background including name, gender, phone number, education level, and research direction. Finally, all the participants introduced themselves briefly, including the moderator and assistant moderator, see Fig. 1(a).

During the review phase, the moderator first presented some of the usability issues that currently exist for older adults when using the calling app of smartphone and showed a video of an older adult using this software for a usability test task. Then, each participant was asked to share the usability problems they knew of when the older adults used the same or similar software. To provide them with a deeper understanding of the design flaws of this software, we distributed a smartphone to each participant, which was the same one used for the usability test, see Fig. 1(b).

In the discussion phase, first, participants used their smartphones to carry out some operational tasks that older adults often encounter when using this type of calling app (i.e., "asking and saving the phone numbers of people around you," "answering or making a call to this number" and "explore this application freely"), so that they could have a better visualization of the difficulties of using this application for older people. Participants were asked to record the problems they encountered or thought older adults would encounter during the task, and then the moderator asked everyone to share and discuss these problems. Next, in response to the operational problems shared by the participants and the usability issues introduced before, the moderator put forward some questions that would lead the participants to improve these design issues (i.e., "What functions in the calling app are useful or useless for older adults?", "How should the existing design problem be improved to resolve the difficulties of elderly users?" and "If we need to design a calling app for older adults now, what functions need to be added, removed, or hidden?"). Again, the moderator asked participants to record, share and discuss their ideas to these questions, see Fig. 1(c).

During the design & presentation phase, participants are required to draw their design concepts on paper and subsequently present them in a random order. The presentations are then subject to a democratic voting process, wherein the two individuals with the highest number of votes are awarded prizes as incentives, see Fig. 1(d).

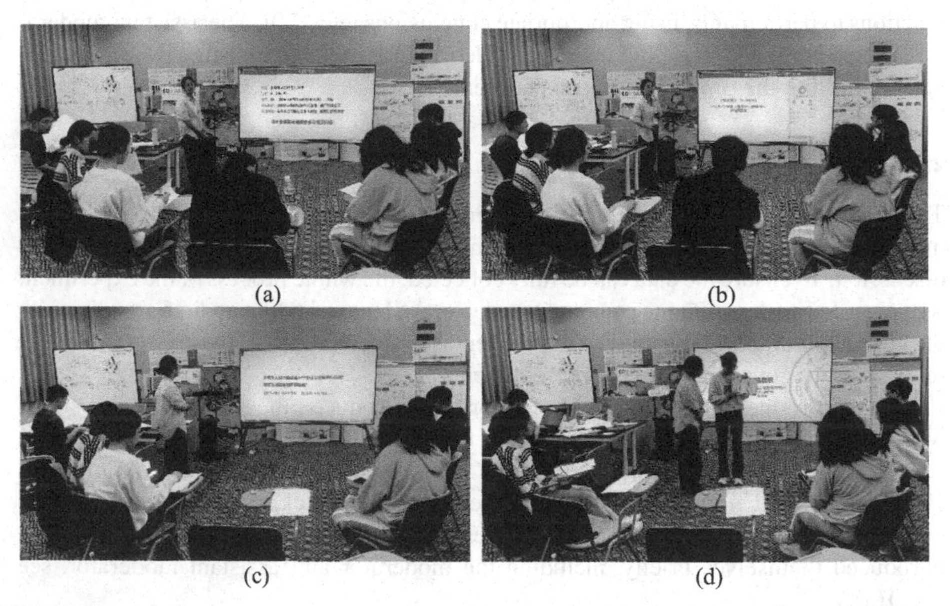

Fig. 1. On-site photos of the focus group conducted: the introduction phase (a), the review phase (b), the discussion phase (c), the design & presentation phase (d)

3 Results

A series of usability problems and design ideas were obtained, which were classified into four categories through data analysis: (a) difficulties encountered; (b) flawed design; (c) design ideas; and (d) idea visualization. Among them, (a) and (b) mainly describe the usability issues of older adults in existing designs. These issues include accidental touch issues and cognitive problems. (c) and (d) represent the ideas and visualizations for solving these usability issues, and the design ideas include interface design, operational design, and functional design. The usability issues and design ideas will be described in detail below.

3.1 Usability Issues

Difficulties Encountered

Accidental Touch: Elderly users may encounter touching issues while using the calling app due to improper operations, and due to the decline of their cognitive ability, they are not easily aware of these accidental touch problems. Therefore, these accidental touches may cause a series of user experience problems and affect their daily life, such as the mute function or hang-up function on the calling interface being accidentally touched.

P3: "When I make a phone call with my grandma, she often accidentally touches the mute button, which causes me to suddenly lose her voice." (see Fig. 2(a))
P4: "When answering the phone in summer, if you put the phone close to your ear, the sweat may cause the keyboard to be touched by mistake." (see Fig. 2(a))
P4: "Elderly users may accidentally touch the home button on the calling interface, but they do not know how to return to the calling interface." (see Fig. 2(b))
P1: "The state after accidentally touching the mute button on the calling interface is not obvious, so elderly users are difficult to notice." (see Fig. 2(a))

Cognitive Issues: Many older adults have not received enough education or training on modern technology like smartphones, and they may not have enough experience using them. Additionally, with the increase of age, their cognitive abilities decline, making it difficult for them to understand the functions of certain icons and programs. Furthermore, some designs of programs and icons may not be user-friendly for older adults, making them even more challenging for them to use.

P5: "Elderly people may have difficulty understanding many icons, especially when they lack accompanying text explanations, which can make them hard to comprehend." (see Fig. 2(c))
P1: "The speaker and recording icons on the call interface are very similar, and older adults may have difficulty distinguishing between them." (see Fig. 2(a))
P1: "Older adults' hearing abilities decline, but some may not know how to use the hands-free function to increase the volume." (see Fig. 2(a))

Design Flaws

Design Flaws: Due to age-related changes in visual acuity, older adults may require larger font sizes and icons to discern information displayed on their phone screens. Furthermore, older people may lack technical knowledge and experience, making it more difficult for them to understand some complex UI designs. This section discusses the existing design flaws that are unreasonable for older people, mainly including the unreasonable design of icons and fonts for the calling APP.

P1: "Older individuals might not understand what the three-dot APP bar on their phone means." (Fig. 2(c))
P2: "Older people may not understand the "My groups" feature in the contact list, which is even rarely used by us." (Fig. 2(c))
P2: "Some fonts and icons may need to be adjusted to make the interface more intuitive." (Fig. 2(a))

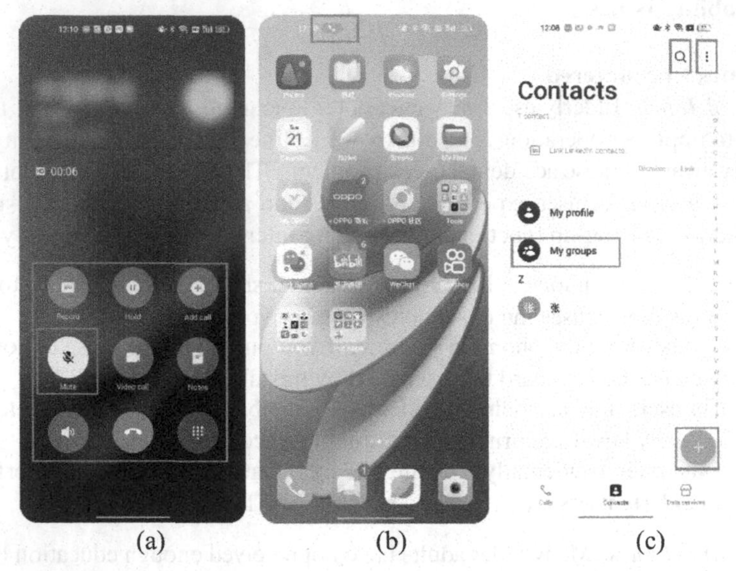

Fig. 2. The existing interface of the phone: Calling interface (a), phone home screen (b), contacts interface (c)

3.2 Design Ideas

Interface Design: The interface design needs to take the visual and cognitive abilities of older adults into consideration, so designers should use larger fonts and icons, and avoid using overly complicated color schemes or flashy designs. This can make it easier for older adults to find the desired content and reduce usage difficulty. In summary, it should be ensured that the design is simple, intuitive, and easy for older adults to use, and in line with the visual habits of the elderly.

Fonts and Icons: For elderly users, larger fonts and icons can make it easier to view information and operate, thereby improving the usability of the application. Adjusting the size of fonts and icons can be achieved by increasing the pixel size of fonts and icons, and better readability and visibility can also be achieved by redesigning fonts and icons, as well as adding text descriptions for some complex icons.

P4: "The search icon on the contact list can be made larger and centered, with added text prompts, and clicking it does not pop up a new page, but stays on the current page, similar to browser search."
P3: "Icons can be simplified and clear, with added text explanations."

Color and Contrast: The vision of older adults may be affected, so increasing contrast can help them distinguish elements on the interface more easily. Using bright colors and high contrast can make it easier for users to differentiate between different elements, thereby increasing usability.

P1: "Contact list can be arranged by frequency of contact, not just alphabetical order, making it easier for them to find contacts."
P2: "The frequency of contacts could be color coded, and a progress bar with some color could be used as a background to indicate the frequency of contacts so that older users could easily find the person they wanted to contact."
P5: "The interface of caller ID can display the number of calls made this month, and also include a progress bar as the background."
P3: "Some buttons can be distinguished by obvious colors such as green and red to indicate their on and off states, thus reminding older adults that they may have accidentally touched them."

Text and Images: The cognitive abilities of older adults may decline, so using simple and clear language and images can help them better understand the function and operation of the application. In addition, using symbolic images can make it easier for older adults to understand the function of the application, thereby improving usability.

P2: "The content in the call logs and contacts list can be separated by lines to make the hierarchy clearer."
P4: "We can add different text labels to indicate the different states of buttons, for example, adding text such as "Speaker on" or "Speaker off" next to a button to make the current state clear to older adults."

Operation Design: Older adults usually encounter difficulties in operation, so a simpler and more user-friendly operation interface should be designed. Large and obvious buttons can be used to avoid confusion and operational errors. Improving the operation design of mobile phones makes it easier for older adults to understand and master. For example, more detailed prompts and instructions can be provided to guide older adults to complete operations through visualization and other means. In addition, voice assistants or other intelligent interaction designs can be considered to make older adults' operations more intuitive and simple, improving user experience.
Layout Design: Optimizing the interface layout and design of the application can help older adults to find and use the functions of the application more easily. For example, in the calling app, placing commonly used functions in more easily accessible positions can improve usability and reduce operational difficulties for the elderly.

P2: "The button on the call interface can be arranged in order of importance, with the most important one in the middle, such as the hands-free button."
P4: "The functional icons on the calling interface can be customized and their positions adjusted."
P4: "We can design a hidden button function for the calling interface to place less frequently used functions inside and prevent accidental touches."
P5: "The edit functions of contacts are all hidden in the "more" setting, which increases interaction costs. They can be directly displayed on the current page, such as clicking on the name and avatar to edit."
P2: "You should avoid mixing multiple features or functions together in a single interface. Instead, display them separately, such as in a contact list or call log interface."

P1: "We should place the same buttons in different interfaces in the same location to enable older adults to identify them better."
P1: "The existing delete button for the dial pad is at the bottom of the screen, but I think it needs to be added to the right of the input number so that older people can find it easily."

Function Design: The focus of function design should be on the needs of older adults, such as adding some functions and services commonly used by the elderly. Based on the needs and usage habits of older adults, functions that are more suitable for them should be designed, for example, better voice recognition and hands-free calling functions can be provided to address the problem of text input and hearing loss in the elderly. It is important to ensure that the design of these functions is simple and easy to use, and does not cause additional difficulties for older adults. In addition, some operational details can be adjusted to a more user-friendly interface, such as more obvious icon prompts and clearer operation prompts.

Feedback Function: Older adults may not be confident enough in their operations, or they may not immediately realize if they accidentally touch the wrong button, resulting in some user experience problems. Therefore, clear and visible feedback should be provided in the application to help them understand whether their operations are successful or not. For example, in a calling application, feedback can be provided by changing button colors or displaying prompt messages to increase usability.

P3: "Remind older adults of accidental touch issues by setting up voice prompts for buttons."
P3: "Elderly people can easily get lost in the interface, so voice control can be added to help them."

Auxiliary Functions: Older adults have individual differences, some have enough experience with smartphones, while others have little experience, and some have good cognitive abilities, while others have significant cognitive decline. Therefore, flexible design is needed to accommodate individual differences among older adults, especially those with cognitive and physiological decline. Participants have proposed some design ideas to address this issue, including custom design and anti-misoperation design.

P2: "We can add recording and text transcription of the call log in the call log details interface so that older adults can review the previous calls."
P3: "A heart can be added to indicate the length of the call, the longer the call, the more the heart will be filled."
P1: "We can design an instructional system to help older adults learn more functions instead of simplifying them."
P5: "A system for identifying and blocking fraudulent calls is also important."

3.3 Design Idea Visualization

During the design and presentation phase of this study, participants generated preliminary design sketches based on their design ideas, exploring how to create a user-friendly and habit-compatible calling app for older adults. These design sketches aimed to better present the participants' design concepts and ideas, and serve as a reference for future feasibility analysis and the development of high-fidelity models. Figure 3 shows the design sketches resulting from some of the design ideas of P4, which included the addition of hidden button functionality in the call screen and improvements in the contact search icon.

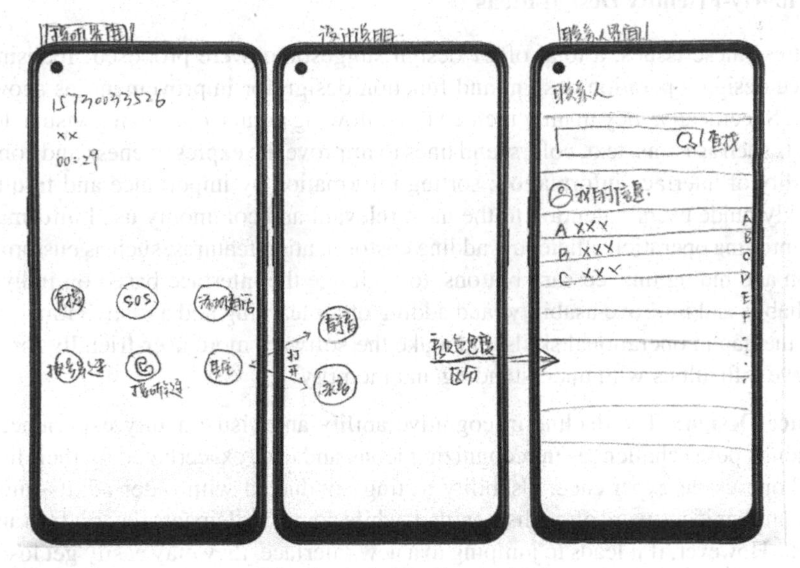

Fig. 3. A design sketch of P4

4 Discussion

4.1 Usability Issues

During the discussion stage, a set of operational tasks was designed for the participants to directly interact with the software in need of improvement. These operational tasks were commonly used by older adults, which helped the participants to identify the problems that older adults would encounter when using this software. Furthermore, to guide the participants in discovering usability issues, they were asked to record the difficulties they encountered while performing the tasks and set a question that they needed to think about, i.e., "What functions in the calling app are useful or useless for older adults?" Participants shared their answers in turn and discussed them with each other, resulting in some usability issues.

This paper identified a total of 10 usability issues, including accidental touch issues, cognitive issues, and design flaws. Two primary reasons were identified for these issues raised: Firstly, the cognitive patterns of older users do not align with the current design, which is typically based on the cognitive habits of younger people. This mismatch may lead to difficulties in understanding and using the software. Secondly, the visual and cognitive abilities of older adults decline with age compared to younger people, resulting in increased susceptibility to distractions, decreased visual perception, and hand-eye coordination. These age-related changes could result in mistakes or oversights during software usage.

4.2 Elderly-Friendly Design Ideas

To address these issues, a total of 21 design suggestions were proposed, focusing on interface design, operation design, and function design for improvement, as shown in Table 1. Specifically, they mainly include the following points: optimizing visual design elements such as icons, text, colors, and lines to improve the expressiveness and comprehensibility of interface information; sorting information by importance and frequency to quickly guide users' attention to the most relevant and commonly used information, thus improving operation efficiency; adding customization features, such as customizing position and hiding unnecessary buttons, to optimize the interface based on individual usage habits and improve usability; and adding other learning and assistive functions to bridge the gap in operational skills and make the software more user-friendly for those who have difficulties with understanding and memory.

Interface Design: The decline in cognitive ability and visual acuity experienced by older adults poses challenges in recognizing icons and text, exacerbated by their limited smartphone usage experience. Usability testing conducted with older adults unveiled that unfamiliar icons were often disregarded, while some participants resorted to random attempts. However, if it leads to jumping to a new interface, they may easily get lost in it. Therefore, to improve the user experience, improvements were implemented specifically for the contact search icon. Firstly, its size was increased to enhance visibility, and its placement was centered for improved discoverability. Secondly, text prompts were added to further help users understand the purpose of the icon. This is consistent with the findings of some studies [21], but we also have adjusted its behavior so that when users click on the search icon, they will not be redirected to a new page but will remain on the current page, making it easier for users to continue browsing. In addition, the color and contrast can be improved to make it easier for older adults to recognize the elements on the interface. Designing bright colors with contrasting differences can help older people recognize easily. For example, showing different colors for different states of important function buttons like speaker and mute, and can also add text labels to indicate the different status of the button, such as adding text "speaker on" or "speaker off" next to the button, so that users can clearly understand the current state of the button. Additionally, contacts can be sorted based on call frequency, prioritizing frequently contacted individuals at the top of the list. This approach proves more convenient for older adults, as it facilitates easier access to their frequently contacted contacts compared to the traditional alphabetical sorting method. Of course, the original alphabetical sorting method can also be retained, allowing users to choose different sorting modes according to their needs. In the contact list, a colored progress bar can be used as the background to indicate the contact's call frequency. This design can also be applied to call logs, caller IDs, and other interfaces. However, designers need to pay attention to setting different

Table 1. Summary of design ideas

	Type	Design idea
Interface Design	Fonts and Icons	Icons are larger and centered
		Text Tips
	Color and Contrast	Contacts are sorted by frequency
		Frequency Visualization
		Display and visualize call count on incoming calling interface
		Use color to distinguish button status
	Text and Images	Line separators
		Using text to distinguish button states
Operational Design	Layout Design	Sort function buttons by importance level
		Customize button positioning
		Hide non-essential buttons
		Click to edit
		simple and concise content for a user interface
		Same button, same position across interfaces
		Delete button next to input box
Functional Design	Feedback Function	"Click" voice prompt
		Voice assistant
	Auxiliary Functions	Call recording and transcription to text
		Display call duration during incoming calls
		Guidance system
		Identify and block harassing calls

levels of progress bar length to correspond to different contact frequency intervals, and also carefully choosing colors. In addition, adding separators between different contacts or call records can also help to make the hierarchy more clear.

Operational Design: Due to the lack of experience in using smartphones and the fact that the interaction design of smartphones may not be very user-friendly for the elderly, they may not fully understand many of the interaction logic of smartphones. Therefore, it is necessary to improve the design of some functions that may be difficult for older adults to operate. Following comprehensive discussions and considerations of usability issues within this category, proposed improvements to the layout design have been put forth. In the call interface, there are often multiple functional buttons, such as mute and hands-free. Several design ideas have been formulated to optimize the arrangement of these buttons. Firstly, they can be sorted by the importance of their functions, placing the most important ones in the middle and allowing users to customize button placement.

Secondly, an "other" button can be added to hide less frequently used functions and prevent older adults from accidentally touching them. Another option is to add a "button lock" feature to lock some buttons and prevent older adults from accidentally touching them. Additionally, the erase button ought to be on the right side of the dial pad rather than at the bottom to make it easier for older adults to remove erroneously entered phone numbers. Moreover, for more intuitive and convenient editing of contact information, older adults can directly click on the corresponding content such as name and avatar, without the need to click on the edit button. Furthermore, on different interfaces, we should place the same buttons in the same position, which can help older adults better remember and use these buttons.

Function Design: In addition to addressing usability issues, the enhancement of user experience for older adults can be achieved through the addition of various features. For instance, the incorporation of feedback and assistance functions proves beneficial. To provide feedback, voice prompts can be implemented for buttons, aiding older adults in understanding the actions they are performing. Additionally, AI-powered voice control capabilities can be introduced to assist them in navigating the interface. In terms of assistance, fostering a sense of connection between older adults and their loved ones can be achieved by incorporating a heart-shaped icon in call records. This visual aid gradually fills up to indicate the duration of the call, enhancing the assisted feature. Given the potential memory decline experienced by older adults, offering call recording and transcription features on the detailed call record interface can assist them in reviewing the content of their conversations. It is also crucial to identify and block scam calls. Implementing flags and warnings for identified scam calls serves as an important preventive measure. Furthermore, considering that older adults often have the time and inclination to learn new things, the inclusion of a guide system and tutorials can facilitate their mastery of additional operations and functions, thereby elevating their overall user experience.

4.3 Limitations

There are some limitations to this focus group. First, although the current sample size met the minimum requirements [20], future studies may require recruiting more participants to obtain more design ideas. Second, due to the purpose of the focus group was to propose design ideas for improving usability issues of older adults, the participants were graduate or undergraduate students with design backgrounds, but one of the tasks of the focus group was to have subjects pretend to be older adults to perform the task, which may be somewhat different from real older adults.

5 Conclusion

This study conducted focus groups on usability issues of the cell phone calling app for the elderly. Through four stages of introduction, review, discussion, and design & presentation, some new usability issues were proposed in addition to the existing usability issues, mainly including accidental touch issues, cognitive issues, and design flaws. And many design ideas were obtained, mainly including interface design, operation design, and function design, which were further divided into fonts and icons, color and contrast, text and images, layout design, feedback function, and design of auxiliary functions.

The proposed design ideas in this study are based on in-depth research and exploration of some common problems encountered by older adults in using the calling app. The implementation of these design ideas can help improve the user experience of older adults in using the calling app, reduce the barriers they may encounter in application usage, and improve their quality of life. Future research should focus on validating the current findings by visualizing the design ideas into high-fidelity prototypes, and conducting usability tests with older adults while continuously iterating the design.

Acknowledgment. The authors would like to acknowledge the support from National Natural Science Foundation of China (72171030).

References

1. Percentage of total population aged 60 years or over. https://www.who.int/data/maternal-newborn-child-adolescent-ageing/indicator-explorer-new/mca/percentage-of-total-population-aged-60-years-or-over. Last accessed 04 Apr 2023
2. Ageing and health. https://www.who.int/news-room/fact-sheets/detail/ageing-and-health. Last accessed 04 Apr 2023
3. Stepler, R.: Smaller share of women ages 65 and older are living alone (2016)
4. Liu, N., et al.: Health-related quality of life among elderly individuals living alone in an urban area of Shaanxi Province, China: a cross-sectional study. J. Int. Med. Res. **48**(4), 0300060520913146 (2020)
5. Bian, M., Leung, L.: Linking loneliness, shyness, smartphone addiction symptoms, and patterns of smartphone use to social capital. Soc. Sci. Comput. Rev. **33**(1), 61–79 (2015)
6. Kim, J.-H.: Smartphone-mediated communication vs face-to-face interaction: two routes to social support and problematic use of smartphone. Comput. Hum. Behavior. **67**, 282–291 (2017)
7. Lapointe, L., Boudreau-Pinsonneault, C., Vaghefi, I.: Is smartphone usage truly smart? A qualitative investigation of IT addictive behaviors. In: 2013 46th Hawaii international conference on system sciences, pp. 1063–1072. IEEE (2013)
8. Kahlon, M.K., et al.: Effect of layperson-delivered, empathy-focused program of telephone calls on loneliness, depression, and anxiety among adults during the covid-19 pandemic: a randomized clinical trial. JAMA Psychiat. **78**(6), 616–622 (2021)
9. Haigh, R.: The ageing process: a challenge for design. Appl. Ergon. **24**(1), 9–14 (1993)
10. Steenbekkers, L.P.A., Dirken, J.M., Van Beijsterveldt, C.E.M.: Design-relevant functional capacities of the elderly, assessed in the delft gerontechnology project. From Experience Innovation-IEA **97**, 612–614 (1997)
11. Takeda, S., Morioka, I., Miyashita, K., Okumura, A., Yoshida, Y., Matsumoto, K.: Age variation in the upper limit of hearing. Eur. J. Appl. Physiol. **65**, 403–408 (1992)
12. Schaie, K.W.: The hazards of cognitive aging. Gerontologist **29**(4), 484–493 (1989)
13. Smith, S., Norris, B., Peebles, L.: The Handbook of Measurements and Capabilities of the Older Adult–Data for Design Safety. Department of Trade and Industry of the United Kingdom, Nottingham, UK (2000)

14. Azuddin, M., Abd Malik, S., Abdullah, L.M., Mahmud, M.: Older people and their use of mobile devices: Issues, purpose and context. In: The 5th International Conference on Information and Communication Technology for the Muslim World (ICT4M), pp. 1–6. IEEE (2014)
15. Nasir, M., Hassan, H., Jomhari, N.: The use of mobile phones by elderly: a study in Malaysia perspectives. J. Soc. Sci. **4**(2), 123–127 (2008)
16. Leung, R., Findlater, L., McGrenere, J., Graf, P., Yang, J.: Multi-layered interfaces to improve older adults' initial learnability of mobile applications. ACM Trans. Accessible Comput. (TACCESS) **3**(1), 1–30 (2010)
17. Hwangbo, H., Yoon, S.H., Jin, B.S., Han, Y.S., Ji, Y.G.: A study of pointing performance of elderly users on smartphones. Int. J. Human-Comput. Interact. **29**(9), 604–618 (2013)
18. Kobayashi, M., Hiyama, A., Miura, T., Asakawa, C., Hirose, M., Ifukube, T.: Elderly user evaluation of mobile touchscreen interactions. In: Campos, P., Graham, N., Jorge, J., Nunes, N., Palanque, P., Winckler, M. (eds.) INTERACT 2011. LNCS, vol. 6946, pp. 83–99. Springer, Heidelberg (2011). https://doi.org/10.1007/978-3-642-23774-4_9
19. Leitao, R., Silva, P.A.: A study of novice older adults and gestural interaction on smartphones (2013)
20. Krueger, R.A., Casey, M.A.: Designing and conducting focus group interviews. Citeseer (2002)
21. Yang, M., Huang, H.: Research on interaction design of intelligent mobile phone for the elderly based on the user experience. In: Zhou, J., Salvendy, G. (eds.) ITAP 2015. LNCS, vol. 9193, pp. 528–536. Springer, Cham (2015). https://doi.org/10.1007/978-3-319-20892-3_51

Effects of Older Adults' Subjective Health Literacy on Health-Oriented Usage Intention of WeChat: Based on Social Media Affordances

Xindi Wang[1](✉), Xiaokang Song[2], and Yuxiang (Chris) Zhao[1]

[1] School of Economics and Management, Nanjing University of Science and Technology, Nanjing 210094, China
wxdkust@163.com

[2] School of Management, Xuzhou Medical University, Xuzhou 221004, China

Abstract. Given the aging population and the rapid development of digital society, concerns about promoting older adults' health literacy are increasing. The broad impact of social media can play a vital role in health empowerment for older adults. Drawing upon the perspectives of social media affordances, we constructed a research model that integrates four affordance types, searching, meta-voicing, recommendation, and communication, to identify the effects of affordances and older adults' subjective health literacy that contribute to their health-oriented usage intention of WeChat. Online survey data from 163 older adults (above 55 years) were collected and analyzed using partial least squares-structural equation modeling. This variable of subjective health literacy was divided into three dimensions: health knowledge, health management, and health skills. The results indicated that older adults' subjective health literacy has significant positive effects on their health-oriented usage intention of WeChat. We also found that meta-voicing affordance, recommendation affordance, and communication affordance have positive influences on health knowledge and health management, and searching affordance, recommendation affordance, and communication affordance have positive effects on health skills. This study enriched the understanding of elders" subjective health literacy on their health-oriented usage intention of social media and contributed to the literature on health-related ICT usage targets of older adults.

Keywords: WeChat · Subjective Health literacy · Older Adults · Social Media Affordance

1 Introduction

With the aging and digitalization of society, the research field of information behavior has gradually begun to focus on health literacy related to the ability of older adults to use information and communication technologies (ICTs) [1]. Social media apps on smartphones provide new digital tools for elder users to obtain health information, especially WeChat, which has become part of Chinese users' daily routine, offering multi-functional features for healthcare purposes and great opportunities for improving health literacy

Q. Gao et al. (Eds.): HCII 2023, LNCS 14055, pp. 217–230, 2023.
https://doi.org/10.1007/978-3-031-48041-6_16

[2]. Nowadays, elders can use WeChat for health-oriented purposes, specifically in the form of accessing health knowledge through searching functions, reading health-related articles or short videos from WeChat official accounts, sharing health information, or discussing health problems with friends. Given the concern about promoting the health literacy of older adults, it is necessary to explore the important role of health-oriented usage of WeChat in improving the health literacy of older adults.

Health literacy has been identified as a public health goal and a significant challenge facing healthcare globally [3]. With the rapid development of digital health, the lack of health literacy blocks older adults' accessibility to professional health knowledge or their engagement in health-related activities online. Social media greatly encourages the public to engage in health information behavior, and this successively attracts the older adult population for health-oriented usage [4]. Chinese elders use WeChat as a necessary social tool, which has become indispensable in their lives, drawing their attention to more health-related activities and increasing their health literacy. To promote older adults' participation in health management, improve their health skills, and facilitate their access to health knowledge, it is essential to explore how to promote older adults' health literacy through WeChat and the mechanisms that influence their health-oriented usage of WeChat.

Affordances are the possibilities of goal-directed actions that an object provides to a goal-oriented actor [5]. Social media affordances enable users to understand what social media is and how it works [6]. The affordances of WeChat can support older adults in their health information behaviors and imperceptibly influence their health literacy. Previous studies have explored whether older adults' assessment of health information differs according to their subjective level of health literacy [7]. Subjective health literacy can evaluate people's confidence in learning, understanding, and using healthcare-related information. This paper aims to identify the factors that contribute to older adults' subjective health literacy and their health-oriented usage intention of WeChat based on social media affordances.

Therefore, we conducted an empirical study of health-oriented usage intention among the older adult population. Specifically, this study aimed to answer the following research questions:

RQ1. How do WeChat's affordances influence older adults' subjective health literacy?
RQ2. How do older adults' subjective health literacy affect their health-oriented usage intention of WeChat?

2 Theoretical Background

2.1 Social Media Affordances

Social media affordances can meet users' specific needs and allow them to utilize social media app features for their purposes [6]. By perceiving social media affordances, users can adjust them to their preferred usage. WeChat, as one of the most widely used social media apps, has great potential for promoting health literacy. With consideration of social media affordances, we developed a research model that incorporates searching affordance, meta-voicing affordance, recommendation affordance, and communication affordance to examine how these affordances affect older adults' subjective health literacy in the context of WeChat.

WeChat's searching affordance refers to the extent to which users believe that WeChat functions offer the opportunity to seek and access the information they need. Previous studies have pointed out that search functions can help users accurately locate relevant information when using social networks [8, 9]. WeChat users can actively locate useful health information by using the searching affordance feature. For instance, users can accurately search for health information by using keywords on the WeChat official accounts they follow. In the context of this study, searching affordance functions can enable older users to acquire the health information they need, locate appropriate information sources, expand their health knowledge, and address health problems. Thus, we believe that WeChat's searching affordance can help older adults obtain health information more easily and effectively, and empower them with the skills to manage their health needs or health hazards. Based on this, we propose the following hypotheses:

H1a: Searching affordance of WeChat positively influences older adults' health knowledge.
H1b: Searching affordance of WeChat positively influences older adults' health skills.

Meta-voicing refers to users' online reactions to others' presence, content, or activities on social media platforms [6]. Scholars identify meta-voicing affordance as the set of functions supporting users in their effort to conduct conversations. Previous studies have shown that meta-voicing affordance can motivate users' engagement on social media and promote knowledge exchange among users [10]. In the context of WeChat, meta-voicing affordance allows users to perceive various functions supporting online interactive reactions, such as "liking", commenting, sharing health information in moments or video channels, labeling "viewing" to health-related articles, or adding them to the floating window. Based on users' actions, we believe that their reactions to health-related content reflect their awareness of health management. In this study, we hypothesize that older adults who are aware of health management would react to health-related content or others' activities on WeChat and engage in health information behaviors, such as saving useful health knowledge in their "favorites" for future reference, complying with health advice, and engaging in exercises or maintaining a balanced diet to improve health. Thus, we hypothesized the following:

H2a: Meta-voicing affordance of WeChat positively influences older adults' health knowledge.
H2b: Meta-voicing affordance of WeChat positively influences older adults' health management.

With the development of technology and information systems, current social media platforms have algorithm technology for accurately recommending useful and attractive content to users based on their operation records. Algorithm-based recommendations of social media can provide users with the health information they need and display helpful knowledge recommended by the algorithm on the user interface of applications. Previous studies have found that recommendation affordance can contribute to users' perceived immersion and trustworthiness and promote their willingness to use social media for health-related purposes [11]. Furthermore, recommendation affordance allows users to obtain useful health information [12]. In the context of WeChat, recommendation affordance can enable users to receive health information relevant to their functions, such as prioritizing information that is more relevant to the user on the search/viewing interface. This helps users proactively or passively acquire health knowledge to deal with health problems, improve health skills, and support users in health management [13]. Additionally, the strategy of professional doctors' teams popularizing health knowledge on WeChat official accounts or video channel accounts increases the proportion of high-quality health information resources in WeChat, which contributes to algorithm-based recommendation affordance to continuously output health knowledge that fulfills users' preferences, especially those that improve older users' health skills and their willingness to manage their health. Thus, we hypothesize the following:

H3a: Recommendation affordance of WeChat positively influences older adults' health knowledge.
H3b: Recommendation affordance of WeChat positively influences older adults' health management.
H3c: Recommendation affordance of WeChat positively influences older adults' health skills.

Communication affordance allows users to directly communicate with each other on a social media app, fulfilling their needs to establish social relationships or obtain information [14]. WeChat integrates communication affordance to empower users with accessibility to health information and the exchange of health information with friends [11]. Communication affordance facilitates the continuous exchange of knowledge among users [10], and provides older adults with valuable health information for health management and enhancing their health skills. Moreover, communication affordance allows older adults to discuss health experiences with friends or seek health-related advice from caregivers. With the help of communication affordance, older adults can access health knowledge while having health-related communication with others, which improves their awareness and abilities of health management and their health skills. Therefore, we hypothesize the following:

H4a: Communication affordance of WeChat positively influences older adults' health knowledge.
H4b: Commendation affordance of WeChat positively influences older adults' health management.
H4c: Commendation affordance of WeChat positively influences older adults' health skills.

2.2 Subjective Health Literacy and Usage Intention

Individuals' health literacy refers to their abilities to obtain, understand, and use health information to enrich health knowledge, improve health skills, and manage health behaviors to maintain their health [15]. In the context of this study, older adults' subjective health literacy refers to the extent of the health knowledge, skills, and behaviors they possess. Previous studies have shown that older users' health literacy can promote their health information behaviors online, such as seeking professional health advice or solutions to health problems [16]. For example, older people's engagement with health information on social media can improve their health literacy and self-healthcare management, and encourage their active interactivity online, such as sharing health information and liking health articles [1]. Nowadays, Chinese elders are increasingly using WeChat for health information engagement, such as browsing health knowledge, subscribing to healthcare-related WeChat official accounts, or having health communication with others. We believe that older adults who have relatively adequate health knowledge, health skills, and abilities in health management are more likely to consciously use WeChat's health-related functions to fulfill their health needs and improve their health literacy. Thus, we hypothesize the following:

H5: Older adults' health knowledge would positively influence their health-oriented usage intention.
H6: Older adults' health management would positively influence their health-oriented usage intention.
H7: Older adults' health skills would positively influence their health-oriented usage intention.

In the end, the conceptual model was built as shown in Fig. 1.

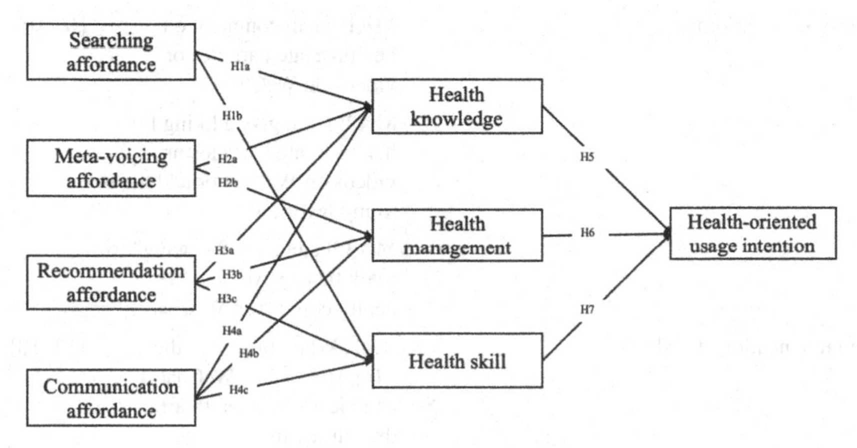

Fig. 1. Research Model.

3 Methodology

3.1 Measures

All construct items in this study were adapted from existing studies. Each item was measured according to a seven-point Likert scale ranging from 1 (strongly disagree) to 7 (strongly agree). There were two stages of questionnaire formation. Initially, we invited 3 senior citizens with health-oriented experience in WeChat usage to participate in the initial questionnaire. Based on their feedback, we revised the questionnaire and obtained the final version. The construct items and references are detailed in Table 1.

Table 1. Research items and references.

Constructs	Items	Source
Searching affordance	SA1: I can easily find health information using WeChat's search functions	[9, 17]
	SA2: I can search for medical and health-related accounts or mini-programs on WeChat	
	SA3: I can find informative articles and videos on health topics through WeChat's search functions	
	SA4: WeChat's search functions allow me to explore health topics that interest me	
Meta-voicing affordance	MA1: I can comment on health-related articles or videos on WeChat	[6, 10]
	MA2: I can give a liking for health-related articles or videos on WeChat or add them to my favorites	
	MA3: I can click "viewing" to mark that I have seen the health content on WeChat	
Recommendation affordance	RA1: When browsing the "Top stories" on WeChat, I can view some health articles that attract my attention	[13, 18]
	RA2: Health-related WeChat public accounts to which I subscribe recommend health knowledge content for me	
	RA3: The health video account I follow on WeChat recommends valuable health information for me	
Communication affordance	CA1: I can discuss some health experiences with others on WeChat	[14, 19]

(*continued*)

Table 1. (*continued*)

Constructs		Items	Source
		CA2: I can communicate some health knowledge with others on WeChat	
		CA3: I can consult with others about health-related advice on WeChat	
Subjective health literacy	Health knowledge	HK1: I know of some WeChat health-related public accounts or video accounts	[20–23]
		HK2: I have knowledge about healthy living	
		HK3: I have knowledge about health topics such as diet, exercise, and more	
	Health management	HM1: I will make lifestyle changes according to the health knowledge I have gained	
		HM2: I will take disease prevention seriously based on the health knowledge I have acquired	
		HM3: I will take action to maintain my health, such as having a balanced diet or exercising regularly	
	Health skill	HS1: I can effectively prevent diseases	
		HS2: I am skilled in using WeChat's health information searching tools	
		HS3: I can utilize health information on WeChat to avoid potential health risks	
Health-related usage intention		HUI1: I will continue to view health-related content on WeChat	[1, 13]
		HUI2: I will search for health knowledge on WeChat	
		HUI3: I will use the medical and health services of WeChat's mini-programs or public accounts	

3.2 Data Collection and Sample

Although the definition of "older adults" varies in the literature [24], the current study selected people over 55 years of age as potential respondents, as this population segment is often studied in relation to health-related usage of social media among older adults. Additionally, this age group is associated with a greater potential need and concern for health literacy. To examine the proposed research model, the study conducted an online survey focused on older adult users over 55 years of age in China and adopted the snowball sampling approach for data collection. A total of 163 questionnaires were collected. Table 2 provides a summary of the demographic information of the participants, with most participants aged between 55 and 60 years. Among the respondents, 52.8% were male and 47.2% were female, and about 23.3% reported being completely healthy.

Table 2. Demographic information of participants (N = 163).

Measure	Items	Frequency	Percentage (%)
Gender	Male	86	52.8
	Female	77	47.2
Age	55–60	105	64.4
	61–65	24	14.7
	66–70	9	5.5
	71–75	12	7.4
	76–80	7	4.3
	Over 81	6	3.7
Health status	Very well	38	23.3
	Good	71	43.6
	Poor	47	28.8
	Very poor	7	4.3

4 Results and the Analysis

The use of partial least squares (PLS) to test the proposed model and Smart PLS to test both the measurement and structural models was utilized in this study. The statistical significance levels of the structural model path coefficients were verified using the bootstrapping technique.

4.1 The Measurement Model

The reliability and validity of the research model were evaluated using various data analyses. Reliability tests the consistency and stability of survey data. Cronbach's alpha values and composite reliability were used to assess the internal consistency of the model constructs. Cronbach's alpha values exceeded the recommended level of 0.6, indicating acceptable reliability [25]. The CR values exceeded the recommended level of 0.7, indicating good reliability. The AVE values were used to assess the convergent and discriminant validity of the model. The AVE values of all constructs exceeded the threshold of 0.5, indicating good convergence validity, and proving that the items effectively represent the corresponding constructs [26]. The reliability and convergence validity results are presented in Table 3. The diagonal of Table 4, which is the square root of AVE, had values that were higher than the inner construct correlations, indicating that the measurement model has good discriminant validity.

Table 3. Reliability and convergence validity

Construct	Composite reliability	AVE	Cronbach's alpha
SA	0.959	0.854	0.943
MA	0.957	0.881	0.932
RA	0.950	0.863	0.921
CA	0.970	0.916	0.954
HK	0.957	0.882	0.933
HM	0.966	0.904	0.947
HS	0.958	0.886	0.936
HUI	0.972	0.919	0.956

Table 4. Discriminant validity

Construct	CA	HK	HM	HS	MA	RA	SA	HUI
CA	**0.957**							
HK	0.772	**0.939**						
HM	0.760	0.866	**0.951**					
HS	0.809	0.907	0.854	**0.941**				
MA	0.807	0.815	0.795	0.813	**0.939**			
RA	0.699	0.797	0.765	0.855	0.778	**0.929**		
SA	0.615	0.681	0.655	0.752	0.678	0.755	**0.924**	
HUI	0.764	0.854	0.855	0.856	0.808	0.778	0.669	**0.959**

4.2 The Structural Model

The test of the structural model included the examination of path coefficients and the corresponding significance levels. Figure 2 presents the results of the PLS analysis (see Fig. 2). The hypothesis testing results are listed in Table 5. We also adopted the bootstrapping technique that can directly test the influence of the independent variable on the dependent variable. The results showed the positive effects of meta-voicing affordance, recommendation affordance, and communication affordance on older adults' subjective health literacy of health knowledge, supporting H2a, H3a, and H4a. In addition, there are positive effects of meta-voicing affordance, recommendation affordance, and communication affordance on elders' subjective health literacy of health management, supporting H2b, H3b, and H4b. Moreover, the results showed the positive effects of searching affordance, recommendation affordance, and communication affordance on older adults' subjective health literacy of health skills, supporting H1b, H3c, and H4c. We also found that older adults' subjective health literacy can positively influence their health-oriented usage intention of WeChat, according to the results about the significant influence of health knowledge (H5), health management (H6), and health skill (H7) on health-related usage intention. Results indicated that the influences of the searching affordance on elder users' health knowledge are not statistically significant. Hence, H1a is not supported.

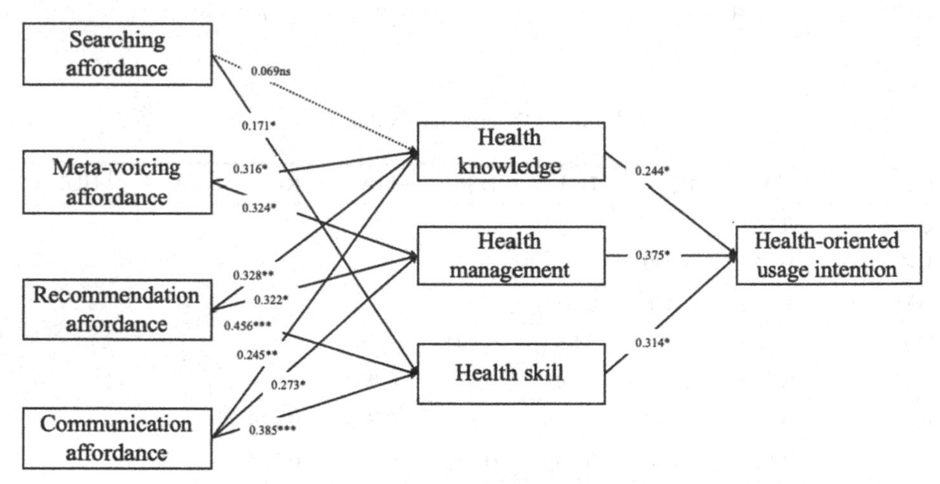

Fig. 2. Structural equation model with standardized coefficients. Note: * $p < .05$, ** $p < .01$, *** $p < .001$, ns = nonsignificant, Nonsignificant paths are presented by a dashed line.

In total, twelve of thirteen hypotheses were supported, indicating a strong relationship between WeChat's affordances, older adults' subjective health literacy, and their health-oriented usage intentions. This suggests that WeChat can be a useful platform for promoting subjective health literacy and facilitating health-oriented behaviors among older adults in China.

Table 5. Results of hypothesis testing

Hypothesis	Paths	Path coefficients	t-value	p-value	Hypothesis validation
H1a	SA->HK	0.069	0.788	0.431	Not Supported
H1b	SA->HS	0.171	2.221	0.027	Supported
H2a	MA->HK	0.316	2.266	0.024	Supported
H2b	MA->HM	0.324	2.412	0.016	Supported
H3a	RA->HK	0.328	2.705	0.007	Supported
H3b	RA->HM	0.322	2.509	0.012	Supported
H3c	RA->HS	0.456	5.144	0	Supported
H4a	CA->HK	0.245	2.643	0.008	Supported
H4b	CA->HM	0.273	2.472	0.014	supported
H4c	CA->HS	0.385	4.909	0	Supported
H5	HK->HUI	0.244	2.049	0.041	Supported
H6	HM->HSI	0.375	2.612	0.009	Supported
H7	HS->HIS	0.314	2.032	0.043	Supported

5 Discussion

5.1 Key Findings

These findings suggest that WeChat can be a valuable tool for promoting health literacy and health-oriented behaviors among older adults in China. Specifically, the searching, meta-voicing, recommendation, and communication affordances of WeChat can contribute to older adults' subjective health literacy, which, in turn, can enhance their health-oriented usage intention of WeChat. This study highlights the importance of considering the affordances of social media platforms in promoting health literacy and health-oriented behaviors among older adults. It also emphasizes the importance of enhancing older adult' subjective health literacy, particularly their awareness of health management, to encourage health-oriented behaviors.

First, the results showed that meta-voicing affordance, recommendation affordance, and communication affordance have significant effects on older adults' health knowledge and their health management, which includes daily health-related lifestyles such as maintaining a balanced diet, engaging in proper exercise, and avoiding smoking and drinking. WeChat's algorithm-based recommendation system can suggest health-related content that aligns with users' interests and needs. Through meta-voicing affordance, users can react to this content by marking it as "viewing" and adding useful health information to their favorite list for review when they conduct health management. Furthermore, communication on WeChat is an effective way for older adults to obtain health knowledge, exchange health information, and share health experiences, thereby enhancing their awareness to manage their health.

Secondly, we found that searching affordance, recommendation affordance, and communication affordance can positively influence older adults' health skills. Health skill refers to one's ability to obtain and understand information related to their health and self-rescue ability. Elder users can use WeChat's searchability functions to seek health knowledge or learn more health skills. Health-related WeChat official accounts or video channels would regularly recommend health-related content to their followers through recommendation affordance. Through meta-voicing affordance, when users browse useful health information, they can comment on the content for a better understanding of the content. They can also give a like or communicate with others about their health problems to acquire more information and enhance their health skills. However, we also found that while searching affordance has a significant effect on older adults' health skills, it does not have the same effect on health knowledge. This may be because elder users who have basic health skills may use WeChat's searchability functions to seek health information but may not be satisfied with the health knowledge they obtained and may not think that WeChat can accurately locate the health information they need.

5.2 Theoretical Implications

Overall, this study has made a significant contribution to the understanding of how social media affordance can impact older adults' subjective health literacy and health-oriented usage intention. By identifying the antecedents of older adults' subjective health literacy, the study provides valuable insights into how social media platforms can be designed to enhance older adults' health knowledge, management, and skills. Additionally, the study's findings establish a clear link between subjective health literacy and health-oriented usage intention, highlighting the importance of designing social media applications that meet older adults' specific health-related needs. The theoretical insights generated by this study can inform the development of more effective and inclusive health-related social media applications for older adults, helping to bridge the digital gap and ensure that older adults can access the benefits of digital health technologies.

5.3 Practical Implications

Our research model on older adults' subjective health literacy has several practical implications. Firstly, it offers ideas for social media apps that can attract older adults to engage in health management, improve their health knowledge, and develop their health skills. Secondly, it reminds social media designers to develop an accessible search engine that can provide adequate and valuable health information and accurately recommend useful health knowledge to elder users using algorithmic techniques. Thirdly, social media platforms should allow elders to freely communicate with healthcare professionals and support them in bookmarking or remembering the health information they need. This will encourage older adults to interact with health-related functions on social media.

6 Limitations and Future Research

This research has several limitations. Firstly, the study mainly focused on older adults' subjective health literacy and explored their self-reported level of health knowledge, health management, and health skills without considering the actual level of participants' health literacy. Secondly, the study only focused on older adults who had experience using health-related functions of social media and did not include elderly individuals who could not use mobile phones. Thirdly, the research questionnaire only investigated elder individuals in the form of text, and the questionnaires were obtained online through self-reports, which may have led to recall bias. Future research should include a wider range of users among the senior population, and a longitudinal study can be conducted to measure the actual health literacy of the elderly and explore the relationship between health literacy and more specific health information behavior, such as seeking or sharing.

Acknowledgment. This study was supported by the National Science Foundation of China (72204210) and Postgraduate Research & Practice Innovation Program of Jiangsu Province (No. KYCX22_0550).

References

1. Zhang, X., Xu, X., Cheng, J.: WeChatting for health: what motivates older adult engagement with health information. Healthcare **9**(6), 751 (2021)
2. Zhang, Y., Xia, T., Huang, L., Yin, M., Sun, M., Huang, J., et al.: Factors influencing user engagement of health information disseminated by Chinese provincial centers for disease control and prevention on WeChat: observational study. JMIR Mhealth Uhealth **7**(6), e12245 (2019)
3. Rootman, I.: Literacy and health in Canada: is it really a problem? Can. J. Public Health **94**(6), 405 (2003)
4. Shang, L., Zhou, J., Zuo, M.: Understanding older adults' intention to share health information on social media: the role of health belief and information processing. Internet Res. **31**(1), 100–122 (2021)
5. Zhao, Y.C., Zhang, Y., Tang, J., Song, S.: Affordances for information practices: theorizing engagement among people, technology, and sociocultural environments. J. Documentation **77**, 229–250 (2020)
6. Karahanna, E., Xu, S.X., Xu, Y., Zhang, N.A.: The needs–affordances–features perspective for the use of social media. MIS Q. **42**(3), 737–756 (2018)
7. An, S., Muturi, N.: Subjective health literacy and older adults' assessment of direct-to-consumer prescription drug ads. J. Health Commun. **16**(sup3), 242–255 (2011)
8. Rice, R.E., Evans, S.K., Pearce, K.E., et al.: Organizational media affordances: operationalization and associations with media use. J. Commun. **67**(1), 106–130 (2017)
9. Chan, T.K., Cheung, C.M., Wong, R.Y.: Cyberbullying on social networking sites: the crime opportunity and affordance perspectives. J. Manag. Inf. Syst. **36**(2), 574–609 (2019)
10. Majchrzak, A., Faraj, S., Kane, G.C., Azad, B.: The contradictory influence of social media affordances on online communal knowledge sharing. J. Comput.-Mediat. Commun. **19**(1), 38–55 (2013)
11. Song, S., Zhao, Y.C., Yao, X., Ba, Z., Zhu, Q.: Short video apps as a health information source: an investigation of affordances, user experience and users' intention to continue the use of TikTok. Internet Res. **31**(6), 2120–2142 (2021)
12. Zhou, Q., Lee, C.S., Sin, S.C.J.: Beyond mandatory use: probing the affordances of social media for formal learning in the voluntary context. Proc. Assoc. Inf. Sci. Technol. **55**(1), 608–617 (2018)
13. Zhang, L., Jung, E.H.: WeChatting for health: an examination of the relationship between motivations and active engagement. Health Commun. **34**(14), 1764–1774 (2019)

14. Junglas, I., Goel, L., Abraham, C., Ives, B.: The social component of information systems—How sociability contributes to technology acceptance. J. Assoc. Inf. Syst. **14**(10), 1 (2013)
15. Ye, X.H., Yang, Y., Gao, Y.H., Chen, S.D., Xu, Y.: Status and determinants of health literacy among adolescents in Guangdong, China. Asian Pac. J. Cancer Prev. **15**(20), 8735–8740 (2014)
16. Tennant, B., et al.: EHealth literacy and web 2.0 health information seeking behaviors among baby boomers and older adults. J. Med. Internet Res. **17**(3), e70 (2015)
17. Hsu, L.C., Wang, K.Y., Chih, W.H., Lin, K.Y.: Investigating the ripple effect in virtual communities: an example of facebook fan pages. Comput. Hum. Behav. **51**, 483–494 (2015)
18. Saad, N.M., Alias, R.A., Ismail, Z.: Initial framework on identifying factors influencing individuals' usage of telehealth. In: 2013 International Conference on Research and Innovation in Information Systems, ICRIIS, pp. 174–179. IEEE (2013)
19. Montanaro, E., Artusi, C.A., Zibetti, M., Lopiano, L.: Complex therapies for advanced Parkinson's disease: what is the role of doctor-patient communication? Neurol. Sci. **40**, 2357–2364 (2019)
20. He, Y., et al.: A reliability and validity study of the electronic health literacy scale among stroke patients in China. Top. Stroke Rehabil. **20**, 1–9 (2021)
21. Stellefson, M., et al.: Reliability and validity of the telephone-based eHealth literacy scale among older adults: cross-sectional survey. J. Med. Internet Res. **19**(10), e362 (2017)
22. Sudbury-Riley, L., FitzPatrick, M., Schulz, P.J.: Exploring the measurement properties of the eHealth literacy scale (eHEALS) among baby boomers: a multinational test of measurement invariance. J. Med. Internet Res. **19**(2), e53 (2017)
23. Chung, S.Y., Nahm, E.S.: Testing reliability and validity of the eHealth Literacy Scale (eHEALS) for older adults recruited online. Comput., Inf., Nurs.: CIN **33**(4), 150 (2015)
24. Zhao, Y.C., Zhao, M., Song, S.: Online health information seeking behaviors among older adults: systematic scoping review. J. Med. Internet Res. **24**(2), e34790 (2022)
25. Jen, W., Hu, K.: Application of perceived value model to identify factors affecting passengers' repurchase intentions on city bus: a case of the Taipei metropolitan area. Transportation **30**(3), 307–327 (2003)
26. Straub, D., Boudreau, M.C., Gefen, D.: Validation guidelines for IS positivist research. Commun. Assoc. Inf. Syst. **13**(1), 24 (2004)

Engagement and Addiction Dilemma Among Older Adults in Short Video Applications: Socio-technical and Self-control Perspectives

Dawei Wu(✉) and Yuxiang (Chris) Zhao

Nanjing University of Science and Technology, Nanjing 210094, China
fyawdw@163.com

Abstract. Short videos are becoming one of the most popular forms of entertainment for older adults and even an integral part of their lives. However, this also raises the dilemma of meaningful engagement and addiction when older adults engage with short video apps. The current research aims to explore the mechanism underlying engagement and addiction dilemma when older adults use short video apps. We employ the socio-technical and self-control perspectives to highlight the influences of social, technical, and individual factors on engagement and addiction dilemma. We constructed the research model and collected survey data from 182 older short video app users for hypothesis testing. The results by partial least squares structural equation modeling (PLS-SEM) show that besides social isolation, other technical factors (i.e., immersion affordance and achievement affordance) and social factors (digital feedback) have a significant impact on satisfaction, which leads to engagement and addiction dilemma. Meanwhile, perceived self-control positively moderates the effects of satisfaction and addiction. Our work advances knowledge by explaining the causes of engagement and addiction dilemma when older adults engage in short video apps, and we contribute the practical insights for short video app practitioners, family members, and older users to cope the engagement and addiction dilemma.

Keywords: Short Video Apps · Older Adults · Socio-technical · Addiction · Perceived Self-control

1 Introduction

In recent years, short video apps, such as TikTok and Kwai, have been developed in full swing. They unseated other traditional apps, like YouTube, to become one of the most sought-after video platforms [1]. With their easy-to-use interface and diverse content types, short video apps have become an essential medium for older adults to stay connected with the digital world. This phenomenon of "short video for pension" has garnered attention from academia and industry alike.

A key issue in the interaction of older adults with short video apps is the engagement and addiction dilemma. Short video app practitioners and the social circles of older adults face the paradoxical problem of promoting the digital inclusion of older adults

Q. Gao et al. (Eds.): HCII 2023, LNCS 14055, pp. 231–245, 2023.
https://doi.org/10.1007/978-3-031-48041-6_17

while minimizing online addiction. On the one hand, short video platforms can provide positive experiences for older users, such as helping them alleviate social isolation, promote digital inclusion, and enrich their spiritual life [2]. On the other hand, as typical hedonic social media, short video apps aim to prolong users' time on their platforms as much as possible [3]. This can lead older users to become addicted to the online world, undermining intergenerational relationships and increasing social isolation [4].

Against this backdrop, we try to understand the formation process of engagement and addiction dilemma among older adults in short video apps. Previous research has attributed engagement and addiction dilemma to system design [5]. However, short video apps are typical socio-technical information systems in which the engagement and addiction dilemma may influence by both technology and social factors [6]. Therefore, this research adopts a socio-technical approach to explore the mechanisms underlying the engagement and addiction dilemma. From a technological perspective, compared to traditional social media such as Facebook and Tweet, short video app features (i.e., live streaming, video editing, personalized recommending designs) can bring users a richer immersion and achievement experience [1]. In addition, regarding social factors, older adults often face a higher level of loneliness and deficient intergenerational communication. We believe that short video apps could provide chances for intergenerational relationships and meet seniors' emotional needs. However, few studies have explored older people's engagement and addiction dilemma in short video apps from a socio-technical perspective. This study can inform an in-depth understanding of two engagement processes in using short videos by older people.

In addition, we are also interested in examining the effects of individual factors on the two engagement outcomes. Self-control refers to people's ability to control their time, thoughts, or behaviors [7]. Unlike stable factors such as habits or traits, which are difficult to change, self-control is often considered malleable literacy [8]. Previous studies have shown that self-control can influence the screen time of user engagement in social media [9]. However, considering the different types of engagement, namely, meaningful engagement and addiction, the compound effect of self-control on them remains understudied. Especially short video apps offer users a stronger immersion engagement than traditional social media [6]. This phenomenon makes the role of self-control in that context for engagement and addiction dilemma more ambiguous and needs further exploration.

To address the above research gaps, we draw on the socio-technical and self-control perspectives to explore the underlying mechanism of engagement and addiction dilemma among older adults in short video apps. We confirmed that technical factors include immersion affordance and achievement affordance; social factors include digital feedback and social isolation. Based on partial least-squares (PLS) modeling, the results show that different socio-technical factors could impact old users' satisfaction with short video apps. Then, users' satisfaction correlates with meaningful engagement and addiction, and the process is moderated by perceived self-control. This study could advance the older adults' social media addiction literature by understanding the engagement and addiction dilemma in the short video context. And our research offers rich insight for social media practitioners and older users' family members to help older adults develop meaningful engagement in short video apps.

2 Theoretical Background

2.1 Engagement and Addiction Dilemma

Engagement and addiction dilemma refers to the concern that the information technology (IT) design can increase engagement but also may lead users to overindulge [5]. Engagement and addiction dilemma have been studied in IT artifacts such as mobile games [5, 10] and social media [11]. Early research was more concerned with guiding users toward IT engagement and continues engagement [12]. In recent years, as the IT industry has grown, researchers have taken up the topic of IT addiction and tried to understand the relationship between engagement and addiction [13].

Technology presents a double-edged sword for older users. On the one hand, most studies approve of the bright side of technology for older people to integrate into the digital society. For example, Wang & Wu (2022) [14] show that older adults' good technology habits positively impact intergenerational relationships. Kim et al. (2019) [15] find older users' adoption of travel websites would increase their well-being. On the other hand, IT does not always show positive results for older adults, some equivocal findings are emerging. For example, Hajek & König (2021) [16] advise older adults should use social media to mitigate loneliness and social isolation. However, research also shows that social media does not reduce social isolation, and problematic social media use will increase social isolation for older adults [4].

Given this, it is necessary to systematically explore the engagement and addiction dilemma of older users, with a particular focus on the dark side (e.g., addiction) of their interaction with social media.

2.2 Socio-technical Approach

The socio-technical approach recognizes that organizational systems are complex and involve not only technical factors, but also human and social factors [17]. It emphasizes the need to consider the interaction between these different elements in the design and understanding of organizational systems [18]. The social system refers to "*people's attributes, relationships, and power structures*" [19], while the technology system refers to "*the technology, processes, and tasks necessary to achieve the system's goals*" [19]. By considering both of these systems, the socio-technical approach can help organizations create more effective and efficient systems that meet the needs of all stakeholders.

Researchers have attempted to use socio-technical approaches to understand the outcomes by which users interact with social media. For instance, Li et al. (2021) found that social and technical factors can trigger different attachment types and facilitate livestreaming stickiness behavior [20]. Hasan et al. (2018) explored socio-technical factors that can exacerbate users' excessive usage behavior with video streaming services [21]. This research used the socio–technical approach to explore older users' engagement and addiction dilemma in short video apps. We identify *immersion affordance* and *achievement affordance* as technical factors [5]. The term *affordance* refers to the action possibilities afforded by the environment [22]. Short video apps afford users related system designs (e.g., live streaming and reward systems), making the immersion and achievement experience easy [1]. In addition, *digital feedback* and *social isolation* are crucial social factors for older adults engaging short video apps [6, 14]. These four factors can all shape older user behavior on short video apps [6, 10, 14]. However, specifically, their nuanced impact on meaningful engagement and addiction has been little studied.

3 Research Model and Hypothesis

This research develops a model to explore the joint effects of socio-technical factors and perceived self-control (see Fig. 1). First, we examine the impact of satisfaction on engagement and addiction dilemma (e.g., meaningful engagement and addiction) (H1 and H2). Second, we propose the effects of technical factors (e.g., immersion affordance and achievement affordance) and social factors (digital feedback and social isolation) on older users' satisfaction with short video apps (H3, H4, H5, and H6). Finally, we explore perceived self-control' moderating effects of satisfaction on meaningful engagement and addiction (H7 and H8).

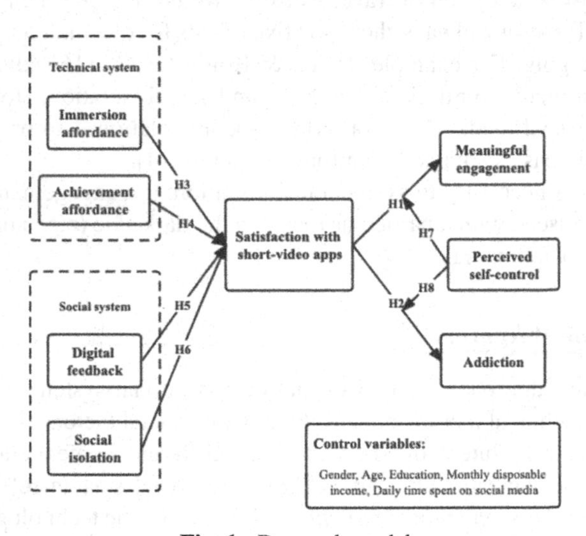

Fig. 1. Research model

3.1 Satisfaction, Meaningful Engagement and Addiction

Satisfaction refers to a positive psychological or affective state resulting from the appraisal of low expectations and high performance [23]. In IT studies, satisfaction plays a critical role in the information systems experience, and it demonstrates both bright and dark outcomes of IT artifacts usage. On the one hand, satisfaction is a positive experience that brings users pleasure [11]. It can promote older users to use technology more actively to improve life well-being [24]. On the other hand, although satisfaction leads to positive affective experiences, it also causes users to use social media more frequently, leading to compulsive behaviors [11]. Wang et al. (2015) claim that satisfaction could positively impact negative affective anticipation, which can lead to psychological dependence on social media [25]. In this research, due to the ease of operation and rich content of short video apps, they can satisfy the innate needs of older adults, which may also facilitate engagement and addiction dilemma. On the one hand, the short video apps allow older users to feel the fun of the virtual world, but on the other hand, it may make older users dependent [16, 26]. Given this, we propose the following hypothesis:

H1: Satisfaction has a positive influence on meaningful engagement in short video apps among older users.

H2: Satisfaction has a positive influence on addiction in short video apps among older users.

3.2 Technical System and Satisfaction

Immersion affordance refers to the possibility of information systems to absorb and engage users [5]. It is considered a critical design for enhancing user engagement in a variety of IT contexts. For example, in mobile games, immersion affordance enhances players' positive emotions while reducing negative ones [10]. In short video apps, personalized recommendations, interactive live streaming, and other functional features afford users unique immersion affordances [1]. These features may also facilitate a positive psychological experience, thus increasing user satisfaction with short video apps.

In addition to immersion affordance, achievement affordance is a basilic determinant for short video engagement [27]. Achievement affordance refers to the potential offered by information systems concerning acquiring a sense of accomplishment [5]. Achievement affordance satisfies the basic need for competence, such as in online games where players can level up, learn skills, and compete with others, which increases players' satisfaction with playing games [10]. Similarly, some short video apps allow users to get bonuses while watching. This achievement design is quite appealing to older users. Meanwhile, short video apps' creation and meta-voicing feedback features may also satisfy the sense of achievement among older users.

This suggests the following hypothesis:

H3: Immersion affordances have a positive influence on satisfaction in short video apps.

H4: Achievement affordances have a positive influence on satisfaction in short video apps.

3.3 Social System and Satisfaction

External interventions are an important way to optimize older adults' digital literacy and increase satisfaction with digital artifacts [28]. *Digital feedback* refers to the process by which younger generations in the family provide digital support levered by helping older adults to learn digital skills and solve digital difficulties [14]. It can help older adults access the internet and provide socio-emotional support [29]. Thus, digital feedback increases older people's identification with new technology and willingness to develop technology habits [14]. This evidence demonstrates the positive impact of digital feedback on technology satisfaction. Users of short video apps cover the entire age range, with older and younger family members able to communicate by "like," commenting, sharing, or posting short videos. This provides more opportunities for digital feedback between the two generations. This leads to the following hypothesis:

H5: Digital feedback has a positive influence on satisfaction in short video apps.

Social isolation is "*a state of lacking social belonging, social engagement, and fulfilling relationships*" [30]. It is a prevalent psychosocial issue among older adults [31]. Studies have shown that social isolation decreases well-being and has been associated with a series of health problems (e.g., hypertension) among older adults [32]. The functional features of social media support conversations, sharing, presence, and building groups between users, which help alleviate the reality of loneliness [33]. Therefore, older adults with social isolation tend to be satisfied with their social media life [6]. Short video apps have richer ways of interaction (e.g., likes, comments, pop-ups, sharing) for helping users develop social relationships. Thus, older adults may place their time and emotions in short video apps and become attached and satisfied with these apps. Therefore, we propose the following hypothesis:

H6: Social isolation has a positive influence on satisfaction with short video apps among older adults.

3.4 The Moderating Effects of Perceived Self-control

Self-control refers to a process allowing reactive regulation of automatic stimuli [34]. It can be seen as a trait or a literacy. Most studies consider it a cultivable digital literacy that can be trained by developing situational and cognitive strategies [35]. Self-control is limited, like human muscle energy that can be easily depleted [7]. Especially in the face of overindulged features and a volume of social cues in social media, users without self-control would focus on the proximal temptations but ignore the *distal benefits* (such as sleeping late because of social media chatting) [35]. Previous research has shown that self-control deficiency is positively associated with social media addiction [13]. Short videos can immediately give users a positive experience [1]. Thus, self-control may occur after satisfaction with short videos. Therefore, in current research, we do not discuss the direct effect of self-control on short video app addiction but focus on its moderating role in the effects of satisfaction on addiction. Self-control could calm and free the mind from emotional bondage [36]. We believe that self-control calms the satisfaction-ridden brain, weakening the potential for addictive behavior. Additionally, self-controlled users do not just control their inappropriate behavior but also reduce their normal social media engagement [9], which may be a preventive mechanism. The immersive designs of short video apps can make self-controlled users vigilant. They may view content in short videos through a critical lens, leading to diminished satisfaction and, in turn, less engagement. Therefore, we hypothesized that:

H8: Higher perceived self-control weakens the relationship between older user's satisfaction and addiction in short video apps.

H8: Higher perceived self-control weakens the relationship between older user's satisfaction and meaningful engagement in short video apps.

4 Research Methodology

4.1 Data Collection

We use the seven-point Likert-type to design construct measurements. From 1 (strongly disagree) to 7 (strongly agree), the number represents the agreement level on items. Our statements of items are all adapted from previous studies. Meaningful engagement and addiction are measured using items adapted from Yang & Gong (2021) [5]. As for technical system, immersion affordance and achievement affordance are adapted from Lee et al. (2021) [10] and Song et al. (2021) [1]. With regard to social system, digital feedback is measured consistently with Wang & Wu (2022) [14], and social isolation is adapted from Zhang et al. (2019) [6]. As for satisfaction, we measure it in keeping with the work of Bhattacherjee (2001) [23]. We measure perceived self-control adapted from the items of Osatuyi & Turel (2018) [9].

The scale is shown in Table 1. This survey was conducted in China, so we adopted the translation approach of Van de Vijver et al. (1997) [37] to process the scale. The first author translated the English items into Chinese, and the second author back-translated the Chinese items into English. We invited two linguistics professors to check the statements of the two scale versions and found no semantic differences. Besides, we conducted a pilot study with 17 older social media users. Their comments helped us revise the scale.

Table 1. Measures of variables

Constructs	Items	Source
Immersion affordance	IA1. Short video apps offer me the possibility to watch livestreaming and interact with others anytime	[1, 10]
	IA2. Short video apps offer me the possibility to lost track of time	
	IA3. Short video apps offer me the possibility to discover and recommend contents that attract me	
Achievement affordance	AA1. Short video apps offer me the possibility to earn some extra money while watching videos	
	AA2. Short video apps offer me the possibility to make my videos commented by others	
	AA3. Short video apps offer me the possibility to get "like" or "collection" by others for my videos	
Digital feedback	DD1. I hope my children and grandchildren at home will encourage me to use short video apps	[14]
	DD2. I hope my children and grandchildren at home will share with me new short videos they find	

(*continued*)

Table 1. *(continued)*

Constructs	Items	Source
	DD3. I hope that my children and grandchildren at home will help me overcome the difficulties which I meet in using short video apps	
Social isolation	SI1. I feel left out	[6]
	SI2. I feel isolated from others	
	SI3. I am unhappy being so withdrawn	
Satisfaction	SA1. I feel very pleased when watching short videos	[23]
	SA2. I feel very contented when watching short videos	
	SA3. I feel very delighted when watching short videos	
Perceived self-control	How much you could resist using SNS in each case?	[9]
	PSC1. How sure are you that you could resist using your short video apps when you are out at dinner?	
	PSC2. How sure are you that you could resist using your short video apps before you sleep?	
	PSC3. How sure are you that you could resist using your short video apps when you want to feel more accepted by friends?	
Meaningful engagement	ME1. I am absorbed intensely in watching short videos	[5]
	ME2. My watching experience with short videos is interesting	
	ME3. My attention is focused on watching short videos	
Short video addiction	SVD1. I sometimes neglect important things because of my interest in watching short videos	
	SVD2. I often fail to get enough rest because of my watch of short videos	
	SVD3. When I am not watching short videos, I often feel agitated	
	SVD4. My social life has sometimes suffered because of my watch of short videos	

We conducted the survey by Tencent wenjuan (https://wj.qq.com/mine.html), which is one of the most professional survey platforms in China. We distributed the questionnaires through several identified social media such as Sina Weibo, Zhihu, and Douban. And we also distributed questionnaires on several social media exclusive to seniors, such as Tangdou and Meipian, which can help us obtain more targeted answers. The survey sustained from November 10 to December 7, 2022, lasted 27 days. 422 questionnaires were collected. We screened samples with several criteria. First, participants must be older than 50 years old. Second, participants must use short video apps for at least 2 years. Third, participants have to use short video apps for at least half an hour a day in recent 2 weeks. Finally, we retained 182 valid questionnaires.

Demographics of the final samples are shown in Table 2. A similar number of male (*N* = 85) and female (*N* = 97) participants. Most participants are younger seniors (50–59, *N* = 136). Their education is mainly bachelor's degree (*N* = 110). Meanwhile, participants' income is high, about half exceeding 6,000RMB per month. Most participants could limit their daily use of short videos to 4 h (*N* = 162).

Table 2. Demographics of participants (N = 182)

Demographic variables		Frequency	Percentage
Gender	Female	97	53.7%
	Male	85	46.7%
Age	50–54	50	27.5%
	55–59	86	47.3%
	60–64	40	22%
	65–69	4	2.2%
	70–79	2	1.1%
	more than 80	0	0%
Education	Senior high school and less	63	34.6%
	Bachelor's degree	110	60.4%
	Master's degree	7	3.8%
	Doctoral degree	2	1.1%
Monthly disposable income (RMB)	less than 1500	20	11%
	1500–2999	20	11%
	3000–4499	31	17%
	4500–5999	25	13.7%
	more than 6000	86	47.3%
Daily time spent on short video apps (Hours)	less than 1	39	21.4%
	1–2	44	24.2%
	2–3	43	23.6%
	3–4	36	19.8%
	4–5	8	4.4%
	more than 5	12	6.5%

4.2 Measurement

We employed SmartPLS 4 and used partial least-squares (PLS) modeling for model testing. PLS is more suitable for theory construction and estimating complicated hypotheses with small sample sizes than co-variance-based (CB) modeling.

We evaluated the reliability and validity of our research model. Cronbach's alpha (α) and composite reliability (CR) values are used to estimate reliability. As shown in Table 3, Cronbach's α and CR values are greater than the recommended threshold (α > 0.6, CR > 0.7) at all constructs [38], and the reliability meets the requirements. As for content validity, we conducted the pilot study and revised the items to make the model's content validity eligible. Regarding convergent validity, the average variance (AVE) extracted from all constructs was higher than 0.5 (see Table 3), and all item loadings exceeded 0.7 [38]. Therefore, the convergent validity of constructs is valid. Regarding discriminant validity, the correlation coefficients between constructs are lower than the square root of the Average Variance Extracted (AVE) for each construct. (see Table 3). Simultaneously, the item loadings for each construct were greater than the loadings for the same items on other constructs. Thus, the discriminant validity is valid in this research.

Table 3. Convergent and discriminant validity

	1	2	3	4	5	6	7	8
1.Immersion affordance	**0.826**							
2.Achievement affordance	0.570	**0.840**						
3.Digital feedback	0.699	0.706	**0.908**					
4.Social isolation	0.473	0.422	0.356	**0.854**				
5.Satisfaction	0.770	0.739	0.757	0.432	**0.874**			
6.Perceived self-control	0.084	0.119	0.089	0.099	0.111	**0.831**		
7.Meaningful engagement	0.733	0.708	0.735	0.482	0.859	0.104	**0.890**	
8.Addiction	0.635	0.578	0.491	0.685	0.592	0.203	0.766	**0.874**
Cronbach's Alpha	0.845	0.861	0.893	0.878	0.938	0.890	0.934	0.922
Composite Reliability	0.853	0.862	0.900	0.904	0.945	0.931	0.937	0.923
Average Variance Extracted (AVE)	0.683	0.705	0.824	0.730	0.764	0.691	0.792	0.764

5 Results and Findings

We tested the hypotheses by Smart PLS 4; the coefficients are shown in Fig. 2. First, the results show that satisfaction can strongly predict both meaningful engagement ($\beta = 0.795, p < .001$) and addiction ($\beta = 0.502, p < .001$). Thus, H1 and H2 are supported. These results are similar to previous studies about user experience's effect on meaningful engagement and addiction in the video game context [5].

Second, as for technical system, immersion affordance ($\beta = 0.280, p < .001$) and achievement affordance ($\beta = 0.297, p < .001$) can positively impact satisfaction. The H3 and H4 are tested. The findings partially corroborate the previous results of affordances that can strengthen users' short video experience [1]. In addition, in terms of social system, social feedback ($\beta = 0.280, p < .01$) can positively influence satisfaction, accepting H5. The result is similar to Wang et al. (2021) in that social feedback is a core predictor of older adults' technology adoption and intergenerational relationships [14]. However, the effect of social isolation ($\beta = 0.061, n.s$) on satisfaction is insignificant. H8 is rejected. A possible conjecture is that short video apps are only helping older adults pass the time, not alleviating true social isolation. Similar findings have been mentioned in the work of Meshi et al. (2020) [4].

Furthermore, as for the moderating effects of perceived self-control, the results indicate that perceived self-control negatively moderates the effect of satisfaction on addiction ($\beta = -0.103, p < .05$), and H8 is supported. Previous studies have demonstrated the direct effect of self-control on inhibiting social media addictive behaviors [35], but research on self-control as a moderating variable is lacking. Our study adds to this gap and shows that satisfaction has a weaker effect on addiction when older adults have higher perceived self-control. However, the interaction effect between satisfaction and perceived self-control on meaningful engagement is insignificant ($\beta = 0.044, n.s$). It is possible that self-control may only serve as an ability to inhibit maladaptive engagement but not further impact meaningful engagement.

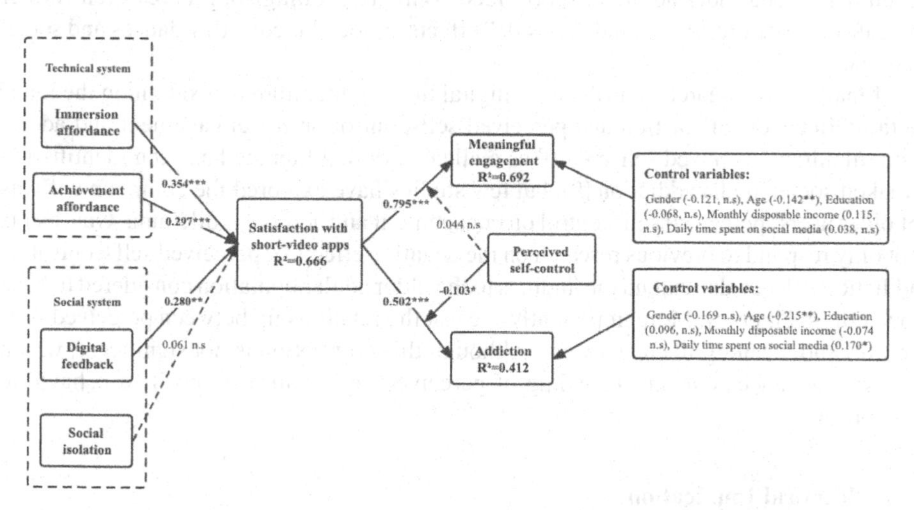

Note: * indicates $p < .05$; ** indicates $p < .01$; *** indicates $p < .001$; n.s.: not significant; two-tailed test.

Fig. 2. Results from the PLS model.

6 Discussion

6.1 Theoretical Implications

Our study explores meaningful engagement and addiction dilemma when older adults use short video apps, which can provide insights for understanding older adults' interactions outcomes with IT artifacts. Older adults are often considered a marginalized population for technology use, so previous research is more likely to encourage them engaging technology to rich their life, but without considering whether this is a beneficial or harmful engagement. In this study, we employed socio – technical approach to investigate the causes of engagement and addiction dilemma related to short video use among older adults. This can provide nuanced insights for understanding older users' different engagement formats in social media context.

Furthermore, this research contributes the older user social media engagement literature by investigating the influences of socio-technical factors on engagement and addiction dilemma. Prior studies have focused on the effect of technological factors on engagement and addiction dilemma [5, 10]. However, few studies have identified the effects of both social and technical factors on engagement and addiction dilemma. Especially for older users, social factors are essential in their technology engagement [14]. By analyzing the older users' socio-technical factors (i.e., immersion affordance, achievement affordance, digital feedback, and social isolation) in the use of short video apps. Our results advance understanding of the causes of engagement and addiction dilemma among older adults in short video context. In doing so, this research further reveals the possible "bright and dark side" effects of social media affordances and social factors.

Finally, this research contributes to digital literacy literature by examining the interaction effects of satisfaction and perceived self-control on the engagement and addiction dilemma. Perceived self-control as malleable digital literacy has been identified to weaken social media addiction [9], but few studies have explored the compound effects of older users' perceived self-control on engagement and addiction dilemma. Our results not only respond to previous research on the negative effects of perceived self-control on addiction [9], but also extend the findings to the older adult population considered to have lower digital literacy. More importantly, we test the relationship between perceived self-control and meaningful engagement. Although this correlation is not significant, which likewise advances our understanding of perceived self-control on positive behavioral outcomes.

6.2 Practical Implications

Our research provides several practical approaches for short video app practitioners, family members, and older adults. First, short video app practitioners should be aware of the engagement and addiction dilemma lurking in system design for older users. While advanced affordances (e.g., immersion affordance and achievement affordance) play a critical role in enhancing user experience. They can also indulge older users in problematic social media use (e.g., addiction) [1, 39]. To alleviate the adverse results, short video app practitioners could consider adding an anti-addiction system (e.g., compulsory in-app warning for time constrain) when making age-appropriate modifications.

Second, family members should consider engagement and addiction dilemma while helping older adults with digital inclusion. The younger generation is helping older adults access short video apps and alleviate social isolation through digital feedback, with little attention paid to addiction in older adults. Our research suggests that family members can give seniors more companionship in real life and balance their online and offline time, thus alleviating their short video addiction.

When using short video apps, older adults should improve their digital literacy comprehensively, especially their self-control capability. When using short video apps, it is essential for older adults to try to engage meaningfully and establish an autonomous "boundary awareness" through self-control. For example, they need to be aware of the adverse effects of algorithmic recommendations and induced content design so that they can effectively control their problematic use to achieve more active engagement in short video apps.

7 Limitations and Future Research

Our research still has several limitations. First, our work's valid sample of older adults is small, and future studies could be conducted on a larger scale. Second, we collected only one wave of data, which may not reveal the causal relationship between the factors. Future work can further explore the effect of socio-technical factors on engagement and addiction dilemma using a longitudinal design. Third, although we considered antecedents of engagement and addiction dilemma from both social and technological factors, our model explains only 41.2% of the variance in short video addiction (In comparison, this model explains 69.2% of the variance in meaningful engagement). Therefore, we encourage scholars to explore other antecedents of short video addiction in older adults, such as considering different social media affordances, personality, or emotional factors of older users.

References

1. Song, S., Zhao, Y.C., Yao, X., Ba, Z., Zhu, Q.: Short video apps as a health information source: an investigation of affordances, user experience and users' intention to continue the use of TikTok. Internet Res. **31**(6), 2120–2142 (2021)
2. Ng, R., Indran, N.: Not too old for tiktok: how older adults are reframing aging. Gerontologist **62**(8), 1207–1216 (2022)
3. Van der Heijden, H.: User acceptance of hedonic information systems. MIS Q. **28**(4), 695–704 (2004)
4. Meshi, D., Cotten, S.R., Bender, A.R.: Problematic social media use and perceived social isolation in older adults: a cross-sectional study. Gerontology **66**(2), 160–168 (2020)
5. Yang, Q., Gong, X.: The engagement–addiction dilemma: an empirical evaluation of mobile user interface and mobile game affordance. Internet Res. **31**(5), 1745–1768 (2021)
6. Zhang, X., Wu, Y., Liu, S.: Exploring short-form video application ad-diction: socio-technical and attachment perspectives. Telematics Inform. **42**, 101243 (2019)

7. Muraven, M., Baumeister, R.F.: Self-regulation and depletion of limited resources: does self-control resemble a muscle? Psychol. Bull. **126**(2), 247–259 (2022)
8. Polites, G.L., Serrano, C., Thatcher, J.B., Matthews, K.: Understanding social networking site (SNS) identity from a dual systems perspective: an investigation of the dark side of SNS use. Eur. J. Inf. Syst. **27**(5), 600–621 (2018)
9. Osatuyi, B., Turel, O.: Tug of war between social self-regulation and habit: explaining the experience of momentary social media addiction symptoms. Comput. Hum. Behav. **85**, 95–105 (2018)
10. Lee, Z.W.Y., Cheung, C.M.K., Chan, T.K.H.: Understanding massively multiplayer online role-playing game addiction: a hedonic management perspective. Inf. Syst. J. **31**(1), 33–61 (2021)
11. Wang, C., Lee, M.K.: Why we cannot resist our smartphones: investigating compulsive use of mobile SNS from a Stimulus-Response-Reinforcement perspective. J. Assoc. Inf. Syst. **21**(1), 175–200 (2020)
12. Agarwal, R., Karahanna, E.: Time flies when you're having fun: Cognitive absorption and beliefs about information technology usage. MIS Q. **24**(4), 665–694 (2000)
13. Gong, X., Zhang, K.Z.K., Cheung, C.M.K., Chen, C., Lee, M.K.O.: Alone or together? Exploring the role of desire for online group gaming in players' social game addiction. Inform. Manag. **56**(6), 103139 (2019)
14. Wang, C.-H., Wu, C.-L.: Bridging the digital divide: the smart TV as a platform for digital literacy among the elderly. Behav. Inform. Technol. **41**(12), 2546–2559 (2022)
15. Kim, J.J., Nam, M., Kim, I.: The effect of trust on value on travel websites: enhancing well-being and word-of-mouth among the elderly. J. Travel Tour. Mark. **36**(1), 76–89 (2019)
16. Hajek, A., König, H.-H.: Social isolation and loneliness of older adults in times of the COVID-19 pandemic: can use of online social media sites and video chats assist in mitigating social isolation and loneliness? Gerontology **67**(1), 121–124 (2021)
17. Baxter, G., Sommerville, I.: Socio-technical systems: from design methods to systems engineering. Interact. Comput. **23**(1), 4–17 (2011)
18. Trist, E., Higgin, G., Murray, H., Pollock, A.: Organizational Choice (RLE: Organizations): Capabilities of Groups at the Coal Face Under Changing Technologies. Routledge (2013)
19. Bostrom, R.P., Heinen, J.S.: MIS problems and failures: a socio-technical perspective, part II: the application of socio-technical theory. MIS Q. **1**(4), 11–28 (1977)
20. Li, Y., Li, X., Cai, J.: How attachment affects user stickiness on live streaming platforms: a socio-technical approach perspective. J. Retail. Consum. Serv. **60**, 102478 (2021)
21. Hasan, M.R., Jha, A.K., Liu, Y.: Excessive use of online video streaming services: impact of recommender system use, psychological factors, and motives. Comput. Hum. Behav. **80**, 220–228 (2018)
22. Majchrzak, A., Faraj, S., Kane, G.C., Azad, B.: The contradictory influence of social media affordances on online communal knowledge sharing. J. Comput.-Mediat. Commun. **19**(1), 38–55 (2013)
23. Bhattacherjee, A.: Understanding information systems continuance: an expectation-confirmation model. MIS Q. **25**(3), 351–370 (2001)
24. Walker, R., Isherwood, L., Burton, C., Kitwe-Magambo, K., Luszcz, M.: Marital satisfaction among older couples: the role of satisfaction with social networks and psychological well-being. Int. J. Aging Hum. Dev. **76**(2), 123–139 (2013)
25. Wang, C., Lee, M.K., Hua, Z.: A theory of social media dependence: evidence from microblog users. Decis. Support Syst. **69**, 40–49 (2015)
26. Han, M., Tan, X.Y., Lee, R., Lee, J.K., Mahendran, R.: Impact of social media on health-related outcomes among older adults in Singapore: qualitative study. JMIR Aging **4**(1), e23826 (2021)

27. Song, S., Zhao, Y.C., Yao, X., Ba, Z., Zhu, Q.: Serious information in hedonic social applications: affordances, self-determination and health information adoption in TikTok. J. Documentation **78**(4), 890–911 (2022)
28. Sriwisathiyakun, K., Dhamanitayakul, C.: Enhancing digital literacy with an intelligent conversational agent for senior citizens in Thailand. Educ. Inf. Technol. **27**(5), 6251–6271 (2022)
29. Haight, M., Quan-Haase, A., Corbett, B.A.: Revisiting the digital divide in Canada: the impact of demographic factors on access to the internet, level of online activity, and social networking site usage. Inf. Commun. Soc. **17**(4), 503–519 (2014)
30. Primack, B.A., et al.: Social media use and perceived social isolation among young adults in the U.S. Am. J. Preventive Med. **53**(1), 1–8 (2017). https://doi.org/10.1016/j.amepre.2017.01.010
31. Khosravi, P., Rezvani, A., Wiewiora, A.: The impact of technology on older adults' social isolation. Comput. Hum. Behav. **63**, 594–603 (2016)
32. Cacioppo, J.T., Hawkley, L.C.: Social isolation and health, with an emphasis on underlying mechanisms. Perspect. Biol. Med. **46**(3), S39–S52 (2003)
33. Hampton, K. N., Sessions, L. F., Her, E. J., & Rainie, L.: Social isolation and new technology. Pew Internet & American Life Project 4 (2009)
34. Baumeister, R.F., Vohs, K.D., Tice, D.M.: The strength model of self-control. Curr. Dir. Psychol. Sci. **16**(6), 351–355 (2007)
35. Brevers, D., Turel, O.: Strategies for self-controlling social media use: classification and role in preventing social media addiction symptoms. J. Behav. Addict. **8**(3), 554–563 (2019)
36. Ho, S.S., Lwin, M.O., Lee, E.W.: Till logout do us part? Comparison of factors predicting excessive social network sites use and addiction between Singaporean adolescents and adults. Comput. Hum. Behav. **75**, 632–642 (2017)
37. Van de Vijver, F.J., Leung, K.: Methods and data analysis for cross-cultural research. Sage, Newbury Park, CA (1997)
38. Fornell, C., Larcker, D.F.: Evaluating structural equation models with unobservable variables and measurement error. J. Mark. Res. **18**(1), 39–50 (1981)
39. Fox, J., Moreland, J.J.: The dark side of social networking sites: an exploration of the relational and psychological stressors associated with Facebook use and affordances. Comput. Hum. Behav. **45**, 168–176 (2015)

StoryLens: Personalizing News Recommendations for Older Adults with Their Life Stories

Jiaoyun Yang[1,2,3,4], Jianguang Lin[1,2], Fang Gui[1,5](✉), Hongdao Meng[6], Honglin Chen[7], and Ning An[1,2,3,8]

[1] School of Computer Science and Information Engineering, Hefei University of Technology, Hefei, China
g_fiona@outlook.com
[2] National Smart Eldercare International S & T Cooperation Base, Hefei University of Technology, Hefei, China
[3] Intelligent Interconnected Systems Laboratory of Anhui Province, Hefei University of Technology, Hefei, China
[4] Key Laboratory of Knowledge Engineering with Big Data of Ministry of Education, Hefei University of Technology, Hefei, China
[5] School of Computer Science and Artificial Intelligence, Chaohu University, Hefei, China
[6] School of Aging Studies, College of Behavioral and Community Sciences, University of South Florida, Tampa, USA
[7] Gerontological Social Work, Faculty of Social Sciences and Business Studies, University of Eastern Finland, Kuopio, Finland
[8] Anhui Province Key Laboratory of Affective Computing and Advanced Intelligent Machine, Hefei University of Technology, Hefei, China

Abstract. Personalizing news recommendations for older adults using their life stories has the potential to enhance their social connectedness, cognitive well-being, and overall quality of life. This approach has the potential to benefit not only older adults but also their family members and professional and informal caregivers who seek to provide human-centric care services. This paper explores this possibility by creating StoryLens—a personalized news recommender system that enables older adults to stay informed about current happenings around them while bringing back cherished memories. The StoryLens comprises four distinct modules: the Life Story Processing module, the News Crawling module, the News Recommendation module, and the News Display module. The Life Story Processing module creates a personalized profile of their news preferences by extracting relevant elements from individuals' life stories. While the News Crawling module continuously crawls news from major news sites, the News Recommendation module deploys a unique algorithm calculating the similarity between the life story elements and the extracted features from the crawled news to personalize news recommendations. Finally, the News Display module displays recommended news with associated life stories to actively engage older adults. A survey shows that the StoryLens recommendations achieved average scores of 4.16 and 4.05 on diversity and relevance based on a 5-point Likert scale questionnaire.

Keywords: News recommendation · Older adults · Life story approach

Q. Gao et al. (Eds.): HCII 2023, LNCS 14055, pp. 246–263, 2023.
https://doi.org/10.1007/978-3-031-48041-6_18

1 Introduction

Social isolation and loneliness are critical yet often overlooked public health risks that plague a significant proportion of the older population [1], with the United States alone spending roughly USD 6.7 billion annually on this issue [2]. With COVID-19 making matters worse for these old adults [3, 4], it is crucial to respond now. To enrich older adults' social connectedness, Waycott et al. proposed a framework with three interrelated dimensions: personal relationships, community connections, and social engagement [5]. News consumption can help social engagement [6], providing older adults with relevant information and fostering social engagement and cohesion [7].

News Recommender Systems (NRS) help users filter information and recommend news of interest to alleviate the problem of information overload [8]. The key idea is to predict users' reading preferences according to their information. Current methods focus on learning users' news reading history, including collaborative filtering, association-rules-based, content-based filtering, deep learning, and hybrid recommendation [9]. The collaborative filtering approach makes recommendations by mining similarities between different users or reading histories, and it has two distinct categories: item-based collaborative filtering and user-based collaborative filtering [10, 11]. While the association-rule-based recommendation predicts news of interest by mining association rules between previously read news and current ones [12], content-based filtering algorithms utilize user-profile information to compare news items regarding content similarity and generate personalized recommendations [8]. Popular deep-learning models for building NRS include DFM, GRU, NPA, NAML, LSTUR, and NRMS [13]. Finally, the hybrid recommendation mixes multiple strategies, including switching back and forth, weighted fusion, feature combination, cascade, meta-level hybrid, and feature augmentation [15]. Unlike content-based and hybrid recommendations, the other three approaches suffer from the "cold start" problem [9], meaning that an NRS struggles to recommend news when there is little reading history data associated with a user. The content-based approach addresses this problem by expanding users' profiles through personal information gathering [16], which can be daunting [17].

To gather personal information for better eldercare services, people have explored the life story approach [18, 19]. This approach [20] refers to capturing, preserving, and sharing the journey of older adults since birth, including cherished moments, educational breakthroughs, work experiences, and personal milestones with heartwarming details, aiming to enhance their well-being and sense of self-identity [21].

Personalizing news recommendations for older adults with their stories has several potential benefits: 1) enhancing social engagement: older adults are more likely to engage with news that resonates deeply with their experiences and recollections [22], as opposed to generic, one-size-fits-all news; 2) strengthening social community connections: older adults are likely to share news stories relevant to their experiences and memories; 3) promoting reflection and self-expression: using their life stories as a basis for news recommendations will encourage older adults to reflect on individual events and moments in time while gaining the opportunity to express themselves [20] through the news content they choose to engage with; 4) exercising cognitive functions: personalizing news recommendations using life stories can stimulate their memory and achieve the effect of reminiscence therapy [23].

This paper presents StoryLens, a personalized news recommender system that taps into the power of life stories to personalize and enhance news recommendations. With StoryLens, older adults can stay informed about current events while also reviving cherished memories—a capability few have explored until now. StoryLens contains four major components: the Life Story Processing module, the News Crawling module, the News Recommendation module, and the News Display module. The Life Story Processing module applies three methods to extract the five keywords [24, 25], including location, school, workplace, hobby, and artwork, viewed as user preference representations [22]. The News Crawling module is to crawl news from major news sites continuously. After extracting news features with the Life Story Processing module, the News Recommendation module proposes a similarity calculation algorithm based on TF-IDF for calculating the similarity between news and life story and generates related news for the corresponding older adult. Finally, the News Display module displays pertinent life stories along with recommendation results to support social engagement.

This paper makes the following contributions:

- We introduce a unique approach, StoryLens, that adopts the life story approach to personalize news recommendations for older adults.
- StoryLens incorporates three methods to extract essential elements from personal life stories to represent users' news preferences.
- To calculate the similarity between personal life stories and news items for personalized news recommendations, we propose Element Frequency-Inverse Document Frequency (EF-IDF), which extends the traditional TF-IDF method.
- To assess the effectiveness of StoryLens, we conducted a survey to measure the relevance and diversity of the recommended news items.

Section 2 will introduce the design and implementation of StoryLens. We evaluate the recommendation results in Sect. 3 and provide a summary in Sect. 4.

2 The Design and Implementation of StoryLens

As shown in Fig. 1, the architecture of StoryLens has four major components: the Life Story Processing module, the News Crawling module, the News Recommendation module, and the News Display module.

The Life Story Processing module stores the stories in the database and extracts the keywords from the life stories using three methods: named entity recognition, rule matching, and Jieba extraction.

The News Crawling module crawls news from major news websites, including URL pool, filter, extraction, and HTML classification.

The News Recommendation module provides recommended news by parsing news, extracting features, calculating similarity, and generating recommendations.

The News Display module has two parts: the first is to collect life stories, and the second displays the recommended results, including a list of resultant news, news content pages, and standard components.

Fig. 1. Illustration of the functional architecture

2.1 The Life Story Processing Module

StoryLens uses the life stories from the Older Adults' Biographies Summarization Dataset (OABS) [26]. The OABS features the life stories of 80 older adults, with 16 collected through in-person interviews and 64 acquired online. The average length of these life stories is about 2000 words. The content of life stories includes the older adults' education experience, work experience, and personal milestones since birth.

The Life Story Processing module consists of four methods: key elements acquisition, named entity recognition, rule matching, and Jieba extracting.

Key Elements Acquisition. This method takes a life story as input and outputs a set of key elements acquired from the input. After examining what could impact the news preferences of older adults, we select five elements to consider: location, school, workplace, hobby, and artwork.

The first three elements draw inspiration from the "place attachment" concept [22], which captures the emotional connection that older adults often have to places where significant events in their life took place [27]. Choosing the hobby element is straightforward, as it is often the information that older adults actively seek [28, 29]. As to the artwork element, we believe artwork appearing in one's life stories carries unique personal value [28].

We implemented three methods to extract these five elements: (1) A named entity recognition model to extract location, school, and workplace; (2) A rule matching algorithm and several Natural Language Process (NLP) techniques to extract the hobby element; (3) the Jieba module to search the name of work, such as the book and the movie in the life story. Story preprocessing aims to extract life stories from the files and provides data for the other three modules.

Named Entity Recognition. Figure 2 shows the flowchart of the named entity recognition in the StoryLens. First, the ELECTRA-Small method extracts the entities in the input life story to construct the entity collection. The Hanlp, which uses the ELECTRA-Small model trained on MSRA with 26 entity types, offers the function of named entity recognition [25]. There are three problems with the entities of location, school, and workplace in the life story:

1) Some location entities are too familiar and too large in scope to characterize the interests of the older adult;
2) The organizations, including schools and workplaces, may change their names and restructure over time;
3) Individual entities suffer from spelling errors.

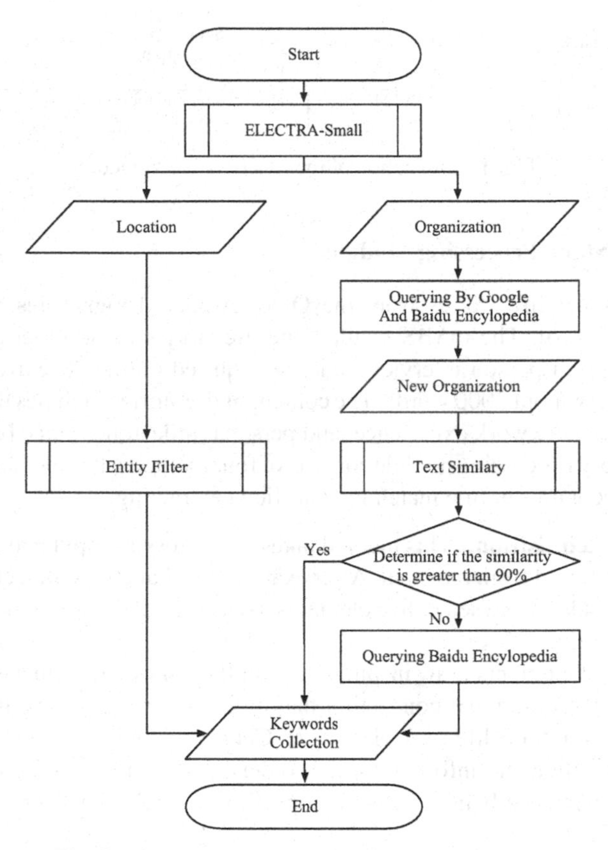

Fig. 2. Flowchart of the Named Entity Recognition

For problem (1), we implement a location filtering method to filter some location entities. We can extract the location entities of Japan and China from the life story by the ELECTRA-Small model. The entities are filtered because their range is too large to reflect the interest of the older adult. However, we also put these location entities into the older adult's interest representation set when less than 3 location entities appear in the life story of the older adult.

For problems (2) and (3), we develop an entity transformation method leveraging Baidu Encyclopedia. This method first attempts to find new organizations with the old organization entities derived from the original life story. However, the renaming of an organization can affect the accuracy of news recommendations, as the news relevant to the old organization may not exist in the news database. Furthermore, life stories could contain organization abbreviations and ambiguous organization names, which can degrade the accuracy of the proposed entity conversion method. To address these issues, we combine location and organization information using an entity distance of fewer than ten characters to form search keywords for querying Baidu Encyclopedia. The first two query results are then considered as new organizations.

The Life Story Processing model uses a verification method to ensure the accuracy of the outcome. First, this method utilizes a text similarity technique to compare the existing and new organization names [25]. If the similarity is more than or equal to 0.9, it selects the new organization; otherwise, it queries the interface of Baidu Encyclopedia for information on the previous organization. StoryLens assesses whether the result is accurate by comparing the data returned from the interface. Text similarity is necessary since some of the organization's entities have incorrect or missing characters. We are unable to obtain results straight from the Baidu Encyclopedia.

We experiment to determine whether the entity transformation method is practical. The experimental design is as follows. The study selects sixteen elderly stories obtained through manual interviews. We find the current organization name corresponding to the old organization name that appears in the stories by manual annotation. Then, the entity transformation method above processes the older adults' story and obtains the predicted organization name. To verify the accuracy of the proposed entity transformation method, we compared the manually labeled and predicted organization names. The method achieved a reasonable accuracy rate of 69.8%, correctly predicting 37 out of 53 manually labeled new organization names. This level of accuracy is deemed acceptable, given that manually labeling new organizations involved querying multiple sources, making it challenging to label new organizations accurately.

Rule Matching Algorithm. We manually constructed a collection of keywords for expressing hobbies, including like, fond, love, and others. After finding the sentences containing these keywords, we use NLP-related techniques to extract the hobby from the sentences. There are three problems in the process:

1) When only personal pronouns appear in the sentence, it is difficult to be sure whether the sentence describes the hobbies of the older adult;
2) The sentence containing the keyword may not necessarily describe the older adult;
3) In a sentence containing multiple predicates, it is difficult to determine the subject in the clause that omits the subject because of the characteristic of omitting the subject in Chinese.

Based on the rule-matching algorithm and HanLP tool, we constructed a hobby extraction method to extract the hobby keywords from the life story. The HanLP is a multilingual NLP library providing several joint tasks: semantic dependency parsing, semantic role labeling, abstract meaning representation parsing, and more. [25]. Figure 3 shows the implementation procedure of hobby extraction. The method includes six steps:

1) Constructing a hobby representation word set and searching the sentences in the life story that contain keywords from the word set;

2) Determining whether the sentence contains the name of the older adult; If not, finding the context of the sentence;
3) Using coreference resolution (COR) technology to process the sentence;
4) Using semantic role labeling (SRL) technology to process the sentence; If the sentence has a subject and the subject is the older adult, skip to step 6);
5) Using dependency parsing (DEP) technology to find the subject of the sentence; If the subject of the sentence is not the older adult, the extraction process concludes;
6) Returning the object of SRL.

We designed steps 2 and 3 to solve the first problem. When only personal pronouns appear in a sentence, we look for the preceding text of the sentence until it contains the older adult. Then, we use the COR technique to find where personal pronouns in the sentence point. The goal of the COR task is to gather the mentions in the text that refer to the same thing in one cluster.

Step 4 solves problem 2 to determine whether the extracted hobbies describe the older adult. The goal of the SRL task is to analyze the predicate-argument structure of a sentence, which answers the semantic question "who did what to whom." In the hobby extraction method, we use the SRL extracted subject to determine whether the extracted hobby belongs to the older adult and thus solve problem 2.

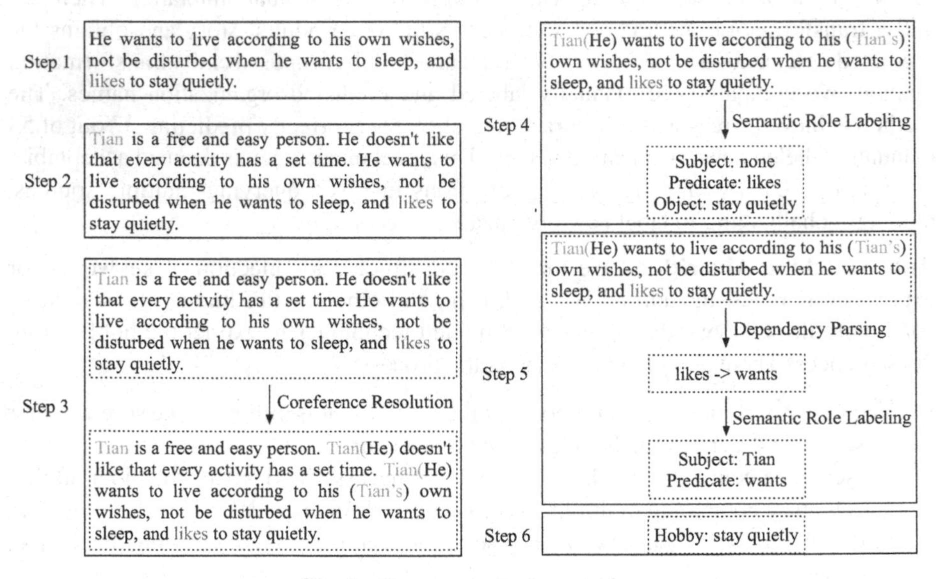

Fig. 3. Flowchart of rule matching

Step 5 uses the dependency parsing technique to solve problem 3. DEP is a task that analyzes the syntactic relations between words in a sentence and represents them as a tree structure.

Jieba Extraction. Jieba is a Chinese word segmentation module of Python. In addition to the word segmentation function, Jieba also provides a part-of-speech tagging (POS) function to annotate the part of speech of each word after sentence splitting. Jieba offers 24 types of part-of-speech tags and four named entity category tags.

In Chinese, two guillemets, i.e., a pair of punctuation marks, identify the name of entities for which one works. Thus, we first use regular matching to find the guillemet in the text and extract the name of the work between the two guillemets. Secondly, based on the POS tagging of Jieba, we extract the titles of the works in the life stories without guillemets.

2.2 The News Crawling Module

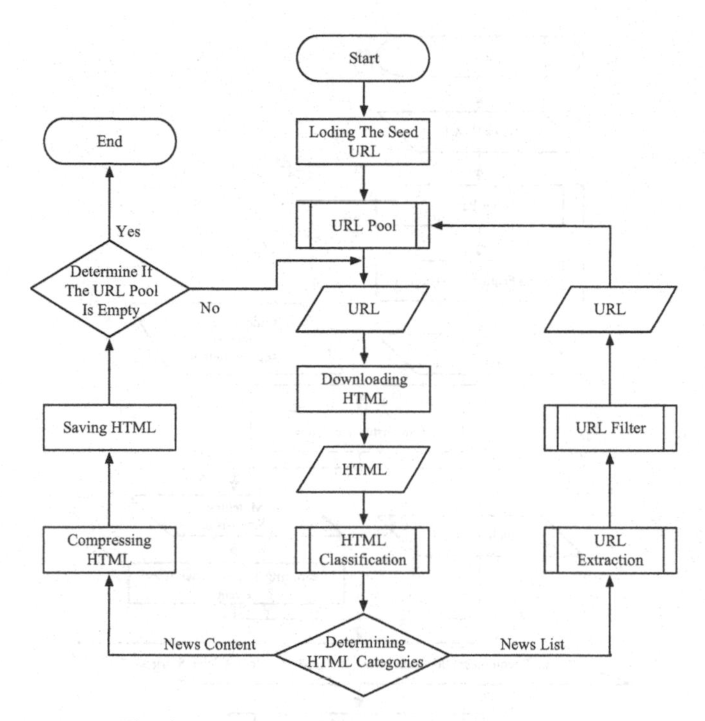

Fig. 4. Flowchart of the News Crawling module

The News Crawling module offers original news data for the News Recommendation module. Our news crawling tasks encounter the following challenges:

1) Because of network failure, the news crawler may time out, which leads to a high risk of missing pages;
2) Because of crawling news from multiple websites, news crawlers are prone to downloading the same news repeatedly;
3) How to extract URLs from HTML pages in different formats;
4) How the news crawler program determines which HTML pages contain the content of the news body.

We have implemented four sub-modules, the URL pool, the URL filter, the URL extraction, and the HTML classification, to solve the four problems, respectively. The URL pool manages URLs and supplies URLs for news crawling, and it prevents missing pages by recording the download status of URLs. It provides the following functions: adding URLs to the pool, removing URLs from the pool to download news HTML, and saving URL status. By mapping URLs into a value through the Hash algorithm, URL Filter can quickly determine whether a URL is in the URL pool and finally achieve the purpose of filtering duplicate URLs. Based on existing technologies for automatically extracting web page information [30], URL Extraction can extract URLs from web pages in different formats. HTML classification then uses the SVM algorithm to classify web pages into List and Content types.

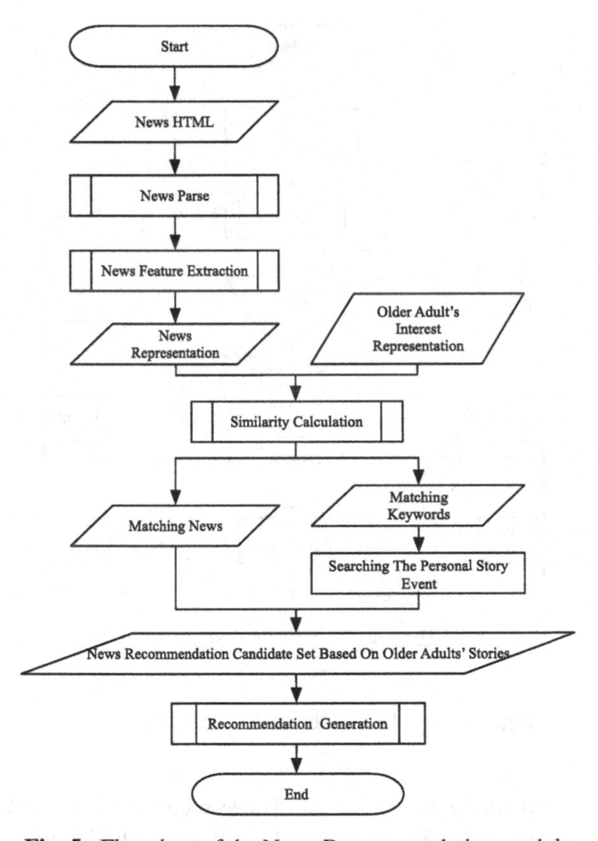

Fig. 5. Flowchart of the News Recommendation module

Figure 4 illustrates the process of the News Crawling module. The URL pool starts by loading seed URLs from the database and initiating downloads of their content. Subsequently, the HTML classification module partitions these downloads into two categories: the News Content and News List pages. The LZMA algorithm compresses the former for storage in the database, while the latter provides URLs that are processed sequentially by the URL extraction module and the URL filter module.

There is also a detailed implementation process, which is listed below.

Here we start with the seed URL. Before the execution of the News Crawling module, the URL pool retrieves the seed URL from the database. Seed URL, the URL of news site index pages, comprises numerous news links. In addition to supplying the initial input to the News Crawling module, the seed URL serves as a filter. StoryLens only crawls news whose URL host is identical to the host in the seed URL, limiting the crawl scope of the crawler module to ensure the correctness of the news source.

As discussed previously, one of the functions of the URL pool is managing URL status. There are four types of URL status: entirely downloaded, abandoned after multiple failed attempts (the default value is five), downloading, and continuing to try after a failed download. We choose LevelDB to store the URLs of the first two types permanently. As soon as StoryLens starts downloading the content of a URL, its status becomes "downloading." Consequently, the DownloadingDict, a Python-supplied container, temporarily records this URL and the current time as its timestamp. When StoryLens retry downloading the content of a previously failed URL, it uses the FailureDict, another Python-supplied container, to temporarily records this URL and the number of failed downloads. If this download fails more than five times, StoryLens will remove it from the FailureDict and store it instead in LevelDB.

2.3 The News Recommendation Module

The purpose of the News Recommendation module is to recommend news for older adults based on the similarity between news features and user interest features. The News Recommendation module comprises four sub-modules: the news parsing module, the news feature extraction module, the similarity calculation module, and the recommendation generation module. Figure 5 illustrates the implementation procedure of the News Recommendation module. Firstly, the news parsing sub-module parses news HTML crawled by the News Crawling module to extract news titles, content, and release times [30]. Secondly, the news feature extraction sub-module uses the partial methods of the Life Story Processing module to extract location entities, organization entities, and work names that appear in the news. Thirdly, the sub-module for calculating similarity computes the similarity between the keyword phrase of news items and user features. A recommendation result includes two parts: the desired news item and its associated life story event matched by the keywords. The recommendation generation sub-module stores recommended results, providing them to older adults.

In the similarity calculation sub-module, the core step of the News Recommendation module, we propose a similarity calculation method based on the Term Frequency-Inverse Document Frequency (TF-IDF) method for calculating the similarity between life stories and news. The TF-IDF refers to a numerical statistic algorithm for determining the importance of a word in a collection or corpus of texts [31]. The TF-IDF consists of two parts. The first part is tf(t,d), which indicates the number of times the word t appears in document d. The second part is idf(t,d), defined as

$$idf(t, d) = \frac{|D|}{|\{d \in D : t \in d\}|} \tag{1}$$

Table 1. Similarity Calculation Algorithm

```
Algorithm: Similarity calculation
Input: A keyword list of the life story KS_i = { k_s^1, k_s^2, ......, k_s^n }
       A keyword list of the news KN_j = { k_n^1, k_n^2, ......, k_n^m }
Output: Similarity value between I_i and N_j : similarity
        The list of identical keywords between I_i and N_j : matching_keyword_list
01. similarity = 0, matching_keyword_list = {}
02. WS_i = { w_s^1, w_s^2, ......, w_s^n }
03. WN_j = { w_n^1, w_n^2, ......, w_n^m }
04. for ( i, k_s ) in KS_i:
05.     w_s^i = tf - idf( k_s )
06. end for
07. for ( i, k_s ) in KS_i:
08.     for ( j, k_n ) in KN_j :
09.         if k_n == k_s :
10.             w_n^j = w_s^i
11.             add k_n in matching_keyword_list
12.         else :
13.             w_n^j = tf - idf( k_n^j )
14.     end for
15. end for
16. if length(matching_keyword_list) == 0 :
17.     return similarity
18. KU = KS_i ∪ KN_j = { k_u^1, k_u^2, ......, k_u^(n+m-l) }
19. // l is the length of matching_keyword_list
20. WUS_i = { w_us^1, w_us^2, ......, w_us^(n+m-l) }
21. WUN_j = { w_un^1, w_un^2, ......, w_un^(n+m-l) }
22. for ( i, k_u ) in KU:
23.     for ( j, k_s ) in KS_i:
24.         w_us^i = 0
25.         if k_s == k_u:
26.             w_us^i = w_s^j
27.             break
28.     end for
29.     for ( j, k_n ) in KN_j :
30.         w_un^i = 0
31.         if k_n == k_u:
32.             w_un^i = w_n^j
33.             break
34.     end for
35. end for
36. dissimilarity = Σ_{i=0}^{n+m-l} |w_us^i - w_un^i|
37. similarity = 1/dissimilarity
```

The |D| in Eq. (1) represents the total number of documents in the corpus, and $|\{d \in D{:}t \in d\}|$ is the number of documents where the word t appears. Thus, the TF-IDF is defined as:

$$tf - idf(t, d) = tf(t, d) \times idf(t, d) \tag{2}$$

Table 1 shows the similarity calculation algorithm. The similarity calculation algorithm consists of 5 steps:

1) Calculating the weights of keywords in life stories;
2) Calculating the weights of keywords in the news;
3) Getting the union set of two lists and computing the two new weights lists;
4) Calculating the dissimilarity;
5) Calculating the similarity.

Fig. 6. News list page

In step 1, we believe that the importance of entities in life stories is different. By improving tf in the TF-IDF algorithm, the similarity calculation algorithm has given different kinds of keywords with different weights. We set the weight of one occurrence of school as 1.5, one occurrence of province entity as 0.8, and the rest as 1. In particular, the weight of the hobby keyword is the average weight of the tf-idf values of each word because the hobby keyword may be a phrase.

In step 2, for each word in the news keyword list, its weight is equal to the word's weight in the keyword list of life stories. If the word does not appear in the keyword list of life stories, its weight is tf-idf value. In particular, if a hobby keyword appears in the news, the weight of the hobby keyword is the average weight of the tf-idf values of each word; Otherwise, the weight of hobby keywords is 0.

In step 3, we take the union of the keyword list of the news and the keyword list of life stories and construct a new keyword list.

In step 4, after getting the two new weight lists, we calculate the dissimilarity of the two weight lists, equal to the sum of the absolute values of the differences of all keywords in the two weight lists.

In step 5, the similarity is equal to the reciprocal of the non-similarity.

Fig. 7. News content page

2.4 The News Display Module

The News Display module allows older adults to read the news from StoryLens. The main pages include the news list and news content page.

Figure 6 shows the news list page that displays the news items that StoryLens recommends based on personal life stories. The header above the news list shows StoryLens's logo and user information. Below the header, on the left side, is the news list featuring the recommended news items' titles, sources, and release times. On the right side, the Hot News column features six recent news items, refreshable by clicking the Refresh button powered by MyBatis-Plus.

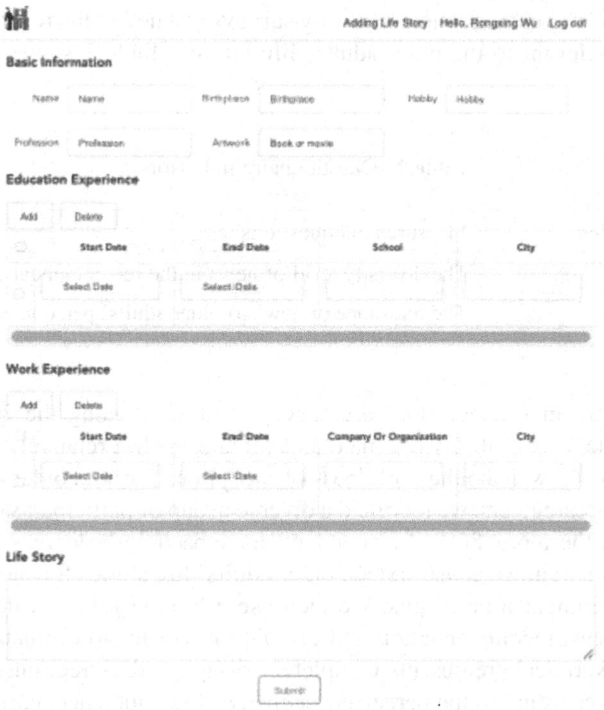

Fig. 8. Story collection page

Figure 7 displays the news content page. The news content page shows both the news and linked personal life events. After clicking on the news list page, StoryLens starts a routing jump in the News Content page and carries the news id as a parameter. The system searches for news content and displays it on the front-end page based on the news id. StoryLens finds personal life events associated with the news by the news trigger keyword.

Figure 8 shows the life story collection page. The life story collection page contains four parts of information, basic information, education experience, work experience, and life story. The first three sections are optional and can be left unfilled by users, while the fourth is required. In the two parts of education experience and work experience, users can add a line of input box by clicking the Add button. The life story input box is the text-area element, a multi-line plain-text editing control used to receive long text entered by the user.

Standard components are code snippets on every page, including the header and hot news subcomponents. The header displays StoryLens's logo and stores the login information of older adults. The hot news component is situated on the right side of the page and shows six pieces of current news at once.

3 Evaluation

We evaluated the recommendation results by surveying whether the recommended news is diverse and relevant to the older adults' life stories. Table 2 shows our evaluation metrics [13].

Table 2. Questionnaire indicators

Evaluation metrics	Measurement questions
Diversity	The diversity level of news in the recommendation list
Relevance	The relevance of news to older adults' personal stories

This study adopted a questionnaire survey method. Among the 30 respondents, approximately 60% and 40% were male and female, with a relatively balanced sample gender ratio. To evaluate the usefulness of StoryLens for both older adults and their family members/caregivers, we recruited a diverse group of participants of varying ages from 18–67. Furthermore, 86% of respondents have bachelor's degrees and above.

For the evaluation, we chose sixteen older adults' life stories for StoryLens to generate news recommendation results. We then use a 5-point Likert scale questionnaire consisting of news recommendation and evaluation metrics to evaluate these results. The 5-point Likert scale represents completely disagree, disagree, unsure, agree, and strongly agree according to the perceived intensity of the audience, corresponding to a score of 1–5, respectively. More miniature scores indicate more disagreement, and more significant scores indicate higher levels of agreement.

We collected thirty valid responses. Two of the responses were missing some data about diversity scores. Therefore, we eventually got thirty answers for the relevance assessment and twenty-eight for diversity. Table 3 shows the statistical results of the evaluation. We can find that the recommendation results achieve average scores of 4.16 and 4.05 on diversity and relevance based on the 5-point Likert scale, respectively. It implies that the recommended news was relevant to the matched personal stories and had a good diversity.

To verify the reliability of the responses, we calculated Cronbach's alpha for the relevance and diversity of the responses separately. Cronbach's alpha measures the reliability of a scale or test. The results show that the reliability score of diversity is $0.91 > 0.7$, and the reliability score of relevance is $0.97 > 0.7$. It proves that the reliability level of the responses is high.

Table 3. Statistics results of the evaluation

Evaluation metrics	Average	Standard deviation	Cronbach's alpha
Diversity	4.16	0.90	0.91
Relevance	4.05	0.98	0.97

4 Conclusion

This paper proposes StoryLens, a personalized news recommendation system that leverages the life stories of older adults to enhance their social connectedness, cognitive well-being, and overall quality of life. With its four modules working in tandem, the StoryLens extracts relevant information from life stories, crawls news articles, calculates similarity scores between life stories and news articles, and finally displays recommended news articles with associated life stories.

Our approach offers a novel way to personalize news recommendations for older adults by incorporating their life stories, enabling them to stay informed about current events while reminiscing about their past experiences. Our system can also help alleviate the problem of information overload faced by older adults by delivering news articles that are personalized and relevant to their interests.

StoryLens has the potential to benefit not only older adults but also their family members and professional and informal caregivers who seek to provide human-centric care services. In the future, we plan to explore additional ways to enhance the personalization of news recommendations for older adults, such as creating new life stories or discovering old life stories after consuming relevant news. We believe that the life story approach has great potential to positively impact the quality of life of older adults and contribute to the development of digital technologies that promote well-being and social connectedness for older adults.

Acknowledgement. This work was partially supported by the National Natural Science Foundation of China (No. 62072153), the Anhui Provincial Key Technologies R&D Program (No. 2022h11020015), and the Program of Introducing Talents of Discipline to Universities (111 Program) (B14025).

References

1. National Academies of Sciences, Engineering, and Medicine. Social Isolation and Loneliness in Older Adults: Opportunities for the Health Care System. National Academies Press (2020)
2. Flowers, L., et al.: Medicare spends more on socially isolated older adults. Insight on the Issues **125**, 1119–1143. AARP Public Policy Institute (2017)
3. Office, E.E., Rodenstein, M.S., Merchant, T.S., Pendergrast, T.R., Lindquist, L.A.: Reducing social isolation of seniors during covid-19 through medical student telephone contact. J. Am. Med. Dir. Assoc. **21**(7), 948–950 (2020)
4. Wu, B.: Social isolation and loneliness among older adults in the context of covid-19: a global challenge. Glob. Health Res. Policy **5**(1), 27 (2020)

5. Waycott, J., Vetere, F., Ozanne, E.: Building social connections: a framework for enriching older adults' social connectedness through information and communication technologies. Ageing and Digital Technology: Designing and Evaluating Emerging Technologies for Older Adults, pp. 65–82 (2019)
6. Xu, B.: Understanding Sticky News: Analyzing the Effect of Content Appeal and Social Engagement for Sharing Political News Online. Ph.D. thesis, University of Maryland, College Park (2019)
7. Bergström, A.: Exploring digital divides in older adults' news consumption. Nordicom Rev. **41**(2), 163–177 (2020)
8. Raza, S., Ding, C.: News recommender system: a review of recent progress, challenges, and opportunities. Artif. Intell. Rev. **55**, 1–52 (2022)
9. Li, M., Wang, L.: A survey on personalized news recommendation technology. IEEE Access **7**, 145861–145879 (2019)
10. Sarwar, B., Karypis, G., Konstan, J., Riedl, J.: Item-based collaborative filtering recommendation algorithms. In: Proceedings of the 10th International Conference on World Wide Web, pp. 285–295 (2001)
11. Zhao, Z.D., Shang, M.S.: User-based collaborative-filtering recommendation algorithms on Hadoop. In: 2010 Third International Conference on Knowledge Discovery and Data Mining, pp. 478–481. IEEE (2010)
12. Kliegr, T., Kuchař, J.: Benchmark of rule-based classifiers in the news recommendation task. In: Mothe, J., et al. (eds.) Experimental IR Meets Multilinguality, Multimodality, and Interaction, pp. 130–141. Springer International Publishing, Cham (2015). https://doi.org/10.1007/978-3-319-24027-5_11
13. Pu, P., Chen, L., Hu, R.: A user-centric evaluation framework for recommender systems. In: Proceedings of the Fifth ACM Conference on Recommender Systems, pp. 157–164 (2011)
14. Wu, F., et al.: Mind: a large-scale dataset for news recommendation. In: Proceedings of the 58th Annual Meeting of the Association for Computational Linguistics, pp. 3597–3606 (2020)
15. Burke, R.: Hybrid recommender systems: survey and experiments. User Model. User-Adap. Inter. **12**, 331–370 (2002)
16. Lika, B., Kolomvatsos, K., Hadjiefthymiades, S.: Facing the cold start problem in recommender systems. Expert Syst. Appl. **41**(4), 2065–2073 (2014)
17. Bobadilla, J., Ortega, F., Hernando, A., Bernal, J.: A collaborative filtering approach to mitigate the new user cold start problem. Knowl.-Based Syst. **26**, 225–238 (2012)
18. Gridley, K., Brooks, J., Birks, Y., Baxter, K., Parker, G.: Improving care for people with dementia: development and initial feasibility study for evaluation of life story work in dementia care. Health Serv. Deliv. Res. **4**(23), 1–298 (2016). https://doi.org/10.3310/hsdr04230
19. Sellers, S.C., Stork, P.B.: Reminiscence as an intervention: rediscovering the essence of nursing. In: Nursing Forum, vol. 32, pp. 17–23. Wiley Online Library (1997)
20. Lind, M., Bluck, S., McAdams, D.P.: More vulnerable? The life story approach highlights older people's potential for strength during the pandemic. J. Gerontol.: Ser. B **76**(2), e45–e48 (2021)
21. Scott, K., DeBrew, J.K.: Helping older adults find meaning and purpose through storytelling. J. Gerontol. Nurs. **35**(12), 38–43 (2009)
22. Rubinstein, R.I., Parmelee, P.A.: Attachment to place and the representation of the life course by the elderly. In: Altman, I., Low, S.M. (eds.) Place Attachment, pp. 139–163. Springer US, Boston, MA (1992). https://doi.org/10.1007/978-1-4684-8753-4_7
23. Woods, B., Spector, A., Jones, C., Orrell, M., Davies, S.: Reminiscence therapy for dementia. Cochrane Database Syst. Rev. **18**(2), CD001120 (2005)
24. Clark, K.L., Le, M., Manning, Q., ELECTRA: Pre-training text encoders as discriminators rather than generators. Preprint at https://arxiv.org/abs/2003.10555 (2020)

25. He, H., Choi, J.D.: The stem cell hypothesis: dilemma behind multi-task learning with transformer encoders. In: Proceedings of the 2021 Conference on Empirical Methods in Natural Language Processing, pp. 5555–5577. Association for Computational Linguistics, Online and Punta Cana, Dominican Republic (2021). https://aclanthology.org/2021.emnlp-main.451
26. An, N., Gui, F., Jin, L., Ming, H., Yang, J.: Toward better understanding older adults: a biography brief timeline extraction approach. Int. J. Hum.-Comput. Interact. **39**, 1–12 (2022)
27. Buffel, T., De Donder, L., Phillipson, C., De Witte, N., Dury, S., Verté, D.: Place attachment among older adults living in four communities in flanders Belgium. Hous. Stud. **29**(6), 800–822 (2014)
28. Wicks, D.A.: Older adults and their information seeking. Behav. Soc. Sci. Libr. **22**(2), 1–26 (2004)
29. Stanziano, S.: Information seeking behavior of older adults. Ser. Libr. **71**(3–4), 221–230 (2016)
30. Gang, C.L.Q.: Web data extraction based on list pages of irregular data. Application Research of Computers **32**(9), 2651–2654, 2658 (2015)
31. Salton, G., Buckley, C.: Term-weighting approaches in automatic text retrieval. Inf. Process. Manage. **24**(5), 513–523 (1988)

Designing and Evaluating MahjongBrain: A Digital Cognitive Assessment Tool Through Gamification

Jiaoyun Yang[1,2,3,4], Richu Jiang[1,2], Huitong Ding[5(✉)], Rhoda Au[5,6,7,8], Jinying Chen[9], Clara Li[10], and Ning An[1,2,3,11]

[1] School of Computer Science and Information Engineering, Hefei University of Technology, Hefei, China

[2] National Smart Eldercare International S&T Cooperation Base, Hefei University of Technology, Hefei, China

[3] Intelligent Interconnected Systems Laboratory of Anhui Province, Hefei University of Technology, Hefei, China

[4] Key Laboratory of Knowledge Engineering with Big Data of Ministry of Education, Hefei University of Technology, Hefei, China

[5] Department of Anatomy and Neurobiology, Boston University Chobanian and Avedisian School of Medicine, Boston, USA

dinghfut@bu.edu

[6] Department of Neurology, Boston University Chobanian and Avedisian School of Medicine, Boston, USA

[7] Framingham Heart Study, Boston University Chobanian and Avedisian School of Medicine, Boston, USA

[8] Department of Epidemiology, Boston University School of Public Health, Boston, USA

[9] Department of Preventive Medicine and Epidemiology, Boston University Chobanian and Avedisian School of Medicine, Boston, USA

[10] Alzheimer's Disease Research Center, Department of Psychiatry, Icahn School of Medicine at Mount Sinai, New York, NY, USA

[11] Anhui Province Key Laboratory of Affective Computing and Advanced Intelligent Machine, Hefei University of Technology, Hefei, China

Abstract. Early detection of cognitive decline is of utmost importance, as research suggests that certain risk factors can be modified to slow down or even prevent the onset of Alzheimer's disease. However, traditional cognitive assessments require a significant amount of time and resources, which can burden both the participants and the clinicians administering the tests. This study developed a new digital cognitive assessment tool called MahjongBrain that incorporates Mahjong elements into eight digital games to improve engagement and interest among older adults during the assessment process. After presenting the software framework, assessment content, and system implementation, we conduct the usability test on 5 participants (mean age 65 years old, 20% women) in Anhui, China. The results demonstrate that the MahjongBrain is user-friendly for older adults, with the majority of participants reporting positive attitudes towards it (mean system usability scale score: 74). Furthermore, we introduce three novel digital measures which could be utilized by machine learning methods to detect subtle changes in cognitive function, including a) the scores and time to completion for each test

Q. Gao et al. (Eds.): HCII 2023, LNCS 14055, pp. 264–278, 2023.
https://doi.org/10.1007/978-3-031-48041-6_19

within each cognitive domain, b) the time-stamped coordinates from the finger tracking, and c) the position of the screen as the participant is playing the games. These initial findings indicate the innovation and transformation of MahjongBrain in cognitive assessment, although further usability and validation tests are needed.

Keywords: Digital Cognitive Assessment · Gamification · Mahjong · Usability Test

1 Introduction

Some individuals may experience cognitive decline as they age, and for some of them, this decline may become clinically significant when it progresses to the point of impairing their normal daily activities. The transition from normal to impaired cognition is often characterized by decreased attention, poor memory, executive dysfunction, and attenuation of other cognitive skills. Mild cognitive impairment (MCI) is the intermediate stage between normal cognitive decline and dementia. Its hallmark feature is a decline in memory, attention, and other cognitive functions that is beyond what is expected based on one's age and level of education [1], yet does not meet the criteria for a clinical diagnosis of dementia. Approximately 35% of participants diagnosed with MCI will progress to more severe levels of cognitive impairment within three years [2].

Cognitive assessment plays a vital role in detecting the deterioration of cognitive skills in older adults [3], with tests measuring performance in domains such as attention, memory, and executive function [4]. Results from cognitive tests can provide older adults and their families with a better understanding of the person's cognitive status from which to determine what cognitive intervention or treatment may be warranted. Many older adults lack a comprehensive understanding of their cognitive ability and do not prioritize their cognitive health, leading to reluctance to spend time and money on cognitive assessments. Early detection of cognitive decline is crucial, as recent advancements in both non-pharmacologic and pharmacologic treatments offer interventions that may be most effective in the early stages. Failing to identify cognitive decline early can increase the risk of irreversible damage and make it difficult for individuals to maintain their independence.

Traditional cognitive screening tests, such as the Mini-Mental State Examination (MMSE) [5], Montreal Cognitive Assessment (MoCA) [6], and clock drawing test (CDT) [7], are typically administered and scored by a trained examiner. However, these approaches are time-consuming, costly, and rely on subjective interpretation. Moreover, most of the existing cognitive test tools are biased towards specific educational and cultural backgrounds, as they are developed for English speakers with a good education in Western cultural contexts.

Gamification is the process of adding game-like elements, such as badges, achievements, rankings, and other features, into non-game scenarios, including educational, daily life, and medical settings [8]. In the field of cognitive health assessment, gamification is gaining popularity as it has the potential to alleviate cultural, educational, and linguistic bias, appealing to the elderly population with racial/ethnic diversity. Evidence shows that gamification can enhance motivation for certain activities [9]. As digital technology continues to disseminate into society, an increasing number of older adults have started to use digital devices like mobile phones and desktop computers. Game-based cognitive assessment tools have increased in the five years from 2018 to 2022, and the cognitive assessment and training market has achieved a growth rate of 32.39% [10]. Compared with the traditional cognitive assessment test methods, digital game-based cognitive assessment tools are novel, more accessible, and less time-consuming. Its pictures, sound effects, and interactive methods make the assessment process more immersive and can better engage older adults. On the other hand, some digital cognitive assessment tools lack interesting features and engaging content for older adults [11–15], resulting in low acceptance and participation [16–18].

To address the limitations of traditional cognitive assessment tools, our team took a gamification approach and developed MahjongBrain, which integrates game-like features with cognitive assessment techniques to enhance engagement, decrease psychological stress, and reduce test anxiety. This approach is in tandem with our previous development of a Digital Mahjong System using Internet of Things (IoT) technologies [19]. Furthermore, MahjongBrain is available on tablets, providing greater accessibility for older adults to assess their cognitive abilities in natural settings.

2 MahjongBrain

2.1 Tool Design

Before commencing the design phase, we met to discuss the game content in the tools and the tools used for development. Each game was designed in three steps: (1) selection of the cognitive domain to be evaluated; (2) identification of the most suitable design approach, and (3) identification of variables to be collected during the application's usage, including the score of each cognitive domain, the time taken, the number of hands raised, and others. To ensure accessibility, MahjongBrain presents all stimuli in the form of text and pictures. We selected Unity from a technological standpoint, as it is commonly used in game development and results in applications that can be run on mainstream computers and touch devices. Compared to more conventional pen-and-paper neuropsychological tests, we designed MahjongBrain to provide added versatility, interactivity, and personalization capabilities. Below, we delve deeper into the key factors we considered during the design process.

Platforms to Deliver the Tool. We selected the tablet device as the operation platform of MahjongBrain due to its touchscreen interface, portability, larger screens, and affordability. Although mobile phones are the most commonly used technology, their small screen size may make it difficult for older adults to see and lead to missed information or incorrect button presses. PCs offer a larger screen but are more expensive and less convenient. Therefore, we decided to use the tablet platform as it balances screen size, portability, and affordability.

2.2 Software Framework

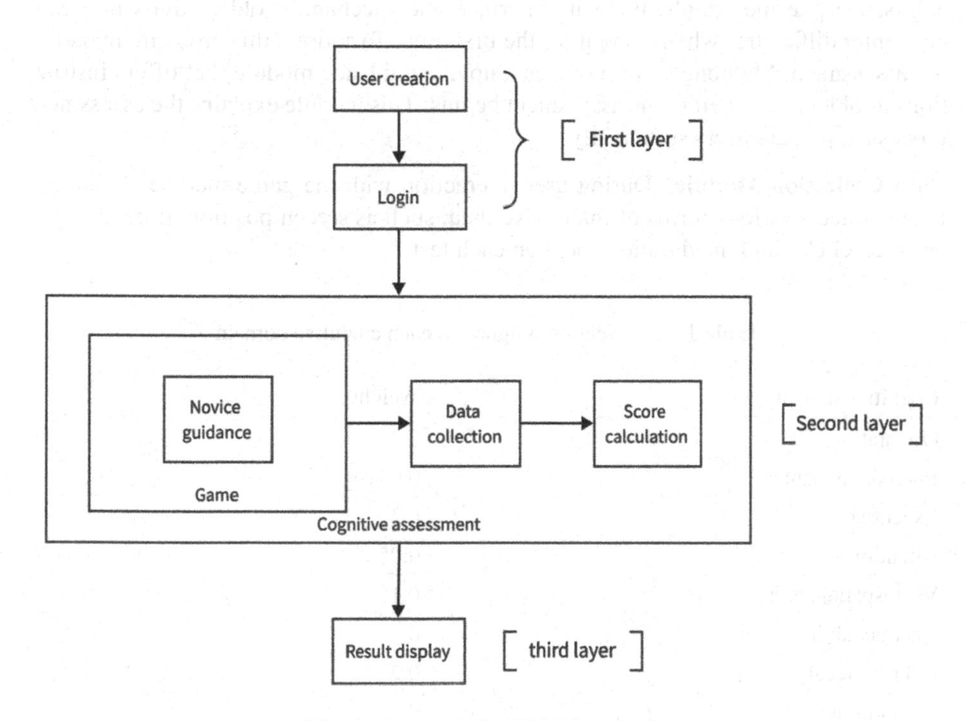

Fig. 1. Framework of MahjongBrain

Figure 1 illustrates the framework of the MahjongBrain system, which outlines the user interaction sequence with the system. It comprises four modules: the user creation module, login module, cognitive assessment module, and assessment result display module. The first layer requires the user to create an account and log in, and the second layer requires the user to complete the cognitive assessment by answering questions and playing games. Scores are obtained based on in-game performance and scoring rules, and the third layer displays the assessment result.

User Creation Module. The user provides an account name and password to create an account and store user information and data.

Login Module. Upon accessing the software, users must enter their username and password to log in, distinguishing individual users.

Cognitive Assessment Module. The main component of MahjongBrain comprises eight digital games for assessing different cognitive domains.

Game Module. This module contains a series of Mahjong games, and users' performance on these games is used to compute their cognitive performance.

Novice Guidance Module. We specifically design the MahjongBrain system for older adults. Despite the simplicity of its interface and mechanics, older adults may still encounter difficulties when using it for the first time. To address this problem, in part of the assessment, MahjongBrain provides a novice guidance module that offers instructions to older adults before the assessment begins. This module explains the assessment process to prepare users sufficiently.

Data Collection Module. During user interaction with the game module, MahjongBrain collects various forms of interactive data, such as screen position, time intervals between clicks, and the duration spent on each test.

Table 1. The weights assigned to each cognitive domain

Cognitive domain	Weight
Orientation	0.2
Immediate memory	0.05
Executive	0.2
Attention	0.05
Visuospatial ability	0.1
Abstract ability	0.1
Delayed recall	0.2
Working memory	0.1

Score Calculation Module. In MahjongBrain, each cognitive domain is separately calculated, with a total score of 100. Correct answers or operations during the game will score points, while incorrect ones will not. The final comprehensive cognitive ability score is calculated as a weighted average of the eight cognitive domains as shown in Table 1. We assigned higher weights to delayed recall, executive ability, and orientation, as we believed these abilities are more closely linked to the daily lives of older adults. Conversely, we assigned relatively lower importance to abstract and visual-spatial abilities. The immediate memory test has a lower weight because the task is relatively simple and easier to accomplish. The attention test only requires participants to evaluate the suit of Mahjong during the process, which is a simple form and easy to score.

Result Display Module. This module displays the overall score for cognitive ability assessment and the individual scores for each of the eight cognitive domains.

2.3 Assessment Content

In this section, after outlining the flow of the cognitive assessment process, we detail each of the eight cognitive domains, each with a screenshot.

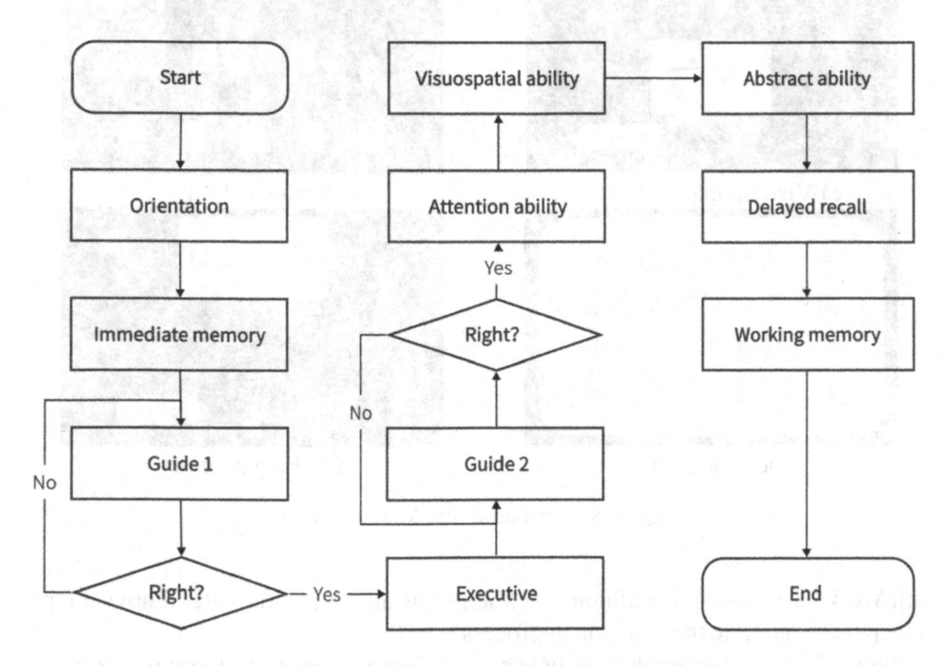

Fig. 2. Cognitive Assessment Flowchart

Figure 2 depicts the complete flow of the cognitive assessment in MahjongBrain. The assessment begins with an Orientation, followed by Immediate memory, Executive function, Attention ability, Visuospatial ability, Abstract ability, Delayed recall, and ends

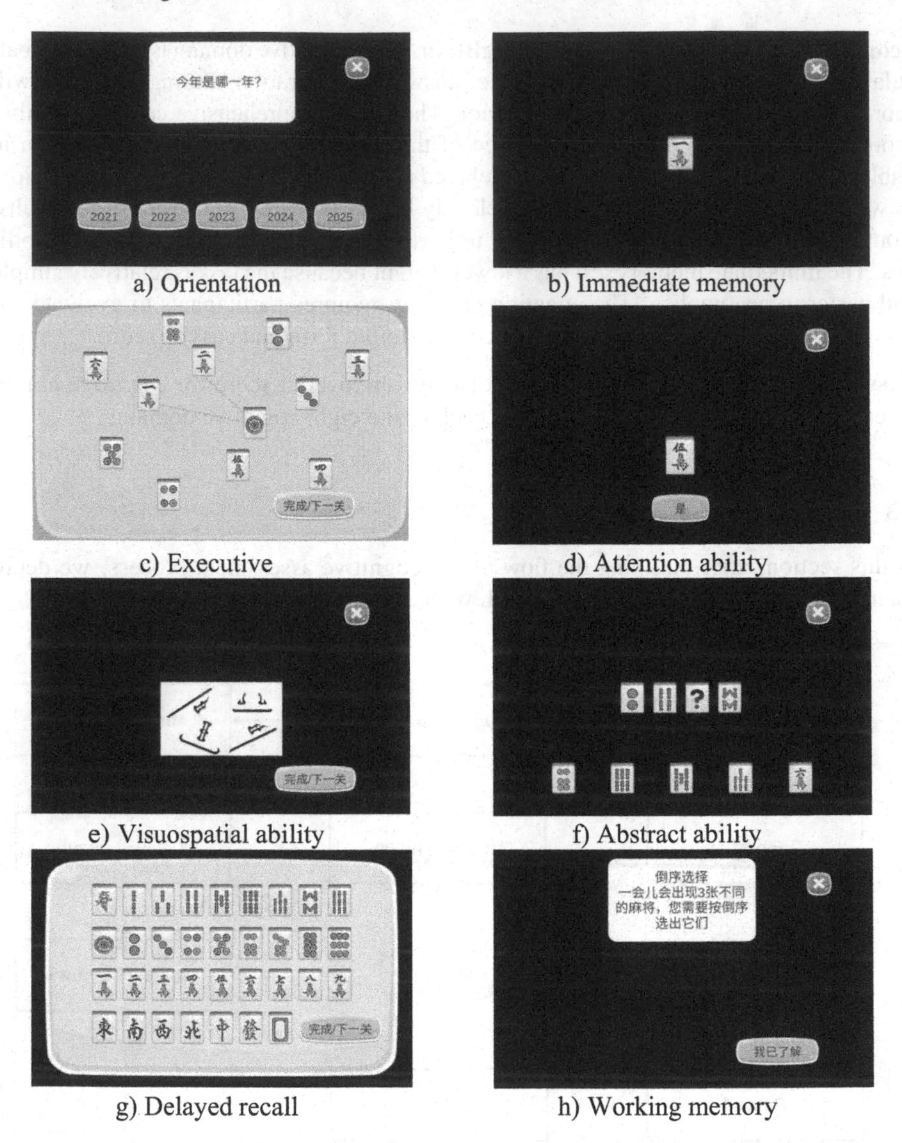

Fig. 3. Screenshots of the MahjongBrain

with Working memory. In addition, the MahjongBrain system provides a novice guide to help users navigate the assessment process.

Figure 3 displays screenshots of eight games corresponding to each cognitive domain. Detailed explanations are as follows:

a) **Orientation: what time now?** Three questions appear sequentially on the screen, asking the older adult to identify the current year, month, and time of the day. The year question provides five options for this year and two years before and after, the month question includes 12 options from 1–12, and the time question has three options:

morning, afternoon, and evening. The user needs to select the correct answer from the available options.

b) **Immediate memory: remember me.** Five different Mahjong tiles appear on the screen one after another (one second apart). The user must remember these five Mahjong tiles and then select them in any order from the entire set of Mahjong tiles once they disappear from the screen.
c) **Executive: draw & connect.** This game involves drawing lines connecting 12 Mahjong tiles arranged randomly on the screen. These tiles include two suits and values of 1–6, with the suits being bamboo, characters, and dots, along with some pictorial tiles. The user must connect the tiles in order, alternating suits from small to large, without raising their hand at any point during the task. Adapted from the Trails B test, this task assesses the visual and executive abilities of older adults.
d) **Attention: dot?** This game requires the user to focus on 15 Mahjong tiles that appear sequentially on the screen. Below each tile is a "yes" button. The user must click "yes" when the Mahjong tile is a single dot. This task is a go-no-go test and assesses simple attention in older adults.
e) **Visuospatial ability: reunion.** This game requires the user to identify a Mahjong tile based on a picture shown on the screen. The picture displays three parts of a Mahjong tile randomly oriented. The user must judge which Mahjong tile it represents and then select the corresponding tile from the whole set of Mahjong tiles.
f) **Abstract ability: Who am I?** This game requires the user to observe a sequence of 3–5 Mahjong tiles that appear on the screen, including one tile with a question mark in a random position. The user must determine what Mahjong tile should appear at the question mark and then choose the corresponding tile from a set of five Mahjong tiles displayed at the bottom of the screen.
g) **Delayed recall: Remember me.** This game requires the user to recall and select five Mahjong tiles shown earlier in the game. The user must choose these five Mahjong tiles from the whole set of Mahjong tiles in any order.
h) **Working memory: Positive and reverse order.** This game presents five Mahjong tiles on the screen, one after the other. Once the Mahjong tile disappears, the user is prompted to select those same five Mahjong tiles from the entire set of Mahjong tiles in the same sequence. Next, three Mahjong tiles appear in a specific order, and after they disappear, the player must select those same three Mahjong tiles from the whole set of Mahjong tiles in reverse order.

2.4 The System Implementation

During the development of MahjongBrain, we held regular meetings to collect feedback and suggestions for improvement. Based on this feedback, we continuously improved the game's task description to ensure greater clarity and comprehension. Additionally, we increased the contrast of the user interface and enlarged the button icon text to improve visibility. We also refined the game's process and mechanics to enhance user engagement and maximize enjoyment.

Game Development. MahjongBrain was developed with the Unity 3D game engine, utilizing its user-friendly operating system and powerful cross-platform capabilities.

Within Unity 3D, We create multiple game objects, including Mahjong tiles and various user interface displays.

Gameplay. The game is a simple click-based game designed to be user-friendly and accessible to individuals without prior experience with tablet games. We set the background at high contrast to enhance screen clarity and evenly distribute the information display. Novice guidance enables users to practice before starting the game, and the total estimated time to complete all games is between 5 to 15 min.

2.5 Usability Test

Participants. Following the widely accepted Nielsen usability principle, which suggests that 5 participants are sufficient to reveal 85% of existing issues in smaller systems [20], we recruited five older adults from the Yuan Tan Community in Qianshan, Anqing City, Anhui province, China for our usability test. The experiment device is the Huawei MatePad 10.8 (model SCMR-W09) with HarmonyOS 3.0.0.

Measure. After recording participants' demographic information, we conducted the usability test in a private room, utilizing the System Usability Scale (SUS) [21], a widely used tool in system usability testing. In addition to SUS, we created a usability testing questionnaire that focused on the design aspects of the system, including the clarity of the screen layout, feedback speed, and the presence of errors. The questionnaire had eight questions and used the Likert scale of 1–5 for answers, with 1 representing "strongly disagree" and 5 representing "strongly agree." At the start of each testing session, the participants received a brief introduction to the functions and content of MahjongBrain. We confirmed that the participants understood the system before asking them to independently complete the cognitive assessment without any assistance from the research staff. Upon completing the test, we ask each participant to complete the SUS and the usability questionnaire. In cases where participants did not comprehend specific questions, they received a default score of 3.

3 Results

3.1 Participant Characteristics

Figure 4 shows the five older adults who participated in the study, and they all completed the usability test successfully.

Table 2 shows the demographic characteristics of the participants (median age: 61, 20% women). One participant had a high school education level, while the other had a junior high school or below education level. Four participants reported having presbyopia and used glasses to correct their vision. In addition, one participant reported having hearing difficulties. All these factors did not appear to affect their performance during the test session.

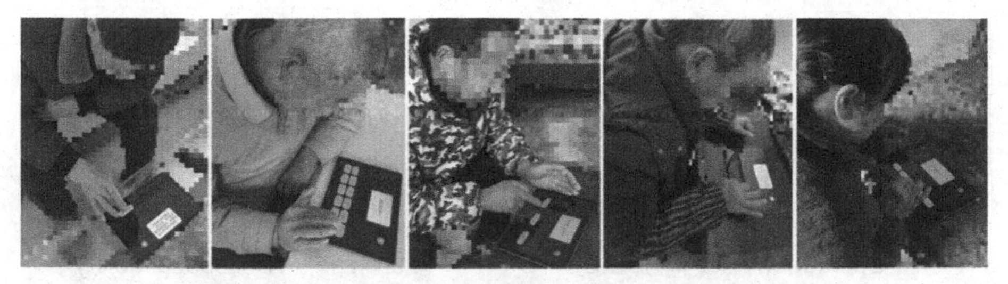

Fig. 4. Participants in this study

Table 2. Demographic characteristics of study participants

Variable	Total(n = 5)
Sex, n (%)	
Men	4(80%)
Women	1(20%)
Age(years)	
Median	61
Max	78
Min	60
Education level, n (%)	
High school and above	1(20%)
Junior high school and below	4(80%)
Vision	
Normal	1(20%)
Presbyopia	4(80%)
Hearing	
Normal	4(80%)
Difficulty in hearing	1(20%)
Frequency of playing Mahjong, n (%)	
Often	2(40%)
Sometimes	1(20%)
Never	2(40%)

3.2 MahjongBrain Usage Statistic

Figure 5 depicts the outcome of the cognitive assessment, which comprised the overall score of cognitive ability and the corresponding score of eight cognitive domains.

Figure 6 shows the novel digital data collected during a cognitive assessment process, which includes a) the scores and time taken to complete each test within each cognitive

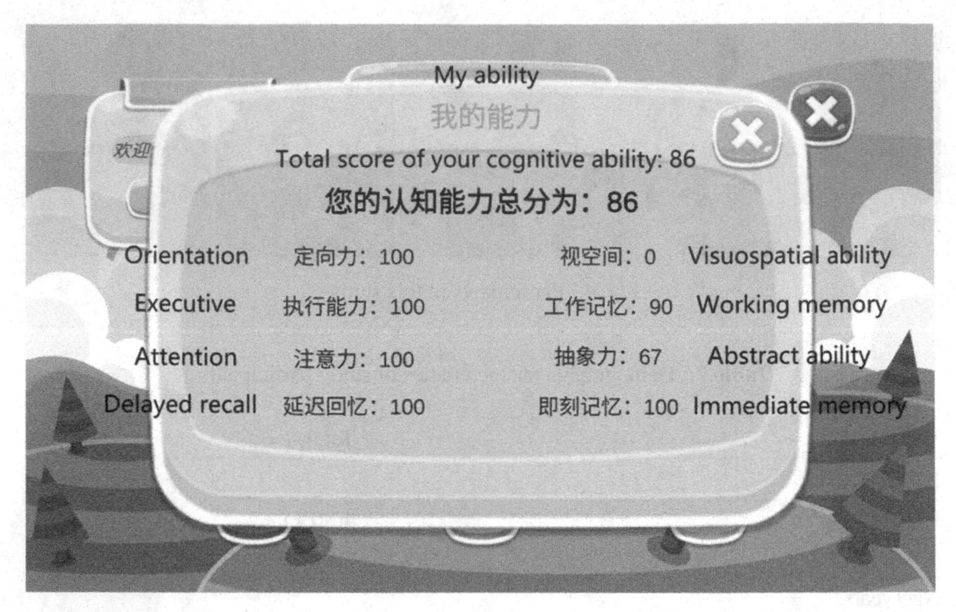

Fig. 5. Assessment results

domain, b) the time-stamped coordinates obtained from the finger-tracking executive function test, and c) the click position of the screen while the participant played the games.

```
24 1999 3 8 1 0  2 2 20 5
定向力得分100
定向力所用时间77.60503
即刻记忆得分100
即刻记忆所用时间42.1738
执行力得分78
执行力所用时间17.18933
注意力得分100
注意力所用时间73.45441
视空间能力得分100
视空间能力所用时间19.73769
抽象力得分100
抽象力 所用时间21.65336
延迟回忆得分100
延迟回忆所用时间8.711143
工作记忆得分100
工作记忆所用时间29.86477
认知能力总分97
评估所用时间29.86477
提笔次数0
提笔时长0
```

a) Score and time used

```
126.9243,759,944
126.9576,759,944
126.991,768.4406,945.1733
127.0243,854.3725,919.7798
127.0576,974.303,889.8901
127.0909,1110.179,882.379
127.1075,1179.418,877.5642
127.1408,1303.72,858.0924
127.1575,1356.794,846.2013
127.1741,1405.636,834.1385
127.2074,1477.091,810.1635
127.2241,1500.001,801.7995
127.2574,1524.292,792.2358
127.2741,1529.552,791.2242
127.2907,1531.795,791
127.324,1533,791
127.3407,1533,791
127.374,1533,791
127.3907,1531.207,792.7933
127.4073,1527.436,795.564
127.4406,1510.338,813.6616
```

b) Finger track

```
1.868893,675,1155
5.699812,1302,1197
8.881159,1747,1211
11.29633,2024,1211
13.9114,1107,1033
17.20936,1889,241
17.99221,1473,1193
20.54057,1458,1037
37.41349,1929,268
38.96253,1166,1188
41.12777,1126,1013
43.54302,1940,202
44.62566,926,1196
50.2389,1504,1189
51.42137,905,1208
57.9839,1494,1197
61.66492,906,1211
66.19551,905,1227
68.67722,1490,1224
71.19237,1877,279
74.02395,1251,336
```

c) Click position

Fig. 6. Data collected in the game

3.3 Usability Test Results

Table 3 presents the results of the SUS scale and questionnaire responses. The Mahjong-Brain system obtained a mean SUS score of 74.0 with a median of 77.5, a standard deviation of 10.3, and a range of scores between 55.0 and 85.0. These results indicate that the usability of the system was high. The questionnaire used a similar scoring algorithm as SUS, but there were eight questions, and the final score was multiplied by 5/4 to match the SUS scale. The average score of the questionnaire was 82.5, the median was 84.3, the standard deviation was 5.4, the maximum was 90.6, and the minimum was 75. Again, Table 2 shows that the system's usability rating was good.

Table 3. The test result

Participants ID	01	02	03	04	05	Mean
Usability measures						
SUS score	55.0	72.5	85.0	77.5	80.0	74.0
Questionnaire score	78.1	84.3	84.3	90.6	75	82.5
Data measures						
N[1]	9	0	0	1	0	2
Task score	26.6	80.0	73.4	71.4	57.8	61.9
Time used (min)						
Orientation test	2.9	0.9	1.9	2.8	0.7	1.8
Immediate memory test	2.3	1.0	1.0	0.9	3.3	1.7
Executive test	4.0	1.6	0.8	1.3	1.9	1.9
Attention test	1.4	0.3	1.2	0.9	1.4	1.1
Visuospatial ability test	1.9	0.7	1.0	0.8	1.9	1.2
Abstract ability test	6.4	0.4	2.4	0.8	1.6	2.3
Delayed recall test	0.8	1.1	0.4	0.3	1.3	0.8
Working memory test	2.2	1.6	1.0	0.7	2.6	1.6
All tests	21.8	7.6	9.8	8.6	14.6	12.5

[1] Number of hands raised in the executive test (Draw & Connect).

Figure 7 presents a radar chart of the scores from the questionnaire, indicating that the system performed well in terms of error rate, feedback speed, and interface and information layout. Nevertheless, there is room for improvement in user experience, overall satisfaction, and step complexity.

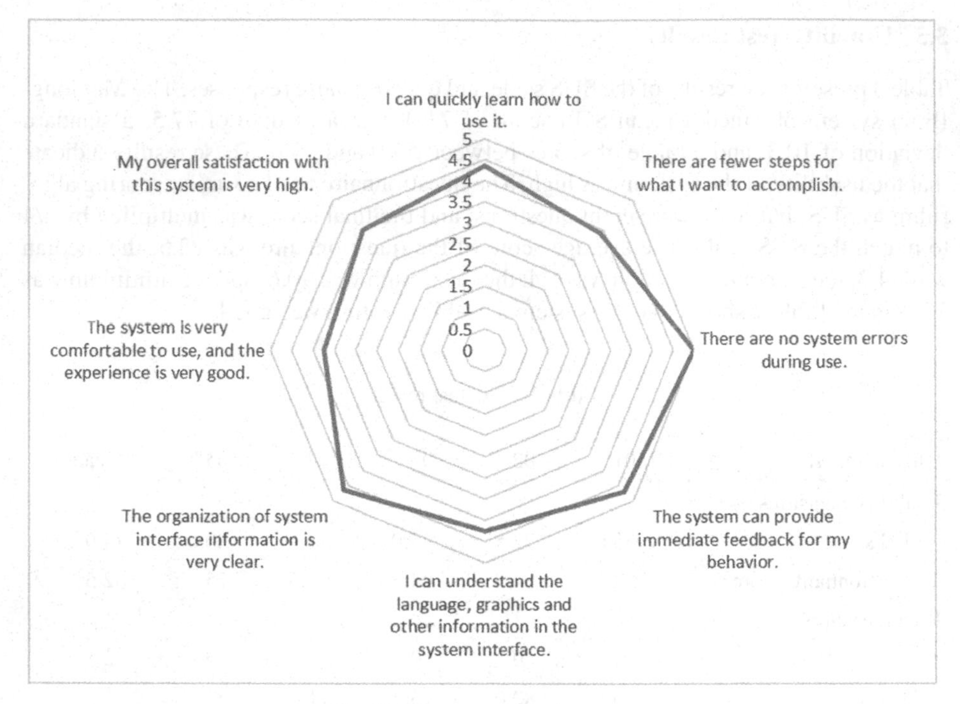

Fig. 7. The questionnaire score

4 Conclusion

This study aimed to address the need for accessible and engaging cognitive assessment tools for older adults by designing and evaluating MahjongBrain, a gamified digital cognitive assessment tool. To address the limitations of traditional cognitive assessments, MahjongBrain uniquely integrates cognitive assessment components with digital game features and Mahjong elements to improve engagement and interest among older adults during the assessment process.

The usability test results indicated that MahjongBrain is simple and easy to use for older adults, with a mean System Usability Scale score of 74.0. Furthermore, MahjongBrain offers three novel digital measures that could assist machine learning methods to detect subtle cognitive function changes. These initial findings suggest that MahjongBrain has the potential to make a significant contribution to the field of cognitive assessment for older adults. Future research will involve enrolling more participants for the usability test and verifying the reliability and validity of MahjongBrain.

Acknowledgment. This work was partially supported by the Wing Tat Lee Fund, the Anhui Provincial Key Technologies R&D Program (No. 2022h11020015).

References

1. Eshkoor, S.A., Hamid, T.A., Mun, C.Y., Ng, C.K.: Mild cognitive impairment and its management in older people. Clin. Interv. Aging **10**, 687–693 (2015)
2. Potter, G.G., Steffens, D.C.: Contribution of depression to cognitive impairment and dementia in older adults. Neurologist **13**(3), 105–117 (2007)
3. Vourvopoulos, A., Faria, A.L., Ponnam, K., Bermudez i Badia, S.: Rehabcity: design and validation of a cognitive assessment and rehabilitation tool through gamified simulations of activities of daily living. In: Proceedings of the 11th Conference on Advances in Computer Entertainment Technology, pp. 1–8 (2014)
4. Lumsden, J., Edwards, E.A., Lawrence, N.S., Coyle, D., Munafò, M.R., et al.: Gamification of cognitive assessment and cognitive training: a systematic review of applications and efficacy. JMIR Serious Games **4**(2), e5888 (2016)
5. Folstein, M.F., Folstein, S.E., McHugh, P.R.: "Mini-mental state": a practical method for grading the cognitive state of patients for the clinician. J. Psychiatr. Res. **12**(3), 189–198 (1975)
6. Nasreddine, Z.S., et al.: The Montreal cognitive assessment, MoCA: a brief screening tool for mild cognitive impairment. J. Am. Geriatr. Soc. **53**(4), 695–699 (2005)
7. Agrell, B., Dehlin, O.: The clock-drawing test. Age Ageing **27**(3), 399–403 (1998). https://doi.org/10.1093/ageing/27.3.399
8. Deterding, S., Dixon, D., Khaled, R., Nacke, L.: From game design elements to gamefulness: defining" gamification." In: Proceedings of the 15th international academic MindTrek conference: Envisioning future media environments, pp. 9–15 (2011)
9. Rohde, L.E., et al.: Health outcomes in decompensated congestive heart failure: a comparison of tertiary hospitals in Brazil and United States. Int. J. Cardiol. **102**(1), 71–77 (2005)
10. Khaleghi, A., Aghaei, Z., Mahdavi, M.A.: A gamification framework for cognitive assessment and cognitive training: qualitative study. JMIR Serious Games **9**(2), e21900 (2021)
11. Lumsden, J., Skinner, A., Woods, A.T., Lawrence, N.S., Munafò, M.: The effects of gamelike features and test location on cognitive test performance and participant enjoyment. PeerJ **4**, e2184 (2016)
12. McPherson, J., Burns, N.R.: Assessing the validity of computer-game-like tests of processing speed and working memory. Behav. Res. Methods **40**, 969–981 (2008)
13. McPherson, J., Burns, N.R.: Gs invaders: assessing a computer game-like test of processing speed. Behav. Res. Methods **39**, 876–883 (2007)
14. Nielsen, J., Landauer, T.K.: A mathematical model of the finding of usability problems. In: Proceedings of the INTERACT'93 and CHI'93 conference on Human factors in computing systems, pp. 206–213 (1993)
15. Ninaus, M., et al.: Game elements improve performance in a working memory training task. Int. J. Serious Games **2**(1), 3–16 (2015)
16. Birk, M.V., Mandryk, R.L., Bowey, J., Buttlar, B.: The effects of adding premise and backstory to psychological tasks. In: Conference on Human Factors in Computing Systems, pp. 18–23 (2015)
17. Lumsden, J., Skinner, A., Coyle, D., Lawrence, N., Munafo, M.: Attrition from web-based cognitive testing: a repeated measures comparison of gamification techniques. J. Med. Internet Res. **19**(11), e395 (2017)
18. Katz, B., Jaeggi, S., Buschkuehl, M., Stegman, A., Shah, P.: Differential effect of motivational features on training improvements in school-based cognitive training. Front. Hum. Neurosci. **8**, 242 (2014)
19. An, N., Hu, E., Guo, Y., Yang, J., Au, R., Ding, H.: Digital mahjong system: towards precise cognitive assessment with IoT technologies. In: HCI International 2022–Late Breaking

Papers: HCI for Health, Well-being, Universal Access and Healthy Aging: 24th International Conference on Human-Computer Interaction, HCII 2022, Virtual Event, 26 June–1 July 2022, Proceedings, pp. 229–241. Springer (2022). https://doi.org/10.1007/978-3-031-17902-0_17
20. Nielsen, J.: Usability Engineering. Morgan Kaufmann (1994)
21. Brooke, J., et al.: Sus-a quick and dirty usability scale. Usability Eval. Ind. **189**(194), 4–7 (1996)

When Seniors Meet Digital: An Investigation on the Antecedents and Consequences of Smartphone Dependence Among Urban Older Adults

Yan Zhang[1](✉), Dawei Wu[2], Yuxiang (Chris) Zhao[2], and Qinghua Zhu[1]

[1] Nanjing University, Nanjing 210023, China
strawberries_z@163.com

[2] Nanjing University of Science and Technology, Nanjing 210094, China

Abstract. With the advancement of digital inclusion, the ability of older adults to use ICT has increased significantly. Smartphone dependence is a pervasive and damaging behavior. With the permeation of smartphones among urban older adults, smartphone dependence is emerging in this population. However, the mechanism underlying smartphone dependence among the older users are still understudied. In this research, we employed the critical incident technique (CIT) method to investment the antecedents and consequences of older users' smartphone dependence. This research gathered and analyzed qualitative data from 9 males and 11 females of older adults aged 55 to 63. The results indicated that antecedents of older adults' smartphone dependence include contextual factors, emotional lift, anxiety sensitivity, and self-regulation. We built the seniors & smartphone pull-out battle model to reveal the process of how these antecedents impact smartphone dependence. In addition, smartphone dependence among older adults would lead to cognitive, psychological, and behavioral consequences. Our work advances older users' smartphone engagement research by exploring the antecedents and consequences of older adults' smartphone dependence behaviors. Meanwhile, this research provides practical insights for smartphone practitioners, family members, and older adults to manage smartphone dependence.

Keywords: Smartphone Dependence · Older Adults · Sensitivity Anxiety · Self-regulation · Intergenerational Dissonance

1 Introduction

The Covid-19 pandemic has accelerated the digital transformation in China, and booming digital industries are enabling more older adults to fully engage with digital technologies. Compared to other digital media, smartphones are portable, instantaneous, and responsive, making it easier for seniors to access, use, share information and interact with others anytime and anywhere. Due to the combined effects of aging-appropriate transformation in internet products and policies for smart senior care, the digital proficiency of older adults has gradually improved [1]. According to the 50th "Statistical

Q. Gao et al. (Eds.): HCII 2023, LNCS 14055, pp. 279–294, 2023.
https://doi.org/10.1007/978-3-031-48041-6_20

Report on the Development of China's Internet" by China Internet Network Information Center (CNNIC), as of June 2022, 99.6% of Chinese Internet users accessed the Internet through mobile phones, with 25.8% of them being aged 50 and above. Moreover, the "2021 Middle-aged and Older People's Internet Behavior Research Report" released by iiMedia Research shows that the average length of internet use for middle-aged and older people has exceeded the national average of 3.74 h spent online per day by internet users.

There are differences in Internet use behaviors and influencing factors between urban and rural older adults, due to reasons such as geography and cross-class [2, 3]. In China, there is evidence that frequent Internet use behavior negatively affects urban older adults [4]. Smartphones are currently an important medium for Internet access. The widespread use of smartphones has changed the way older adults live their daily lives, such as keeping in touch with friends and family, gaining knowledge, social inclusion and support, being more autonomous, and having a better quality of life through the smartphone [5–7]. However, excessive smartphone use can lead to negative consequences [8], such as problematic use, addiction, and other behaviors that can be seen as manifestations of smartphone dependence [9, 10]. Smartphone dependence can be considered as the downside of technological advancements [11]. It's a state of uncontrolled behavior in which the user might experience different degrees of physiological and psychological consequences, leading to social dysfunctions [12]. One of the typical symptoms of smartphone dependence is compulsive checking of missed calls and messages [13–15]. While most of the research on smartphone dependence focuses on adolescents and college students, there have been fewer studies carried out on adults over the age of 30, especially on older adults [8, 16, 17]. This may be because people believe that the consequences of Internet and smartphone use by older adults over 50 are not as devastating as those for adolescents and college students, and that adults have more self-control. However, recent studies have shown that even older adults experience an uncontrollable and incessant desire to use their smartphones due to emotional absences, fear of missing out (FoMO), and social influences, which can affect their daily life [17].

Although previous studies have explored the factors that influence smartphone dependence in adolescents and college students, there are natural differences between older adults and younger generations. If adolescents and college students are considered digital natives, then older adults are digital immigrants. Therefore, the antecedents and consequences of smartphone dependence cannot be generalized. Given China's senior population and the pervasiveness of smartphones, as well as the epidemic prevention and control policies implemented in the last three years, investigating smartphone dependence in the Chinese context is appropriate. Moreover, considering the difference in digitalization levels between urban and rural areas [17], we chose urban older adults as the research target.

2 Methods

For this line of research, we used critical incident technique (CIT) to explore the antecedents and consequences of smartphone dependence among urban older adults. CIT, which is derived from industrial psychology, is an empirical research method for analyzing observed and collected human behavior and is often used to analyze factors that promote and hinder informational behavior [18]. In HCI-related research, this approach is applied to investigate the important events or activities that occur during HCI, such as analyzing the features, process and influencing factors associated with users' engagement in Snapchat APP [19]. The wide usage of CIT shows that this method has provided a systematic procedure to collect and analyze the incidents that influence the older adults' smartphone dependence behaviors. Figure 1 presents the research process of our research. In-depth interviewing was selected because of its strength in establishing rapport with participants to make them feel more comfortable and at-ease, which can generate insightful responses. In-depth interviewing also allows the researcher to ask follow-up questions, probe for additional information, and circle back to key questions later on in the interview to generate a rich understanding of attitudes, perceptions, and motivations [20].

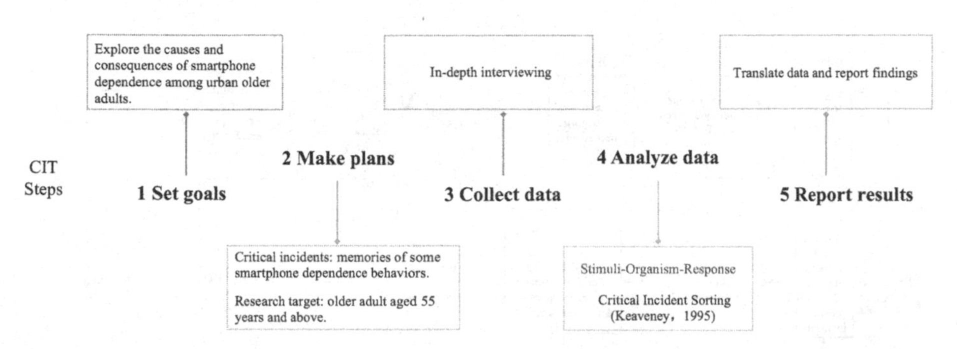

Fig. 1. The Research Process with CIT

The researcher interviewed 20 smartphone users to analyze individuals' smartphone usage habits in their lives to probe how they develop smartphone dependence and how it affects their daily functions. Firstly, through snowballing and social platform invitations, the researchers recruited 25 older adults aged 55 years and above who self-assessed as smartphone dependent. Second, the researchers screened participants by asking them how long they used their smartphones and how often they used them. In the end, 20 older adults were selected. The interviews were conducted from September to December in 2022. Each interview lasted about 45 min. In addition, we conducted interviews with family members of 2 older adults as a supplement to the data.

The interview included three parts. The first part was to guide the older adults to recall the process and experience of their smartphone use, and provide as much detail as possible about their smartphone dependence behaviors. In the second part, we asked about the antecedents that influence older adults' smartphone behaviors. The third part was going to ask about the influences and changes of smartphone dependence on their lives.

Of these participants, 9 (45%) are male and 11(55%) are female. Participants' age ranged from 55 to 63 years, with a mean of 57.8. Ten interviewees had bachelor's degrees. Six had a graduate or higher degree, and four had high school diplomas. All participants were retired. Most participants use their smartphones more than seven times a day. The average time spent on the smartphone daily was 5 h.

We transcribed and organized the interviews and invited five PhD candidates (Judges A, B, C, D, and E) to thematically categorize and conceptually identify 212 critical incidents that influence older adults' smartphone dependence behavior. Following an approach recommended by Keaveney for classifying critical incidents [21], the judges classified the first 2/3 of critical incidents as a classification sample (numbered 1–141) and the rest as a test sample (numbered 142–212). Figure 2 illustrates the classification process. Inter-judge reliability was assessed using the Holsti formula (Eq. 1) [22].

$$R = \frac{M}{(N_1 + N_2)/n} \tag{1}$$

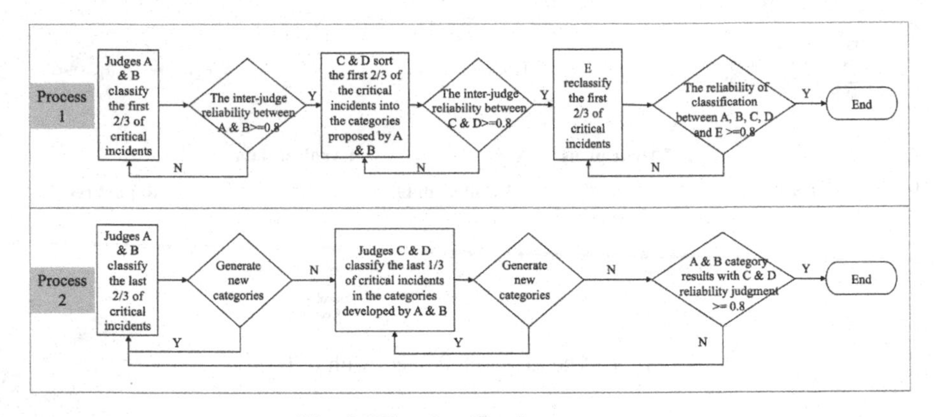

Fig. 2. The classification processes

R represents the confidence index, M is the number of identical classifications, n is the number of classifiers, and N1 and N2 are the number of judges' respective classifications. If the calculation result is greater than 0.8, it indicates that the consistency of this classification result is high; if the confidence is less than 0.8, the judges need to compare and discuss repeatedly to determine the final classification result.

First of all, A and B classified the critical incidents. The inter-judge reliability between A and B was 0.96. After discussing the categories where differences existed, A and B identified 5 categories and 10 subcategories. In the process of checking the existing classification topics, C and D found that there were some incidents that could not be classified into the current classification scheme proposed by A and B. Therefore, they respectively added 1 and 2 subcategories. The inter-judgment reliability between C and D was 0.92. Moreover, Judge E reclassified the first 2/3 critical incidents and no new categories were found. The reliability of classification between A, B, C, D and E was 0.93. Eventually, during the subsequent sample test, Judges A–D sorted the remaining 1/3 incidents according to the classification scheme obtained by Process 1 and did not find any new categories. This indicates that the classification results reached saturation. Following steps consistent with those described above, we classified 156 critical incidents of consequences arising from smartphone dependence behaviors in older adults. The reliabilities of the inter-judge classification results were all greater than 0.8. In addition, the content validity of this research was judged by experts to be satisfactory. In summary, the high inter-judges' reliabilities and content validity of the classification scheme demonstrate that categories provide a good insight into the antecedents and consequences of smartphone dependence among older adults.

As summarized in Table 1, the classification scheme for the antecedents of smartphone dependence among older adults consisted of 5 categories and 13 subcategories, mainly involving contextual factors, emotional gain, anxiety sensitivity, smartphone dependence, and self-control. Likewise, the classification scheme for the consequences of smartphone dependence among older adults included 3 main categories and 6 subcategories, as shown in Table 2. The results of the analysis contained three aspects: cognitive, psychological, behavioral.

Table 1. The antecedents of smartphone dependence among older adults

Category	Subcategory
Contextual factors	Individual factors
	Social-psychology factors
	Social-cultural factors
	Technology factors
Emotional lift	Mood modification
	Autonomy
	Relatedness
Anxiety sensitivity	Attachment anxiety
	FoMO
Self-regulation	Mindfulness
	Perceived self-control of time
Smartphone dependence	Functional dependence
	Existential dependence

Table 2. The consequences of smartphone dependence among older adults

Category	Subcategory
Cognitive	Information cocoon
	Insufficient risk perception
Psychological	Abatement of social connectedness
	Intergenerational dissonance
Behavioral	Scheduling disorders
	Sleeplessness

3 Findings

3.1 The Situation of Smartphone Daily Use Among Older Adults

Through our analysis of the interview contents, we have summarized the characteristics of seniors and their smartphone usage scenarios. Smartphone-dependent older adults are proactive in embracing new technologies and have acquired various digital skills. They also have a high sense of necessity for digital inclusion and take an active role in learning online operating skills to enhance their information capabilities. Furthermore, they are motivated to integrate into the internet life. Figure 3 illustrates the primary smartphone usage scenarios of older adults, including entertainment information, social communication, lifestyle services, health care, and e-commerce shopping. Based on the critical incidents, 90% of the participants' daily smartphone use behavior includes reading news and information, 85% read articles, 80% chat, and 82% watch videos (including short videos).

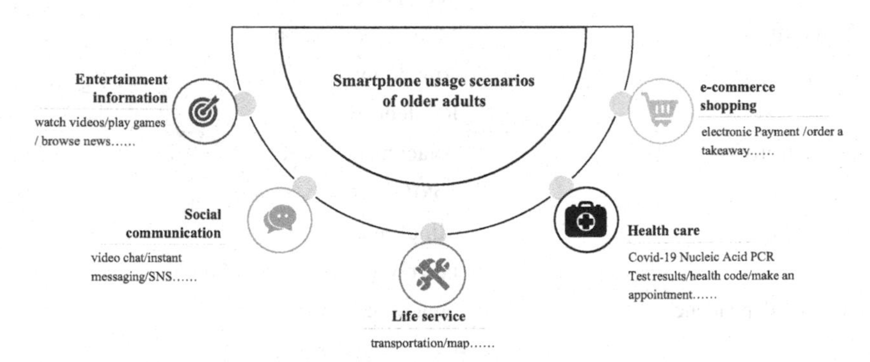

Fig. 3. Smartphone usage scenarios of older adults

3.2 The Smartphone Dependence Among Older Adults

Drawing reference to Davis and Park for the typology of Internet dependence and the definition of smartphone dependence [12, 23], there are two categories of smartphone dependence among older adults in this research. One is functional dependence, where it refers to the targeted use of smartphones by older adults to meet their specific needs. For example, looking for news and information, listening to music, e-commerce shopping, making video calls, and so on. This is a dependence triggered by the tool properties of smartphones. Many participants described instances where they necessarily use their smartphones to accomplish specific tasks on a daily basis. For example, P1 and P7 said they "*rely on their smartphones to find news and information.*" P3 and P20 "*like to use their smartphones to play music.*" P11 and P16 "*are used to shopping online through their smartphones.*" Meanwhile, P14 and P19 "*use their smartphones to video chat with their family members every day.*"

Another is existential dependence, in which older adults spend an unconscionably large amount of time connected instantly or continuously through their smartphones. In this circumstance, older adults do not use smartphones to exploit their utility as a tool. While many of the interviewees shared that they were using their smartphones purposelessly, the P20 mentioned that they "*check their phones habitually every day even though they have nothing to do.*" Similarly, the P7 and P12 described their mindless smartphone usage as follows,

If I don't use my [smart] phone, it's like I'm lacking a part of my life. Even if I watch ads or even some junk news, I still don't want to turn off my [smart] phone. (P7).

3.3 The Antecedents of Smartphone Dependence Among Older Adults

Figure 4 depicts the Seniors & Smartphone Pull-out Battle. More specifically, older adults' smartphone dependence implicates a dynamic tug amongst three categories: emotional lift, anxiety sensitivity, and self-regulation. These are the direct factors that initiate smartphone dependence among older adults. Besides, contextual factors are indirectly influencing smartphone dependence.

Emotional Lift. Emotional lift refers to the use of smartphones by older adults to meet their emotional needs and social desires. As older adults retire, they experience a steep shrinking of their social network and an increase in free time. By using smartphones seniors can mitigate loneliness or sadness and pass the time of boredom. Smartphones are a "shelter" for a range of emotions in seniors, increasing their perception of heightened emotions and leading to dependent behaviors. As P3 described,

Retirement has led to a sudden increase in time and fewer people to be able to contact. Using my smartphone makes me feel calm and forget about the troubles of life. It is my emotional anchor. (P3).

In addition, many participants mentioned the warmth and relatedness that smartphones bring to them, and P15 said that they "*don't have a plan for their old age and feel bored. But the personalized recommendations of the smartphone will constantly push content that meets the interests of seniors. It feels like there is someone who knows you very well and cares about you.*" *Older adults have not been online for very long and are* "*curious about what smartphones can do*" (P18). This sense of exploration satisfies the autonomy of older adults.

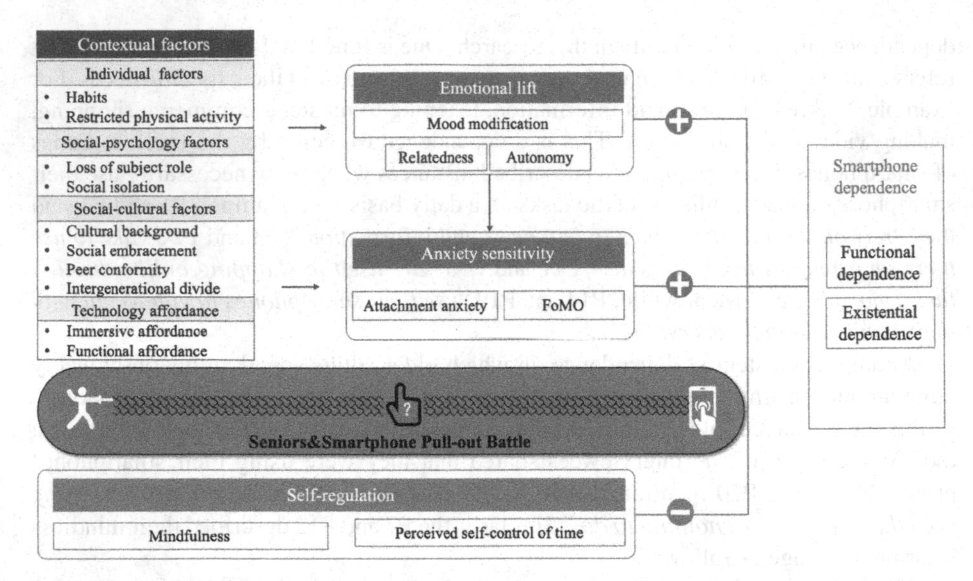

Fig. 4. The Seniors & Smartphone Pull-out Battle: The antecedents of smartphone dependence

Anxiety Sensitivity. Using a smartphone satisfies the inner enjoyment of older adults. When seniors are not accessing smartphones, they feel anxious and uncomfortable. Anxiety sensitivity mainly relates to older adults' perception of something unpleasant that may happen in the future, including fear of missing out (FoMO) and attachment anxiety. The older population could re-establish social communities through smartphones. Also, they become attached to the social relationships online. When they do not have access to the smartphone, they will worry about missing out on people or new things in the social network Anxiety sensitivity is an important factor that trigger the development of psychological dependence on smartphones among older adults. As P1 mentioned,

I usually check my smartphone every once in a while. I'd like to know what my friends are watching or doing every day. I'm afraid that if I don't check it for a while, I'll lose the shared conversation with my friends. (P1).

In addition, emotional lift enhances older adults' attachment to online social relationships and information content. Furthermore, emotional gain increases older adults' attachment to online social relationships and information content. As P5 stated,

I have gotten a lot of joy from my friends online. I can't imagine what life would be like without these friends. (P5).

Self-regulation. Self-regulation is defined as the ability of older adults to change their behavior towards smartphone dependence. This may involve modifying, abandoning, or escaping to change current behavior patterns so that one's smartphone usage progresses in the desired direction. In our research, older adults controlled their behavior mainly through mindfulness and perceived self-control of time. When older adults realize that their smartphone usage is problematic, they will intentionally control or remediate their behavior. Self-regulation reflects an older adult's appraisal of the self-containment state and the adoption of strategies to maintain regulation. Sustaining adequate self-regulation supports older adults in winning the tug-of-war with their smartphones. As P6 commented,

Sometimes I will consciously control the time of smartphone use. Once I let my guard down, I may have to spend most of the day on my phone. (P6).

Moreover, our findings show that self-regulation is a critical factor that moderates the relationship between contextual factors and smartphone dependence. Older adults with strong self-control tend to limit their smartphone use, even when they encounter contextual factors that trigger their emotional needs and anxiety. On the other hand, older adults with weak self-regulation tend to succumb to their smartphone dependence, even when they encounter only minor contextual triggers.

Contextual Factors. Contextual factors include individual factors, social-psychological factors, social-cultural factors, and technology affordance. For older adults, the decline in physical function makes them dependent on their smartphones to carry out many activities. Habits are developed through repeated training of older adults in their daily usage activities. The usage of smartphones has become a routine and automatic function performed by older adults, leading to dependence on them. For example, while P10 wakes up, she uses her smartphone for morning news every morning to catch up on changes around the world, and P2 plays music on her smartphone to start the day. P4 described to us how she uses her smartphone to have fun throughout the day.

I used to go to the park every day to sing and dance with my friends. Now I can't go there every day because my legs are not strong enough. But with my smartphone, I can sing with my friends online. I can sing pretty well, and I have gained some fans. Now I turn on my phone every night at 7 p.m. and sing with my friends. (P4).

Social-psychological factors are important triggers for feelings of anxiety and depression in older adults, such as loss of subject roles and social isolation. The reduction of social roles and weakening of social networks that older adults experience in preparation for and during retirement. P13 emphasized that the online interaction and community engagement provided by smartphones can contribute to alleviating loneliness in older adults.

When I used to work, I had tasks to complete every day, and it was very busy. Now there is no one who needs me to do anything anymore either. I feel like I'm going to be eliminated from society...... Smartphones can expand my social circle and meet like-minded people from other places. (P13).

Moreover, P12 mentioned that using smartphones for entertainment and games can temporarily forget the worries and anxieties about the future. These are the reasons that predispose to smartphone dependence.

Mobile games nowadays give me a high level of realism. I can talk and fight with other users through avatar. I don't think I'm getting old. (P12).

Social-cultural factors are external stimuli that induce smartphone dependence, in terms of cultural background, social embrace, peer conformity, and intergenerational divide. In the past, household items were purchased from offline supermarkets. In the context of the Covid-19, all these activities are transformed to be done online through smartphones to minimize person-to-person contact. China's epidemic prevention policy requires everyone to use health codes and travel codes, which must be implemented through smartphones. The cultural context silently advances smartphone dependence. This was also brought up by P14 who described that:

Because of the Covid-19 lockdown, you can't buy food offline, you have to rush on your smartphone. Registration must also be reserved in advance on WeChat...... Without the health code cannot go anywhere. You also have to check the color of the health code to identify whether you are in touch with the Covid-19 patients. You really can't do anything without a smartphone. (P14).

Social embrace refers to the use and prevalence of smartphones in society, especially in the intimate social networks of older adults. For example, many participants reported a high level of acceptance of smartphones among older adults, with P11 stating, "*All my friends have switched to smartphones now.*" Similarly, P10 emphasized that "*I use smartphones every day to connect with people around me.*" There is a high level of acceptance and recognition of smartphones as a communication and entertainment tool in society. Therefore, the trend toward widespread smartphone usage has prompted seniors to accept and spend a lot of time learning how to use smartphones.

The large use of smartphones by older adults is also affected by the behavior of people around them, especially their peers, both online and offline. One participant said that the reason she first bought and learned to use a smartphone was because "*a friend recommended it*" (P16), and P8 described how she started learning to use a smartphone with the support of a friend by saying, "*My best friend guided me to download and sign up for common apps.*" Simultaneously, if people around them were actively using their smartphones at offline gatherings, they would follow suit to maintain a sense of connection with others. As P10 said,

When we go to public square dancing, our friends use their smartphones to take videos and post them on social media. I do the same thing because we are a group. Besides, we compare ourselves to each other to see who gets more likes. (P10).

The intergenerational divide is a major issue among the seniors. In the face of fast-paced urban life, the strong sense of loneliness between the younger generation and the older adults in the family, even when they coexist face-to-face in the same space and time, is magnified by mutual neglect. Many seniors describe the lack of intergenerational interaction and the absence of care from their children. The intergenerational divide also obliged the older adults to prefer the emotional comfort of virtual networks via smartphones. For example, P13, who moved from the countryside to live with his son in the city, reveals that he spends most of his time with his smartphone. He ascribed smartphone dependence to the gap between the offspring and the parental generation.

My son bought a flat in the city and invited me to live with him. I thought we would get to know each other better when we live together. But in fact, we didn't have much to share. He [his son] has to work during the day, and after work we each play on our own phones. I want to get to know his life, but he doesn't seem to have much patience...... Playing on my phone allows me to forget these worries for a while. (P13).

The progress of digital technology and the features it offers have had a significant impact on the daily behavior of older adults. The implications of technology affordance on older adults' smartphone dependence are both immersive and functional. Immersive affordance, such as personalized algorithmic control and game-designed motivational strategies, provide a certain degree of emotional lift for older adults, which in turn leads to functional dependence on smartphones. Both P6 and P9 specified in their interviews that their smartphones engrossed them and they could not feel the passing of time. They feel anxious when they can't use their smartphones.

I focus more on Chinese history, and my smartphone often pushes me articles or topics that I like to read. Sometimes I feel a struggle. I think about reading this one and then stop reading it [turn off him phone], while wondering what the next one will be about. Time went by while I was wrestling with that. (P6).

The first thing I do when I wake up every morning is to sign in. Because continuous sign-in will give me a reward. For fear of missing or forgetting, I set an alarm clock to remind myself. (P9).

As well as the many functions of smartphones that empower seniors to freely explore new knowledge and interact with others, P2 credits the likes in smartphone socialization with providing her with an extremely important sense of ceremony.

Liking is telling people "I'm following you" or "I'm getting attention and recognition from others". My friends will enthusiastically like each of my friends' circle, which gives me a feeling of being noticed and respected. So, I always pay attention to my friends' latest status updates. I sometimes took a nap with my smartphone in my hand, and I also watched TV. (P2).

3.4 The Consequences of Smartphone Dependence Among Older Adults

Cognitive. Firstly, smartphone dependence among the seniors can have an impact on cognition, like Information cocoon and Insufficient risk perception. The traditional reading practices of the older adults make them dependent and reliable on the media. This leads them to have faith in every piece of information on their smartphones. The precise algorithmic push of the Internet makes the seniors increasingly closed and isolated in the huge online world. Moreover, due to the lack of ability to filter and identify effective information, the seniors are easily caught in the online information field built by pseudoscience, extremist thinking, online financial scams and other false information, which lure them to buy financial products and health care products, resulting in heavy losses. They have inadvertently become the main group of people who believe and spread rumors. In a supplementary interview, P16's daughter told us that the older adults had a limited experience with the Internet and were unable to effectively identify false information on the Internet, so they inadvertently became the main group of people who believed and spread rumors.

My dad believes everything he can find on the Internet and clicks on it. He doesn't believe in the existence of false information at all. Moreover, he shares these messages in family groups. (P16's daughter).

Psychological. Secondly, an overreliance on smartphones may reduce the interaction between the seniors and others, which may cause adverse psychological effects. P8 depicted that as they become more and more dependent on smartphones, they will have difficulties in communicating and interacting with others in real life.

Smartphones have become a part of my life. Sometimes friends will ask me to go out with them. I might have gone according to my previous habit, but now I prefer to stay home and play with my phone. (P8).

In this research, we found that older adults' smartphone dependence does not repair the intergenerational divide. On the contrary, it can foster intergenerational dissonance. Many participants indicated that their children complained about their excessive smartphone dependence and would try to reduce older adults' dependence on their smartphones by persuasion and coercion. The stalemate between the persistent nagging of the young and the stubborn rebellion of the old seems to be an interchange of roles between the two parties regarding adolescence. The sons of P2 and P2 recalled the incident of the quarrel for us.

My son and I had a quarrel about my dependence behavior. He didn't understand why I was spending every moment swiping short videos. But my life is so boring that I have nothing else to do without my smartphone. Funny videos on my smartphone one after another, I just can't stop. (P2).

During the epidemic, my dad barely left home. Sometimes he didn't even get out of bed and spent all day and night looking at his smartphone. The taijiquan that he was once passionate about was all but cast aside. Whenever I nagged him, he asked me why I didn't have time for him. (P2's son).

Behavioral. Smartphone dependence among older adults also posed behavioral consequences, like scheduling disorders, sleeplessness. Many interviewees pointed out that smartphone dependence made it difficult to follow their daily life plans. For example, P4 mentioned that they forgot the time by playing with their phones, which led to irregular diet. p7 said, "*When I was playing with my smartphone while cooking, I forgot to turn off the heat and burnt the pot.*" In addition, the results of the interviews also revealed that smartphone dependence among the older adults tend to cause problems such as lack of sleep and poor sleep quality.

I play with my phone until late at night every day, and the number of hours of sleep has decreased significantly. (P6).

4 Discussion

In this study, we examined the antecedents and consequences of smartphone dependence among older adults using CIT. Based on interviews with 20 older adults and 2 family members, we characterized dependence behaviors as both functional and existential dependence. Furthermore, these behaviors were found to be a result of a competition between the emotional lift and anxiety sensitivity associated with smartphone use, and the self-regulation of seniors. Contextual factors acted as triggers for the emotional needs and anxiety of older adults. Additionally, smartphone dependence caused cognitive, psychological, and behavioral effects on older adults.

4.1 Theoretical Implications

This study makes three significant contributions to the study of smartphone use. First, we utilized the concept of "smartphone dependence" instead of "smartphone addiction" to better understand the smartphone use behavior of older adults. The findings of this study demonstrate that older adults who are dependent do not experience symptoms that threaten their physical and psychological health. Therefore, while urban seniors may still exhibit compulsive smartphone use, their dependence is much weaker than addiction. Through the analysis of interview data, our research analyzed both functional and existential attributes of dependence as defined by Park [12]. Additionally, we examined the antecedents of the emergence of both sorts of dependence. We found that there appears to be a specific association between anxiety sensitivity and existential dependence. Anxiety-sensitive people tend to continuously check their smartphones [24], resulting in a permanent connection [25].

Second, this study illustrates that technological advances, represented by smartphones, have two sides. On the one hand, they bring emotional lift for older adults, and on the other hand, they enhance anxiety sensitivity. In order to overcome their social isolation, seniors have a strong desire to keep up with the times and integrate into their children's lives. Smartphones and virtual networks have become important tools for re-socialization, emotional bonding, and socialization. Previous studies have considered technology affordance as a positive factor and explored its impact on user experience [26], whose findings have informed the optimization of product design. However, in recent years, studies have also discussed the possible negative effects of technology affordance, such as addiction [27]. Older adults prefer to cultivate smaller, tighter social circles than younger people [17]. They will be attentive to maintaining online social relationships and, in parallel, will worry about disconnection and other issues related to virtual socialization.

Third, we have discovered that the antecedents and consequences of older adults' smartphone dependence behaviors are somewhat intersectional. By diagnosing the antecedents of older adults' smartphone dependence behaviors, we are able to understand the process of older adults escaping from their real dilemmas and reconstructing their digital lives. However, the intersectionality of antecedents and consequences suggests that while older adults may initially use smartphones to escape from reality, their real needs or problems are not solved through virtual networks. On the contrary, smartphone dependence even has the potential to exacerbate real problems. We can describe this phenomenon as 'drinking poison in the hope of quenching one's thirst'. For example, the generational divide may drive older adults to use smartphones for emotional support. However, smartphone-dependent behavior among older adults can also lead to intergenerational dissonance. Based on a review of literature on problematic smartphone use, we found that some factors are treated as antecedents in some studies and appear as outcomes in others. For instance, loneliness has been used as an independent variable in some studies [28, 29], while other studies explore loneliness as an outcome variable [30].

4.2 Practical Implications

Our research offers several practical alternatives for smartphone practitioners, family members, and older adults. To begin with, smartphone practitioners should be aware of the existential dependence that lurks in the design of systems for older users. While immersive affordance plays a critical role in enhancing user engagement, it can also lead to dependent behavior among older users. Smartphone practitioners could add a series of "time management" features for seniors, which could provide pop-ups or forced interruptions for all older users who watch longer. In addition, smartphone practitioners should be concerned about the dangers of false information on the internet for seniors. Special content curation for seniors should be carried out to combat malicious baiting and fraudulent behaviors.

Next, family members should pay more attention and be more patient with older adults. While the younger generation is focused on improving the digital inclusion level among older adults, little attention is given to the dependence dilemma that arises from smartphone use. Our findings suggest that if family members can strengthen mutual communication and understanding with older adults in real life, it can compensate for the emotional loss that older adults may experience. Besides, family members should also encourage and support older adults in pursuing offline activities, such as hobbies or social events. This can help them stay socially connected and engaged with their communities, which can reduce their reliance on virtual networks for emotional support. Moreover, family members can help older adults to learn and use digital tools in a responsible and healthy way, which can improve their digital literacy and prevent negative outcomes associated with excessive smartphone use.

At last, seniors should focus on improving their self-regulation and information screening abilities. In their daily lives, older adults should consciously limit their smartphone usage. It is also crucial to increase seniors' awareness of false information on the internet. One way to achieve this is by participating in digital literacy programs, where they can learn about internet safety and responsible smartphone use.

Acknowledgment. This work was funded by the Key Projects of the National Social Science Foundation of China under Grant (No. 22&ZD327).

References

1. Bevilacqua, R., et al.: EHealth literacy: from theory to clinical application for digital health improvement. Results from the ACCESS training experience. Int. J. Env. Res. Public Health **18**(22), 11800 (2021). https://doi.org/10.3390/ijerph182211800
2. Berner, J., et al.: Factors influencing Internet usage in older adults (65 years and above) living in rural and urban Sweden. Health Inform. J. **21**, 237–249 (2014). https://doi.org/10.1177/1460458214521226
3. Mack, E.A., Dutton, W.H., Rikard, R.V., Yankelevich, A.: Mapping and measuring the information society: a social science perspective on the opportunities, problems, and prospects of broadband Internet data in the United States. Inf. Soc. **35**, 57–68 (2019). https://doi.org/10.1080/01972243.2019.1574526
4. Sun, K., Zhao, Y.C., Tao, X., Zhou, J., Liu, Q.: Examining urban-rural differences in the impact of Internet use on older adults' depression: evidence from China. Data Sci. Manag. **5**, 13–20 (2022). https://doi.org/10.1016/j.dsm.2022.03.003
5. Barnes, D.E., et al.: The mental activity and eXercise (MAX) trial. JAMA Intern. Med. **173**, 797 (2013). https://doi.org/10.1001/jamainternmed.2013.189
6. Cotten, S.R., Ford, G., Ford, S., Hale, T.M.: Internet use and depression among retired older adults in the United States: a longitudinal analysis. J. Gerontol. Ser. B: Psychol. Sci. Soc. Sci. **69**, 763–771 (2014). https://doi.org/10.1093/geronb/gbu018

7. Rowe, J.W., Kahn, R.L.: Successful aging 2.0: conceptual expansions for the 21st century. J. Gerontol. Ser. B: Psychol. Sci. Soc. Sci. **70**(4), 593–596 (2015). https://doi.org/10.1093/geronb/gbv025
8. Busch, P.A., McCarthy, S.: Antecedents and consequences of problematic smartphone use: a systematic literature review of an emerging research area. Comput. Hum. Behav. **114**, 106414 (2021). https://doi.org/10.1016/j.chb.2020.106414
9. Elhai, J.D., Levine, J.C., Dvorak, R.D., Hall, B.J.: Non-social features of smartphone use are most related to depression, anxiety and problematic smartphone use. Comput. Hum. Behav. **69**, 75–82 (2017). https://doi.org/10.1016/j.chb.2016.12.023
10. Loredo e Silva, M.P., de Souza Matos, B.D., da Silva Ezequiel, O., Lucchetti, A.L.G., Lucchetti, G.: The use of smartphones in different phases of medical school and its relationship to internet addiction and learning approaches. J. Med. Syst. (2018). https://doi.org/10.1007/s10916-018-0958-x
11. Genta, G., Riberi, P.: The dark side of technology. In: Technology and the Growth of Civilization. SPB, pp. 172–182. Springer, Cham (2019). https://doi.org/10.1007/978-3-030-25583-1_9
12. Park, C.S.: Examination of smartphone dependence: functionally and existentially dependent behavior on the smartphone. Comput. Hum. Behav. **93**, 123–128 (2019). https://doi.org/10.1016/j.chb.2018.12.022
13. van Deursen, A.J.A.M., Bolle, C.L., Hegner, S.M., Kommers, P.A.M.: Modeling habitual and addictive smartphone behavior: the role of smartphone usage types, emotional intelligence, social stress, self-regulation, age, and gender. Comput. Hum. Behav. **45**, 411–420 (2015). https://doi.org/10.1016/j.chb.2014.12.039
14. Chen, C., Zhang, K.Z.K., Gong, X., Zhao, S.J., Lee, M.K.O., Liang, L.: Understanding compulsive smartphone use: an empirical test of a flow-based model. Int. J. Inform. Manag. **37**(5), 438–454 (2017). https://doi.org/10.1016/j.ijinfomgt.2017.04.009
15. Lee, Y.-K., Chang, C.-T., Lin, Y., Cheng, Z.-H.: The dark side of smartphone usage: psychological traits, compulsive behavior and technostress. Comput. Hum. Behav. **31**, 373–383 (2014). https://doi.org/10.1016/j.chb.2013.10.047
16. Nahas, M., Hlais, S., Saberian, C., Antoun, J.: Problematic smartphone use among Lebanese adults aged 18–65 years using MPPUS-10. Comput. Hum. Behav. **87**, 348–353 (2018). https://doi.org/10.1016/j.chb.2018.06.009
17. Busch, P.A., Hausvik, G.I., Ropstad, O.K., Pettersen, D.: Smartphone usage among older adults. Comput. Hum. Behav. **121**, 106783 (2021). https://doi.org/10.1016/j.chb.2021.106783
18. Flanagan, J.C.: The critical incident technique. Psychol. Bull. **51**, 327–358 (1954). https://doi.org/10.1037/h0061470
19. Piwek, L., Joinson, A.: "What do they snapchat about?" Patterns of use in time-limited instant messaging service. Comput. Hum. Behav. **54**, 358–367 (2016). https://doi.org/10.1016/j.chb.2015.08.026
20. Johnson, J.M.: In-Depth Interviewing (2002). https://doi.org/10.4135/9781412973588.n8
21. Keaveney, S.M.: Customer switching behavior in service industries: an exploratory study. J. Mark. **59**, 71–82 (1995). https://doi.org/10.1177/002224299505900206
22. Parker, E.B., Holsti, O.R.: Content analysis for the social sciences and humanities. Am. Sociol. Rev. **35**, 356 (1970). https://doi.org/10.2307/2093233
23. Davis, R.A.: A cognitive-behavioral model of pathological Internet use. Comput. Hum. Behav. **17**, 187–195 (2001). https://doi.org/10.1016/s0747-5632(00)00041-8
24. Hussain, Z., Griffiths, M.D., Sheffield, D.: An investigation into problematic smartphone use: the role of narcissism, anxiety, and personality factors. J. Behav. Addict. **6**, 378–386 (2017). https://doi.org/10.1556/2006.6.2017.052
25. Katz, J.: Handbook of Mobile Communication Studies. The MIT Press (2008). https://doi.org/10.7551/mitpress/9780262113120.001.0001

26. Song, S., Zhao, Y.C., Yao, X., Ba, Z., Zhu, Q.: Short video apps as a health information source: an investigation of affordances, user experience and users' intention to continue the use of TikTok. INTR. **31**, 2120–2142 (2021). https://doi.org/10.1108/intr-10-2020-0593
27. Fox, J., Moreland, J.J.: The dark side of social networking sites: an exploration of the relational and psychological stressors associated with Facebook use and affordances. Comput. Hum. Behav. **45**, 168–176 (2015). https://doi.org/10.1016/j.chb.2014.11.083
28. Bian, M., Leung, L.: Linking loneliness, shyness, smartphone addiction symptoms, and patterns of smartphone use to social capital. Soc. Sci. Comput. Rev. **33**, 61–79 (2014). https://doi.org/10.1177/0894439314528779
29. Mahapatra, S.: Smartphone addiction and associated consequences: role of loneliness and self-regulation. Behav. Inf. Technol. **38**, 833–844 (2019). https://doi.org/10.1080/0144929x.2018.1560499
30. Mosalanejad, L., Nikbakht, G., Abdollahifrad, S., Kalani, N.: The prevalence of smartphone addiction and its relationship with personality traits, loneliness and daily stress of students in Jahrom University of medical sciences in 2014: a cross-sectional analytical study. J. Res. Med. Dental Sci. **7**, 131–136 (2019)

Innovative Design of Aging-Friendly Household Cleaning Products from the Perspective of Ergonomics

Lige Zhang, Minghan Sun, and Yeqing Pei(✉)

School of Fashion Accessory, Beijing Institute of Fashion Technology, Princeton University, Beijing, China
caupyq@126.com

Abstract. The rapid development of an aging society has highlighted the importance of meeting the basic needs of the elderly in their daily lives, especially in terms of living conditions. To ensure the safety and comfort requirements of the elderly, home products must take into account their physical, cognitive and psychological characteristics. Therefore, a key aspect of designing age-friendly products is to consider their usability and accessibility in the home environment. This emphasizes the importance of creating user-friendly home products for older adults to improve their quality of life. The goal of this study is to improve the ease of use of cleaning products by examining specific forms of operation during product use. Based on ergonomic design principles, this study aims to provide universal design guidelines for older adults when using home cleaning products. By considering the ergonomic requirements and emotional preferences of users, the researchers aim to improve the overall user experience and promote the adoption of cleaning products by older consumers. Guided by ergonomics, specific experimental results of muscle fatigue were analyzed to determine the ideal grip and operating angle of the product handle to ensure the comfort of use of senior-friendly household products. The size and structure of the product was ergonomically designed to meet the daily needs of the elderly while satisfying their physical and psychological needs for ease, safety and comfort. Ultimately, this helps create a happier home lifestyle for seniors.

Keywords: Ergonomic · design of age-friendly · User Centered Design · Electromyogram

1 Introduction

1.1 Overview of Relevant Theories

Overview of Ergonomics/Human Factors Theory and Research Methods. Ergonomics and Human Factors is an interdisciplinary research field that aims to investigate the interactions between humans and their work environment in order to improve the efficiency, safety, and comfort of work systems. This field combines theories and

Q. Gao et al. (Eds.): HCII 2023, LNCS 14055, pp. 295–312, 2023.
https://doi.org/10.1007/978-3-031-48041-6_21

methods from disciplines such as engineering, psychology, and physiology to gain a deeper understanding of human physiological and psychological characteristics, with the ultimate goal of designing and optimizing work systems and products to enhance productivity and human well-being. The theories and research methods of Ergonomics and Human Factors provide a theoretical basis and practical guidance for the design of more humane and efficient work systems, which can enhance efficiency and staff satisfaction, while reducing the risks of workplace accidents and health issues.

This paper mainly focuses on using the theory of ergonomics and human factors as the main theoretical foundation and experimentation-based research as the primary method to design household cleaning products that are user-friendly.

Age-Friendly Design. Age-friendly design involves the improvement of products, environments, and services based on the unique needs and abilities of elderly individuals, aiming to enhance their quality of life and independence. With an increasing aging population, age-friendly design has become increasingly important in society.

Design Methodology Construction. Within the framework of ergonomics, age-friendly design involves considering the physical, cognitive and psychological characteristics of older adults to ensure that products and environments are more friendly and easier to use for them. Ergonomics provides a range of theoretical and research methods that can be used to assess the needs and limitations of older adults in terms of human-computer interaction, ergonomics, and cognitive load.

This study will use empirical research methods, including user studies and observations, to understand the behaviors and needs of older adults during in-home cleaning tasks. Anthropometric and other methods will also be used to collect feedback and physiological data from older adults about the product. This data will provide an important basis for designing age-appropriate products to meet the needs of older adults and promote their independent living.

1.2 Aging-Friendly Home Products Research

Current Status. Research on aging-friendly home products is one of the current hot topics in the field of ergonomics and design. As the global trend of population aging increases, more and more research is focused on how to design and improve home products to meet the special needs of older adults and to enhance their quality of life and independence. Current research focuses on the following areas:

Safety and Protection. Research aims to design home products with a high level of safety to prevent accidents in the home for older adults, such as slips and falls. This includes the use of non-slip materials, safety handrails, non-slip flooring, non-slip bathtubs, etc., as well as the application of smart home technologies such as smart cameras and sensors for monitoring and early warning.

Functionality and Ease of Use. The research looks at designing home products that are functional and easy to use to meet the daily needs of older people. This involves research on the human-machine interface design of home devices, the legibility of symbols and signs, and the simplified operation of home appliances.

Ergonomics and Comfort. Research focuses on how to design home products that meet ergonomic principles based on the physical characteristics and abilities of older adults to provide better comfort and use experience. This may include adjusting seat heights, optimizing button layouts for appliances, providing easy-to-grip handles, etc.

Accessibility and Adaptability. The research aims to improve the accessibility of home products so that older adults can easily access and use areas of the home. The research also explores how to design adaptable home products to accommodate the changing needs of older adults, such as height-adjustable beds, folding armrests, etc.

Smart and Remote Monitoring. The research explores combining smart home technologies and remote monitoring systems with age-appropriate home products to provide 1additional support and safety. This includes research and application of smart lighting systems, remote health monitoring devices, smart home control systems, etc.

Trends. The future trends of aging-friendly home products will be influenced by technological innovation, aging population trends and changing user needs. The following are a few possible trends in the future development of age-appropriate home products:

Smart and IoT Technology. With the advancement of IoT technology, age-appropriate home products will become more intelligent and interconnected. Smart home devices and sensors will be able to automatically monitor and regulate the home environment and provide more personalized support and services, such as smart lighting, smart temperature control, remote monitoring, etc.

Virtual and Augmented Reality Technologies. Virtual reality (VR) and augmented reality (AR) technologies are expected to provide richer experiences and features for seniors. Through virtual reality technology, seniors can experience activities such as virtual travel, social interaction and cognitive training. Augmented reality technology can provide older adults with features such as assisted navigation, memory aids and object recognition.

Health Monitoring and Telemedicine. Aging-friendly home products will increasingly focus on health monitoring and telemedicine. Intelligent health monitoring devices and sensors will be able to monitor the physiological indicators, activities and sleep of the elderly in real time, and communicate with medical institutions or doctors remotely to achieve telemedicine and health management.

Personalized Customization and Adaptable Design. Future aging-friendly home products will focus more on personalized customization and adaptable design. Through artificial intelligence and machine learning technology, products can be customized and optimized according to the individual differences and needs of the elderly. Adaptive design will allow products to adapt and change according to the changing needs and abilities of older adults.

Social Interaction and Emotional Support. Age-appropriate home products will provide more social interaction and emotional support. Smart assistants, virtual social platforms and remote interaction tools will help seniors stay socially connected and provide emotional support and recreational activities.

In research on aging-friendly home products, a common issue is insufficient user participation, resulting in products that do not meet the needs of older adults. Given the special needs and abilities of older adults, their involvement and feedback are essential for product design and evaluation. When designing aging-friendly home cleaning products, it is worth studying the grip posture of older adults during product use. Starting from this issue, this author aims to provide practical design guidelines and suggestions on grip posture and size of cleaning products, combining the theory of ergonomics and aging-friendly design principles to improve older adults' home life. The ultimate goal is to create products that are more friendly and responsive to older adults' needs and to design a better life for them.

2 Research Methodology

2.1 Characteristics of the Elderly

Physiological Characteristics. Physical characteristics of older adults refer to the physical and physiological changes that occur as we age. The following are common physiological characteristics of older adults:

Changes in the Muscular and Skeletal Systems. Changes in the muscular and skeletal systems occur with age. Muscle mass and strength may decrease, and bone density may decrease, leading to muscle atrophy and osteoporosis.

Changes in the Cardiovascular System. The cardiovascular system is also affected in older adults. The heart's ability to pump blood may decrease, the walls of blood vessels become more rigid, and the coronary artery supply to the heart may decrease, increasing the risk of cardiovascular disease.

Respiratory System Changes. The respiratory system may become less functional in the elderly. Lung capacity and respiratory muscle strength may decrease, and the elasticity and clearance capacity of lung tissue may diminish, leading to breathing difficulties and susceptibility to infection.

Changes in the Digestive System. The elderly may also experience some changes in their digestive system. Oral health may be affected with reduced saliva production and increased dental and gum problems. Gastrointestinal motility slows down and digestion and absorption may decrease.

Neurological Changes. As the elderly age, there are some changes in the nervous system. The number of neurons may decrease, the speed of nerve conduction may decrease, and cognitive function and attention may decline.

Changes in the sensory system: The sensory system of older adults may also be affected. Vision and hearing may decrease, and color perception and sensitivity to high frequency sounds may be diminished. The senses of smell and taste may also be diminished.

Psychological Characteristics. Psychological characteristics of older adults refer to the psychological and cognitive changes that occur with age. The following are common psychological characteristics of older adults:

Memory Decline. Older adults may experience a decline in memory, especially working memory and short-term memory. They may forget newly learned things more easily or lose memory coherence.

Slower Processing. Older adults may have slower information processing, and they may need more time to process and understand new information or perform cognitive tasks.

Reduced Attention Span. Older adults may become more easily distracted and have difficulty staying focused for long periods of time. They may be more susceptible to distractions and have higher attention demands for complex tasks.

Decreased Abstract Thinking and Flexibility. Older adults' abstract thinking and flexibility may be affected. They may be more accustomed to traditional ways of thinking and problem solving and may find it difficult for novel or complex concepts and tasks.

Emotional and Psychological Adjustment. As older adults age, they may experience challenges with emotional regulation. They may be more likely to feel anxious, depressed, or lonely, especially in the face of life changes, physical health problems, or reduced social networks.

Self-Identity and Identity Shifts. Older adults may experience a process of self-identity and identity shifts. They may face situations such as role changes, retirement, and changes in family structure that require redefining their identity and goals.

The Influence of Psychological Characteristics on Design. The psychological characteristics of older adults have an important impact on the design of in-home products, and designers should take these characteristics into account to provide a better user experience and meet the needs of older adults. The following are some specific areas of influence:

Simplicity and Ease of Use. Since the information processing speed and memory of the elderly may decrease, the design of in-home products should focus on simplicity and ease of use. Clear interfaces, concise steps and intuitive instructions can help older adults understand and use products more easily.

Emotional Design. Older adults may be more susceptible to emotional and psychological influences, so the design of in-home products can consider elements of warmth and emotional support. For example, products can provide friendly voice prompts, approachable interface design and encouraging feedback to enhance the positive emotions and motivation of older adults to use them.

Ease of Reading and Visibility. Older adults may have reduced vision and be sensitive to fine print or low contrast designs. Therefore, the design of in-home products should consider appropriate font size, high-contrast colors and clearly visible icons to ensure that older adults can easily read and identify relevant information.

Provide Cognitive Support. Older adults may have reduced attention span and abstract thinking skills, and product design can provide cognitive support. For example, by using clear and concise instructions, step-by-step guidance and providing help functions to help older adults complete complex tasks or solve problems.

Emphasize Personalization and Autonomy. Older adults may experience challenges in self-identification and identity transformation, and the design of in-home products can emphasize personalization and autonomy. Products can provide personalized setting options, memory functions for user preferences, and opportunities for older adults to participate in decision-making and control to enhance their self-esteem and sense of autonomy.

Social Interaction and Connectivity. Older adults may face reduced social interaction and feelings of isolation, and the design of in-home products can provide features for social interaction and connectivity. For example, products can support remote communication, virtual social networks and online communities to help older adults stay connected with family, friends and communities.

2.2 Characteristics of the Elderly

Based on the analysis of the physiological and psychological characteristics of the elderly, the product was positioned as a safe and caring household cleaning product. The user interacts mainly with the product's handle and the designed grip angle is emphasized. Due to the unique physiological characteristics of the user, the product's original cleaning power system has been transformed from relying solely on human strength to a combined effort between the user and the product. The product also guides the user in the cleaning process and addresses the psychological desire for independent use, while considering human factors and designing the product's size and structure for stability and cost reduction. Additionally, an entertainment mode was added to make cleaning less tedious and increase user engagement.

2.3 Product Structure Size Determination

Elderly Body Size Reference. Physical characteristics of older adults refer to the physical and physiological changes that occur as we age. The following are common physiological characteristics of older adults:

Sitting Height. The sitting height of the elderly may vary, generally you can refer to the sitting height of the elderly is about 400–500 mm.

Seat Width. The width of the hips of the elderly may be wider, generally can refer to the elderly seat width of about 450–500 mm.

Seat Depth. The thigh length of the elderly may be shorter, generally can refer to the elderly seat depth of about 400–450 mm.

Seat Height. The elderly may have limited knee mobility, you can generally refer to the elderly seat height of about 400–450 mm.

Armrest Height. When the elderly use armrests, the armrest height should be moderate, generally you can refer to the height of the armrests for the elderly is about 650–750 mm.

Desktop Height. When the elderly are standing up, the desktop height should be suitable for their height, generally can refer to the desktop height of the elderly is about 900–1000 mm.

Elderly Walker Size Reference. According to the research data, the minimum height of the adjustable walker is 875 mm, the maximum height is 1075 mm, the width is 400 mm, and the side leg spacing is 390 mm. To achieve the purpose of getting up comfortably, the sitting elbow height should be 210 mm higher than the seat, the seat surface height is 430 mm, the seat width is 390 mm, the seat depth is 400 mm, and the highest armrest height at the side of the seat corresponds to the sitting elbow height. Elbow height Take 640 mm.

2.4 Experiments Related to the Way Products are Used

Purpose of the Experiment. The main objective of this experiment was to assess the effect of different handle angles on the fatigue level of the hand muscles. Based on the collected EMG signals, the activity levels and fatigue levels of hand muscles can be measured at different handle angles. By verifying the more energy-efficient handle angle, it can be determined which handle angle can be selected to reduce hand muscle fatigue and improve user comfort and work efficiency in a specific task or operation. This is important for the design of humane aging-friendly tools, equipment or products.

Experimental Principle. Electromyography detects muscle fatigue status by measuring muscle electrical activity. This is based on the special electrical signals, called myoelectric signals, that are generated by the muscles during movement and contraction.

EMG signals are made up of weak electrical currents generated by the motor units in the muscle. When the nervous system sends signals to control muscle movement, the bundles of muscle fibers in the muscle contract and generate electrical activity. EMG signals can be detected and recorded by electrodes placed on the skin surface.

In the experiment, adhesive surface electrodes will be used to connect the EMG sensor to the muscle under test. These electrodes will record the electrical signal produced by the muscle and convert it into an analog or digital signal that can be measured and analyzed. The electromyograph will amplify and filter the muscle electrical signal to improve the quality and accuracy of the signal, and the signal can be transmitted to a computer for analysis in real time. In the case of muscle fatigue, the characteristics of the EMG signal change. As muscle fatigue increases, the amplitude of the EMG signal may decrease and the frequency characteristics may change. These changes reflect the degree of muscle adaptation and fatigue to continuous exercise or loading. By analyzing the EMG signal, muscle activity level, fatigue and recovery can be assessed as a way to infer a more energy-efficient handle angle.

It is important to note that the interpretation and analysis of EMG signals requires consideration of several factors, including electrode placement, muscle anatomy, and signal processing methods, so a rigorous approach and appropriate data analysis techniques are needed to interpret the meaning of EMG signals in experiments.

Experiment Content. The experiments were conducted to detect the surface EMG signals of the upper limb muscles in the pushing posture for a period of time under the same weight-bearing condition, and the left arm was chosen as the force-applying arm:

Continuous pushing of a model vehicle with a 15° handle for 60 s and recording of its surface EMG characteristic signals.
Continuous pushing of a model cart with a 90° handle for 60 s and recording of its surface EMG signal.
Continuous pushing the shopping cart for 60 s and recording its surface EMG signal.

Firstly, prepare the instruments and models required for the experiment, and debug the EMG instrument to make sure it can work properly. Next, explain the experimental content and procedure to the subject. After recording the basic information of the subject (age, gender, height, weekly cleaning time), the electrode sheet was attached to the correct position and the subject was guided to try the model cart to adjust it to the appropriate height. After the subject and the model car were ready, the electrode sheet, wire and transmitter were connected, and the switch was turned on ready to start the measurement experiment.

All three experiments were conducted continuously for 60 s, with 30 min between each experiment as a rest to allow the muscle state to recover. The third experiment served as a control group for the level of muscle fatigue in the normal pushing state. During the 60 s of pushing, the EMG signals were recorded throughout, but in the later experimental processing, they were divided into 6 periods equally, as 0–10 s, 10–20 s, 20–30 s, 30–40 s, 40–50 s and 50–60 s moments, to observe the fatigue level over time.

Pre-experimental Preparation *Subjects' Situation.* Five elderly subjects with a mean age of 57.2 years, one male and four female, were selected for the experiment. The subjects cleaned for 3.7 h per week, usually with a one-handed vacuum cleaner. All five subjects had no upper limb injuries or related diseases, and had not performed any strenuous exercise related to the upper limbs in the last three days, and the upper limbs were in good condition to ensure a certain degree of experimental accuracy. After the demonstration the subjects understood and mastered the purpose of the experiment and the experimental essentials (Table 1).

Table 1. Basic statistics of experimental subjects.

	Age (years)	Gender	Height (cm)	Weight (kg)	Weekly cleaning time (h)
Subject1	58	Female	165	65	4
Subject2	55	Female	168	68	6
Subject3	60	Female	168	70	2.5
Subject4	58	Female	172	72	4
Subject5	55	Male	178	78	2

Equipment. The device used in this experiment is Biopac's EMG, a portable EMG instrument suitable for measuring and recording muscle electrical activity. It has high resolution and low noise signal acquisition, allowing simultaneous measurement of a single muscle or multiple muscles. The device can be connected to a computer via a USB interface and uses AcqKnowledge software for data acquisition and analysis.

Table 2. Electromyography comparison of muscle force application magnitude.

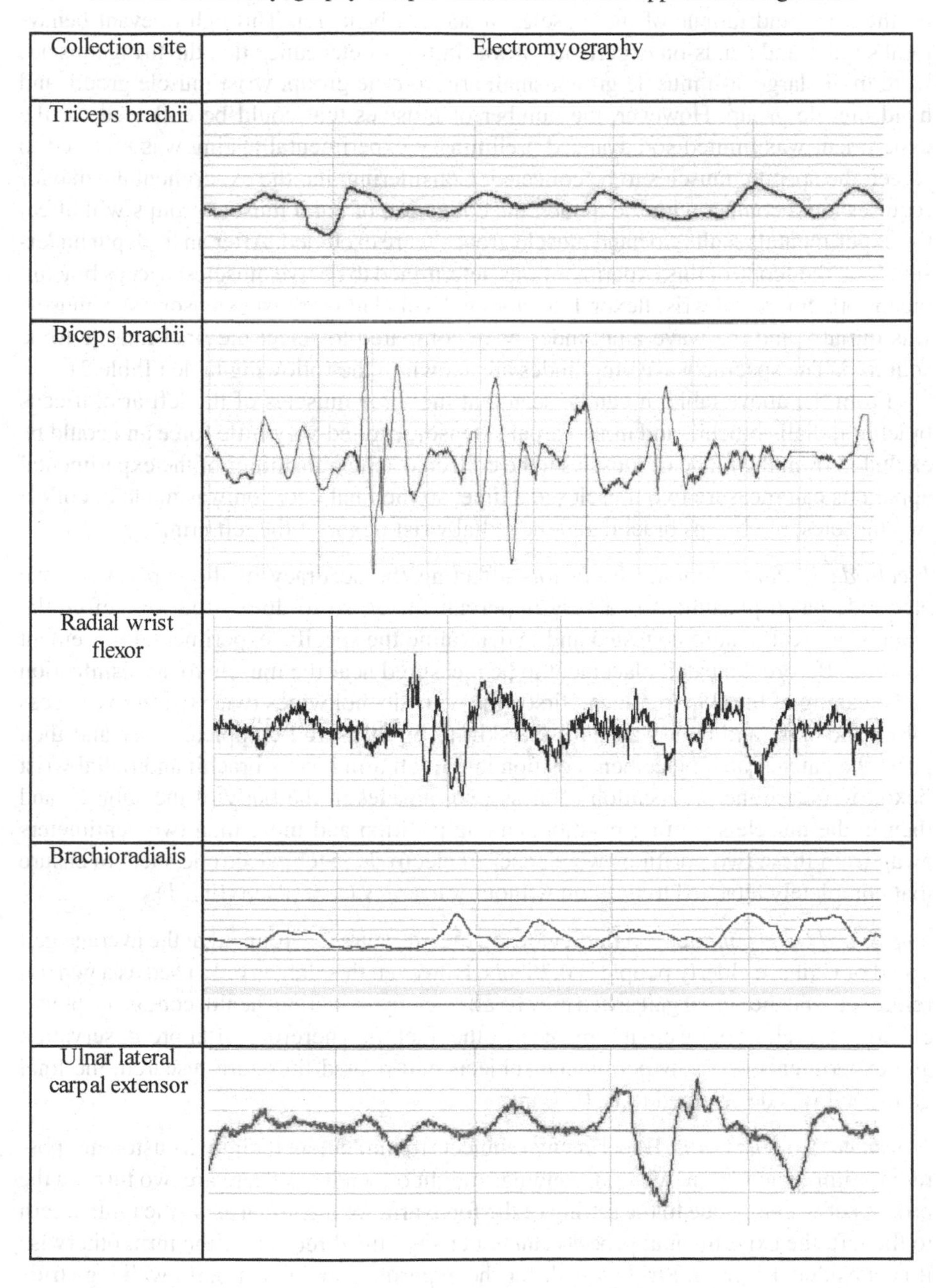

Collection site	Electromyography
Triceps brachii	
Biceps brachii	
Radial wrist flexor	
Brachioradialis	
Ulnar lateral carpal extensor	

Muscle Determination. The muscles to be collected for this experiment were determined by the force and fatigue of the muscles under this behavior. Through relevant behavioral studies and hands-on experience, it was initially determined that the firing muscles were in the large arm muscle group, small arm muscle group, wrist muscle group, and hand muscle group. However, the number of muscles that could be collected for the experiment was limited so advanced preliminary experimental testing was required to screen the specific muscles to be collected. Considering that the experimental behavior requires hand contact with the model, the collection of hand muscle groups will affect the experimental results, so hand muscle groups were excluded. After an in-depth understanding, the scope of this experiment was determined to be five muscles: triceps brachii, biceps brachii, radial wrist flexor, brachioradialis, and ulnar wrist extensor. Each muscle was initially and the wave amplitudes were compared to select the final muscle to be acquired. The specific wave amplitudes are shown in the following table (Table 2):

From the above table, it can be seen that the three muscles of the left arm, triceps brachii, radialis brachii, and ulnar carpal extensor, exerted very little force and could be excluded from the range of muscles to be collected. The transmitter of the experimental apparatus can measure two muscles at a time, so the final decision was made to collect two muscles, the biceps brachii and the radial wrist flexor of the left arm.

Electrode Posting. Among the factors affecting the accuracy of the experiment, the electrode patch placement is a very important factor, so to do a good job before the patch skin treatment to be tested and to determine the specific experimental placement position. Before the patch placement to be measured near the muscle to do disinfection and cleaning of the skin treatment, first wipe with alcohol wipes twice to remove excess oil on the skin, and then wait until the skin to be measured completely dry and then paste the patch. Patch placement position in the left arm biceps brachii and radial wrist flexor, to determine the location of these two muscles in the body of the subject, and then in the muscle's starting position, ending position and more than two centimeters away from these two positions were attached electrode patch, electrode sheet to ensure that completely attached to the skin without warping vacant place (Fig. 1).

Step Speed Determination. After reviewing the literature, we found that the average gait speed of Chinese elderly people is 0.76 m/s. However, this data is only used as a general reference, and the actual gait speed may be affected by individual health condition, physical fitness level, walking environment and other factors. Therefore, after pre-observation and experiments on the experimental subjects and related literature research, the final gait speed was determined to be 0.60 m/s.

Movement Specification. Experimental subjects to implement their own customary posture for implementation, without standing straight or bending. There are two turns in the process of walking, due to the setting of the force arm for the left arm, so the unified turn to the left, the experimental process can not change the direction of the turn, otherwise it is considered invalid. Stride length for the experimental subject daily walking stride length, can not be deliberately too large or too small, as far as possible to maintain the same in each step.

Movement Specification. Experimental subjects to implement their own customary posture for implementation, without standing straight or bending. There are two turns in the

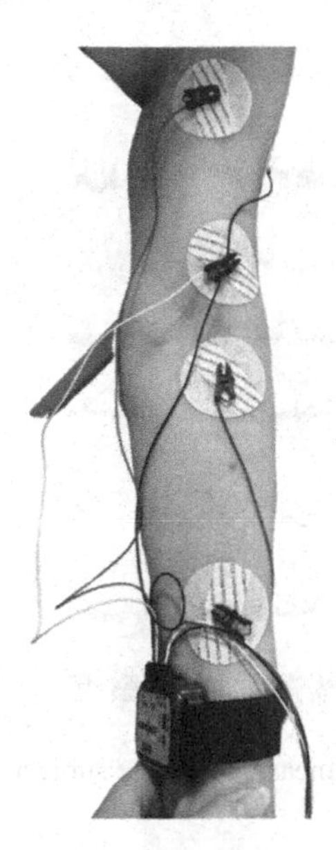
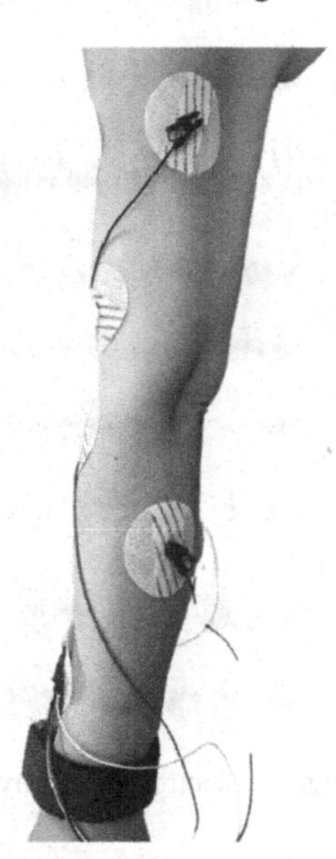

Fig. 1. Electrode patch placement position

process of walking, due to the setting of the force arm for the left arm, so the unified turn to the left, the experimental process can not change the direction of the turn, otherwise it is considered invalid. Stride length for the experimental subject daily walking stride length, can not be deliberately too large or too small, as far as possible to maintain the same in each step.

Experimental Environment. To ensure the accuracy of the experiment and to reduce the influence of various factors on the experimental results, this experiment was conducted in a flat and open closed room with a quiet environment without noise. The experimental travel area was 5.20 m long and 2.10 m wide with a wooden floor and no protrusions or obstructions throughout.

Model Introduction. Experimental research for the hands to push the posture of cleaning products, so the model car for the double rod support, and the ground angle to simulate the tilt angle of cleaning products at work, two rod spacing for the elderly shoulder width. Considering the lack of weight at the bottom of the model car leading to its low stability, so the two main rods behind the addition of auxiliary support, and taking into account the friction, so the main rod under the addition of a small auxiliary wheel to help push. Since the experimental subjects have different heights of men and women, there is a structure for adjusting the height of the main bar, and the same structure for adjusting the angle of the handle.

Data Recording. The electromyograph recorded a waveform plot of the electromyographic signal for a segment of the muscle measured for each subject as follows (Fig. 2):

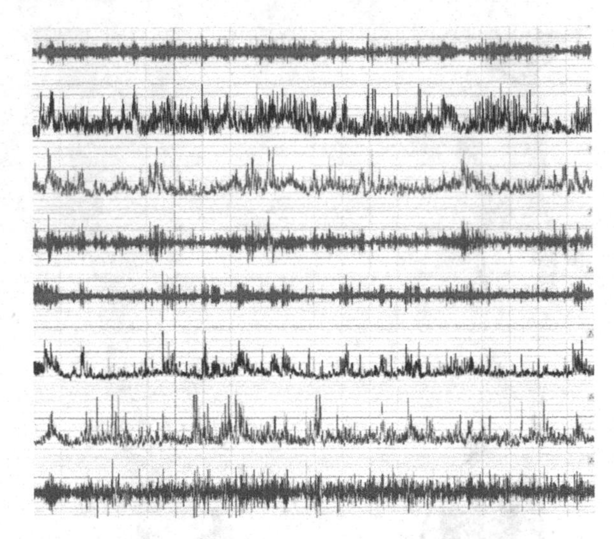

Fig. 2. Electromyography of the muscles measured by the subject

3 Analysis of Results

3.1 Subjective Evaluation Analysis

Subjective Scale Development. The subjective evaluation scale is the subject's self-assessment of the experimental physical fatigue level. The subjective fatigue level evaluation is to consider the subject's subjective self-perception after using different handle angles for a sustained period of time, so as to make preliminary assumptions about which handle angle is relatively effortless and to corroborate with the experimental data results (Table 3).

Table 3. Subjective physical fatigue evaluation scale

Rating	1	2	3	4	5	6	7	8	9	10
	No effort at all									Very laborious
Posture 1										
Posture 2										
Posture 3										

The subjective evaluation scale was set in the range of 1–10 points to assess the self-perception of each angle of the handle, and the higher the score, the higher the fatigue level.

Table 4. Statistical table of subjective physical fatigue evaluation

	Posture	Rating
Subject1	Posture 1	4
	Posture 2	5
	Posture 3	7
Subject2	Posture 1	5
	Posture 2	5
	Posture 3	7
Subject3	Posture 1	4
	Posture 2	4
	Posture 3	6
Subject4	Posture 1	3
	Posture 2	5
	Posture 3	6
Subject5	Posture 1	3
	Posture 2	4
	Posture 3	5

Data Statistics and Analysis

The statistics of the data collected from the 5 experimental subjects are presented in the table above. Based on calculating the mean of the subjective assessment scores of the 5 subjects under each handle angle for comparison, it was tentatively inferred that angle 1 was more effortless (Table 4).

3.2 Experimental Data Analysis

Data Processing. Since the EMG instrument records a segmented waveform map, it is not feasible to use these waveforms directly for data analysis. In order to perform the analysis, the original waveform needs to be segmented first. The segmentation was performed by dividing the waveform into segments every 10 s, and each segmented waveform could be considered as an interval, and a total of six intervals of data were extracted. Subsequently, the data of each interval was exported to digital format, and next, the text file was processed using a pre-written data conversion program to obtain the final metric used for experimental analysis, i.e., the root mean square (RMS) value of the EMG signal. Again, since there was a large amount of data in each interval, the RMSACT was obtained by averaging the data for each segment.

Data Standardization. In order to allow comparison and analysis between different muscles and between subjects, and because of the large individual variability of EMG signals, they need to be standardized. A common standardization method is to divide the actual measured EMG amplitude (RMS_{ACT}) by the EMG amplitude at maximum voluntary contraction (RMS_{MVC}):

$$MVE\% = \frac{RMS_{ACT}}{RMS_{MVC}} \times 100\%$$

The meaning of MVE% is the percentage of muscle loading equivalent to that during maximal voluntary contraction in a given movement or posture. For a specific muscle in the same subject, the change in MVE% over time can reflect the change in muscle load.

Table 5. Variation process of applied force magnitude and fatigue degree

Subject 1 biceps	B1	B2	B3	B4	B5	B6
Posture 1 RMS	0.138849	0.153993	0.182182	0.129566	0174913	0182928
Posture 2 RMS	0.157126	0 155363	0.178556	0.176719	0.165669	0.169940
Control group	0.186490	0.179353	0.226611	0.181734	0 203837	0.197688
Subject 1 radial wrist flexor	B1	B2	B3	B4	B5	B6
Posture 1 RMS	0.090338	0.100703	0.085152	0.090804	0.107306	0.088214
Posture 2 RMS	0.164578	0.185701	0.186047	0.216156	0.206593	0.197902
Control group	0.049717	0.042763	0.055617	0.064662	0.067598	0.052574
Subject 2 biceps	B1	B2	B3	B4	B5	B6
Posture 1 RMS	0.169708	0.160377	0.205741	0.137862	0.167828	0.148058
Posture 2 RMS	0.164653	0.106925	0.119025	0.136640	0.136611	0.108861
Control group	0.345995	0.395623	0.417319	0.331650	0.329758	0.334275
Subject 2 radial wrist flexor	B1	B2	B3	B4	B5	B6
Posture 1 RMS	0.159724	0.154571	0.194709	0.160356	0.166001	0.142535
Posture 2 RMS	0.293389	0239854	0.291266	0.315183	0.226807	0.179980
Control group	0.227961	0.204597	0.287915	0.217081	0.210242	0.211884
Subject 3 biceps	B1	B2	B3	B4	B5	B6
Posture 1 RMS	0.113747	0.132822	0.149508	0.129351	0.145129	0.144118
Posture 2 RMS	0.121113	0.157422	0.191429	0.159034	0.173287	0.166451
Control group	0.225625	0.246938	0.258017	0.261902	0.254782	0.264667
Subject 3 radial wrist flexor	B1	B2	B3	B4	B5	B6
Posture 1 RMS	0.158238	0.115484	0168965	0.158860	0128149	0140852

(continued)

Table 5. (*continued*)

Subjcct 1 biceps	B1	B2	B3	B4	B5	B6
Posture 2 RMS	0.191814	0.199401	0.279086	0.191768	0.233796	0.222971
Control group	0.274492	0.242839	0.258697	0175835	0.219075	0.224311
Subject 4 biceps	B1	B2	B3	B4	B5	B6
Posture 1 RMS	0.095843	0.054663	0.096890	0.074961	0.072623	0.093473
Posture 2 RMS	0.147632	0.121067	0.161914	0.185946	0.137967	0.128397
Control group	0.099035	0.128157	0.128076	0.147785	0.130297	0158575
Subject 4 radial wrist flexor	B1	B2	B3	B4	B5	B6
Posture 1 RMS	0.049149	0.031074	0.065440	0.049662	0.046796	0.039211
Posture 2 RMS	0105072	0.098586	0.105237	0.073151	0.084066	0.090133
Control group	0.802810	0.866206	0.996297	0.989640	1.114463	1 230154
Subject 5 biceps	B1	B2	B3	B4	B5	B6
Posture 1 RMS	0.076842	0.075842	0.082469	0.067446	0.075492	0.068310
Posture 2 RMS	0.098567	0.095428	0.085567	0.095743	0.104329	0.079957
Control group	0.120043	0.100542	0.098975	0.098842	0.100043	0.099854
Subject 5 radial wrist flexor	B1	B2	B3	B4	B5	B6
Posture 1 RMS	0.062501	0.050041	0.048237	0.042697	0.065574	0.059972
Posture 2 RMS	0.067842	0.056742	0.088852	0.054287	0.068849	0.057334
Control group	0.105685	0.125668	0.100247	0.098852	0095557	0.100025

Applied Force Magnitude and Fatigue Change Process
Reflects the magnitude of force applied and the process of fatigue change in the pushing posture during each time period. The RMS values for each time period in the above table are plotted as line graphs to better visualize the changes and contrast (Fig. 3 and Table 5):

The Results. Based on the RMS values for each time period, it can be seen that the overall RMS value of the shopping cart as a control group was higher than that of posture 1 and posture 2. In a few cases, the RMS value of the radial wrist flexor control group was lower than that of posture 1 and 2, which may be influenced by the individual's implementation habits. This also indicates that the shopping cart as a control group is the most easily fatigued muscle, i.e., the angle and position that is more strenuous in comparison. The RMS values of posture 1 and posture 2 were lower in posture 1 than in posture 2, mostly in the radial wrist flexors, and the biceps, although not as pronounced as in the radial wrist flexors, were also lower in posture 1. The above analysis shows that posture 1, which is the handle angle of 15° from the horizontal position, has the lowest muscle fatigue over time and exerts less force, which is a more energy-efficient pushing angle and posture in comparison.

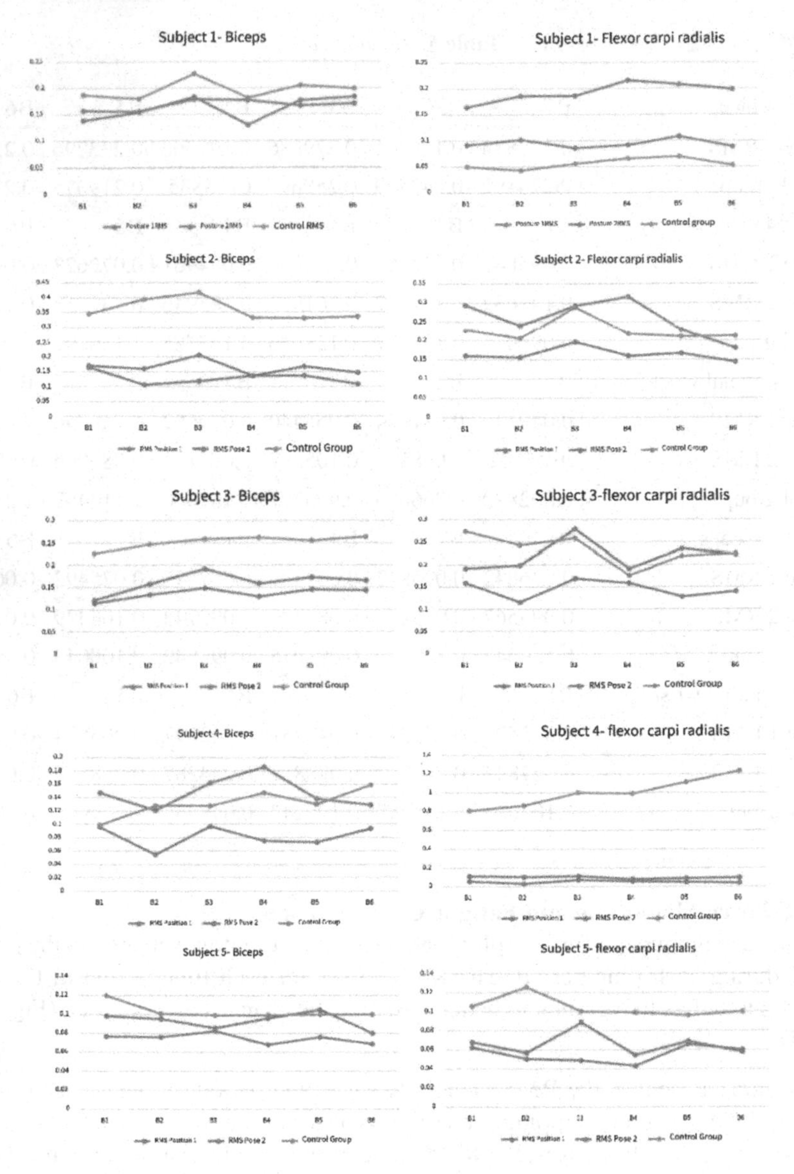

Fig. 3. Subjects muscle RMS

4 Conclusion

Provide ergonomic design guidance: By studying the grip angle of the elderly, we can determine the shape and size of the product handle that is suitable for the mechanical characteristics of the elderly's hands. This helps to design humanized products, improve the comfort of holding and reduce hand fatigue.

Optimize the experience of using products for the elderly: the elderly usually face problems such as decreasing hand strength and dexterity. By understanding the research results of hand grip angle of the elderly, the shape and angle of the product handle can be adjusted to better match the hand characteristics of the elderly, provide better grip support, reduce inconvenience and pain when using, and improve the ease of use and comfort of the product.

Reduce the risk of elderly people using the products: The use of inappropriate product handles by the elderly may increase the risk of accidental falls or slips. By studying the grip angle of the elderly and designing product handles that meet their grip needs, we can reduce the sliding and loss of control during the use of the products and improve the safety of the elderly.

Promote the development of elderly-friendly products: With the arrival of an aging society, the demand for elderly-friendly products is growing. Understanding the conclusion of the grip angle of the elderly can help design more suitable products for the elderly to meet their special needs and improve their autonomy and quality of life in daily life.

Acknowledgements. The authors are particularly grateful to all participants in the study. This work was funded by the Special funds for high-level teachers in Beijing Institute of Fashion Technology, with support from Beijing Institute of Fashion Technology, under Grant BIFTXJ202212.

In this study, we successfully performed experimental analysis of EMG signals and obtained important data regarding EMG waveforms and root mean square values. We would like to express our sincere gratitude to all those who provided support and assistance for the completion of this study.

First of all, we would like to thank the participants in the experiment whose active participation and cooperation were crucial for us to obtain valid EMG signal data. Their dedication and patience enabled us to conduct the experiment smoothly and provided a reliable data base for the study.

We would also like to thank Ms. Yeqing Pei and Ms. Jiurui Yang, who provided valuable guidance and advice, and gave us continuous support and encouragement during the experimental design, data acquisition and analysis. Their expertise and experience have been an important impetus to our study.

In addition, we would like to thank the suppliers of EMG instrumentation (e.g. Biopac Systems), who provided quality EMG instrumentation equipment and provided reliable tools and technical support for our experiments.

Finally, we would like to thank all our family members and friends who provided help and support during this study. Their understanding, encouragement and assistance provided us with invaluable support and enabled us to complete this study successfully.

We thank all those who contributed to this study, and it is your support and assistance that made it possible to conduct this study smoothly and achieve meaningful results. We are deeply grateful for your support!

References

1. Ye, J., Wu, Z., Wang, Y., Yang, T., Li, X.: China health statistics. Journal **39**(4), 494–498 (2022)
2. Han, C.F., He, Z.F., Yang, J.R.S.: A study of human-machine performance of pruner handle based on myoelectric measurement technology. Design **11** (2013)

3. Wang, Z.F.: Study on the characteristic signals of human surface electromyography during hand weighted walking (2015)
4. Chen, Y.F., Ye, J.F., Yu, D.S.: Research on the sustainable design of elderly walker based on the concept of inclusiveness. Packag. Eng. Art Edn. **41**(18), 101–108 (2020)
5. Song, C.F.: Research on ergonomics-based assisted transfer design (2019)
6. Liu, J.F.: Analysis of muscle fatigue during prolonged use of computer mouse (2013)
7. Du, X.F.: Research on the design of mobility assistance products for the elderly based on user experience (2021)

Impact of Optical Flow Cues and Slope Gradient on Risk Perception and Balance Ability of Older Adults

Yanling Zuo[1], Shunji Wu[2], and Jia Zhou[1](✉)

[1] School of Management Science and Real Estate, Chongqing University, Chongqing, China
jiazhou@cqu.edu.cn
[2] Huawei Digital Technologies (Cheng Du) Co., Limited, Sichuan, China

Abstract. In an aging society, falls are an important cause of injury among older adults. This study aimed to investigate the perceived risk characteristics of falls among older adults from the perspective of risk perception, and to provide environmental intervention guidelines for preventing falls. A within-group experiment involving 32 older adults and 30 young adults was conducted to examine the effects of optical flow cues and slope gradient on postural sway, perceived balance, and perceived likelihood of falling. The results showed that the type of optical flow cues did not affect the risk judgment or postural sway of older adult participants in the virtual reality environment, while local optic flow induced greater risk perception of falls among young participants. In addition, for older adults, when the slope gradient increased from 10° to 20°, the percentage difference in risk perception showed a downward trend, while the percentage difference in balance ability showed an upward trend. This mismatch between subjective assessment and objective risk carried with it a greater risk of falls. Below 10° might be considered for slope design in the virtual reality environment. The conclusions drawn from this study could provide design experience and further optimization ideas for intervention design to address the problem of falls among older adults in future age-friendly environment renovation.

Keywords: Aging · Optical Flow · Slope Gradient · Prevention of Falls · Risk Perception · Balance Ability · Virtual Reality

1 Introduction

In an aging society, falling is one of the significant health hazards for older adults. According to the United Nations projections, the proportion of people aged 65 and above will reach one-sixth of the global population by 2050 [1]. As aging populations continue to increase globally, improving the issue of falls has become a major focus of attention. Data from the Centers for Disease Control and Prevention (CDC) in the United States indicated that one-quarter of older adults aged 65 or above have experienced falls [2]. After a fall, older adults may face a range of injuries, including hip fractures, other bone fractures, traumatic brain injuries, chest and abdominal organ injuries, spinal and nerve

Q. Gao et al. (Eds.): HCII 2023, LNCS 14055, pp. 313–330, 2023.
https://doi.org/10.1007/978-3-031-48041-6_22

injuries, joint sprains, and dislocations, among others [3]. Additionally, falls might lead to a decline in physical function and emotional problems, such as a decrease in the ability to perform daily activities, restricted activity, depression, decreased social abilities, fear of falling, increased caregiving dependence, and an overall decline in quality of life [4].

The falls of older adults are influenced by both visual and environmental factors. Previous studies have often investigated these two factors separately. However, considering the interactive nature of vision and environment, it is necessary to explore variables that integrate both elements (such as optical flow cues) and their impact on falls in older adults. From a physiological perspective, the visual system is one of the crucial guarantees of body balance. The visual system perceived optical flow information during the interaction between humans and the environment [5]. Optical flow serves as a fundamental information source that enables successful direction recognition for almost all human movement processes [6]. Regarding falling, older adults were more susceptible to visual changes, and those with poor balance were more vulnerable to optical flow information [7]. The research on how the combination of optical flow visual information and environmental information affects the risk of falls in older adults is still limited. Considering the importance of optical flow stimulation in self-motion perception and posture control, a deeper study of the components of optical flow cues will help understand the fall risk caused by visual aging in older adults.

In the environmental factors influencing falls, slope gradient is one of the key points, but related research is scarce. According to survey data from CPSC, slopes, stairs, stair platforms, and floors were the most common locations for injuries in the population aged 65 years and older in the United States [8]. Research on urban spatial structures and walkability for older adults indicated that outdoor slopes are one of the essential elements affecting accessibility for older adults [9]. Currently, related research mainly focused on the design of stairs and stair platforms [10] or floors [11], but there is little research on age-friendly design for slopes [12]. A small number of studies involving slopes mostly focused on roof slopes or building construction scenarios [13]. Other studies focused on the special pathological needs group of patients with lumbar disc herniation [14]. However, there is a lack of research that takes the needs of healthy older adults as the research subject and investigates the age-friendly extent of slopes in living environments.

Therefore, this study aims to investigate two main questions. Firstly, considering the role of visual information in maintaining body balance in older adults, it is necessary to clarify the effects of optical flow cues on fall risk perception and posture control. Secondly, in order to promote age-friendly research on slopes, it is valuable to explore the impact of slope angle on fall risk perception and posture control. This research can provide a theoretical basis and practical guidance for fall prevention and management in older adults, as well as references for designing age-friendly architectural environments.

2 Literature Review

2.1 Optical Flow Cues

With the emergence of new technologies such as virtual reality, people now have the opportunity to explore the impact of more fundamental visual cues on motion in a more efficient way. Optic flow is one unique perspective of visual intervention. When an individual is in motion, the external environment projected on the retina will shift, which is called optic flow [5]. From the perspective of ecological psychology, optic flow information is a property of information in the interaction process between humans and the environment [15]. It could provide humans with movement guidance and direction localization, which can help humans to avoid obstacles timely.

From the perspective of the initiation mode, current research about the influence of optical flow cues on cognitive or postural control could be mainly classified into two categories: external-induced and self-initiated [6]. External-induced optic flow refers to additional optic flow information added to the existing environment. For example, Higuchi et al. [16] used the optic flow generated by a superimposed dot matrix motion as artificial optic flow, and the optic flow information generated by vehicle motion attributes as natural optic flow. Self-initiated optic flow refers to the optic flow induced by changing the physical properties of the environment or the motion properties between humans and the environment, such as environmental perturbation speed [17], perturbation direction [18], optic flow pattern [19], etc. Compared with the external-induced optic flow, self-initiated optic flow is more frequently used in postural control research [6, 19].

2.2 Slope Gradient

In current studies investigating slopes, there have been significant variations in scene settings, resulting in differences in the selection of slope angles. For instance, King et al. [12] clarified the effect of slope on postural stability and set the slope at 30°, 0°, and 25°. The results showed that the objective posture sway of young participants presented a "U"-shaped trend with the increase of slope. Simeonov et al. [20] studied the risk of falling among workers when working on roofs and set the slope at 0°, 18°, 26°, and 34°. They found that visual references could significantly reduce the instability of postures caused by increasing slope angles when the slope was 18° or higher. Wade et al. [21] researched the effect of altitude on slope selection and chose a 26° slope determined by the United States Occupational Safety and Health Administration (OSHA) as "steep". Guo et al. [13] investigated workers' perceived postural stability during lifting tasks and set the slope at 0° and 18°. Meanwhile, these studies mainly explored the impact of environmental characteristics on the falling or balance ability of elderly people from either subjective [13] or objective perspectives [12, 21]. There is a lack of research that simultaneously examines the subjective and objective aspects of environmental features and their impact on the balance and falls of older adults.

2.3 Balance Ability and VR

Balance ability is the fundamental ability to maintain human posture. Balance dysfunction was a significant cause of falls in older adults, while postural sway was the most critical indicator of balance ability [22]. Currently, the measurement and assessment methods of human postural sway mainly included the observational method, scale test method, and experimental test method [23]. In the analysis of postural sway under various working conditions, the experimental test method based on a force platform or pressure plate was the most widely used. For example, it involved studies on the stability of posture in young people [12] and roof slopes [8, 9]. However, due to the high cost of force platforms, scholars have begun to explore using VR devices as a means of balance evaluation. Based on built-in sensors and development kits, researchers enable to capture motion data from the built-in sensors of VR headsets. These motion data include linear displacement indicators in the x, y, and z directions, as well as angular rotation indicators in the roll, pitch, and yaw directions. The effectiveness of postural sway indicators of VR headsets for postural sway assessment has been confirmed on multiple devices such as the HTC Vive [24], The Oculus Rift [25], and Microsoft Hololens [26]. Compared with angular rotation measurement indicators, the linear displacement measurement indicators of VR devices have a higher correlation with postural sway indicators such as force platforms. In linear displacement measurement, the Medio Lateral (ML) direction showed better stability than the Anterior Posterior (AP) direction in various studies.

2.4 Fall Risk Perception

In order to study the influence of various factors on public risk perception and risk adaptation behavior, Slovic [27] proposed a psychological measurement paradigm to attempt to directly investigate people's perception of risk through questionnaires. Current methods of measuring risk perception included general item coding or scale coding, and focused on the cognitive and affective components of risk perception. In the study of fall risk perception, the perceived likelihood of falling was often used to measure older adults' subjective perceived risk of falling [28]. It was typically assessed using a 5-point Likert scale or percentage slider to have participants report the perceived likelihood of falling in a specific environment [29].

3 Materials and Methods

3.1 Participants

Convenience sampling was used to recruit participants by disseminating information and calling for volunteers from a collaborative older adult community in the laboratory. The inclusion criteria for older adult participants were 60 years old or above, while younger participants were 18–54 years old. Participants with a history of concussion or any other neurological functional disorders that could affect balance were excluded [30].

Thirty-two older adult participants (age range 62–80 years, M = 68.93, SD = 3.244) and thirty younger adult participants (age range 20–27 years, M = 23.97, SD = 1.873) were formally recruited for the experiment, with a total of 62 participants. After data collection, it was found that data from two older adult participants were partially missing due to equipment issues. Due to the data missing rate reaching 40%, these two participants were excluded. Eventually, data from 60 participants were included in the formal analysis. All participants were native speakers of Chinese.

3.2 Variables

Independent Variables: Optical Flow Cues and Slope Gradient. A 5 (slope gradient) × 2 (optical flow cues) experimental design was used in this experiment, with both slope inclination and optical flow cues being designed as within-subject variables.

Optical flow cues included two conditions which were local condition and global condition. Different types of optical flow reflect different correspondences between motion information and retinal positions. In the global condition, the optical flow field pointed to the center and periphery of the retina (using the moving room paradigm [31] including conditions of front wall, side walls, floor, and ceiling as shown in Fig. 1). In the local condition, the optical flow field mainly pointed to the peripheral region of the retina (using the moving room paradigm [31] including only the floor condition as shown in Fig. 1).

Slope gradient was defined as the ratio of the height difference to the radial length of the slope, with five levels including 0°, −10°, 10°, −20°, and 20°. Negative slope angles indicated the downhill process. Due to the definition of the low-slope roof by the United States Occupational Safety and Health Administration as 18° [20], and the previously defined slope upper limit of 25° in a study on posture instability on road slopes by King et al. [12], this study ultimately chose 20° as the slope upper limit. In order to further compare the effect of slope changes on posture stability, the midpoint of 0° and 20°, 10°, was added as one of the levels. As previous studies have demonstrated different effects of posture orientation on the ability of the human control system to maintain vertical stability of the center of mass [32], the polarity of the slope was also taken into consideration.

Dependent Variables: the Standard Deviation of Postural Sway, the Range of Postural Sway, Perceived Balance, and Perceived Likelihood of Falling. The first two were objective variables, while the latter two were subjective variables.

Based on the correlation between traditional postural sway measurements and the stability in various studies, the standard deviation (SD) and range of lateral coordinate values in head-mounted devices were ultimately chosen as the postural sway indicators to represent participants' balance ability and fall risk.

The perceived balance represents the subjective feeling of stability and was evaluated using a 1 (worst) to 10 (best) score [33]. During the experiment, a score of 0.25 and 0.5 was allowed to distinguish minor differences [34]. The widely used subjective fall risk perception [35] was also chosen as another subjective indicator of fall risk perception.

3.3 Apparatus

The HTC Vive Pro 2 system was used as the hardware development device, with Unity2019.3.13f1 and C# scripting language as the software development tools to build the high-fidelity VR experimental prototype. During the experiment, the position data from the built-in sensors in the VR headset were captured through C# code for final data analysis. The data were recorded at a sampling rate of 50 Hz, and the visual scene was presented at a refresh rate of 120 Hz. The system had a dual-eye resolution of 4896 × 2448 pixels and a field of view of 120°.

3.4 Experiment Scenes

Based on the literature review, a model of the walking process on a ramp was established as shown in Fig. 1. The elements of the ramp walking process model included geometric parameters and the walking process. The walking process mainly consisted of two stages: the approaching stage and the climbing stage. The paradigm of the ramp environment was based on the VR moving room paradigm used by Winkel et al. [36]. A total of 10 scenes were created. During the experiment, the standard walking speed of the participants in the virtual environment was set to 1 m/s, and the participants were allowed to adjust their walking speed according to their feelings using a joystick during the experiment.

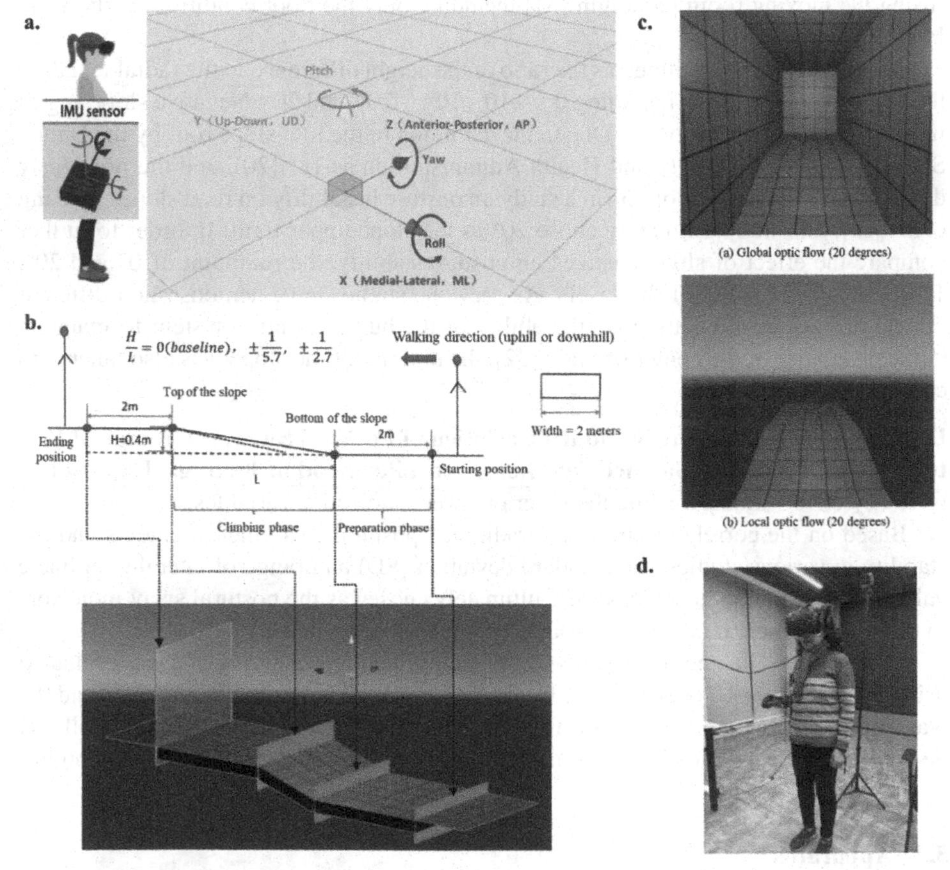

Fig. 1. Experimental Scene Design. **a.** The measurement parameters of the sensor of the head-mounted equipment and the human anatomical axis and tangent plane. **b.** Modeling and virtual reality prototype of walking process on different slopes. **c.** Examples of virtual reality high-fidelity prototypes (Global vs Local). **d.** Experimental environment

3.5 Procedure

Training Phase. Participants were guided to use the equipment for walking in a virtual environment. The training scenes were designed differently from the formal experiments, with scenes of varying sizes and materials to minimize interference with the formal experiments. The sign of successful training was when the participants used the joystick to navigate through the training scene and reach the designated location.

Test Phase. Participants used the joystick to move their view in the virtual environment while standing still. Participants were required to maintain stability throughout the experiment. The sequence of scenes in the experiment was balanced using a Latin square design to control for learning effects. Each participant completed 10 trials, and before each trial, the experimenter asked the participants to rate their perceived likelihood of falling in the current environment. After completing each trial, the experimenter asked the participants to rate their perceived balance during the movement process. Participants were given the choice to rest after each trial to relieve visual and physical fatigue.

3.6 Data Analysis

After testing for normality, as the standard deviation and range of posture sway were not normally distributed, an Aligned Rank Transform was used for the analysis of differences. If the main effect was significant, post-hoc pairwise comparisons of all levels were performed using Wilcoxon signed-rank tests. Perceived likelihood of falling and perceived balance were normally distributed, and a repeated-measures analysis of variance was used for the analysis of differences. If the ANOVA showed a significant main effect, post-hoc pairwise comparisons of all levels were conducted using paired t-tests, with sphericity assumed and p-values corrected using the Greenhouse-Geisser or Huynh-Feldt correction based on epsilon values [37]. Data processing and analysis were performed using SPSS Statistics (version 25) and R 4.0.5 software in this study.

4 Results

4.1 Background Information

The results revealed that among older adults, 93.3% did not experience any falls in the past 180 days. A small fraction of older adults reported experiencing two or more falls without any injuries. In comparison, the proportion of young adults who did not experience any falls was 76.7% (as shown in Table 1).

Table 1. Description of background information of participants

Variables	Categories	Participants		%
		Older adults	Younger	
Recent falls	No fall	28	23	85.0
	One fall, no injury	0	3	5.0
	Two or more falls, no injury	2	3	83.3
	One or more falls, injuries occur	0	1	16.7
Gender	male	11	19	50.0
	female	19	11	50.0

4.2 Performance of Objective Variables

The Standard Deviation of Postural Sway. For the older adult group, there were significant differences in postural sway (standard deviation) among the five different slope levels ($F(4, 25) = 6.706$, $p < .001$). Similarly, for the young adult group, there was a significant main effect of slope inclination ($F(4, 26) = 3.848$, $p < .01$) on postural sway (standard deviation). Overall, for both the older and young adult groups, as the slope angle increased, the participants' postural sway (standard deviation) gradually increased regardless of uphill or downhill conditions, indicating a decrease in their objective stability during the experiment (as shown in Fig. 2).

Post-hoc analysis showed that compared to the −10° slope, postural sway significantly increased by 1.86% under the −20° slope. Compared to the 10° slope, postural sway significantly increased by 1.48% under the 20° slope. In contrast, significant differences in postural sway were only observed between 0° and 10° slopes for the young adult group.

In the same experimental environment, the postural sway (standard deviation) of the older adult group was about 1.01 to 1.06 times higher than that of the young adult group, and the age difference was significant ($F(1, 58) = 16.731$, $p < .001$).

The Range of Postural Sway. For the older adults, there were significant differences in the range of postural sway among the five different slope levels ($F(4, 25) = 11.128$, $p < .001$). Similarly, for the younger group, there was a significant main effect of slope incline on the range of postural sway ($F(4, 26) = 5.937$, $p < .01$). Both younger and older adults showed a decrease in objective stability with increasing slope incline, reflecting a similar pattern as the standard deviation of postural sway (as shown in Fig. 3).

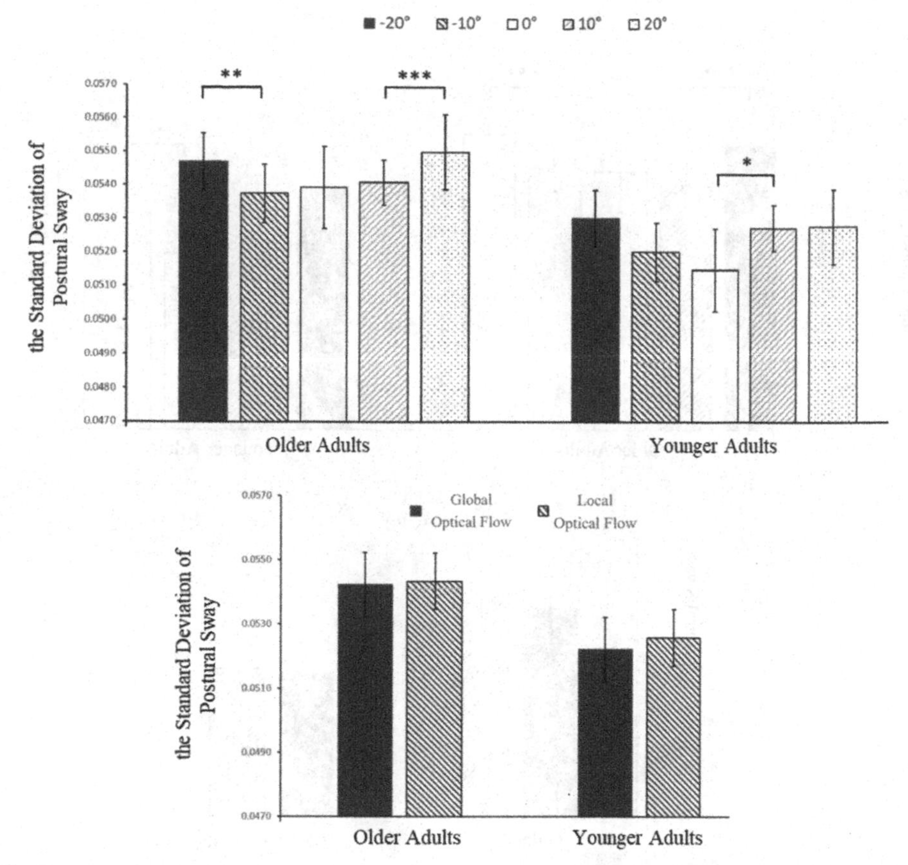

Fig. 2. The Standard Deviation of Postural Sway under Different Slope and Optical Flow Condition Based on Age Groups (*p < .05, **p < .01, ***p < .001).

Post-hoc tests revealed that postural sway was significantly increased by 2.16% at the −20° slope compared to the −10° slope. Additionally, postural sway was significantly increased by 1.51% at the 20° slope compared to the 10° slope. Differences in the younger group were only observed between the 0 and 10° slopes.

In the same experimental environment, the range of postural sway for the older adults was approximately 1.00–1.05 times greater than that of the younger adults, and the age difference was significant ($F(1, 58) = 12.733$, $p < .001$).

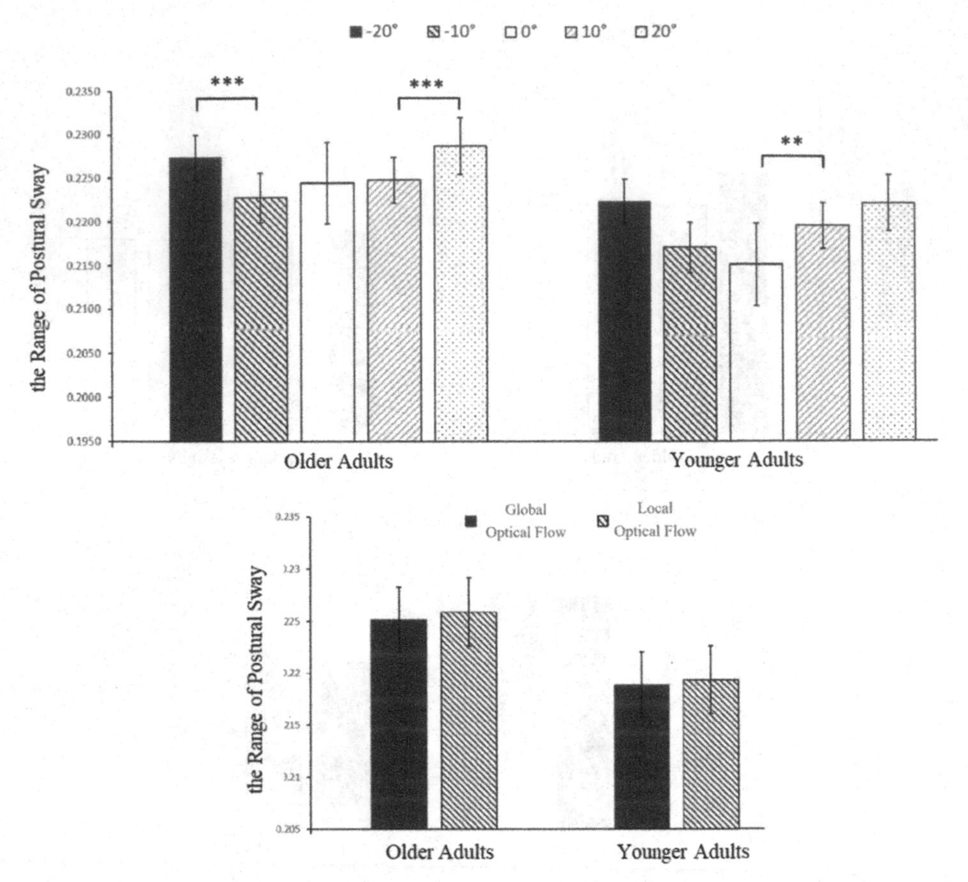

Fig. 3. The Range of Postural Sway under Different Slope and Optical Flow Condition Based on Age Groups (*$p < .05$, **$p < .01$, ***$p < .001$).

4.3 Performance of Subjective Variables

Perceived Balance. For the older adult group, there were significant differences in the perceived balance scores across the five different slope levels ($F(4,14) = 6.380$, $p < .001$, $\eta^2 = 0.150$). Similarly, for the younger adult group, there was a significant main effect of slope on perceived balance scores ($F(4,14) = 8.560$, $p < .001$, $\eta^2 = 0.191$). As the slope of the ground increased in either positive (0° to 20°) or negative (0° to −20°) direction, perceived balance gradually decreased for both older and younger adults, indicating a U-shaped trend in their perceived stability during the experiment (as shown in Fig. 4).

Post-hoc analysis of differences between pairs of levels revealed that the perceived balance ratings of older adults differed significantly across all slope levels, while the pattern for the younger adult group was similar to that of the older adults.

In the same experimental environment, the perceived balance scores of the younger adult group were approximately 1.02 times higher than those of the older adult group, and the age difference was significant ($F(1,58) = 5.879$, $p < .05$).

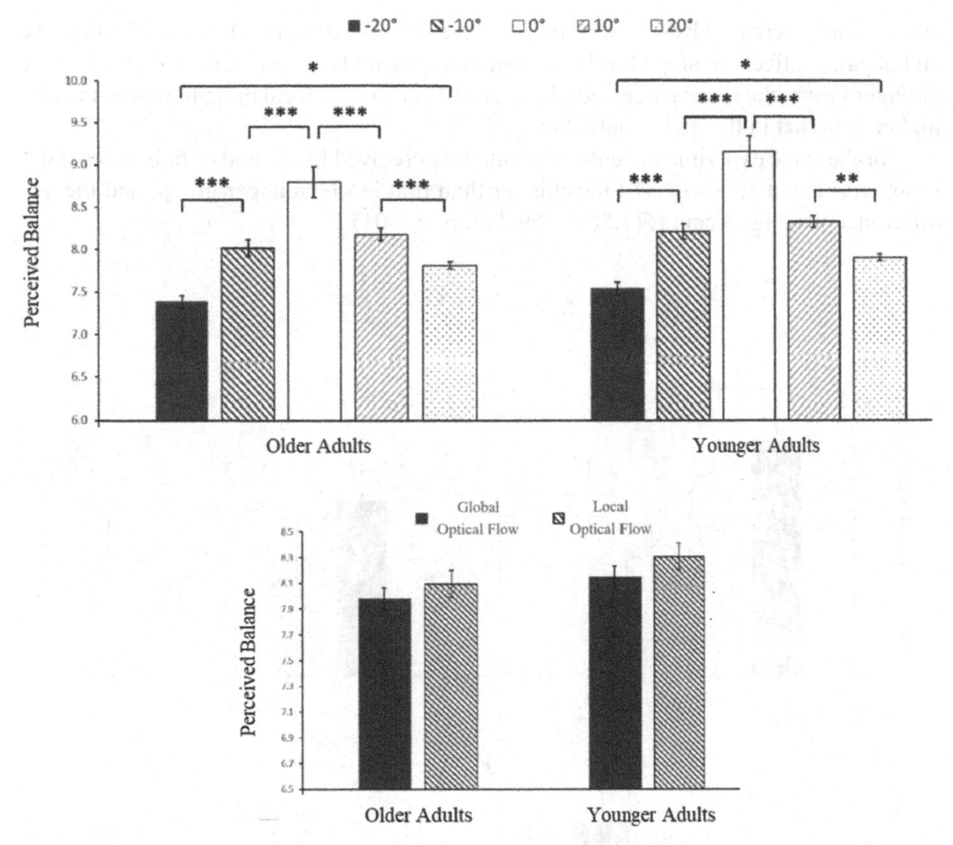

Fig. 4. The score of Perceived Balance under Different Slope and Optical Flow Condition Based on Age Groups (*$p < .05$, **$p < .01$, ***$p < .001$).

Perceived Likelihood of Falling. For the older adults group, there was a significant difference in the perceived likelihood of falls among the five different slope levels (F(4,14) = 6.326, p < .001, $\eta^2 = 0.149$), while the effect of optic flow on the perceived likelihood of falls was not significant. For the younger group, both slope level (F(4,14) = 11.639, p < .001, $\eta^2 = 0.243$) and optic flow (F(1,14) = 8.449, p < .01, $\eta^2 = 0.055$) had significant main effects on the perceived likelihood of falls. For both older and younger groups, the perceived likelihood of falls gradually increased as the slope level increased, indicating an increased perception of the risk of falling in the environment. For the younger group, the perceived likelihood of falls in the local optic flow (Mean = 33.4, SD = 22.85) was significantly higher than that in the global optic flow (Mean = 29.9, SD = 22.58) (as shown in Fig. 5).

Post-hoc analysis revealed that for the older group, there were significant differences in the perceived likelihood of falls for different slope levels, and as the slope level decreased in the negative direction, the perceived likelihood of falls significantly increased by 64.0% and 18.6%, respectively, compared to the 0° level and -10° level. When the slope level increased in the positive direction, the perceived likelihood of falls significantly increased by 47.3% at the 10° level compared to the 0° level. The positive and negative effects of slope level were only significant between −20° and 20°. For the younger group, the mean perceived likelihood of falls in the local optic flow was 11.53% higher than that in the global optic flow.

For the same experimental environment, the perceived likelihood of falls in the older group was about 1.18 to 2.37 times higher than that in the younger group, and the age difference was significant ($F(1,58) = 69.743$, $p < .001$).

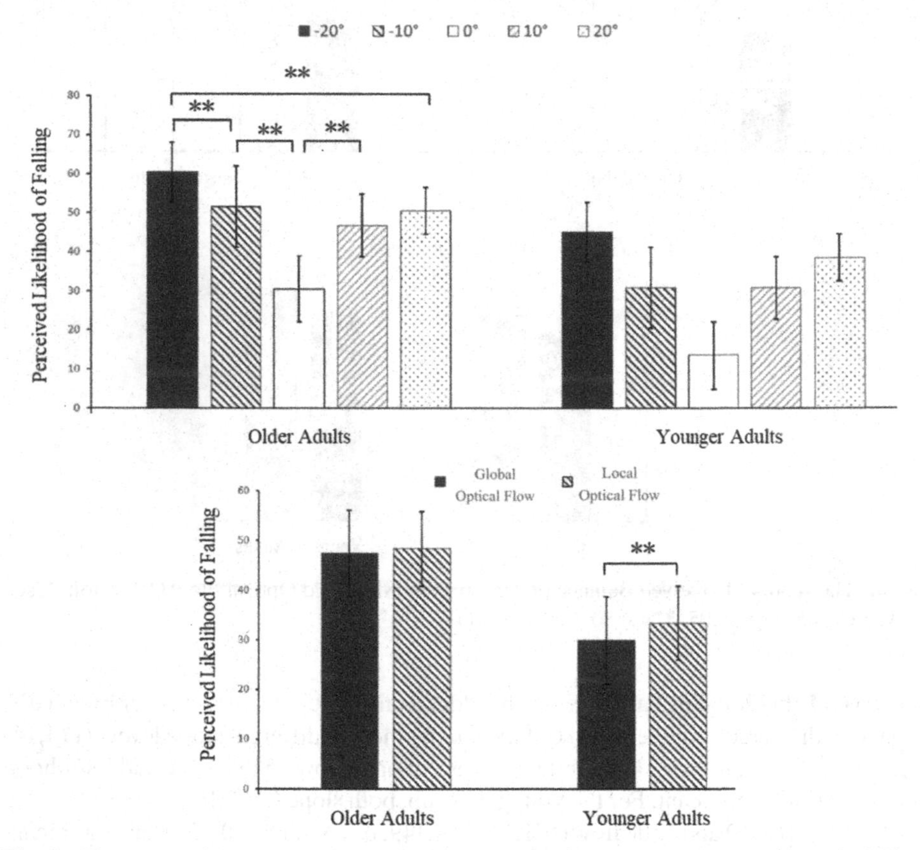

Fig. 5. The score of Perceived Possibility of Falling under Different Slope and Optical Flow Condition Based on Age Groups (*$p < .05$, **$p < .01$, ***$p < .001$).

4.4 The Change Difference Between Subjective and Objective Indicators

It was valuable to further compare the difference between subjective index and objective index in the process of slope change. Therefore, percentage difference [38] was calculated respectively to reflect the growth between the two levels (as shown in the formula below).

$$PD_{A \to B} = \frac{2|D_B - D_A|}{D_B + D_A} \times 100\% \tag{1}$$

In the formula, *PD* was percentage difference. *A* and *B* represented different levels of slope. D_A and D_B represented the mean values of dependent variables at two levels respectively.

For the older adult group, the percentage differences in perceived likelihood of falling and perceived balance during the 10 to 20° slope showed a decreasing trend compared to 0 to 10°, while the percentage differences in the standard deviation and range of postural sway showed an increasing trend (as shown in Table 2). The same pattern was observed as the slope angle increased in the negative direction. This indicated that as the slope increased, the subjective assessment of environmental risk and the mismatch between subjective and objective risks gradually increased in older adults. This mismatch may have led to a greater risk of falls, especially when the slope was greater than 10°. The younger group did not show a similar trend.

Table 2. The percentage difference of dependent variable between two levels of slope.

Age group	Slope°	Objective swing percentage difference (%)		Subjective rating percentage difference (%)	
		Postural sway (SD)	Postural sway (range)	Perceived balance	Perceived likelihood of falling
Older Adults	0° → −10°	0.91	1.21	9.03	48.42
	−10° → −20°	1.80	2.14	8.12	17.14
	0° → 10°	0.23	0.28	7.31	38.19
	−10° → 20°	1.65	1.73	4.69	9.86
Younger	0° → −10°	1.03	0.91	10.96	78.35
	−10° → −20°	1.91	2.40	8.55	37.85
	0° → 10°	2.38	2.05	9.57	78.38
	−10° → 20°	0.07	1.20	5.28	22.30

4.5 The Influence of Personal Characteristics

The influence of personal characteristics was analyzed on objective and subjective variables among older adults (as shown in Table 3). The results showed that recent fall incidents affected the objective balance of older participants, but did not affect their perception of falls. Conversely, young adults were more sensitive to fall-related perceptions, although their objective balance was not affected. Based on the lack of correlation between age and balance, older women rated their stability higher, while no gender differences were found in the young group.

Table 3. Results of correlation analysis of characteristics and dependent variables

Group	Items	Postural sway (SD)	Postural sway (range)	Perceived balance	Perceived likelihood of falling
Older adults	Year	0.092	0.089	0.093	−0.119*
	Gender	0.108	0.105	−0.158**	−0.015
	Height	0.068	0.101	−0.132**	−0.101
	Recent falls	−0.154**	−0.164**	0.040	0.075
Younger	Year	0.034	0.039	−0.041	−0.137*
	Gender	0.063	0.044	−0.080	−0.089
	Height	0.002	−0.017	−0.001	−0.073
	Recent falls	−0.061	−0.049	0.193**	−0.151**

5 Discussion

This study found that in the VR environment, global optical flow led to greater subjective risk perception in young participants, while self-generated optical flow had no effect on older adults. These results differ from previous studies in real environments. Wade et al. [19] previously demonstrated, based on the moving room paradigm, that global optical flow environments lead to greater postural sway for older adults compared to local optical flow. They suggested that older users are more unstable in global optical flow environments because they lack visual anchors for maintaining postural balance. These visual anchors refer to motion perceived in certain positions on the retina, which can be canceled out by information from other parts of the retina that do not detect motion. However, the same effect was not observed in the VR environment, possibly because the reduced distance perception in VR environments weakens or even eliminates the role of the light flow field in maintaining postural balance for older adults. Distance perception in the VR environment was found to be only 71% accurate, compared to 99.9% accuracy in the real world [39]. Other intervention methods need to be explored to compensate for this weakening effect. For example, in future studies, it may be possible to explore the effects of more externally induced optical flow interventions in VR environments, which contain more artificially added optical flow than self-generated optical flow, on the balance of older adults.

The slope angle associated with an objective increase in fall risk for older adults was found to be 10°. In comparison to level ground (0°), there were no significant changes in postural sway range or standard deviation during uphill (0° to 10°) or downhill (0° to −10°) walking in older participants, indicating that the slope changes at this stage did not significantly increase fall risk. However, as the slope angle increased further, both postural sway range and standard deviation during uphill (10° to 20°) and downhill (−10° to −20°) walking showed significant changes, indicating a significant increase in fall risk. Therefore, particular attention should be paid to the objective fall risk associated with slope angles above 10° for older adults. The Occupational Safety and Health Administration in the United States defines a slope angle of 26° (1:2.05) as "steep" for health workers in rooftop work scenarios [40]. For healthy older adults, the VR environment slope angle critical threshold recommended by this study is 10° (1:5.67).

In terms of the magnitude of differences, this study found some differences in the objective postural sway between older adults and previous studies. For example, the range of postural sway for the young group was 1.02 and 1.03 times that of the flat ground at −20° and 20°, respectively. Although the differences were significant, in King et al.'s study [12], the range of postural sway for −30° and 25° was 1.83 and 1.59 times that of the flat ground, respectively, and in Simeonov et al.'s study [20], the range of postural sway at 34° was 1.86 times that of the flat ground. Apart from environmental factors, there are two reasons for the differences in the analysis, one being the floor effect, which means that the effect of slope on postural sway only becomes apparent when the slope reaches a certain critical value; the other being differences in experimental conditions, including the altitude of the participants [21] and differences in measuring devices. In the analysis of the impact of personal characteristics on objective postural sway, no significant differences were observed in the influence of height, so in future studies, it is necessary to further consider the influence of altitude (rather than height) on postural stability, and to explore the use of VR devices as a means of balance assessment, for different populations and specific usage scenarios.

This study has three limitations. Firstly, the recruited participants in the experiment were relatively homogenous, which may affect the external validity of the study. The participants were mainly Chongqing University students and older adults living around the campus, and future experiments could include more young and older adults with different educational backgrounds and from different regions. Secondly, due to the constraints of the VR experiment's realistic conditions, the age entry criteria for older adults in this study were appropriately relaxed to 55 years old, although the average age of the participants was still above 65 years old, there are still limitations. Thirdly, the fidelity of the virtual reality scenes used in this study was relatively low, and future research is necessary to study more and more realistic scenes to obtain comprehensive environmental design recommendations.

6 Conclusion

Based on a virtual reality environment, this study selected a more specific high-risk falling scenario - the slope scene, with different slopes (−20, −10, 0, 10, 20°) to investigate the effects of optical flow cues design (global, local) and environmental geometric parameters on older adults' fall risk perception and objective balance ability. The study recruited 32 older adults and 30 younger adults as participants for laboratory experiments. Through the analysis of the data collected from the experimental tests, the study mainly drew the following conclusions: Firstly, the type of optical flow cues in the virtual environment had no significant effect on older adults' subjective risk perception and objective postural sway. For younger adults, the type of optical flow cues had a significant effect on the probability of fall perception scores, with local optic flow having significantly higher scores than global optic flow. Secondly, the slope angle in the virtual environment had a significant effect on older adults' fall risk perception and perceived balance. Specifically, as the absolute value of the slope angle increased, older adults' perceived balance scores significantly increased with every 10° change. Compared with the situation where the slope increased from 0° to 10°, the mismatch between the subjective risk assessment and the objective balance ability of older adults was deepened when the slope increased from 10° to 20°, revealing that the slope of 10° and above might cause older adults to have a greater fall risk.

Acknowledgment. The authors would like to acknowledge the support from the National Natural Science Foundation of China (72171030) and the Project supported by graduate research and innovation foundation of Chongqing, China (Grant No. CYB23067).

References

1. Nations, U.: World Population Prospects 2019: Highlights. https://www.un.org/en/desa/world-population-prospects-2019-highlights. Accessed 12 March 2023
2. CDC: Facts About Falls | Fall Prevention | Injury Center | CDC. https://www.cdc.gov/falls/facts.html. Accessed 12 March 2023
3. Jensen, J., Lundin-Olsson, L., Nyberg, L., Gustafson, Y.: Falls among frail older people in residential care. Scand. J. Public Health. **30**, 54–61 (2002)
4. Suzuki, M., Ohyama, N., Yamada, K., Kanamori, M.: The relationship between fear of falling, activities of daily living and quality of life among elderly individuals. Nurs. Health Sci. **4**, 155–161 (2002). https://doi.org/10.1046/j.1442-2018.2002.00123.x
5. Gibson, J.J.: The Perception of the Visual World. Houghton Mifflin, Oxford, England (1950)
6. Agathos, C.: Reliance on the visual frame of reference in ageing across different sensorimotor tasks: from perception to walking (2016)
7. Phillips, D., dos Santos, F.V., Santoso, M.: Sudden visual perturbations induce postural responses in a virtual reality environment. Theor. Issues Ergon. Sci. **23**, 25–37 (2022). https://doi.org/10.1080/1463922X.2020.1870052
8. NEISS Data Highlights (Top 20 Product Groups by Age Group) | NFSI. https://nfsi.org/neiss-data-highlights-top-20-product-groups-by-age-group/. Accessed 12 March 2023
9. Amaya, V., Moulaert, T., Gwiazdzinski, L., Vuillerme, N.: Assessing and qualifying neighborhood walkability for older adults: construction and initial testing of a multivariate spatial accessibility model. Int. J. Environ. Res. Public Health **19**, 1808 (2022). https://doi.org/10.3390/ijerph19031808
10. Gosine, P., Komisar, V., Novak, A.C.: A kinematic analysis of balance recovery following an unexpected forward balance loss during stair descent. Appl. Ergon. **92**, 103317 (2021). https://doi.org/10.1016/j.apergo.2020.103317
11. Redfern, M.S., Moore, P.L., Yarsky, C.M.: The influence of flooring on standing balance among older persons. Hum. Factors **39**, 445–455 (1997). https://doi.org/10.1518/001872097778827043

12. King, A.C., Patton, J., Dutt-Mazumder, A., Newell, K.M.: Center-of-pressure dynamics of upright standing as a function of sloped surfaces and vision. Neurosci. Lett. **737**, 135334 (2020). https://doi.org/10.1016/j.neulet.2020.135334
13. Guo, L., Xiong, S.: Effects of working posture, lifting load, and standing surface on postural instability during simulated lifting tasks in construction. Ergonomics **63**, 1571–1583 (2020). https://doi.org/10.1080/00140139.2020.1807614
14. Li, J., et al.: Dynamical analysis of standing balance control on sloped surfaces in individuals with lumbar disc herniation. Sci. Rep. **10**, 1676 (2020). https://doi.org/10.1038/s41598-020-58455-z
15. Richardson, M.J., Shockley, K., Fajen, B.R., Riley, M.A., Turvey, M.T.: Ecological psychology: six principles for an embodied–embedded approach to behavior. In: Calvo, P. and Gomila, A. (eds.) Handbook of Cognitive Science. pp. 159–187. Elsevier, San Diego (2008). https://doi.org/10.1016/B978-0-08-046616-3.00009-8
16. Higuchi, Y., Inoue, S., Hamada, H., Kumada, T.: Artificial optic flow guides visual attention in a driving scene. Hum. Factors **62**, 578–588 (2020). https://doi.org/10.1177/0018720819847022
17. Dokka, K., Kenyon, R.V., Keshner, E.A.: Influence of visual scene velocity on segmental kinematics during stance. Gait Posture **30**, 211–216 (2009). https://doi.org/10.1016/j.gaitpost.2009.05.001
18. Raffi, M., Piras, A., Persiani, M., Perazzolo, M., Squatrito, S.: Angle of gaze and optic flow direction modulate body sway. J. Electromyogr. Kinesiol. **35**, 61–68 (2017). https://doi.org/10.1016/j.jelekin.2017.05.008
19. Wade, M.G., Lindquist, R., Taylor, J.R., Treat-Jacobson, D.: Optical flow, spatial orientation, and the control of posture in the elderly. J. Gerontol. B Psychol. Sci. Soc. Sci. **50B**, P51–P54 (1995). https://doi.org/10.1093/geronb/50B.1.P51
20. Simeonov, P.I., Hsiao, H., Dotson, B.W., Ammons, D.E.: Control and perception of balance at elevated and sloped surfaces. Hum. Factors **45**, 136–147 (2003). https://doi.org/10.1518/hfes.45.1.136.27232
21. Wade, C., Davis, J., Weimar, W.H.: Balance and exposure to an elevated sloped surface. Gait Posture **39**, 599–605 (2014). https://doi.org/10.1016/j.gaitpost.2013.09.017
22. Rimland, J.M., et al.: Effectiveness of non-pharmacological interventions to prevent falls in older people: a systematic overview. The SENATOR Project ONTOP Series. PLoS One **11**, e0161579 (2016). https://doi.org/10.1371/journal.pone.0161579
23. Panjan, A., Sarabon, N.: Review of methods for the evaluation of human body balance. Sport Sci. Rev. **19** (2010). https://doi.org/10.2478/v10237-011-0036-5
24. Sylcott, B., Lin, C.-C., Williams, K., Hinderaker, M.: Investigating the use of virtual reality headsets for postural control assessment: instrument validation study. JMIR Rehabil Assist Technol. **8**, e24950 (2021). https://doi.org/10.2196/24950
25. Marchetto, J., Wright, W.G.: The validity of an oculus rift to assess postural changes during balance tasks. Hum. Factors **61**, 1340–1352 (2019). https://doi.org/10.1177/0018720819835088
26. Lee, E.-Y., Tran, V.T., Kim, D.: A novel head mounted display based methodology for balance evaluation and rehabilitation. Sustainability. **11**, 6453 (2019). https://doi.org/10.3390/su11226453
27. Slovic, P.: Perception of risk. Science **236**, 280–285 (1987). https://doi.org/10.1126/science.3563507
28. Ahn, S., Oh, J.: Effects of a health-belief-model-based osteoporosis- and fall-prevention program on women at early old age. Appl. Nurs. Res. **59**, 151430 (2021). https://doi.org/10.1016/j.apnr.2021.151430

29. Twibell, R.S., Siela, D., Sproat, T., Coers, G.: Perceptions related to falls and fall prevention among hospitalized adults. Am. J. Crit. Care **24**, e78-85 (2015). https://doi.org/10.4037/ajcc2015375
30. Cruz, C.F., et al.: Parkinson's disease does not alter automatic visual-motor coupling in postural control. Neurosci Lett. **686**, 47–52 (2018). https://doi.org/10.1016/j.neulet.2018.08.050
31. Lee, D.N., Lishman, J.R.: Visual proprioceptive control of stance. J. Hum. Mov. Stud. **1**, 87–95 (1975)
32. Dutt-Mazumder, A., Slobounov, S.M., Challis, J.H., Newell, K.M.: Postural stability margins as a function of support surface slopes. PLoS ONE **11**, e0164913 (2016). https://doi.org/10.1371/journal.pone.0164913
33. Kim, S., Madinei, S., Alemi, M.M., Srinivasan, D., Nussbaum, M.A.: Assessing the potential for "undesired" effects of passive back-support exoskeleton use during a simulated manual assembly task: muscle activity, posture, balance, discomfort, and usability. Appl. Ergon. **89**, 103194 (2020). https://doi.org/10.1016/j.apergo.2020.103194
34. Schieppati, M., Tacchini, E., Nardone, A., Tarantola, J., Corna, S.: Subjective perception of body sway. J. Neurol. Neurosurg. Psychiatry **66**, 313–322 (1999). https://doi.org/10.1136/jnnp.66.3.313
35. Wilson, R.S., Zwickle, A., Walpole, H.: Developing a broadly applicable measure of risk perception. Risk Anal. **39**, 777–791 (2019). https://doi.org/10.1111/risa.13207
36. e Winkel, K.N., Pretto, P., Nooij, S.A.E., Cohen, I., Bülthoff, H.H.: Efficacy of augmented visual environments for reducing sickness in autonomous vehicles. Appl. Ergon. **90**, 103282 (2021). https://doi.org/10.1016/j.apergo.2020.103282
37. Girden, E.R.: ANOVA: Repeated Measures. Sage Publications Inc, Thousand Oaks, CA, US (1992)
38. Cole, T.J., Altman, D.G.: Statistics notes: what is a percentage difference? BMJ **358**, j3663 (2017). https://doi.org/10.1136/bmj.j3663
39. Waller, D., Richardson, A.R.: Correcting distance estimates by interacting with immersive virtual environments: effects of task and available sensory information. J. Exp. Psychol. Appl. **14**, 61–72 (2008). https://doi.org/10.1037/1076-898X.14.1.61
40. Occupational Safety and Health Administration: Plain Language Revision of OSHA Instruction STD 3.1, Interim Fall Protection Compliance Guidelines for Residential Construction | Occupational Safety and Health Administration, https://www.osha.gov/enforcement/directives/std-03-00-001. Accessed 28 March 2023

Accessibility and Design for All

Building an Inclusive Metaverse: Opening Doors to a Brighter Digital Future

Andrew Bedard(✉) and Qiping Zhang

Long Island University Post Campus, 720 Northern Blvd, Greenvale, NY, USA
andrew.bedard@my.liu.edu

Abstract. ***Description of Methods:*** The focus of this research is the identification and comprehensive analysis of salient scholarly literature, using content analysis to ascertain the capabilities of various assistive technologies and devices that could benefit people with disabilities, and ultimately enhance their Extended Reality (XR) and Metaverse experiences. To this end, the paper will provide definitions and characterizations of the 'Metaverse', according to its implications for Augmented Reality (AR), Virtual Reality (VR), and Mixed Reality (MR) respectively. It will also address how key implementations of interactive hardware and software technologies, applicable to these environments, can effectively benefit prospective users with various mobility, hearing, visual and cognitive encumbrances.

Discussion of Results: The paper highlights the unique accessibility features necessary to support four types of disability: visual, mobility, hearing, and cognitive. For each kind of disability, we discuss corresponding key assistive technologies, alternative input recognition devices, and behavioral use of those technologies. Specific alternative input recognition systems include White-cane-controller interfaces for the visually impaired. At the same time, speech-to-text, gesture-tracking hardware such as multisensorial rings and sign-language tools are used for individuals with hearing impairments. Behavioral tracking software potentially affords avenues for training and rehabilitation purposes. This technology may also provide the capability to digitally construct virtual environments to facilitate the management of those with cognitive challenges. This may enable individuals, such as people with Autism Spectrum Disorder (ASD), to accomplish fundamental daily living tasks, as well as support the evaluation of psychological tendencies, in order to devise more comprehensive plans of treatment.

Keywords: Metaverse · Virtual Reality · Extended Reality · User Experience · Online Accessibility · HCI · Assistive Technologies · Usability

1 Introduction

It is important to consider how digital accessibility barriers can hinder the online experiences of under-represented groups, especially those with disabilities such as physical, sensory, auditory, and cognitive impairments. According to data collected by the World Health Organization (WHO), there are approximately 1.3 billion disabled people, diagnosed with a variety of visual, cognitive, audiological, and mobility impairments, globally. HCI efforts, in the context of accessible and inclusive design features, have been

Q. Gao et al. (Eds.): HCII 2023, LNCS 14055, pp. 333–351, 2023.
https://doi.org/10.1007/978-3-031-48041-6_23

concerned with evaluating the experience of accessing and interacting with technology, while also addressing mitigating barriers associated with fully utilizing these related devices. Research on accessibility in virtual reality (VR) has been on the rise, especially in the discussion of platforms such as the Metaverse. As we explore the influence of Extended Reality (XR) hardware and software applications to enhance web interactivity, developing human-centered technologies is vital. The consideration of assistive devices, prototyped systems, and personalized VR applications, is crucial, especially in the field of Human-Computer Interaction (HCI).

Some have argued that the characteristics of the Metaverse, due to its core configuration and design, pose inherent exclusionary risks for people with varying degrees and types of physical and cognitive challenges. The primary goal of this research is to address potential accessibility implications and impediments for prospective users of the Metaverse who have various disabilities. It will focus on modifications that can improve the approachability and usability of digital interfacing technologies, while ultimately facilitating usability through personalized modes of interaction for each type of disability stated above. More specifically, it intends to investigate and highlight some of the key hardware and software input alternatives of extended reality technologies. Many have claimed that the incorporation of digital technologies has had a profound effect on expanding the depth and breadth of interactions. The ensuing benefits have expanded and enhanced the potential capability to deliver greater societal impacts and opportunities in key industrial sectors such as education, healthcare, and business. The Metaverse fundamentally revolutionizes how we communicate and disseminate information. While the conceptualization of Extended Reality is evolving on the theoretical horizon, much of the discussion surrounding this innovative platform has emphasized the importance of achieving a desirable user experience for the population at large who may be interacting with it.

2 An Overview of the Metaverse

The Metaverse is a collective virtual shared space, created by the convergence of the real and the cybernetic. It is a virtual world that encompasses many different virtual environments and allows users to interact with each other and with virtual objects and experiences in real time [1]. The term was coined by Neal Stephenson in his 1992 science fiction novel, *Snow Crash,* and has since been used to refer to a wide range of virtual worlds and online communities [2]. In some cases, it is seen as a potential successor to the internet as we know it, offering more immersive and interactive online experiences. "The metaverse offers a great opportunity to overcome many of the challenges people face in the physical world, from physical disabilities, limited access to places, social exclusion due to lack of exposure to the diversity of human beings, to opportunities to enable new sensorial experiences for people who have sensory or cognitive impairments" [3]. In these regards, the benefits of the Metaverse are two-fold: Firstly, it can grant these marginalized groups access to places that may have otherwise been inaccessible based on a myriad of factors such as limited transportation, socioeconomic status, and other associated barriers. Secondly, a focus on accessibility can expand the known functionality of business-to-consumer relationships by affording users new opportunities to interact with products and services.

While scholars have discussed a plethora of investigative avenues for the functionality and conceptualization of the Metaverse, there has not been a universally accepted characterization of the term. Numerous, diverse elements can be included in the contextual scope of the Metaverse including simple and complex computing, which can dictate the representation of a truly immersive experience:

> *"The Metaverse is the post-reality universe, a perpetual and persistent multiuser environment merging physical reality with digital virtuality. It is based on the convergence of technologies that enable multisensory interactions with virtual environments, digital objects, and people such as virtual reality (VR) and augmented reality (AR). Hence, the Metaverse is an interconnected web of social, networked immersive environments in persistent multiuser platforms. It enables seamless embodied user communication in real-time and dynamic interactions with digital artifacts* [4].

In describing the Metaverse as a "post-reality", it seems the Metaverse will seemingly be able to enhance our level of interactivity between virtual and physical environments to the extent that both coincide with one another. In these regards, implementing digital technologies applicable to the virtual world would aspire to enhance familiar experiences through the use of more sophisticated hardware and software, such as Virtual Reality (VR) and Augmented Reality (AR), while perhaps expanding the capabilities of socially-defined activities, by providing access to personalized, software-generated tools and environments.

3 Definitions

3.1 Augmented Reality (AR)

AR attempts to combine both physical and virtual interactive elements through the use of computer or software-generated stimuli, facilitated through sound, touch, or another combination of the five senses, to perceive digital artifacts to simulate the experience of the physical environment. "AR allows the user to see the real world, with virtual objects superimposed upon or composited with the real world. Therefore, AR supplements reality, rather than completely replacing it" [5]. More specifically, AR can leverage the use of wearable technologies such as "glasses" and "gloves" that facilitate activities such as drawing [6] and gaming through the use of various input and output sensors that can track articulated movements of the hands (gripping) and eyes (blinking) [7].

3.2 Virtual Reality (VR)

VR is primarily three-dimensional or simulated in nature. The purpose of these types of technologies is to recreate, simulate or mimic activities and spaces as they would be accomplished in the physical or real world [8]. "Virtual Reality (VR) can be defined as the "use of computer modeling & simulations which help a person in interacting with the artificial 3D environment. This 3D artificial environment shows reality with the help of some interactive devices which can send and receive information and are worn in the form of goggles, headsets, gloves or body suits, etc." [9] The wearable equipment and devices are not only used to allow users to interact with the environments but they help to reproduce 3D personas, such as avatars [10]. VR hardware is not only capable of tracking the inputs and gestures of users but also can generate "Digital Twin" environments. Digital Twins attempt to recreate closely-scaled or otherwise familiar models or artifacts, identifiable in traditional or physical environments [11].

3.3 Mixed Reality (MR)

There are many different types of Mixed Reality (MR) devices, which can utilize a combination of video displays (such as monitors) or head-mounted displays in an attempt to portray computer-generated or otherwise 3D-rendered objects and environments [12]. Hence, MR (sometimes referred to as XR), exists along a spectrum that persists between both augmented and virtual reality applications. "MR describes the interaction between an AR and a VR user that are potentially physically separated. Also, this notion includes mapping spaces, i.e., for a remote user, the environment of a local AR user is reconstructed in VR" [13] In some cases, this may include using an object existing in the physical environment as a point of reference, via spatial recognition tools and software to dictate a given user scenario, as opposed to simply providing an overlay using pass-through technologies, such as a camera included with a head-mounted display.

4 AR, VR, and MR in the Context of the Metaverse

There is no single qualification or description that can be used to articulate the entirety of the Metaverse. Rather, it ought to be considered a platform through which AR, VR, and MR are used to create meaningful experiences [14]. They can individually or collectively leverage the affordances of AR, VR, and MR, to promote and facilitate the delivery of quintessential products and services to underrepresented groups such as people with disabilities:

> *"The Metaverse differs from augmented reality (AR) and virtual reality (VR) in three ways. First, while VR-related studies focus on a physical approach and rendering, Metaverse has a strong aspect as a service with more sustainable content and social meaning. Second, the Metaverse does not necessarily use AR and VR technologies. Even if the platform does not support VR and AR, it can be a Metaverse application. Lastly, the Metaverse has a scalable environment that can accommodate many people [and] is essential to reinforce social meaning* [15]

Traditional objectives of digital spaces were previously fixated on facilitating physically rendered movements and animations with limited external motivations. However, with the advent of the Metaverse and other associated technologies, the implications of VR and AR appear to have expanded the depth and breadth of socialization, communication, and even more sophisticated service orientations, which may perhaps influence the diversification of many industries including business, healthcare, and education. Moreover, they seem to suggest that the Metaverse may exist independently from VR and AR, and may instead be implemented to carry out specific user requests or scenarios, when these types of technologies are not adequately supported. Hence, its multidimensionality may be used to construct even more complex systems in many social or professional contexts. Lastly, they assert that the scalability of these environments should feasibly be able to support interactions between more users to allow for more meaningful interactions.

For instance, businesses can take advantage of newly-defined retail strategies by introducing large or small-scale "virtual malls," [16] or digital shopping which traditionally would have required an individual to be geographically present to effectively view or purchase a product [17]. But despite differences in how AR features are implemented, they essentially result in altering an environment with virtual representations. These would include head-mounted displays such as VR headsets, haptic gloves, or other equipment used to detect, track, or replicate the movements of the body, through a close representation of one's physical body posture, represented through an avatar. AR would instead focus primarily on the generation of artifacts that are meant to blend in with a user's visible background or foreground. Software implementation relates to the output of digitized signals and stimuli that the users would rely on to acclimate themselves to their surroundings – with any or all of their five senses. The final technical component of the Metaverse used in this characterization is the content, which considers how the value of an experience could be enhanced by uniquely generating objects for users to deliver a truly personalized experience. User-generated content could potentially have meaningful applications offering new modes of interaction in several common social domains in the real world, such as education, [18], gaming, [19], and remote work conditions [20] etc.

The contextual scope of the Metaverse with regard to its technological capabilities has even been purported as the "next internet". "Metaverse has been viewed as a new type of online social network, and arguably NextG Internet. It would be the convergence of digital second life (to "escape" to) and virtual reality (for exploration), mimicking user interaction in the real world" [21]. This description of Metaverse boldly claims the advent of digital alternatives, which would perhaps supersede the current modes of information generation and use, which would allow its adopters to 'escape' to the online environment, but also approximate specific types of interaction common to the real world.

They further describe the integral role of various enabling technologies, such as edge and wireless computing, which aid information professionals in exploring auxiliary development options such as Blockchain and Machine Learning in simulating communication and data transmission between online users. However, they argue that the constraints and current limitations of wireless computing and network transfer protocols act as barriers to harnessing the true potential of these technologies.

Another research endeavor developed a Canetroller, which featured an array of tactile and audio sensors and was prototyped as an input alternative for completely blind users to simulate the experience of navigating the natural and physical world, as they would with a White Cane [22]. Some activities included spatial recognition for crossing the street and detecting objects and other potential environmental hazards. Text magnification, while mostly applicable to those with only minor vision loss explores the significance of lens modifications to allow for greater visibility of content that appears on-screen, as well as in the user interface and menus [23].

This would be particularly insightful, as it would allow for the design flexibility to develop both users with any grade of vision loss, including those who simply rely on glasses to read and see objects. Text-to-speech alternatives in VR would allow users to initiate gesture-based responses by reading text aloud to them, according to where the cursor is positioned on the screen. However, a common issue with prolonged exposure to a gestured interface is that users may experience symptoms of nausea due to the frequency of orientation changes, such as body movements and other factors [24].

5 Disability and Social Participation

This section will provide a contextual overview of the key considerations that the CDC incorporates into defining different severity levels of disability, according to the lack of capability that such individuals tend to experience. While these definitions are quite broad in scope, there are some distinctions that can be made between the description of a person's disability and their need for customized modifications, in order for them to perform specific tasks, or to participate in social events and activities of daily living, in addition to physical and social barriers that affect the ways they circumvent their known challenges in the Metaverse.

According to the CDC, disabilities exist along a theoretical spectrum wherein a person's disability can be considered according to three specified dimensions:

- **Impairment**: Is regarded as severe, with the significant diminishment or total loss of a person's ability to perform a certain function (e.g. loss of vision, memory, or mobility,)
- **Activity Limitation**: Refers to a potential barrier presented by a person's sensory perception, which may include difficulty with hearing, vision, or walking
- **Participation**: Denotes an inability to engage in social or otherwise recreational activities, such as working, or attending events.

As of May 15, 2023, the CDC reported that more than a quarter, (approximately 27%) of all Americans have some type of disability [25] and that Mobility impairment is the most common of all disabilities, representing 13.7% of the entire population in the USA [26]. This category represents an even more diverse cohort of individuals. Depending on the etiology of their mobility challenge, each may require a very different approach to their technological accommodation needed. For example, an individual with paraplegia, quadriplegia, or another neurologically-based disability would need a completely different assistive device than an individual like an amputee who is missing a limb.

The term "people with disabilities" tends to be a catch-all phrase that refers to a large, homogenous group. However, as is evident above, the disabled population is a complex and diverse group. Therefore, completely different technologies, modalities, and degrees of accommodation will likely need to be customized in order to provide them with a satisfactory user experience. Cognitive impairments are the second most common disability, representing 10.8% of the US population [25]. These categories include individuals with memory impairment and autism spectrum disorder (ASD). Similarly, hearing impairment ranges from volume and tone deficits to total loss of sound. Loss of vision exists along a broad spectrum, from decreased visual acuity, to near-sightedness, far-sightedness, cataracts and legal, or total blindness.

5.1 Physical Barriers

Virtual Reality technologies have proven to play an integral role in defining the modes of communication and interaction in digital environments, and potentially even the Metaverse. While the interest and focus on commercialized alternate reality technologies have led to the design and proliferation of various head-mounted displays such as Microsoft HoloLens, MetaQuest 2, HTC Vive, and many other types, it has been argued that the scope of implementation of these devices has been limited and indirectly excludes people with mobility, auditory, visual, and cognitive challenges. For example, the traditional scope of virtual reality technologies makes a glaring assumption that all prospective users possess normal visual acuity, as well as hearing and sensory perception within the normal range. They then utilize this as the basis for the majority of its features and experiences. The subsequent sections of this paper, discussing impairments, not only attempt to conceptualize potential barriers of entry for people with specific types of disabilities but also explore the prospect of several different hardware and software accommodations that could potentially enhance their experience while interacting in these virtual environments.

5.2 Social Barriers

The aspects of "Accessibility," "Social Equity", and Inclusion are some of the quintessential elements of understanding and developing the Metaverse [27]. More specifically, focus and attention placed on these facets of interaction will promote a greater sense of belonging for these marginalized groups and more importantly foster the development of more socially applicable modes of interaction to accommodate more diverse user scenarios and populations. "However, the current metaverse, especially with VR, has not yet addressed accessibility and representation for humans with disabilities" [28]. While investigating the Decentralands virtual reality platform, which allows users to customize the appearance of their personalized avatars, the authors were unable to substantiate any elements of disability representation given the absence of crucial assistive devices in the database. The nonexistence of virtual gadgets like walkers, canes, wheelchairs, etc., that people with mobility challenges would typically utilize, could conceivably compromise personal aspects of social identification and immersion through their avatars (Tables 1 and 2).

Table 1. Overview of Virtual Reality and Metaverse Technologies to Accommodate Visual and Mobility Impairment

Types of Accessibility	Sources	Types of Interaction	Heuristic Evaluation	HCI Application
Visual impairment	Zhao et al. (2018), Zhao et al. (2019)	White Cane remote control	Vibrotactile and audio output for cane	Navigation of the virtual world using a White Cane, similar to the assistive device used by people with total blindness
	Isewon et al. (2014)	Text-to-speech Interaction	Evaluation of Natural Language Processing	Synchronization of captions correlating with people speaking in video for people with minor vision loss
	Teofilio (2018)	Image and text magnification	Consistency and appearance of text	Magnification of on-screen content in virtual reality for people with minor vision loss
	Valesquez (2010)	Vibrotactile Interaction for Braille	Evaluation of Tactile input device	Braille-based touch interface to read on-screen content
Mobility Impairment	Mott et al. (2020),	VR interaction Design for Accessibility	Barriers in using Head-mounted display	Using the touch interface Google Glass as an alternative to heavier VR headsets
	Budziszewski et al. (2016)	Workspace Modification	Simulated Workplace environments	Constructing a workspace for people in wheelchairs to be able to navigate effectively

(*continued*)

Table 1. (*continued*)

Types of Accessibility	Sources	Types of Interaction	Heuristic Evaluation	HCI Application
	Malu et al. (2015)	Customization of Wearable Device	Touch and Gesture input alternatives	Gesture tracking through wearable devices
	Wentzel (2020)	Gesture Tracking for Mobility Impairment	Evaluating multimodal input for people with physical disabilities	Alternative input using different parts of the body (mouth, tongue, hands) for playing different genres of video games

6 Inclusive Accessibility Design for the Metaverse

6.1 Mobility Impairment

The current landscape and technical capabilities of commercially available Virtual Reality headsets such as the Meta Quest 2 and PICO 4 are limited in their functionality and design, to actuate and record movements, gestures, and other inputs that were designed based on an "ideal" bodily structure, which inadvertently excludes people with disabilities who are hoping to take advantage of the provisions of the Extended Reality experience. In these regards, users with physical constraints may perhaps struggle with performing physically or neurologically complex movements. This could be especially significant when considering the compromised mobility in the upper and lower extremities of a person in a wheelchair, who might not be able to perform the postural movements and gestures necessary to accomplish tasks in certain interactive scenarios. Wentzel et al. (2020) identified more than 20 issues concerning chosen input methods and control schemes when playing different genres of video games [29]. Their experiment concluded that users experienced a diverse array of encumbrances associated with gripping, holding, and articulating precise movements involving both small and large muscle groups.

While some research studies that include prototyped design functionality allow for more user-dynamic input schemes, the ubiquity of these interfaces appears to be limited to research domains. In some instances, scholars have concluded, that the current design limitations of VR headsets distributed to consumers may result in significant challenges for people with limited mobility, such as people with gait and posture issues, people in wheelchairs, or those with limited strength in their upper or lower extremities. Challenges in fully utilizing VR hardware and software are further exacerbated by a lack of customizable controllers and sensors which are seemingly not made to accommodate different levels of body functionality, which acts as an inherent barrier for people with disabilities.

Table 2. Overview of Virtual Reality & Metaverse Technologies to Accommodate Visual and Mobility Impairment

Types of Accessibility	Sources	Types of Interaction	Heuristic Evaluation	HCI Application
Hearing impairment	Rothe et al. (2020)	Text-to-Speech Recognition	Evaluation of Text-to-Speech for video and cinema	Determining the placement of captions for real time video and cinematic experiences
	Cho et al. (2022)	Gesture Interaction for sign language	Using Machine learning to codify the recognition of sign language	Simulating the use of sign language for interpersonal and human-machine communication
	Narashiman (2013)	Modeling and Rendering Virtual Avatars	Evaluating the perception and Representation of sign language in Tamil by virtual avatars	Representation of sign language in Tamil by virtual avatars
	Sun et al. (2022)	Gesture tracking using lightweight wearable technologies	Evaluating the use of wearable ring sensors to record gestured sign language	Explored the use of rings to track the accuracy of gestures when performing sign language
	Kanza et al. (2020)	People and object detection and recognition for users with hearing impairment	Visual and Vibration feedback to help familiarize user with their environment	Contextual Filters replace sound with vibration
Cognitive Impairment	Standen & Brown (2006)	Simulating Social and Environmental Interaction	Behavior tracking and observation for therapeutic intervention	Evaluation of cognitive impairment by tracking social behaviors

(*continued*)

"Because the expectation that VR technology has in terms of bodily involvement is extensive, it can therefore create accessibility barriers for people who lend their bodies differently to the system. For example, many wheelchair users would find bodily involvement of the legs or the trunk unsuitable… and "might find it difficult to involve

Table 2. (*continued*)

Types of Accessibility	Sources	Types of Interaction	Heuristic Evaluation	HCI Application
	Garzotto et al. (2018)	Cognitive Walkthrough	Using Virtual Assistance for learning daily tasks	Virtual assistance to help with memorization of activities of daily living
	Calabrò et al. (2022)	Customization of Wearable Device	Potential Applications for Human Behavior Tracking	Using artificial intelligence to screen for the potential clinical diagnosis of psychological disorders

large parts of their body over longer periods of time" [30]. Here, the authors suggest that rather than providing a truly personalized experience for each prospective VR user, the commercial availability of products that are purchasable by consumers are instead, better suited for use and access by the general public. They particularly call attention to specific user scenarios wherein people with mobility, balance, posture, or stability constraints may struggle to perform necessary actions. Hardware appears to be the biggest hindrance to promoting an acceptable experience for people within this diversely unique group.

However, smaller and gesture-specific input technologies, like those implemented in Google Glass can be used as alternatives to larger models of HMDs in the VR market. Google Glass is not only lighter but can utilize touch interfaces and sensors in scenarios where users would have issues performing necessary movements [31]. An interesting prototyped combination sought to combine the feasibility of the touch interface provided in Google Glass, with a series of body-mounted nodes and sensors to facilitate the different types of interaction commonly associated with VR controllers and headsets. The goal appeared to be to offer a lighter alternative to traditionally cumbersome headsets and controllers commercially available to consumers [32].

Without the customization of hardware and software components to suit a broad array of potential modalities and input methods, exploration of the Metaverse for people with these circumstances may be hindered in their ability to experience the virtual world, to the same degree that others without disabilities or physiological constraints would. The primary concern of accessibility in these contexts should be to develop and refine technologies and analysis techniques to collect more data on supplemental tools that lessen the gap and ensure a truly accessible experience, even if limited physical constraints may persist.

6.2 Hearing Impairment

Research areas have aimed to articulate enabling modes of interaction for deaf and hard of hearing (DHH) people via personalized approaches to audio modification and spatial rendering applications, in addition to the use of tactile and gesture-based interfaces to facilitate interpersonal and system-oriented communication for people with auditory limitations. For example, "For people with hearing impairment, visual display, vibrations, and captions might replace sounds and voices. Note, however, that AID is not just personalization, it is a suite of tools to test and support accessibility and inclusion." [33] Contextual filters can aid those with compromised hearing to navigate their environment by ultimately circumventing sound queues with vibration feedback, or in other cases, providing supporting captions to indicate when people are speaking and other accompanying sounds and dialogue.

In these regards, Most of the research in this area has focused on the use of natural language processing (NLP) to provide text-to-speech (TTS) accessibility to improve the functionality of virtual interfaces. Some of these applications include implementing machine-readable software capable of interpreting sign language inputs prompted by users [34, 35]; or contextualizing the representation of signed gestures by a virtual avatar in another language [36].

6.3 Sign-Language Reading and Recognition

One prototyped experiment evaluated the utilization of wearable ring devices placed on the hands, wrist, and fingers to simulate the activity of accurately performing sign language. They concluded that these applications offer a close approximation of the action of performing sign language to an acceptable degree "where the object in the real space of one user could be recognized and reconstructed into the virtual format, and remotely felt in real time by another user in the same metaverse virtual space through the simulated stimuli and the feedback, giving people a face-to-face like immersive virtual social experiences" [35]. With regards to the aspect of the digital presence of virtual avatars, being able to achieve an ideal approximation of this type of interaction in the real world is an important milestone in emphasizing that the needs and concerns of marginalized populations are accounted for in the construction of a truly accessible virtual world. This would not only afford DHH users the flexibility of using sign language in human-machine interaction but may allow them to converse with others who haven't formally learned sign language.

The DAVE system [34] is yet another example of a system that aimed to evaluate the interactivity of tactile and gesture interfaces in facilitating interpersonal and system-oriented communication for DHH users. Translating sign language could be important for ensuring users can communicate with other people who rely on sign language for comprehension. Moreover, this could feasibly allow users without hearing deficits to converse with others without the need to formally study sign language to communicate.

7 Visual Impairment

Prior research in the area of visual accessibility has suggested the design of haptic and auditory interfaces for people with low vision: "Besides being considered a predominantly visual experience... VR can be expanded to, not only include impaired people as a target but also when several constraints of common displays are put aside, enhance the current accessibility tools expanding technology and information access" [37]. Here, the authors suggest that the current limitations of the Metaverse are centered around the necessity of a head-mounted display to navigate either the virtual world of settings that would make the experience more manageable for people with visual constraints, or construct touch interfaces for users that need braille to read content displayed on their screen [38]; or facilitate text-to-speech assistance through the application of machine learning [39].

However, research avenues have attempted to evaluate the feasibility of text-to-speech to assist with both spatial and user interface navigation [40].This ultimately reduces the complexity of search and retrieval tasks by removing the redundancy of certain interface actions such as clicking and inputting multiple keystrokes [41]. Similarly, the VRIO system is a voice-operated interface capable of recording physical or virtual keyboard inputs or even the movement of their virtual avatar via commands such as "step forward" or "step back".

Alternative input devices, such as the "Canetroller" [22] demonstrate a comprehensive solution for people with visual impairments that could simulate the experience of using a "White Cane", which is commonly necessary for them to navigate both indoor and outdoor environments. Some activities included spatial recognition for crossing the street and detecting objects and other potential environmental hazards. This could eliminate the need for their reliance on additional assistance in exploring or navigating unfamiliar territory. Furthermore, the device was able to replicate the vibrotactile feedback that a "White Cane" user might receive if their cane made contact with the object in the physical environment.

7.1 Acoustic and Spatial Audio

Dynamic sound presentation can provide prospective users with visual challenges with contextual information that can be crucial to acclimating them to virtual environments. More specifically, these technologies can enhance the experience of using VR by providing the opportunity to identify the proximity of people and objects within a given radius of the user. These applications can be expanded to provide more meaningful interactions. In the context of the Metaverse, for example, "bubbles" can be implemented to acclimate users to virtual environments, and allow them to identify the proximity, direction, or relative position of objects and people in the environment [42]. Similar audio-mapping techniques have been applied to enhance the experience of enjoying virtual concerts in virtual environments and could eventually expand to Metaverse platforms [43].

7.2 Alternative Text

Text input and format can influence the presentation of contextual information to users and can even help to acclimate users to their environment [44]. They suggest that "contextual augmented reality language" (CARL) can be useful in providing salient information that could potentially identify distinct locations through object-description relationships, dictated through text-to-speech applications. A similar prototyped experiment sought to evaluate the effectiveness of utilizing text-to-speech descriptions to identify scene objects and avatars, which they suggest contribute to the overall immersive experience: "While size, shape, or colour convey the visual look, animations, and movements mediate how objects or avatars behave, embedding them into the living virtual scene and contributing to a convincing VR simulation. In the context of social interactions, personal objects of avatars, such as a guitar, may disclose a person's personality trait and enhance social connectedness" [45]. In these regards, alternative text descriptions can not only help users recognize traditional objects that would otherwise be present in the physical environment but in the case of contextual descriptions of avatars, help to identify people close by. By embedding descriptions of objects clothing and accessories, prospective users could make inferences about an individual's personality, facial features, and hair color.

8 Cognitive Impairment

According to the Centers for Disease Control (CDC), "Cognitive impairment ranges from mild to severe. With mild impairment, people may begin to notice changes in cognitive functions but still be able to do their everyday activities. Severe levels of impairment can lead to losing the ability to understand the meaning or importance of something and the ability to talk or write, resulting in the inability to live independently" [26]. Cognitive impairment includes a spectrum of challenges in comprehension, which can affect a person's ability to complete daily tasks and activities and can even affect a person's ability to live independently. For instances of severe impairment, individuals may require the use of memory aids, and personal assistants to accomplish basic life activities. Much of the literature concerning the understanding of cognitive and mental health in the Metaverse suggests the development of personalized systems. For people with cognitive disabilities AR, VR, and MR can provide opportunities to enhance the use of complex digital platforms such as the Metaverse much easier. Generally, the goals of implementing AR and VR technologies to aid people with cognitive disabilities have been primarily directed toward two main outcomes: 1) Using Virtual Learning Environments as education settings for children with autism spectrum disorder and 2) Developing simulations used for Training and Rehabilitation for people with cognitive disabilities to improve their performance of daily living activities and social acuity.

AR can help children with intellectual disability and autism spectrum disorder (ASD). Other prospective technologies can help dyslexic people decipher text-based content that may appear in the environment, via either text-to-speech or speech-to-text options [46]. AR can also help to facilitate dynamic location-based assistance to aid users needing navigation tracking of guidance when traveling from one setting to another, especially locations of interest such as job site locations, schools, and other important desirable places [33]. For example, combining the use of AR and GPS features could allow people with cognitive barriers the ability to independently navigate to and from social spaces such as employment sites and educational institutions [47]. Training and virtual assistance programs especially can be used to "create the opportunity for people with intellectual disabilities to learn by making mistakes but without suffering the real, humiliating or dangerous consequences of their errors" [48]. VR removes some of the barriers for people looking for training alternatives that would otherwise have deeper social implications [49].

8.1 Virtual Learning Environments

As the implications of introducing digital tools in education continue to evolve, innovative strategies hope to harness the capabilities to improve the prospect of collaborative learning, assessment, and evaluation. "VR offers new ways to develop social skills, socialize and interact with others via customizable, realistic, 3D, fully textured, and animated avatars. The user can attend and participate in live events like lectures and conferences, build communities – including learners' communities and patient support groups – relax and visit new places, browse document collections in 3D virtual libraries" [50]. Virtual Learning Environments (VLE) can provide some new avenues for both qualitative and quantitative assessments, through artificial intelligence (AI). Simulated scenarios can be developed, including one-on-one teaching, presentation practice, and information and technical glossary to help acclimate users to their tasks and environment [51]. This area of research can also be particularly advantageous for information professionals looking to explore the transference or translation of certain social skills from the virtual environment to the physical spaces [52].VLEs can potentially aid information, health, and other supporting fields to develop tools and resources that can help acclimate people who struggle with the variability of digitized assistive programs. For example, the prototype platform iSocial [53], attempts to provide an evaluation framework of various social competencies for people with Autism; while others have explored the pertinence of verbal and non-verbal articulation software to improve the comprehension of various tasks in long and short-form scenarios.

8.2 Training and Rehabilitation

In recent developments following the COVID-19 pandemic, research in telehealth systems has been done to explore aspects of preventative care and treatment that could be facilitated remotely [54]. This can be especially significant when evaluating how to provide care in scenarios where face-to-face interaction may not be necessary or even required [55]. In the context of the Metaverse, these methods of evaluation aim to utilize VR to "create a virtual experience that people can manipulate and explore as if they were there." In other words, VR technology tries to predict the sensory consequences of users' actions by displaying the same outcome that our brains expect in the real world" [56]. Similarly, one experiment sought to enhance the reinforcement of social skills training using games in VR, particular for people with Schizophrenia by observing common verbal and non-verbal communication and cues [57]. To this end, mediating clinical interventions in virtual reality could perhaps allow health professionals to perceive the events of their clients by digitally reconstructing the experience for a more effective evaluation strategy and ultimately provide predictive or calculable data and substantiate the use of more objective methodologies [58, 59].

9 Limitations of Research

This content-focused analysis aimed to discuss and identify the notable accessibility challenges that people with disabilities may face when indulging in virtual experiences. While there are many other suitable areas of research investigation concerning both the types of accessibility and disabilities that could have been explored, there is no all-encompassing solution for each physical or social barrier these individuals may face. Furthermore, this research does not include qualitative or quantitative data, through the use of an auxiliary VR or AR hardware available in consumer markets today. With adequate access to Extended Reality hardware and software, a future investigation in this particular area of scholarly interest would perhaps prioritize the recruitment of people in this unique population along with the procurement of head-mounted displays to ascertain how these individuals circumvent their known limitations to perform tasks in specific environments.

10 Trends for Future Research and Conclusion

Ultimately, this paper underscores the current and future research trends in digital accessibility design and their applicability to the Metaverse. Accessibility features in digital and socially-driven environments will be an important facet of ensuring that future technologies are inclusive, i.e. developed for impaired, disabled, and non-disabled users. One of the promising areas is Brain-Computer Interfaces (BCIs) which could offer additional modes of interaction that may apply to more diverse disability groups than those outlined in this paper. It would be beneficial for future trends in research to focus on designing potentially non-invasive technologies such as Brain-Computer Interfaces (BCIs). Added benefits include a myriad of human-centered, computer-integrated solutions that can accommodate the needs of all who intend to harness the full potential of the Metaverse, regardless of the type or degree of disability they might be experiencing. In addition, concurrently designing, prototyping, and integrating the development of artificial intelligence algorithms could facilitate more well-defined approaches, which may apply to resolving ubiquitous or user-specific concerns. Finally, it is important to consider how innovation in this burgeoning field of scholarly and commercial interest may change as newer VR, AR, and MR hardware and software become more open-source and usable by the general pub.

References

1. Kraus, S., Kanbach, D.K., Krysta, P.M., Steinhoff, M.M., Tomini, N.: Facebook and the creation of the metaverse: radical business model innovation or incremental transformation?. Int. J. Entrepren. Behav. Res. (2022)

2. Laeeq, K.: Metaverse: Why, How and What. How and What (2022)
3. Zallio, M., Clarkson, P.: Inclusive Metaverse. How businesses can maximize opportunities to deliver an accessible, inclusive, safe Metaverse that guarantees equity and diversity (2022)
4. Mystakidis, S.: Metaverse. Encyclopedia **2**(1), 486-497 (2022)
5. Azuma, R.T.: A survey of augmented reality. Presence: Teleoper. Virtual Environ. **6**(4), 355–385 (1997)
6. Bach, B., Sicat, R., Pfister, H., Quigley, A.: Drawing into the AR-CANVAS: Designing embedded visualizations for augmented reality. In: Workshop on Immersive Analytics, IEEE Vis (2017)
7. Arena, F., Collotta, M., Pau, G., Termine, F.: An overview of augmented reality. Computers **11**(2), 28 (2022)
8. Rauschnabel, P.A., Felix, R., Hinsch, C., Shahab, H., Alt, F.: What is XR? Towards a framework for augmented and virtual reality. Comput. Hum. Behav. **133**, 107289 (2022)
9. Gandhi, R.D., Patel, D.S.: Virtual reality–opportunities and challenges. Virtual Reality **5**(01), 2714–2724 (2018)
10. Xu, M., et al.: A full dive into realizing the edge-enabled metaverse: Visions, enabling technologies, and challenges. IEEE Commun. Surv. Tutor. (2022)
11. Duan, H., Li, J., Fan, S., Lin, Z., Wu, X., Cai, W.: Metaverse for social good: A university campus prototype. In: Proceedings of the 29th ACM International Conference on Multimedia, pp. 153–161 (2021)
12. Milgram, P., Kishino, F.: A taxonomy of mixed reality visual displays. IEICE Trans. Inf. Syst. **77**(12), 1321–1329 (1994)
13. Speicher, M., Hall, B.D., Nebeling, M.: What is mixed reality?. In: Proceedings of the 2019 CHI Conference on Human Factors in Computing Systems, pp. 1–15 (2019)
14. Faraboschi, P., Frachtenberg, E., Laplante, P., Milojicic, D., Saracco, R.: Virtual worlds (Metaverse): From skepticism, to fear, to immersive opportunities. Computer **55**(10), 100–106 (2022)
15. Park, S.M., Kim, Y.G.: A Metaverse: taxonomy, components, applications, and open challenges. IEEE Access **10**, 4209–4251 (2022)
16. Kovacova, M., Machova, V., Bennett, D.: Immersive extended reality technologies, data visualization tools, and customer behavior analytics in the metaverse commerce. J. Self-Govern. Manage. Econ. **10**(2), 7–21 (2022)
17. Kliestik, T., Novak, A., Lăzăroiu, G.: Live Shopping in the metaverse: visual and spatial analytics, cognitive artificial intelligence techniques and algorithms, and immersive digital simulations. Linguist. Philosoph. Invest. **21**, 187–202 (2022)
18. Tlili, A., et al.: Is Metaverse in education a blessing or a curse: a combined content and bibliometric analysis. Smart Learn. Environ. **9**(1), 1–31 (2022)
19. Nevelsteen, K.J.: Virtual world, defined from a technological perspective and applied to video games, mixed reality, and the Metaverse. Comput. Anim. Virtual Worlds **29**(1), e1752 (2018)
20. Budziszewski, P., Grabowski, A., Milanowicz, M., Jankowski, J.: Workstations for people with disabilities: an example of a virtual reality approach. Int. J. Occup. Saf. Ergon. **22**(3), 367–373 (2016)
21. Cheng, R., Wu, N., Chen, S., Han, B.: Will metaverse be nextg internet? vision, hype, and reality. arXiv preprint arXiv:2201.12894 (2022)
22. Zhao, Y., et al.: Enabling people with visual impairments to navigate virtual reality with a haptic and auditory cane simulation. In: Proceedings of the 2018 CHI Conference on Human Factors in Computing Systems, CHI 2018, pp. 1–14. Association for Computing Machinery, New York, NY, USA. (2018)
23. Knaack, L., Lache, A.K., Preikszas, O., Reinhold, S., Teistler, M.: Improving readability of text in realistic virtual reality scenarios: visual magnification without restricting user interactions. In: Proceedings of Mensch und Computer 2019, pp. 749–753 (2019)

24. Memo, A., Zanuttigh, P.: Head-mounted gesture-controlled interface for human-computer interaction. Multimedia Tools Appl. **77**(1), 27–53 (2018)
25. Centers for Disease Control: FastStats. Disability Impacts All of US (2023). Accessed 18 June 2023
26. Centers for Disease Control: Cognitive Impairment: A Call to Action Now. Alzheimer's Disease Facts and Figures 2010 (2010)
27. Yang, F.X., Wang, Y.: Rethinking metaverse tourism: a taxonomy and an agenda for future research. J. Hosp. Tourism Res. 10963480231163509 (2023)
28. Seigneur, J.M., Choukou, M.A.: How should metaverse augment humans with disabilities? In: 13th Augmented Human International Conference Proceedings. ACM (2022)
29. Wentzel, J., Junuzovic, S., Devine, J., Porter, J., Mott, M.: Understanding how people with limited mobility use multi-modal input. In: CHI Conference on Human Factors in Computing Systems, pp. 1–17 (2022)
30. Gerling, K., Spiel, K.: A critical examination of virtual reality technology in the context of the minority body. In: Proceedings of the 2021 CHI Conference on Human Factors in Computing Systems, pp. 1–14 (2021)
31. Mott, M., Tang, J., Kane, S., Cutrell, E., Ringel Morris, M.: "I just went into it assuming that I wouldn't be able to have the full experience" Understanding the Accessibility of Virtual Reality for People with Limited Mobility. In The 22nd International ACM SIGACCESS Conference on Computers and Accessibility, pp. 1–13 (2020)
32. Malu, M., Findlater, L.: Personalized, wearable control of a head-mounted display for users with upper body motor impairments. In: Proceedings of the 33rd Annual ACM Conference on Human Factors in Computing Systems, pp. 221–230 (2015)
33. Kanza, Y., Krishnamurthy, B., Srivastava, D.: Geospatial accessibility and inclusion by combining contextual filters, the metaverse, and ambient intelligence. In: Proceedings of the 30th International Conference on Advances in Geographic Information Systems, pp. 1–4 (2022)
34. Cho, Y., Hong, S., Kim, M., Kim, J.: DAVE: deep learning-based asymmetric virtual environment for immersive experiential metaverse content. Electronics **11**(16), 2604 (2022)
35. Sun, Z., Zhu, M., Shan, X., Lee, C.: Augmented tactile-perception and haptic-feedback rings as human-machine interfaces aiming for immersive interactions. Nat. Commun. **13**(1), 1–13 (2022)
36. Narashiman, D., Mala, T.: An avatar rendering hand gestures for Tamil words. Methodology **4**, 3 (2013)
37. Teófilo, M., Nascimento, J., Santos, J., Albuquerque, Y., Souza, A.L., Nogueira, D.: Bringing basic accessibility features to virtual reality context. In: 2016 IEEE Virtual Reality (VR), pp. 293–294. IEEE (2016)
38. Velázquez, R.: Wearable assistive devices for the blind. In: Lay-Ekuakille, A., Mukhopadhyay, S.C. (eds.) Wearable and autonomous biomedical devices and systems for smart environment, pp. 331–349. Springer Berlin Heidelberg, Berlin, Heidelberg (2010). https://doi.org/10.1007/978-3-642-15687-8_17
39. Isewon, I., Oyelade, J., Oladipupo, O.: Design and implementation of text-to-speech conversion for visually impaired people. Int. J. Appl. Inform. Syst. **7**(2), 25–30 (2014)
40. Fernandes, F., Werner, C.: Accessibility in the metaverse: are we prepared?. In: Anais do XIII Workshop sobre Aspectos da Interação Humano-Computador para a Web Social, pp. 9–15. SBC (2022)
41. Alateeq, A., Roantree, M., Gurrin, C.: Voxento 2.0: a prototype voice-controlled interactive search engine for lifelogs. In: Proceedings of the 4th Annual on Lifelog Search Challenge, pp. 65–70 (2021)
42. Schirosa, M., Janer, J., Kersten, S., Roma, G.: A system for soundscape generation, composition and streaming. In: Xvii CIM-Colloquium of Musical Informatics (2010)

43. Jot, J.M., Audfray, R., Hertensteiner, M., Schmidt, B.: Rendering spatial sound for interoperable experiences in the audio metaverse. In: 2021 Immersive and 3D Audio: from Architecture to Automotive (I3DA), pp. 1–15. IEEE (2021)
44. Rumiński, D., Walczak, K.: Carl: a language for modelling contextual augmented reality environments. In: Technological Innovation for Collective Awareness Systems: 5th IFIP WG 5.5/SOCOLNET Doctoral Conference on Computing, Electrical and Industrial Systems, DoCEIS 2014, Costa de Caparica, Portugal, April 7–9, 2014. Proceedings 5, pp. 183–190. Springer Berlin Heidelberg (2014). https://doi.org/10.1007/978-3-642-54734-8_21
45. Sun, Y., Stellmacher, C., Kaltenhauser, A., Wagener, N., Neumann, D., Schöning, J.: Alt Text and Alt Sense in VR: Engaging Screen Reader Users within the Metaverse Through Multisenses (2023)
46. Caute, A., Cruice, M., Marshall, J., Monnelly, K., Wilson, S., Woolf, C.: Assistive technology approaches to reading therapy for people with acquired dyslexia. Aphasiology **32**(sup1), 40–42 (2018)
47. McMahon, D., Cihak, D.F., Wright, R.: Augmented reality as a navigation tool to employment opportunities for postsecondary education students with intellectual disabilities and autism. J. Res. Technol. Educ. **47**(3), 157–172 (2015)
48. Standen, P.J., Brown, D.J.: Virtual reality and its role in removing the barriers that turn cognitive impairments into intellectual disability. Virtual Reality **10**(3), 241–252 (2006)
49. Moon, H.J., Han, S.: Perspective: present and future of virtual reality for neurological disorders. Brain Sci. **12**(12), 1692 (2022)
50. Pensieri, C., Pennacchini, M.: Overview: virtual reality in medicine. J. Virtual Worlds Res. **7**(1) (2014)
51. Sghaier, S., Elfakki, A.O., Alotaibi, A.A.: Development of an intelligent system based on metaverse learning for students with disabilities. Front. Robot. A **I**, 9 (2022)
52. Ke, F., Moon, J., Sokolikj, Z.: Virtual reality–based social skills training for children with autism spectrum disorder. J. Spec. Educ. Technol. **37**(1), 49–62 (2022)
53. Jovanović, A., Milosavljević, A.: VoRtex Metaverse platform for gamified collaborative learning. Electronics **11**(3), 317 (2022)
54. Usmani, S.S., Sharath, M., Mehendale, M.: Future of mental health in the metaverse. General Psych. **35**(4), e100825 (2022)
55. Reay, R.E., Looi, J.C., Keightley, P.: <? covid19?> Telehealth mental health services during COVID-19: summary of evidence and clinical practice. Australas. Psych. **28**(5), 514–516 (2020)
56. Riva, G., et al.: Virtual reality therapy in the Metaverse: merging VR for the outside with VR for the inside. Ann. Rev. Cyber. Telemed **19**, 3–8 (2021)
57. Park, K.M., et al.: A virtual reality application in role-plays of social skills training for schizophrenia: a randomized, controlled trial. Psych. Res. **189**(2), 166–172 (2011)
58. Cerasa, A., Gaggioli, A., Marino, F., Riva, G., Pioggia, G.: The promise of the metaverse in mental health: the new era of MEDverse. Heliyon e11762 (2022)
59. Calabrò, R.S., et al.: The arrival of the metaverse in neurorehabilitation: fact, fake or vision? Biomedicines **10**(10), 2602 (2022)

Evaluation of the Accessibility of Mobile Applications: Current Approaches and Challenges

Maria Matos, Letícia Seixas Pereira(✉), and Carlos Duarte

LASIGE, Faculdade de Ciências, Universidade de Lisboa, Lisbon, Portugal
lspereira@ciencias.ulisboa.pt

Abstract. The World Health Organization estimates that around 1.3 billion people worldwide are affected by some form of impairment. Ensuring accessibility of mobile applications has become imperative to meet the requirements of this group. Mobile accessibility involves the process of making mobile applications more inclusive for individuals with disabilities using mobile devices. This paper investigates the strong need for effective methodologies to evaluate the accessibility of mobile applications, particularly with the recent implementation of the Web Accessibility Directive in Europe. By reviewing existing research, analyzing monitoring reports from European Union Member States, and conducting interviews with mobile accessibility evaluators, this study identifies limitations in current evaluation methodologies and provides some insights into the challenges faced by evaluators. The findings reveal that there is no universally adopted methodology for evaluating the accessibility of mobile applications. Evaluators either adapt existing methodologies designed for web accessibility or develop their own approaches. The absence of specific guidelines for mobile accessibility poses a challenge, with evaluators often having to interpret web-focused documents. The lack of comprehensive automated tools for mobile accessibility evaluation further complicates the process. Through this research, it is anticipated that improvements in mobile application accessibility evaluations will contribute to creating more inclusive mobile experiences for all individuals.

Keywords: Accessibility · Mobile Accessibility Evaluation · Mobile Accessibility Monitoring · Accessibility Evaluation Methodologies · Mobile Applications

1 Introduction

According to the World Health Organization, approximately 1.3 billion people worldwide are affected by some sort of impairment [24]. Developers must consider these individuals' particular requirements and build accessible solutions. Accessibility refers to everyone's right to experience the environments, products, services, and information that come with living in society, regardless of

Q. Gao et al. (Eds.): HCII 2023, LNCS 14055, pp. 352–371, 2023.
https://doi.org/10.1007/978-3-031-48041-6_24

their sensorial, motor or cognitive skills, or social and cultural backgrounds. To be considered accessible, an information system should not include barriers that prohibit users, regardless of disability, from using it [27].

The term "mobile accessibility" refers to the process of making websites and applications more accessible to individuals with disabilities who use mobile phones and other mobile devices [14]. Smartphones, as a technological resource, are extremely beneficial to people with disabilities [27], affording them some independence. However, these devices bring with them new challenges [27]. Mobile devices are smaller than traditional desktops or laptops devices, which makes them challenging in a variety of ways, like tapping the right target, as discussed in Gonçalves et al. [23]. The vast number of applications and tasks, along with the small display size, makes them cognitively demanding [13]. Mobile devices and their applications have been evolving at a fast pace, driven by huge corporations. The lack of convergence and standards also marks this industry driven progress. Thus, impacting the treatment of accessibility [13].

The need to ensure accessible mobile applications is a pertinent, current issue, especially in Europe, where the Web Accessibility Directive (WAD) [6] has been recently implemented. This directive requires regular monitoring of public sector websites and mobile applications, demonstrated with periodical reports of accessibility evaluations. These reports [9] have revealed different methodologies and tools used by Member States to evaluate the accessibility of mobile applications, as well as challenges faced by monitoring bodies.

Although researchers have proposed evaluation methodologies, these have certain limitations. For instance, most of these methodologies do not provide complete information to conduct a thorough accessibility evaluation of mobile applications [3,27], and they are not able to identify all types of accessibility barriers [1,22]. To address these issues, an effective accessibility evaluation methodology for mobile applications is necessary. To obtain a more comprehensive understanding of the challenges faced by mobile application evaluators and address some of the issues of existing evaluation methodologies, we combined a review of the research on the subject with a thorough examination of the reports of the first period of monitoring from European Union (EU) Member States. Additionally, we conducted interviews with five mobile accessibility evaluators to understand the methods, tools, and challenges faced during evaluations.

This article is organized as follows: in Sect. 2, we discuss accessibility guidelines applicable to mobile applications, how accessibility is evaluated, methodologies to evaluate the accessibility of mobile applications, and existing tools to help in the evaluation; in Sect. 3, we analyze the monitoring reports provided by the EU Member States, the procedures followed in the monitoring activities, and the results from the accessibility evaluations; in Sect. 4, we report on the findings from a set of semi-structured interviews with mobile accessibility evaluators; in Sect. 5, we discuss all the findings in the context of existing guidelines, past evaluation studies and available evaluation methodologies; and finally in Sect. 6 we conclude the article.

2 Related Work

This research is related to prior work on accessibility guidelines, accessibility evaluation, methodologies and tools for accessibility evaluation.

2.1 Accessibility Guidelines

The W3C Web Accessibility Initiative (WAI) develops guidelines and resources to help make the Web accessible to all types of disabilities [19]. Among them, the Web Content Accessibility Guidelines (WCAG) [30] stand out, with versions that have evolved over the years. The WCAG 2.0 provides little guidance on creating accessible content for mobile devices. To fill this void, the Mobile Web Best Practices (MWBP) [26] were released. MWBP is a document that defines rules to make websites more usable in a mobile device. Similar to the WCAG, the MWBP defines a set of checkpoints that should be considered to guarantee that online content is suitable for access from mobile devices.

Another effort is the Guidance on Applying WCAG 2.0 to Non-Web Information and Communications Technologies (WCAG2ICT) document [16]. This document provides guidance on how to apply the concepts, guidelines, and success criteria of WCAG 2.0 to non-web documents and software. It was developed to give interpretations of how to use WCAG 2.0 in various contexts. WCAG2ICT addresses a broad variety of issues, however, it also acknowledges that it is unable to meet the needs of all individuals with disabilities. Because WCAG 2.0 was created for the web, addressing accessibility for non-web documents and software may need additional steps beyond those specified in the document [16].

Shortly after the MWBP was released, an update to the WCAG was also released. WCAG 2.1 has one new guideline and 17 new success criteria to address mobile accessibility, people with low vision, and people with cognitive and learning disabilities [17].

There is now a public draft of the WCAG 2.2 with 9 new success criteria. These new success criteria enhance users' experiences by ensuring easy access to support resources and allowing for a wider range of assistive technologies. Related to mobile, there are two new success criteria: one about movements to facilitate drag and drop actions, and another about target size to prevent people from clicking on the wrong button due to lack of space between buttons [15].

Besides WCAG, there are other guidelines that can be applied to the mobile context. The User Agent Accessibility Guidelines (UAAG) 2.0 [29] are intended for user agent developers working on desktop or mobile operating systems. A user agent that follows UAAG 2.0 improves accessibility through its own user interface, options for rendering and interacting with content, and the ability to communicate with other technologies, including assistive technologies. Its support documentation contains numerous mobile examples. The Authoring Tool Accessibility Guidelines (ATAG) 2.0 [28] provide guidelines for developers of authoring tools for desktop or mobile operating systems. An authoring tool that adheres to ATAG 2.0 will be more accessible to authors with disabilities while also enabling, supporting, and promoting the creation of more accessible online content by all authors. The support document to implement ATAG 2.0 contains multiple examples of mobile authoring tools [31].

2.2 Accessibility Evaluation

An accessibility evaluation aims to verify how well websites or mobile applications can be used by as many people as possible [25]. There are different methods for conducting an accessibility evaluation. One of them is automated testing, a starting point to evaluate the accessibility of websites or mobile applications with an automatic tool. This tool detects accessibility problems in the code of each page or screen. Usually, it follows a checklist of points that should be verified to ensure compliance [2,22]. This testing technique is not capable of finding every problem in the website or mobile application being tested, so these need further testing. On the other hand, it is a fast method, saving time and effort [25].

There is also manual testing. In this, an inspection of the website or mobile application is done by an expert to check for issues that may cause problems for users with disabilities. Experts have to interpret the guidelines being used and determine if they are fulfilled by the mobile application [2,22]. This is the method that allows evaluators to find the largest amount of errors (ideally all, depending on the expertise of the evaluator), especially the ones that cannot be programmatically detected, although it's a more time consuming method and prone to human error [25].

Another testing method that can be used is user testing. User testing should involve users with disabilities. It allows us to have a better understanding of the users' perspectives, including any issues they may encounter using or not using assistive technologies while navigating the website or mobile application. It also helps us understand if the accessibility criteria address all the issues that people with disabilities may face [25].

Combining these different methods, we can obtain different methodologies for evaluation.

2.3 Methodologies Used for Accessibility Evaluation

A review of the most relevant methodologies for evaluating web and mobile applications was conducted.

European Standard (EN) Methodology. The Web Accessibility Directive [6] is a work of the European Commission to ensure an inclusive Europe, accessible to all. The goal is to enable people with disabilities to better use websites and mobile applications of public services, by ensuring these meet all the requirements of the European Standard EN 301 549 [5]. In the monitoring process, member states must use the methodology chosen by the Commission to monitor compliance [6]. The methodology defines:

- The frequency with which the monitoring of website and mobile application is carried out;

- The sampling of web pages, their content, and the content of mobile applications;
- Provisions for automated, manual and usability testing;
- The guidelines used for determining compliance;
- A mechanism to assist public sector bodies in correcting any deficiencies discovered.

The WAD also defines two evaluation processes, simplified testing and detailed testing, to perform audits using some of the methods already mentioned [6]. Simplified testing uses automated tools and manual checks to examine a small section of the website or mobile application's pages. Detailed testing takes a more in-depth look at the website or mobile application. This monitoring method tests the platform against the WCAG success criteria, using assistive technology along with manual testing combined or not with automated testing to ensure compliance. To monitor the accessibility of mobile applications, WAD only requires the detailed testing method. It is important to note that, in the mobile context, different operating systems must be taken into account [7].

WCAG-EM. The Website Accessibility Conformance Evaluation Methodology (WCAG-EM) [18] is a methodology to determine how well a website, including web applications and mobile websites, complies with the WCAG. The conformance evaluation procedure is divided into five major steps, each broken out with recommendations, best practices, and guidance for evaluators:

1. Define the scope of the evaluation – in this step, the scope of the evaluation, the evaluation's goal, and the WCAG conformance level are defined.
2. Explore the website – the key web pages, key functionality, types of web content, designs, functionality, and required web technologies are all identified here.
3. Select a representative sample – when it is impossible to evaluate every web page on a website, guidance is given to choose structured and random samples of web pages.
4. Evaluate the selected sample – WCAG success and failure are determined in this phase, website features are checked for accessibility, and evaluation steps are documented.
5. Report the evaluation findings – here are the aggregation and reporting of evaluation findings, the formulation of evaluation statements, and the calculation of overall scores.

Appt-EM. The Appt-EM methodology [11] is based on the WCAG-EM, but instead of being developed for websites, the Appt-EM was developed for mobile applications. Out of the 50 A and AA success criteria from the WCAG 2.1, 6 are not applied in this methodology, 13 have undergone minor adjustments to the notes or definitions, and the other 31 are applied without changes.

The evaluation procedure is also divided into five steps, each broken out into activities to guide the evaluators:

1. Define the scope of the evaluation – in this step, you start by determining the scope of the application by specifying the URL for downloading the application and the version to be tested, and knowing which screens are available to be evaluated; then you determine which compliance level to use; and finally you determine the scope of the hardware and software by defining screen sizes, system settings, operating system version, among other things.
2. Research mobile application – the most frequently used screens, the most critical flows, the most used elements, the techniques used, and other relevant screens are all identified here.
3. Select the sample to be evaluated – determine the screens to be assessed, both the structured sample and the random sample, and since the applications consist mainly of flows, add the flows to the scope.
4. Evaluate the selected sample – classify the screens, evaluate the flows, and compare the structured sample with the random sample.
5. Report the evaluation results – report must meet specific formal requirements of WCAG-EM.

This methodology also provides additional recommendations [11], such as providing sufficient context about the evaluation; for example, by saving screenshots of the application screen when some error occurs – since the application can be updated and the error can be gone. Another recommendation is that reports should be organised by success criteria and screen, making it easier for developers to understand how to correct the errors identified.

The authors also provide a list of the WCAG success criteria [12] with additional content tailored to the mobile context. This additional content includes a description of each success criteria, the impact it may have, a way to check if the requirements are being met, and some ways for developers to solve the problems, considering different operating systems.

Evaluation Methodologies in Academic Literature. In addition to the previous methodologies, there are also some that have been developed and used in studies to evaluate mobile applications. Acosta-Vargas *et al.* [1] explored a combination of automatic testing using an automatic tool with manual testing based on the WCAG 2.1 guidelines. After choosing a mobile application, the methodology goes through six phases:

1. Explore, interact, and navigate through each application.
2. Define activities and tasks for users to do in each application.
3. Define a list of accessibility barriers based on the four principles of WCAG 2.1.
4. Select users based on the barriers established in the previous phase.
5. Run the automatic test and review each guideline manually. The parameters selected to be evaluated by the authors in the automatic test were the number of elements, touch target, text contrast, item label, and image contrast.
6. Record the automatic and manual evaluation data and analyze it.

Using this methodology, the authors were able to determine which accessibility principles were being infringed the most in the applications, such as small touch targets, low text contrast, missing item labels, and low image contrast. The authors highlight the reliance on the expertise of the evaluator as a limitation of the method, but it can be mitigated by replicating the manual process with different people. This paper shows that automatic testing still needs some adaptations and tools to be effective on mobile devices, but there is the option to combine it with manual testing.

Ferreira da Silva *et al.* [27] used an observation method in the context of usage of mobile applications to assess their accessibility for people with visual impairment, based on a protocol tested in a previous study [10]. After choosing one mobile application, the methodology included the following stages: participant selection, equipment definition, task list definition, case study implementation, and results analysis. Difficulties and problems were analyzed and compared with the WCAG 2.0 guidelines. Overall, it was possible to observe that most of the users' difficulties are related to the way information and interface components are presented. Besides revealing some of the problems users with visual impairments face using mobile applications, this study supports the idea that designers and developers have difficulties understanding accessibility guidelines, which does not contribute to better accessibility in mobile applications.

Joshi *et al.* [21] proposes a methodology with four different testing approaches that can be applied throughout the mobile app development lifecycle. Authors argue that simple approaches can be carried out by any member of the development team because they do not require advanced knowledge of accessibility testing. The four testing approaches are: automated test, screen reader test, magnification/zooming test, and switch access and keyboard test. The authors report that adopting this methodology during the development phase can produce the most accessible application without incurring additional costs or time. It is simple to plan and implement without the use of expensive tools, and it can help people with visual, motor, and cognitive challenges avoid accessibility concerns. According to their findings, major issues can be identified and resolved if the appropriate testing procedures are employed at the appropriate development phase. Although these are promising developments, the fact is that mobile applications continue being inaccessible. This is, probably, a consequence of these suggestions not being applied by developers. They are, nonetheless, a set of recommendations that are useful for mobile accessibility evaluation even outside the scope of development.

Acosta-Vargas *et al.* [3] recognize that there is a lack of adequate methods to test mobile applications' accessibility and that has become a challenge for accessibility experts. To address this problem, they proposed a method of manual testing using WCAG 2.1 combined with automatic testing using the Accessibility Scanner [4]. The authors only worked with Android applications in this study. After choosing and installing the mobile applications that are going to be tested, the proposed method follows these steps:

- Install the Accessibility Scanner validator and activate the accessibility test;

- Interact with the mobile applications being tested running the accessibility test;
- Record the results in a Microsoft Excel spreadsheet;
- Analyze the problems identified by the tool;
- Review the barriers identified and propose some improvements.

The authors conclude that the information found can be helpful for designers, developers, and evaluators, giving some recommendations to overcome the most common problems encountered in their evaluation, such as lack of item labels, poor text contrast, or even issues with touch targets. They also suggest that to evaluate mobile applications, the process should use a combination of multiple methods, consider users with different disabilities, the different barriers raised by different disabilities, and the diverse usage scenarios of the mobile application. This study sustains the idea that combining methods is the best option to obtain a more accurate assessment and for providing better information to all parties involved in the creation and development of mobile applications.

Mateus *et al.* [22] presents a study that compares different methodologies used to evaluate mobile applications, using problems encountered only by users and problems encountered by both tools and users. It reveals that automated tools can only encounter a small portion of problems while users find a more significant number of problems. The authors came to the conclusion that, despite the fact that automated evaluation techniques might encounter a small but significant portion of difficulties, they cannot replace user testing, which is still a safe way of detecting accessibility barriers. Tools do not identify all of the issues that users describe, but they can be valuable for developers and evaluators in the early stages. They are an evaluation method that identifies a great number of problems at a lower cost and with greater agility.

2.4 Existing Tools for Accessibility Evaluation

Using an automated tool can help verify criteria in a faster way, but they can have disadvantages, depending on the tool, operating system, and even the task performed. Examples of automatic tools used for testing mobile applications are:

Accessibility Scanner: This tool checks Android apps against a set of rules that identify possible problems for people with disabilities. When opened, it scans the screen of the application and gives suggestions for improving its accessibility. It is a tool that can be used directly in a mobile application by anyone since all functions are user-friendly; it can evaluate any screen element; it allows people to leave suggestions about possible alterations for the developers; and it shows the code that is generating accessibility problems. It tests content labels, touch target size, clickable items, text and image contrast. On the downside, this tool only works for Android, and it does not replace manual testing; it only complements it [4].

Accessibility Inspector: This tool inspects an iOS application, looking for potential optimizations that allow people with disabilities to use the app.

Accessibility Inspector makes it possible to conduct automatic audits on any page; to see all element properties at once; to explore switch control, braille boards, and alternative input devices; to help develop apps more accessible to VoiceOver (Apple's voice assistant) and other accessibility technologies; and to run the application as if it were running with VoiceOver but using a mouse to see the elements' labels. On the other hand, this tool is only for iOS, only tests on the source code, and its automatic audits must be manually reviewed due to false positives [20].

Apart from automatic tools, there are other types of tools, called support tools, used to evaluate some specific aspects of mobile applications. These support tools are used to help in the manual testing of applications. The most common support tool used to help evaluate the accessibility of mobile applications is color contrast analyzers, which allow you to determine the contrast between two colors.

For websites, there are many more support tools for other functionalities, for example, a tool that helps to check if there are any issues with the content or functionality of your website after increasing the line, paragraph, letter, and word spacing according to the "text spacing" success criterion of the WCAG or even another tool to examine the HTML markup on a web page for syntax and lexical mistakes. These tools do not exist for mobile.

3 Monitoring Reports

In the monitoring process defined by the European Commission's methodology [6], member states describe the results in reports. These monitoring reports are reports of accessibility evaluations of websites and mobile applications done by each member state, showing some of the shortcomings and difficulties faced when evaluating the applications [9]. From these reports, it is possible to draw some conclusions about what is missing in order to make evaluations more accurate and complete toward achieving more accessible mobile applications.

3.1 Review of Monitoring Reports

To understand what methods were used by member states to assess the accessibility of their platforms, the problems they have faced, and the conclusions they have reached, the monitoring reports [9] were analyzed.

Table 1 shows the methods used by each country to evaluate websites and mobile applications. This table does not contain the reports from Hungary, whose report was difficult to analyze due to a lack of information and structure, and France and Cyprus, who had not published a report by the time of this analysis.

To evaluate websites, almost every country employed a methodology combining both automated and manual testing for a more efficient and accurate evaluation. To evaluate mobile applications, the most common method is manual testing, with some countries also using automatic testing. In general, user

Table 1. Evaluation Methods used by each country

Country	Evaluation Method for					
	Website			Mobile Applications		
	Automated Testing	Manual Testing	User Testing	Automated Testing	Manual Testing	User Testing
Belgium	✓	✓	—	—	—	—
Bulgaria	✓	✓	✓	✓	✓	—
Czechia	✓	✓	—	✓	✓	—
Denmark	✓	✓	—	—	✓	—
Germany	✓	✓	—	✓	✓	—
Estonia	✓	✓	—	—	✓	—
Ireland	✓	—	—	✓	✓	—
Greece	✓	✓	—	✓	✓	—
Spain	✓	✓	—	—	✓	—
Croatia	✓	✓	—	—	✓	—
Italy	✓	✓	—	✓	✓	—
Latvia	✓	✓	✓	—	✓	✓
Lithuania	✓	✓	✓	—	✓	✓
Luxembourg	✓	✓	—	—	✓	—
Malta	✓	✓	—	✓	✓	—
Netherlands	✓	✓	—	—	✓	—
Austria	✓	✓	—	—	✓	—
Poland	✓	✓	✓	✓	✓	—
Portugal	✓	✓	✓	—	✓	✓
Romania	✓	✓	—	—	✓	—
Slovenia	✓	✓	—	—	✓	—
Slovakia	✓	✓	—	—	✓	—
Finland	✓	✓	—	—	✓	—
Sweden	✓	✓	—	—	✓	—
United Kingdom	✓	✓	—	✓	✓	—

testing is not widely used to assess websites or mobile applications. Still, we can see that there are some countries, although few, that make use of this technique combined with others to ensure that the users' point of view is taken into consideration when evaluating mobile platforms.

Overall, the two evaluation processes defined by the WAD were used to perform the audits. For websites, the evaluation processes mostly used were simplified and detailed testing, while for mobile applications, only detailed testing was used.

When it comes to mobile applications, Table 2 shows that the samples differ slightly between countries. According to the methodology defined by the European Commission, the sample size should be proportional to the size of the country's population, consisting of one application per million inhabitants plus six applications. Therefore, there are larger and smaller samples, some of them too small to draw any significant conclusions. According to the Study support-

Table 2. Number of mobile applications per country (* Countries reporting only the total number of mobile applications).

Country	Android Apps	iOS Apps	Total
Belgium	0	0	0
Bulgaria	13	0	13
Czechia	17	0	17
Denmark	4	4	8
Germany	23	34	57
Estonia	4	3	7
Ireland	2	2	4
Greece	17	17	34
Spain	8	10	18
Croatia	8	0	8
Italy	11	11	22
Latvia	–	–	8*
Lithuania	10	8	18
Luxembourg	1	1	2
Hungary	12	12	24
Malta	2	2	4
Netherlands	4	4	8
Austria	3	2	5
Poland	8	7	15
Portugal	8	8	16
Romania	25	0	25
Slovenia	–	–	3*
Slovakia	3	3	6
Finland	2	2	4
Sweden	0	2	2
United Kingdom	2	2	4

ing the review of the WAD [8], the countries with small samples are Luxembourg, Ireland, and Sweden. There is one country (Belgium) that, at the time of this analysis, had yet to conduct mobile application evaluation. Latvia's and Slovenia's reports did not state how many mobile applications of each operating system were evaluated, only the total number. Based on the number of mobile applications evaluated in the countries that have monitored them, the average is 13 mobile applications evaluated per country.

The reports show the contrast between Android and iOS. Table 2 presents how many Android or iOS applications were evaluated in each country. There are some that do not evaluate iOS because it is not the most used operating system by people with disabilities in the country, or because the countries language is not supported by the screen reader. There is only one country that does not evaluate Android mobile applications, Sweden, but they do not explain why.

Looking at the reports, it is possible to see that some mobile apps do not have any issues complying with all the criteria. Still, other problems were identified in the monitoring of mobile applications:

- The applications miss some criteria;
- There is a lack of information about the results or conclusions;
- Mobile applications are given little importance compared to websites;
- There is no fixed methodology that can be used by everyone in the same way to draw the best possible conclusions;
- There is a lack of accessibility statements.

On the bright side, some reports show detailed conclusions about the accessibility of the applications monitored, and the user testing allows the users to give their perspective on problems they face daily, including some that people without their disabilities wouldn't think of.

3.2 Problems Identified in the Reports

In the reports of the member states of the European Commission it is possible to see which methods were used in the evaluation process of mobile applications. Starting with automated testing, out of the 24 countries that evaluated mobile applications, only nine of them conducted this type of testing. We can deduce the reasons why this strategy is not widely used based on what was said in these reports:

- Not having coding skills to be able to use a certain tool;
- Not testing all the criteria desired to be tested, since these tools cannot identify all problems listed in the guidelines [22];
- Automatic tools continue to face challenges in accurately identifying false positives and handling dynamic content [8]. This further contributes to the existing limitations of automated tools, as discussed in previous sections. Additionally, the majority of these tools only support one of the two major mobile operating systems (Android or iOS), which adds another layer of complexity to automated testing.

Regarding manual testing, as reported by the countries that conducted this type of evaluation:

- There are success criteria that are difficult to evaluate in mobile applications for lack of support tools or an easier process to do it;
- Manual testing increases the time and cost of operations, which are worsened by the difficulties encountered when interpreting the directive's guidelines [8].

About user testing, we can see in Table 1 that only 3 countries conducted this test. This can be partially explained due to:

- User testing takes work to plan and execute and time to do it all;
- It can be hard to find people with disabilities to participate in these tests, either because of deadlines for submitting results, a lack of funds to be able to compensate the participants or a lack of people available to do so.

4 Interviews with Accessibility Evaluators

To better characterize the issues faced when monitoring and evaluating mobile applications, for the following stages, we established two research questions:

- What are the main problems evaluators face when evaluating the accessibility of mobile applications?
- Why they choose the methodologies and tools they use for evaluations?

To answer the research questions we conducted semi-structured interviews with accessibility evaluators to discuss their experience with accessibility evaluations. These interviews aimed to understand the problems they face when assessing mobile applications, the methodologies and tools they use and why, and what they would change to make this process easier and more reliable.

4.1 Participants

Five accessibility evaluators (Table 3) from four different European countries were interviewed remotely. The evaluators had between 1 to 9 years of experience, with an average of three years. All of them had experience evaluating Android, and only one didn't have with iOS. The only requirements for the choice of participants were that they should be of legal age and have previous experience evaluating mobile applications.

Table 3. Characterization of the evaluators

Evaluator	Country	Years of experience with mobile accessibility	Operating Systems used in accessibility evaluations
P1	Portugal	9 years	Android and iOS
P2	Denmark	3 years	Android and iOS
P3	Norway	1 year	Android and iOS
P4	Portugal	1 year	Android
P5	Netherlands	2 years	Android and iOS

4.2 Procedure

Participants were recruited through the research team's network. An email was sent to them with information about the study and an Informed Consent Form to be signed. A convenient time was arranged for both the researcher and the participant to conduct the interview. Sessions were conducted through Zoom and were recorded with the permission of the participants. One of them did not authorize recording the session, so the researcher took notes.

The interview started with a brief introduction about the study. It was checked if there were any questions regarding the study and if the participant authorized the interview recording. It was explained that the participant would be asked a few questions about their experience evaluating mobile applications and to provide feedback on anything they felt relevant to the study. Next, questions were asked related to the problems faced during mobile applications accessibility evaluation, methodologies used in the evaluations along with tools, their thoughts on the ideal methodology, and what they would change in the evaluation process to make it easier. They were still asked if they would like to add anything. In the end, they were thanked for their participation and time. This procedure was approved by the Ethics Committee of the Faculty of Sciences of the University of Lisbon.

4.3 Data Analysis

To analyse the data from the interviews we conducted a thematic analysis. We started by transcribing and coding the recorded interviews. Notes from the non-recorded interview were also coded. Multiple iterations of the codes and themes were discussed among the researchers until a final consensus was reached. The thematic analysis was used to reach conclusions about the research questions established and to understand common problems, methodologies, and tools.

4.4 Findings

From the five interviews with the evaluators, six themes emerged: "Lack of a common methodology for mobile accessibility assessment", "Automation of methodology processes", "Methodologies are not adapted for mobile applications", "Main accessibility flaws found in mobile applications", "Reporting errors to developers in a perceivable way is not easy", "Lack of information and guides to assess mobile accessibility".

Through the coding it is possible to understand that there is no methodology for evaluating the accessibility of mobile application that is common to all evaluators. Some of them developed their own methodology based on an existing one (P5: "so we are testing 44 criteria and besides that we rewrote the WCAG-EM and did some pointers as well") or from scratch (P2: "we've actually built out our own methodology"), arguing that there should be a common methodology to all European Union countries (P3).

Given the problems of the existing methodologies, some ideas emerge that automating the processes of the methodology (P4: "Ideally it would be all automatic, that's impossible, but automating as much as possible") would be positive to decrease time and resources (P3), even if the evaluation process was only semi-automatic, and some specific criteria had to be manually evaluated (P3). Still, there are some who say that the evaluation process they use does not present major problems (P4: "I don't think we had any major problems in the evaluation process").

To automate methodology processes one can resort to the use of tools, both automatic and support tools since both help in the evaluation process. However, evaluators agree that there is a lack of tools to evaluate mobile application accessibility. Automatic tools are either non-existent (P3), or they only test some problems and the results may not even be right (P1: "sometimes you find things that turn out to be right"). Still, evaluators say that an automatic tool for everything would be ideal (P2: "I mean anyone would wish that there was an automatic tool that could do anything"), or that, at least, a tool that could detect errors that are not always detected manually (P1: "Detect errors that are not so noticeable in manual validation"). Support tools are either not used or limited in their scope, with the usual mention being the color contrast analyzer (P2: "we use color contrast checkers"). Another idea given by the evaluators is the possible use of Artificial Intelligence (AI) (P2: "I also believe that we can use the power of AI to some extent, but still it will require manual assessments").

Evaluators reported that there is a lack of guidelines to evaluate mobile accessibility (P3) and that the documents that do exist are geared towards the web (P3) which leads to everyone having to interpret these documents differently (P3). The evaluators feel that there is lack of information (P1: "There is no specific thing for native apps") and of examples regarding the evaluation of mobile apps (P3). As much as they may use a certain methodology, they don't know if it is the right one (P1: "I can use my methodology all right, but for what it's worth, there is no standard") because there is no concrete document for mobile applications (P1: "what applies to mobile? There is no specific thing for native applications"). They also mention that there are mismatches between the European Standard and the WCAG (P3), that user needs differ in the two documents (P3), and that it would be important to make an accurate interpretation of the standard and the WCAG (P5: "I think you should first start with EN standard with a good interpretation of WCAG, because otherwise it doesn't make sense"). Some evaluators argue that the user's perspective can provide some important information in the evaluation process (P2: "what we have to do then is to put ourselves in the place of the user, which is in principle really, really good because what we are evaluating is not so much compliance but more the actual user experience").

One of the biggest difficulties of the existing methodologies is the fact that they are not adapted for mobile devices (P4: "as it is not adapted, as it was not made on purpose for mobile applications, there are some things that do not make so much sense"), having differences between operating systems, both in terms of the criteria that the operating system itself requires to be met (P1: "I think Apple does something better, which is that when they make an application they have to meet certain criteria") and in terms of automatic tools available for each one (P2: "I mean they are only available for Android primarily"). Participants also mentioned it could be advantageous to have access to the code to inspect some problems that may go unnoticed when using only the app (P3).

Some evaluators also discussed the way the problems are reported to the developers, which may not be understandable by developers if they don't have some knowledge of accessibility (P2: "typically the recipient of an evaluation report like this, they don't have knowledge enough about, you know, what the reasons would be for that symptom"). They also argue that the methodology should be oriented to solving the problems, not just finding them (P5: "it's all about WCAG and finding the issues. And I think that's wrong because it's about fixing the issues").

Finally, some of the accessibility flaws still found in mobile applications were also mentioned, the most common being the lack of labels on elements (P1: "Labels, labels of the fields and the buttons"), contrast between elements (P5: "about contrast elements, contrast of text"), problems related to navigation in the application (P4: "the navigation, the fact that they are adapted from web pages makes the navigation a lot worse") and with the use of screen readers (P5: "The focus order for the screen reader that goes wrong quite often").

5 Discussion

From the problems identified in the reports and the findings of the interviews, the most pressing issues preventing effective and efficient mobile accessibility evaluations emerged.

- Both the reports and the interviews indicate that there is no agreed upon methodology to be used when evaluating mobile applications. This originates from a clear lack of accessibility guidelines for mobile applications, which could be seen from several of our interviewees referring to WCAG. Unlike the web, with the WCAG, there is no set of guidelines to orient the development of accessible mobile applications. The European Standard has adopted the WCAG for the mobile context, but what is expressed in the reports and by our interviewees is that is not the proper solution. Our findings show that even if mobile accessibility evaluation methodologies exist, they were originally designed for the web and require adaptation, or are being developed independently by the evaluators or monitoring bodies themselves driven by their necessity.
- Our findings highlight that there is a lack of documentation about how the existing mobile accessibility guidelines should be applied. This problem is compounded by the fact that these guidelines have been originally developed for the web and, consequently, most documentation available was created for the web platform. It should be noted that, while our focus is on the evaluation

and the impact that the lack of documentation has on accessibility evaluators, this issue also applies to designers and developers that lack an understanding of how to avoid accessibility barriers during the design and development process. The way guidelines are presented right now leaves space for different interpretations and lacks descriptions of how they should be applied in the mobile context, therefore preventing consistent and effective mobile accessibility evaluations.
- There is a discrepancy in the availability of tools to evaluate the accessibility of web and mobile applications. There are a lot of tools, automatic or support, available for the web, while there is a lack of tools for mobile. Many web accessibility evaluation tools rely on the inspection of the DOM. This is usually not an issue, given that many web user agents make the DOM accessible for inspection. However, mobile platforms operate differently and it is much harder to programmatically access the underlying representation of the interface elements. For that reason, having access to the source code of the mobile application makes the evaluation process easier. But it is not always possible to access the source code of mobile applications when you are not their developer, which is the situation of monitoring agencies. Therefore, this is still an added limitation for mobile accessibility evaluation. Ideally, a methodology to monitor and evaluate the accessibility of a mobile application would be fully automatic. While this does not happen, developing automated or support tools to help with the evaluation would minimize the resources used.
- Since evaluations of mobile applications are conducted to understand how accessible they are for people with disabilities, it is important to make sure they are as accurate and complete as possible. There is no better way to understand their point of view than to listen to their feedback while using the application. Automatic accessibility evaluations are know to be limited in the type of barriers they can find. Manual evaluations depend on the expertise of the evaluator, which means that they also do not guarantee the identification of every possible barrier. For that reason, complementing automated and manual evaluations with user testing with participants with disabilities increases the changes that as many barriers as possible are identified. Still, the EN methodology only enforces automated and manual evaluations, leaving user testing as optional. Additionally, of the methodologies reviewed, those that mention user testing are rare. Although a manual evaluation will try to identify every possible barrier, this might not be possible every time, so, complementing accessibility evaluations with user tests should be further encouraged and incorporated in future methodologies.

Even though these are not directly related to the evaluation methodologies or processes, our study also allowed us to find what are the most often identified mobile accessibility problems in the reports and by the evaluators interviewed. These problems are often related to basic accessibility principles, such as elements without labels, low contrast between elements, text size that cannot be changed, missing language for screen readers, wrong focus setting, or navigation that does not work properly, with and without an external keyboard. These problems impact elements which support basic tasks that users need to perform and, thus, are not able to. Most of these problems are easy to solve at the source if designers and developers are educated and aware of mobile accessibility.

6 Conclusion

Ensuring the accessibility of mobile applications is a critical concern in today's digital landscape, particularly for the 1.3 billion people worldwide affected by disabilities. Mobile accessibility involves addressing the unique needs of individuals with disabilities using mobile devices. While smartphones offer benefits in terms of independence, they also present challenges due to their smaller screens and evolving nature. The lack of convergence and standards in the mobile industry further complicates accessibility efforts. However, the implementation of the Web Accessibility Directive in Europe highlights the importance of monitoring and evaluating the accessibility of public sector websites and mobile applications. Through periodic reports, Member States have shed light on various evaluation methodologies, tools, and challenges faced by monitoring bodies.

To better characterise these methodologies and challenges, we performed a review of existing research on mobile accessibility, analyzed monitoring reports from EU Member States, and conducted interviews with mobile accessibility evaluators. This procedure provided valuable information about the limitations of the current evaluation practices and the challenges faced by evaluators. The results of the reports and interviews highlight the absence of a methodology designed specifically for mobile applications, which leads to inconsistent evaluations. To improve the evaluation process, it is crucial to develop a standard methodology that takes into account the unique characteristics of mobile platforms. In addition, the limited supply of automated and support evaluation tools for mobile applications complicates the process by requiring more resources. Efforts should be made to improve existing tools and create new ones to meet the specific needs of mobile accessibility evaluations. By addressing these challenges and promoting collaboration between evaluators, developers, and users, we can contribute to a world more accessible and inclusive for all.

References

1. Acosta-Vargas, P., Guaña-Moya, J., Jadán-Guerrero, J., Alvites-Huamaní, C., Salvador-Ullauri, L.: Towards accessibility assessment with a combined approach for native mobile applications. In: Advances in Human Factors and System Interactions, vol. 265, pp. 234–241 (2021). https://doi.org/10.1007/978-3-030-79816-1_29
2. Acosta-Vargas, P., Salvador-Acosta, B., Salvador-Ullauri, L., Villegas-Ch, W., Gonzalez, M.: Accessibility in native mobile applications for users with disabilities: a scoping review. Appl. Sci. (Switzerland) **11**, 5707 (2021). https://doi.org/10.3390/app11125707

3. Acosta-Vargas, P., et al.: Accessibility Assessment in Mobile Applications for Android, pp. 279–288 (2019). https://doi.org/10.1007/978-3-030-20040-4_25
4. Android: Accessibility scanner (2022). https://play.google.com/store/apps/details?id=com.google.android.apps.accessibility.auditor&hl=en&gl=US
5. CEN, C., ETSI: En 301 549 v3.2.1 (2021). https://www.etsi.org/deliver/etsi_en/301500_301599/301549/03.02.01_60/en_301549v030201p.pdf
6. European Commission: Web accessibility directive (2016). https://eur-lex.europa.eu/eli/dir/2016/2102/oj
7. European Commission: Commission implementing decision (EU) 2018/1524 (2018). https://eur-lex.europa.eu/eli/dec_impl/2018/1524/oj
8. European Commission and Directorate-General for Communications Networks, Content and Technology, et al.: Study supporting the review of the application of the Web Accessibility Directive (WAD): VIGIE 2020–0656: executive summary in English. Publications Office of the European Union, Luxembourg, UE (2022). https://doi.org/10.2759/25194
9. Member States of EU: Web accessibility directive - monitoring reports (2022). https://digital-strategy.ec.europa.eu/en/library/web-accessibility-directive-monitoring-reports
10. Ferreira, S.B.L., da Silveira, D.S., Capra, E.P., Ferreira, A.O.: Protocols for evaluation of site accessibility with the participation of blind users. Procedia Comput. Sci. **14**, 47–55 (2012). https://doi.org/10.1016/j.procs.2012.10.006
11. Appt Foundation: Appt evaluation methodology (Appt-EM) (2022). https://appt.nl/toolkit/appt-em
12. Appt Foundation: Appt web content accessibility guidelines (WCAG) (2022). https://appt.org/en/guidelines/wcag/principle-1
13. Guerreiro, T., Carriço, L., Rodrigues, A.: Mobile Web. Springer, London (2019). https://doi.org/10.1007/978-1-4471-7440-0_37
14. Henry, S.L.: Mobile accessibility at W3C (2021). https://www.w3.org/WAI/standards-guidelines/mobile/
15. Henry, S.L.: What's new in WCAG 2.2 draft (2022). https://www.w3.org/WAI/standards-guidelines/wcag/new-in-22/#257-dragging-movements-aa
16. Henry, S.L., Brewer, J.: WCAG2ICT overview (2022). https://www.w3.org/WAI/standards-guidelines/wcag/non-web-ict/
17. Henry, W.S.L.: What's new in WCAG 2.1 (2020). https://www.w3.org/WAI/standards-guidelines/wcag/new-in-21/
18. Henry, W.S.L., Abou-Zahra, S.: WCAG-EM overview: Website accessibility conformance evaluation methodology (2020). https://www.w3.org/WAI/test-evaluate/conformance/wcag-em/
19. Henry, W.S.L., McGee, L.: Web accessibility initiative (WAI) at W3C (2018). https://www.w3.org/standards/webdesign/accessibility#wai
20. Apple Inc: Testing for accessibility on OS X (2018). https://developer.apple.com/library/archive/documentation/Accessibility/Conceptual/AccessibilityMacOSX/OSXAXTestingApps.html
21. Joshi, P., Bhagat, S.: Effective accessibility testing methodologies and seamless accessibility integration in mobile applications. In: ICEGOV, pp. 449–455. ACM, New York (2022). https://doi.org/10.1145/3560107.3560175
22. Mateus, D.A., Silva, C.A., Eler, M.M., Freire, A.P.: Accessibility of mobile applications: evaluation by users with visual impairment and by automated tools. In: IHC. ACM, New York (2020). https://doi.org/10.1145/3424953.3426633

23. Nicolau, H., Guerreiro, T., Jorge, J., Gonçalves, D.: Mobile touchscreen user interfaces: bridging the gap between motor-impaired and able-bodied users. Univ. Access Inf. Soc. **13**, 303–313 (2014). https://doi.org/10.1007/s10209-013-0320-5
24. World Health Organization: Disability (2022). https://www.who.int/news-room/fact-sheets/detail/disability-and-health
25. ProfessionalQA: Accessibility testing: Complete guide (2020). https://www.professionalqa.com/accessibility-testing
26. Rabin, J., McCathieNevile, C.: Mobile web best practices 1.0 (2008). https://www.w3.org/TR/mobile-bp/#d0e128
27. da Silva, C.F., Ferreira, S.B.L., Sacramento, C.: Mobile application accessibility in the context of visually impaired users. In: IHC. IHC 2018, ACM, New York (2018). https://doi.org/10.1145/3274192.3274224
28. W3C: Authoring tool accessibility guidelines (ATAG) 2.0 (2015). https://www.w3.org/TR/ATAG20/
29. W3C: User agent accessibility guidelines (UAAG) 2.0 (2015). https://www.w3.org/TR/UAAG20/
30. W3C: WCAG 2 overview (2022). https://www.w3.org/WAI/standards-guidelines/wcag/
31. W3C Kim Patch, Jeanne Spellman, K.W.: Mobile accessibility: How WCAG 2.0 and other W3C/WAI guidelines apply to mobile (2016). https://www.w3.org/TR/mobile-accessibility-mapping/

Challenges, Tensions, and Opportunities in Designing App-Based Orientation and Mobility Tools for Blind and Visually Impaired Students

Jennifer Palilonis[1](✉), Caitlin Cambron[2], and Mianda Hakim[2]

[1] Ball State University, Muncie, IN 47304, USA
jageorge2@bsu.edu
[2] GoodMaps, Louisville, KY 40206, USA

Abstract. Individuals who are blind and/or visually impaired (BVI) face several challenges related to orientation and mobility (O&M), including orienting to new environments, finding and navigating routes, effectively using mobility aids, identifying landmarks, and obstacle avoidance, to name a few. To develop independent travel skills, BVI students often receive instruction from O&M specialists. O&M instruction includes development of spatial awareness, understanding cardinal direction, knowledge of environments, leveraging senses (i.e., sound, touch, smell), protective techniques, and learning to navigate routes. Assistive technologies are also introduced to provide additional O&M support and to foster effective technology adoption and use. This paper chronicles a task-based user experience study that engaged students from six schools for BVI students with GoodMaps *Explore,* a smartphone navigation app that provides turn-by-turn navigational support. The study uncovered challenges and opportunities for apps designed to support BVI users, particularly O&M teachers and students.

Keywords: User-centered design · accessibility · blindness · visual impairment · orientation and mobility curricula · user evaluation

1 Introduction

In 2021, The International Agency for the Prevention of Blindness reported that 338 million people worldwide are visually impaired, of which 43 million are blind and 295 million have moderate-to-severe visual impairment [1]. These individuals confront a number of challenges related to orientation and mobility, including orienting to new environments, finding and navigating routes to desired locations/destinations, effectively using mobility aids, identifying landmarks, and obstacle avoidance, to name a few [2]. Thus, comprehensive orientation and mobility (O&M) instruction is critical to ensuring safe, efficient, and effective travel skills for blind and visually impaired (BVI) individuals of all ages. O&M includes being able to walk without tripping or falling, the ability to cross streets and use public transportation, and the use of assistive aids–such as a cane

Q. Gao et al. (Eds.): HCII 2023, LNCS 14055, pp. 372–391, 2023.
https://doi.org/10.1007/978-3-031-48041-6_25

or a guide dog–to navigate a route. "Consequently, wayfinding becomes a particularly challenging skill for people with visual impairments to develop, making navigation–especially in unknown indoor scenarios–a long-standing research challenge in the field of O&M techniques" [2].

Moreover, to develop independent travel skills, BVI children often require special instruction from O&M specialists. These specialists typically work with students over several years to develop a scaffolded O&M plan that is personalized to meet an individual's unique needs and abilities. Independent travel fosters self-esteem and confidence and improves quality of life as students learn to move freely about. Thus, O&M instruction involves working with students on concept development, including spatial awareness, cardinal direction, laterality, knowledge of environments, leveraging other senses (i.e., sound, touch, smell), and protective techniques. O&M specialists also help students learn routes to and from classrooms and offices within school settings.

In Spring 2022, a research team partnered with six schools for BVI students across the U.S. to explore how GoodMaps *Explore* – an indoor and between building navigation app could be used to support students learning orientation and mobility and teachers in their O&M instructional efforts. To do so, the six schools were mapped with a Light Detection and Ranging (LiDAR) scanning process during the 2021–22 academic year, and teachers and students were recruited to participate in a usability and user experience study that included observation and interviews to explore their perceptions of the efficacy of *Explore* as a navigational tool. The goals for the study were twofold: 1) to determine the ways in which an indoor and between building app can help improve navigation experiences for BVI students, and 2) to discover whether a navigation app can help instructors more effectively teach navigation skills to students. Findings illuminate key challenges, tensions, and opportunities in designing app-based orientation and mobility tools for these audiences. Limitations and future research and development opportunities are also discussed.

2 Review of Background

This section provides an overview of recent literature focused on orientation and mobility research and technology-enhanced O&M instruction, as well as a review of related state-of-the-art in app-based assistive technology for BVI users. For context, *orientation* refers to the ability to know where you are and want to go, to sense whether you're moving from one room to another, or to effectively navigate a crosswalk using pedestrian traffic signals; whereas *mobility* refers to the ability to move safely, efficiently, and effectively from one place to another [3].

2.1 The Need for Novel Technologies that Support Curriculum for BVI Students

Instructors of children who are blind or visually impaired are responsible for teaching students a wide range of concepts and skills in addition to the core curriculum, including orienting to their surroundings, independent navigation, and general life skills [4]. BVI children face significant challenges learning and practicing orientation and mobility skills, such as determining where they are in a building or outdoor setting, understanding and identifying cardinal direction, navigating routes, using assistive tools like white canes or guide dogs, and using residual visual, auditory, and other sensory information to understand their environments. "Well-designed technologies can provide an alternative to prescriptive teaching approaches by providing access to the world through alternative perceptual modalities to enable self-exploration" [5].

Technologies that support independent travel require novel approaches that allow kids learning O&M skills to engage thoroughly and confidently with their surroundings [6]. Additionally, although technology-enhanced instruction can provide teachers with innovative support for O&M instruction, technology can also be a distraction that impedes a BVI user from effectively implementing traditional O&M skills like sensory techniques, self-protective strategies, cane operation, critical thinking, and independent problem solving [7]. Thus, new technologies to support independent navigation for BVI users require considered effort to effectively foster safe, logical, and meaningful use in the context of O&M curriculum [6]. Likewise, for educators to understand how they might effectively integrate new technologies within their O&M lessons, curricular support, as well as evidence of technology efficacy, must also be provided [8].

2.2 Orientation and Mobility Aids

In the past 25 years, there has been a significant increase in the number of technological solutions developed specifically for BVI users. When it comes to navigation, perhaps the greatest accessibility advancement to date for people who are blind is rideshare, which provides greater access to independent transportation [9]. Also popular are technology-enhanced canes and smartphone apps that use GPS and other positioning technology to assist with navigation, orientation, and mobility. For example, in 2021, Stanford researchers introduced a $400 self-navigating smart cane that uses sensors and wayfinding principles from robotics and self-driving vehicles [10]. The augmented cane helps people detect and identify obstacles, move easily around objects, and follow routes both indoors and outside. A host of other researchers and developers have explored GPS-enhanced technology for BVI users [11, 12], including navigating systems that use ultrasonic proximity sensors [13], haptic or tonal feedback [14, 15], and technologies that integrate face identification [16, 17], to name a few. Other assistive tools have also been widely adopted in recent years, especially smartphone apps (some very accessible and others less so) that act as a portal from everything from banking to appliances. Assistive technology facilitates BVI users' ability to access information, promotes safety, and supports mobility and an improved quality of life, which has a direct effect on social inclusion [18]. However, research has indicated that BVI individuals are often dissatisfied with the latest assistive technologies, largely because they fail to address their unique needs [19]. Furthermore, although most mapping apps like Google Maps and Apple Maps provide some assistive navigation features for BVI users, they were designed first for a sighted experience with BVI features added later.

The importance and pervasiveness of assistive technology has led O&M instructors to integrate assistive technologies into lessons with students. It has become increasingly popular, for example, for them to integrate apps like Apple Maps, Google Maps, and Transit into lessons that involve practicing navigation. Likewise, O&M instructors report exposing students to other assistive apps for BVI people like Be My Eyes, BlindSquare, and Seeing AI when appropriate [20]. However, little to no research exists that examines the extent to which technology is integrated in O&M curricula. There is no evidence that O&M lesson plans include systematic integration of app-based technology as an instructional tool or that any app-based assistive technologies have been designed and developed specifically with O&M instruction in mind. Thus, many advocates for inclusive advancements in assistive technology have championed a user-centered approach to design and development that aims to address key requirements of BVI people, including students learning many O&M strategies for the first time [21].

The introduction of accessible GPS devices in the past 15 years–including development of smartphone and navigation applications–have enabled people with visual impairments to identify their locations and navigate to desired destinations. However, GPS-enabled apps and devices are limited to outdoor navigation, rendering them ineffective for indoor O&M training, especially for students who are also trying to master traditional O&M skills. Significant obstacles stand in the way of widespread adoption of technological solutions for BVI children, including that they are often too complex for children to use [22], they do not effectively integrate O&M instructional strategies and skills, and they are sometimes too expensive or otherwise difficult to access for BVI youth [23]. Despite these challenges, studies have demonstrated that when students with disabilities use assistive technology devices and apps in educational settings, the technologies often promote heightened engagement [24].

2.3 State-of-the-Art in App-Based Assistive Technology for BVI Users

Several assistive technologies have been developed and studied to help people with visual impairments navigate a variety of environments [25–27]. However, most require renovations to the environment or installation of custom proprietary devices that can be expensive or cumbersome [27]. About 50% of BVI users have smartphones (likely fewer children), and the use of assistive apps to help them reach heightened levels of autonomy is on the rise [28]. Some integrate artificial intelligence or allow voice control; others are designed to assist with navigation or object identification using the phone's camera. Studies have shown that BVI individuals frequently use apps specifically designed to help them accomplish daily activities [21]. Table 1 describes apps in use within the BVI community and includes an evaluation of how each differs from the *Explore*. As previously noted, however, we found no comprehensive research that examines the extent to which these types of apps are integrated in O&M curricula.

3 Methodology

This study applied multiple qualitative methods–observation and interviews–to explore the ways in which an indoor and between building navigation app can help improve navigation experiences for BVI students. Researchers also hoped to discover whether this app can help instructors more effectively teach O&M skills to students.

Table 1. Navigation and orientation apps for individuals who are blind or visually impaired.

App name	Description	Differentiation
Aira	Live, on-demand visual interpreting service that connects users to human assistants that provide on-demand, skilled, reliable visual interpreting for a variety of tasks using a phone camera	• Requires connection to live agents to talk blind users through a situation • No built-in navigation support
Be My Eyes	Free app that connects blind and low-vision people with sighted volunteers for visual assistance through a live video call	• Requires connection to sighted volunteers to provide assistance • No built-in navigation support
BlindSquare	GPS-app for blind, deafblind, and partially sighted users that gathers info about surroundings on Foursquare and OpenStreetMap to deliver information about points of interest, intersections	• Provides info about surroundings but not routing support
Clew	Path retracing app designed to help BVI users independently return to a location; app records path and guides user back to starting location with voice directions, sound effects, haptic feedback	• Requires user to record a route before providing return navigation support • Built only for iOS 11 devices
CamFind	Image recognition app allows users to take a picture of any object; app uses mobile visual search technology to communicate what the object is	• No built-in navigation support
EnvisionAI	Object recognition app that uses phone's camera to speak written information, describe surroundings and objects, and communicate who is nearby	• No built-in navigation support
Lazarillo	Intelligent app that guides users through city and building environments with real-time voice messages; connects users with businesses through accessible online shopping and notification services	• Requires Bluetooth beacons for navigation support

(continued)

3.1 Participants

A total of 17 students (11 male, 6 female; aged 13 to 21) and 11 O&M instructors and teachers of students with visual impairments (TVIs) from six schools participated in this pilot study. Although this small sample size does not generate statistically significant

Table 1. (*continued*)

App name	Description	Differentiation
Lazarus	Android app that helps people move through cities and perform simple tasks without human assistance through geolocation, voice recognition, and the phone's camera	• No built-in navigation support • Android-only app
Nearby Explorer	Free outdoor and indoor location app that supports onboard maps from OpenStreetMap and augments maps with data from Google Places or Foursquare; announces information about locations, including street names, addresses, nearby places, and distances and directions to them	• Limited built-in navigation support • Sunsetted in 2019
RightHear	System that includes a mobile app, beacons to be installed by companies/organizations in venues, and an online portal for writing and providing audio descriptions of a location	• Requires Bluetooth beacons for audio descriptions and navigation support
Seeing AI	Microsoft's artificial intelligence app; uses device camera to identify people, objects, and text and then audibly describes items to user	• No built-in navigation support
SoundScape	3D audio app that helps users build mental maps and audio-enhanced awareness of surroundings	• Requires headphones for optimal performance • Sunsetted in 2022
TapTapSee	Mobile camera app that uses smartphone camera to take a picture or video of objects and identify them for users; accurately analyzes and identifies any 2- or 3-dimensional object at any angle	• No built-in navigation support

results, narrative summary results provide insights that will be useful to designers and developers of orientation and mobility aids for BVI users.

School administrators first reached out to O&M instructors and TVIs to identify individuals interested in participating. Then, O&M instructors shared information about the study provided by the research team with BVI students currently enrolled in O&M instruction to solicit student participants. Teacher participants, parents of students younger than 18, and students over the age of 18 were provided with detailed information about the nature of the user experience study and consent forms to sign and return.

Prior to engaging in the study, students younger than 18 were also provided with detailed information about the study and child assent forms to sign and return. All participants were assured that the researcher was *not* testing them. Rather, the research involved observing students' use of *Explore* to study how effective the app is in helping them navigate walking routes.

Of the 17 student participants, visual acuity fell into two categories: 1) individuals who are totally blind and 2) individuals who are significantly visually impaired but *can* discern *light*, basic shapes, or other figures. All teacher participants had 10+ years of O&M or TVI experience.

3.2 GoodMaps *Explore*

First launched in September 2020, GoodMaps *Explore* is a smartphone app for both iOS and Android devices that provides turn-by-turn navigation for indoor spaces. To date, *Explore* has amassed just over 15,000 users worldwide, and GoodMaps has mapped more than 100 indoor buildings around the world, including seven schools for BVI students in the U.S. The *Explore* app uses camera-based positioning (CPS), which implements geo-referenced images to determine a user's position and can locate where a user is standing in a room within one meter of accuracy. This is a substantial improvement over the accuracy provided by GPS (which is eight to 10 m outdoors), Bluetooth trilateration (which is four to five meters), and other approaches. Additionally, *Explore* is designed to help people who are BVI to navigate safely and efficiently with dynamic routing instructions, orientation aids, and landmark recognition. The mapping system allows venue owners to update and customize indoor maps, ensuring that points of interest data are always up to date. The system also includes GoodMaps *Studio*, which gathers, processes, and stores the map data associated with an indoor space.

There are four steps to creating an accessible building map with *Studio*. First a GoodMaps technician scans a facility with a LiDAR camera scanner. The scan takes about as long as it would to walk the entirety of the building. The equipment records 360-degree images, measurement data, and video footage to compile the building map. Second, an accurate and detailed map is created from the scan and image data. All points of interest–such as restrooms, offices, dining, AED devices, IT closets, fire exits, etc.– are tagged in *Studio*, which processes and hosts all the map data. *Studio* also generates three different map views: a 2D floorplan, a LiDAR point cloud, and a 3D model. Third, building supervisors edit the map in *Studio*. They can add location names in multiple languages, update points of interest, and set up access permissions for various sections of the map. Fourth, the building map is published to the *Explore* navigation app. GoodMaps also offers an SDK to facilitate third-party app development.

Data from *Studio* powers the *Explore* application. Users can navigate indoor spaces using the app along with voice, tactile, or text prompts to find their desired destinations. Once the building map is added to the GoodMaps "indoor venues list," an *Explore* app user can enter a mapped building and begin navigating. Buildings mapped with this technology are fully explorable via the app, which includes step-by-step navigation to selected destinations. A user's location inside a building is determined with GoodMaps' camera-based positioning (CPS) technique (CPS video). *Explore* also offers detailed information about indoor points of interest, describing individual rooms and features

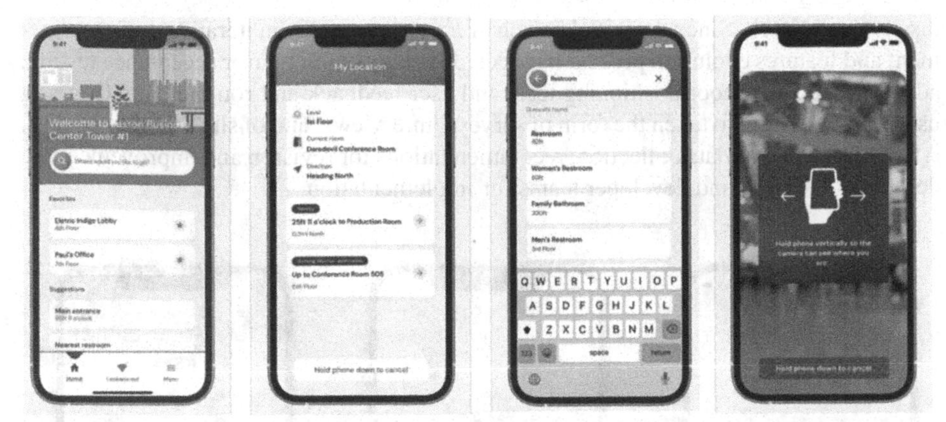

Fig. 1. Upon entering a mapped building, the user is alerted they are inside the building and provided with a home screen (image one) that includes a destination search field, any favorite destinations the user has previously established, a "Lookaround" feature that provides information about immediate surroundings, and a menu that includes additional settings. The user can also access additional information about current location (image two). To engage the app for navigation from one location to another, the user must search a destination via dictation or text input (image three) and hold up the phone so the camera can scan the environment (image four).

like water fountains, information desks, restrooms, and more. *Explore* relies on visually distinct surroundings–typically architectural in nature–such as patterned carpets, ceiling paneling, and art so that it can provide hyper-accurate location information. *Studio* can create highly accurate digital maps that rely on camera positioning to navigate users through spaces without the need for infrastructure installation. It is important to note here that f a user wishes to navigate from a location in one building to a location in a different building, they must switch to a GPS-based mapping app, such as Google Maps or Apple Maps. This is because the primary *Explore* navigation experience is built on camera-based positioning as opposed to GPS technology. This limitation will be discussed at greater length in the sections that follow. The app also includes a searchable directory that allows users to select destinations within a building *Explore* also provides general information about the user's current location. Then, to engage the app for navigation from one location to another, the user must hold the phone up so the camera can scan the environment and locate where the user is standing. Once the app has oriented to the current location, it provides dynamic, turn-by-turn instructions for how to get to the selected destination. The app then alerts the user when they have arrived at the desired location. Figures 1 and 2 provide a visual account of this user process.

The GoodMaps team implemented a variety of user-centered processes for design and development of *Explore*. During the discovery phase (in 2019), subject matter experts from the Charles W. McDowell Center for the Blind in Louisville, KY helped identify necessary features and functionality. BVI users of several other navigation apps–including Nearby Explorer, BlindSquare, Lazarillo, and SoundScape–were also interviewed to understand strengths and weaknesses related usability, feature sets, design, and functionality. Initial *Explore* features and functionality were guided by findings from this discovery research. Since the initial launch of *Explore* in 2020, an iterative design refinement and features evolution process has been driven by ongoing user acceptance testing, advancements in indoor positioning tech, and user feedback and routing data. Ongoing user research has also taken the form of surveys, interviews, and onsite usability studies. After each round of data collection, recommendations for revision and improvement are delivered to design and developer teams for implementation.

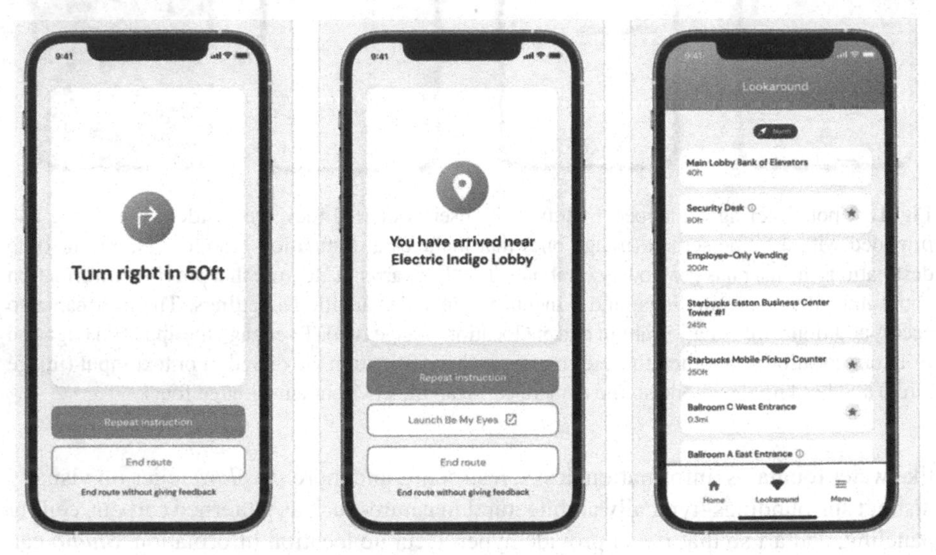

Fig. 2. Once *Explore* has identified the user's location, it provides turn-by-turn instructions to the desired destination (image one). Voiceover, tones, and haptics provide positive reinforcement throughout a route. The user is alerted when they have successfully completed of a route (image two). A "Lookaround" feature offers additional orientation support by providing information about nearby points of interest (image three).

3.3 Procedures

Students and teachers were encouraged to try *Explore* prior to a user experience research session in which a researcher visited their school to observe students' use of *Explore* during navigation. Familiarizing themselves with the app ahead of time ensured that participants possessed a basic understanding of app functionality. Novice users were not chosen for this study because there was not enough time to provide the level of training necessary (two to three hours minimum) to ensure observational sessions could be completed in the time allotted. A UI/UX researcher then visited each school for two days between April 22 and May 22, 2022, to observe students' use of the app during a task-based navigation session and subsequent interview.

During the task-based navigation experience, student participants were first asked to complete a series of indoor and outdoor walking routes around their schools using *Explore* as a guide. In addition to the researcher, an O&M teacher chaperone accompanied students during navigation tasks to observe how they used the app and to assist if necessary. During the walking tasks, the researcher asked student participants to share any thoughts they had about the experience, with the intent of providing honest feedback about their experience using the app as a navigation aid. Accompanying O&M teachers were also encouraged to share thoughts about the experience. The complete set of walking tasks was tailored to the school/campus layout, with each task focused on a route from one predetermined location to another. For example, tasks might require participants to use the app to guide them from a restroom to a classroom, a classroom to a gymnasium, a gymnasium to a cafeteria, a cafeteria to an outdoor point of interest, and so on. The complete set of walking tasks took 40 to 80 min to complete, depending on the size of the school building and/or campus and the relative distances from one location to another. Upon completion of each task, students were asked to rate how difficult the task was to complete on a scale of one to three: (1) easy, (2) neutral (neither easy nor difficult), (3) difficult. This simple scale was used primarily to stoke conversation rather than as a quantitative measure.

3.4 Interview

After students completed the walking tasks, they were asked to answer 15 questions about the navigation experience. The interview portion of the research took about 40 min. Interview questions were designed to elicit feedback about user perceptions of the navigation experience with *Explore*, what they liked and disliked about the app, what significant challenges they faced, successes they experienced when navigating with the app, and how they think the app might be improved for use by BVI students and O&M teachers.

O&M instructors and TVIs also engaged in a 20-item interview after the observation sessions to explore their perceptions about the potential for *Explore* to support O&M instructional strategies they typically use when working with BVI students, perceptions of the observed student experience with *Explore* during navigation, and how the app might be improved to better support them during O&M instruction with students.

3.5 Data Conversion and Analysis

Two types of data were collected for this research: 1) observational notes taken by the primary onsite researcher and 2) participant responses collected during post-observation interview sessions. The observer noted participants' actions and comments made during navigation tasks, including challenges faced with app operation, tensions between app functionality and user perceptions of how it works, and general questions and comments made during navigation. Observational and interview data was coded and analyzed through the process of Interpretive Phenomenological Analysis (IPA), designed to illuminate the experiences individuals had with the app to identify summative, salient, and/or essence-capturing attributes of the navigation experience [29].

4 Results

App observation and interview sessions provide a glimpse into how students who are learning O&M skills navigate with GoodMaps *Explore,* as well as how O&M teachers envision its use within the O&M curriculum. Findings from these sessions are presented as narrative summary results supported by the number of students who experienced specific challenges at each site. Key themes emerged to solve navigation challenges for BVI students and their teachers, specifically around travelling indoors and on school campuses. Fundamental ergonomic and technical issues have also surfaced that provide app designers with insight about the specific usability and user experience concerns that must be addressed. The sections that follow provide a deeper look at these results.

4.1 General Observations and Key Themes from App Observation and Interview Sessions

Six key themes emerged from observational data and interviews, which are discussed in the following sections. Behaviors and/or experience attributes observed for at least one-fourth of participants were considered pervasive. Given the small number of participants for this study, behaviors and/or experience attributes observed for fewer than one-fourth of participants were noted for future exploration but eliminated from these findings due to their limited presence in these findings. For each key theme, we report the number of students (n) across all schools that had a related experience, and we report in how many and in which schools each theme surfaced (SC).

Indoor/Outdoor Navigation. Students and instructors expect a navigation app to function outdoors similarly to the way it functions indoors. During sessions at all six schools, participants were confused when they had to move from indoor tasks to tasks that required them to navigate outdoors and/or from building-to-building across a campus. Because *Explore* primarily provides indoor maps and relies on GPS data for outside navigation, the transition from indoors to outdoors does not support the same turn-by-turn experience. However, students almost always expected the app to provide turn-by-turn instructions outdoors (n = 10), and when they realized it would not, they were disappointed (n = 6) and indicated they thought the transition from indoor to outdoor navigation must be smoother than it currently is.

Likewise, during outdoor navigation tasks, teachers (n = 2) and students (n = 3) at two schools (SC2, SC3) indicated that having to switch to Google Maps is not a good work around for BVI users. They noted that in general, Google Maps does not work as well on campuses because although campus perimeter streets are generally mapped, internal walkways, paths, and minor streets are not as likely to be mapped. "I don't like that the app is sending me to a less friendly app that is designed for sighted people," one participant shared. "That's where the app is falling short for me."

Routing. At times, the app provides a less desirable route when there was more than one possible option for getting to a single destination. This issue presented in four schools (SC1, SC2, SC3, SC4). For example, at one school (SC2), the resource center/library has two entrances. The first is a main, glass-doored entrance that students and teachers use daily, and it is about 15 feet from the main librarian counter. The second is a back door to the same hallway located along the wall of a back room that includes equipment used by resource center staff. When one student tried to exit the school's resource center during a route, *Explore* routed her through the back room to the back door instead of through the main entrance. The accompanying O&M teacher shared that this would be considered "incorrect," as students generally aren't allowed to wander freely through the back room.

A similar challenge surfaced in SC3, when a student and teacher attempted to walk to the occupational therapy office using *Explore*. They explained that they were routed to the wrong entrance to the office. In this case, there are two entrances down the hall from one another about 20 feet apart. One is the "main" entrance, and the other is not used by anyone because it is blocked on the other side. The teacher also indicated that there are a couple similar locations on that school's campus, and he would like to ensure that routes in *Explore* led students to the main entrances, not back doors or unused or "off limits" entrances, as that could present potential safety hazards and/or rules violations when areas are considered "off limits" to students.

Holding the Device While Routing. Properly holding the device during navigation is, at times, difficult for BVI users. In several instances, participants indicated their arms became tired from having to hold the phone vertically during walking tasks (n = 4). This feedback was offered at varying degrees of severity. One student indicated that he felt his arm "might get a little tired" if he had to hold it up during the entire session or for a long period of time. Another student shared the same sentiment with a little more force, noting "this app is great for short trips. But if I were using it for a longer trip, I think my arm would get sore and tired." Two students (SC1) indicated multiple times during their sessions that having to hold the phone up while walking was extremely problematic. By the end of his session, one student said, "My arm is really killing me. I love the accuracy of this app. But I don't think I would want to use it a lot if my arm is going to hurt like this." Some participants also struggled to hold the phone properly (n = 7) at a vertical position in front of them as they walked (SC1, SC3, SC6). In some cases, users held the phone so the top drooped toward the floor. In other cases, participants held the phone vertically, but pointing it to the left or right, not facing forward. The instructors and researcher gently corrected students when this happened. However, some students who had this problem soon reverted to incorrect positioning (n = 6), making it difficult for the camera to effectively "see" it's surroundings and the route.

Additionally, one student (SC1) is a guide dog handler and illuminated the challenges he and individuals like him will have when it comes to trying to manage the phone and, at the same time, effectively handle a dog. "My arm is getting really tired," he said. "If I could move the phone back and forth between two hands, it would be easier. But because I have to handle the dog, that's not possible." Specifically, guide dog owners may struggle to balance holding a phone properly along with the attention required to effectively handle the dog. Nearly every time a new task began, the following process unfolded: 1) while the student searched for a location in *Explore,* the dog laid down next to him; 2) when a destination was selected in the app, the student had to interact with the dog to get her up and moving; 3) interaction with the dog required the student to bend down, which, in turn, caused the phone to reset and request the student "scan" his surroundings to orient to the current location again; 4) while the student re-scanned the area, the dog laid back down, and the tedious process began again.

Ultimately, students in three schools (SC2, SC3, SC4) indicated they would prefer a hands-free option for navigating with *Explore*, both for convenience and for safety (n = 6). This sentiment was also supported by teachers (n = 7). Significantly, several students cited this as more of a safety issue than one of convenience. For example, when in a stairwell during one navigation task, one participant (SC2) said, "There's no way I can use proper cane skills and hold the phone in a stairwell. The app is telling me to be safe. But I'm still trying to juggle the phone, and my cane, and hold the railing."

Interpreting Turns In-route. Students often struggled to correctly interpret instructions related to turns. In a few schools (SC1, SC2, SC3), hallways included 15- to 45-degree bends, narrow corridors, and/or plain white walls, causing confusion for the app and the user during navigation. For example, in SC1, when users encountered bends in corridors, *Explore* directed them to "turn" left or right. However, students interpreted "turn" to mean a 90-degree turn (n = 4). Thus, when a turn was only 45 degrees, users often made a full 90-degree turn, resulting in the participant walking toward a wall and then getting confused when the app attempted to correct them. This confusion resulted in the student assuming the app gave bad directions rather than recognition of a misstep in interpreting the app's instructions. Likewise, walking tasks in several schools (SC1, SC3, SC5) included routes along narrow, bended hallways or through areas with several obstacles along the way. During some of those sessions (n = 6), students struggled to navigate those spaces, as the app did not account for obstacles like pillars in the middle of the room, tables, or chairs, to name a few.

Properly scanning the environment so the app could orient to the users' location was also a challenge in some settings. Scanning challenges often seemed to be related to certain types of spaces (n = 5). Specifically, when participants in one school (SC3) encountered narrow and/or long hallways, *Explore* had trouble maintaining and/or regaining orientation. Older buildings on a couple campuses (SC3, SC6) with narrow hallways and low ceilings were especially challenging. In SC3, for example, *Explore* lost orientation easily when students scanned the environment along routes in long, narrow brick hallways.

Students in three schools (SC3, SC4, SC6) also had difficulty navigating complex stairwells using *Explore* (n = 6). Students and teachers generally preferred to take routes that included stairs, even when *Explore* directed them to take elevators. For example, at one school (SC4) teachers shared that otherwise able-bodied BVI students are discouraged from using elevators. Rather, they are encouraged to practice using stairs because as one teacher put it, "the world is full of stairs and our students need to be comfortable using them." However, when stair routes include navigating multiple floors with stairwells that include landings and turns, navigation was sometimes challenging. As a matter of safety, *Explore* encourages users to stop using the app when in stairwells so they can more safely use handrails and pay closer attention to their footing. However, in the absence of turn-by-turn instructions on routes that require users to ascend or descend multiple floors (SC2, SC3, SC6), areas between floors with flat ground and stairs were sometimes confusing for users (n = 7).

Balancing O&M Skills. Users may inadvertently abandon traditional O&M skills while using an app. Both student participants (n = 5) and teacher participants (n = 4) at several schools (SC1, SC, SC, SC5) emphasized the need for users to balance their traditional O&M skills (e.g., proper cane techniques, consistent use of other senses to make judgments about the environment, or rote memory) when using *Explore* for navigation. For example, one student participant noted that she likes *Explore* because she doesn't have to focus as much on "using only my brainpower. I can just listen [to the app] and let it guide me." She went on to note that she and her classmates often must memorize routes or ask for directions from others and then rely on rote memory to navigate. However, she explained that she knows she "can't trust the app entirely" and still must use other O&M skills to get around. This sentiment was echoed by O&M teachers (n = 9), one of whom (SC2) shared that he is concerned when he sees students rely so heavily on an app to guide them that they stop using safe/proper cane skills or are distracted away from "using their ears" to listen to the environment for safety clues. "I think that if we are to integrate this app into our O&M curriculum in the future–which I want to do–we will need to make sure we actively teach kids how to balance use of technology with use of their O&M skills and senses," he said. Likewise, in one school (SC3) participants struggled to follow the instructions the app was giving them because they didn't understand what to do or why (i.e., sometimes students were confused by the definition of "turn" and "rotate," misunderstanding when a 90-degree turn vs. a smaller angle or more nuanced rotation was required). When this occurred, O&M teachers expressed concern that students were either "relying too much on the app and not paying attention to their surroundings" or "not listening carefully enough to what the app was telling them."

Supplemental Curriculum Needs. Teachers and students alike expressed a desire for an app to provide O&M curriculum that is custom-made for teaching O&M and technology use together. In all six schools, teachers expressed a strong desire to integrate *Explore* into their daily O&M curricula (n = 9). One teacher (SC2) indicated that he would like app developers to consider creating a special curriculum packet to accompany *Explore* that includes specific lessons O&M teachers could implement. "Teachers love ready-made curriculum," he said. "I think many of us would love to have pre-made lessons we could draw from" that integrate *Explore* as an assistive technology. Likewise, teachers at SC3 and SC5 indicated that this type of offering would increase their motivation to integrate *Explore* into the regular O&M curriculum at their school. Three teachers at two different schools also volunteered to help build custom O&M lessons designed for integration with *Explore*. Likewise, teachers at one school (SC6) noted that there would be great value–especially for teaching new and younger students O&M skills–associated with an app that would provide turn-by-turn instructions and related O&M lesson plans.

5 Discussion

Overall, using *Explore* as a navigation tool provides added O&M benefits for student users, and there is potential for integration of the app with O&M curriculum to enhance instruction and support O&M instructors in significant ways. However, this study also yields valuable insights for the greater design and development communities, and findings can be used to understand the challenges, tensions, and opportunities in designing app-based O&M solutions for BVI students. Practitioners can use these user-centered findings to envision new products and/or to improve existing products. Specifically, we propose viewing these results through the lens of three main categories: 1) navigation functionality and app design, 2) user interaction with the device, and 3) O&M

educational opportunities for navigation app technology. Following are discussion and recommendations for future development and exploration in each category.

5.1 Navigation Functionality and App Design

Certainly, accuracy is imperative for BVI users of assistive technology, especially for successful independent navigation in complex indoor spaces. Students and instructors alike described their experiences with *Explore* favorably when it was accurate and worked as intended, i.e., the app got them where they wanted to go efficiently and with precision in terms of their relative distance to the desired endpoint. They shared that it empowers students with a sense of independence and confidence to travel safely. Navigation apps like *Explore* also have the potential to make traveling more accessible and to enable young people to orient to buildings, learn routes, and improve navigation skills quickly. From instructors' perspectives, there is a greater level of engagement from students, increased motivation, and excitement when using accurate technologies [22], which can make teaching and learning O&M easier and fun. Unsurprisingly, when an app is not functioning as planned or as expected, the opposite effects are likely to occur. Confusion, emotional stress, and frustration may increase; and inaccurate or missing information in different kinds of spaces and settings can lead to disappointment and decrease users' trust in a product [30].

Specific to this study, participants highlighted several areas in which functional accuracy and easy-to-understand design is central to a favorable user experience. First, location orientation (i.e., figuring out where you are) and destination identification (i.e., figuring out where you want to go) are, perhaps, the two most important navigation goals for a user. Although this would seem to be an obvious and simple concept, there are a wide variety of ways that location directories within an app may be designed (e.g., categorical, alphabetical, locational) and several ways a user could input and receive that information from a device (e.g., keyboard, dictation, voiceover, etc.). To complicate matters, different users may prefer different methods as a matter of personal choice or as a matter of circumstance. Thus, landing on a universally accepted and preferred design for an indoor navigation app is unlikely. Rather, it is likely that two things must occur: 1) additional research should explore directory design and interaction in isolation to identify optimal design structures, and 2) well-designed, intuitive methods of customization should be developed to meet the needs of different users in different navigational scenarios and settings.

Additionally, navigation often include travel both indoors and outdoors during a single route. There is currently no single app solution that provides a streamlined building-to-building navigation experience due to limitations of differing technologies required for each (i.e., GPS for outdoor mapping vs. cellular positioning system for indoor mapping). However, for a BVI navigation app to be widely accepted and adopted–especially as an O&M teaching and learning tool–there is a need to fulfill user expectations that the app will function the same in both indoor and outdoor settings [31]. In this study, the stark difference between the indoor and outdoor navigation experience left participants feeling disappointed, confused, stressed, and frustrated with the app. Students and instructors alike shared that the outdoor mode was inaccurate, and inferior compared to the precise turn-by-turn walking instructions provided along indoor routes. Thus, developers should continue to work on solutions that sync indoor and outdoor maps within a single app to provide a consistent and accurate navigation experience.

Finally, built maps must be highly customizable so that the people who regularly work, live, and travel in them are able to adapt routes, entrances, and locations to reflect the nuances of their culture and practice. For example, in this study, the app did not know that some entrances or areas are "off limits" to students. In those cases, students and teachers were confused by what the app was telling them to do and what they know to be true about the rules set forth by their schools. This concept could easily be applied to other types of budlings, such as airports or hospitals, where as a matter of safety and/or security, it's necessary for areas to be restricted, modified, or otherwise hidden within the app to certain types of travelers.

5.2 User Interaction with the Device

Just as app functionality must be tailored to the needs of users and the businesses or organizations that use it, users are often required to learn and adapt to the interaction requirements of a device. In this study, participants learned that the phone must be held a certain way for it to function properly, which was sometimes uncomfortable or even impossible. Of course, app design is, in some ways, limited by the design of the devices on which they are installed. For example, *Explore* must rely on the phone's camera to collect information about a participant's location and route. Thus, the phone must be held at a specific position and angle for the camera to effectively do its job. However, BVI kids may encounter obstacles that would make holding the phone properly more difficult. They may walk with a cane or a guide dog that requires use of one or both hands. They may also have other disabilities, like ataxia, that make it challenging to hold a phone steady while walking. Or their spatial awareness in relation to body positioning may not be as developed. Researchers have suggested development of hand-free devices for safe and comfortable navigation [32–34] to alleviate the physical constraints that holding a device may cause. Thus, future research and development should explore hands-free options or other solutions that mitigate this concern.

Additionally, the ability for the phone's camera to discern the environments and objects it is focused on may be limited by how close the user is to a wall or an object, as well as how detailed that object is. For example, in this study, plain white walls in tight corridors or stairwells were sometimes hard for the camera to identify. As previously noted, this is because *Explore* relies on visually distinct surroundings–typically architectural in nature–to provide hyper-accurate location information. Likewise, in tight spaces, it was sometimes hard for BVI students to position themselves far enough away from a setting for the camera to quickly recognize and orient. In these cases, navigating those spaces was challenging, and often stopped students from being able to continue or complete a route quickly and efficiently. Thus, there exists a need to improve upon app design and CPS implementation in ways that make navigation more accurate and efficient in tight spaces.

5.3 O&M Educational Opportunities for Navigation App Technology

According to participants, customization of lessons for each unique student is the biggest challenge in teaching O&M. Instructors teach children of all ages, who often have a variety of behavioral and medical needs and varying levels of cognitive physical ability instructors must consider when planning lessons. Often, O&M instructors also have large caseloads. This supports prior research advocating for supporting educators with curriculum that helps them "understand how they might productively use these technologies in meaningful ways within their educational environments" [5, 35, 36]. Thus, developing personalized O&M plans is time consuming and can be very challenging and stressful. Add to that a desire to integrate new technologies into O&M lessons, and teachers are faced with the burdensome task of both learning new technology *and* building their own lesson plans around it [37]. This expectation is unrealistic and unfair.

Perhaps one of the most exciting opportunities that arose from this research lies in the desire by O&M instructors and their students to have well-designed, preplanned curricula that is specifically designed for integration with a navigation app like this. Having the opportunity to participate in tech training on new apps along with ready-made curricula and supplementary materials to incorporate into O&M lessons would be immensely helpful, especially for those who are short on time and must frequently revise their curricula. However, it is important that this type of curricula be designed with input from O&M teachers who can provide expertise and insight to ensure that the technology supports and enhances development of traditional O&M skills.

5.4 Limitations and Future Work

Some challenges encountered during observation sessions likely affected feedback gathered from student participants, including technical glitches, mapping inaccuracies, timing of app updates over the five weeks during which research site visits occurred, and general connectivity issues. For example, some technical glitches occurred on the first day of the first site visit to a school (SC1) resulting from an update to *Explore* two days prior to the site visit. Specifically, for the first 45 min of the first student session, the location coordinates for various rooms outlined in the protocol were incorrect. As a result, the researcher was unable to complete all nine tasks in the time allotted. App developers were able to reset the coordinates remotely once the problem was discovered; however, the indoor tasks resumed with only 40 min left in the two-hour observation session. From that point forward, the app functioned perfectly for all remaining tasks and participants. It is worth noting, however, that the first participant had quite a bit of experience with *Explore* prior to the research visit and was still able to give feedback based on indoor tasks completed during prior navigation experiences.

At another school (SC5), an errant "stand still and rotate the phone" message appeared on several occasions while participants walked, stopping them from being able to complete a route. Participants could not recover from this error without restarting the app. Likewise, although participants at the final school (SC6) did not experience any major issues on day one, significant technical difficulties prevented them from completing indoor tasks on day two. Finally, a weak Internet connection and poor cellular service inside buildings of two schools (SC4, SC6) made it challenging to successfully complete indoor walking tasks and slowed down several sessions. In this case, the researcher and lead O&M teacher both agreed that for *Explore* to work effectively, the school will need to address weak Wi-Fi issues in all campus buildings.

5.5 Conclusion

As the number of assistive apps for BVI smartphone users continues to increase, so too must our understanding of the specific needs and challenges this population faces when navigating indoor spaces. This is especially important as we consider how assistive technology can be most effectively integrated in O&M instruction for young people with visual impairments. Smartphones have the potential to serve as an alternative assistive tool, especially when it comes to navigation of large, complex indoor spaces. As such, this paper makes the following contributions to the assistive technology design and development communities:

- introduces a novel indoor navigation app that includes indoor mapping capabilities for several schools for BVI students in the U.S.;
- illuminates the need for seamless integration of turn-by-turn navigation instructions when traveling between indoor and outdoor locations;
- presents findings from a task-based observational study that explored user experience for BVI students using the app; and
- makes key recommendations for the design and development of future tools intended to support O&M instructional efforts.

Based on these results, future research and development in this area should explore improved functionality and additional features that make indoor and outdoor navigation more streamlined, accurate, and easy for BVI users. Additionally, future designs should address the specific functional challenges BVI learners face when integrating technology into navigation experiences. Finally, an opportunity exists to better support O&M teachers and learners by providing age-appropriate, scaffolded curricula to accompany the use of technology in the classroom.

References

1. International Agency for the Prevention of Blindness. https://www.iapb.org/learn/vision-atlas/. Accessed 11 June 2023
2. Façanha, A.R., Darin, T., Viana, W., Sánchez, J.: O&M indoor virtual environments for people who are blind: a systematic literature review. ACM Trans. Accessible Comput. **13**(2), 1–42 (2020)
3. Kaiser, J.T., Cmar, J.L., Anderson, D.L.: What's in a definition? Reflections on the scope of orientation and mobility. J. Visual Impair. Blind. **113**(1), 89–92 (2019)
4. Kish, D., Hook, J.: Echolocation and FlashSonar. APA, American Printing House for the Blind (2016)
5. Morrison, C., et al.: Enabling meaningful use of AI-infused educational technologies for children with blindness: learnings from the development and piloting of the PeopleLens curriculum. In: Proceedings of the 23rd International ACM SIGACCESS Conference on Computers and Accessibility, pp. 1–13 (2021)

6. Freeman, E., Wilson, G., Brewster, S., Baud-Bovy, G., Magnusson, C., Caltenco, H.: Audible beacons and wearables in schools: helping young visually impaired children play and move independently. In: Proceedings of the 2017 CHI Conference on Human Factors in Computing Systems, pp. 4146–4157 (2017)
7. Giudice, N.A., Legge, G.E.: Blind navigation and the role of technology. The Engineering Handbook of Smart Technology for Aging, Disability, and Independence, pp. 479–500 (2008)
8. Morrison, C., et al.: Physical programming for blind and low vision children at scale. Hum.-Comput. Interact. **36**(5–6), 535–569 (2019)
9. Brewer, R.N., Kameswaran, V.: Understanding trust, transportation, and accessibility through ridesharing. In: Proceedings of the CHI Conference on Human Factors in Computing Systems, pp. 1–11 (2019)
10. Slade, P., Tambe, A., Kockenderfer, M.J.: Multimodal sensing and intuitive steering assistance improve navigation and mobility for people with impaired vision. Sci. Robot. **6**(59), eagb6594 (2021)
11. Nazri, N.M., Fauzi, S., Gining, R.A., Razak, T.R., Jamaluddin, M.: Smart cane for visually impaired with obstacle, water detection and GPS. Int. J. Comput. Digital Syst. **10**, 2–8 (2021)
12. Ahmed, F., Tasnim, Z., Rana, M., Khan, M.M.: Development of low cost smart cane with GPS. In: IEEE World AI IoT Congress (AIIoT), pp. 715–724. IEEE (2022)
13. Guerrero, J. C., Quezada-V, C., Chacon-Troya, D.: Design and implementation of an intelligent cane, with proximity sensors, GPS localization and GSM feedback. In: IEEE Canadian Conference on Electrical & Computer Engineering (CCECE), pp. 1–4. IEEE (2018)
14. Zhao, Y., et al.: Enabling people with visual impairments to navigate virtual reality with a haptic and auditory cane simulation. In: Proceedings of the CHI Conference on Human Factors in Computing Systems, pp. 1–14 (2018)
15. Khusro, S., Shah, B., Khan, I., Rahman, S.: Haptic feedback to assist blind people in indoor environment using vibration patterns. Sensors **22**(1), 361 (2022)
16. Jin, Y., Kim, J., Kim, B., Mallipeddi, R., Lee, M.: Smart cane: face recognition system for blind. In: Proceedings of the 3rd International Conference on Human-Agent Interaction, pp. 145–148 (2015)
17. Nishajith, A., Nivedha, J., Nair, S.S., Shaffi, J.M.: Smart cap-wearable visual guidance system for blind. In: International Conference on Inventive Research in Computing Applications (ICIRCA), pp. 275–278. IEEE (2018)
18. Cazini, J., Frasson, A.C.: Voices project: technological innovations in social inclusion of people with visual impairment. J. Technol. Manag. Innov. **8**, 13 (2013)
19. Bhowmick, A., Hazarika, S.M.: An insight into assistive technology for the visually impaired and blind people: state-of-the-art and future trends. J. Multimodal User Interfaces **11**(2), 149–172 (2017)
20. Goldschmidt, M.: Orientation and mobility training to people with visual impairments. Mobility of visually impaired people: fundamentals and ICT assistive technologies, pp. 237–261 (2018)
21. Griffin-Shirley, N., et al.: A survey on the use of mobile applications for people who are visually impaired. J. Visual Impair. Blind. **111**(4), 307–323 (2017)
22. Gori, M., Cappagli, G., Tonelli, A., Baud-Bovy, G., Finocchietti, S.: Devices for visually impaired people: high technological devices with low user acceptance and no adaptability for children. Neurosci. Biobehav. Rev. **69**, 79–88 (2016)
23. Uslan, M.M.: Barriers to acquiring assistive technology: cost and lack of information. J. Visual Impair. Blind. **86**(9), 402–407 (1992)
24. Depountis, V., Okungu, P., Molloy-Daugherty, D.: The development of an application that supports body awareness for children with visual impairments and additional disabilities. Vision Rehabil. Int. **10**(1), 1–8 (2019)

25. Faria, J., Lopes, S., Fernandes, H., Martins, R., Barroso, J.: Electronic white cane for blind people navigation assistance. In: World Automation Congress, pp. 1–7. IEEE (2010)
26. Nakajima, M. Haruyama, S.: Indoor navigation system for visually impaired people using visible light communication and compensated geomagnetic sensing. In: 1st IEEE International Conference on Communications in China (ICCC), pp. 524–529. IEEE (2012)
27. Ahmetovic, D., Gleason, C., Ruan, C., Kitani, K., Takagi, H., Asakawa, C.: NavCog: a navigational cognitive assistant for the blind. In: Proceedings of the 18th International Conference on Human-Computer Interaction with Mobile Devices and Services, pp. 90–99 (2016)
28. Abraham, C. H., Boadi-Kusi, B., Morny, E.K.A., Agyekum, P.: Smartphone usage among people living with severe visual impairment and blindness. Assist. Technol. 1–8 (2021)
29. Saldana, J.: Fundamentals of Qualitative Research. Oxford university press (2011)
30. Pohjolainen, S., Chaudary, B., Arhippainen, L., Pulli, P.: Development of cooperative assistive technology user experience evaluation model for blind and visually impaired people. Submitted to 13th ICDVRAT with ITAG, pp. 8–10. Serpa, Portugal (2021)
31. Real, S., Araujo, A.: Navigation systems for the blind and visually impaired: past work, challenges, and open problems. Sensors **19**(15), 3404 (2019)
32. Zhang, J., Lip, C.W., Ong, S.-K., Nee, A.Y.: A multiple sensor-based shoe-mounted user interface designed for navigation systems for the visually impaired. In: 2010 The 5th Annual ICST Wireless Internet Conference (WICON), pp. 1–8. IEEE (2010)
33. Shoval, S., Ulrich, I., Borenstein, J.: NavBelt and the Guide-Cane [obstacle-avoidance systems for the blind and visually impaired]. IEEE Robot. Autom. Mag. **10**(1), 9–20 (2003)
34. Velázquez, R., Maingreaud, F., Pissaloux, E.: Intelligent glasses: a new man-machine interface concept integrating computer vision and human tactile perception. In: Proceedings of EuroHaptics, pp. 456–460. Citeseer (2003)
35. Metatla, O., Bardot, S., Cullen, C., Serrano, M. Jouffrais, C.: Robots for inclusive play: Co-designing an educational game with visually impaired and sighted children. In: Proceedings of the CHI Conference on Human Factors in Computing Systems, pp. 1–10 (2020)
36. Sacks, S., Gaylord-Ross, R.: Peer-mediated and teacher-directed social skills training for visually impaired students. Behav. Ther. **20**(4), 619–640 (1989)
37. Lohman, M.C.: Environmental inhibitors to informal learning in the workplace: a case study of public school teachers. Adult Educ. Q. **50**(2), 83–101 (2000)

Haptic Mobile Application to Develop Pre-braille Skills

J. Andrés Sandoval-Bringas(✉), Mónica A. Carreño-León, Rafael Cosío-Castro, Italia Estrada-Cota, and Alejandro Leyva-Carrillo

Universidad Autónoma de Baja California Sur, La Paz, B.C.S, Mexico
{sandoval,mcarreno,r.cosio,iestrada,aleyva}@uabcs.mx

Abstract. Attention to people with disabilities has been a topic of interest for different areas of science and technology. A large percentage of all information available to people comes from vision. That is why people with visual disabilities are seriously affected and must seek means and alternatives that allow them to access this information. Currently, technology has allowed the introduction of new forms of education and communication with the people who have a disability and, there is interest in the incorporation of these technologies in teaching methods. The main objective of this work is the design of a mobile application that incorporates gamification elements that can be used by children to learn braille signs. Gamification is an important trend for education, which is used as a method to encourage students to perform certain activities or tasks that they generally would not do. The preliminary results obtained are considered favorable.

Keywords: Visual impairment · Braille system · Mobile app · educational inclusion

1 Introduction

According to reports from the World Health Organization (WHO), there are around 2.2 billion people in the world with conditions of visual impairment, of which 80% are in developing countries, among the causes of blindness. In the world, non-communicable visual diseases represent 12% to 15% of these (glaucoma, diabetic retinopathy, degenerative myopia, age-related macular degeneration, non-surgical cataracts) [1].

Visual impairment is a condition that directly affects the perception of images in whole or in part. Sight is a global sense that allows to identify at a distance and at the same time an object already known or presented for the first time. Visual impairment is defined based on visual acuity and visual field. Visual disability is considered when a significant decrease in visual acuity is detected, which persists even with the use of glasses. Also when a significant decrease in the visual field is detected. Visual acuity is the ability of a subject to clearly perceive the shape of objects at a certain distance. The visual field refers to the portion of space that an individual can see without moving their head or eyes [2].

Q. Gao et al. (Eds.): HCII 2023, LNCS 14055, pp. 392–403, 2023.
https://doi.org/10.1007/978-3-031-48041-6_26

Of the five senses, sight is the most dominant and plays a crucial role at every stage of people's lives. It is an integral part of interpersonal and social interactions in face-to-face communication, where information is conveyed through non-verbal signals, such as gestures and facial expressions [3, 4].

Vision allows easy access to educational materials, from childhood to adolescence, and is critical to achieving educational goals [5, 6]. The vision supports the development of social skills to foster friendships, build self-esteem and maintain well-being, as well as participation in sports and social activities that are essential for physical development, physical and mental health, personal identity and socialization [7].

According to a report by the World Health Organization (WHO), people with disabilities have historically not been included in education. Although this has improved in recent years, the probability of people with disabilities entering educational institutions is still very low, with high dropout rates [8, 9].

Technology has brought great benefits to humanity, and is present in practically any area of society. Its evolution has been very fast and it has become a fundamental tool for day to day. For many researchers, the development of inclusive technologies to support people with special needs has been a topic of special interest, since through these developments their quality of life can be improved and their incorporation into society easier.

Failure to meet the needs or fulfill the rights of people with disabilities, including blindness, has far-reaching consequences.

1.1 Visual Impairment and Braille system

In Mexico, in the 2020 Census, INEGI counted 20 million 838 thousand 108 people in the category of disability, a figure that represents 16.5% of the population of Mexico. This figure results from the sum of the 6 million 179 thousand 890 (4.9%) who were identified as people with disabilities, plus the 13 million 934 thousand 448 (11.1%) who said they had some limitation to carry out activities of daily living (walking, seeing, hearing, self-care, speaking or communicating, remembering or concentrating), and 723,770 (0.6%) with some "mental problem or condition". Visual impairment is slightly higher than the number of people with walking limitations or motor disabilities. In previous measurements, motor disability always grouped the largest number of people, with a wide distance in relation to other disabilities: visual, hearing, cognitive or intellectual and mental condition. Within the group of people with visual disabilities, 63.5% do not use any type of technical aid, and only 4.6% use the Braille system [10].

People who are visually impaired or blind use the braille system or language for the blind to write and read. The blind read by touch, sliding their fingers over an alphabet specially designed for them [11].

The Braille method is a reading system for people with visual disabilities through the sense of touch, it consists of 6 raised dots (generative sign), whose combination produces all the letters of the alphabet, mathematical signs and musical notes. limes. The generator sign is made up of 6 points organized in two columns of 3 points each, the measurement units of each point are 5 mm high by 2.5 mm wide and the horizontal separation between one point and another is approximately 6.30 mm, in such a way that the 6 points can be perceived by the fingertips [12]. The different combinations of these

6 points make it possible to obtain seventy-three signs or characters [11]. This system limitation allows the same character to have more than one meaning depending on the context in which it is applied or the predecessor cell [13].

Braille is a very helpful tool for blind people to acquire all the information they need and to develop at a cognitive and intellectual level, as well as providing great autonomy [14]. It is their usual form of contact with culture and the written media and their main channel of learning. A blind child can, through Braille, gain access to the same degree of knowledge as students of the same age and with a similar learning rate. However, despite its effectiveness in accessing information, reading and study for blind people, the Braille method is rarely used [10].

To learn to read Braille, you basically need three things: tactile development, learning the code, and reading animation [11]. In order to read and write Braille, children need to learn not only each letter of the Braille alphabet, but also its mirror image. Also, you only know if they have spelled it correctly when you turn the page. The whole process represents a great challenge for young children who are learning to read and write.

Learning and familiarization with the Braille method is done progressively. At the beginning, children work exercising sensory development and especially touch, handling sheets and puzzles that help them distinguish textures and simple shapes [15, 16].

Little by little, children begin to learn the reading sequence from left to right, to handle basic number concepts, and to coordinate both hands to distinguish three-dimensional shapes. The first contacts are in the form of a game.

The most common methods used in the process of teaching the Braille system are: Alborada, Bliseo, Pergamo, Thyme [17].

However, the recommended method for working with children is the Thyme method. This method is used to address it with children, taking into account uniqueness and learning pace, materials with a lot of motivating, didactic and pertinent to learning relief content are included, phrases and sentences of interest to the student are included. Letter order: a, o, u, e, l, p, á, b, c, d, m, capital letter, period, i, n v, ó, s g, t, f, r í, ll, j, z, ñ, é, h, y, ch, ú, q, rr, r, gu.

Reading and writing supposes the opening to the world and with it the feeling of an integral part of it. Por ello, un objetivo prioritario en la educación básica es la adquisición de la lectura. Reading is the main means for the acquisition of new learning, and it does not always happen in the same way [18]. Through literacy, social relationships are enriched, knowing oneself and others and developing skills that prepare them for life: memory, languages, imagination, and the ability to abstract [19].

Technology has brought great benefits to humanity and is present in practically any area of society. Its evolution has been very rapid, and it has become a fundamental tool for day-to-day use. For many researchers, the development of inclusive technologies to support people with special needs has been a topic of special interest, because through these developments their quality of life can be improved and their incorporation into society easier.

For there to really be social integration, it is essential that children and young people with special needs be accepted in regular educational institutions.

1.2 Haptic Perception and Technology

In the teaching and learning process it is important to communicate meanings, concepts, ideas and generate appropriate educational situations that lead to an adequate learning environment. Many of these educational situations and settings are based on visual representations. However, the process of teaching and learning blind people is a challenging practice because information and communication technologies (ICT), and conventional visual materials can be ineffective [20].

Modern computing technologies include virtual reality and so-called haptic systems, which add the sense of touch to human-computer interaction and provide information about the dimensional and physical properties of virtual objects. Consequently, digital touch can be used to generate mental representations of virtual objects [20].

Research papers related to virtual technologies with digital tactile feedback show that visually impaired people can practically perceive spaces through virtual applications and devices with audio-haptic feedback. These works have examined the ability of participants to represent space after having studied an audio-haptic map [21].

The areas in which the educational intervention with students with blindness or severe visual impairment should focus are mainly three: (a) personal autonomy (b) communication and access to information and (c) manipulation and exploration. For the development of the first area, it is very important that the students have previously improved certain requirements or skills, among which are the use of the haptic-tactile system.

Some researchers suggest that through the use of virtual environments, users can practice skills safely, avoiding the consequences of the real world that can become dangerous, mainly for users with special needs. In [22] it is mentioned that Information and Communication Technologies (ICT) can decisively improve the quality of life of people with disabilities, in addition to being one of the few options to access the school curriculum, helping to communication and facilitating social and labor integration. For people with autism, the use of ICT can be considered a powerful tool to enhance and improve communication [23].

Various studies show that tangible interfaces are useful because they promote active participation, which helps in the learning process. These interfaces do not intimidate the inexperienced user and encourage exploratory, expressive and experimental activities.

In recent decades, education has undergone important changes brought about by the development of technologies. There is an interest in designing and putting into practice new methods, strategies and didactics in the development of classes, in order for students to achieve competitive results.

Research on the use of mobile devices in education is a widespread trend. This trend is mainly due to the characteristics of mobile devices that allow flexible learning since it is possible to use them anywhere and at any time. The United Nations Educational, Scientific and Cultural Organization (UNESCO) considers that mobile technologies can expand and enrich educational opportunities in different contexts [24].

Screen readers on the mobile device are one of the most important tools for visually impaired people, allowing them to interact with the device through voice. This consists of listening to the information aloud through a screen reader, while the user moves their fingers over the screen of the device.

Mobile devices have other interaction functions that can be used: vibrations and voice recognition.

The main objective of this work is the design of a mobile application that incorporates gamification elements that can be used by children to learn braille signs. Gamification is an important trend for education, which is used as a method to encourage students to perform certain activities or tasks that they generally would not do.

This project was developed in the laboratory of the Research and Development Group for Inclusive Technologies and Educational Innovation (GIDTIITEC, by its Spanish initials), at the Autonomous University of Baja California Sur (UABCS, for its Spanish initials).

2 Methodology

For the construction of the mobile application, a user-centered methodology was adopted. This methodologies is an iterative design process in which designers focus on users and their needs throughout the design process. They draw on a variety of research and design techniques to create highly usable and accessible products. This methodology consists of 4 stages: 1) Understanding the user's context; 2) Specify user requirements; 3) Design solutions; 4) Evaluate the results [25].

2.1 User Context

In order to understand the user's context, work meetings were held with special education and basic education teachers, in order to learn about the characteristics of people with visual disabilities, as well as the strategies used for the process of teaching-learning. Touch is the fundamental sense for blind children to collect information about their environment and perform daily life tasks, so haptic skills are essential for them to function as independently as possible [26].

2.2 Specification of Requirements

To gather the requirements for the design of the mobile application, work meetings were held with special education teachers, as well as with basic education teachers. In the meetings, the most convenient strategies for children to learn the braille symbols were analyzed. As a result of the meetings, a document was generated with the specifications and characteristics required for the construction of the mobile application.

The identified requirements for the mobile application are as follows:

- 3D sound: The mobile application should consider the use of binaural sound to aid spatial orientation within the mobile application. Binaural sounds are sounds of different frequencies from one ear to the other when listening with the aid of a stereophonic hearing aid.
- Voice recognition: The mobile application should allow users to perform tasks using voice commands that understand natural speech.

- Game mechanics: The mobile application must use game mechanics to encourage the user to solve the proposed activities. The use of rewards is considered through points for activities that result correctly.
- Auto-generated activities: The activities will be generated automatically by the mobile application considering the thyme method, and according to the degree of general progress.
- Feedback: Every time the user solves an activity, the mobile application must indicate whether it is correct or not.

The requirements identified for the teacher module are as follows:

- Manage users for students: The system will allow the edition, creation and deletion of users, who can access the student module.
- Activity editor: It must be possible for the teacher to incorporate activities into the system, as well as edit the stored activities.
- Student monitoring: The system will allow the teacher to monitor the performance of each of the students.
- Manage levels: The system will allow the teacher to assign the activities corresponding to each of the levels.

Figure 1 shows the use case diagram for the User and Teacher actors.

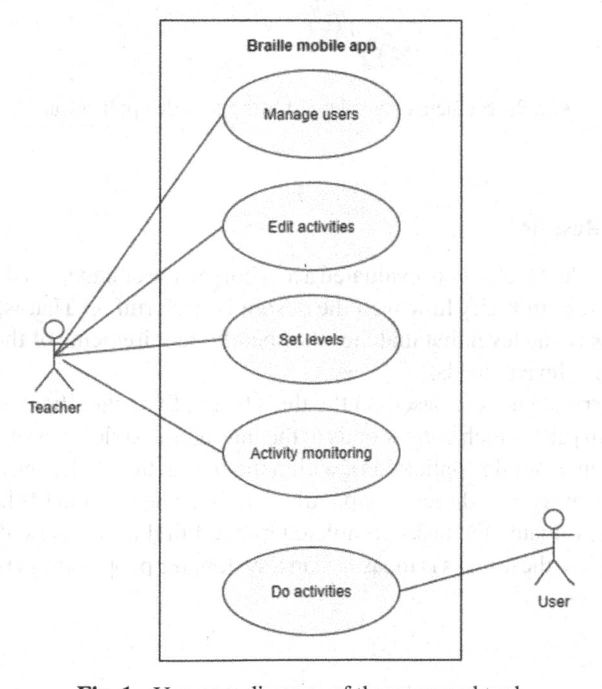

Fig. 1. Use case diagram of the proposed tool.

2.3 Design Solutions

For the construction of the application, specific characteristics that an interactive system must meet must be considered, depending on the disability to which the development is focusing. The characteristics that must be considered for an application, depending on the type of disability, are the size of the buttons, sound, ergonomics, among others [27].

Figure 2 shows the elements considered for the operation of the mobile application: 1) Vibrations, 2) Binaural sound and 3) Voice recognition. High-quality headphones are required, essential for handling binaural sound, allowing the user to locate the columns of the Braille generator sign.

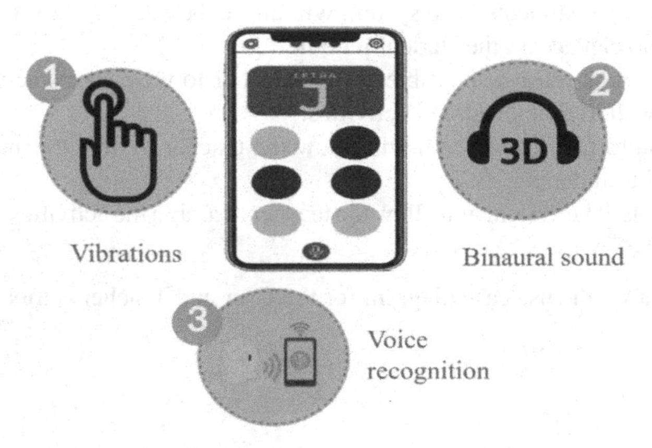

Fig. 2. Elements considered for the mobile application.

2.4 Evaluate Results

During this stage the results were evaluated according to the context and the requirements of the users in order to verify how well the design is performing. That is, it is displayed how close it was to the level that matches the specific requirements of the users and if it satisfies all their relevant needs.

The tests carried out were based on the third level of the classification proposed by: Cañas and Waern [28], which corresponds to the interaction styles of a single person with a computer system (mobile application), within the interaction styles they are: command line, menus and navigation, direct manipulation, assisted interaction [29]; and in Álvarez et al. [30], who evaluated the tasks completed by the blind user, where the time it takes the user to complete these tasks is measured in a system for people with visual disabilities and using a survey.

3 Results

The mobile application provides a gamified environment, which can be used by visually impaired children to learn Braille symbols. To use the mobile application, it is necessary to have a username and password that identifies the user within the mobile application.

In Fig. 3 can see on the left side the interface for entering the application which can be done through facial recognition, to facilitate its entry. On the right side are the options available to interact with the application: practice mode or game mode.

Fig. 3. Mobile app home interface.

1) Practice mode. This option allows you to learn each of the symbols of the Braille system, which are displayed on the screen of the mobile device. Through audio, the mobile application indicates the Braille symbol displayed on the screen, and the user, through touch and binaural sound, learns the location of the dots of the Braille-generating signal. That represent the symbol shown. With this option, the child becomes familiar with the location of the dots on the Braille generator sign.
2) Game mode. This option allows user interaction in the form of a game, to confirm that it identifies and recognizes the Braille symbols. The mobile application randomly, through an auditory instruction, asks the user to identify the symbol that is displayed on the screen. The user must move his finger on the screen with the help of the binaural sound to recognize the symbol that is being displayed, and through the microphone the user indicates his answer. The user receives immediate feedback, indicating whether the answer is correct or incorrect. If the answer was incorrect, the user will be prompted to try again. If the answer is correct, points are accumulated and the user is notified. The user can be tracked through the mobile application, this is because each of the sessions is recorded, including the Braille symbols that were reviewed, the hits and misses.

Figure 4 shows the interface where the Braille generator symbol is shown. Enabled points are shown in dark color and disabled points in light color. To identify the symbol displayed on the screen, the user must slide their finger over the points. Passing your finger over an activated point emits a vibration and a sound. On the contrary, when passing over a deactivated point, a vibration is not emitted and the sound is different.

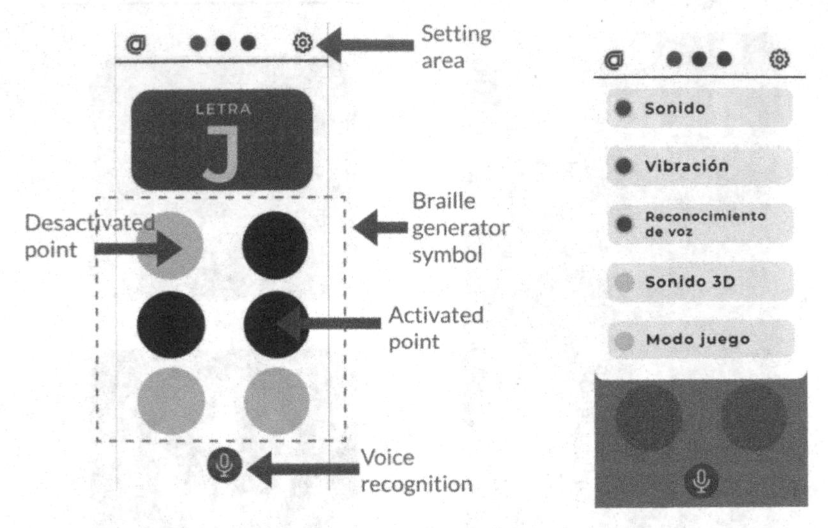

Fig. 4. Braille generator symbol interface and settings.

The teacher or the person in charge of the teaching-learning process of braille symbols can configure the mobile application so that it can be adapted to the needs of the visually impaired user. On the right side of Fig. 4, the interface that allows configuring the functionalities available in the mobile application is shown. This interface is activated by pressing the upper right button.

To know the degree of usability and compliance with the objectives set at the beginning of the development of the mobile application, two case studies were designed and implemented.

In the first case, the mobile application was evaluated by two experts from the special education area, who first focused on evaluating aspects of usability, design, and functionality. Checklists, surveys and interviews were used as instruments to collect expert assessment. The results obtained were positive, since the experts agreed that the use of the mobile application is convenient for children with visual disabilities to teach braille symbols (Fig. 5).

To verify the functionality of the technological prototype from the user's perspective, an intervention was designed with an 8-year-old girl with visual impairment. The mobile app was given to a special education teacher so that during her scheduled sessions with the girl she could do activities using the mobile app. The study period was 3 months, with two sessions per week. In the study preparation meetings, the order in which the braille symbols would be used was defined. The girl's mother accepted an informed

Fig. 5. Session using the mobile application.

consent stating that the rights to confidentiality and privacy of personal data would be respected and that it would only be used for research purposes.

During the test period, 24 sessions of 30 min were carried out. The initial session of each week was carried out in test mode, introducing the symbols in braille for the letters: a, o, u, e, l, p, b, c, d, m, i, n, according to the method thyme. The second session of each week was carried out in game mode to reinforce the learning of the symbols worked on.

4 Conclusions

In this research work, the use of tactile perception through a mobile device has been proposed and evaluated as a strategy for children with visual disabilities so that they can learn Braille symbols.

The mobile application developed aims to be an aid for people with visual disabilities, also providing help to tutors, managers or managers of them, since through the mobile application the learning of Braille symbols is facilitated, for later Start with the read and write process.

The results obtained confirm that the incorporation of technology can be of great help during the teaching-learning process.

References

1. World Health Organization: World Report Vision, World Health Organization 2019, Switzerland (2019)
2. Saucedo, A., Heredia, F., Martínez, R.: Discapacidad visual. Cultura Científica y Tecnológica, no **51**, 193–205 (2016)
3. World Health Organization: Framework on integrated, people-centred health services. World Health Organization (2016)
4. Muir, K.: Lee, P.: Health literacy and ophthalmic patient education. Surv. Ophthalmol. **55**(5), 454–459 (2010)

5. Schillinger, D., et al.: Association of health literacy with diabetes outcomes. JAMA **288**(4), 475–482 (2002)
6. Frick, K.D., Foster, A.: The magnitude and cost of global blindness: an increasing problem that can be alleviated. Am. J. Ophthalmol. **135**(4), 471–476 (2003)
7. Armstrong, K.L., Jovic, M., Vo-Phuoc, J.L., Thorpe, J.G., Doolan, B.L.: The global cost of eliminating avoidable blindness. Indian J. Ophthalmol. **60**(5), 475–480 (2012)
8. Bautista Molina, J.D., Espitia Beltrán, A.: Teclado Braille de 8 puntos con conexión USB. Revista Latinoamericana en Discapacidad, Sociedad y Derechos Humanos **4**(1), 160–171 (2020)
9. Organización Mundial de la Salud: Información mundial sobre la discapacidad (2011)
10. INEGI: Censo de Poablación y Vivienda 2020, INEGI (2020)
11. Jawasreh, Z.; Ashaari, N.; Dahnil, D.: Braille tutorial model using braille fingers puller. In: de 6th International Conference en Electrical Engineering and Informatics (ICEEI) (2017)
12. Xie, L.; Antle, A.; Motamedi, N.: Are tangibles more fun?: comparing children´s enjoyment and engagement using physical, graphical and tangible user interfaces,. In: 2nd International Conference on Tangible and Embedded Interaction. Bonn, Germany (2008)
13. Zaman, B.; Abeele, V.: How to measure the likeability of tangible interactin with preschoolers, de CHI Nederland (2007)
14. O'Malley, C.: Literature Review in Learning with Tangible Technologies, NESTA Futurelab (2004)
15. Price, S.: A representation approach to conceptualizing tangible learning environments, de TEI'08, Bonn, Alemania (2008)
16. Marshall, P.: Do tangible interfaces enhance learning?, de TEI'07. Baton Rouge, LA, USA (2007)
17. Carreño-León, M.A., Sandoval-Bringas, J.A., Estrada-Cota, I., Leyva-Carrillo, A.A., Durán-Encinas, I., Sandoval-Carreño, A.: Herramienta tecnológica como recurso didáctico en niños para el aprendizaje de símbolos de braille: casos de estudio., de Avances Tecnológicos en la educación y el aprendizaje, Ciudad Real, Castilla-La Mancha, España, CIATA.org - UNACAR, pp. 106–116 (2022)
18. Solé, I.: Estrategias de lectura. España, Barcelona (1992)
19. Colina, C.: La lectoescritura, un beneficio comunicacional. Procesos de lectura y escritura (2012)
20. Espinosa-Castañeda, R., Medellín-Castillo, H.I.: Percepción táctil digital para enseñanza de personas con discapacidad visual. Prisma Social, Revista de Ciencias Sociales, no **36**, 195–219 (2021)
21. Konstantinos, P., Panagiotis, K., Eleni, K., Marina, M., Asimis, V., Valari, E.: Audio-Haptic Map: an orientation and mobility aid for individuals with blindness. Procedi Comput. Sci. **67**, 223–230 (2015)
22. Tortosa, N.: Tecnologías de ayuda en personas con trastornos del espectro autista: guía para docentes, Murcia, España: CPR (2004)
23. Tecno-autismo, Tecno-autismo, [En línea]. https://autismoytecnologia.webnode.es/investigando-/marco-teorico-autismo-y-nuevas-tecnologias/. [Último acceso: 18 noviembre 2022]
24. UNESCO: Turning on mobile learning in Latin America (2012)
25. Asociación Española de Normalización y Certificación: Norma UNE-EN ISO 13407: Procesos de diseño para sistemas interactivos centrados en el operador humano, AENOR (2000)
26. Withagen, A.; Vervloed, M.P.J.; Jannsen, N.M.; Knoors, H.; Verhoeven, L.: Funcionamiento táctil en niños que son ciegos: una perspectiva clínica, Integración: Revista sobre discapacidad visual, nº 60, pp. 63–81 (2011)

27. Esparza-Maldonado, A.L., Margain-Fuentes, L.Y., Álvarez-Rodríguez, F.J., Benítez-Guerrero, E.I.: Desarrollo y evaluación de un sistema interactivo para personas con discapacidad visual. TecnoLógicas **21**(41), 149–157 (2018)
28. Cañas, J. J.; Waerns, Y.: Ergonomía cognitiva. Aspectos psicológicos de la interacción de las personas con la tecnología de la información., Editorial Médica Panamericana (2001)
29. Muñoz-Arteaga, J.; Bustos-Amador, V.: Temas de Diseño en Interacción Humano-Computadora, LATIn (2014)
30. Álvarez, T., García, A.S.A.: Hacia una metodología de interfaz móvil basada en audio para recorridos en interiores como apoyo a personas con discapacidad visual., Educação Especial na Perspectiva da Educação Inclusiva: concepções e práticas educativas, pp. 167–176 (2016)
31. W. H. Organization: Blindness and vision impairment. [En línea] (2018). https://www.who.int/news-room/fact-sheets/detail/blindness-and-visual-impairment

New Universal Design Heuristics for Mobile Augmented Reality Applications

Attila Bekkvik Szentirmai[1](✉) and Pietro Murano[2]

[1] Faculty of Architecture and Design, Department of Design Mustad, Norwegian University of Science and Technology, Bygg 118, 315, Gjøvik, Norway
attila.b.szentirmai@ntnu.com

[2] Department of Computer Science, Oslo Metropolitan University – OsloMet, Postboks 4, St. Olavs Plass, 0130 Oslo, Norway
pietro.murano@oslomet.no

Abstract. This paper presents new, novel and useful Universal Design principles in the context of mobile augmented reality (AR) applications. The principles can be used in an evaluative and/or design setting. The design of the principles was undertaken through experience-based practice. The new universal design principles for Mobile AR were then tested in an evaluation with four well known educational-type AR applications found in the Google Play store. The results of the evaluation closely matched public user comments about each application. Further, the evaluative activity using the new principles fostered design solutions for the problems found in the evaluation. From our activity, the new principles are very useful. It is suggested that these principles, if used, will help to develop better and more user friendly mobile AR applications.

Keywords: Universal Design · Design for All · Education · Augmented Reality · E-Learning · Heuristic Evaluation · Usability · Accessibility

1 Introduction

Augmented Reality (AR) is the technology that extends, enhances and combines the user's real-world environment with additional computer-generated digital information in real time. (Aukstakalnis 2016; Furht 2011; Azuma 1997). Despite its recent reappearance, AR is an over 50-year-old technology (Billinghurst, Clark, & Lee 2015) striving for a technological breakthrough into establishing itself in the mainstream markets with no success (Gartner 2018). The rapid development of mobile technologies provides a widely available and cost-effective platform. However, the human factors, accessibility, usability and user satisfaction are often overlooked and under-represented in AR research and development. Due to a need for digital inclusion (Dobransky, & Hargittai 2016), which is an international (United Nations General Assembly 2007) and national (Lovdata 2018) ICT (Information and Communication Technologies) requirement in many regions, more user-centred views or approaches are required.

Q. Gao et al. (Eds.): HCII 2023, LNCS 14055, pp. 404–418, 2023.
https://doi.org/10.1007/978-3-031-48041-6_27

Furthermore, in recent times more attention is being given to computer systems being universally designed. This being the case, one would expect that AR systems would also be universally designed.

Since its appearance in the 1960s Universal Design (UD) grew to become a national (Lovdata 2018) and international (United Nations General Assembly 2007) requirement. UD and its seven principles stood the challenge and its abstract nature made it suitable for multipurpose use cases as the design of environments, products, services and ICT solutions (Darzentas & Miesenberger, 2005; Björk, 2009; Story 1998). However, new emerging technologies such as Augmented Reality (AR), require a defined interpretation of the conceptual principles to deliver reliable evaluation results.

Therefore, the indications are that AR application designers are lacking enough or good enough guidelines or heuristics for design and evaluation. To contribute to this area we present new and novel universal design principles for mobile AR. They have been developed to particularly help with designing and evaluating mobile AR user interfaces and user experiences.

In this paper we will begin with a brief literature review which will indicate that there is still a deficiency in approaches to evaluating AR user interfaces and user experiences. Next, the new seven principles will be presented. This will be followed by a section detailing the results involving the use of the new principles in the context of mobile AR for educational purposes. Finally, the paper will conclude with an overall discussion and conclusion.

2 Related Works

Over a number of years, different researchers have designed various heuristics or guidelines to help with design and evaluation of user interfaces, software systems and web sites. One of the most well-known and used set of heuristics are by Nielsen (1994). These aim to help with Discount Usability Engineering.

Other researchers have tried to address specific issues and have therefore devised yet more guidelines, e.g. Gong and Tarasewich (2004) devised guidelines aiming to specifically help with the design of mobile user interfaces. They based their guidelines on Shneiderman's 'Eight Golden Rules of Interface Design' (Shneiderman, Plaisant, Cohen, Jacobs and Elmqvist 2018).

In another example, Wheeler Atkinson, Bennett, Bahr and Walwanis Nelson (2007) combined several well-known sets of guidelines into a single more unified set of guidelines. Some of their aims were to make the guidelines easier to access and also to update them.

The above brief examples from the literature indicate that the area of heuristics and guidelines for general user interfaces is quite mature, despite it continually evolving. However, when it comes to heuristics or guidelines that are useful for AR user interfaces and incorporate elements of Universal Design, to our knowledge this specific area is still immature and requires more work. This is particularly so, as good interaction design practice in AR systems is sometimes neglected, e.g. Swan II and Gabbard (2005) surveyed 1104 articles about AR and found that only approximately 3% of these looked at some Human Computer Interaction (HCI) issues.

Some AR studies propose the use of user-centred studies and refined evaluation methods (Yilmaz 2018; Akçayır & Akçayır 2017; Radu 2014). However, the lack of available literature and the required multidisciplinary expertise to conduct such studies poses some challenges. Researchers and developers are currently relying on generic evaluation methods that are focusing only on certain parts of the technology (e.g. system usability, GUI design, etc.), instead of evaluating the applications as a whole, including the human factors and requirements of broad audiences.

Another drawback of using traditional evaluation methods is that they are intended for evaluating generic, well-established ICT solutions. Two widely taught and used approaches involve WCAG (W3C 2019) and Nielsen's usability heuristics (Nielsen 1994). These, are mainly focusing on accessibility and interface/usability issues of traditional two-dimensional GUI systems where interaction buttons and design elements are usually static and predefined by the developers.

AR by nature tends to provide novel dynamic multimodal information presentation (e.g. visual, auditory, tactile), that is not limited to the graphical user interface only (i.e. can include the user's real-time surroundings and objects, etc.), and interaction styles that go beyond conventional WIMP and post-WIMP interactions (Jo, Lee & Seo 2017).

Traditional evaluation methods, therefore, have to be adjusted, specified and extended to be capable to cover a wider spectrum of application features.

Universal Design of ICT is an international requirement for ICT systems and its abstract nature makes it capable to become an all in one framework to evaluate AR systems (Story 1998), with specifications and clarifications of each principle in accordance with AR requirements.

Livingston (2005) suggested that AR systems have problems with 'human factors' issues and at times the hardware used. Further, three years later, Gabbard and Swan II (2008) were in agreement with Livingston, by suggesting that it is an Usability Engineering challenge to design good user interfaces in, e.g. AR contexts. Gabbard and Swan II (2008) suggested that using a 'user-based study' would help with usability issues. Their approach was to use 'user-based studies to inform design by iteratively inserting a series of user-based studies into a traditional Usability Engineering life cycle to better inform initial user interface designs (Gabbard and Swan II 2008).'

Despite our observations concerning immaturity in this area, some work has been done in relation to providing guidelines or heuristics for AR application design and evaluation. D¨unser, Grasset, Seichter and Billinghurst (2004) try to put forward key design principles which would be applicable to AR systems. Their aim was to give the reader examples on using HCI principles within an AR context. However, by their own admission at the time of writing, the result was a perhaps too general outcome needing further work.

In Ko, Chang and Ji (2013) an effort was made to develop 22 usability principles for AR applications in a smartphone context. While this work is a step in the right direction, it would be good to see it expanded. Some examples include coverage of AR applications beyond smartphone contexts and including some aspects in the guidelines concerning the 'exterior environment'. Further, more explicit linkage with universal design would also improve the guidelines.

A similar effort was carried out by Kourouthanassis, Boletsis and Lekakos (2013). They devised five broad areas of principles for interaction design for mobile AR applications. Their effort tried to ground these principles in both theory and practice with the authors positing that the principles could be used during design activities and/or evaluative activities. As stated by the authors, more evidence would need to be gathered to show that these principles actually make a difference. Further, we would suggest that the principles could be improved by being more relevant to applications beyond the mobile context and to universal design.

One final and quite recent work that will be considered is that of Endsley, Sprehn, Brill, Ryan, Vincent and Martin (2017). The authors acknowledged that in designing and developing AR applications, usability is important and that a failure in usability will lead to more errors and accidents. This in turn will lead to users' reduced trust in such technologies. They then went on to develop a nine point set of 'design heuristics for AR' aiming to address design aspects in AR systems.

While the nine point heuristics are a good attempt and a step in the right direction, we would suggest that there is room for improvement. In our examination of the nine point heuristics we judge them to be rather 'abstract' in nature and not specific enough. This in turn leads to the potential issue of them being interpreted in multiple ways by multiple evaluators/designers. Further, in some countries, such as Norway it is already a requirement for public systems and web sites to be universally designed. The nine heuristics do not fully address universal design issues or at the very least are too 'abstract' to be clear about this.

In the next section we present the new novel principles.

3 New Universal Design Principles for Mobile Augmented Reality

1. Equitable Use (Accessibility)

The design and evaluation of multimodal communication of the presented information is useful and marketable to people with diverse abilities.

1a. Communicate visual information in auditory form.
1b. Make auditory information available in a visual form.
1c. Multimodal information presentation must be useful.
1d. Make the application accessible to users with sensory (e.g. visual, auditory) impairments.

2. Flexibility of Use (Accessibility & Usability)

The design of inbuilt functions can adapt to the user needs and different user environments.

2a. Support portrait/landscape modes.
2b. Support head-mounted/handheld view.
2c. GUI design facilitates indoor/outdoor visibility.
2d. Make the application compatible with inbuilt assistive technologies (e.g. screen readers, voice command).

2e. Make the application accessible to users with motor impairments.

3. Simple and Intuitive Use (Usability)

Provided affordances and symbols are easy to understand, logical and intuitive. Inbuilt tutorials and user guidance must be present and easy to understand. Information overload and/or visual stress must be avoided.

3a. Application functions and features must be self-explanatory.
3b. Inbuilt user guidance of the application must be included.
3c. Application functions must be predictable.
3d. The system must react to user interactions in line with common user expectations.
3e. The user interface must not cause information overload and confusion.
3f. The application must provide audio, visual or haptic feedback on user interaction in accordance with user expectations and context.
3g. The application must be usable by users with cognitive impairments (e.g. reduced working memory, dyslexia and dyscalculia).

4. Perceptible Information (Accessibility & Usability)

All presented information, including information architecture and visibility must be clearly perceptible.

4a. Information must be distributed and presented in accordance with its importance (e.g. more important information should be more prominent).
4b. Foregrounds and backgrounds must be distinguishable from one another.
4c. Labelled interface elements must remain readable in dynamically changing backgrounds (e.g. live camera stream).
4d. The graphical user interface must provide satisfactory contrast (e.g. low screen brightness, direct sunlight, etc.).
4e. The application must be usable by users with sensory impairments (e.g. visual, auditory, etc.).

5. Tolerance for Error (Usability)

The design must have inbuilt safety and self-correction mechanisms to secure the users' safety and provide self-correction for unintentional user interactions.

5a. The application must provide inbuilt self-correction mechanisms (e.g. undo, rewind).
5b. The application should prevent possible user errors by design.
5c. There must be inbuilt warnings, notification systems to warn and alert the users preventing accidents and user harm.

6. Low Physical Effort (Accessibility & Usability)

The application should foster a minimum level of effort and complexity whilst maximising accuracy.

6a. The application must be controllable without complex gestures or interaction inputs (e.g. one finger gesture, switch support).

6b. The application must not require an unreasonable operation force.
6c. The application must be operable by users with motor impairments (e.g. reduced dexterity).

7. Size and Space for Approach (Accessibility & Usability)

The reach, manipulation, and use, regardless of a user's body size, posture, or mobility must maximise physical comfort whilst being flexibly usable on different devices.

7a. Interface elements must be comfortably reachable.
7b. The interface must be usable for various hand and finger sizes.
7c. The interface must be usable for different sizes of devices (e.g. smartphone, phablet, tablet, etc.).
7d. The interface must be usable and scalable whilst remaining usable under different screen aspect ratios (e.g. 16:9, 4:3, 21:9).
7e. The application must be fully operable in different body positions (e.g. sitting or lying down).
7f. To minimise motion sickness, the application should not require the user to walk whilst using the app in headset/head-mounted mode.

4 Using the New Universal Design Principles

To test the relevance of our new Universal Design principles, we tested them on mainstream educational AR applications from the Google Play store. We set the scope of four, popular, rated and reviewed applications as a representative sample, to examine how our findings complied with user feedback. We chose to compare our findings with public user feedback because to our knowledge there are no other sets of results available for comparison. This would allow for an informal benchmark. Table 1 gives an overview of the applications we evaluated with the new principles.

Table 1. Sample Applications – Overview

Application	Required hardware	Operating system	Additional hardware support	Public user score
TH!NGS for MERGE Cube/Holo Body (1.06) (GooglePlay 2019c)	Smartphone, Merge Cube	Android / IOS	VR/AR headset	4/5
AR Medical (0.2) (GooglePlay 2019a)	Smartphone, Merge Cube	Android / IOS	-	3.5/5
AR solar system (1.03) (GooglePlay 2019b)	Smartphone, Image target	Android	-	3.8/5

(*continued*)

Table 1. *(continued)*

Application	Required hardware	Operating system	Additional hardware support	Public user score
Twinkl AR Book (2.4) (GooglePlay 2019d)	Smartphone, Augmentable book	Android	-	3.1/5

4.1 Evaluation Process

Once the above applications were identified and made available, the following process was followed in conjunction with our new Universal Design principles.

1. We used the applications freely and tested all provided functions, features and interaction methods to get an overview of the applications, so we could get an overview of the complexity and scope of the applications.
2. We used our specified UD AR principles, tested and observed how they pass or violate certain requirements during application walkthroughs.
3. Recorded our discoveries on observation protocols.
4. We compared our findings with common AR inclusion barriers from previous works (e.g. Endsley et al. (2017) and Gabbard and Swan (2008)) and analyzed user feedback, ratings, and comments from the Google Play store and searched for matches, differences and recurring patterns. The authors' expertise was also used in this context.
5. We summarized the findings and classified the applications as approved or not approved in accordance with UD requirements, with suggestions for improvements.

5 Findings and Results

All applications had some severe flaws which were identified by the above process and using our new Universal Design Principles as an evaluative checklist.

Tables 2, 3, 4 and 5 show our findings for each of the four applications we tested. Each table outlines the problems found, which Universal Design principles were violated, the consequences for the users of such violations and finally, possible design changes to mitigate the problems.

5.1 TH!NGS for MERGE Cube/Holo Body AR App

Table 2. TH!NGS for MERGE Cube/Holo Body AR App Results Summary

Identified issues	UD-Principle(s) not met	Consequence and severity level	Suggested design changes
Instruction for cube scanning using symbolism and instructions that are hard to understand for first time users	P4-Perceptible information P3-Simple and Intuitive use	High - users cannot use the application	Using realistic representation of the Merge cube Providing step by step guidance
Barely visible hamburger menu, with the usage of unconventional icon	P4-Perceptible information P3-Simple and Intuitive use P6-Low Physical Effort	Low - users can easily overlook menu functions The application still remains usable	Implementation of responsive menu buttons that scale and can adopt a high variety of screen resolutions and aspect ratios
An on-screen pointer (crosshair) has to be aligned with the clickable object to be able to execute touch interactions This default interaction style on mobile view requires two hand usage, accuracy and precision	P3-Simple and Intuitive use P6-Low Physical Effort P7-Size and space for approach	Medium - users can tap on the physical cube or tap the screen However, if the position of the crosshair is a little bit off the clickable object, touch interactions will not be registered. This makes the application appear unresponsive	Eliminating the usage of pointers and implement widely used and predictable post-WIMP touch interaction style
Application plays background music, mute button is not implemented, changing volume in mobile mode would be difficult because the application requires two hand usage Volume control in headset mode is unresolvable	P6-Low Physical Effort P7-Size and space for approach	Low - Users require extra effort and attention to change system volume	Implementation of Mute and/or volume control options in both mobile and headset view

(continued)

Table 2. (*continued*)

Identified issues	UD-Principle(s) not met	Consequence and severity level	Suggested design changes
Background music stops playing immediately after target object lost. This can happen multiple times within a second	P3-Simple and Intuitive use P5-Tolerance for error	Low - users can get scared or annoyed, because of the unpredictable sound toggling	Tolerance for object lost, that does not break the audio or application flow
Poor visibility and contrast on augmented text labels, especially on bright backgrounds	P4-Perceptible information	Medium - users cannot see and read labels to learn certain body parts	Using background or transparent background for label text, that secures high contrast (7:1) and visibility on foreground (text) and background, despite the color theme of the camera stream
Difficult and non-intuitive navigation between application layouts	P3-Simple and Intuitive use P5-Tolerance for error P6-Low Physical Effort P7-Size and space for approach	Medium - Navigation back to the main menu requires extra precision and effort to hit the small target. On accidental user interaction the application swaps the superimposed 3d object with a new one, instead of navigating back to the main menu	Simplified navigation mechanism that does not demand accuracy and effort from the users. Objects that can be interacted with should be separated from each other to minimize accidental user interactions. On user error, the application should implement a self-correction mechanism
The application promotes compatibility with third party AR/VR headsets. However, the app requires additional button inputs	P2-Flexibility in Use	Medium - On 3rd party AR/VR headset, because of the missing control buttons the application becomes unusable in headset mode	Implementation of simplified interaction style that does not require additional buttons in headset mode

5.2 AR Medic AR App

Table 3. AR Medic AR App Results Summary

Identified issues	UD-Principle(s) not met	Consequence and severity level	Suggested design changes
The application boots up into a live camera stream, without informing the users about inbuilt functions, use-cases, or required external hardware elements (i.e. target object)	P3-Simple and Intuitive Use	High - users cannot figure out how to use the application The application can foster false mental models and make users believe they are using a camera application	Warning the users about the need for Merge Cube, providing a tutorial about its usage Suggest and communicate application functions
Barely visible hamburger menu, with the usage of unconventional icon	P4-Perceptible information P3-Simple and Intuitive use P6-Low Physical Effort	Low - users can easily overlook menu functions The application still remains usable	Implementation of responsive menu buttons that scale and adopt a high variety of screen resolutions and aspect ratios
Hamburger menu is hard to reach and interact with	P6-Low Physical Effort	Low - the menu only contains a non-functioning flashlight option – potentially disappointing users	Refine the design without the need for a hamburger menu (Contains only one function) or position it in accordance with Fitts law to support reachability
Flashlight function doesn't work. Tested on (LG V20, V30, V40, Google Pixel2)	P3-Simple and Intuitive use	Low - users cannot use flashlight function that aims to increase the visibility of the Merge Cube in dark environments	Push an update that resolves the issue, eventually remove the function, which also removes the necessity of usage of hamburger menus
Confusing interaction methods and GUI representations	P3-Simple and Intuitive use	High - users' expectations might not meet application requirements. Users might try to perform touch interactions on the Merge Cube	Redefine GUI implementation and differentiate the 3D GUI from the 3D content to reduce confusion. And do not force users to explore the interface before they can use it

(continued)

Table 3. *(continued)*

Identified issues	UD-Principle(s) not met	Consequence and severity level	Suggested design changes
Inconvenient interaction with the 3D content. Some interactive objects provide visual feedback on user interaction, whilst some do not	P3-Simple and Intuitive use	Low - users can easily overlook the fact some 3D organs are animated on user interaction	Inbuilt narration, explanation or suggestion of application functions
The oversized "Close" button despite the name does not close the application, it navigates back to the main menu	P3-Simple and Intuitive use	Low - The application suggests one function but does something else, by using the label "close" on the application's "home" button	Renaming the label of "Close" button into "Home" button. Eventually support the message with a conventional icon

5.3 AR Solar System App

Table 4. AR Solar System App Results Summary

Identified issues	UD-Principle(s) not met	Consequence and severity level	Suggested design changes
The application loads without any information, description or tutorial	P3-Simple and Intuitive use	High - users cannot use the application	Implement help functions, tutorials and application guides
The futuristic Space theme and the provided futuristic user interface is not self-explanatory and not all functions are working	P3-Simple and Intuitive use	Medium - users have to try and discover application functions. Some functions remain unusable without the image target	Implement labels or audio narration to explain interface functions
Unpredictable menu behavior. Clicking on the options icon searching for help, hides all on screen buttons	P3-Simple and Intuitive use	Low - some users can potentially be annoyed and surprised	Implement option menu where users can change theme or activate guidance or narration

(continued)

Table 4. (*continued*)

Identified issues	UD-Principle(s) not met	Consequence and severity level	Suggested design changes
Buttons are small and arranged close to each other, which can potentially lead to accidental clicks	P5-Tolerance for error P7-Size and Space for Approach and Use	Medium - the app requires accuracy and the probability for accidental interaction is very likely	Place and group buttons in accordance to their functions. Support reachability but prevent accidental hits
The power off icon exits the application	P3-Simple and Intuitive use	Low - Power off button on a spaceship theme suggests turning off the spaceship and not exiting the application	Implementing convenient exit button, optionally support the symbol with text label
Share button is not functioning. Green and Red interface button does nothing without the image target being detected	P3-Simple and Intuitive use	Low - the unpredictable interface can affect user experience	Hide buttons that are inactive, support buttons with text labels
There is only a link on the Google Play store that communicates the requirement for an image target	P3-Simple and Intuitive use	High - without the image target the application is unusable	Provide download link and warning in the application about the necessity of an image target, to use the application
The image target is a black and white marker. Users who see the marker first might have problems in figuring out how to activate it	P3-Simple and Intuitive use	High - users might not know what to do with the image target, so the application is potentially unusable	Provide a QR code or a link or a short explanation about how to use the image target and how to download the related application

5.4 Twinkl Augmented Reality Book App

As stated above, we then compared our findings with the public comments written by users and left at the Google Play store. Our aim was to see if the public comments matched in any way the findings we had by using our extended Universal Design principles. We discovered a very strong overlap between the two.

In summary, we identified recurring design flaws in all applications in accordance with Simple and Intuitive use (UD Principle 3), Perceptible Information (UD Principle 4), Flexibility in Use (UD Principle 2), Tolerance for Error (UD Principle 5) and Low Physical Effort (UD Principle 6). These were also evident in negative public user

Table 5. Twinkl Augmented Reality Book App Results Summary

Identified issues	UD-Principle(s) not met	Consequence and severity level	Suggested design changes
The superimposed 3D content can be offset and displaced from the image target	P4-Perceptible information	High - The augmented experience can be useless	Use multiple image targets and secure accuracy for positioning the content
The application does not provide support for Portrait / Landscape mode	P2-Flexibility in use	Low - The application remains still usable; however, the screen does not orient	Implement screen rotation and support for portrait/landscape mode
The application does not provide headset view	P2-Flexibility in use	Low - Users are limited to mobile view only. The nature of AR books would benefit from the usage of stereoscopic view	Implement headset view

comments. Some users inaccurately claimed an application did not work as they had problems with the touch buttons and other interaction issues involving navigation. Some accused the developers of 'cheating' because the applications did not communicate inbuilt functions, thus giving the impression that the app was not real. Other users faced major problems with accuracy and aspects of control whilst interacting with the cube. These applications clearly neglect users with diverse abilities. Overall, the applications are not intuitive, they do not communicate their functions and interaction styles are not as expected. These issues make some users believe they are faulty or even fake applications.

6 Discussion and Conclusions

Our work discussed in this paper makes very strong and novel contributions to the area of Universal Design and Usability Engineering. We have designed new Universal Design principles to more easily facilitate the evaluation and design of AR applications.

Our new principles aim to close two gaps currently in existence (see above Related Works section) concerning such guidelines or heuristics. The first gap concerns the issue that to our knowledge no one has devised guidelines or heuristics that have a strong Universal Design slant. The second gap our work deals with, is that despite several attempts by other researchers in developing new or extended AR guidelines or heuristics (see above Related Works section), several of these have the shortcoming that they are too abstract in nature and thus potentially open to all kinds of interpretation.

Our guidelines aim to be completely linked with Universal Design and Usability while being more specific in nature regarding what should be present in AR applications for them to be effective and user friendly. Our guidelines also have the strength of building on existing Universal Design principles thus keeping the original guidelines relevant.

In the discussion above we have shown that where AR apps have usability and Universal Design failures, use of our guidelines uncovers a multitude of these. Although this paper is focusing on the evaluative side of our new guidelines, the results above show that the use of these can also bring benefits during design activities. Tables 2, 3, 4 and 5 above show for each failing that has been uncovered possible re-design solutions that could be immediately implemented.

Through the results we have presented in this paper, we believe that the extended guidelines are a step in the right direction. However, we would suggest that some future work should concentrate on the following factors. The first is that our sample set of AR applications all had an educational flavour. Future evaluations should go beyond the educational type AR applications to provide more evidence for their flexibility and far-reaching scope in the AR context. The second aspect would be to gather more evidence for their applicability and practicality during design phases of AR app development. A third area concerns our use of four mobile AR applications from the Google Play store. Four applications is a somewhat small amount of applications which cannot cover every eventuality. However, the selected suite of four applications were strategically selected to reflect the most design and interaction styles possible within a small set of applications. Therefore, future work could increase the set of applications evaluated for comparison purposes. Finally, a fourth area concerns the fact that although we successfully identified accessibility and usability flaws, the whole process could have been executed with a larger number of evaluators. Therefore, future work in this area could include more evaluators in the process.

References

Akçayır, M., Akçayır, G.: Advantages and challenges associated with augmented reality for education: a systematic review of the literature. Educ. Res. Rev. **20**, 1–11 (2017)

Aukstakalnis, S.: Practical Augmented Reality: A Guide to the Technologies, Applications, and Human Factors for AR and VR. Addison-Wesley Professional (2016)

Azuma, R.T.: A survey of augmented reality. Presence: Teleoperators Virtual Environ. **6**(4), 355–385 (1997)

Billinghurst, M., Clark, A., Lee, G.: A survey of augmented reality. Foundations and Trends® in Human–Computer Interaction, **8**(2–3), 73–272 (2015)

Björk, E.: Many become losers when the Universal Design perspective is neglected: exploring the true cost of ignoring Universal Design principles. Technol. Disabil. **21**(4), 117–125 (2009)

Darzentas, J., Miesenberger, K.: Design for all in information technology: a Universal Concern. In: Andersen, K.V., Debenham, J., Wagner, R. (eds.) Database and Expert Systems Applications. DEXA 2005. Lecture Notes in Computer Science, vol. 3588. Springer, Heidelberg (2005). https://doi.org/10.1007/11546924_40

Dobransky, K., Hargittai, E.: Unrealized potential: exploring the digital disability divide. Poetics **58**, 18–28 (2016)

Dünser, A., Grasset, R., Seichter, H., Billinghurst, M.: Applying HCI Principles to AR Systems Design. University of Canterbury, New Zealand, HIT Lab NZ (2004)

Endsley, T.C., Sprehn, K., Brill, R.M, Ryan, K.J., Vincent, E.C., Martin, J.M.: Augmented reality design heuristics: designing for dynamic interactions, human factors and ergonomics society. In: 2017 International Annual Meeting, Austin, TX, 9–13 October 2017

Furht, B. (ed.): Handbook of Augmented Reality. Springer Science & Business Media (2011)
Gabbard, J.L., Swan II, J.E.: Usability engineering for augmented reality: empliying user-based studies to inform design. IEEE Trans. Visual. Comput. Graph. **14**(3), May/June 2008
Gartner: 3 Reasons Why VR and AR Are Slow to Take Off. Retrieved March 8 2018. https://www.gartner.com/smarterwithgartner/3-reasons-why-vr-and-ar-are-slow-to-take-off/. Accessed May 2020
Gong, J., Tarasewich, P.: Guidelines for handheld mobile device interface design. In: Proceedings of DSI 2004 Annual Meeting, pp. 3751–3756 (2004)
GooglePlay: AR Medical (2019a). https://play.google.com/store/apps/details?id=de.nextreality.medicalcube. Accessed May 2020
GooglePlay: AR Solar System (2019b). https://play.google.com/store/apps/details?id=com.ar.solar, Accessed May 2020
GooglePlay: TH!NGS for MERGE Cube (2019c). https://play.google.com/store/apps/details?id=com.MergeCube.Things. Accessed May 2020
GooglePlay: Twinkl Augmented Reality (2019d). https://play.google.com/store/apps/details?id=co.uk.twinkl.twinklaugmentedrealitys. Accessed May 2020
Jo, J., L'Yi, S., Lee, B., Seo, J.: TouchPivot: blending WIMP & post-WIMP interfaces for data exploration on tablet devices. In: Proceedings of the 2017 CHI Conference on Human Factors in Computing Systems, pp. 2660–2671, May 2017
Ko, S.M., Chang, W.S., Ji, Y.G.: Usability principles for augmented reality applications in a smartphone environment. Int. J. Hum.-Comput. Interact. **29**(8), 501–515 (2013)
Kourouthanassis, P.E., Boletsis, C., Lekakos, G.: Demystifying the design of mobile augmented reality applications. Multimedia Tools Appl. **74**, 1045–1066 (2015). (2013)
Lovdata: Act relating to equality and a prohibition against discrimination (Equality and Anti-Discrimination Act), (1 January 2018). https://lovdata.no/dokument/NLE/lov/2017-06-16-51#KAPITTEL_3. Accessed May 2020
Livingston, M.A.: Evaluating human factors in augmented reality systems. IEEE Comput. Graph. Appl. **25**(6), 6–9, November–December 2005
Nielsen, J.: 10 Usability Heuristics for User Interface Design (1994). https://www.nngroup.com/articles/ten-usability-heuristics/. Accessed May 2020
Radu, I.: Augmented reality in education: a meta-review and cross-media analysis. Pers. Ubiquit. Comput. **18**(6), 1533–1543 (2014). https://doi.org/10.1007/s00779-013-0747-y
Shneiderman, B., Plaisant, C., Cohen, M., Jacobs, S., Elmqvist, N.: Designing the User Interface: Strategies for Effective Human-Computer Interaction, Sixth Edition Global Edition. Pearson (2018)
Story, M.F.: Maximizing usability: the principles of universal design. Assist. Technol. **10**(1), 4–12 (1998)
Swan II, J.E., Gabbard, J.L.: Survey of user-based experimentation in augmented reality. In: Proceedings of First International Conference Virtual Reality (VR 2005), July 2005
United Nations General Assembly, Convention on the Rights of Persons with Disabilities: resolution / adopted by the General Assembly, 24 January 2007, A/RES/61/106. https://www.refworld.org/docid/45f973632.html. Accessed 7 March 2019
W3C: W3C Accessibility Standards Overview. Retrieved 7 March 2019. https://www.w3.org/WAI/standards-guidelines/. Accessed May 2020
Wheeler Atkinson, B.F., Bennett, T.O., Bahr, G.S., Walwanis Nelson, M.M.: Development of a Multiple Heuristics Evaluation Table (MHET) to support software development and usability analysis. In: Stephanidis, C. (eds.) Universal Access in Human Computer Interaction. Coping with Diversity. UAHCI 2007. Lecture Notes in Computer Science, vol. 4554. Springer, Heidelberg (2007). https://doi.org/10.1007/978-3-540-73279-2_63
Yilmaz, R.M.: Augmented reality trends in education between 2016 and 2017 years. In: State of the Art Virtual Reality and Augmented Reality Knowhow. IntechOpen (2018)

HandiMathKey-Device

Frédéric Vella[1(✉)], Nathalie Dubus[2], Eloise Grolleau[2], Marjorie Deleau[2], Cécile Malet[2], Christine Gallard[2], Véronique Ades[2], and Nadine Vigouroux[1]

[1] UMR CNRS 5505, IRIT, Paul Sabatier University, 118 Route de Narbonne Cedex 9, 31062 Toulouse, France
frederic.vella@irit.fr

[2] ASEI, Jean Lagarde Center, 1 Avenue Tolosane, 31520 Ramonville-Saint-Agne, France

Abstract. Typing mathematics is sometimes difficult with text editor functions for students with motor impairment and other associated impairments (visual, cognitive). Based on the HandiMathKey software keyboard, a user-centred design method involving the ecosytem of disabled students was applied to design the HMK-D physical keyboard for mathematical input. We opted for the Stream Deck device because of its multimedia features and its appeal to young students to the HMK-D. Preliminary tests with 8 students (5 in secondary school and 3 in high school) shows that HMK-D is highly accepted, accessible and fun for mathematical input by students with impairments. A longitudinal study of the usability and acceptability of HMK-D is planned for the 2023–2024 school year.

Keywords: User Centered Design · Students with impairments · Text entry of mathematical symbols · Physical keyboard · HMK-D

1 Introduction

Information and communication technologies on computers, or tablets, can become an assistive technology that makes the learning process more accessible. Indeed, handwriting is a difficult and tiring task for students with grapho-motor deficits. Benoit and Sagot [1] have analyzed and identified the difficulties encountered by students with neurodevelopmental disorders in order to determine special educational needs.

There is a poorly addressed input area in the accessibility field that deals with the input of scientific elements including mathematical formulas. For students, the ability to produce written work is an essential activity when they start secondary school. For those who have not acquired this autonomy in writing, they are accompanied by a secretary or by a companion of students with impairment who provides the written transcription. For others, the computer is an assistive tool used to compensate for handwriting that may be dysorthographic, slow and tiring. There are many text input solutions for motor impairment [2]. The work carried out during occupational therapy sessions enables the student to gradually acquire more functional typing, with or without the help of word prediction software with or without voice synthesis, and/or voice recognition software.

Q. Gao et al. (Eds.): HCII 2023, LNCS 14055, pp. 419–433, 2023.
https://doi.org/10.1007/978-3-031-48041-6_28

In this way, students gradually develop autonomy in their schoolwork, being able to produce more independently when taking notes, doing homework and so on.

However, when it comes to typing mathematics, the computer is not an easy tool. Observations by occupational therapists at Centre for inclusive schooling Jean Lagarde of ASEI have shown that word-processor equation editors (Microsoft Office, Open Office, Libre Office, etc.) make it difficult for students with motor impairment to enter mathematical data. These include motor impairments (combining keys on the physical keyboard, bimanual coordination, multiple movements of the mouse to access symbols), visual and visuospatial difficulties (spatial location and localization of symbols in an environment overloaded with information and of small size, little contrast) and memory difficulties (memorizing shortcuts or writing codes).

Typing in these editors has proved to be demanding both functionally (motor impairment) and cognitively (attentional, visuo-spatial, memory), generating fatigue at every level for little productive and effective gain [3].

To avoid this fatigue when typing mathematical formulas, we co-designed the HMK mathematical input application [3]. The Centre for inclusive schooling Jean Lagarde of ASEI conducted a multidisciplinary workshop with 23with different disabilities to evaluate its effectiveness and usefulness in three classes [4]. The use of the HMK (virtual HandiMathKey application) in the classroom favours its acceptability and appropriation. However, many students identified the need for a physical HMK-D keyboard for those who have difficulty pointing.

In this paper, we will first look at the various existing solutions for entering mathematical formulae, then describe the genesis of HMK and report on the main conclusions drawn from its use. We will then detail the design process used to develop the HMK-D physical keyboard and describe the various prototypes produced. Finally, we will report on the initial feedback from observation of use by nine students with impairment.

2 Related Work

Inputting mathematical formulae is a question of accessibility that can unfortunately be addressed.. According to Akpan and Beard [5] writing mathematical symbol is important in their learning. However, Smith [6] have shown that teaching mathematics with a computer-like digital artifact does not work well. In addition, handwriting is a difficult and tiring task for students with grapho-motor deficits [7]. Benoit & Sagot [1] have analyzed and identified the difficulties encountered by a student with neurodevelopmental disorders in order to determine special educational needs. This is why keystroking on the computer keyboard, combined with word processing software, is recommended for text entry.

Few studies have addressed this issue although Word and Open Office editors offer input interfaces consisting of button bars associated with mathematical symbols and an "input sheet". The analysis of input activity with these tools with disabled children has revealed that the use of these bars is complex and tiring. Bertrand *et al.* [3] have conducted an introspective study of some interactive applications (Dmaths [8], MathType[9], MathMagic Lite [10], MathCast [11]) to create mathematical notation. Windsteiger [12] has designed a graphical user interface based on the possibility to have dynamic objects (sliders, menus, checkboxes, radio buttons, and more) but within the specific framework of the Mathematica programming environment. Their goal was to facilitate the use of the Mathematica programming environment. Elliott and Bilmes [13] proposed the CamMath application that allows the creation and manipulation of mathematical formulas using a speech recognition system. They reported that this input modality is useful for students or professionals with motor disabilities. In addition, the use of this modality results in fewer errors and faster input of mathematical formulas than when using a keyboard and pointing device [14]. Indeed, Anthony *et al.* have explored a multimodal input method combining handwriting and speech. Their hypothesis is that the multimodal input may enhance computer recognition and aid user cognition. They reported that novice users were indeed faster, more efficient and enjoyed the handwriting modality more than a standard keyboard and mouse mathematics interface, especially as equation length and complexity increased. Bouck et al. [15] explored a developed computer-based voice input, speech output calculator for students with visual impairments. They reported positive perceptions of the calculator, particularly noting the independence.

However, although speech recognition is a useful modality for people with motor and visual impairment, it could be on the one hand intrusive in crowded environments (schools, etc.) and on the other hand, it would have degraded performance in noisy environments.

Bertrand *et al.* [3] developed the HMK application for typing the mathematical formula to reduce the fatigue reported by the same authors during the use of applications [8–11], etc.. The HMK application was accessible for students with motor and speech impairments [4]. ElSheikh and Najdi [16] studied the use of special math hardware keyboard. Their study reported that the math keyboard supports well the goal of mathematic communication for learning mathematics.

This related work shows that some studies are looking into more efficient interaction methods, hardware solutions or input applications that are independent of editors.

3 HMK Background

3.1 Description of HandiMathKey (HMK)

HandiMathKey is an application for inputting mathematical formulae. It has been designed separately for lower and upper secondary schools. It was co-designed in collaboration with teachers and occupational therapists [3].

The HMK interface consists of three sub-keyboards (see Fig. 1):

- at the top, the Latin alphabet versus Greek sub-keyboards, which is used to enter utterances or responses of a mathematical exercise,
- in blue, the operators block and the numeric keypad common to all mathematical concepts
- and finally the mathematical concept sub-keyboard, accessible by tabs. They are four mathematical concepts (probability, trigonometry, functions and geometry).

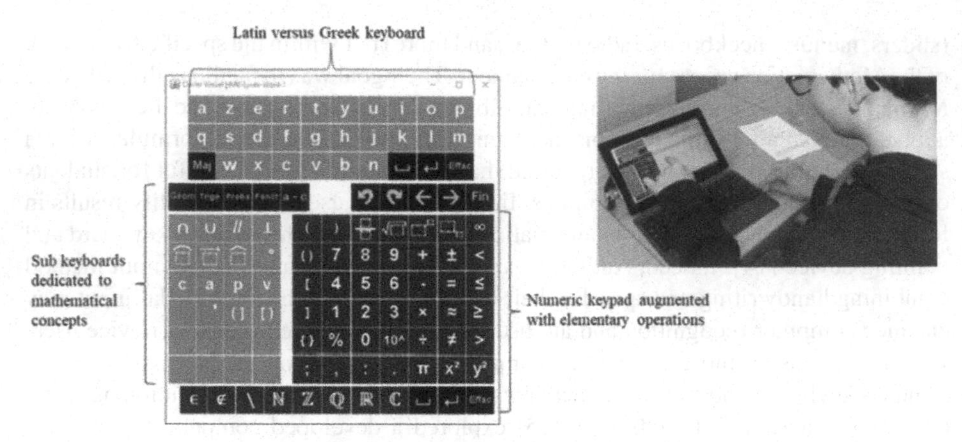

Fig. 1. HandiMathKey used by a student

3.2 Description of the HMK Multidisciplinary Study

A multidisciplinary team (a mathematics teacher, an occupational therapist and a special education assistant) led an interdisciplinary workshop to observe how students used HMK. This field study began in September 2018 at Centre for inclusive schooling Jean Lagarde of ASEI (Toulouse, France). HMK was pro-posed to a small group of students in three middle school classes (two 4th grade classes and one 5th grade class) during one school year. The study population consisted of 23 students: 19 with upper limb motor impairments, 3 with visual impairments and 1 with dyspraxia and dysgraphia. Every three weeks, the students used the HMK application during one hour of mathematics lessons. Each teacher taught both the mathematical concept and the associated mathematical symbols. The students' tasks consisted of copying mathematical formulae. Two classes used HMK with Microsoft Office, the third with Libre Office. We used written observations reports and a use log file of HMK as evaluation tools.

Observations of the three workshops [4] for each class confirmed the value of involving teams of mathematicians and occupational therapists in the HMK appropriation phase. The use of the HMK in the classes encouraged its acceptability and appropriation. No disability-related difficulties were reported. In all the classes, the students volunteered, but during the first two or three workshops they had not perceived any immediate interest in HMK. The students adopted HMK because of the easy access to mathematical symbols. However, this workshop demonstrated the need to first learn how to use the text editor to type mathematical formulae. Typing with HMK and Libre Office is similar to reading the mathematical formula, which makes it easier for students with planning and visual-spatial difficulties. Using the HMK application with the Libre Office editor made it easier to learn its commands. Since in Microsoft Office the typing order is not similar to reading, typing with HMK application has to be planned and requires more visual attention on the part of the student.

This workshop revealed a new need to use a physical keyboard for the following reasons: difficulties with pointing, use of numeric operators out of routine. The aim of Sect. 4 is to implement a user-centred design method for an HMK-D physical keyboard, based on the structuring of HMK into sub-keyboards.

4 User Centered Design

A user-centered co-design method [17] was implemented by three occupational therapists, two mathematics teachers, three computer science students and two senior researchers in human-computer interaction.

4.1 Expression of Needs

During workshops on using the HMK application with lower secondary students, teachers and occupational therapists [4], it emerged that some students needed a physical HMK keyboard to enter mathematical formulae. Some of them had difficulty using the software application HMK with a pointing device. We also observed different input strategies: some used the physical keyboard to enter alphabetic characters for operators and numbers and the HMK application for the more complex mathematical symbols. These students expressed the need to have everything on one physical keyboard for mathematical input rather than having to juggle with the two input devices.

The device we had to design had to be USB-connected to the computer. It would either complement the physical keyboard-or replace it. We will refer to this solution as HMK-D in the remainder of this article.

4.2 Design Cycles

Three co-design cycles were carried out, as described below. At each end of the design cycle, focus groups or user tests were carried out by occupational therapists and students with disabilities. These tests were carried out on several prototypes, first on very low-fidelity prototypes in the form of images, then on medium-fidelity prototypes implemented on physical keyboards and finally on high-fidelity prototypes implemented on a Stream desk.

Low Fidelity Prototypes

We planned to use two types of input device: a physical keyboard with mechanical buttons on which mathematical symbols would be associated, and a touch-sensitive tablet. The choice of the second medium was to free up the computer's field of vision so that only the text editor would be on the screen and the HMK keyboard on the entire tactile surface.

This expression of requirements led to six prototypes designed using a 3D modelling tool:

- Proposal 1: A touch-sensitive tablet with an interface for inputting mathematic symbols. Above this is a zone for typing the mathematical formula. This provides visual continuity between the formula entered and the keys. Navigation between the interface is via tabs on the left of the interface (see Fig. 2);

- Proposal 2: This is identical to proposal 1, except that navigation between the interfaces is via navigation arrows on either side of the interface (see Fig. 3);
- Proposal 3: A physical keyboard with mechanical keys containing mathematical symbols, the Greek and Latin alphabets and numeric operators. Above these keys, we have placed 3 switch keys enabling you to switch from one symbol to another for the same key (see Fig. 4); for example, the orange switch key enables you to switch from the Latin character block to the Greek symbol block.
- Proposal 4: Proposal 3 without the alphabetic keys (see Fig. 5);
- Proposal 5: Proposal 1 without the mathematical formula input area (see Fig. 6);
- Proposal 6: Proposal 2 without the mathematical formula input area (see Fig. 7).

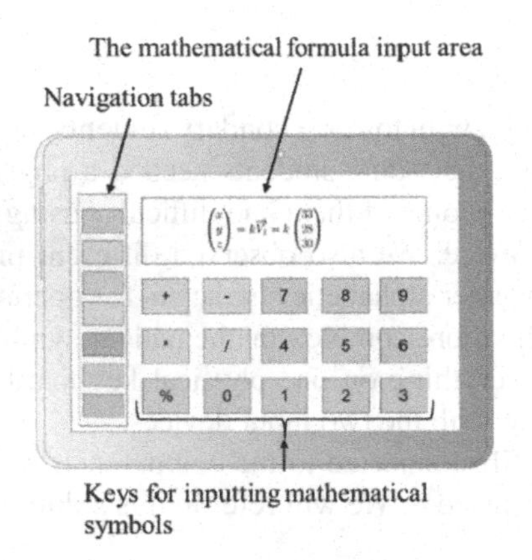

Fig. 2. Proposal 1 on touchpad.

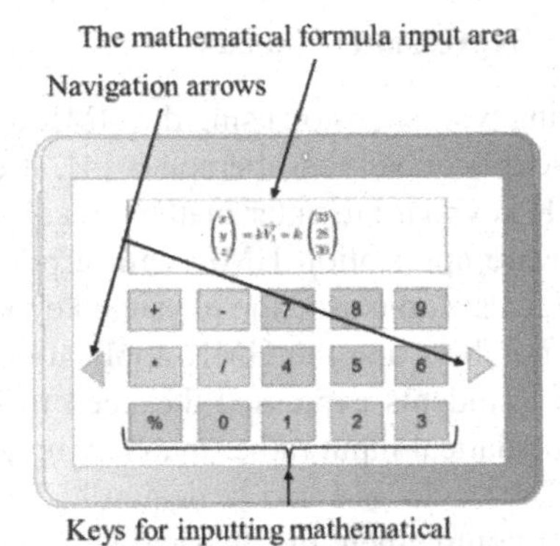

Fig. 3. Proposal 2 on touchpad

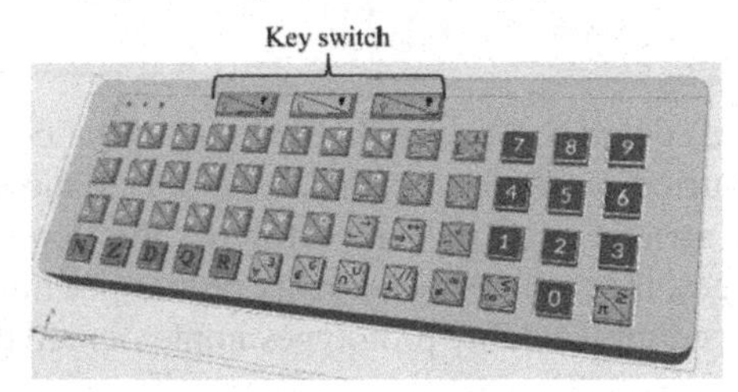

Fig. 4. Proposal 3

Fig. 5. Proposal 4

The chosen solution is proposal 3. This is the most complete solution compared with the HMK software version. Proposals 1, 2, 5 and 6 were not retained because of the high risk of occlusion during tactile interaction for children with neuromotor disorders of the upper limbs. The coexistence of the two keyboards (standard physical keyboard and solution 3 keyboard) means that the numeric keypad, for example, is redundant. In addition, the use of two large keyboards is cumbersome and generates significant motor movements. These drawbacks led us to design a prototype on an existing keyboard.

Co-Design Cycles for a Physical Keyboard

The focus group conducted during the previous cycle/step led us to the design of a

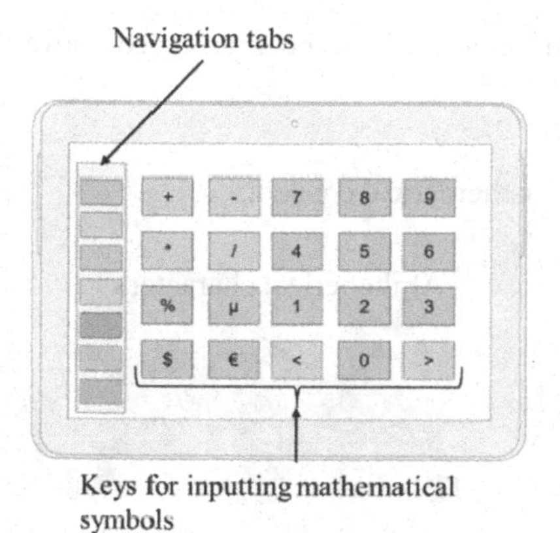

Fig. 6. Proposal 5 on touchpad

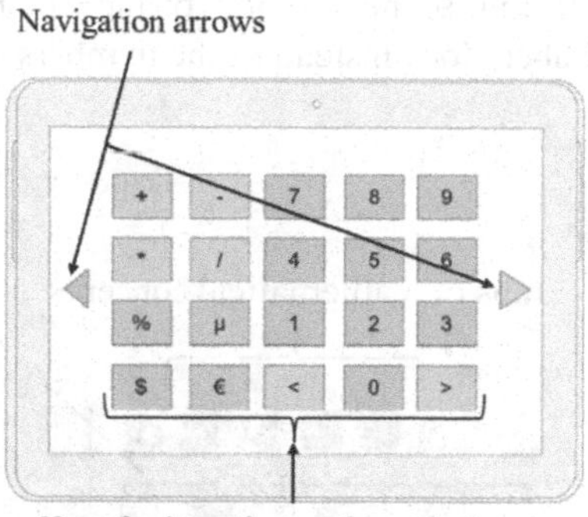

Fig. 7. Proposal 6 on touchpad

physical keyboard with mechanical keys. However, to avoid manufacturing costs and implementation time, we preferred to start with a conventional physical keyboard. In this cycle, we will successively present the mock-ups in paper format to be more representative of reality in relation to the size scale and then the physical solution of the paper mock-up.

Paper Prototypes

In Fig. 8 the static symbols (operators, numbers, symbols common to the four concepts, etc.) have been placed around the alphabet block. The numeric keypad, on the other hand, forms the dynamic part and has been replaced here by the symbols of the mathematical concept of trigonometry.

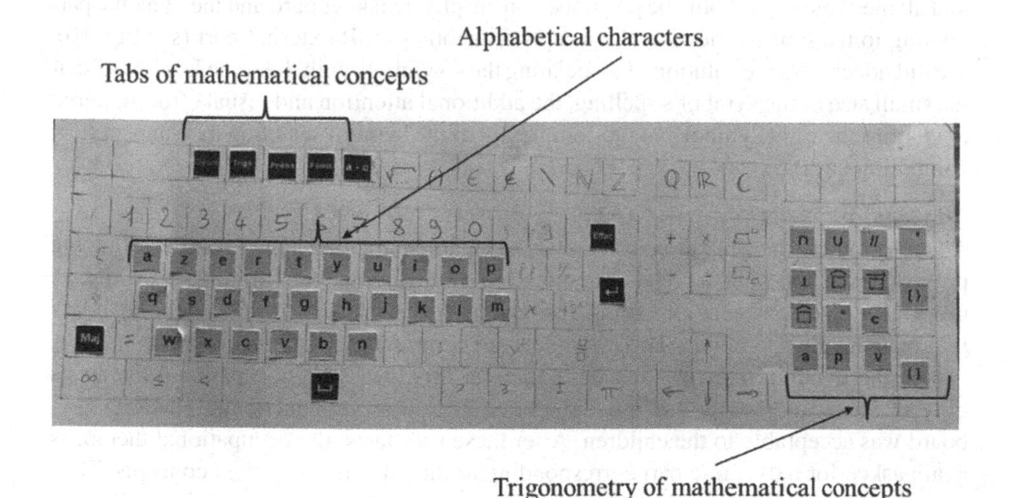

Fig. 8. Paper mock-up version 1

In Fig. 9, the symbols of the trigonometry concept have been arranged above the alphabet block instead of the numbers.

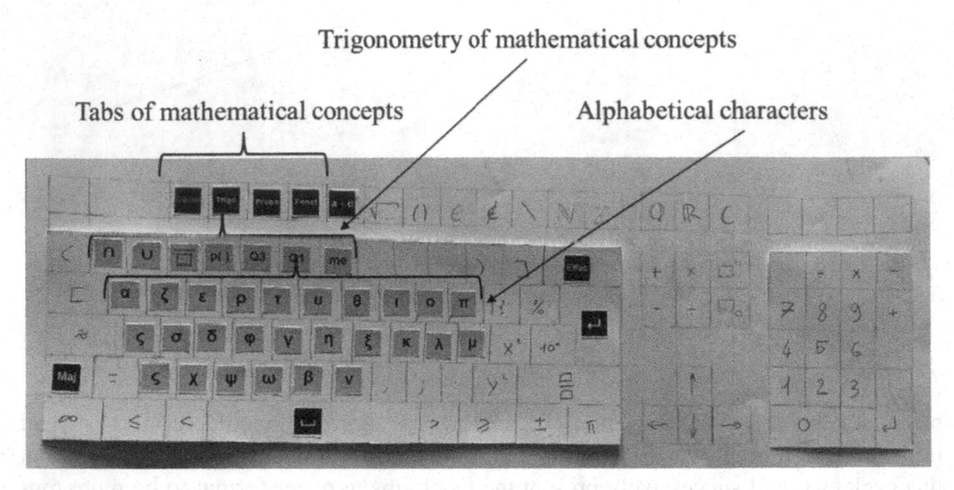

Fig. 9. Paper mock-up version 2

The most difficult part of these two mock-ups was defining the position of the 4 mathematical concepts. The geometry concept was either placed where the numeric keypad was (see Fig. 8), or where the numbers were located above the alphabetical section (see Fig. 9). This was not a good choice because of the children's acquired habits regarding the layout of the keyboard. At the end of the focus group between the occupational therapists and the human computer interaction researchers, it was suggested that all the static keys should be positioned on the physical keyboard and the dynamic part relating to the four mathematical concepts on another USB external port (see Fig. 10). We did not choose the solution of associating the 4 symbols with the same key because of the small size of the symbol's spelling, the additional attention and visual effort required to identify the right symbol and the complexity of the symbol selection mechanism (e.g. combining keys).

Physical Prototypes

A focus group with occupational therapists and mathematics teachers led to the following proposal (see Fig. 11) for the representation of mathematical formulae in white. A transducer based on Teensy version 4.1[1] converts the keys labelled white on the keyboard into mathematical symbols. These symbols are common to all mathematical concepts.

As the dynamic part was not designated at this level, the occupational therapists only evaluated the static part with students. This first version of the HMK-D keyboard was acceptable to the children. After these user tests, the occupational therapists again asked for a dynamic part corresponding to the four mathematical concepts. They strongly emphasized that the solution had to be integrated to limit the number of devices (ergonomic improvements: cluttering up the student's desk and cumbersome installation

[1] https://www.pjrc.com/teensy/.

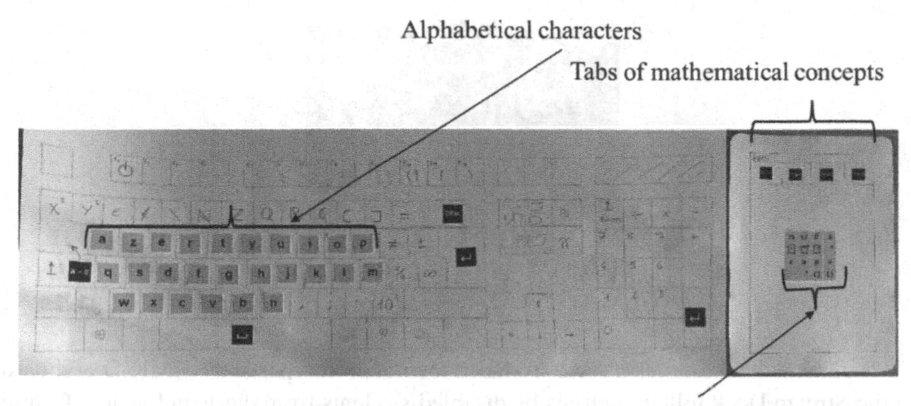

Fig. 10. Paper mock-up version 3.

Fig. 11. Labelled physical keyboard

of the two devices, etc.), fun and playful. We explored the technologies used in video games and multimedia. They also said that the characteristics (color or background) of the buttons should change according to the mathematical concept.

Stream Deck Prototype

We selected the stream deck[2] of the company Elgato© composed of 32 fully customizable LCD (Liquid Crystal Display) keys (see Fig. 12). For each keys it is possible to design its content (textual, sound, running a media, visual and sound feedback…). The first version of HMK-D on the Stream Deck has been designed as closely as possible to the sub-keyboard structure of the HMK software application (see Fig. 1). The tests were carried out using Microsoft.

[2] https://www.elgato.com/us/en/s/welcome-to-stream-deck.

Fig. 12. Stream Deck

Together with the therapists, we produced several prototypes of the HMK-D keyboard on the Stream Deck following trials by disabled students from the Jean Lagarde Centre for Inclusive Education in secondary school (fifth and fourth) and high school (from seconde to terminale).

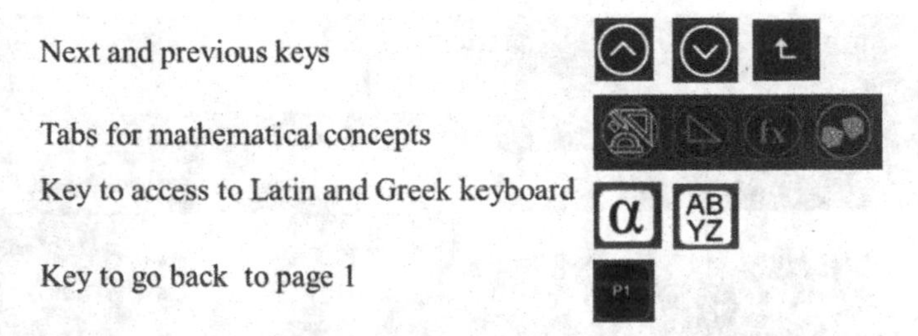

Fig. 13. Page change keys

A page corresponds to a Stream Deck interface change. Pages are navigated by means of the buttons illustrated in Fig. 13.

We present below the changes per page that we have made to HMK-D from the first version that was tested (noted 'a' in the figures) to the latest version (noted 'b' in the figures). These changes were introduced following the consensus reached at focus group meetings between teachers, researchers and occupational therapists. One of the changes from page two was to add a button called P1 for returning to page one, to facilitate rapid access to operators.

Page 1 consisted of the numeric keypad, operators and functionalities (see Fig. 14a). User tests identified the need to add the membership symbols, the alphabetic keyboard access key and the equations key (see Fig. 14b). This layout makes it easier to enter basic mathematical formulas.

Page 2 has undergone a number of changes. In fact, this first version (see Fig. 15a) required a lot of navigating through the pages due to the incorrect structuring of HMK-D and the arrangement of symbols within the pages, as revealed during testing with children. So, in the latest version (see Fig. 15b), we prefer to integrate the common functions (fraction, square root, etc.) with all the mathematical concepts by integrating the arrows for navigating formulas, spacing, the equal key and parenthesis.

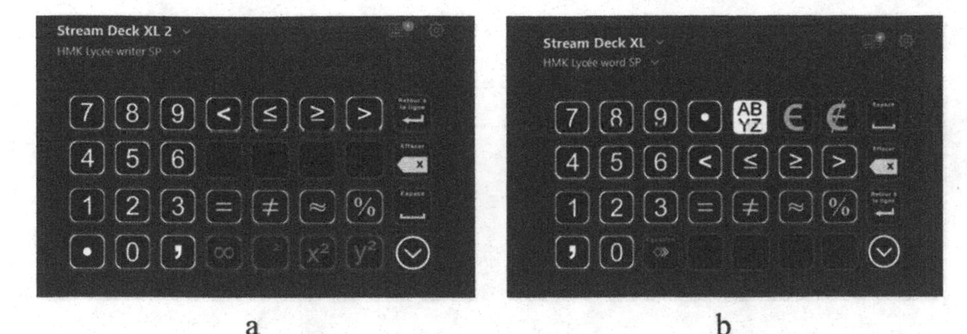

Fig. 14. Page 1

Fig. 15. Page 2

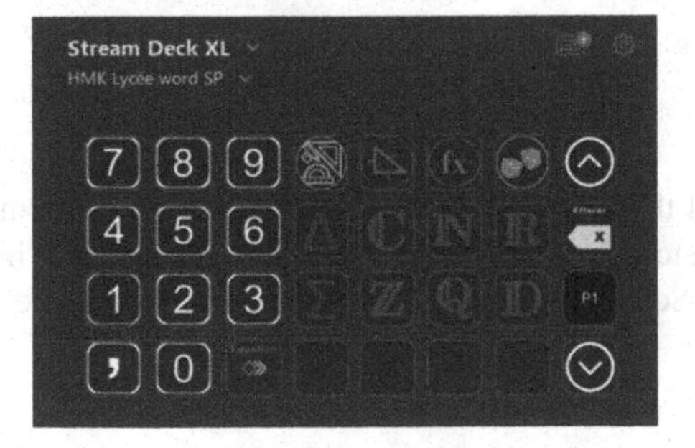

Fig. 16. Page 3

No changes have been made to page 3 (see Fig. 16). However, the pages of the mathematical concepts have been modified by adding navigation arrows in the formula to simplify its input. For example, on the page related to the mathematical function concept, the navigation arrows have been added to the bottom right-hand section (see Fig. 17b).

Page 4 was initially used to navigate mathematical formulas and to add the rest of the symbols (see Fig. 18a). The modifications made concerned the addition of the symbols

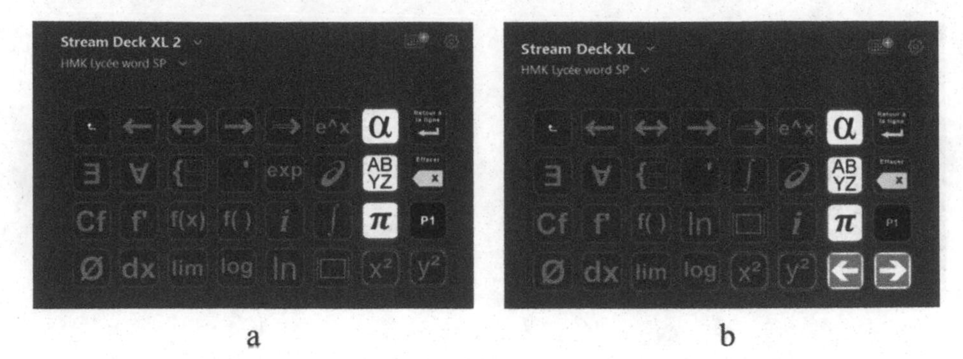

Fig. 17. Page function concept

“;” and the quotation mark, and a rearrangement of the operators. The navigation arrow were not considered useful on this page.

Fig. 18. Page 4

The occupational therapists had the HMK-D solution implemented on the Stream Desk empirically tested by 9 students of middle school and high school from the Centre for Inclusive Schools Jean Lagarde. This user experience was done during the rehabilitation session.

5 Preliminary Results and Perspective

8 students (5 in secondary school and 3 in high school) took part in tests using the HMK adaptation on the Stream Deck during the occupational therapy session at 7 students have a motor disability and one has a neurodevelopmental disorder. 3 of them have associated learning disorders and two others have visual-spatial disorders. All 8 used a physical azerty keyboard. 7 of them had already used the HMK software version [3]. For these user tests we used a Thing Aloud type method [18] as the students expressed their feelings and comments verbally. The HMK version designed for the Stream Deck was generally accepted by the students. They also appreciated the visual feedback following

the press of a key, the absence of noise unlike the HMK software version where click noise is present all the time and the possibility of tilting the Stream Deck which facilitates the spatial layout of the student's working environment (see Fig. 19).

Fig. 19. Students using HMK-D on the Stream Deck

The verbatims collected attest to the degree of satisfaction of the students: "*It's too good. I was tired with HMK and now it's better*", "*It's easy to learn*", grade 4 student. "*It's very good and better than HMK*", students from second. "*It's satisfying to press*", another grade 4 student. "*It's good and practical*", final year student. Stream Deck is also fun. "*It's more fun and easier*", a grade 4 student who is a regular user of the HMK application. Some students expressed an interest in using it in class. "*I'd prefer Stream Deck HMK-D for the classroom*", grade 4 student. "*I'm motivated to learn maths*", grade 4 student.

The Stream Deck's multimedia features enabled the HMK-D application to be designed in a more ergonomic, attractive and customisable way, and it was well accepted by the students during the series of pre-tests.

The first feedback from HMK-D users has been very promising. However, there are still improvements to be considered: the possibility of configuring the backlighting to take account of glare (students with visual-spatial disorders); the integration of an azerty keyboard rather than an alphabetical keyboard on the page for text input; the addition of character sound associated to the key. We also propose to make better use of the user profile function available in the Stream Deck environment to offer several profiles depending on the impairment of the students.

A multidisciplinary longitudinal study over the school year (empirical observations, HMK-D usage logs, usability questionnaires) on secondary school classes is planned for the start of the 2023–2024 school year on a population of pupils with motor impairment with or without associated other disorders.

6 Conclusion

We used a user-centered design method to design the HMK-D mathematical input solution for secondary school students with impairment at Centre for inclusive schooling Jean Lagarde of ASEI. This co-design was carried out with occupational therapists, mathematics teachers and researchers and students in human-computer interaction.

Several HMK-D co-design cycles were implemented. Cycle 2 proposed a physical keyboard, but this was not chosen because of the size of the solution due to the addition of an extra device to implement the sub-keyboards corresponding to the mathematical concepts. We opted for the Stream Deck device because of its multimedia features and its appeal to young students. Initial feedback shows that HMK-D is highly accepted and accessible for mathematical input by students with impairments. A longitudinal study of the usability and acceptability of HMK-D is planned for the 2023–2024 school year.

Acknowledgement. We would particularly like to thank the Centre for inclusive schooling Jean Lagarde of ASEI f(Toulouse, France) or enabling us to implement the co-design method as part of the Hand'Innov agreement between the IRIT laboratory and ASEI. We would also like to thank all the students with impairment who took part in the first user experiments with HMK-D.

References

1. Benoit, H., Sagot, J.: L'apport des aides techniques à la scolarisation des élèves handicapés. La nouvelle revue de l'adaptation et de la scolarisation **3**, 19–26 (2008)
2. Polacek, O., Sporka, A.J., Slavik, P.: Text input for motor-impaired people. Univ. Access Inf. Soc. **16**, 51–72 (2017). https://doi.org/10.1007/s10209-015-0433-0

3. Bertrand, E., Sauzin, D., Vella, F., Dubus, N., Vigouroux, N.: HandiMathKey: mathematical keyboard for disabled person. In: Miesenberger, K., Bühler, C., Penaz, P. (eds.) ICCHP 2016. LNCS, vol. 9759, pp. 487–494. Springer, Cham (2016). https://doi.org/10.1007/978-3-319-41267-2_68
4. Vella, F., et al.: Multi-disciplinary experience feedback on the use of the HandiMathKey keyboard in a middle school. Lecture Notes in Computer Science book series (LNCS), 12376, pp.393–400, 2020, ICCHP 2020: International Conference on Computers Helping People with Special Needs, 978-3-030-58795-6. ⟨https://doi.org/10.1007/978-3-030-58796-3_46⟩. ⟨hal-03013160⟩. https://hal.archives-ouvertes.fr/hal-03013160
5. Akpan, J.-P., Beard, L.A.: Assistive technology and mathematics education. Univ. J. Educ. Res. **2**(3), 219–222 (2014). http://www.hrpub.org. https://doi.org/10.13189/ujer.2014.020303
6. Smith, G.: Student attrition in mathematics e-learning. Australas. J. Educ. Technol. **3**, 323–334 (2005)
7. Paz-Villagrán, V., Gilhodes, J.-C., Velay, J.-L.: Les enfants dysgraphiques sont-ils réellement plus lents que les autres? Développements **13**, 38–44 (2012). https://doi.org/10.3917/devel.013.0038. https://www.cairn-int.info/revue-developpements-2012-4-page-38.htm
8. https://www.dmaths.org
9. http://www.dessci.com/en/products/mathtype
10. http://www.mathmagic.com
11. http://mathcast.sourceforge.net/home.html
12. Windsteiger, W.: Theorema 2.0: a graphical user interface for a mathematical assistant system. arXiv preprint arXiv:1307.1945 (2013)
13. Elliott, C., Bilmes, J.: Computer based mathematics using continuous speech recognition. Striking a C[h]ord: Vocal Interaction in Assistive Technologies, Games and More (2007)
14. Anthony, L., Yang, J., Koedinger, K.R.: Evaluation of multimodal input for entering mathematical equations on the computer. In: CHI 2005 Extended Abstracts on Human Factors in Computing Systems, pp. 1184–1187 (2005)
15. Bouck, E.C., Flanagan, S., Joshi, G.S., Sheikh, W., Schleppenbach, D.: Speaking math—a voice input, speech output calculator for students with visual impairments. J. Spec. Educ. Technol. **26**(4), 1–14 (2011)
16. ElSheikh, R.M., Najdi, S.D.: Math keyboard symbols and its effect in improving communication in math virtual classes. Int. J. Inf. Educ. Technol. **3**(6) (2013)
17. ISO (2019, ISO 9241-210:2019, Ergonomics of human-system interaction — Part 210: Human-centred design for interactive systems ISO 9241-210:2019
18. Lewis, C.: Using the "thinking-aloud" method in cognitive interface design. IBM TJ Watson Research Center, Yorktown Heights (1982)

Bridging the Communication Rate Gap: Enhancing Text Input for Augmentative and Alternative Communication (AAC)

Hussein Yusufali(✉), Stefan Goetze, and Roger K. Moore

Department of Computer Science, The University of Sheffield, Sheffield, UK
{hsayusufali1,s.goetze,r.k.moore}@sheffield.ac.uk

Abstract. Over 70 million people worldwide face communication difficulties, with many using augmentative and alternative communication (AAC) technology. While AAC systems help improve interaction, the communication rate gap between individuals with and without speaking difficulties remains significant, and this has led to a low sustained use of AAC systems. The study reported here combines human computer interaction (HCI) and language modelling techniques to improve the ease of use, user satisfaction, and communication rates of AAC technology in open-domain interactions. A text input interface utilising word prediction based on BERT and RoBERTa language models has been investigated with a view to improving communication rates. Three interface layouts were implemented, and it was found that a radial configuration was the most efficient. RoBERTa models fine-tuned on conversational AAC corpora led to the highest communication rates of 25.75 words per minute (WPM), with alphabetical ordering preferred over probabilistic ordering. It was also found that training on conversational corpora such as TV and Reddit outperformed training based on generic corpora such as COCA or Wikipedia. Hence, it is concluded that the limited availability of large-scale conversational AAC corpora represent a key challenge for improving communication rates and robust AAC systems.

Index Terms: Text Input Prediction, Language Modelling, Augmentative and Alternative Communication (AAC), Speech Synthesis

1 Introduction

Speech impairments can have significant inhibiting effects on affected individuals. It is estimated that over 0.5% of the UK population and 7.5 million individuals in the United States have a specific type of vocal impairment [14,36]. The effects of speech impairments can vary significantly depending on the severity and extent of the individual's impairment. The degree of impairment determines whether an individual may benefit from an AAC device. The primary objective of the AAC strategy or device is to assist or facilitate a user's communication ability [41,42].

An inhibiting factor in the adoption of AAC is the significant gap in communication rates between standard spoken conversational interaction and that

Q. Gao et al. (Eds.): HCII 2023, LNCS 14055, pp. 434–452, 2023.
https://doi.org/10.1007/978-3-031-48041-6_29

experienced by AAC device users [8]. AAC devices have been shown to reach communication rates of approximately 10–16 WPM whereas conversational rates can surpass 140–150 WPM [38,46]. Communication rates measure the rate at which individuals exchange information during an interaction; whereas conversational rates indicate the pace of a conversation between two or more individuals which incorporates turn-taking and the flow of a dialogue. The significant gap between these two rates restricts individuals with communication difficulties from effective participation in multiparty interactions with minimal delay [22]. Overall, current assistive technologies cannot enable AAC users to participate successfully in multiparty interactions due to large time delays and a lack of expressivity, naturalness and personalisation [17,46,48].

Prediction and predictive technologies are integral to the development of AAC devices, as these techniques have the potential to decrease the communication gap between participants by using text or character predictions (as in Dasher [52], a graphical user interface (GUI) based system presenting animated character predictions as an innovative text input interface at the time of its publication). However, for these techniques to be effective, the phrase, word or character prediction mechanisms must be accurate and have a minimal delay to ensure that the device is not detrimental towards the user or interaction [24,44]. If prediction mechanisms are not accurate, they can amplify the communication gap by increasing delays in the exchange of information. Nevertheless, AAC users widely use Pictureboards, Pragmatic Organisation Dynamic Display (PODD), speech generation AAC devices and predictive systems such as *Predictable*[1] [22,49], depending on an individual's unique communication abilities. The implementation of advanced text prediction techniques such as language modelling, topic modelling, using semantic or syntactic information and conversational context has significantly improved AAC devices [8,16,22,27].

In the design and evaluation of user interfaces, including assistive technologies like AAC devices, HCI plays a critical role. User modelling is essential to determine the efficacy of a system that is aimed at users with a diverse range of abilities and circumstances. Various models are utilised to understand how individuals interact with interfaces and systems, and these generate effective design and evaluation justifications for developing systems, specifically AAC systems. For instance, 'task analysis models' have been used to capture a user's ability to achieve a specific task outside of a computer system or interface [1]. In particular, AAC system designs are able to benefit from HCI modelling as they can inform the development of personalised and effective AAC strategies and devices. Furthermore, HCI modelling can identify potential barriers to device usage as well as be used to design interfaces that are intuitive and accessible to users with different requirements [1]. Indeed, it has been shown that by considering the needs and abilities of diverse users, AAC designers can create more inclusive and effective assistive technologies [2]. However, despite these advances, there is still a need for improved prediction-based interfaces for AAC users.

[1] https://therapy-box.co.uk/predictable - Available on June 2023.

This paper addresses these issues and is structured as follows: Sect. 2, discusses modelling techniques for user interface design. Section 3 describes the experimental method and interface designs used in modelling user behaviour for text prediction interfaces and the results are presented in Sect. 4. Section 5 concludes the paper. The main contributions of this paper are four-fold:

1. A general model for user predictive text-entry has been introduced based on established HCI laws.
2. Three word-prediction selection interfaces for text input have been modelled.
3. Choice vs. human response time (HRT) has been investigated for word selection, concluding in the number of optimal choices presented to the user in a text-input interface.
4. Fine-tuning large language models (LLM) for increased text-entry for AAC devices have been examined, with conversational data and testing text input user interfaces across four communication scenarios.

2 User Behaviour Modelling and Text Prediction for Increased Text Entry

Within the field of HCI there are specific models relating to how users interact with movements within an interface and how users interact with choices provided. Models such as 'Fitts' Law' [15] and the 'Hick Hymen Law' [21] provide designers with predictability information about user behaviour, which can be used to justify design decisions and enhance the user experience [45]. Additionally, predictive models allow for the calculation of metrics in an analytical manner [35], eliminating the need for time-consuming and resource-intensive experimentation.

HCI is intrinsically linked to human-motor movement. Therefore, when designing interfaces and systems, models of movement can be utilised to inform the best approaches in the design of systems. An early example of such an HCI modelling is the keystroke level model (KLM) [5]. KLM predicts the approximate time it takes the user to perform a specific task using a system, assuming that there are no errors. However, users differ significantly, and some factors have more impact on performance than others [30]. For example, users have different ways to use their hands and motor skills. The topic of bimanual (the use of both hands simultaneously) and laterality (preference of the use of one hand) has been extensively studied with Guiard's model [18] being one of the most notable. The examination of Guiard's model is critical, due to enhancing user experience and developing efficient interfaces. This model proposes a framework for understanding preferred and non-preferred hand movements. Guiard's model proposes that individuals have a preferred hand (usually the dominant hand) that performs tasks that require precision and fine motor control, and a non-preferred hand that performs tasks that require less precision and forceful movements. This understanding is important when analysing the efficacy of user interfaces, particularly for tasks involving fine motor movements.

Furthermore, other factors are also critical, such as the variety of goals that can be achieved with a system and the ability to recall a specific function after a period of not using a system [23]. There are also associated factors such as user fatigue, concentration, and satisfaction [30].

2.1 Interface Modelling

Fitts' Law: Fitts' law [15] states that the time taken for a cursor to move in a user interface is directly related to the area and width of the target on the interface. Fitts defines an Index of Difficulty (ID) as a function of the Euclidean distance D between two points on the screen $\mathbf{p}_1 = [x_1, y_1]^T$ and $\mathbf{p}_2 = [x_2, y_2]^T$ and width W of a target.

$$\mathrm{ID} = \log_2\left(\frac{2D}{W}\right) \tag{1}$$

The ID is a measure of complexity or difficulty for a movement in an interface, such as clicking or selecting a widget via using a cursor or on a touchscreen. The ID is directly related to a prediction of a Movement Time (MT) as follows:

$$\mathrm{MT} = a + b \cdot \mathrm{ID} \equiv a + b \cdot \log_2\left(\frac{2D}{W}\right) \tag{2}$$

The constants a and b reflect the efficiency of the interfaces and systems, in particular pointing and mouse cursor movements. They are constants that are determined empirically via regression analysis.

Fitts' Law (and its variants) have become ubiquitous in predicting the performance and difficulty of movement in interface designs; it is one of the most widely adopted models for human performance prediction and behaviour modelling [19,45].

Hick Hymens Law: A second model ubiquitous in HCI is the Hick-Hymens law [21,45], which states that the reaction time of an individual T will be logarithmically correlated to the number of choices n presented to the user. This model was investigated to determine the optimal number of words presented to a user in a text-input word prediction interface as follows:

$$T = b \cdot \log_2(n+1) \tag{3}$$

The constant b is determined empirically via experimentation. There are several time latencies related to human motor and cognitive behaviour that must be examined to justify design interfaces and layouts.

2.2 Text Entry Speeds

A significant limiting factor for the sustained use of AAC devices is the difference between text input rates and spoken conversational rates. The QWERTY keyboard has become predominant in text-entry layout interfaces, both in physical text-entry and touchscreen interfaces [33]. Text-entry rates for a typical QWERTY keyboard can be predicted using a variation of Fitts' law (the Shannon formulation [32]) as follows:

$$\mathrm{MT}_{i,j} = a + b \cdot \log_2 \left(\frac{D_{i,j}}{W} + 1 \right) \tag{4}$$

In (4), i and j are the indices of the separate keys and $D_{i,j}$ is the distance between key i and key j. However, this model does not take into account if a key is repeated. This was investigated in [33] which predicted a text input rate of 30.1 WPM for a typical soft QWERTY keyboard. This model is in accordance with studies [26] representing entry speeds aligning to the predictive model established by [33].

Spoken conversational rates and text entry rates are considerably different [3]. There are also consequential differences between spoken and written language [6]. This was investigated by [29] establishing that the highest text entry rates that can be achieved are not only dependent on the text entry method, but also on the user transferring thoughts and information to written text. An 'inviscid' text-entry rate of 67 WPM was determined by [29], establishing a grand goal for text entry input methods. Table 1 summarises text entry rates reported in the state-of-the-art literature and the respective references.

Table 1. Comparison of text entry rates with varying text input methods.

Text Entry Method	WPM Rate	Reference
Inviscid Upper Bound	67	[29]
QWERTY Physical Keyboard	51.56 ± 20.2	[13]
QWERTY Touchscreen Keyboard	45	[26]
Gesture Keyboards (Swype)	45	[25]
Dasher	17.26 (Upper Bound)	[52]

2.3 Language Modelling

Statistical language modelling techniques are utilised in the predictive text input to increase communication rates [7]. These techniques are thus essential for text input into AAC devices. Prediction mechanisms can be character-based, word-based, or phrase-based (multiple words), demonstrated by the Dasher interface [52], where character predictions are presented to the user in a streaming interface with low latency. Prediction with gesture keyboards such as Swype (virtual touch-based keyboard allowing users to join characters by a sliding gesture) [25] and phrase prediction techniques such as [27] have demonstrated the efficacy of language modelling techniques for AAC devices. LLMs have the ability to generate text based on user input with the incorporation of contextual history and semantic correctness. LLMs, such as transformer-based models, Bidirectional Encoder Representations from Transformers (BERT) [12,43] and Robustly Optimized BERT (RoBERTa) [55] can be fine-tuned (adapting the pre-trained model to a specific task) for specifically the use case in conversational open-domain AAC devices (cf. Sect. 3.3 for corpora used for fine-tuning). These language models are chosen because they have been shown to achieve high accuracy on language generation tasks and to score high on commonly used metrics such as General Language Understanding Evaluation (GLUE) and BiLingual Evaluation Understudy (BLEU) [39,51]. RoBERTa has proven to be effective in language generation due to dynamic masking in model training.

To increase text entry rates and decrease the communication gap between AAC users and their conversational partners, predictive language modelling is utilised in this work (cf. Sect. 3.3), together with various input methods and interfaces (cf. Sect. 3.1).

The Process of Predictive Text Input: There are associated time latencies involved when utilising a system. To optimise a system, a functional component analysis can be conducted to optimise the controllable parameters [38]. A functional structure, i.e. decomposition of the components of the system into sub-functions to analyse the system either as a whole or at the component level, can be critical in analysing certain time latencies and shortcomings of a system. Figure 1 visualises a general overview of the functional flow and associated time components in a predictive text input system, which can be summed to equal the time per utterance (i.e. a sequence of written text):

- T_{Type}: time to enter the initial word and type characters for a word, if a word prediction is not selected by the user
- $T_{\text{Prediction}}$: time necessary for language model to predict the next word
- T_{Look}: time for the user to scan the search space of word predictions
- T_{React}: decision time of the user to decide if the word predictions are satisfactory
- T_{Select}: time for the user to select a word prediction or revert to typing.

This functional system flowchart, when used in conjunction with envelope analysis [28], i.e. analysing each sub-component with a user-centric approach, can be instrumental in improving the efficiency and effectiveness of system designs. Please note, that timings in Fig. 1 do not correspond to the time T in (3).

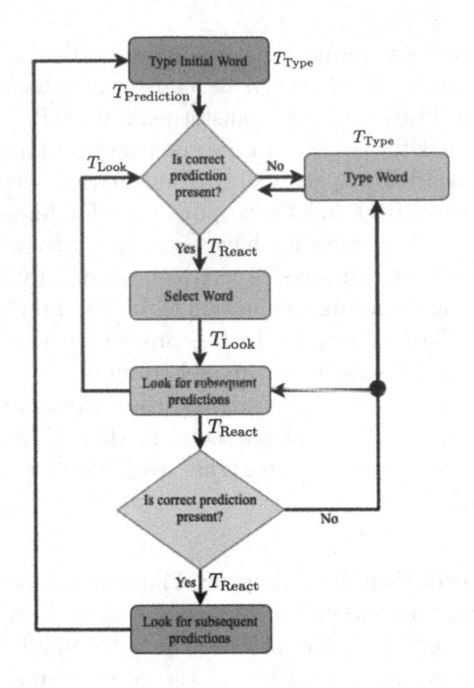

Fig. 1. Functional system flowchart for the developed interface to select predictive words, including time delays introduced by system and user.

3 Experimental Method

Informal experiments were conducted by the main author, being an AAC user for many years.

3.1 Fitts' Law Modelling and Experimentation of User Interfaces

To model the impact of layout changes, Fitts' law [15] in (2) is utilised and tested to predict the time of movements, i.e. the time required to move to a target position on an interface, performed by users during use of the interface. Three interfaces are tested with differing button sizes, and distance lengths across the screen which influence the ID.

amazing	chilly	fantastic	great	nice
awesome	cloudy	fine	horrible	ok
awful		gloomy	hot	perfect
bad	cool	good	humid	pleasant
beautiful	crazy	gorgeous	lovely	raining

(a) Alphabetical Ordering

nice	cold	awesome	gorgeous	horrible
beautiful	hot	fine	pleasant	terrible
great	cool	bad	cloudy	improving
good	wonderful	sunny	perfect	awful
lovely	warm	amazing	chilly	gloomy

(b) Probabilistic Ordering

Fig. 2. Ordering strategies: Predicted words are presented to the user either in (a) alphabetical or (b) probabilistic order, i.e. sorted based on the confidence score of the LLM text prediction model. The word predictions are generated after the phrase 'The weather is' has been entered.

Further to this, two different ordering strategies of the predicted words are investigated as visualised in Fig. 2: (i) alphabetical ordering (cf. Fig. 2a) and (ii) ordering via probabilities of the generated words (cf. Fig. 2b). The probabilities are the confidence scores (likelihood of this word prediction following the utterance) which are generated together with the word predictions and which can be interpreted as confidence scores of the prediction.

Figure 3 shows the three layouts under test. The list layout interface in Fig. 3a was chosen as this is similar to the list style of the Dasher Keyboard [52], a grid layout (cf. Fig. 3b), since it is similar to the auto-predict selection above a QWERTY keyboard (QWERTY) on a smartphone, with a similar width to a smartphone auto-predict interface, and the radial interface (cf. Fig. 3c), since it is similar to a hexagonal keyboard, such as e.g. the TYPEHEX or Hookes Keyboard [40,54]. Coefficients a and b in (2) are determined by regression analysis with x and y values empirically measured, where x and y are scalar coordinates on the Fitts' plots (Movement Time (MT) vs ID) which are empirically measured, correlated to the distances moved by the user in the interfaces.

Additionally for accurate measurements, the cursor origin must remain constant for each distance measurement when empirically evaluating an interface. For each interface layout in Fig. 3, three cursor origin positions were tested; top of the interface, middle centre and bottom centre of the interfaces. The purpose of investigating the origin cursor positions was to determine which cursor origin reduces the ID in (2) for the user and, thereby, increase efficiency. Cursor movements can vary between different users due to dexterity, fine-motor movement and also the concentration of the user. However, Fitts' law provides a foundation for the predictability and efficacy of user interfaces, which is utilised to determine an efficient interface for predictive text input.

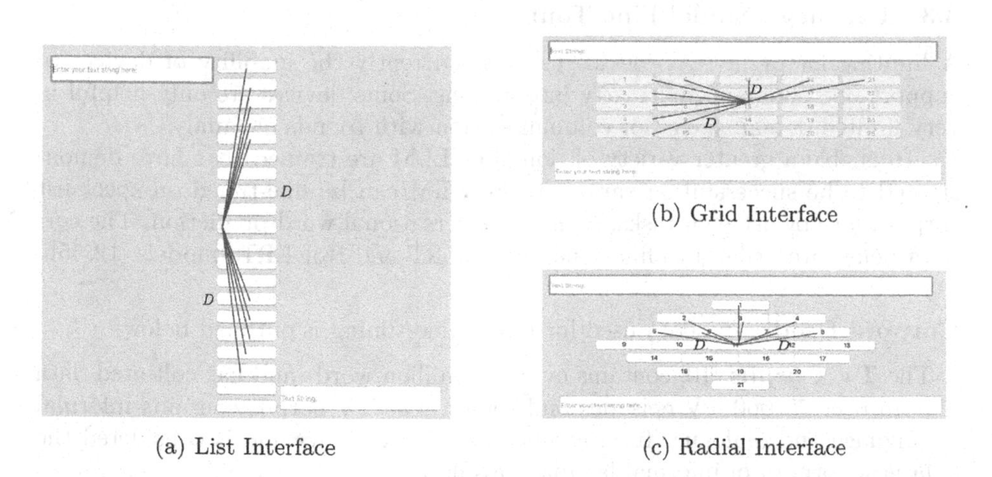

(a) List Interface

(b) Grid Interface

(c) Radial Interface

Fig. 3. GUI Interface Designs.

3.2 Number of Choice of Words vs Human Response Time

To optimise the time latencies for text entry, controllable parameters in the system can be refined. An initial experiment is conducted to investigate the relationship between the number of word choices and the HRT. Users were provided with lists containing varying numbers of words, denoted as n in (3), and their reaction times to select a specific word from the list were measured. To ensure accurate time measurements and to minimise human errors, an automatic timer was used.

Hick-Hymen's law according to (3) is commonly used to investigate the choice paradigm. However, this experiment aimed to investigate word choices given a list, which is not covered by the choice paradigm. Therefore, the experiment focused on this aspect. The word *"the"* was chosen as the target word for selection from the list. *"The"* was chosen as it is a common English word that is easily comprehensible to all users. Furthermore, the experiment aimed to validate and predict the optimal number of words to present to the user for predictive text input. Human response times were measured with different numbers of words presented to the user. Random word lists were created, lists consisting of common English words and users were instructed to select the word *"the"* from each list. Each trial, corresponding to each list size, was repeated 3 times to ensure fairness and accuracy. The lists increased in length by 5 word increments.

To accurately represent human response times for word selection, factors and environmental conditions such as screen size, brightness, location, mouse or cursor speeds, font and button sizes and text colour were kept constant. Additionally, users were given practice instructions and a warm-up period of 3 minutes enabling them to familiarise themselves with the task.

3.3 Language Model Fine-Tuning

A limiting factor in AAC device usage is currently the inability of devices to support open-domain multiparty interactions. Some devices are only helpful in very limited domains, e.g. for communication with friends or family.

To enable a greater variety of domains, LLM are trained that have demonstrated to be successful on various tasks. LLM can be fine-tuned on specialist corpora for downstream tasks, such as conversational word prediction. The corpora below are utilised to fine-tune both BERT and RoBERTa models [12,55].

Corpora Used: The data used for model fine-tuning is outlined below:

- The **TV Corpus** [10] contains over 325 million words and has collected data from over 75,000 TV episodes and shows. The TV corpus contains informal language and dialogues from a collection of TV shows and is considered the largest corpora of informal language available.
- The **Switchboard Corpus** [4] consists of spontaneous telephone conversations between American-English speakers of over 300 h of recorded and transcribed multi-gender and multi-topic speech. There is a total of 2300 conversations covering 70 topics.

- **The Corpus of Contemporary American English (COCA)** [9] is a widely used American English corpus and contains over one billion words, spanning eight genres: fiction, popular magazines, newspapers, academic texts, TV, Movies and blogs.
- The **Wikipedia Corpus** [11] is one of the largest corpora based upon a large Wikipedia collection from 2014. The corpus contains over 2 billion words, covering a variety of genres and topics, together with over 4.4 million pages of data.
- The **AAC Corpus** [50] is one of a limited amount of specialist AAC corpora available for AAC applications, especially to train large-scale models on. The corpus consists of imagined sentences and responses from users who imagine themselves using AAC devices. The AAC corpus is small in size, with approx. 6,000 messages from 289 unique workers on glsAMT. However, it is considered to be beneficial when training language models for specific AAC applications.
- The **Reddit Corpus** [34] is a collection of cross-domain text, scraped from Reddit and containing over 256M conversational threads across a variety of unspecified domains, ranging from 2015–2018.
- The **Daily Dialog** [31] corpus is a smaller, fully annotated corpus utilised for multi-turn dialogues, with 13k dialogues and the average speaker turns per dialogue of 7.9 turns. It is an open-domain corpus with utterances being more formal than other widely used corpora, such as Twitter or Reddit corpora.

The training times for fine-tuning times vary depending on the size of the training data, between 4 hours to 7 days on 2 NVIDIA V100 GPU's (each with 32 GB RAM). Table 2 summarises parameters for the model adaptation. The learning rate, weight decay and Adam weights were utilised as the same as fine-tuning BERT or RoBERTa models in the original tuning parameters.

Table 2. Hyperparameter values used during fine-tuning of LLMs.

Hyperparameter	Value	Hyperparameter	Value
Learning Rate	$5 \cdot 10^{-5}$	Adam Beta_1	0.9
Batch Size	16	Adam Beta_2	0.99
Number of Training Epochs	50	Adam Epsilon	$1 \cdot 10^{-8}$
Weight Decay	0.01		

3.4 Interface Testing for AAC Scenarios

An informal study was conducted to evaluate the interfaces together with the fine-tuned language models by the first author of this work. To mimic close-to-realistic situations, four communication scenarios and tasks were defined: a scripted dialogue for ordering coffee, a half-scripted dialogue where topics were provided but the responses were not scripted an open-ended question, and a picture description.

Task 1 - Scripted Dialogue

- **AU:** *A coffee with cream and sugar, please.*
- **CP:** *Which size?*
- **AU:** *A small, please. Thanks.*
- **CP:** *Here you are.*
- **AU:** *I think I have some change somewhere; let me check.*
- **CP:** *Thanks.*
- **AU:** *Thanks, have a nice day.*

AU is the AAC user utilising the interface and responding to the utterances given by CP, the conversational participant.

Task 2 - Half Prompted Dialogue
Task 2 aims to simulate a workplace scenario where the participants are asked to engage in small talk. They are prompted to start with a general greeting, sustain the conversation, transition to discussing an after-work event and conclude by talking about their workload. This dialogue intends to total 9 utterances in the conversation, between both the AAC user and conversation participant and mimic a realistic situation.

Task 3 - Open-Ended Scenario
Task 3 aims to test the accuracy and capability of the language model by instructing the participant to utilise the interface, the participant is instructed to answer the following question with the interface: *Please describe a weekend when you have had fun memories.*

Task 4 - Picture Description
Task 4 is primarily aimed at testing the open-domain capabilities of the fine-tuned language models, as well as assessing their ability to construct long sentences effectively. To accomplish this, an image depicting a cat trapped on a tree [20,37] was used. This was chosen due since it allows for the description of various topics and is commonly used in testing aphasia patients.

During the study of the interfaces, two metrics, i.e.

$$\text{WPM} = \frac{\text{number of words typed}}{\text{time taken in seconds}} \cdot 60, \tag{5}$$

and

$$\text{Accuracy} = \frac{\text{number of words selected in utterance}}{\text{total number of words in utterance}} \cdot 100 \tag{6}$$

were calculated for each utterance. Subsequently, the average WPM and accuracy rates were computed across all utterances in the given communication scenario.

To minimise and mitigate any unnecessary delays during the use of the AAC system, the predictions generated from the language models are processed through a stemmer [47] to remove any individual punctuation predictions. The decision to remove individual punctuation predictions is in line with previous work [27]. By this, the AAC system offers a more efficient and streamlined user experience.

4 Results

The results of the initial experiments conducted by the main author to investigate the speed of text input and the various factors involved in users' text entry are presented in the following.

4.1 Fitts' Law Experimentation for User Interfaces

Figure 4 shows movement time in seconds over ID for the interface layouts shown in Fig. 3, determined by the methodology described in Sect. 3.1. The interface buttons have a constant size (width W). Points in Fig. 4 represent ID for each button on the interfaces, and the time MT necessary for the user to move towards the target selection area of the button according to (2). The coefficients of Fitts' law, a and b, were determined by regression analysis and are summarised in Table 3.

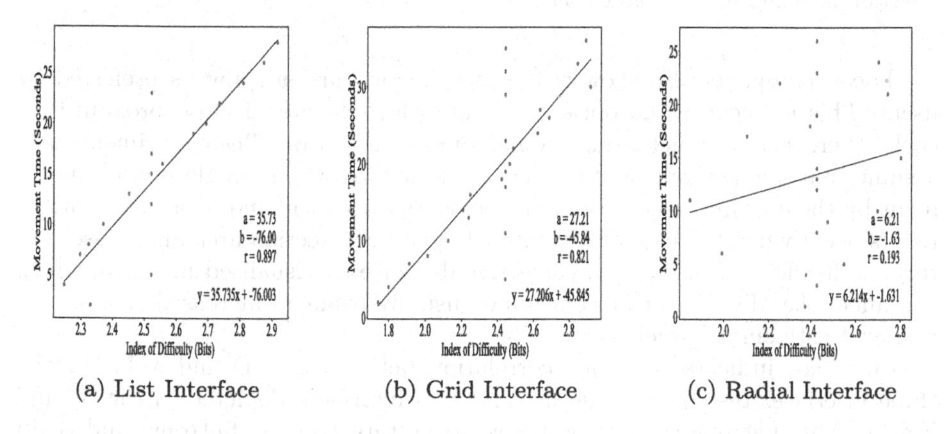

(a) List Interface (b) Grid Interface (c) Radial Interface

Fig. 4. Comparison of movement time in seconds over ID for the three user interfaces shown in Fig. 3.

Table 3. Fitts' law's parameters for the user interface layouts.

Interface Layout	Cursor Position	Equation of Regression Line
List	Middle	MT = 35.73 – 76.00 ID
Grid	Middle	MT = 27.21 – 45.84 ID
Radial	**Middle**	**MT = 6.21 – 1.63 ID**

The results indicate that the list interface Fig. 3a is the slowest and most difficult for the user. The results align with Fitts' law; the user has to move further in the list interface and cover longer distances to reach the target selection area, consequently resulting in higher ID and MT. The grid interface (cf. Fig. 3b) is less efficient for text entry. Fitts' law is indicative of preferring radial layouts (as in Fig. 3c) over list layouts, which is reflected in Fig. 4. Radial layouts offer shorter and closer movement distances for the users, resulting in lower ID.

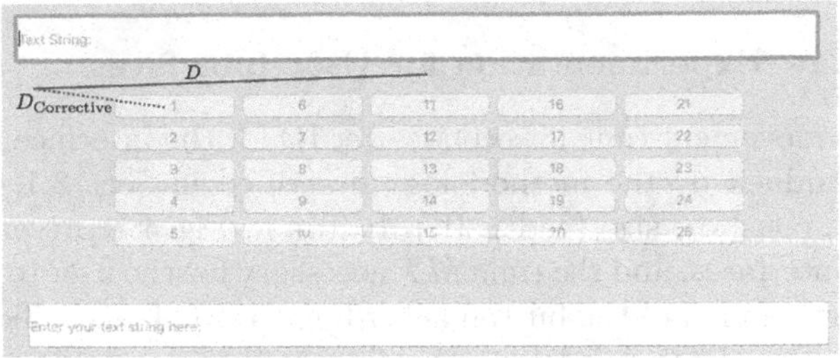

Fig. 5. Representing a corrective distance by a user if the user has missed the target selection area and has to revert back.

The experiments also show that radial layouts are not always preferred by users. This is because the options in radial layouts are in close proximity to each other, therefore increasing the risk of error selection. The experiments also assume that the distances and timings measured follow one single smooth movement by the user and no corrective movements are considered. Corrective movements occur when the user moves towards a target selection area and misses the target; therefore introducing a corrective distance as visualised in Fig. 5, which can affect the MT. Faster movements do usually result in increased errors, particularly with small target widths [53].

Fitts' law indicates a strong correlation between the ID and MT. For the three interfaces tested, only the list and grid interfaces depicted in Fig. 3a and Fig. 3b show a strong correlation between the target areas (buttons) and ID in Fig. 4. The list layout interface shows the strongest correlation. The radial layout shown in Fig. 4c shows a weaker correlation, however, the Fitts' law coefficients a and b were also low, indicating a radial layout is effective, if the target selection areas (i.e. the buttons for selecting the word predictions) are closely aligned in the interface. The distances between the buttons are in close proximity in the interface, so the user's MT is reduced, therefore decreasing the ID.

4.2 Number of Choice of Words vs Human Response Time

The graph depicted in Fig. 6 analyses results generated from the methodology described in Sect. 3.2. The results indicate that the HRT increases as the number of words presented to the user increases, which is consistent with Hick-Hymen's law as expressed in (3). However, it is noteworthy that the observed relationship is not logarithmic, deviating from Hick-Hymen's law in (3). While the correlation between the number of words presented and the HRT does appear to be linear, there are noticeable outliers that become prominent when the number of words exceeds a search space of 200.

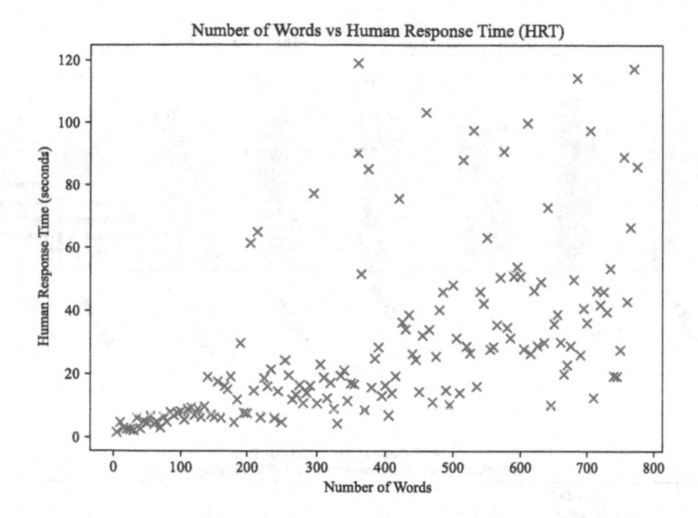

Fig. 6. Relationship between the number of words presented to a user in a list, and the response time taken to select a specific word from the list.

Figure 6 show a strong correlation between HRT and the number of words presented for a small search space, below 100 words. However, as the search space becomes larger, there is an increased number of observed outliers. Thus, for efficient text entry, the search space n must be limited to mitigate and minimise latency.

4.3 Language Model Fine-Tuning and Interface Testing for AAC Devices

Results for fine-tuning of the LLM as described in Sect. 3.3 are presented in Fig. 7, highlighting the advantages of utilising conversational corpora for fine-tuning language models, particularly for AAC systems. Results show that the baseline models BERT and RoBERTa show lower performance and are therefore less suitable for predictive text entry, both, in terms of accuracy and WPM rates. The results for the baseline models can be attributed to the model's inability to provide accurate or satisfactory predictions across the four communication scenarios. In comparison, fine-tuning with conversational corpora produces higher accuracy and WPM rates compared to using more generic corpora such as the Wikipedia or COCA Corpus. However, results also show that specific corpora, such as the Switchboard and Reddit corpora, were not especially useful for open-domain applications (across the four communication scenarios when testing the interfaces) because of their limited domain applications.

To determine the best ordering of the word predictions, i.e. alphabetical or probabilistic (cf. Fig. 2), subsequently, interface testing was conducted across the four communication scenarios. Initial experiments and use of the interfaces indicated that alphabetical ordering via the first character of the word predictions

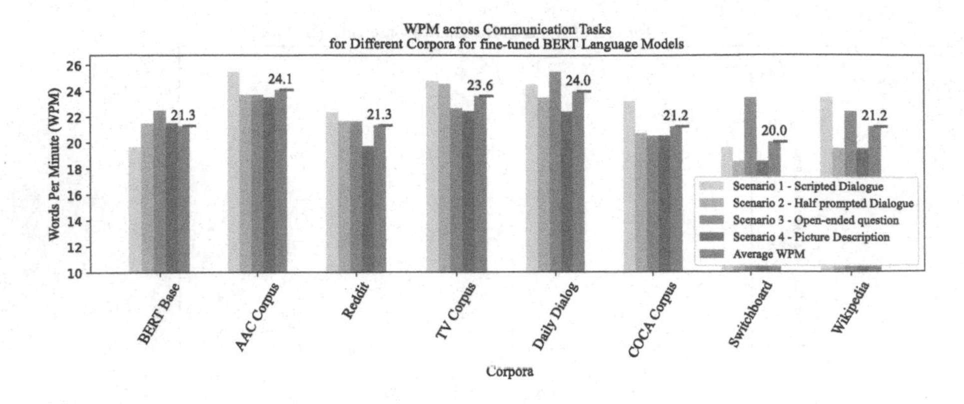

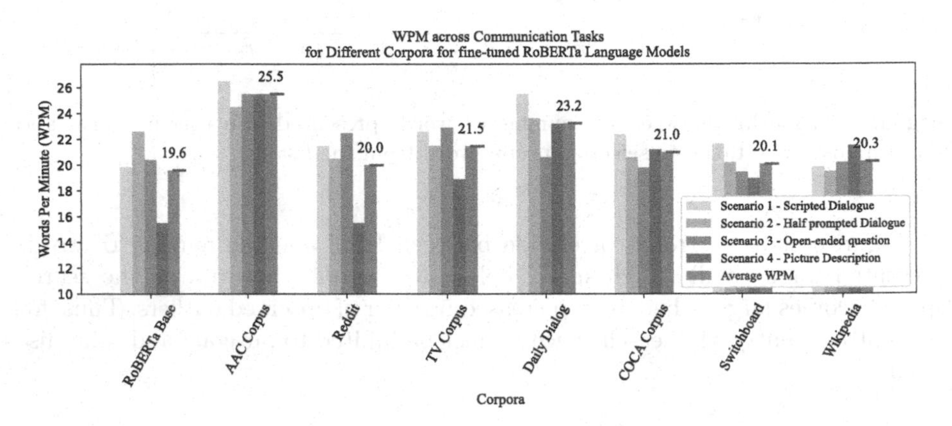

Fig. 7. Comparison of WPM across four communication scenarios utilising a radial interface with BERT and RoBERTa fine-tuned language models.

was preferred over probabilistic order (ordering via the confidence scores of the generated predictions). The alphabetical ordering preference did result in higher communication rates. However, further experimentation is necessary to investigate the impact of changing the layout or style of how the word predictions appear to the user on text input rates.

The results presented in Fig. 7 indicate that RoBERTa models outperformed BERT models, with higher resulting communication rates, primarily due to RoBERTa models having higher prediction quality. Consequently, the RoBERTa models outperformed certain fine-tuned BERT models. However, the difference in certain fine-tuned models is marginal. This study emphasises the importance of selecting appropriate corpora for specific applications. While conversational corpora are useful for open-domain applications, domain-specific corpora may be more suitable for limited certain tasks, specifically helpful for long-term AAC usage. The limited robustness of AAC systems and the lack of adaptability of AAC systems in various domains pose challenges. However, the lack of available and open-source AAC corpora makes training such open-domain models challenging. The results also showed that both fine-tuned BERT and RoBERTa models that were fine-tuned on the smaller specialist AAC [50] corpora achieved higher communication rates, compared to other generic corpora fine-tuned models. These fine-tuned models consistently outperformed the other models across the four communication scenarios.

Experiments also show that the fine-tuned models achieve higher accuracy rates in both scripted and prompted communication tasks, as described in Sect. 3.4. This higher accuracy can be attributed to the specific communication scenarios being scripted, allowing the models to generate more accurate predictions. However, when tested on open-domain communication scenarios, the fine-tuned models did not perform as well. Resulting in consistently lower communication rates. This emphasises a limitation in AAC devices, where the systems are more effective in short scripted or prompted dialogues and not open-domain tasks.

The four communication scenarios described in Sect. 3.4 aimed to simulate realistic situations and varied topics. However, these experiments are still not indicative of the long-term usage of AAC systems. The study could benefit from a long-term longitudinal study, to gain a comprehensive understanding of the capabilities of the system and to test the robustness of the interface. Overall, this study highlights the benefits of leveraging conversational data and fine-tuning language models for improving the performance and usability of AAC systems.

5 Conclusion

The limited communication output rates of individuals using AAC systems significantly hinder their ability to engage in multiparty open-domain interactions. This paper proposed a solution by combining techniques from HCI and language modelling to bridge the communication rate gap between AAC users and typical speakers. The preliminary results demonstrate that a radial text input interface integrated with a RoBERTa language model fine-tuned on conversational corpora, specifically fine-tuned on AAC, outperforms other text input interfaces, such as a grid or list interface. This approach achieves a communication rate output of 25.75 WPM across four simulated communication scenarios. Although the text input methods do not match the typical typing rate of a QWERTY keyboard, the communication rates surpass those of other AAC devices. Future research has to focus on refining user interfaces by minimising redundant time latencies and improving language prediction capabilities in conjunction with HCI modelling.

References

1. Benyon, D., Murray, D.: Applying user modeling to human-computer interaction design. Artif. Intell. Rev. **7**(3–4), 199–225 (1993)
2. Biswas, P., Robinson, P.: Automatic evaluation of assistive interfaces. In: Proceedings of the 13th International Conference on Intelligent User Interfaces, pp. 247–256 (2008)
3. Cai, S., et al.: Speakfaster observer: long-term instrumentation of eye-gaze typing for measuring AAC communication. In: Extended Abstracts of the 2023 CHI Conference on Human Factors in Computing Systems, pp. 1–8 (2023)

4. Calhoun, S., et al.: The NXT-format switchboard corpus: a rich resource for investigating the syntax, semantics, pragmatics and prosody of dialogue. Lang. Resour. Eval. **44**(4), 387–419 (2010)
5. Card, S.K., Moran, T.P., Newell, A.: The keystroke-level model for user performance time with interactive systems. Commun. ACM **23**(7), 396–410 (1980)
6. Chafe, W., Tannen, D.: The relation between written and spoken language. Annu. Rev. Anthropol. **16**(1), 383–407 (1987)
7. Copestake, A.: Augmented and alternative NLP techniques for augmentative and alternative communication (AAC). In: Natural Language Processing for Communication Aids (1997)
8. Curtis, H., Neate, T., Vazquez Gonzalez, C.: State of the art in AAC: a systematic review and taxonomy. In: Proceedings of the 24th International ACM SIGACCESS Conference on Computers and Accessibility, pp. 1–22 (2022)
9. Davies, M.: The corpus of contemporary American English as the first reliable monitor corpus of English. Lit. Linguist. Comput. **25**(4), 447–464 (2010)
10. Davies, M.: The TV and Movies corpora: design, construction, and use. Int. J. Corpus Linguist. **26**(1), 10–37 (2021)
11. Denoyer, L., Gallinari, P.: The Wikipedia XML corpus. In: Fuhr, N., Lalmas, M., Trotman, A. (eds.) INEX 2006. LNCS, vol. 4518, pp. 12–19. Springer, Heidelberg (2007). https://doi.org/10.1007/978-3-540-73888-6_2
12. Devlin, J., Chang, M., Lee, K., Toutanova, K.: BERT: pre-training of deep bidirectional transformers for language understanding. In: Proceedings of naacL-HLT, vol. 1, p. 2 (2019)
13. Dhakal, V., Feit, A.M., Kristensson, P.O., Oulasvirta, A.: Observations on typing from 136 million keystrokes. In: Conference on Human Factors in Computing Systems - Proceedings, vol. 2018-April. Association for Computing Machinery (2018)
14. Dupré, D., Karjalainen, A.: Employment of disabled people in Europe in 2002. Stat. Focus 3–26 (2003)
15. Fitts, P.M.: The information capacity of the human motor system in controlling the amplitude of movement. J. Exp. Psychol. **47**(6), 381–391 (1954)
16. Garay-Vitoria, N., Abascal, J.: Text prediction systems: a survey. Univ. Access Inf. Soc. **4**(3), 188–203 (2006)
17. Goetze, S., Moritz, N., Appell, J.E., Meis, M., Bartsch, C., Bitzer, J.: Acoustic user interfaces for ambient assisted living technologies. Inform. Health Soc. Care SI Ageing Technol. **35**(4), 161–179 (2010)
18. Guiard, Y.: Asymmetric division of labor in human skilled bimanual action: the kinematic chain as a model. J. Mot. Behav. **19**(4), 486–517 (1987)
19. Guiard, Y., Olafsdottir, H.B., Perrault, S.T.: Fitt's law as an explicit time/error trade-off. In: Proceedings of the SIGCHI Conference on Human Factors in Computing Systems, pp. 1619–1628 (2011)
20. Hameister, I., Nickels, L.: The cat in the tree-using picture descriptions to inform our understanding of conceptualisation in aphasia. Lang. Cogn. Neurosci. **33**(10), 1296–1314 (2018)
21. Hick, W.E.: On the rate of gain of information. Q. J. Exp. Psychol. **4**(1), 11–26 (2008)
22. Higginbotham, D.J., Shane, H., Russell, S., Caves, K.: Access to AAC: present, past, and future. Augment. Altern. Commun. **23**(3), 243–257 (2007)
23. John, B.E., Kieras, D.E.: The GOMS family of user interface analysis techniques: comparison and contrast. ACM Trans. Comput.-Hum. Interact. (CHI) **3**(4), 320–351 (1996)

24. Krause, J., Taliaferro, A.: Supporting students with autism spectrum disorders in physical education: there's an app for that. Palaestra **29**(2), 45 (2015)
25. Kristensson, P.: Discrete and continuous shape writing for text entry and control. Ph.D. thesis, Linköping University (2007)
26. Kristensson, P.O., et al.: Grand challenges in text entry. In: CHI 2013 Extended Abstracts on Human Factors in Computing Systems, pp. 3315–3318. Association for Computing Machinery, ACM (2013)
27. Kristensson, P.O., Lilley, J., Black, R., Waller, A.: A design engineering approach for quantitatively exploring context-aware sentence retrieval for nonspeaking individuals with motor disabilities. In: Proceedings of the 2020 CHI Conference on Human Factors in Computing Systems, vol. 20, pp. 1–11. Association for Computing Machinery (ACM) (2020)
28. Kristensson, P.O., Müllners, T.: Design and analysis of intelligent text entry systems with function structure models and envelope analysis. In: Proceedings of the 2021 CHI Conference on Human Factors in Computing Systems, pp. 1–12 (2021)
29. Kristensson, P.O., Vertanen, K.: The inviscid text entry rate and its application as a grand goal for mobile text entry. In: Proceedings of the 16th International Conference on Human-Computer Interaction with Mobile Devices & Services, pp. 335–338 (2014)
30. Kurosu, M.: Human-Computer Interaction: Human-Centred Design Approaches, Methods, Tools and Environments: 15th International Conference, HCI International 2013, Las Vegas, NV, USA, July 21–26, 2013, Proceedings, Part I, vol. 8004. Springer, Heidelberg (2013). https://doi.org/10.1007/978-3-642-39232-0
31. Ma, K., Jurczyk, T., Choi, J.D.: Challenging reading comprehension on daily conversation: passage completion on multiparty dialog. In: NAACL HLT 2018–2018 Conference of the North American Chapter of the Association for Computational Linguistics: Human Language Technologies - Proceedings of the Conference 1, 2039–2048 (2018)
32. MacKenzie, I.S.: Fitts' law as a research and design tool in human-computer interaction. Hum.-Comput. Interact. **7**(1), 91–139 (1992)
33. Mackenzie, I.S., Zhang, S.X., Soukoreff, R.W.: Text entry using soft keyboards. Behav. Inf. Technol. **18**(4), 235–244 (1999)
34. Medvedev, A.N., Lambiotte, R., Delvenne, J.-C.: The anatomy of reddit: an overview of academic research. In: Ghanbarnejad, F., Saha Roy, R., Karimi, F., Delvenne, J.-C., Mitra, B. (eds.) DOOCN 2017. SPC, pp. 183–204. Springer, Cham (2019). https://doi.org/10.1007/978-3-030-14683-2_9
35. Moore, R.K.: Modeling data entry rates for ASR and alternative input methods. In: Interspeech (2004)
36. Morris, M.A., Meier, S.K., Griffin, J.M., Branda, M.E., Phelan, S.M.: Prevalence and etiologies of adult communication disabilities in the united states: results from the 2012 national health interview survey. Disabil. Health J. **9**(1), 140–144 (2016)
37. Nicholas, L.E., Brookshire, R.H.: A system for quantifying the informativeness and efficiency of the connected speech of adults with aphasia. J. Speech Lang. Hear. Res. **36**(2), 338–350 (1993)
38. Ola Kristensson, P., Müllners, T.: Design and analysis of intelligent text entry systems with function structure models and envelope analysis. Analysis **12** (2021)
39. Papineni, K., Roukos, S., Ward, T., Zhu, W.J.: Bleu: a method for automatic evaluation of machine translation. In: Proceedings of the 40th Annual Meeting of the Association for Computational Linguistics, pp. 311–318 (2002)

40. Pritom, A.I., Mahmud, H., Ahmed, S., Hasan, M.K., Khan, M.M.: TYPEHEX keyboard: a virtual keyboard for faster typing in smartphone. In: 2015 18th International Conference on Computer and Information Technology (ICCIT), pp. 522–526. IEEE (2015)
41. Rackensperger, T., Krezman, C., Mcnaughton, D., Williams, M.B., D'silva, K.: "When I first got it, I wanted to throw it off a cliff": the challenges and benefits of learning AAC technologies as described by adults who use AAC. Augment. Altern. Commun. **21**(3), 165–186 (2005)
42. Rennies, J., Goetze, S., Appell, J.E.: Personalized acoustic interfaces for human-computer interaction. In: Ziefle, M., C.Röcker (eds.) Human-Centered Design of E-Health Technologies: Concepts, Methods and Applications, chap. 8, pp. 180–207. IGI Global (2011)
43. Rogers, A., Kovaleva, O., Rumshisky, A.: A primer in BERTology: what we know about how BERT works. Trans. Assoc. Comput. Linguist. **8**, 842–866 (2021)
44. Schepis, M.M., Reid, D.H., Behrman, M.M.: Acquisition and functional use of voice output communication by persons with profound multiple disabilities. Behav. Modif. **20**(4), 451–468 (1996)
45. Seow, S.C.: Information theoretic models of HCI: a comparison of the Hick-Hyman law and Fitt's law. Hum.-Comput. Interact. **20**(3), 315–352 (2005)
46. Shane, H.C., Blackstone, S., Vanderheiden, G., Williams, M., DeRuyter, F.: Using AAC technology to access the world. Assist. Technol. **24**(1), 3–13 (2012)
47. Sharma, D., Cse, M.: Stemming algorithms: a comparative study and their analysis. Int. J. Appl. Inf. Syst. **4**(3), 7–12 (2012)
48. Shire, S.Y., Jones, N.: Communication partners supporting children with complex communication needs who use AAC: a systematic review. Commun. Disord. Q. **37**(1), 3–15 (2015)
49. Todman, J., Alm, N., Higginbotham, J., File, P.: Whole utterance approaches in AAC. Augment. Altern. Commun. **24**(3), 235–254 (2008)
50. Vertanen, K., Kristensson, P.O.: The imagination of crowds: conversational AAC language modeling using crowdsourcing and large data sources. In: Proceedings of the 2011 Conference on Empirical Methods in Natural Language Processing, pp. 700–711 (2011)
51. Wang, A., Singh, A., Michael, J., Hill, F., Levy, O., Bowman, S.: GLUE: a multi-task benchmark and analysis platform for natural language understanding. In: Proceedings of the 2018 EMNLP Workshop BlackboxNLP: Analyzing and Interpreting Neural Networks for NLP, pp. 353–355. Association for Computational Linguistics, Brussels (2018)
52. Ward, D.J., Blackwell, A.F., MacKay, D.J.C.: Dasher-a data entry interface using continuous gestures and language models. In: Proceedings of the 13th Annual ACM Symposium on User Interface Software and Technology, pp. 129–137 (2000)
53. Wobbrock, J.O., Cutrell, E., Harada, S., MacKenzie, I.S.: An error model for pointing based on Fitts' law. In: Proceedings of the SIGCHI Conference on Human Factors in Computing Systems, pp. 1613–1622 (2008)
54. Zhai, S., Hunter, M., Smith, B.A.: Performance optimization of virtual keyboards. Hum.-Comput. Interact. **17**(2–3), 229–269 (2002)
55. Zhuang, L., Wayne, L., Ya, S., Jun, Z.: A robustly optimized BERT pre-training approach with post-training. In: Proceedings of the 20th Chinese National Conference on Computational Linguistics, pp. 1218–1227. Chinese Information Processing Society of China (2021)

Design and Research of Intelligent Walking Aid Products for Visually Impaired Individuals

Huijuan Zhu(✉) and Meiyu Zhou

School of Art Design and Media, East China University of Science and Technology, No. 130, Meilong Road, Xuhui District, Shanghai, People's Republic of China
1774155579@qq.com

Abstract. *Background:* According to the results of the second China Disability Sample Survey, there are about 12.33 million visually impaired people in China, and the number of visually impaired people is increasing year by year as China's society is aging. Therefore, it is becoming more and more urgent to solve their most basic travel problems. In the complex urban road environment, it becomes extremely difficult for visually impaired people to travel, not only by their own experience and sense of direction, but also by their efforts to identify various obstacles on the road through assistive devices. Traditional travel aids are mainly guide canes and guide dogs, but guide canes have many limitations for detecting obstacles, for example, obstacles above the chest are usually difficult to be detected, while guide dogs are very expensive to train and not suitable for general promotion. With the progress of sensors and computer technology, more and more intelligent products have entered the lives of visually impaired people, such as through wearable However, most of these products are not only expensive and very complicated to use, but also change the original habits of the blind and create a sense of resistance.

Aim: This paper focuses on exploring a travel assistance product that does not change the travel habits of visually impaired people and does not burden them psychologically, which not only provides timely feedback to visually impaired people about obstacles, but also protects their travel safety.

Methods: In this paper, we first analyzed the global smart travel products for visually impaired people, discussed the advantages and shortcomings of these products, and analyzed the living habits and behavioral characteristics of some visually impaired people by means of literature research and questionnaire survey, and based on the analysis results, we designed the smart mobility products, selected and installed suitable sensors, and programmed them. Finally, we tested the usability of the designed product in outdoor environment.

Conclusion: The test results show that the product design has certain usability and shortcomings, and further optimization is still needed in the future, but this design and research can provide reference advice for such smart product design.

Keywords: Intelligent products · People with visual impairment · human-computer interaction · multisensor fusion

Q. Gao et al. (Eds.): HCII 2023, LNCS 14055, pp. 453–467, 2023.
https://doi.org/10.1007/978-3-031-48041-6_30

1 Introduction

People with disabilities have always been the key objects of care in China, and among them, the life of visually impaired people is particularly difficult. These people are those who have very serious defects in visual perception and cannot be corrected by existing medical means[1], and because they have lost the primary way to obtain information about the outside world, it is difficult for them to integrate into the social group, which has a deeper impact on their life, study, and work. Deep impact on their life, study and work, and even also affect the degree of development of our society, so the problems related to visually impaired people are something that cannot be ignored by social development.

According to the Second China Disability Sample Survey, there are about 12.33 million visually impaired people in China as of 2007, accounting for 14.86% of the total number of people with disabilities, of which about 5.23 million are blind and about 7.1 million are low-vision. China currently has the largest number of blind people in the world, accounting for about 18% of the world's blind population [2]. Recent statistics also show that the number of visually impaired people in China has been increasing year after year, and the percentage of visually impaired people is also on the rise as Chinese society ages [3]. The large base of visually impaired people and their rapid growth are the actual national conditions that China must face.

In fact, as early as after the Second World War, international attention began to be paid to issues related to people with disabilities, the United Nations organization and in 1974 proposed the barrier-free design, the basic principle of barrier-free design is equality, and in the design process to the use of product performance as the primary consideration, to remove those factors that make users feel confused product barriers, easier for regular people to use, or can meet the physiologically impaired people's relevant needs and provide them with convenient design [4]. With the spread of the concept of barrier-free design in the international arena, China has also started its urban accessibility renovation program, and in the construction of public facilities and public environment planning, blind corridors have been paved, blind signs have been added, etc. The progress of technology has led to more and more accessible products to help the visually impaired, but no matter the blind corridors in the society or the products designed by individuals, the utilization rate is not high, and many of them even hinder the However, the utilization rate of both socially and personally designed products is not high, and many of them even hinder the normal life of visually impaired people, making their personal safety and psychological aspects affected.

This study is based on the concept of human-centered design from the perspective of caring for the safety and psychological health of blind people, and redesigning the travel aid for blind people through ergonomic and sensual engineering design methods, and adding multiple sensors to enable blind people to quickly obtain obstacle information. This paper firstly researches the development of international products for the blind through literature review, and secondly obtains some information about the characteristics of blind people through visits, questionnaires and data collection. Finally, through the data analysis results, we designed the travel aid for the blind and added smart sensors for human-computer interaction. After the design was completed, we tested the product, and the test results showed that the product can identify obstacles and provide positioning information, but there are also some problems. It is hoped that this paper will help the development of guide products for the blind, and that more designers will pay attention to these visually impaired people and give them more and better designs in the future.

2 Literature Review

Guiding aids for the visually impaired play an important role in the daily travel of the visually impaired. Currently, most visually impaired people will rely on traditional guide canes to travel, which are basic in function and simple in structure, and the visually impaired person judges the obstacles around them by tapping [5], which not only requires the blind person to practice repeatedly, but also makes it difficult for the traditional guide cane to detect all obstacles when there are multiple obstacles or obstacles in special locations such as the head, and in unfamiliar places, the situation will be even more In unfamiliar places, the situation can be even more complicated and the blind person can be exposed to a variety of hazards. Guide dogs are an alternative to assisted travel for blind people. They can guide visually impaired people to walk and avoid obstacles on the road through special training, but the selection and training of guide dogs requires a lot of human, material, and financial resources [6], and they are not feasible for some blind people with dog hair allergies, so guide dogs are not suitable for all blind people.

With the development of computer technology and sensor technology, mobility aids for the visually impaired are becoming more and more diverse and versatile. They can be divided into three types according to their forms: guide cane form, robot form, and wearable form. In most of these three types of assistive mobility devices, multi-sensor assistance systems such as radar, ultrasonic, and infrared sensing are incorporated, especially the electronic device based travel assistance systems are the most common [7], aiming to ensure the safety of visually impaired people. Different intelligent travel assistance systems have different ways of information acquisition and information transfer, usually using ultrasonic sensors, infrared sensors, etc. to obtain information about the surrounding environment, using embedded processing chips, microcomputers, and other devices for information processing and information transfer through sound perception or tactile perception [8].

The smart guide cane form can be seen as an extension of the traditional cane by adding sensor devices to the cane to increase the functionality of the traditional cane. The GuideCane, a collaborative project developed by the University of Michigan and Carnegie Mellon University, is an expanded and enhanced device based on the traditional cane [9], which operates on the system shown in Fig. 1. 10 ultrasonic distance measurement devices are installed on the GuideCane, eight of which face forward and are capable of reaching a detection range of 120 degrees, and two of which are located on either side of the cane to help The GuideCane, as an early representative of the smart cane, is functionally complete, but it is not minimalistic enough, and the wheels in front of the cane increase the risk of falls for the blind.

The Ultrane Cane, released on the Disability Horizons website, is a simpler, intelligent guide cane. The Ultra Cane has two modes, one for short range detection: to detect obstacles up to two meters and the other for long range detection: to detect obstacles up to four meters (Fig. 2), while the upper sensor can detect higher obstacles to avoid hitting the user's head [10]. When an obstacle is detected, it gives information back

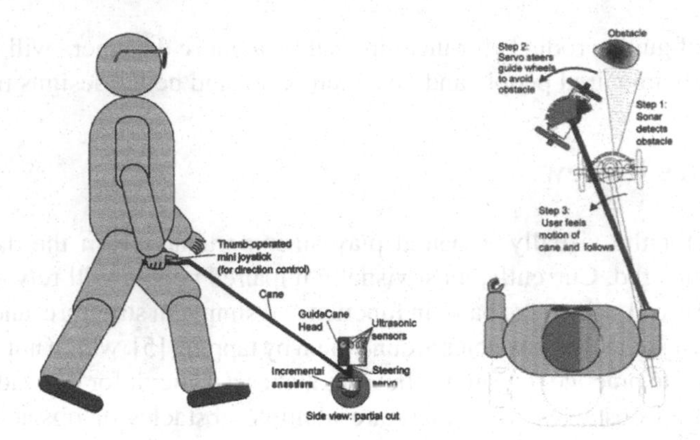

Fig. 1. Schematic diagram and usage scenarios of GuideCane [9]

to the visually impaired person in the form of a grip vibration. However, the Ultrane Cane is expensive and visually impaired people with average income rarely purchase this product.

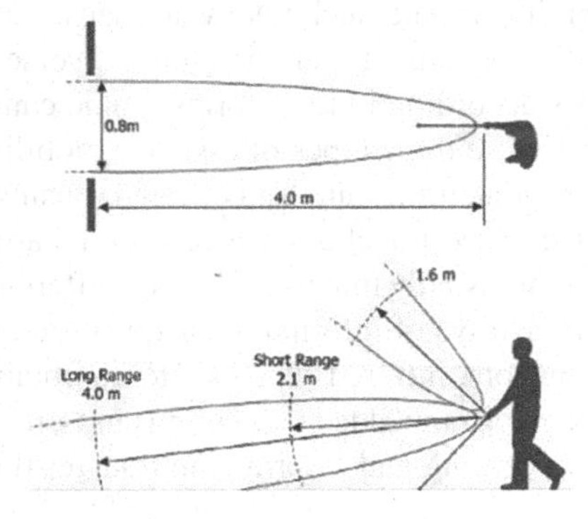

Fig. 2. Two modes of Ultrane Cane obstacle detection [10]

The mobile guide robot is another form of guide product, Rentsctde developed a mobility aid VA-PAMAID (Veterans Affairs Personal Adaptive Mobility Aid) [11] which can correctly avoid obstacles and can assist the user's body to maintain balance However, the size is too large and not suitable for the visually impaired. The University of Yamanashi, Japan, developed an intelligent cart ROTA (Robotic Travel Aid) [12]. It is mainly equipped with a vision system and visual and sound sensors to guide visually impaired people safely across the road, but it is also not suitable for daily travel. A robot developed by Carnegie Mellon University in Pittsburgh, USA, to help visually impaired people [13]. This robot uses multiple sets of tactile sensors and a series of software programming to locate and navigate the robot. However, it is quite expensive to build and is not suitable for the average consumer.

A wearable guide product is a guide system fitted to the clothing, glasses, and backpack of a visually impaired person, freeing the hands of the blind and allowing the blind to walk more freely on the street [14]. In China, Zhongchao Wei et al. [15] invented a head-mounted product with an ultrasonic sensor on the head of the visually impaired person and an infrared sensor on each side, with the detection direction changing as the visually impaired person's head turns. Ram S et al. [16], USA, developed a wearable product with ultrasonic and thermoelectric sensors on the chest of a visually impaired person to distinguish pedestrians and objects on the road. The product developed by Filipe V et al. [17], Portugal, is equipped with a Microsoft Kinetic camera on the chest of a visually impaired person to shoot at an oblique downward angle of 45°, and uses a neural network to classify the depth information extracted from the image and compare it with a predefined environmental pattern to identify obstacles and stairs within a two-meter range in front of them.

For example, most smart crutches are not foldable or retractable, so the height of the visually impaired person is not compatible with the length of the crutches, and the use of shorter crutches by taller people increases the risk of wrist and arm muscle damage. This will increase the risk of wrist and arm muscle damage. The same wearable smart devices will not only increase the travel burden of the visually impaired but also make them feel uncomfortable and nervous. In the face of the increasing number of visually impaired people year by year, ensuring their travel safety and solving their travel difficulties is an urgent problem to be solved in order to promote social equality, but before designing products, we should understand the travel conditions, living habits and consumption level of visually impaired people in order to design smart products that are really suitable for visually impaired people. In the next chapter, we will convert the collected questionnaires into data to analyze the characteristics of the visually impaired group.

3 Analysis of the Characteristics of the Visually Impaired Group

3.1 Questionnaire

The research content of this questionnaire includes personal socio-economic attributes, travel habits, and experiences of using assistive travel products are three aspects of the content. Since the audience of the questionnaire is visually impaired people, only some basic questions are set. In order to expand the sample size, the questionnaire was distributed in both online and offline forms, and offline mainly used the form of surveyors reading the questions aloud and recording the answers of the visually impaired people. When conducting the visit survey, we found that some visually impaired people are able to operate online access through the voice broadcast function of cell phones and computers, and some visually impaired people have their own small groups such as WeChat groups, which not only made the efficiency of our questionnaire distribution improved, but also made the distribution of online questionnaires one of the feasible solutions. The questionnaire survey finally collected data from 145 visually impaired people, of which 130 were valid data (Table 1). The reasons for invalid samples were as follows: 1. Filling in errors 2. Duplicate filling in the online questionnaire 3. Subjects dropping out in the middle of the offline survey.

Table 1. Description of data from the questionnaire for the visually impaired (N = 130).

Variable name	Variable classification	Quantity	Percentage
Gender	Male	66	50.77%
	Female	64	49.23%
Age	Under 18 years old	4	3.08%
	19–40 years old	32	24.62%
	41–60 years old	50	38.46%
	60 years old and above	44	33.85%
Height	Less than 160 cm	34	26.15%
	160-180 cm	73	56.15%
	180–190 cm	19	14.62%
	190 cm or more	4	3.08%
Educated or not	Educated	87	66.92%
	No education	43	33.08%
Degree of visual impairment	Blind	58	44.62%
	People with low vision	72	55.38%
Causes of visual impairment	Congenital	71	54.62%
	Non-congenital	59	45.38%
Monthly household income (RMB)	Less than 3,000	13	10%
	3,000–5,000	66	50.77%
	5,000–10,000	45	34.62%
	More than 10,000	6	4.62%
Frequency of solo trips (times/week)	0	37	28.46%
	1–3	53	40.77%
	4–6	34	26.15%
	More than 7 times	6	4.62%
Length of time away from home	Less than 30 min	35	26.92%
	30 min–1 h	45	34.62%
	1 h–3 h	30	23.08%
	More than 3 h	20	15.38%
Whether to use a guide cane	Use	98	75.38%
	Not used	32	24.62%

(continued)

Table 1. (*continued*)

Variable name	Variable classification	Quantity	Percentage
The experience of not being able to find the way	Always	10	7.69%
	Often	57	43.85%
	Occasionally	38	29.23%
	Never	25	19.23%
Use of intelligent products	Used	105	80.77%
	Never used	25	19.23%
Which features of the product are more important (multiple choice)	Portability	81	62.31%
	Practicality	83	63.85%
	Aesthetics	86	66.15%
	Price advantage	84	64.62%

3.2 Analysis of the Physiological Characteristics of Visually Impaired People

People with visual impairment are mainly divided into those with low vision and those who are totally blind. The criteria for blindness and low vision vary from country to country, and the World Health Organization established criteria for blindness and low vision in 1973 [18] (Table 2). Low vision people are only those who have poor vision and cannot see clearly the shape of objects look like, etc., but they can see the presence of light, but totally blind people not only cannot see any object or see light, they cannot even feel the presence of their eyes, the life of totally blind people is very difficult, they cannot read and write like our normal people, and according to the survey, only about 10% of blind people in China can use Braille to get information [19], and the rest of blind people can only rely on other senses to get information.

Table 2. Diagnostic criteria for blindness and low vision set by WHO

Category	Level	Best corrected visual acuity (good eye in both eyes)	
		Optimal visual acuity below	Optimal visual acuity equal to or better than
Low vision	1	0.3	0.1
	2	0.1	0.05 (3m index)
Blind	3	0.05	0.02 (1m index)
	4	0.02	Light Sensitivity
	5	No sense of light	

In the survey study, it was found that most of the subjects only knew that they were blind or low vision, but they did not know the grade, and according to Mascetti's research, it is more valuable to classify the visually impaired people into two categories: blind and visually impaired [20], so when designing the questionnaire, it was only divided into two categories and not into grades. When investigating about the causes of visual impairment, it was found that some of the visually impaired people were born with visual impairment and some of them had visual impairment due to accidents, accidents, etc. Also, according to the analysis of the questionnaire data, most of the totally blind people were congenital (probably related to heredity, genes, etc.), while most of the low vision people were non-congenital (Fig. 3).

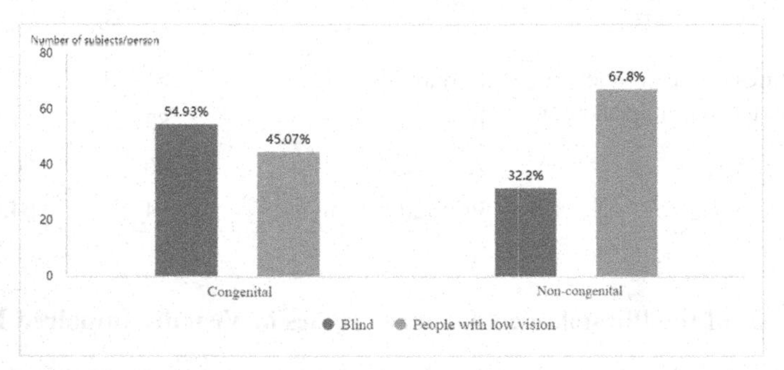

Fig. 3. Relationship between congenital and non-congenital in blind and low vision individuals

3.3 Analysis of Travel Characteristics of the Visually Impaired

The analysis of the frequency of trips made by visually impaired people of different genders and ages (Fig. 4) revealed that more men than women were among the subjects who did not travel, and significantly more women than men made more than seven trips. At the age level, those aged 41–60 years traveled more frequently, which may be related to their jobs, and commuting trips may be their main reason for traveling. Therefore, when designing or making related auxiliary outbound travel products, not only the physiological differences between women and men (such as strength size, etc.) should be taken into account, but also the travel needs of different age groups, and the difference in needs may affect their choice of products.

An analysis of the height of males and females (Table 3) revealed that both males and females had the highest number of people between 160 cm and 180 cm in height. Visually impaired people often use their hands to touch to obtain information, and the size of their touch range has an impact on the amount of information they can obtain. According to the survey, if the touch range of visually impaired people is based on a female of 160 cm height and a male of 172 cm height, the forearm is extended diagonally to the ground at an angle of 45 degrees and the height between the fingers is 70 cm according to the ground [21]. Therefore, it is most appropriate to set up touch aids to help the blind within this range.

Visually impaired people can walk without relying on facilities such as walking sticks when they are familiar with indoor areas, but when walking alone in unfamiliar outdoor areas, they must rely on guide sticks and handrails, otherwise they can easily get

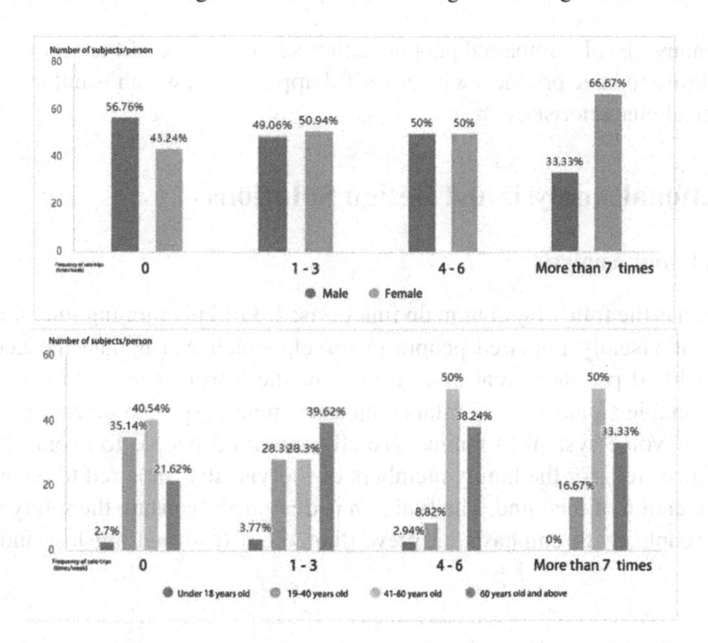

Fig. 4. Frequency of travel for people with visual impairment by gender and age group

Table 3. Male and female height analysis

Height	Male	Female	Total
Less than 160 cm	16	18	34
160 cm–180 cm	36	37	73
180 cm–190 cm	12	7	19
190 cm or more	2	2	4

injured or lost. The questionnaire survey shows that more than 50% (43.85%) of visually impaired people often (43.85%) or always (7.69%) get lost, and the results of the data survey also show that there are 75.38% of visually impaired people use a guide cane to get information about the road by sweeping the cane from side to side, for example, when they pass through the grass, they will first use the cane to find out if the soil is walkable. And 80.77% of the visually impaired people themselves or others around them have used intelligent mobility aids, probably because our survey was conducted in Shanghai, a more developed city in China, where they have more access to intelligent products. In the analysis of the product features that visually impaired people are concerned about, we found that the four features of portability, practicality, aesthetics and price advantage are almost all the key concerns of visually impaired people, and to our surprise, the concern for aesthetics (66.15%) exceeds the price advantage (64.62%), through the analysis, we found that although many visually impaired people cannot see the product they are using, they still desire to have the product. Through analysis, we found that although many visually impaired people cannot see the shape of the products they use, they still desire to have products with beautiful appearance, which is influenced by their psychological characteristics.

4 Functional Analysis and Design Solutions

4.1 Functional Analysis

The design has the following four main functions: 1. GPS positioning function to ensure the safety of visually impaired people in travel, which can update the geographical location of blind people in real time to prevent them from getting lost or encountering unpredictable situations; 2. Distance measurement system to detect the distance of obstacles; 3. Voice system to remind visually impaired people to avoid obstacles; 4. Information system for the family members of the visually impaired to obtain the geographical location of the blind. The function is designed to ensure the safety of visually impaired people, with emphasis on preventing them from getting lost and detecting obstacles.

4.2 Intelligent System Design

According to the system analysis, the internal system is divided into three main parts: the GPS module for positioning, the range module for detecting obstacles and the information module for providing positioning information (Fig. 5).

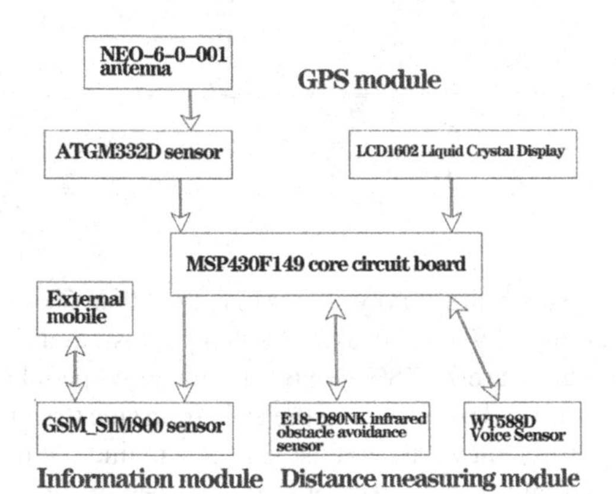

Fig. 5. Intelligent system overall module design

The MSP430F149 microcontroller was chosen for the core processing of the data, which uses a precise yet simple instruction set structure with seven source operand addressing, four destination operand addressing, 27 kernel instructions, and a large number of analog instructions, and it is fast, capable of 40ns instruction cycles, and also capable of multiplying and adding forms of operations [22].

The GPS module uses the NEO-6–0-001 antenna to determine the position information and uses the ATGM332D sensor to locate and store the position information of the visually impaired, which supports both GPS and BDS single system positioning and dual system joint positioning, and supports a variety of satellite navigation systems, and is a true six-in-one satellite navigation chip that contains 32 tracking channels This chip is used in the field of cell phones, tablet PCs and car navigation, for example [23]. The geographical location latitude and longitude of the positioning information is displayed through the LCD1602 display. Also, if the family of the visually impaired person wants to get their geographic location information, they can use the cell phone SMS to get the latitude and longitude of the geographic location of the visually impaired person, which is mainly used by the GSM_SIM800 sensor to receive and return the information from the cell phone end of the module.

The distance measurement module uses the E18-D80NK infrared obstacle avoidance sensor used to detect obstacles, which has a potentiometer knob at the end of the sensor to adjust the detection distance, and can detect obstacles up to 80 cm, but the detection distance will be different due to different colors of obstacles [24], but it can effectively avoid the interference of visible light, and is widely used in obstacle avoidance robots, floor sweeping robots and other fields. The obstacle information will be played through the ISD1820 voice sensor after the obstacle is detected. The intelligent system flow is shown in Fig. 6.

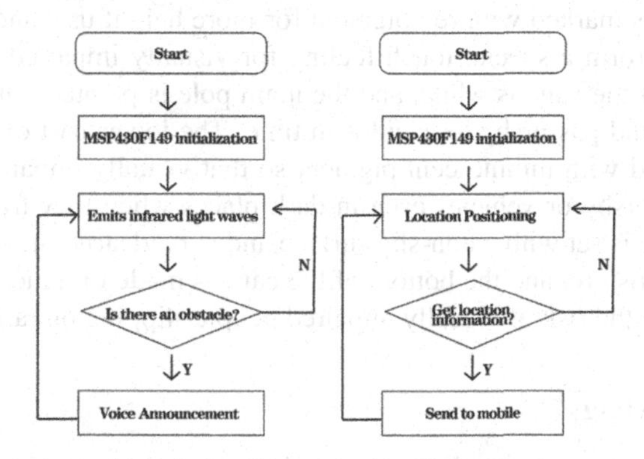

Fig. 6. Intelligent System Flow Chart

The circuit design of the intelligent system was drawn using Altium Designer software, an electronic product development system introduced by Altium, which mainly uses a computer to handle the various tasks in circuit design and can greatly improve the quality and efficiency of circuit design [25]. The initial circuit design required the USB port to be connected to the power supply all the time, and since it was considered very inconvenient for the outdoor use of the crutches, it was changed to the use of lithium battery power supply, i.e., Fig. 7, and the lithium battery can be charged with the USB power cable, solving the problem of outdoor power supply for the crutches.

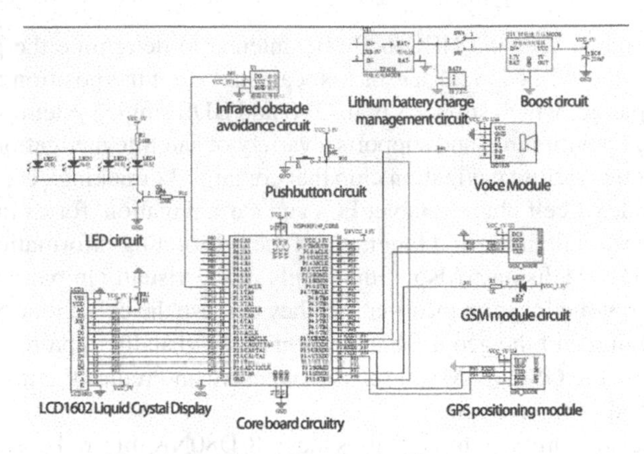

Fig. 7. Circuit design for intelligent systems

4.3 Product Shape Design

The overall design of the cane is shown in Fig. 8. The cane is designed as a telescopic structure, which can adjust the height of the main pole for visually impaired people from 1.4 m to 1.9 m high. The telescopic structure of the cane is similar to the telescopic umbrella pole of an umbrella, with each hole spaced at 2 cm, and the length position of the main pole is marked with red pigment for more height use, and the thickness of the pigment will form a special touch feeling for visually impaired people to adjust. The main color of the cane is white, and the main pole is painted with red pigment as a warning to remind passersby to avoid it in time. The lower part of the main pole of the cane is painted with luminescent pigment so that visually impaired people can be observed by passersby or vehicles even in dark places when they travel at night. The handle of the cane is set with a non-slip surface and curved structure, more in line with the manual grip posture, and the bottom of the cane is made of a more non-slip rubber material to reduce the risk of visually impaired people slipping on rainy days.

4.4 Outdoor Testing

The test environment is an open-air outdoor environment where the GPS can fully receive the signal without interference. There are various obstacles in the outdoor area, such as steps, fences, gates, stones, etc., of different sizes and distances, which are ideal for testing. Because the E18-D80NK sensor is less interference by visible light, so do not have to consider the weather conditions, the test weather is sunny, the light is relatively strong, the cane detects obstacles will be "please pay attention to the obstacles" prompt voice (test Fig. 9), the test for obstacles is relatively smooth, but for some relatively too low or However, for some relatively low or very narrow aisles, accurate information could not be detected.

After repeated tests, the GPS navigation system can receive signals and will be displayed on the LCD screen, the cell phone to send information keyword "JW" that will immediately return to the location of the crutches latitude and longitude information, but into the indoor or basement places, GPS will be interfered with, the signal is weak,

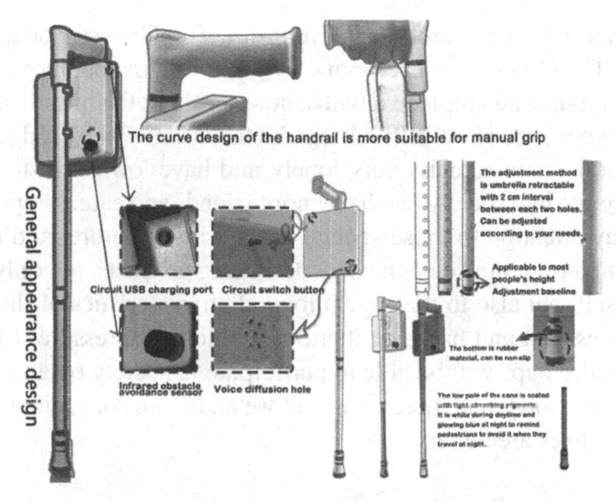

Fig. 8. Overall design of crutch shape

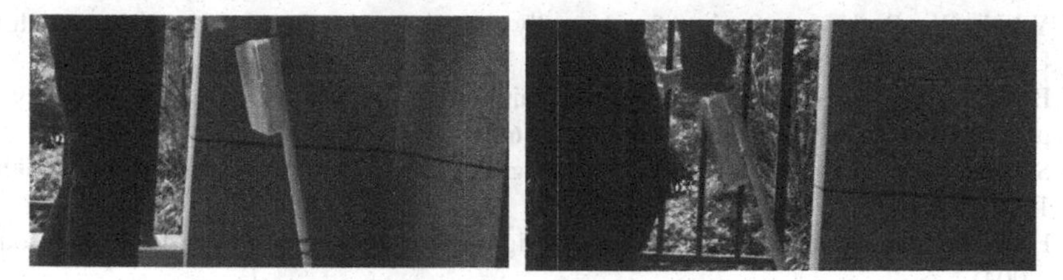

Fig. 9. Outdoor Testing

can not display positioning information, receive and send SMS in the outdoor all normal, but because into the indoor or basement GPS will sometimes fail, so the SMS can not provide timely positioning information.

5 Conclusion

This research is based on the human-centered design concept from the perspective of caring for the safety and psychological health of the visually impaired, and redesigning the travel aid for the visually impaired through ergonomic and perceptual engineering design methods, and adding multiple sensors to enable the blind to quickly access obstacle information. Although the final product is able to truly detect obstacles and provide feedback in the form of voice, this design still has many shortcomings: 1. The questionnaire and study were conducted in Shanghai, a more developed city in China, and most visually impaired people in the survey had used smart products before, but if in other poorer areas, many visually impaired people may have never been exposed to smart products, their The psychological situation will change, so this study is not applicable to all areas.2. After this product design was completed, due to time and funding problems, no large-scale testing was conducted, but only simple testing, so no data analysis was formed in response to the feedback from the testing, and the usability aspect of this product still needs further research in the future.3. The GPS sensor used can only be used outdoors to The GPS sensor used can only get the signal outdoors, so we still need to study the GPS module and replace it with a new sensor in the future. After this study, I have personally experienced how difficult it is for the visually impaired to live, especially to travel, and that they are actually very lonely and have low self-esteem, but they are also eager to integrate into society and have more friends and care. I hope more and more designers will pay attention to these special groups in the future, and pay attention to the concept of human-oriented design when designing products, not only to the function of the product itself, but also to the psychological characteristics of the group to avoid hurting their self-esteem and bringing them psychological pressure. I hope that in the future these special groups will be able to participate in society on an equal footing, no longer have fear and worry, and there will be more and more convenient products to help them, so that their lives are better.

References

1. Yahui, W.: Packaging Design for Visually Impaired Nut-Based Snack Foods. Hunan University of Technology (2014)
2. Bao, T.: Comparison and analysis of the main data of the two national sample surveys on people with disabilities. Spec. Educ. China **86**(8), 54–56 (2007)
3. Shiyun, L.: Wearable-based intelligent navigation design for the blind. Ind. Des. **000**(3), 102–103 (2018)
4. Lianxin, L.: Introduction to Barrier-Free Design. China Construction Industry Press, Beijing (2004)
5. Xiaoyu, Z.: An analysis of the future realization of intelligent guide products. Consum. Electron. **12**, 38–44 (2022)
6. Huiling, L.: Animal behavior applications - an introduction to the training and application of guide dogs for the blind. Lab. Anim. Sci. **27**(4), 81–82 (2010)
7. Shiheng, W.: Research on the Guide Device Based on multi-Information Fusion Technology. Zhejiang University of Technology, Zhejiang (2013)
8. Wenqin, S.: Research on the Key Technology of Machine Vision-Based Outdoor Support System for the Blind. Zhejiang University, Zhejiang (2012)
9. Ulrich, I., Borenstein, J.: The guidecane-applying mobile robot technologies to assist the visually impaired people. IEEE Trans. Syst. **31**(2), 131–136 (2001)
10. Zhuling, W.: User Experience-Based Design of Mobility Aids for the Blind: A Study of Blind People in Edinburgh UK. Shanghai Jiaotong University, Shanghai (2013)
11. Andrew, J.: Intelligent walkers for the elderly: performance and safety testing of VA-PAMAID robotic walker. Rehabilitation Research and Development Service, pp. 423–431 (2003)
12. Mori, H.: The matching fund project for practical use of robotic travel aid for the visually impaired. Adv. Robot. 453–472 (2004)
13. Aaron, M.: A RoboticWalker that provides guidance. In: Proceedings of International Conference on Robotics and Automation, pp. 25–30 (2003)
14. Xuewen, R.: A review of the current status of research on guide robots for the blind. Comput. Eng. Appl. **56**(14), 1–13 (2020)
15. Zhongchao, W.: An intelligent voice guide based on ultrasonic distance measurement and PSD infrared distance measurement. Mod. Elec. Technol. **36**(10), 115–118 (2013)
16. Ram, S.: The people sensor: a mobility aid for the visually impaired. In: Second International Symposium on Wearable Computers, pp. 166–167 (1998)

17. Filipe, V.: Blind navigation support system based on Microsoft Kinect. Proc. Comput. Sci. 94–101 (2012)
18. World Health Organization. International Classification of Impairment, Disabilities and HandicapsWH.O Geneva (1980)
19. Li, C.: A study on the use of Braille in China. Lang. Writ. Appl. **2**, 42–48 (2013)
20. Mascetti, S.: Sonification of guidance data during road crossing for people with visual impairments or blindness. Int. J. Hum. Comput. Stud. **85**(C), 16–26 (2016)
21. Zhimin, L.: Barrier-Free Architectural Environment Design. Huazhong University of Science and Technology Press, Wuhan (2011)
22. Yinhong, L.: Universal controller for stepper motors with MSP430F149 microcontroller. Elec. Prod. World **22**, 71–72 (2002)
23. Saba, F.: Blind's eye: employing Google directions API for outdoor navigation of visually impaired pedestrians. Mehran Univ. Res. J. Eng. Technol. **36**(3), 693–706 (2017)
24. Hongbin, M.: Design and implementation of a microcontroller-based intelligent cart obstacle avoidance system. Inf. Technol. **19**(10), 76–78 (2018)
25. Qiang, F.: Application of Altium Designer software in circuit design. Sci. Technol. Commun. **14**, 165–166 (2011)

Designing for Health and Wellbeing

Design Considerations for Virtual Reality (VR) Vaping Applications: Co-Designing Persuasive Computing Scenarios

Fatima Adem[1(✉)], Noor Alsaadoun[1,2], Hoda Elsayed[3], and Areej Al-Wabil[2,3]

[1] College of Medicine, Alfaisal University, Riyadh, Saudi Arabia
{fadem,naalsaadoun}@alfaisal.edu, fadem056@gmail.com

[2] AI Research Center, College of Engineering, Alfaisal University, Riyadh, Saudi Arabia
awabil@alfaisal.edu

[3] Game Innovation Lab, College of Engineering, Alfaisal University, Riyadh, Saudi Arabia
helsayed@alfaisal.edu

Abstract. Tobacco smoking and vaping remain a global public health concern, causing millions of premature deaths and imposing substantial economic losses. In spite of persistent efforts to combat the health risks, smoking continues to persist, necessitating the exploration of innovative interventions or technology solutions such as mobile applications, wearables, virtual reality, and more. Despite being included in public health programs worldwide, vaping or smoking awareness and/or cessation campaigns face barriers as they pertain to scalability and accessibility. Virtual reality (VR) experiences could potentially contribute towards remedial programs, but virtual reality experiences, that cater for both pre-vaping awareness, cessation and post cessation awareness, are scarce. Co-design, involving public health policy makers and subject matter experts is crucial for creating meaningful technology solutions. However, few researchers have explored this approach in VR contexts, despite its potential for authentic public health campaign support. Recognizing the need for a holistic approach, this paper used a co-design approach, collaborating with public health policy makers and subject matter experts to design and evaluate a VR experience for the contexts of pre-vaping, cessation and post cessation awareness. In this paper, we present necessary design guidelines and an evaluation framework for the creation of virtual reality experiences in persuasive computing contexts for public health.

Keywords: Extended Reality · XR · Smoking Cessation · Persuasive Computing

1 Introduction

In recent years, advances in technologies at the intersection of persuasive computing and medicine have revolutionized the healthcare sector. These rapid changes, marked by advanced diagnostic tools, robotic surgical support, data-driven patient care, and

Fatima Adem, Noor Alsaadoun, Areej Al-Wabil: These authors contributed equally to this work as co-first authors.

Q. Gao et al. (Eds.): HCII 2023, LNCS 14055, pp. 471–481, 2023.
https://doi.org/10.1007/978-3-031-48041-6_31

telemedicine, have led to a new era in healthcare provision, distinguished by precision, inclusiveness, and effectiveness. At the heart of this change is the seamless integration of technology with medical expertise. The co-design approach embodies this union. By promoting collaboration between technologists and healthcare experts, co-design fosters tailored healthcare solutions, reflecting the practical requirements of patients and medical systems. This methodology does more than speed up the development of medical tools—it ensures their relevance in real-world clinical settings. One of the notable hallmarks of this integrative momentum is the ascent of Virtual Reality (VR) in the realm of healthcare, especially its potential for public health initiatives. The essence of VR embodies a pioneering and transformative shift in the domains of patient care and health-centric education. In this paper, we explored the process that underpins the co-design of VR solutions, ensuring they are in sync with public health objectives.

This study delves into the co-design process of VR experiences for public health, specifically focusing on interventions for smoking and vaping. It revolves around three pivotal research inquiries: (1) What challenges and barriers are prevalent in public health awareness campaigns and interventions targeting smoking and vaping? (2) How can VR experiences be collaboratively designed in conjunction with stakeholders engaged in public health initiatives? (3) To what extent can VR technology bolster promotional and intervention programs in this context?

Our investigative approach encompasses focus group sessions involving experts in both public health and VR technology, followed by a series of co-design workshops aimed at exploring VR design considerations. From these activities we aim to derive a set of guidelines for the design of VR experience specific to the scope of interventions for vaping and/or smoking.

We thus make the following contributions by: (1) Identifying and characterizing barriers to effective promotional campaigns; (2) Demonstrating the efficacy of inclusive co-design activities involving subject-matter experts, advocating the co-creation of innovative VR technologies for immersive experiences; and (3) Presenting a comprehensive outline and discussion of guidelines governing the development of VR experiences within the domain of public health programs.

2 Related Work

In the field of virtual health interventions, co-design is becoming an increasingly important approach. Our own work on co-design has been influenced by previous studies that have developed an understanding of public health in virtual settings. We drew on the knowledge and insights from these foundational works to create our own collaborative design process for immersive VR experiences, ensuring that our methods were informed and enriched by the precedents set before us.

2.1 Co-Design for Public Health

Co-design in the context of health applications is a collaborative approach to developing health interventions. It involves working with the people who will be affected by the intervention, such as patients, healthcare providers, and policy makers, to design an intervention that meets their needs. Co-design has been used in a variety of health interventions, including programs to improve patient care, reduce chronic diseases, and promote healthy lifestyles [1]. The goal of co-design is to create interventions that are more effective and sustainable than those developed by experts alone [2]. By involving the people who will be affected by the intervention, co-design can ensure that the intervention is tailored to their needs and that they are more likely to adopt and use it [1].

In previous years, co-design methods have been used to develop awareness campaigns [2, 3], interventions [4, 5] and reflections [6, 7]. Research has also demonstrated that co-designing technology with stakeholders is valued for creating meaningful technology solutions as well as for enriching and empowering the public in their own wellbeing [8]. Researchers are now actively seeking to involve subject matter experts (SMEs) in the design of new technologies (e.g. [9, 10]). However, little research has explored inclusive co-design involving SMEs of public health for VR contexts. This is particularly important when aiming to support public health campaigns in order to more authentically understand the context [11, 12] An example of co-design for public health is a workshop that is shown in Fig. 1 which brought together public health officials with designers and developers to collaboratively explore creative solutions for problems in the local context that are related to vaping and smoking in the general population.

Co-Design Workshops for Ideation

Collaborative Sketching and Brainstorming

Fig. 1. Contextual images of the co-design activities that were conducted in the project.

2.2 Smoking as a Public Health Concern

Tobacco smoking, whether it is via a cigarette or via heated or electronic delivery systems, is an international public health concern claiming over 8 million lives yearly as noted in [13]. The morbidity and mortality caused by smoking is preventable and is considered a modifiable risk factor [14–16]. Beside its devastating impact on health, the World Health Organization (WHO) reports the global economy's expenditure on healthcare and lost productivity to surpass 1 trillion US dollars each year [17].

Globally, various measures have been taken to regulate smoking and mitigate its adverse effects. These measures include increased taxation, commercial advertisement bans, public and workspace smoking restrictions, age restrictions, and international agreements such as the WHO Framework Convention on Tobacco Control [18, 19]. However, studies have demonstrated despite the impact of these measures, smoking still remains among the leading causes of death and a contributing factor to many diseases [20]. Recent advances in technology have provided health professionals with new opportunities for exploring innovative approaches to address the smoking epidemic issue and that is where mobile health applications, wearable devices, virtual reality, automated voice responses, smoking detectors, vape trackers, and games among others have emerged [5, 21–26].

2.3 VR Technologies for Public Health

Virtual Reality (VR) is defined as "a computer-generated digital environment that can be experienced and interacted with as if that environment were real" [27]. VR experiences are increasingly being considered in the realm of healthcare. Previous research has addressed the need to create immersive experiences in promotional campaigns and remedial programs. VR has also been reported to be an efficacious intervention in the treatment of various conditions such as in the treatment of phobias, management of pain, management of psychological disease, and physical rehabilitation [28–30].

Within the smoking domain, VR has been observed to either advocate or oppose the culture of smoking. This is evident from the body of literature present online. It has been reported that the tobacco industry spends more than 22.5 million dollars each day on their products' marketing plans and it has now leveraged VR technologies in the creation of video games with scenes that promote smoking [31–35]. This is quite concerning for the youth who are often the target audience of such video games, as evidence suggests that behaviors in the virtual realms can shape the behaviors in the real world [36, 37]. Furthermore, a simple search using search engines often leads to a wealth of discussions, images and videos that support the existence and promote the culture of smoking in VR games. On the other hand, research over the past two decades has shown VR technologies to be successfully used to promote smoking cessation and vaping cessation through exploring VR usage as interventions (via cue exposure therapy, cognitive behavioral therapy, approach avoidance task / gamified behavior training) as cue reactivity, and as anti-smoking campaigns, among other tools [24]. The success of VR utilization was due to several reasons including the ability of the VR to create a user specific immersive experience and the ability of VR to enable smokers to practice different ways of responding to a temptation within a safe environment that resembles the real world [38, 39].

3 Framework for VR Experiences in Persuasive Computing

3.1 Presence and Immersion in VR

Research has particularly focused on frameworks for presence, immersion and persuasive computing designs in the virtual realm [40]. Presence within the context of virtual reality is defined as one's sense of being in the virtual world whereas immersion is defined as the framework where place illusion occurs. We emphasize immersion and presence and this includes awareness of self, awareness of others and awareness of the environment as noted in [40, 41].

3.2 Persuasive Computing Design Considerations in the VR

Previous approaches involved creating real world scenarios in which participants had options to consider for responding to peer-pressure and other stimuli as depicted in role-playing user experiences. Research has shown that VR successfully contributed towards added realism and interactivity, increased knowledge and ultimately a change in behavior and/or attitude as evidenced in these studies [42, 43]. In this study, we explore the pivotal role of human factors in the design of VR applications, with a particular focus on the design factors that are relevant for immersion and presence during interactions in the real world and the virtual realm Five key design considerations are discussed, emphasizing their relevance in crafting immersive and effective VR experiences.

3.2.1 Design Considerations for VR Experiences

In this section, we describe the design constraints that are relevant for public health programs in general, with a specific focus on one use case for smoking cessation to highlight the applicability of the concepts and constraints in the VR context.

User Constraints

- Personalization: Allow users to customize their virtual smoking cessation experience, from choosing the appearance of their virtual environment to setting their own pace for use cases or scenarios (e.g. quitting).
- Behavioral Tracking: Implement user data tracking to provide tailored feedback and reminders based on individual smoking habits and progress in the VR experience (e.g. levels, scoring).
- Accessibility: Ensure the application is usable by individuals with varying levels of familiarity with VR technology, including those with physical or cognitive limitations.

Hardware Constraints

- Device Compatibility: Optimize the application to run on a range of VR headsets, from high-end devices to more affordable options, to maximize accessibility.
- Performance Optimization: Streamline graphics and interactions to maintain a consistent frame rate across different VR hardware, preventing motion sickness.
- Battery Management: Design power-efficient features and provide clear notifications to users about how long they can expect to use the application on a single charge.

Graphics Constraints

- Realistic Visuals: Create a visually immersive virtual environment with realistic smoking scenarios to trigger cravings while also offering persuasive nudges or communication embedded within the VR experience.

- Simplicity: Balance realism with simplicity, ensuring sufficient salience and that complex graphics do not overwhelm users or hinder interactions.
- Visual Feedback: Use graphics to visualize health improvements over time, reinforcing the benefits of quitting smoking.

3.2.2 Scale and Space

- Virtual world's scale: The scale in virtual realms has been shown to impact user engagement. A confined, controlled space can improve concentration, replicating real-world smoking and/or vaping scenarios. Alternatively, an expansive, infinite environment can encourage exploration and distraction, potentially harnessing the medium's potential for immersive distraction therapy. Hybrid approaches can be considered, in which designers can explore both of the above features by creating a confined virtual space with realistic smoking triggers for intense cravings, and an expansive, serene landscape for relaxation and distraction from cravings.
- Power of the Medium: Leveraging VR's capabilities enhances effectiveness. Realistic sensory feedback (haptic, olfactory) can replicate smoking sensations, aiding habit replacement. Simulating the tactile sensation and smell of smoking when users attempt to vape in the virtual world, reinforcing the association between vaping and smoking cessation.

These design considerations contribute towards a framework for understanding the user experience in VR experiences that are designed for smoking cessation, which consequently aids designers in optimizing the virtual environment's scale and sensory fidelity for persuasive computing scenarios.

3.2.3 Interaction Design Considerations

- Tools for Interaction: Provide users with intuitive tools for virtual interaction, such as handheld controllers or gestures, allowing them to navigate the virtual environment and engage with smoking cessation, stress reduction exercises.
- Tolerance: Ensure user-friendly controls with a forgiving tolerance for input errors, reducing frustration during critical cessation moments.
- User-System Interaction: Facilitate user-system interaction that is seamless and responsive, enabling users to control their virtual actions effectively.

These interaction design considerations guide the development of VR vaping applications, promoting effective user engagement and support in the journey to quit smoking as using handheld controllers, users can pick up and manipulate virtual cigarettes, reinforcing the tactile experience of smoking while gradually reducing nicotine levels.

3.2.4 Navigation Design

- Limit Navigation: Restrict excessive movement to maintain user immersion and focus on the cessation narrative.
- Free vs. Controlled Movement: Balance free exploration with controlled guidance in specific smoking awareness or cessation scenarios.

- Teleportation: Implement teleportation for user convenience and controlled transitions between scenes.
- Orientation: Ensure clear spatial orientation cues to prevent disorientation and maintain a smooth user experience.

Users can freely explore a tranquil virtual park for relaxation but are guided through controlled movements in therapy sessions focused on quitting smoking. Teleportation is available for seamless transition between these scenarios.

3.2.5 Designing for the Senses - Spatial Audio, Haptics and Olfaction

- Spatial Audio: Spatial audio is utilized to immerse users in the environment, guiding their attention or signaling actions. For instance, the sound of a calming breeze or support messages can encourage users to stay engaged.
- Haptics: Haptic feedback enhances immersion mimicking sensations related to vaping. Users can feel the simulated act of vaping as a tactile reminder.
- Olfaction: Olfactory cues are incorporated to evoke positive or aversive sensations, reinforcing the association between vaping and smoking cessation. For example, the smell of burnt cigarettes vs fresh air.

3.3 EO2 First Prototype Design for Virtual Reality (VR) Interventions on Smoking Perceptions

For our pilot study phase, termed EO2, we co-designed and developed three immersive VR scenarios tailored for distinct focus groups:

- Pre-Smokers Scenario: Targeting individuals who have never engaged in smoking. This scenario simulates various situations where participants practice declining offers to smoke, focusing particularly on handling peer pressure and the allure of curiosity.
- Current Smokers Scenario: Addressing those actively smoking, this scenario portrays the multifaceted consequences of continued smoking. It sheds light on the health repercussions, economic implications, familial burdens, and the eventual somber fate awaiting persistent smokers, presenting these realities in a compelling virtual setting.
- Ex-Smokers Scenario: Geared toward those who have quit smoking, this scenario is designed to bolster their resilience against relapses. It provides strategies to handle temptations and manage delayed gratifications, fortifying their commitment to a smoke-free life.

Each VR intervention is designed as an interactive game. Participants navigate these scenarios using external hardware, voice recognition, and hand gestures, making pivotal decisions at various junctures. Post-interaction, participants undergo interviews with a validated questionnaire, aiming to discern the VR intervention's impact on their smoking-related perceptions, knowledge, attitudes, and behaviors.

4 Conclusion

The interaction between humans and computers in virtual environments is a fundamental concept in human-computer interaction (HCI), but the co-design of health interventions for the virtual realm has been rarely studied. In this paper, we used co-design methods to investigate how this interaction can be explored in the context of public health programs with a focus on smoking and vaping as a use-case. We found that VR can be a powerful tool for both public health education and behavior change. The design considerations provide a framework for designers to consider the various constraints and design opportunities that can provide users with a realistic and immersive experience which consequently contribute toward understanding health risks and learning new behaviors. The co-design process highlighted opportunities for persuasive computing techniques which can be used to make VR experiences more effective for different demographics and to personalize health interventions to the individual user's needs.

Persuasive computing is a field of study that focuses on using technology to influence human behavior. By using persuasive computing techniques in the virtual realm, immersive VR experiences can be designed to amplify the salience of cues which are often embedded to motivate users to change their behavior. Our findings suggest that the fusion of VR and persuasive computing has the potential to contribute towards innovative programs for public health education and behavior change through leveraging these technologies. Future directions of research need to explore the various approaches for creating personalized, immersive, and persuasive VR experiences that are well aligned with public health objectives.

Acknowledgments. We would like to thank our colleagues in the MIT Solve program at Alfaisal University and the CoCreate program for their thoughtful discussions and feedback. Research assisted by Alfaisal University's Solve grant for 2023.

References

1. Slattery, P., Saeri, A.K., Bragge, P.: Research co-design in health: a rapid overview of reviews. Health Res. Policy Sys. **18**, 17 (2020). https://doi.org/10.1186/s12961-020-0528-9
2. Thorn, P., et al.: Developing a suicide prevention social media campaign with young people (The #Chatsafe Project): co-design approach. JMIR Mental Health **7**(5), e17520 (2020). https://doi.org/10.2196/17520
3. Chan, L., et al.: Evaluation of 'Shisha No Thanks' - a co-design social marketing campaign on the harms of waterpipe smoking. BMC Publ. Health **22**(1), 386 (2022). https://doi.org/10.1186/s12889-022-12792-y
4. Yadav, U.N., Lloyd, J., Baral, K.P., et al.: Using a co-design process to develop an integrated model of care for delivering self-management intervention to multi-morbid COPD people in rural Nepal. Health Res. Policy Sys. **19**, 17 (2021). https://doi.org/10.1186/s12961-020-00664-z
5. El Ali, A., Matviienko, A., Feld, Y., Heuten, W., Boll, S.: VapeTracker: Tracking vapor consumption to help e-cigarette users quit. In: Proceedings of the 2016 CHI Conference Extended Abstracts on Human Factors in Computing Systems, pp. 2049–2056, May 2016
6. Tong, C., et al.: Lessons and reflections from an extended co-design process developing an mHealth App with and for older adults: multiphase Mixed Methods Study. JMIR aging **5**(4), e39189 (2022). https://doi.org/10.2196/39189
7. Moll, S., et al.: Are you really doing 'codesign'? critical reflections when working with vulnerable populations. BMJ Open **10**(11), e038339 (2020). https://doi.org/10.1136/bmjopen-2020-038339

8. Sharpe, D., Green, E., Harden, A., Freer, R., Moodambail, A.: Towndrow S. 'It's my diabetes': co-production in practice with young people in delivering a 'perfect' care pathway for diabetes. Res. All **2**(2), 289–303 (2018). CrossRef
9. Threatt, A.L., et al.: The Design, prototyping, and formative evaluation of an Assistive Robotic Table (ART) for stroke patients. HERD **10**(3), 152–169 (2017). https://doi.org/10.1177/1937586716687802
10. Wray, T.B., Kahler, C.W., Simpanen, E.M., Operario, D.: User-centered, interaction design research approaches to inform the development of health risk behavior intervention technologies. Int. Interv. **15**, 1–9 (2018). https://doi.org/10.1016/j.invent.2018.10.002
11. Tabbaa, L., Ang, C.S., Siriaraya, P., She, W.J., Prigerson, H.G.: A reflection on virtual reality design for psychological, cognitive and behavioral interventions: design needs, opportunities and challenges. Int. J. Hum.-Comput. Interact. **37**(9), 851–866 (2021). https://doi.org/10.1080/10447318.2020.1848161
12. Mohamad, U.H., Ahmad, M.N., Benferdia, Y., Shapi'i, A., Bajuri, M.Y.: An overview of ontologies in virtual reality-based training for healthcare domain. Front. Med. **8**, 698855 (2021). https://doi.org/10.3389/fmed.2021.698855
13. Tobacco Fact Sheet. World Health Organization website. Accessed April 16, 2023. https://www.who.int/news-room/fact-sheets/detail/tobacco
14. Gleerup, H.B., et al.: Smoking is the dominating modifiable risk factor in younger patients with STEMI. Eur. Heart J. Acute Cardiovasc. Care **9**(1), 70–75 (2020). https://doi.org/10.1177/2048872618810414
15. Wannamethee, S. G., Shaper, A. G., Perry, I. J., & British Regional Heart Study: Smoking as a modifiable risk factor for type 2 diabetes in middle-aged men. Diabetes Care **24**(9), 1590–1595 (2001). https://doi.org/10.2337/diacare.24.9.1590
16. Ng, R., Sutradhar, R., Yao, Z.: Walter P Wodchis, Laura C Rosella, Smoking, drinking, diet and physical activity—modifiable lifestyle risk factors and their associations with age to first chronic disease. Int. J. Epidemiol. **49**(1), 113–130 (2020). https://doi.org/10.1093/ije/dyz078
17. U.S. National Cancer Institute and World Health Organization. The Economics of Tobacco and Tobacco Control. National Cancer Institute Tobacco Control Monograph 21. NIH Publication No. 16-CA-8029A. Bethesda, MD: U.S. Department of Health and Human Services, National Institutes of Health, National Cancer Institute; and Geneva, World Health Organization, CH (2016)
18. Sandford, A.: Government action to reduce smoking. Respirology **8**(1), 7–16 (2003). https://doi.org/10.1046/j.1440-1843.2003.00436.x. PMID: 12856736
19. Who framework convention on tobacco control overview World Health Organization. World Health Organization. https://fctc.who.int/who-fctc/overview. Accessed 16 April 2023
20. WHO Report on the Global Tobacco Epidemic, 2021: Addressing New and Emerging Products.World Health Organization (2021). https://www.who.int/publications/i/item/9789240032095
21. Ortis, A., Caponnetto, P., Polosa, R., Urso, S., Battiato, S.: A report on smoking detection and quitting technologies. Int. J. Environ. Res. Public Health **17**(7), 2614 (2020). https://doi.org/10.3390/ijerph17072614
22. Munafo, M.: How can technology support smoking cessation interventions? Nicotine & Tobacco Research: Official J. Soc. Res. Nicotine Tobacco **19**(3), 271–272 (2017). https://doi.org/10.1093/ntr/ntx019
23. Mahoney, M.C., et al.: Leveraging technology to promote smoking cessation in urban and rural primary care medical offices. Prev. Med. **114**, 102–106 (2018). https://doi.org/10.1016/j.ypmed.2018.06.016
24. Keijsers, M., Vega-Corredor, M.C., Tomintz, M., Hoermann, S.: Virtual reality technology use in cigarette craving and smoking interventions (I "Virtually" Quit): systematic review. J. Med. Internet Res. **23**(9), e24307 (2021). https://doi.org/10.2196/24307

25. Adams, A.T., Mandel, I., Shats, A., Robin, A., Choudhury, T.: PuffPacket: a platform for unobtrusively tracking the fine-grained consumption patterns of E-cigarette users. In Proceedings of the 2020 CHI Conference on Human Factors in Computing Systems, pp. 1–12, April 2020
26. Veronica, U., Weser, Kimberly, D., Hieftje: Invite only VR: a vaping prevention game: an evidence-based VR game for health and behavior change. In: ACM SIGGRAPH 2020 Talks (SIGGRAPH2020). Association for Computing Machinery, New York, NY, USA, Article 57, pp. 1–2 (2020). https://doi.org/10.1145/3388767.3407355
27. Jerald, J.: The VR Book: Human-Centered Design for Virtual Reality, vol. 8. Morgan & Claypool, San Rafael (2016). ISBN: 978-1-97000-115-0
28. Li, L., et al.: Application of virtual reality technology in clinical medicine. Am. J. Transl. Res. **9**(9), 3867–3880 (2017)
29. Grogna, D., Stassart, C., Servotte, JC., Bragard, I., Etienne, AM., Verly, J.G.: Some novel applications of VR in the domain of health. In: Bagnara, S., Tartaglia, R., Albolino, S., Alexander, T., Fujita, Y. (eds.) Proceedings of the 20th Congress of the International Ergonomics Association (IEA 2018). IEA 2018. Advances in Intelligent Systems and Computing, vol. 827. Springer, Cham (2019). https://doi.org/10.1007/978-3-319-96059-3_49
30. Amirthalingam, J., et al.: Virtual reality intervention to help improve motor function in patients undergoing rehabilitation for cerebral palsy, Parkinson's disease, or stroke: a systematic review of randomized controlled trials. Cureus **13**(7), e16763 (2021). https://doi.org/10.7759/cureus.16763
31. Tobacco industry marketing (2021) Centers for Disease Control and Prevention. Centers for Disease Control and Prevention. https://www.cdc.gov/tobacco/data_statistics/fact_sheets/tobacco_industry/marketing/index.htm. Accessed 17 April 2023
32. McDaniel, P.A., Forsyth, S.R.: Exploiting the "video game craze": a case study of the tobacco industry's use of video games as a marketing tool. PLoS ONE **14**(7), e0220407 (2019). https://doi.org/10.1371/journal.pone.0220407
33. Forsyth, S., McDaniel, P.A.: Cease and desist?' the persistence of Marlboro brand imagery in racing video games. Tob. Control. **29**(e1), e31–e40 (2020). https://doi.org/10.1136/tobaccocontrol-2019-055300
34. Forsyth, S.R., McDaniel, P.A.: Tobacco Imagery in the 20 Best-Selling Video Games of 2018. Nicotine & Tobacco Res. Off. J. Soc. Res. Nicotine and Tobacco **23**(8), 1341–1348 (2021). https://doi.org/10.1093/ntr/ntaa233
35. Forsyth, S.R., Malone, R.E.: Tobacco imagery in video games: ratings and gamer recall. Tob. Control. **25**(5), 587–590 (2016). https://doi.org/10.1136/tobaccocontrol-2015-052286
36. Hull, J.G., Brunelle, T.J., Prescott, A.T., Sargent, J.D.: A longitudinal study of risk-glorifying video games and behavioral deviance. J. Pers. Soc. Psychol. **107**(2), 300–325 (2014). https://doi.org/10.1037/a0036058
37. Kim, A.E., et al.: Influence of tobacco displays and ads on youth: a virtual store experiment. Pediatrics **131**(1), e88–e95 (2013). https://doi.org/10.1542/peds.2012-0197
38. Pericot-Valverde, I., Secades-Villa, R., Gutiérrez-Maldonado, J.: A randomized clinical trial of cue exposure treatment through virtual reality for smoking cessation. J. Subst. Abuse Treat. **96**, 26–32 (2019). https://doi.org/10.1016/j.jsat.2018.10.003
39. Machulska, A., et al.: Promoting smoking abstinence in smokers willing to quit smoking through virtual reality-approach bias retraining: a study protocol for a randomized controlled trial. Trials **21**(1), 227 (2020). https://doi.org/10.1186/s13063-020-4098-5
40. Berkman, M.I., Akan, E.: Presence and immersion in virtual reality. In: Lee, N. (eds.) Encyclopedia of Computer Graphics and Games. Springer, Cham (2019). https://doi.org/10.1007/978-3-319-08234-9_162-1

41. Yassien, A., Agroudy, P.E., Makled, E., Abdennadher, S.: A design space for social presence in VR. In: Proceedings of the 11th Nordic Conference on Human-Computer Interaction: Shaping Experiences, Shaping Society (2020)
42. Weser, V.U., et al.: Evaluation of a virtual reality E-cigarette prevention game for adolescents. Addict. Behav. **122**, 107027 (2021)
43. Ebrahimi, E., Hajj, D., Jarrett, M., Ferrell, A., Haddad, L., Chelala, M.: Designing virtual environments for smoking cessation: a preliminary investigation. In: Chen, J.Y.C., Fragomeni, G. (eds.) Virtual, Augmented and Mixed Reality: Design and Development. HCII 2022. Lecture Notes in Computer Science, vol. 13317. Springer, Cham (2022). https://doi.org/10.1007/978-3-031-05939-1_28

Supporting Schizophrenia PatiEnts' Care wiTh Robotics and Artificial Intelligence

Ilaria Amaro[1], Rita Francese[1(✉)], Genoveffa Tortora[1], Cesare Tucci[1], Lorenzo D'Errico[2], and Mariacarla Staffa[3]

[1] University of Salerno, Fisciano, Italy
{iamaro,francese,tortora,ctucci}@unisa.it

[2] University Federico II, Naples, Italy
lorenzo.derrico@unina.it

[3] Parthenope University of Naples, Naples, Italy
mariacarla.staffa@uniparthenope.it

Abstract. People with schizophrenia generally have different speech disorders, such as tangentiality, dissociation of thought, or perseveration. These disorders can be classified using the Thought and Language Disorder (TALD) scale, which measures the intensity of the different disorders based on the presence of particular characteristics of the speech. At present, the current practice to measure speech disorders through the TALD scale involves specialized clinicians who administer specific interviews to assess the degree of TALD's sub-scales with no technological support. Conducting the interviews is a very time consuming activity and an automatic support for the interview administration and the identification of the language disorders may be useful. In this paper, we propose an approach named RoboTald in which a robot is adopted for formulating questions to patients by following the TALD guidelines and to record their answers. The audio files are then automatically transcripted and inputted to a deep-learning-based system aiming at assessing the speech disorders basing on the TALD classification. Faced with the need to improve and speed up the classification and quantification of disorders we adopt NLP models for analyzing the speech characteristics. In particular, the robot dialogues with the patient and collects her speech. Starting from the transcription of patient's speech, TALD Item measurements are computed by Transformer models, able to recognize the semantic meaning of sentences and to understand the similarity between two inputs using the "Cosine Similarity" technique. This technique identifies the semantic distance between two inputs based on the features extracted from the text provided to the Transformer. The distances are then used to evaluate the elements of the scale by analyzing how far the various sentences deviate from the initial question or how far apart they are from each other. In this preliminary work we focus our attention on two elements of the TALD scale: Tangentiality and Derailment.

Keywords: Speech Disorder · Robotics · Artificial Intelligence · BERT · Schizophrenia · TALD · NLP

Q. Gao et al. (Eds.): HCII 2023, LNCS 14055, pp. 482–495, 2023.
https://doi.org/10.1007/978-3-031-48041-6_32

1 Introduction

Schizophrenia (SZ) affects approximately 24 million people, or 0.32% of the global population [16]. This incidence rate is 1 in 222 adults (0.45%). SZ causes psychosis and may result in severe disability that compromises all facets of life, including the personal, familial, social, and educational. It also has a significant impact on the employability and economic status of schizophrenics and their families. SZ is a complex disorder characterized by several distinct disorders which can be assimilated to SZ (for this named "group of schizophrenias" [3]), with partially overlapping phenomenology and neural correlates [4]. This disease has numerous symptoms, including persistent hallucinations, disorganized behavior, extreme agitation, and slowed movement. One other characteristic is the disorganized thought, which is frequently manifested in speech that is jumbled or irrelevant. Often people with SZ are discriminated and their human rights are violated. According to [16] more than two out of three people are not treated at all by psychiatrists.

There are care options for people with SZ, and in many cases, they can recover completely with the right care. Therefore, obtaining an early diagnosis may significantly improve the Quality of Life (QoL) of these patients.

Language and speech are the main sources of data for clinicians to diagnose and treat mental disorders [7], evaluated by analyzing the eventual presence of particular speech characteristics, which may emerge during an interview with the patient, and classifying their severity using the Thought and Language Disorder (TALD) scale [13]. These measurements represent a time-consuming task performed manually and without technological support by specialized physicians. Thus, an automated support for the administration of interviews and the identification of language disorders could be advantageous. AI methods and techniques may be a useful diagnostic aid for SZ.

In this paper, we present an on-going research in which Natural Language Processing (NLP) techniques are adopted to support the clinicians in the classification of the SZ patients degree of speech disorders according to the TALD scale by examining the definition of each element of the scale and by providing an algorithm for scoring the single items. Moreover, to reduce the time spent by the clinicians to administer the interviews, a humanized social robot is used to formulate questions according to the TALD scale to patients. A human-in-the-loop approach is adopted to permit the specialist to provide a direct feedback to the robot to correct sentences or suggest additional ones more suitable for the particular patient. The robot, given its physical presence and the possibility of movement, represents an added value compared to the classic monitoring systems as it can pro-actively provide services to the user, improving patient acceptance on the one hand, being equipped with the ability to both verbal and non-verbal communication and on the other hand representing a sort of mobile and hidden active sensor. The robot's sensors, such as cameras and microphones, are adopted to record the interview data during the administration of the TALD scale. This data are then transcripted to assess the presence of speech disorders.

Starting from the transcription of people's speeches, TALD item measurements are computed by the BERT model, able to recognize the semantic meaning of sentences and understand the similarity between two inputs using the "Cosine Similarity" technique. This technique identifies the semantic distance between two inputs based on the features extracted from the text provided to the Transformer. The distances are then used to evaluate the elements of the scale by analyzing how far the various sentences deviate from the initial question or how far apart they are from each other. Some examples of scoring of human-robot interaction according to the TALD scale are also reported.

The paper is organized as follows: Sect. 2 discusses background and related work. Section 3 presents the RoboTald methodology. Finally, Sect. 4 concludes the paper.

2 Background and Related Work

This section considers the main aspects of interest for this paper: NLP processing technique for assessing SZ, sentence embedding with BERT, and the use of robots for supporting clinicians in SZ diagnosis. The main concepts related to the TALD scale are also introduced.

2.1 ML Speech Analysis for Detecting Schizophrenia

Traditionally, the analysis of language for the diagnosis of schizophrenia it is not an easy task: it is relied on subjective measurements on which even the expert clinicians often disagree. In recent years, thanks to research advances in machine learning (ML) and NLP, it has been possible to demonstrate the effectiveness of automated natural language analysis for supporting the diagnosis of schizophrenia (e.g., [7,11,22]). In particular, these models automatically extract and analyze natural language features for the detection speech disorders which are characteristics of SZ patients, as described in the following.

Iter et al. [11] proposed an approach based on the analysis of speech coherence through the detection of ambiguous pronouns. Their model adopted speech analysis to classify healthy people belonging to the control group (HC), first-episode psychosis patients (FEP) and chronic schizopherenia patients. This model is the result of the improvement made on two existing algorithms, one for assessing tangentiality [9] and the other for assessing speech incoherence [2]. The Tangentiality Model compares responses to similar questions in fixed-sized word windows using the coherence metric. The slope of the linear regression line for the cosine similarity of the sliding window is used to calculate the coherence of a response. Steeper slopes indicate that the response is diverging from the query and becoming less comprehensible. By calculating the semantic coherence of each adjacent pair of sentences in a text to get a global coherence independent of the question, or First Order Coherence, what we will refer to as the Incoherence Model [2] quantifies the coherence of a speaker. Sentences are preprocessed to handle conversational aspects, and the representation is improved by using contemporary word and phrase embeddings. Phrases containing only stop words and any filler words (such as the many versions of uh, um, you know, etc.) are deleted. In order to capture semantically significant portions of the response without having to change the window size parameter, they secondly substituted sentence tokenization for the sliding window of the tangentiality model. The accuracy obtained in classifying the three groups was 80.97% (HC vs SZ), 85.93% (HC vs FEP + SZ), and 91.11% (HC vs FEP).

Huang et al. [10] considered two scales traditionally used for the diagnosis of schizophrenia to detect schizophrenia in Chinese patients: the Scale for the Assessment of Thinking, Language and Communication (TLC) [1], and the Positive and Negative Syndrome Scale (PANSS) [12]. Speech analysis detects the presence of negative and positive symptoms of schizophrenia. Long-Short Term Memory (LSTM) and pre-trained transformer-based models were adopted to analyze speech using three categories of features: two textual (semantic and syntactic) and one acoustic. In particular, BERT [8] was used for syntactic feature extraction while ELECTRA [6] was used for syntactic analysis of speech, and TERA [15] performed acoustic analysis. A two-layered neural network was finally trained for the prediction of the item scores, using the ratings of expert psychiatrists as a ground truth. The dataset used for the testing of the algorithms is composed by the speech (both in audio and textual formats) of 26 people diagnosed with schizophrenia. The model for the TLC scale items achieved an accuracy of 88% in classifying High-TLC disorder vs. low TLC disorder patients. The PANSS scale items including other information in addition to speech characteristics achieves a lower overall accuracy (80%). Specifically, an accuracy of 74% in the assessment of positive symptoms and an accuracy of 82% in the assessment of negative symptoms.

In [9], Elvevåg et al. developed a model for detecting speech incoherence in SZ patients, using Latent Semantic Analysis [14] (LSA). LSA was able to quantify incoherence, identify differences between patient and control groups, and predict clinical ratings. It was sensitive to subtle deviations and elevated levels of thought disorders. To reach such result, the authors set up 4 different experiments: a single word association task, a verbal fluency task, a structured interview, and a story-telling task. The authors propose LSA's potential for analyzing discourse across various patient groups and neuropsychological disorders, thereby facilitating treatment monitoring and increasing comprehension of language abnormalities.

2.2 The TALD Scale

The "Thought and Language Dysfunction Scale" (TALD) [13] aims at assessing in both objective and subjective way dysfunctions in language and thinking during clinical observation. The exploration lasts 50 min. Since specific language disturbs generally occur in stress conditions the interviewer has to afford emotional topics. The patient should have the time to speak freely. The scale is composed of 30 items that are scored considering the scale reported in Table 1.

Table 1. The TALD scores.

Value	Description
0	not present
1	doubtful (not definitely pathological; may also occur in healthy individuals)
2	mild
3	moderate
4	severe

Specifically, for this study, two of the thirty items on the TALD scale were considered Tangentiality and Derailment. A description of the items is provided in Table 2.

2.3 Sentence Embedding with BERT

The BERT model's capacity to capture contextual information in natural language processing tasks has garnered considerable attention, as it provides a robust framework for the generation of sentence embeddings, i.e., numerical representation of some text that is capable of capturing the semantic meaning and contextual information of sentences or larger writings. These representations enable NLP models to comprehend text data's nuances, relationships, and subtleties, useful to perform tasks such as sentiment analysis, text classification, query answering, and machine translation.

The BERT's sentence embedding production algorithm is shown in Fig. 1. The first step involves encoding the input sentences [17]. BERT tokenizes the

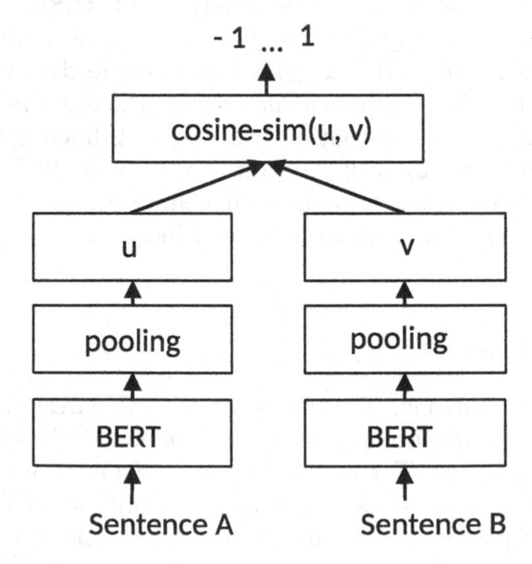

Fig. 1. SBERT architecture to compute similarity scores between two sentences. [17]

sentences into subword tokens and incorporates special tokens, such as [CLS] to mark the beginning of the sequence and [SEP] to separate sentences. The tokenized sentences are then transformed into input embeddings.

Next, BERT applies a stack of transformer layers to the input embeddings to capture the contextual relationships between the tokens and generate contextualized representations. This allows the system to model complex linguistic dependencies and produce robust embeddings. To obtain a fixed-sized embedding, a pooling operation is performed on the output of the transformer layers. In the case of BERT, the [CLS] token is typically used for pooling. The output representation of the [CLS] token captures the overall meaning and contextual information of the entire sentence.

For the specific objective of measuring the similarity between pairs of sentences, a regression objective function was used. Besides, BERT derives the similarity score by using the cosine similarity measure, which computes the cosine of the angle between two sentence embeddings. The cosine similarity between two sentence embeddings denoted as u and v is defined as follows:

$$cos(u, v) = \frac{u \cdot v}{||u|| * ||v||} \quad (1)$$

where $u \cdot v$ represents the dot product between the two vectors, and $||u||$ and $||v||$ represent their respective Euclidean norms. The output range of the function is [-1, 1].

The BERT model has been trained with a regression objective function by using pairs of sentences with known similarity scores as training data. The model is optimized by minimizing the mean squared error (MSE) loss between the predicted cosine similarity and the ground truth similarity score. Fine-tuning BERT with the regression objective function and minimizing the MSE loss enables the model to generate sentence embeddings that capture the semantic relatedness between pairs of sentences. This approach facilitates the creation of semantically meaningful sentence embeddings, which can then be used for various downstream tasks, such as similarity scoring or information retrieval.

2.4 Robot for Supporting SZ Detection

Assistive social robotics are receiving great attention from the scientific community, technological and industrial for their potential value not only in improving the QoL of large sections of the population [1–3], but also in supporting Doctors in time consuming and repetitive activities [19].

During last years, the use of social robots has been in fact explored to provide assistance to clinicians to the administration of pshycological/phsycometric assessment of patients with diverse disorders [19], and specifically tailored for a personalized interaction, taking into account personality and emotional aspects of the involved patient, as a human doctor would do [18].

Despite, as far as we know, the actual approach to SZ disorders assessment is realized exclusively by traditional paper-and-pencil tests, several studies have been conducted on the employment of social robots as screening tool for mental impairment. In [19] the authors explore the possibility of using social robots to assess different cognitive functions derived directly from the Montreal Cognitive Assessment test (MoCA) and adapted to be managed by a Softbank Pepper robot. Chang etn al. [5] investigated the possibility to assess Mild Cognitive Impairment (MCI), a risk factor for dementia in older adults, by using a social robot, examining the utility of five cognitive tests focused on language, episodic memory, prospective memory, and aspects of executive function to classify age-associated cognitive changes versus MCI.

In this work, we proposed the employment of a humanoid social robot to administer TALD scales to SZ Patients, that up to our knowledge is a completely new way of conducting the assessment in this particular medical field. The advantages of using this type of technology are various: first of all, according to recent research trends in HRI [20,21], our hypothesis is that non-verbal cues can provide a more natural interaction, with respect to interfaces that only produces a verbal interaction. In particular, a humanoid robot, due to its physical presence and similarity with human beings has the potential to portray a rich repertoire of non-verbal behaviors, which can make the interaction more credible and engaging since these behaviors express a social meaning that is very familiar to human users. Additionally, a robot can serve as an active sensor able to monitor and record the patients during the interaction, permitting to maintain the data of the interview also after the administration of the scales, with the two-fold intent to construct a new domain dataset and to permit clinicians to perform an in depth analysis of the patients peculiarity also a posteriori. This can be very useful both to maintain the history of each patient and also to identify a posteriori some details that can be missed during the interaction.

Table 2. The considered TALD-items [13].

Item	Description
Tangentiality	The speaker responds tangentially to the interviewer's question. The content of the speech is far from the original question
Derailment	A slow and steady slippage of the conversation with no awareness on the part of the speaker that his answer no longer has any connection with the question asked by the interviewer. Derailment should be coded objectively as if the interviewed were unaware of personal associative connections between thoughts

3 Methodology

We propose an approach called RoboTald in which a robot is used to ask patients scale-based questions and record their responses. The audio files are then automatically transcribed and fed into a deep-learning system designed to evaluate speech disorders based on TALD classification. Artificial Intelligence (AI) models have been implemented in an effort to improve and accelerate the classification and quantification of disorders. In particular, we compute the scores of the items of the TALD scale. This approach has two main motivations: (i) by using NLP techniques such as the cosine similarity between sentences we can provide a logical explanation of the produced score, (ii) working on the language characteristics without the need for a dataset that may be created by using the proposed system with the aid of the clinicians (Human-in-the-loop).

As shown in Fig. 2, RoboTald has three main components:

- the Questionnaire subministration module, running on the Pepper robot. It dialogs with the patient by proposing questions according to the TALD subministration protocol;
- the NLP module, which exploits NLP techniques together with Deep Learning models to compute the TALD scores;
- the clinician Web App, which enables the clinicians to listen to the audio track of the dialog between the patient and Pepper and provides a detailed description of the automatically computed scores of the TALD items.

In the remaining of this section we describe in detail these modules.

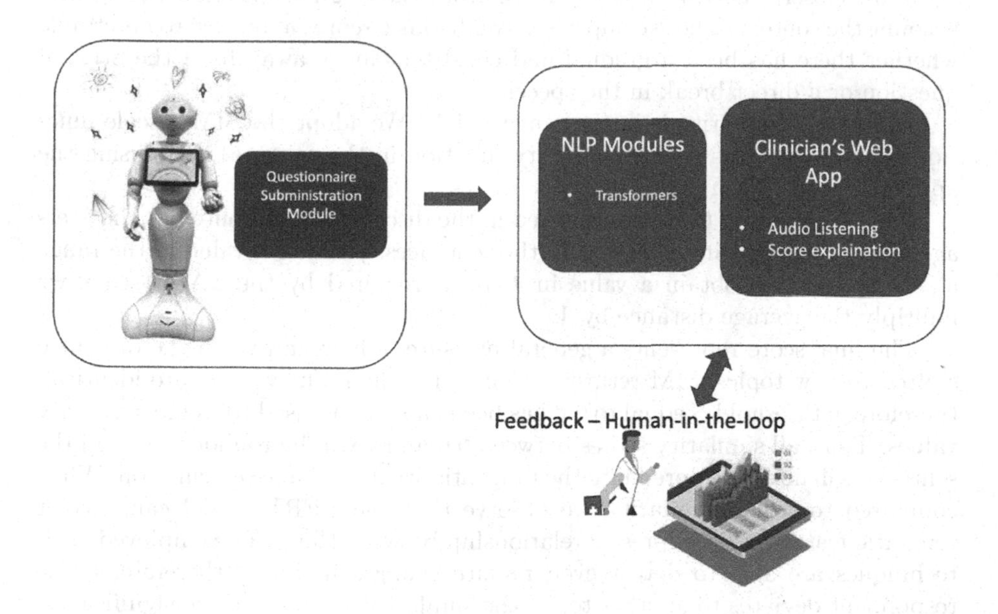

Fig. 2. Main RoboTald modules.

3.1 The NLP Module

In order to implement the NLP functionalities, we employed the *distiluse-base-multilingual-cased-v1* model[1], a language representation model based on the *distilBERT* architecture, a compact version of *BERT*. BERT computes the cosine similarity between two sentences, as described in Sect. 2.3.

The Tangentiality Scoring Algorithm. Tangentiality occurs when content suddenly drifts away from the interviewer question and the patient does not return to the initial topic 2. An example of tangentiality affected conversation with SZ patient is reported below:

> **Example of tangentiality affected conversation with SZ patient.**
>
> - What pizza do you like?
> - My favorite is certainly the Neapolitan pizza. In fact, I eat it almost all the time. Like everybody I listened to the radio in the sixties. They had a garage band down the street. I couldn't understand why the shoes were up on the wire. They said that the cloud was grey becose of the smog."

The Tangentiality algorithm (Algorithm 1) iteratively computes for each sentence s_i the similarity SIM between s_i and the previous two sentences s_{i-1} and s_{i-2}, and between s_i and the original question s_0. Thus, the algorithm evaluates how closely the *i-th* sentence is far from the original question taking into account the context. These comparisons of distance scores allow one to determine whether there has been a gradual and consistent move away from the original question or a direct break in the speech.

The cosine similarity is in the range [−1,1]. We adopt the SIM rescale function that rescales the cosine similarity function in the range [0,1] by using the approach proposed in [23].

The tangentiality that has occurred in the discourse is computed as the average of the tangentiality scores of all the sentences, yielding a value in the range [0, 1]. In order to obtain a value in [0,4], as required by the TALD scale, we multiply the average distance by 4.

The final score represents a general measure of how and when the discourse shifted to new topics. SIM returns 1 only when the input vectors are identical; therefore, a threshold S equal to 0.6 has been chosen and used to round similarity values. Thus, all similarity scores between 0.6 and 1 will be rounded up, and the sentence will not be factored into the tangentiality disturbance calculation. When compared to cosine similarity, we observe that the BERT model can extract semantic features that express a relationship between them. The employed NLP techniques are able to detect even minute changes in topic; therefore, if the respondent deviates to another topic, the similarity score would be significantly

[1] https://www.sbert.net/docs/pretrained_models.html, accessed on 22 June 2023.

Algorithm 1 kern-3pt. Pseudocode for the tangentiality assessment.

1: scores ← []
2: **for** $i \leftarrow 2$ to N **do**
3: $question\_similarity \leftarrow SIM(question\_embeddings, sentence\_embeddings[i])$ *question_embeddings is the clinician's question*
4: $first\_similarity \leftarrow SIM(sentence\_embeddings[i], sentence\_embeddings[i-1])$
5: $second\_similarity \leftarrow SIM(sentence\_embeddings[i], sentence\_embeddings[i-2])$
6: **if** $question\_similarity > S$ **then**
7: $question\_similarity \leftarrow 1$
8: **end if**
9: **if** $first\_similarity > S$ **then**
10: $first\_similarity \leftarrow 1$
11: **end if**
12: **if** $second\_similarity > S$ **then**
13: $second\_similarity \leftarrow 1$
14: **end if**
15: $question\_distance \leftarrow 1 - question\_similarity$
16: $first\_distance \leftarrow 1 - first\_similarity$
17: $second\_distance \leftarrow 1 - second\_similarity$
18: $scores$.append($question\_distance$)
19: $scores$.append($first\_distance$)
20: $scores$.append($second\_distance$)
21: **end for**
22: $meanTan \leftarrow$ mean($scores$)
23: $tangentiality \leftarrow \lceil 4 \times meanTan \rceil$

lower than 0.6. This method enables to attain more reliable scores in situations involving no or minimal tangentiality. Considering the example of conversation above reported, RoboTald produced a tangentiality score of 3.0.

The Derailment Scoring Algorithm. Derailment is defined as *a slow and steady slippage of the conversation.* Below is reported an example of a conversation with SZ patient affected by derailment.

Example of a derailment affected conversation with SZ patient.

- Which city do you belong to?
- Well, it's hard to say. I was born in Marburg, but my parents met in Cologne. It was a difficult period, they faced many financial difficulties. It was during war and we were forced to leave our town. The trip was very long. I met a very beautiful girl.

For the assessment of the derailment score, it was deemed necessary to consider two speech characteristics:

- The rate at which the patient departs from the main topic.
- The frequency with which she returns to the original topic after deviating from it.

Let's formalize these two traits. Let X be a question sentence, and let $Y = y_1, y_2, ..., y_N$ be a set of N sentences corresponding to the answer, where y_i is the *i-th* period in the answer. Finally, let T_1 be a threshold. When k is in $[1, N]$ and

$$SIM(X, yk) \leq T_1 \tag{2}$$

derailment is detected in the discourse at the k_{th} sentence of the response. For every index k that meets this condition, y_k is stored in a vector. To avoid a disproportionate impact on the derailment score, we wish to identify the sentences in the response resulting in a significant detachment from the main topic of the discussion. When a patient completely changes the topic of the speech, they may demonstrate speech disorders other than derailment, such as tangentiality or cognitive dissociation. For this reason, it is important to be able to discern between strong and slight topic deviations. Let T_2 be a new threshold. For some k, we will say that the patient's answer has strongly distanced from the original topic when

$$SIM(X, y_k) < T_1 \cap SIM(X, y_{k-1}) > T_1 \tag{3}$$

and

$$SIM(X, y_{k-1}) - SIM(X, y_k) > T_2 \tag{4}$$

In order to obtain a score to classify the presence of strong deviations, we divide the total number of strong deviations by the number of sentences in the speech. We obtain a value between 0 and 1 that we refer to as the strong detachments score. Since abrupt pauses are not a symptom of derailment, but can also characterize other disorders, we derive in this way a value that has a diminishing effect as the number of strong detachments increases. In practice, the score has minimal effect on the calculation of derailment if the patient abruptly detaches her speech multiple times.

To reliably classify the results, it is also needed to determine how frequently the patient returns to the original topic of the question. Returning to the original topic of the conversation results in a less severe derailment score. When in an answer Y, for some k such that derailment was detected in y_k, and

$$SIM(X, y_{k+1}) > T_1 \tag{5}$$

a return to the original topic is detected. The metric of topic return provides an indication of whether the patient has effectively resumed discussing the original topic. A lower quotient is derived when the patient demonstrates only sporadic returns to the topic. By subtracting this quotient from 1, we enhance the scoring of patient returns, thereby accentuating derailment. The evaluation of derailment is aided by the patient's ability to consistently return to the initial theme. If the patient repeatedly veers off topic without returning, the degree of derailment is considered severe. Conversely, if the patient frequently strays from the subject matter, the score remains low. In the algorithm's final step, we acquire three intermediate scores: one reflecting the frequency of detachment from the original topic (q_d), another representing significant digressions (q_s), and a third denoting returns to the initial topic (q_r). More details about the computations of these scores are presented in Algorithm 2.

As equal weightage is assigned to the three quotient in the calculation of the final derailment score, they all are divided by 3, yielding a range of $[0, 0.33]$ for each component. The sum of these calculated scores is a value between 0 and 0.99. Multiplying this value by 4 produces the ultimate outcome of the algorithm, specifically the TALD derailment score.

Algorithm 2 kern-3pt. Pseudocode for the derailment score assessment.

1: $X \leftarrow question$
2: $Y \leftarrow answer$
3: $deviations \leftarrow []$
4: **for** i ← 1 to N **do**
5: $similarities[i] \leftarrow SIM(X, y_i)$
6: **if** $similarities[i] \leq T_1$ **then**
7: $deviations.append(i)$
8: **end if**
9: **end for**
10: **for** i ← 0 to length(deviations) **do**
11: **if** $similarities[i-1] \geq T_1$ **then**
12: **if** $similarities[i-1] - smilarities[i] > T_2$ **then**
13: strong_deviation ← strong_deviations + 1
14: **end if**
15: **end if**
16: **end for**
17: returns ← []
18: **for** j ← 0 to length(deviations) **do**
19: **if** $similarities[deviations[j]+1] \geq T_1$ **then**
20: returns.append(j + 1)
21: **end if**
22: **end for**
23: $deviation\_score \leftarrow 1 - (length(deviations)/N)$
24: $strong\_deviation\_score \leftarrow 1 - (strong\_deviations/N)$
25: $returns\_score \leftarrow 1 - (length(returns)/N)$
26: $deviation\_score \leftarrow deviation\_score/3$
27: $strong\_deviation\_score \leftarrow strong\_deviation\_score/3$
28: $returns\_score \leftarrow returns\_score/3$
29: $derailment \leftarrow (deviation\_score + strong\_deviation\_score + returns\_score) * 4$

RoboTald produced 3 as derailment score for the initial example.

4 Conclusion

In this paper we present RoboTald, a system integrating a Robot with speech to text and NLP features to stimulating conversation with patients according to the TALD SZ assessment methodology and supporting the clinicians in the identification of speech disorders. In this preliminary phase, we concentrated our attention on two subscales of the TALD methodology, namely derailment and tangentiality.

We observed that RoboTald has difficulty when patients doesn't speak in clear way or when they use dialect. For this kind of patients other metrics are more effective, such as poverty of speech, logorrhoca, slowed thinking and pressured speech, based on the number of the word pronounced. Thus, in future work we will aim to implement algorithms that are able to analyze and evaluate other language disorders considered by TALD for the diagnosis of schizophrenia. In addition, since the proposed algorithms are intended to assist clinicians during diagnostic evaluation, we aim to conduct future studies on an extended sample of patients diagnosed with schizophrenia.

Acknowledgement. We acknowledge financial support from the Research Projects of Significant National Interest (PRIN) 2022 PNRR, project n. D53D23017290001 entitled "Supporting schizophrenia PatiEnts Care wiTh aRtificiAl intelligence (SPECTRA)".

References

1. Andreasen, N.C.: Scale for the assessment of thought, language, and communication (TLC). Schizophr. Bull. **12**(3), 473 (1986)
2. Bedi, G., et al.: Automated analysis of free speech predicts psychosis onset in high-risk youths. npj Schizophr. **1**(1), 1–7 (2015)
3. Bleuler, E.: Dementia praecox or the group of schizophrenias (1950)
4. Brugger, S.P., Howes, O.D.: Heterogeneity and homogeneity of regional brain structure in schizophrenia: a meta-analysis. JAMA Psychiat. **74**(11), 1104–1111 (2017)
5. Chang, Y.L., Luo, D.H., Huang, T.R., Goh, J.O., Yeh, S.L., Fu, L.C.: Identifying mild cognitive impairment by using human-robot interactions. J. Alzheimers Dis. **85**(3), 1129–1142 (2022)
6. Clark, K., Luong, M.T., Le, Q.V., Manning, C.D.: ELECTRA: pre-training text encoders as discriminators rather than generators. arXiv preprint arXiv:2003.10555 (2020)
7. Corcoran, C.M., et al.: Language as a biomarker for psychosis: a natural language processing approach. Schizophr. Res. **226**, 158–166 (2020)
8. Devlin, J., Chang, M.W., Lee, K., Toutanova, K.: BERT: pre-training of deep bidirectional transformers for language understanding. In: Proceedings of the 2019 Conference of the North American Chapter of the Association for Computational Linguistics: Human Language Technologies, vol. 1 (Long and Short Papers), pp. 4171–4186. Association for Computational Linguistics, Minneapolis, Minnesota (2019). https://doi.org/10.18653/v1/N19-1423. https://aclanthology.org/N19-1423

9. Elvevåg, B., Foltz, P.W., Weinberger, D.R., Goldberg, T.E.: Quantifying incoherence in speech: an automated methodology and novel application to schizophrenia. Schizophr. Res. **93**(1–3), 304–316 (2007)
10. Huang, Y.J., et al.: Assessing schizophrenia patients through linguistic and acoustic features using deep learning techniques. IEEE Trans. Neural Syst. Rehabil. Eng. **30**, 947–956 (2022)
11. Iter, D., Yoon, J., Jurafsky, D.: Automatic detection of incoherent speech for diagnosing schizophrenia. In: Proceedings of the Fifth Workshop on Computational Linguistics and Clinical Psychology: From Keyboard to Clinic, pp. 136–146 (2018)
12. Kay, S.R., Fiszbein, A., Opler, L.A.: The positive and negative syndrome scale (PANSS) for schizophrenia. Schizophr. Bull. **13**(2), 261–276 (1987)
13. Kircher, T., et al.: A rating scale for the assessment of objective and subjective formal thought and language disorder (TALD). Schizophr. Res. **160**(1–3), 216–221 (2014). https://doi.org/10.1016/j.schres.2014.10.024. https://www.sciencedirect.com/science/article/pii/S0920996414005933
14. Landauer, T.K., Foltz, P.W., Laham, D.: An introduction to latent semantic analysis. Discourse Process. **25**(2–3), 259–284 (1998)
15. Liu, A.T., Li, S.W., Lee, H.Y.: TERA: self-supervised learning of transformer encoder representation for speech. IEEE/ACM Trans. Audio Speech Lang. Process. **29**, 2351–2366 (2021)
16. World Health Organization: Schizophrenia. https://www.who.int/news-room/fact-sheets/detail/schizophrenia
17. Reimers, N., Gurevych, I.: Sentence-BERT: sentence embeddings using Siamese BERT-networks. arXiv preprint arXiv:1908.10084 (2019)
18. Rossi, S., et al.: The role of personality factors and empathy in the acceptance and performance of a social robot for psychometric evaluations. Robotics **9**(2), 39 (2020). https://doi.org/10.3390/robotics9020039. https://www.mdpi.com/2218-6581/9/2/39
19. Rossi, S., Santangelo, G., Staffa, M., Varrasi, S., Conti, D., Di Nuovo, A.: Psychometric evaluation supported by a social robot: Personality factors and technology acceptance. In: 2018 27th IEEE International Symposium on Robot and Human Interactive Communication (RO-MAN), pp. 802–807. IEEE Press (2018). https://doi.org/10.1109/ROMAN.2018.8525838
20. Rossi, S., et al.: Robot head movements and human effort in the evaluation of tracking performance. In: RO-MAN, pp. 791–796. IEEE (2015). http://dblp.uni-trier.de/db/conf/ro-man/ro-man2015.html#RossiSGGRTV15
21. Rossi, S., Staffa, M., Tamburro, A.: Socially assistive robot for providing recommendations: comparing a humanoid robot with a mobile application. Int. J. Soc. Robot. **10**(2), 265–278 (2018). https://doi.org/10.1007/s12369-018-0469-4. A correction to this article is available https://doi.org/10.1007/s12369-018-0489-0
22. Tang, S.X., et al.: Natural language processing methods are sensitive to sub-clinical linguistic differences in schizophrenia spectrum disorders. npj Schizophr. **7**(1), 25 (2021)
23. Zhang, T., Kishore, V., Wu, F., Weinberger, K.Q., Artzi, Y.: BERTScore: evaluating text generation with BERT. arXiv preprint arXiv:1904.09675 (2019)

Can the Use of Avatars Contribute to Human Well-Being?

Hideyuki Ando(✉) and Nagi Ono

Osaka University of Arts, 469 Higashiyama, Kanan-cho, Minamikawachi-gun, Osaka, Japan
Hideyuki.a@osaka-geidai.ac.jp

Abstract. In this paper, we discuss the effect of using an avatar on interpersonal communication. Past research has confirmed that changes in communication and cognition such as the "Proteus effect" and "disappearance of stereotypes" occur. In this research, we are discussing whether we can improve our own wellbeing. Users with a tendency to stutter cannot speak well face-to-face, but wearing an avatar reduces the number of times they stutter, and it was confirmed that stress was reduced from the biological response. Based on this, we discuss the impact of avatars on communication-related wellbeing.

Keywords: Avatar · Stuttering disorder · face-to-face communication

1 Introduction

Numerous studies have investigated the possibility of improving the level of human well-being using information technology [1, 2], and developed techniques to promote interpersonal communications via the metaverse, a cutting-edge technology [3]. Virtual reality (VR) technology helps users immerse in a virtual world. The essence of VR technology is that it allows users to perceive computer-generated objects and scenes as if they are real. This technology manipulates subconscious physical responses to create an illusion of reality [4]. For example, in a study, participants were shown a VR environment wherein a wooden plank was placed between two high-rises. The participants were then asked to walk across the plank. The VR environment induced the participants to react as if they faced an emergency—their legs trembled and they became petrified—although they were aware that the plank was only a few centimeters above the floor [5]. It implies that VR environments temporarily affect the way the human brain processes information.

In face-to-face communications, the inflection and speech style of an individual change depending on whom they interact with. The tone of voice an individual uses to converse with their partner differs from that used to talk to their children. The phenomenon in which humans subconsciously change their speech patterns during interpersonal communications is consistent with the phenomenon of "individualism" [6].

According to the literature [3], males choose female avatars, instead of male avatars, 76% of the time, while females choose female avatars 79% of the time. This indicates

Q. Gao et al. (Eds.): HCII 2023, LNCS 14055, pp. 496–505, 2023.
https://doi.org/10.1007/978-3-031-48041-6_33

that the number of female avatars is higher than that of male avatars. This is probably because females are generally considered more receptive and softer than males are. In the metaverse space, where establishing an effective communication is important, users do not usually choose avatars that appear domineering or awe-inspiring to others.

Proteus effect [7, 8] describes the effect of avatars on interpersonal communication. Research reveals that users are likely to disclose information when they interact with attractive avatars. Additionally, users feel a sense of heightened self-esteem and other psychological effects when their avatars are taller than they are.

In conclusion, the Proteus effect induces a user to associate a set of character traits to an avatar based on its appearance and to conform to predictable attitudes and behaviors. Furthermore, according to a similar study [9], the uniform of an avatar influences the behavior response it evokes.

Moreover, a study [10] was conducted on the possibility of using avatars to change "stereotypes." The study found that interacting with a black avatar in a VR space for three days reduced implicit racial bias, as evidenced by the results of a race implicit association test. Stereotyping is often considered a subconscious behavior. This is because the prejudices, values, and experiences humans encounter for long periods are ingrained in the brain. They shape human behavior and thought processes, thereby creating prejudices and biases toward certain groups and individuals.

However, people can improve their stereotypical behavior by identifying the subconscious stereotypes they believe about others.

Hence, numerous studies have suggested that VR avatars can be used to treat various psychological problems [11]. The Proteus effect and stereotyping are often considered subconscious behaviors. This is because humans are unaware of the influences perceptions and impressions exert on their behavior and thoughts. However, in certain cases, individuals may deliberately attempt to conform to the opinions and actions of a group under the influence of the group.

"Stuttering disorder" is a condition in which stuttering occurs when interpersonal communication in daily life is accompanied by tension, which inhibits the patient from communicating with others. Some scholars believe that the disorder is caused by social anxiety.

The symptoms for this disorder can vary significantly depending on the speaker, the context of the conversation, and other factors. Therefore, it is possible that the disorder is related to the aforementioned phenomenon in which humans subconsciously change their speech patterns. It may be possible to solve "stuttering" problems by effecting the subconscious change in speech patterns using external stimuli.

Alternatively, using an avatar can improve self-confidence and self-esteem, and reduce stress and anxiety; hence, the use of avatars is a potential avenue for curing stuttering, which in most cases is caused by stress and other psychological factors.

This paper discusses the possibility of using avatars to improve the quality of human-to-human communications.

2 Reduction of Stuttering and Psychological Loads

Reference [12] investigated the conditions that predispose an individual to stuttering and demonstrated that the likelihood of an individual developing stuttering was high when the individual was exposed to high psychological loads, such as high stress or tension. Reference [13] demonstrated the effectiveness of shadowing in reducing stuttering.

On the basis of these findings, we hypothesized that stuttering in an individual could be reduced using avatars, through which the individual can pretend to be a character who could speak fluently.

3 Experiment: The Effect of Using Avatars on Stuttering [14]

In this section, we discuss the experiments [14] that were conducted to investigate the effects of using avatars on stuttering and the possibility of using avatars to improve the quality of communication.

In the experiment, we counted the number of times subjects tended to stutter when they were talking face-to-face with a person who exhibited no speech impairments. We counted the number also when the subjects were talking in a VR space with an avatar with whom the subjects felt comfortable. Subsequently, the change in the number was noted. The psychological load of the subjects was measured using galvanic skin response [15].

3.1 Preparation for the Experiment

The avatar used in the experiment (Fig. 1: right) was designed to be amiable and approachable. The avatar was equipped with a lip-sync function and a function to switch facial expressions to ensure that the subjects would feel comfortable during their conversation.

The VR space used for the experiment was designed with a typical layout and an atmosphere suitable for the avatars, to ensure that the participants would feel comfortable in the environment (Fig. 1: left). In addition, mirrors were placed on the walls so that the subjects could view their avatars synchronizing with them. This was intended to accentuate their feeling of having a total physical control over the body of their avatar. The avatar and experimental environment were uploaded to VRChat [16] for the experiments.

3.2 Stuttering Frequency Measurement

OculusQuest2 was used as the VR device. Subjects who had a tendency to stutter (A) and normal subjects (B) interacted with each other under two modes. In the first mode, the A and B subjects interacted with each other using VR avatars ("avatar" mode). In the second mode, the A and B subjects engaged in face-to-face interactions without using avatars ("face-to-face" mode). In the avatar mode (Fig. 2, 3), the A subjects wore an HMD, whereas the B subjects interacted with a PC screen. Their conversations under the two modes were recorded. The number of times the A subjects stuttered under the avatar and face-to-face modes was assessed using the recorded tapes.

Fig. 1. The experimental environment in the VR space (left) and Avatar (right)

In this experiment, one A subject was asked to interact with twelve B subjects. This was done to address the possibility that the number of times an A subject stuttered depended on whom the subject interacted with. One B subject was asked to interact with twelve A subjects because the frequency of stuttering might differ between each A subject. In addition, to investigate the effect of the order of the modes, six B subjects participated in the avatar mode first and then in the face-to-face mode, whereas the remaining six participated in the opposite mode order.

Fig. 2. Avatar user of Experiments.

To examine the psychological load of the A subjects under the two modes, we measured the electrodermal activity in the A subjects using an E4 wristband (Empatica) during the interactions. The measurements were obtained before conducting the experiment in the avatar mode and during the face-to-face mode. To investigate the influence of the avatar, we instructed the B subjects to answer a questionnaire using the SD method after the experiment. All subjects were asked about the ease of talking to each other

Fig. 3. Avatar in VR space.

face-to-face and talking to an avatar. A 5-point rating scale was used, wherein 1 indicated that interactions were considerably easy and 5 indicated that they were extremely difficult. The questionnaire included a comment box for providing optional answers.

4 Experimental Results

4.1 Comparison of the Frequency of Stuttering

Table 1 shows the number of times the A subjects stuttered in the experiment. The results were analyzed using Wilcoxon's signed-rank sum test (5% significance level) (Fig. 4). On average, the number of times the A subjects stuttered under the avatar mode is 6.67 and under the face-to-face mode is 9.33. The median frequency of stuttering under the avatar and face-to-face modes are 6.50 and 9.50, respectively. This confirms that the frequency of stuttering can be decreased using avatars.

Table 1. Frequency of stuttering.

Number of Participants	1	2	3	4	5	6	7	8	9	10	11	12
Via Avatar	7	4	6	4	3	8	6	8	10	10	10	4
Face-to-face	10	6	9	6	6	13	8	12	13	11	11	7

Subsequently, we examined the effect of the mode order on the frequency of stuttering. We investigated whether the frequency of stuttering recorded when the (a) face-to-face mode was performed first, followed by the avatar mode, differed from that when (b) the avatar mode was performed first followed by the face-to-face mode. As shown in Fig. 4, under (a), the average frequencies of stuttering in the face-to-face and avatar modes are 9.17 and 6.33, respectively. Under (b), the average frequencies of stuttering in the face-to-face and avatar modes are 9.50 times and 7.00, respectively. The frequency under the avatar mode is lower than that under the face-to-face mode, regardless of the order of the modes (Fig. 5).

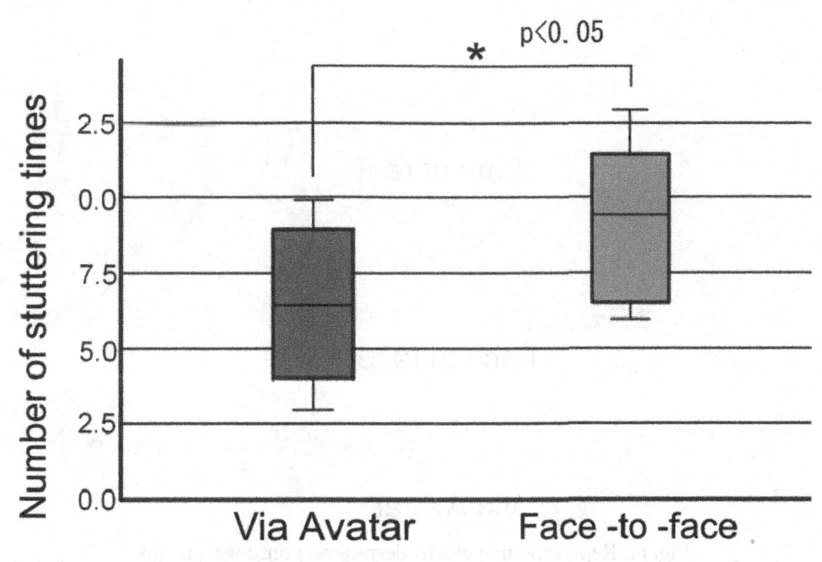

Fig. 4. Difference in the frequency of stuttering between the avatar and face-to-face modes

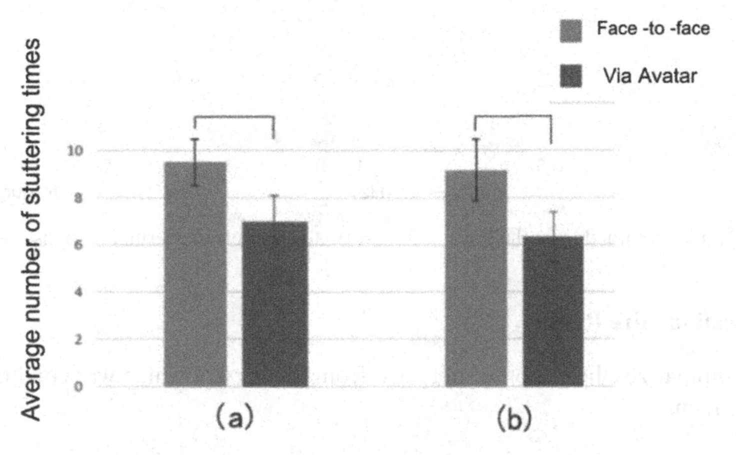

Fig. 5. Experimental results illustrating the order effect

4.2 Comparison of Psychological Loads Obtained Using Electrodermal Responses

Figure 6 shows the representative electrodermal response waveforms obtained from the A subjects. All electrodermal responses were analyzed using fast Fourier transform. As shown in Fig. 7, compared with the avatar mode, the face-to-face mode exhibits higher frequency components, and the responses from all the twelve subjects exhibit this trend. According to literature [6], high frequency components tend to appear under high psychological loads. Evidently, the psychological load is lower in the avatar mode than in the face-to-face mode.

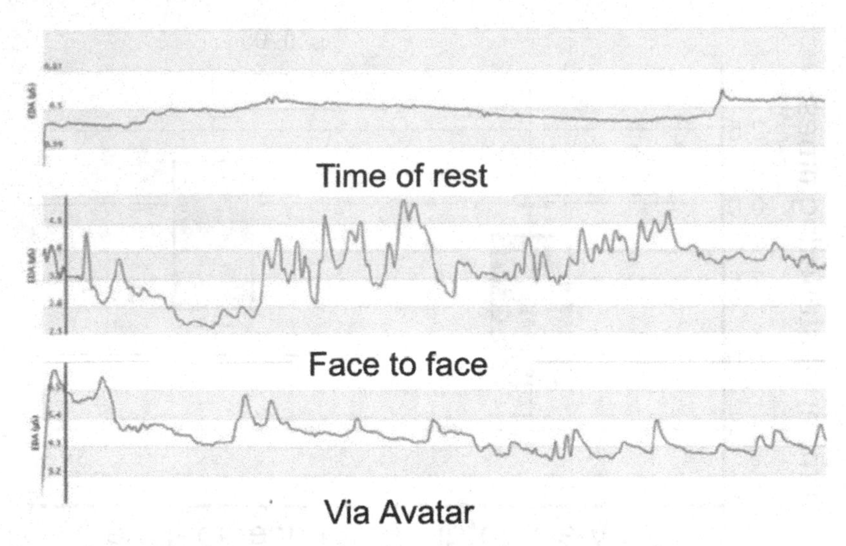

Fig. 6. Representative electrodermal response waveforms

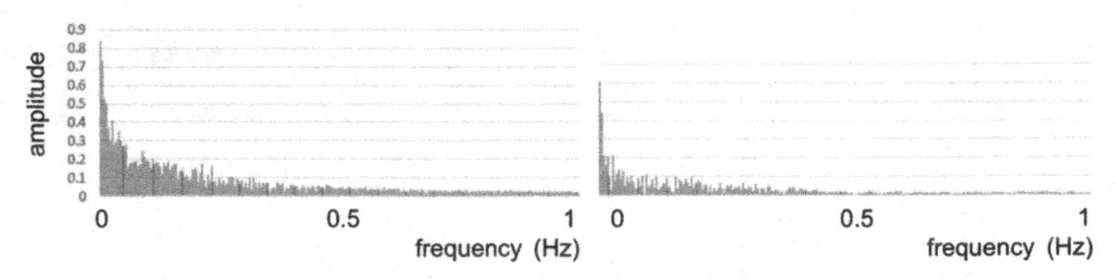

Fig. 7. Results obtained from the Fourier transformation of electrodermal response waveforms

4.3 Questionnaire Results

Table 2 summarizes the responses obtained from the survey, which was conducted after the experiment.

Table 2. Questionnaire results

Number of Participants	1	2	3	4	5	6	7	8	9	10	11	12
Via Avatar	5	2	1	1	3	3	1	1	4	3	2	5
Face-to-face	4	1	1	4	2	2	3	3.5	2	1	2	3

The questionnaire scores were structured such that the scores were inversely correlated to the ease of conversation. As shown in Table 2, the scores provided by seven subjects are lower for the avatar mode than those for the face-to-face mode. By contrast, scores provided by the remaining five subjects are lower for the face-to-face mode than those for the avatar mode. This implies that five subjects prefer the face-to-face mode and seven subjects the avatar mode.

Original comments provided by nine subjects are given below.

"I didn't know where to look when I had to talk face-to-face. I did not need to be as careful with the avatars."

"I thought the avatar's gestures were better; however, the feeling that we were strangers was stronger when I was talking to the avatar."

"The avatar's reactions were a little confusing because they were formulaic. They were as annoying as when someone uses thumbs up and the peace sign in a normal conversation."

"I felt more comfortable interacting face-to-face because I am used to it and I can see facial expressions. It would be better if the avatars could establish eye contact."

"I felt that the hurdle I feel whenever I talk to someone for the first time was lowered. I could talk like myself. It is strange but in a good way."

"It was easy to talk under both situations; however, I felt more alive with the avatar."

"It was easier to look people in the eye when I used my avatar."

"It was easier to talk to the avatar because I could not see the other person's facial expressions. I am nervous about looking people in the eye. It was easy to talk to the avatar because it was smiling all the time."

"I am a gamer; it is much easier to have in-depth conversations with an avatar. Others' eye contact and body language make me nervous; hence, it is difficult for me to discuss in-depth topics with them."

"It was easier to talk to the avatar. I was surprised to see how different this was. I have to try hard to make eye contact with people whenever I talk to them face-to-face, and I think it is better to use an avatar because it does not require such norms."

The above comments demonstrated that seven subjects felt more comfortable talking to the avatar than talking face-to-face to with the B subjects. However, one subject expressed an aversion to interacting through the avatar.

5 Discussion

This experiment suggests that communicating through an avatar in a VR space can reduce stuttering. Electrodermal responses indicate that avatars can reduce the psychological load generated during conversations.

Furthermore, the questionnaire survey results indicated that some normal subjects found it easier to communicate with the A subjects when the avatars were used.

The extent to which this effect can be reproduced is unclear as only one subject had stuttering in this experiment. Therefore, an experiment is currently being conducted with the cooperation of a medical institution and another subject who exhibits stuttering symptoms. It was crucial to examine the changes in the brain activity between the avatar and face-to-face modes.

The latent cause model [16] can be applied to model the changes in the speech patterns that occur during interpersonal communications, which is described in Sect. 1.

The model can be conceptualized as a module that switches on for a person when the person is comfortable interacting with another. Furthermore, if the relationship between sensory stimuli and switching threshold can be observed using fMRI, it may be possible to control "individualism" in the metaverse space.

This may solve the problem of stuttering and facilitate smooth communication with whom conversations may be inhibited by generation gap. It may also function as an effective interface that eliminates discrepancies in human-to-human communication, for example, by generating sustained conversations with people of differing perspectives. However, unintentional changes may have the same effect as brainwashing. It may be misused for undesirable solicitation or persuasion. Therefore, ethical regulations may be required in particular cases, and sufficient verification is necessary.

6 Conclusion

In this paper, we discussed the effect of using an avatar on interpersonal communication. We demonstrated that avatars could be used to treat people who stutter.

Subsequently, we discussed the positive and negative aspects of developing and implementing the proposed technique. We plan to examine the implications of the proposed technique further to ensure that it will not be misused.

Acknowledgments. This work is supported by CREST JPMJCR22P4.

References

1. Calvo, R.A., Peters, D.: Positive Computing: Technology for Wellbeing and Human Potential. The MIT Press, 28 November 2014
2. A life of wellbeing. http://wellbeing-technology.jp/. Accessed 31 Jan 2023
3. Virtual Beautiful Girl Nemu: Metaverse Evolution Theory (in Japanese), Gijutsuhyoronsha, 16 March 2022
4. Bailenson, J.: Experience on demand: what virtual reality is, how it works, and what it can do. W. W. Norton & Company, 30 January 2018
5. Richie's Plank Experience. https://store.steampowered.com/app/517160/Richies_Plank_Experience. Accessed 31 Jan 2023
6. Hirano, K.: What is a Person? https://youtu.be/0waGGRA3El0. Accessed 31 Jan 2023
7. Yee, N., Bailenson, J.: The proteus effect: the effect of transformed self-representation on behavior. Hum. Commun. Res. **33**, 271–290 (2007)
8. Yee, N., Bailenson, J.N., Ducheneaut, N.: The proteus effect: implications of transformed digital self-representation on online and offline behavior. Commun. Res. **36**(2), 285–312 (2009)
9. Praetorius, A.S., Görlich, D.: The proteus effect: how avatars influence their users' self-perception and behaviour. In: tom Dieck, M.C., Jung, T.H., Loureiro, S.M.C. (eds.) Augmented Reality and Virtual Reality. PI, pp. 109–122. Springer, Cham (2021). https://doi.org/10.1007/978-3-030-68086-2_9
10. Peck, T.C., Seinfeld, S., Aglioti, S.M., Slater, M.: Putting yourself in the skin of a black avatar reduces implicit racial bias. Conscious. Cogn. **22**(3), 779–787 (2013)
11. Diener, E., Ryan, C.: The digital divide: how the online environment affects well-being. Int. J. Hum. Comput. Interact. **25**(6), 531–547 (2009)

12. Kim, S.-Y., Sakuma, R., Sakai, N., Houjou, T., Mori, K., Oiji, A.: Psychiatric comorbidities in adult patients who stutter. Kitasato Med J **51**, 117–127 (2021)
13. A-Rong-Na, Sakai, N., Mori, K.: Short-term effects of speech shadowing training on stuttering. Jpn J. Logopedics Phoniatrics **56-4**, 326–334 (2015). (in Japanese)
14. Ono, N., Miyashita, T., Shinozawa, K., Hagita, N., Ando, H.: Effects of avatars in VR space on stuttering. In: The 27th Annual Conference of the Virtual Reality Society of Japan, 1C3-2 (2022). (in Japanese)
15. Montagu, J.D., Coles, E.M.: Mechanism and measurement of the galvanic skin response. Psychol. Bull. **65**(5), 261–279 (1966)
16. VRChat Inc: VRChat. https://hello.vrchat.com/
17. Gershman, S.J., Niv, Y.: Exploring a latent cause theory of classical conditioning. Learn. Behav. **40**, 255–268 (2012)

Medics: An Interdisciplinary Proposal to Create a Medical Data Collection Device to Empower the Patient

Leonardo Bautista Gómez, Victor Liceaga Ríos, Juan Carlos Ramírez González(✉), and Rocío Abascal Mena

Universidad Autónoma Metropolitana unidad Cuajimalpa, 4871 Ciudad de México, Mexico
{leonardo.bautista,victor.liceaga,juan.c.ramirez}@cua.uam.mx,
mabascal@dccd.mx

Abstract. This article shows the progress of the Medics, a tool that seeks to facilitate the recording, analysis, and interpretation of medical results, vital signs, and mental health, using a device and an application. This tool arises from the need of people with a medical situation to have a centralized log for health care that is simple to use. In that sense, the target user is a person who has the basic knowledge of using a smartphone or tablet and with the willingness to use technology as an ally in medical treatments. The first approach was given by interviewing three patients to detect the most pressing needs: the care of their health through periodic reviews and records of vital signs, medical appointments, and moods. Subsequently, a person scenario was generated by following the User-Centered Design (UCD) methodology. The next step was the elaboration of a storyboard that showed the frustrations of the user and their ideal solutions. The development of a pretotype was essential in the process of finding a possible solution; the survey method was also used, which showed relevant information on the aspects to be improved in the user experience. Finally, a prototype was developed which approaches the final tool that supports patients in the process of the registration and monitoring of a medical situation empowering the patient with the correct storage and visualization of their medical data.

Keywords: Health · application · patient · log · User-Centered Design · usability · evaluation

1 Introduction

There is without doubt that technology has transformed the way people relate to the world. Nowadays, applications are used for almost everything: shopping, entertainment, transportation, socialization, moreover, health care. In this way, an application is software that stores information and enables interaction and can be used on different devices. In recent years, an endless number of applications have been developed to facilitate daily activities, and the health app market is estimated to grow from $8.2 billion in revenue by 2022, to $35.7 billion by 2030 [1].

Q. Gao et al. (Eds.): HCII 2023, LNCS 14055, pp. 506–518, 2023.
https://doi.org/10.1007/978-3-031-48041-6_34

A topic that should be considered a fundamental part of the daily routine is health. Especially, when there are medical conditions that require more detailed observation. According to the World Health Organization (WHO), the use of mobile and wireless technologies to support the achievement of health goals has the potential to transform the delivery of health services worldwide [2].

The use of mobile applications empowers and turns the patient into a more active subject by allowing more independent management with the care of their health. Self-care is especially useful applied to patients with chronic diseases, as it facilitates adherence to treatment and its follow-up.

Empowerment covers a wide range of meanings, definitions, and interpretations. In general, the term refers to being able to make decisions about personal and collective circumstances; a process through which people gain greater control over decisions and actions that affect their health [3].

In that sense, chronic diseases are conditions that usually last about three months or more. The most common types of chronic diseases are cancer, heart disease, stroke, diabetes, and arthritis [4].

These conditions require punctual and constant follow-up, since, if they are not monitored, it can bring consequences, even fatal. According to National Institute of Statistics and Geography, in Mexico (INEGI) [5] the main causes of death in Mexico are COVID-19, cardiovascular diseases, diabetes, and malignant tumors.

COVID-19 accelerated the trend of self-care of health, this virus generated uncertainty in the world population and the need to take better control of health. In addition, isolation made evident the need to be able to share medical data easily.

The rest of the article is organized as follows: in Sect. 2 the related work is presented at each step of the UCD methodology, and the results are provided in Sect. 3. A heuristic evaluation was made with some patients resulting in several observations that encourage us to change and adapt the prototype.

By using the User Centered Design (UCD) methodology, user participation is involved in both stages of the evaluation process. Of the improvements obtained in the user interface, the one achieved in the process execution certainty heuristics, the standardization of terms in Spanish, the centralization of navigation on a single screen, the adjustments in the categories to maintain coherence with clinical metaphors, data protection with password activation and fingerprint recognition to protect medical and personal information.

In addition, functions are incorporated to increase the readability of the interface, such as adjusting the size of the fonts, brightness and contrast of the device, and changing the range of colors for users with color blindness. Both visual and audio alerts were also added to notify users without having to access the main screen. In turn, an emergency button was enabled to make medical emergency calls, and the option to view archived studies by date, type, and name was implemented. And a section has been included to indicate the emotional state of the users, since this can influence decisions and actions related to medical treatment. In this way, Sect. 4 shows the final prototype. Finally, conclusions and further work are provided.

2 Related Work

Within the market, there are thousands of applications for health care that can be downloaded today [6] (see Fig. 1). Most of them are dedicated to wellness and sports, however, approximately 30% are exclusive to patients and doctors. During the research conducted, four applications were discovered that address issues like the problem identified for resolution in this project. These applications include *Medisafe* [7], Omron Connect [8], and *VeSync* [9], which primarily focus on facilitating access to health data, monitoring functionalities, and reminders.

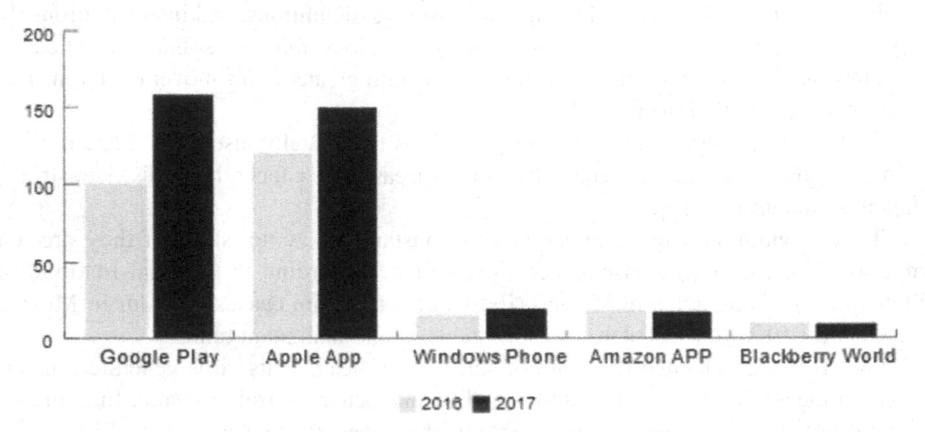

Fig. 1. Number of Health apps displayed in different App Stores. (Figures in thousands).

The main purpose of this section is to analyze some of the most popular applications, their use, and the differences with the solution proposal. The proposed prototype, Medics, is not an application but an interface that achieves the following aims: 1) that the user is not distracted by messages or other applications, 2) An adequate font size is essential to ensure that the content is readable by users and 3) that allows portability.

Considering medication reminders, Medisafe stands out, its interface is clear and simple, it takes up the metaphor of a digital pillbox, and warns the patient to take a pill and to fill the prescription in the pharmacy.

There are also several applications for pregnancy that allow weight monitoring, baby activity logs, tips, and useful information for those expecting a child. Other options are for weight tracking, and glucose, these applications are related to brands of devices for monitoring vital signs that can be linked to a smartphone, such as the case of Omron Connect and VeSync.

To save and organize clinical analyzes there are options of private laboratories such as Poplar, Médica Sur [10], and Grupo Angeles [11]. However, the problem is that they are focused only on receiving medical results and not to keep a history of these. The absence of a centralized and comprehensive repository for medical results presents a substantial impediment to patients in monitoring their health and discerning patterns or trends within their medical data. Consequently, this impediment restricts their capacity to proactively manage their well-being and make informed decisions pertaining to their treatment modalities and lifestyle adjustments.

Within the realm of academic research focused on developing applications to support patient self-care, two notable examples are *CanSelfMan* and *Stress Proffen*, both designed to address the specific needs of distinct patient groups.

CanSelfMan [12] is a self-management system developed to assist children with cancer and their caregivers in Iran. Its primary objective is to provide information, education, and self-management skills, enabling users to generate self-assessment reports and engage in health-related inquiries while receiving reminders for medication intake and medical appointments. Evaluations of CanSelfMan have demonstrated its utility in offering reliable cancer information, facilitating patient-provider communication, and enhancing medication adherence through reminder functionalities. The active involvement of patients, caregivers, and oncologists in the design process has significantly contributed to the system's usability enhancements.

On the other hand, it is an eHealth psychosocial intervention application tailored for cancer survivors. Its cognitive-behavioral intervention approach supports stress management in patients via mobile applications. Evaluations of Stress Proffen have shown significant improvements in stress reduction, anxiety alleviation, self-regulatory fatigue reduction, and enhanced health-related quality of life following the interventions. Børøsund *et al.* [13] emphasize that eHealth interventions can provide valuable support for cancer survivors, with user-friendly interfaces playing a crucial role in reducing stress levels and improving emotional well-being.

Notably, Kip *et al.* [14] have made significant contributions to the eHealth research field by addressing the need to synthesize existing knowledge concerning research activities in participatory and iterative design for product development. Their work emphasizes the importance of involving participants throughout the eHealth development process, utilizing data collection methods such as focus groups, interviews, and questionnaires. Similarly, Derksen et al. [15] assert that the user-centered design process should prioritize the evaluation of application usability, as involving end users helps to identify specific usability issues within the target population. Additionally, Birkhoff and Smeltzer [16] emphasize the significance of comprehending the motivating factors that foster sustained engagement among users of mobile applications for accurate health monitoring purposes.

Notwithstanding the proliferation of numerous health applications available in the marketplace, there remains a paucity of offerings that encompass a comprehensive solution aligned with the central requirements of end users. The advent of the pandemic has brought to light a multitude of individuals who have been confronted with the reality of significant medical conditions, necessitating their adherence to a regimen of medications and diligent self-care practices.

Medics gather in a single device, laboratory results, recording and monitoring vital signs, data visualization, medical appointments, medication doses and reminders, health status monitoring, contacts in case of emergency, in addition to the possibility of sharing medical data. All this is presented, in Medics, in a simple and easy-to-use way which is incorporated into the normal habits of the patient.

In this regard, it should be noted that eHealth can increase access to specialized care in developing countries, as well as improve clinical outcomes and quality of care measures. Berrouigue *et al.* [17] highlight that eHealth has the potential to transform mental health care by shifting it from a reactive discipline to a proactive and personalized one. These apps have proven effective in improving clinical outcomes and providing real-time feedback from clinicians. In addition, they facilitate the medication of patients and allow instant changes in medication regimens based on glucose readings. For their part, Lee, *et al.*, [18] expose how through the active participation of users through eHealth, access barriers to disease detection resources can be overcome.

For their part, Luo and White-Means [19] mention that eHealth empowers patients by requesting accessible and low-cost resources for self-management of their disease. This is why as digital healthcare interventions advance, it is critical to engage specific populations in the design and development of technologies, as patients can be guided in real time to improve their medical decision-making with a focus proactive and personalized.

eHealth are powerful tools that improve the care and quality of life of patients from user participation and customization in their design, which is why the adjustments related to the user experience are relevant and go beyond their appearance. In summary, studies of experiences that empower patients in health are essential to create effective and user-centered tools. These tools improve the patient experience, facilitate access to health information and services, promote active patient participation, and increase adherence to treatment.

3 Methodology

The design of interfaces has a great potential to solve problems and improve the user experience (UX) and navigability (UI), with this tool it will be possible to solve the specific needs of storage, organization, and accessibility to medical data of the patients. That is why a device was developed using the UCD methodology.

Medics is an approach to the design of products and applications that places the user at the center of the process. In this project, the UCD was applied as a philosophy, whose premise is to guarantee the success of a product considering the user in all phases of the design. In addition, the UCD can also be understood as a development methodology: a way of planning projects and a set of methods that can be used in each of the main phases [20].

Each step was developed systematically and with the possibility of going back to update and improve the tool, with the purpose of potentiating the result. The steps to follow to develop a prototype are listed below:

3.1 Observation and Detection of Needs

Through conducting interviews with three participants, a discernment of the primary needs encountered by individuals grappling with health issues or diseases was attained. The identified needs encompassed a range of aspects, including the facilitation of data registration, the provision of accessible and secure information, the capability to visualize one's health status without relying solely on medical consultations, and the centralization of all health-related information, such as medical appointments, medication regimens, and test results. Additionally, a comprehensive analysis of the participants' objectives was conducted, considering their personal context and the strategies they employ to address their challenges, as well as an examination of the underlying factors impeding their task completion.

3.2 Build a Persona

Pruitt and Adlin [21] mention that one of the tools of the UCD is Persona: these are fictional characters whose representations are concrete and specific to end-users. This tool allowed us to define what type of user is contemplated in the use of the final product (archetypes). Not only does it show a physical characteristic, but it gives us a user with emotions that require solutions to their needs. In this case, three people with different characteristics, goals, motivations, and frustrations were defined for the design of an ideal archetype.

3.3 Storyboard

The storyboard is a key instrument for the visualization of scenes of an essential itinerary in the process of creating cartoons. The realization of a storyboard involves a narrow boundary between visualization and narration because storyboards explain the story in images [22].

This communication element allows generating a scenario that shows the interaction of the product, how it satisfies the needs of the user, and how the user could perform its tasks in an agile way. In this case, three scenarios were produced that showed possible visual solutions to the needs of the archetype.

3.4 Inspiration and Point of View Board

As a result of the storyboards, a point of view was created that clearly expressed the problem and the opportunity for improvement. It is important to make clear what a good solution should achieve.

Based on the needs of the users, the following point of view was conceptualized: Having the relevant medical information allows the patient to make better decisions. The interface will empower the user as it improves access and registration of their medical data.

The inspiration board was based on keywords that will conceptualize what the user should feel when using the product:

- Peace of mind: You feel that your information is complete and protected.
- Convenience: Quickly obtain and query your relevant information.
- Help: Feel safe sharing information with your family and friends.
- Empower: Make better decisions by having the necessary and important data.
- Understandable: Detects and analyzes significant information in a simple and accurate way.
- Attractive: Experience a harmonious design that makes it easier for you to consult the information.

3.5 Pretotype

The pretotype is a useful tool to define the user's interest in the product and their willingness to acquire it. With a minimum budget and in a short time people can develop a simplified version of the product to test it and anticipate the possible problems that the final prototype may have.

Accordingly, two techniques were used: The first is YouTube, which uses "the magic of cinema" to show something that does not yet exist and know how much interest it generated in the public. The second is the imposter, this technique consists of using an existing product to simulate the use and functions of the pretotype.

Subsequently, a usage survey was conducted that determined the functions that they liked the most to the public and those that would change based on the video they observed, as well as an opinion on the cost of the device.

3.6 Prototype and Heuristic Evaluation

Through the analysis of feedback obtained from 49 visualizations and the evaluation questionnaires completed by 30 participants, the necessary adjustments were implemented within the Figma platform. Figma, an application designed for user experience (UX) and user interface (UI) purposes, proved instrumental in generating a scenario and presenting a prototype of commendable quality.

The prototype underwent testing with core users who possess the potential to utilize the final product. Notably, the prototype adhered to Jakob Nielsen's ten heuristics, with particular emphasis on fortifying the aspects of system status visibility, help, and feedback. Users positively perceived the heuristics related to the system's adequacy in relation to the real world, as well as consistency and conformity to established standards.

During the application testing phase, users encountered an initial drawback upon entering their information to create a profile. They noted the lack of certainty regarding the successful completion of the process due to prolonged waiting times, thereby instilling a sense of frustration and resentment towards the system. A similar circumstance arose when users attempted to send medical results via email. The prototype failed to display a confirmation message indicating the successful completion of the task or offer an option to cancel the action to avoid erroneous submissions.

Furthermore, it was observed that the system employed terms in different languages. This decision aimed to facilitate the learning process by utilizing terminology commonly found in Facebook systems. However, users reported confusion during the evaluation tests, as they were unable to ascertain whether they had correctly configured the language settings.

The results of user evaluations also highlighted discomfort arising from the requirement to create a password for system access. Elderly users expressed difficulty in remembering yet another password distinct from those used in other applications. However, they acknowledged the importance of safeguarding their medical information. To address this concern, a fingerprint recognition feature was integrated, enabling users to bypass password authentication for emergency tasks.

4 Results

With the guidelines obtained from the analysis carried out on the functionality of the prototype, some functions were updated to facilitate the use of the user interface.

First, to avoid confusion and give users certainty of the execution of their processes, confirmation messages and the states of their processes were added to comply with the heuristic of visibility of the state of the system (see Fig. 2).

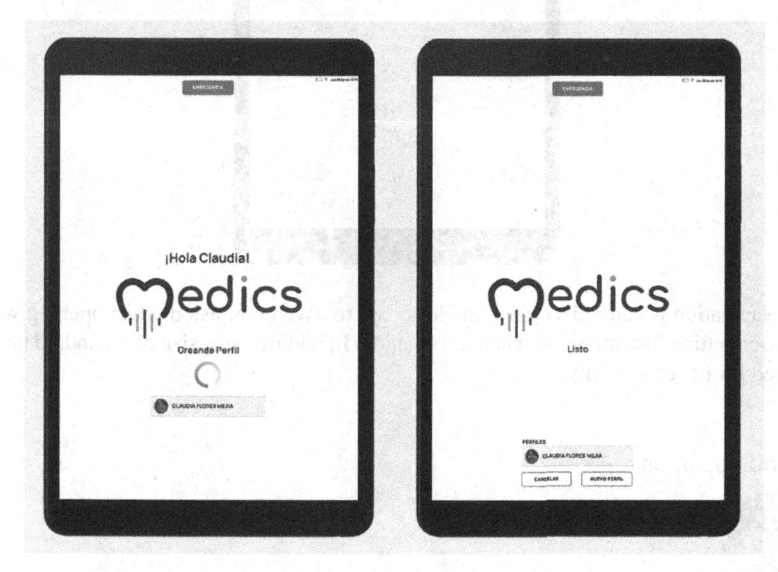

Fig. 2. Screens that show the creation of a new profile (left) and a confirmation screen (right) that shows that the action was completed successfully.

Also, the use of Spanish in the language of the system screens was standardized, to avoid misinterpretations and comply with the heuristics of consistency and standards.

In addition, this focused information helps the user to have control over the clicks and not generate too many screens, since having too many display screens and with the large amount of data, their navigation within the Medics application could be lost (see Fig. 3).

On the other hand, some names were adjusted in the categories to continue with the coherence in the metaphors of the clinic (see Fig. 4).

Finally, to protect the medical and personal information of users, the use of passwords to access the system was activated. To facilitate access and avoid the confusion generated by the increase in the use of passwords, the option of entering by reading a fingerprint was incorporated (see Fig. 5).

In a self-assessment of the team, other functions were found that could be improved and it was decided to update them.

Functions were incorporated that allows for increasing the readability of the interface according to the needs of each user. First, an option was added to adjust the size of the fonts for ease of reading.

Fig. 3. Navigation is centralized on a single screen to avoid confusion when opening windows and the user getting lost among so much information. In addition, the size of a standard tablet was considered for better visibility.

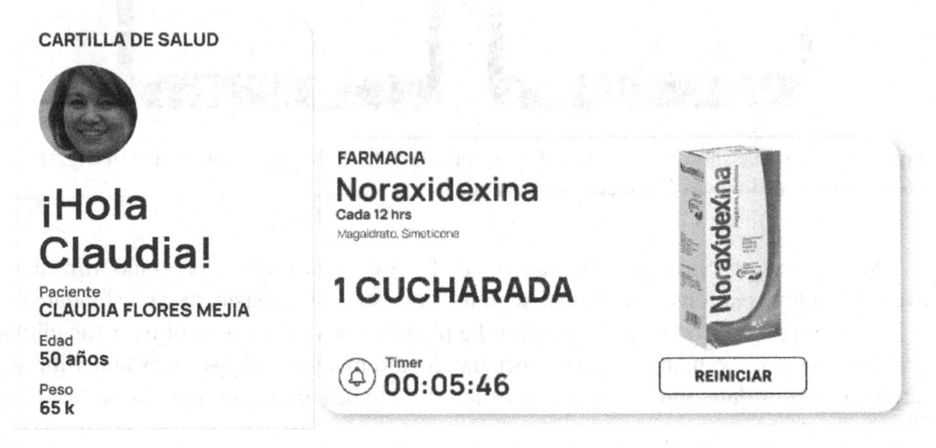

Fig. 4. To name the categories, the use of metaphors was thought to facilitate the understanding of clinical terms.

Moreover, a function was enabled to adjust the brightness and contrast of the device. In turn, the color gamut was changed to avoid confusion for colorblind users, and the option to change this range completely if the user needs it was added (see Fig. 6). Finally, audible, and visual alerts were added to give notice to users without the need to access the home screen.

An emergency button, present on all interface screens, was enabled to facilitate users' medical emergency calls. By activating the button, the system contacts up to four people

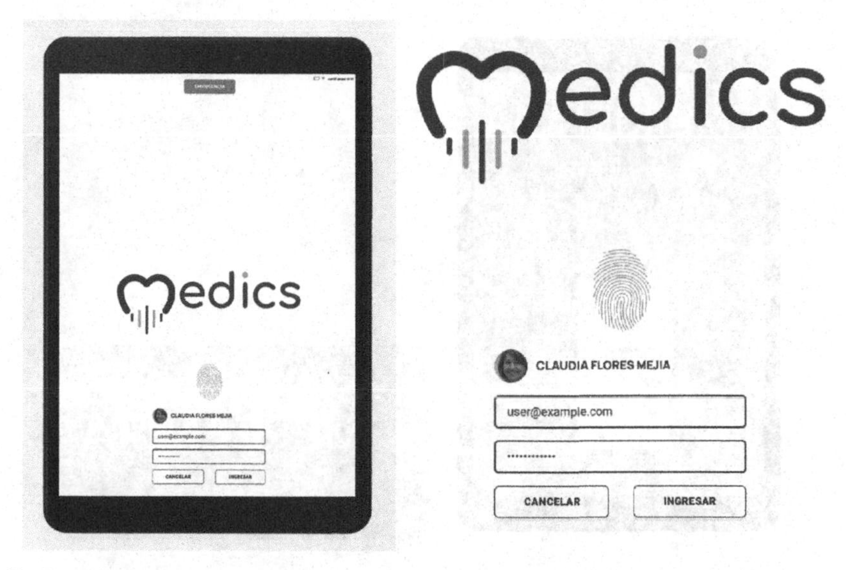

Fig. 5. One change made after evaluating Jakob Nielsen's heuristics was to be able to log into medics via fingerprint reading.

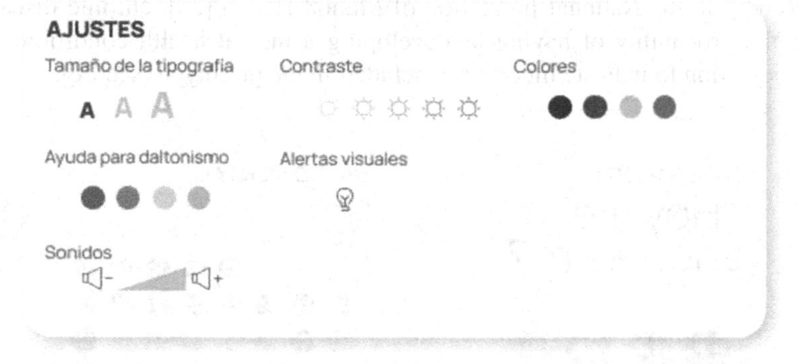

Fig. 6. One change made after evaluating Jakob Nielsen's heuristics was to be able to log into medics via fingerprint reading.

already defined by the user, and to avoid false calls an error prevention confirmation was added (see Fig. 7).

The option to view the archived studies by date, type and name was incorporated, to facilitate the user to find their information in a clearer and more precise way.

At the beginning, considering a section within Medics that would allow expressing the user's emotional state was not among the priorities, however, some users showed interest in being able to indicate how they felt every day, since the emotional state can influence decisions and actions when following a medical treatment, also in elderly people they considered this section as an interaction with someone close, and despite living alone, this was a way of expressing themselves even with a machine.

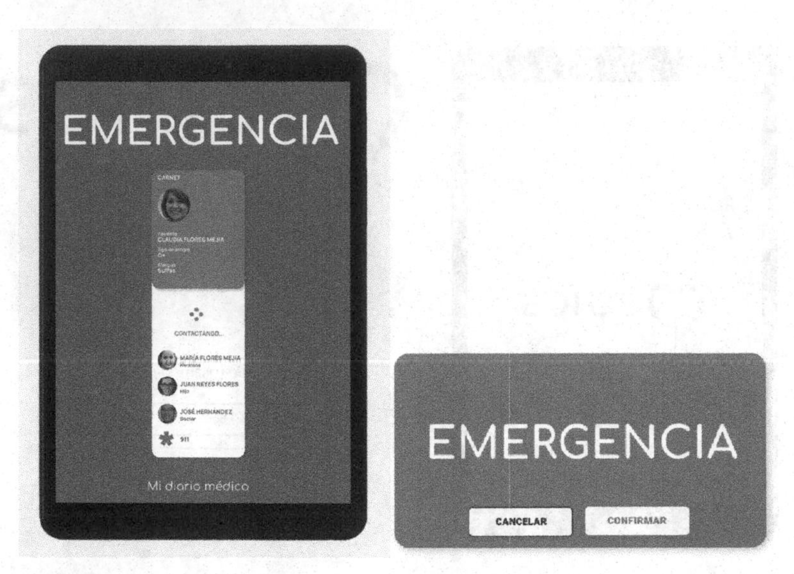

Fig. 7. Having the emergency button on the whole screen was exposed to false calls, so the confirmation button is added.

According to the National Institution of Mental Health [23], chronic diseases can increase the probability of having or developing a mental health condition; for this reason, the option to indicate mood was included in the prototype (see Fig. 8).

Fig. 8. Monitoring Mental Health is also considered important for Medics because it can influence the follow-up of medical treatments.

5 Conclusion and Future Work

This article presents the process for creating a mobile device that helps people better cope with a disease or that for some reason requires better medical follow-up.

It was based on the UCD methodology in which the user participates in all stages of the process. This was able to meet the needs and frustrations of users when it came to supporting their medical documents, vital signs records, and reminders to take their medications.

As users were involved in the whole process, the project was modified, and functions were incorporated to easily share data, accessibility issues, and a special button in case of an emergency.

The prototype underwent testing with individuals who expressed interest in the solution presented by the project, as it pertains to supporting healthcare. These users can be considered potential adopters of the system. Their evaluations underscore the efficacy of the interface, which not only exhibits clarity and simplicity but also effectively addresses their fundamental self-care needs in relation to their medical conditions.

Furthermore, the evaluations revealed that users possess information that holds significance not only for themselves but also for their immediate support network, which aids them in their healthcare journey. The ability to share their medical data facilitated heightened vigilance and knowledge, enabling swift responses to change in health status or emergencies.

As a part of future endeavors, it is imperative to underscore the incomplete nature of the design and development of the electronic device, as the application was tested on commercial tablets. However, the proposed objective entails transforming it into a dedicated healthcare device, exclusively tailored for this purpose and available at an affordable cost. This necessitates a comprehensive examination of feasible costs that enable device acquisition, alongside conducting tests that exclusively focus on device programming with the Medics system as the singular application.

Regarding the Medics system, further work encompasses the development and integration of an operating system specifically designed for the application. Additionally, a concise user guide should be created within the application itself to streamline the learning process and enhance system navigation. Lastly, it is crucial to evaluate the implementation of accessibility features catering to individuals with restricted physical capabilities.

Medics can certainly be a fundamental tool for health care, empowering the patient with the correct storage and visualization of their medical data. That is why the approach will be sought from a foundation, hospital, or medical association that is willing to adopt it.

References

1. Business of apps. https://www.businessofapps.com/data/health-statistics. Accessed 20 June 2023
2. World Health Organization: mHealth: new horizons for health through mobile technologies. Global Observatory for eHealth series, pp. 66–71 (2011)
3. World Health Organization: 7th Global Conference on Health Promotion (2013)
4. National Center for Chronic Disease Prevention and Health Promotion. https://www.cdc.gov/chronicdisease/about/index.htm. Accessed 20 June 2023
5. INEGI. https://www.inegi.org.mx/investigacion/covid/ligas.html. Accessed 22 May 2023

6. R2G. https://research2guidance.com/product/mhealth-economics-2017-current-status-and-future-trends-in-mobile-health. Accessed 22 June 2023
7. Medisafe. https://www.medisafe.com. Accessed 22 June 2023
8. Omron México. https://omronhealthcare.la/mx/connect. Accessed 22 June 2023
9. Vesync. https://www.vesync.com/app. Accessed 22 June 2023
10. Médica Sur. https://medicasur.com.mx. Accessed 22 June 2023
11. Hospital Angeles. https://hospitalangeles.com. Accessed 22 June 2023
12. Mehdizadeh, H., Asadi, F., Nazemi, E., Mehrvar, A., Yazdanian, A., Emami, H.: A mobile self-management app (CanSelfMan) for children with cancer and their caregivers: usability and compatibility study. JMIR Pediatr. Parent. **30**(6) (2023)
13. Børøsund, E., et al.: Pilot testing an app-based stress management intervention for cancer survivors **10**(3), 770–780 (2020)
14. Kip, H., Keizer, J., da Silva, M., Beerlage-de Jong, N., Köhle, N., Kelders, S.: Methods for human-centered eHealth development: a narrative scoping review. J. Med. Internet Res. **24**(1) (2022)
15. Derksen, M., Jaspers, M., van Strijp, S., Fransen, M.: Mobile health for smoking cessation among disadvantaged young women during and after pregnancy: user-centered design and usability study. JMIR Form Res. **5**(8) (2021)
16. Birkhoff, S.D., Smeltzer, S.C.: Perceptions of smartphone user-centered mobile health tracking apps across various chronic illness populations: an integrative review. J. Nurs. Scholarsh. **49**(4) (2017)
17. Berrouiguet, S., Perez-Rodriguez, M., Larsen, M., Baca-García, E., Courtet, P., Oquendo, M.: From eHealth to iHealth: transition to participatory and personalized medicine in mental health. J. Med. Internet Res. **20**(1) (2018)
18. Lee, D., Hutchens, M., George, T., Wilson-Howard, D., Cooks, E., Krieger, J.: Do they speak like me? Exploring how perceptions of linguistic difference may influence patient perceptions of healthcare providers. Med. Educ. Online **27**(1) (2022)
19. Luo, J., White-Means, S.: Evaluating the potential use of smartphone apps for diabetes self-management in an underserved population: a qualitative approach about chronic diseases. Int. J. Environ. Res. Public Health **18** (2021)
20. Garreta Domingo, M., Mor Pera, E.: Diseño centrado en el usuario. UOC (2011)
21. Pruitt, J., Adlin, T.: The persona lifecycle (2006)
22. Wells, P.: Fundamentos de la animación. Parramón, Barcelona (2007)
23. National Center for Chronic Disease Prevention and Health Promotion: Chronic illnesses such as cancer, heart disease, or diabetes may make you more likely to have or develop a mental health condition. NIH Publ. **21** (2021)

P5 Medicine and BI for Monitoring Moderate Neurocognitive Disorders

Karim Elia Fraoua[1(✉)] and Stéphane Mouly[2]

[1] Université Paris Est Marne-La-Vallée, Equipe Dispositifs d'Information et de Communication à l'Ere Numérique (DICEN IDF), Conservatoire national des arts et métiers, Paris-Est Paris-Ouest, EA 7339, Paris, France
fraoua@u-pem.fr

[2] Université Paris Cité, INSERM UMR-S1144, Département de Médecine Interne, DMU INVICTUS, APHP.Nord - Groupe Hospitalier Lariboisière-Fernand Widal, 75010 Paris, France

Abstract. The evolution of mental disorders during this last decade and the future evolution with a lack of medical and social structure will put our society in a harmful situation. In the absence of curative treatment, it seems very hard to define a pathway to help the patient and his family for the management of autonomy of the patient. We will discuss the question of the Data shared by the patient himself or his entourage and we will develop the notion of quality of care through indicators as PREMS, PROMS (Patient-reported outcomes measures), HrQol (Health related Quality of Life), and the role of Business Intelligence (BI) tools in a perspective of P5 Medicine. This new approach would be analyzed in term of Technology Acceptance Model (TAM) by actors considering to implement this tools from the point of view of Perceived Usefulness (PU), Perceived Ease of Use (PEOU).

Keywords: Neurocognitive disorders · P5 Medicine · Business Intelligence · situation · information

1 Introduction

According to INSEE in 2022, life expectancy at 65 years is currently 88.1 years for women and 84,2 years for men, it continues to progress despite a noticeable slowdown in recent years [1]. The health system is encountering significant difficulties, as in many countries, in providing care but also in providing quality care. The aging of the population also causes the development of chronic diseases which considerably increases the need for personnel, we see that the Covid-19 crisis has increased this tension and with the current epidemics the system is on the verge of implosion. In this context, there is an explosion in the amount of information in organizations, which contributes to the current strong tension in the health system. This new dimension of production of information in a perspective of communication from and to patients, must put into perspective a new form of production in what we can consider as a new structuring of the information offer in order to support organizations in improving their effectiveness, it can and must accompany the actors in their actions [2]. This choice we're wishing to confront it

Q. Gao et al. (Eds.): HCII 2023, LNCS 14055, pp. 519–535, 2023.
https://doi.org/10.1007/978-3-031-48041-6_35

with the management of patients with neurodegenerative diseases in view of the current situation. Moreover, to show that this organizational structure based on the question of data, is so significant on the question of health, that a recent reform has made it possible to concentrate the organization around Data Health Hub [3], which brings together the main actors and which is supposed to allow simplified access to data. There are various competing reasons for this, including GDPR rules (General Data Protection Regulation) [4], due to the risk of data theft and the risks inherent in their use. Another question arises, namely the use of certain data processing tools by the medical profession, which is not intrinsically in practice today. The health professional will be able to use tools for analyzing the data collected in a decision-making process on the future of the patient's health and for the care provided to patients, which could not be obtained with a physical examination. These data will eventually lead to the digitization of clinical pathways [5].

This approach seems necessary to us, given that the cost of public health in France is already high with a cost of 12.8% of GDP (current health expenditure in the international sense) [6] and which will increase even more, and consequently impacts the care of patients with neurocognitive diseases with the corollary of a decline in quality of life. The system will no longer be able to meet everyone's needs with the same quality of care. This work is part of the prospects for possible solutions [7, 8] with the implementation of new systems that will allow partial availability of the health system, thanks to remote monitoring. The objective is to make the life of the patient and his entourage more adequate with his state of health, especially when we know the heaviness of the course of care for a person with Alzheimer's disease. According to the Mederic Alzheimer Foundation, the cost of care amounts to 5.3 billion euros per year, between the cost of diagnosis and the care of sick people at home, and their care in a health establishment [9, 10]. The important element to visualize in these expenses, is represented by the cost of hospitalizations, not for the direct management of Alzheimer's disease (diagnosis, treatment), but for its complications (falls, behavioral disorders, malnutrition, depression...). In addition, the report specifies that the informal cost is around 14 billion euros per year, which is the caregiver management of the daily life of the patient. In addition, there is the question of the autonomy of these people, with health establishments such as EHPAD (Accommodation establishment for dependent elderly people) already overloaded and unable to accommodate all patients. To respond to this complex and urgent situation, the French State has established 6 axes within the framework of the national health strategy with axis 3 which aims to guarantee the quality, safety and relevance of care [11]. The axis 1 aims to innovate to transform our health system by reaffirming the place of citizens, which corresponds to our thinking, in particular with the integration of quality indicators which are integrated into our vision of P5 medicine which will be discussed below. We also discussed like other authors the contribution of the Internet of Things (IOT) [12–14], Blockchain [15] and other systems that could intervene in the improvement of the quality of life, knowing that there is still no cure for neurodegenerative diseases, even if progress has been made and hopes for new treatments are emerging.

Consequently, given all the above and given that the managerial approaches have not made it possible to make the system more efficient in view of the current difficulties, it seems to us that one of the solutions would be the increased use of tools from information systems that could improve certain processes, such is our hypothesis, considering that the vision of systems as approached by Simondon could be justified. In this vision, of which Herbert Simon was a forerunner with the "artificial sciences" [16]. According to Simon and summarized by Forest [17], a device or artefact is not only a technical object, it is "any entity which has the purpose of meeting needs, designed by Man in this sense". Indeed, in his vision of the devices, Simondon considers that these contribute to the improvement of practices and does not fit into the constrained vision of Foucault, who considers that the artefact would be a form of confinement linked to coercion and discipline [18]. This vision allows us to think that we should not consider only the technical determinism of society or the social determinism of technology. We must consider the evolution of technical systems as a dynamic process where technical and non-technical, human and non-human elements interact with each other by modifying themselves [19]. This view is also shared by Wartofsky who considers a type of abstract artifact that "transcends the necessities of productive praxis". This is also in line with B. Guyot's thinking. We already see that artifacts are present in the human environment and participate in all collaborative activities between humans, which will bring us to actor-network theory, since the artifact is generally designed intentionally, which is our case according to a goal, which here would be to allow to put a place for digital medicine. To do this, we have relied on changes in uses which are justified by requests for improved care through the use of technologies, while analyzing how these practices must be installed so as not to be in a constrained approach as it was rightly analyzed by Foucault. For this, we must think of the dynamics of appropriation that other authors mean by affordance [20]. We relied on the concept of the TAM (Technology Acceptance Model) to analyze the implementation of this type of device [21].

2 Evolution of the Care of the Elderly and the Use of Technologies

According to the report "Supporting the autonomy of the elderly by 2030" several issues are emerging according to current trends:

- An increase in the demand for care and the number of people needing assistance with autonomy
- Caregiver progression
- Stay at home
- Continuation of the development of alternative forms of housing
- The continued specialization of EHPADs in neurocognitive diseases with models open to the outside world and the home.
- The attractiveness of social, medico-social, care and improvement of working conditions professions.

Several points mentioned take into account the evolution of patient/medical space relationships and in particular the desire to maintain a quality of life for someone in good health. We can therefore think that there is a need for a way to link the doctor and his patient with an object or a process allowing quality of care and remote monitoring. However, diagnoses often require the two to meet to carry out tests or other protocols. Today there are approximately 1 million people with Alzheimer's disease or a related disease. Including caregivers, 3 million people are affected by the disease. It is in this context that we believe that home hospitalization must evolve significantly if we can provide sufficient autonomy to the elderly through technological solutions. From these questions, we can clearly see that there are new lines of thought which would be effective and which are located around the uses of technologies, which could constitute new information systems, whose appropriation must be designed through the question of the TAM. One can wonder about the use of robots or even Cobots [22] to compensate for the lack of staff available to take care of the elderly, including in retirement homes or cognitive care homes, which could be a third place, which would make it possible not only to relieve hospitals but also to create an adequate space where the course of care would be represented in situ, or through interfaces, in which caregiver would be pivotal in the actions carried out in favor of people with dementia neurocognitive diseases. Technological innovations seem to be an increasingly relevant solution to support these people in their daily lives. Robotic solutions are a new way to develop home help and assistance [23].

The resistance of people to new tools and practices is well known and a whole approach has developed on resistance to change in technology, and the elderly in particular, can constitute a hindrance in the acceptance of these new objects. The Internet of Things constitutes a very interesting way already discussed [14] and which must be included in the solutions, in particular when maintaining people at home. The literature reveals a rather positive view of technological innovations among the over 50s [24]. It also shows the role of the entourage, and more generally of the ecosystem of the elderly person, can play an important role in the process of adoption of technological innovation by people who are no longer autonomous in their actions or decisions. In addition, "Elderly people with loss of autonomy have a positive perception of robotic solutions insofar as they offer the possibility of gaining autonomy, independence, mobility and provide them with easier communication with their loved ones and services emergencies [25]. According to a study "Can robotic solutions promote the aging well of the elderly person with loss of autonomy?" carried out on people aged 65 to 91 and their caregiver, we can find several needs expressed as well as their priority. The needs mainly relate to questions of safety and reminders in the event of a dangerous situation.

We are thinking of simple solutions to implement with connected objects that make it possible to respond effectively to these questions such as the risk of falling, problems related to the use of communication such as being able to telephone, answer the telephone, or as mats to track bedroom exits, pillows to track sleep, coffee makers to track breakfast intake, water bottles to best track hydration, as these are considered a concern for caregivers as well as doctors. There are now a plethora of objects that make it possible to better monitor the autonomy of people with tools for reminding people to take medication and also solutions to monitor their cognitive abilities with simple games and cognitive exercises. We list in the following table the connected objects and their usefulness in the context of monitoring patients with neurocognitive disorders and which are defined in an IoMT (Internet of Medical Things) [26] reading.

Here are different categories of devices of IoMT:

- **Portable devices for the general public:** Connected devices such as mobile phones, connected watches including on the mobile network, which make it possible to monitor a set of activities as physical activities and also the evolution of the state of health.
- **Connected devices:** Devices that allow the patient to be monitored remotely thanks to home automation (refrigerator, coffee maker, carpet, etc.). These devices make it possible to monitor the daily life and analyze the autonomy of patients.
- **Medical-grade wearable devices:** Regulated clinical-grade products used to manage pain or address other health concerns under the direction of a doctor.
- **Remote Patient Monitoring (RPM) devices:** Chronic disease management support systems. These devices are used in the context of hospitalization at home and are therefore often placed in the patient's home.
- **Personal Emergency Response Systems (PERS):** Wearable devices that allow a patient to call a healthcare professional for help in an emergency situation.

We are thinking of adding a new category to it, namely robotic solutions which make it possible to a lesser extent to fight against isolation by compensating for the absence of a caregiver. The robot can also make possible to maintain a state of comfort by being present and by acting as a communicating element, thus making it possible to reduce the state of stress, but also to see the evolution of the speech of the patients in order to better assess their situation. We see that this solution is structured around two aspects, namely telehealth which is "the use of digital information and communication technologies, such as computers and mobile devices, for remote access to health services and management of health care". Improving patient-doctor communications and diagnostics, but also telemedicine, which uses technological tools to carry out care, to make the diagnosis at a distance and the monitoring of patients. These sets of tools cannot be followed individually and it is obvious that a global solution is needed which will make it possible to assess the patient's state of health but also to recommend actions which would be effective in meeting the needs or to critical situations such as a fall, problems with hydration, nutrition, etc. If the presence of applications is useful in the management of the curative approach of the disease by considering that certain activities have a benefit on the evolution of the disease or that a general way certain activities like the visit of its neighborhood, gardening, reading activities adapted to the patient's condition, or even the psychoeducation and rehabilitation of social cognition project aimed at improving the social interaction capacities of sick people and providing them and caregivers a better understanding of social cognition, led by the team of doctor Lisette Volpe-Gillot [27].

It seems obvious that the solution based on Business Intelligence (BI) tools is very relevant because not only can we have simple dashboards to visualize, but also permanent monitoring according to a time frame to be defined to better predict patient evolutions. And thus to plan meetings with the appropriate people defined during the path of care in the house dedicated to the reception of sick people. We are indeed considering defining a dedicated space to allow patients with their caregivers to meet where they could meet the necessary person who has been alerted by negative developments observed in the dashboard, and who would issue an alert to the person concerned. In order to take charge of this evolution, such as for example the project of Adaptation of the speech therapy and language adjustment to a population presenting an Alzheimer's disease at an advanced stage presented by Clotilde Caillet-Gipeaux [27]. This can be detected by the robot which would be triggered by interaction with the patient or by the caregiver remotely. And in order to better build this new digital communication space, it is useful to visualize the difficulties of use and to build relevant tools in the sense of ease. To this end, new approaches to UX/UI [28] define new approaches that must be combined with theories such as TAM (Technology Acceptance Model) [29], PU (Perceived Usefulness) [29] or PEOU (Perceived Ease of Use) [29].

3 TAM (*Technology of Acceptance Model*)

In order to build a new technology, it is important to understand its reception by users, and as such it is useful to explain the behavior of an individual with respect to a new technology. A first reading comes with Azjen's theory [30] of reasoned action. Davis later developed his so-called technological acceptance model based on this theory of reasoned action [31]. Indeed, the emergence of information systems that were initially very technical did not consider this point of view of use, which made them very technical tools and for which it was necessary to train individuals who had the ability to use them. With the emergence of the digitization of our societies and the adoption of digital platform structures, constitute major difficulties, in particular because of the area not covered by the internet network, but also by the difficulties of use due to the lack of consideration of the capacities of the users.

Nowadays efforts are made in the field of UX/UI without however having a technical reading related to the TAM or the PU or the PEOU [29]. In the reasoned theory of Azjen and "the absolute conviction that personal decisions are purely rational". The behavior of individuals is then correlated to their intention "to emit said behavior". This intention depends on two variables: motivation (personal interest and social influence of others) and capacity (what is achievable according to the efforts to be made). The first variable is defined by the positive or negative attitude of an individual concerning a given behavior, the second shows the social pressure sustained by an individual in the decision-making process. In a second step, Davis relies on this model to develop the "Technology Acceptance Model" or TAM which he uses to show the reasons why people accept or not accept new technologies. The objective of this model is to specify the determinants of the acceptance of new tools and the role of human behavior in terms of technological acceptance" (Fig. 1).

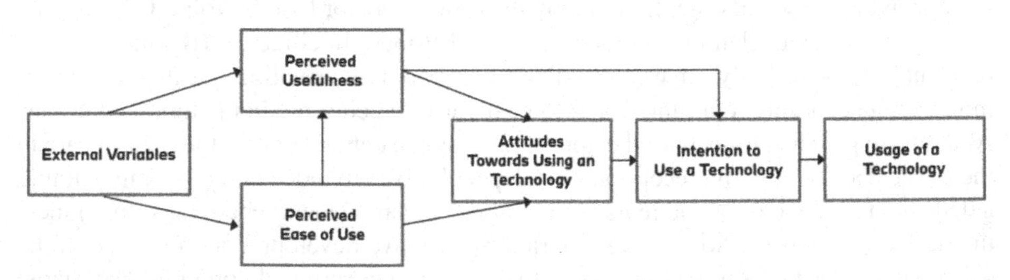

Fig. 1. TAM from Davis (The Technology Acceptance Model (Davis 1989))

3.1 The TAM2 Model

Venkatesh and Davis suggested that the TAM model was unsatisfactory and evolved it to take more into account the concept of Perceived Usefulness (PU) and especially Perceived Ease Of Use (PEOU). They highlighted the determinants of these concepts. This approach has enabled structures and organizations to better support users, which would increase the acceptance and use of new systems by users [32].

The TAM 2 has two major determinants within its model:

- Perceived utility (PU): The level of performance that using a system can bring to a user.
- Perceived ease of use (PEOU): The level of effort the system requires from a user in his or her opinion and thus the cost/benefit ratio.

This model highlights the constraints that may appear in the use of new tools or connected objects that could deviate from their initial use. It is therefore necessary to ensure that end users, whether they are elderly or sick, are informed about the real usefulness of these objects. An object can therefore only be presented with a pure data collection approach without providing any help to the user. This model also makes it possible to anticipate behaviors and possible rejections in the introduction of a new technology. These authors indicated that the cognitive determinants of perceived usefulness in TAM2 could be described as perceived ease of use, outcome, outcome quality, and appropriateness of use.

4 The TAM 3 Model

The continuation of the evolution of the reflection of Davis was to lead to the TAM 3 model which was developed by Venkatesh and Bala [33] by indicating the innovations compared to the TAM 1 and TAM 2 model, by adding the perceptions of the external control, computer anxiety and computer self-efficacy and also incorporating objective usability and perceived user enjoyment (Fig. 2).

Our approach to developing new tools integrated into this ecosystem should take into account these aspects of TAM, PU and PEOU, in order to better support "sick" people but also caregivers.

5 RGPD

Indeed with all these connected objects, users are permanently connected. This evolution naturally implies a certain mistrust of consumers regarding the use of their personal data. Thus, according to an Internet Society survey, approximately 65% of consumers questioned have concerns about the use of their data [34]. The French are vigilant about the use of data, but we can think that if the data is shared as part of the care pathway, it would be easier to share it. It is in this context that the General Data Protection Regulation (GDPR) appeared, adopted by the European Union on April 27, 2016 with the following obligations:

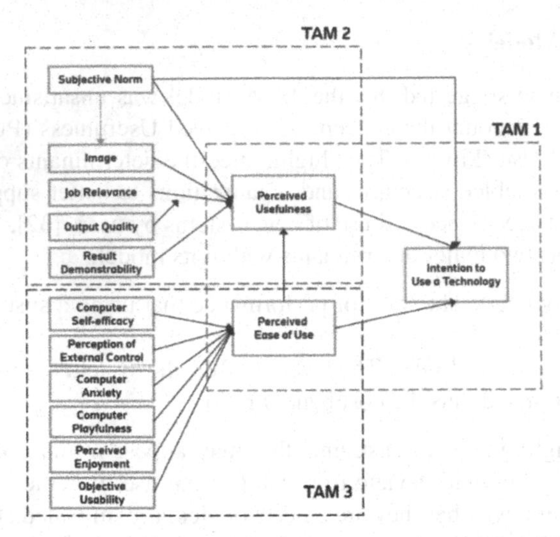

Fig. 2. TAM, TAM2 et TAM3 (The Technology Acceptance Model (Davis 1989))

(1) "Privacy by Design et accountability"
(2) Establishment and maintenance of a register
(3) Notification des fuites de données
(4) Realization of impact studies
(5) Data Protection Officer
(6) Rights of individuals

All connected objects are therefore subject to the requirements of the GDPR. However, the main obstacle to these technologies and the IoT is the level of security achievable for the process to be viable. We discussed all these elements because today should develop the concept of P4 medicine which has evolved into P5 medicine, which would be an interesting approach in the context of monitoring people with neurocognitive disorders. Indeed, the development of the digitization of medicine cannot take place without there being a framework encouraging the use of data.

6 Medicine P4 et P5

P4 medicine (predictive, preventive, personalized and participatory) is implemented thanks to new tools which make it possible to predict, in healthy subjects, the occurrence of such disease and, in patients, to predict the evolution of their disease [35]. With this vision of medicine, we see that this new approach makes it possible to treat both the quality of care and the quality of life of patients. It is certain that modern medicine has focused more on illness than on health. New vision through P5 medicine emerges [36]:

- **Personalized:** Considers the genetic and epigenetic profile of the individual, in order to take this aspect into account in the treatment of the patient.
- **Preventive:** To prevent the onset or worsening of the disease more than its treatment, and to make it possible to provide medical advice.
- **Predictive:** By adapting the appropriate treatments for the patient and to avoid drug reactions.

- **Participative:** Patients are responsible for their health and care.
- **The fifth P would be positive medicine as a proof:** The prognosis for recovery depends on the patient, compliance with the treatment, his state of mind and in our case, the studies show that one of the aspects of positive evolution of certain neurodegenerative diseases will depend a lot on the patient but also on his career.

7 Connected Objects

A connected object is an ordinary object capable of communicating with the world around it, almost all objects can become connected. Tools allow you to connect any object with Wi-Fi switches. The use of smartphones has facilitated the use of connected objects, the telephone itself being a connected object capable of taking data, which is then returned in the form of information and sometimes in the form of knowledge. To better contextualize these definitions, we considered this definition [37]:

- Data is the "raw" material of information designed more for machines.
- Information could be defined as data that has been interpreted to make sense to humans.
- By giving meaning to information, we obtain knowledge
- By giving meaning to knowledge we obtain wisdom.

The development of home automation has meant that our homes are and will become more connected. These are a whole system of communicating objects that tend to revolutionize our way of life with the aim of facilitating it and better controlling our uses. You have to see, for example, the security or energy control equipment that is democratized these days. Few consider that data stored in the cloud or with private hosts is an invasion of privacy. The connected watch which collects several data related to heart rate or blood pressure is mainly intended for private use or by the entourage, including by the medical profession if authorized to do so. In the same way, certain objects record the times of entry and exit from the home or the conversations within the home. We clearly see that these objects are already part of our daily lives for the vast majority of us.

8 Alzheimer's Disease

According to the definition adopted by the French Ministry of Health, Alzheimer's disease is a neurodegenerative disease characterized by a progressive loss of memory and of certain intellectual functions, in particular cognitive, leading to repercussions in the activities of daily life. It should be noted that our perspective of use of the IoMT and the BI is relevant, indeed the symptoms evolve over time and especially that this evolution varies from one individual to another. The major symptom remains memory disorders and even if it is very painful for the patient and his entourage, a certain number of disorders weigh heavily in the daily life of the patient and his entourage such as:

- Language disorders (aphasia).
- Difficulty performing certain gestures (apraxia).
- Loss of recognition of objects or people (agnosia);
- Loss of executive functions, i.e. the ability to adapt one's behavior to a given context.

These symptoms evolve over time according to stages ranging from 1 to 7:

- Stage 1: Normal operation
- Stage 2: Very mild cognitive decline
- Stage 3: Mild cognitive decline
- Stage 4: Moderate cognitive decline
- Stage 5: Moderately severe cognitive decline
- Stage 6: Severe cognitive decline
- Stage 7: Very severe cognitive decline

8.1 Early Diagnosis of Alzheimer's Disease

The objective is to help diagnose of the disease early in order to anticipate and preserve people's quality of life and autonomy for as long as possible. Indeed, the final diagnosis can only be established by the medical profession. This approach aims to alert whether it is the person himself, or his entourage that signs of the disease are manifesting and that the agglomeration of these data in the form of information must lead to the next stage, namely the knowledge, and validation of the diagnosis, which must be made by a doctor. Indeed, the diagnosis is established on the basis of analysis and medical imaging and there are no other alternatives to date. The diagnosis is based on the dosage of biomarkers in the CSF, hippocampal atrophy on MRI, and significant hypometabolism of the hippocampal regions confirming the diagnosis [38]. It is necessary to remember and because of the medical nature of the diagnosis, that the place of the doctor in this ecosystem is imponderable. It is the only one today to be able to differentiate a person suffering from Alzheimer's disease from another dementia and which could resemble Alzheimer's disease in certain respects.

8.2 Spotting the First Signs

According again to the definition of French Ministry of Health, The following signs should alert, without being specific to Alzheimer's disease, since as previously stated other diseases may present similar signs:

- A change in behavior and/or personality.
- Forgetting about recent events.
- Loss of objects;
- Language disorders (common words forgotten, or used in place of another).
- Difficulty performing familiar tasks.
- Loss of orientation in space and time.
- Difficulties performing abstract reasoning.
- Impaired judgment.
- A loss of motivation.

In addition, if we want to improve disease management in the coming years, we must be able to intervene as soon as possible. We see that our instrumental approach makes it possible to follow the evolution of the disease as well as its appearance on a temporal scale, by providing caregivers in these dedicated centers with the devices listed above in order to situate themselves in relation to the disease. Itself, knowing that these dedicated centers are piloted by doctors, including remotely, given that our reading of the problem integrates the question of medical deserts, which are only rural or peri-urban, because in fact monitoring and piloting are will be done remotely, including with access to dashboards that are extracted from patient databases. We are not going to show our technical approach in depth in this article, our approach here is more on the definition of the ecosystem with the analysis of the IOT, the IoMT, the use of robots, by defining new health spaces, themselves connected, thus allowing the definition of a favorable environment in which caregivers can also play a crucial role, bearing in mind that everything is done to help keep people in their care for as long as possible at home, independently. It is in this space that we will be able to validate the tools put in place to validate this information with PREMS (Patient-Reported Experience Measures), PROMS (Patient-reported outcomes measures), HrQol (Health related Quality of Life). PROMS [39], measure the outcome perceived by the patient through usually a questionnaire and the patient's answers can be entered by a caregiver, a close friend or a family member. PREMS are used to measure the Patient's experience. This is why we believe that these technological solutions will improve the follow-up and the experience of the patient, thanks to this personalized follow-up. The medical profession will have access to a certain amount of information and will be alerted automatically as part of the monitoring of the disease, which implies stronger interaction with the medical profession. That said, and according to the indications and recommendations of the HAS (Haute autorité de santé, High Authority for Health), a functional assessment can be carried out on site or remotely to measure the impact of cognitive disorders on activities of daily living using scales already defined as the Instrumental Activities of Daily Life (IADL) [40] scale and which could be observed through connected devices and their daily uses. We also have a simplified scale covering four items with the use of the telephone as a connected object, measurable mobility thanks to GPS,... taking medication with the use of a connected pill dispenser or the connected pill, the physical activity with the connected watch, connected mats, etc. It is possible, thanks to the presence of a robot, to perform cognitive evaluation tests on the 5-word recall test, measure verbal fluency [41], or any other test that would have previously validated such as the 7-min test [42], the Memory Impairment Screen (MIS) [43], the GPCog [44],... Finally we will also be interested in the context of IoT and IoMT in the thymic and behavioral evaluation with the objects which seem relevant to us such as the mattress or connected cushion to measure sleep disorders, just like the absence of activity can be a sign of apathy,... Some signs can only be reported by caregivers thanks to the platform that will be put in place, such as signs of irritability, hallucinations, anxiety,... Indeed, it is necessary to refer to the scales used in this part such as the Neuropsychiatric Inventory (NPI) [45] or the frontal dysfunction scale (FDS) [46] because there are other types of dementia than Alzheimer's disease such as dementia with Lewy body, frontotemporal dementia or vascular dementia.

9 Le Bigdata

The appearance of the "Internet of Things" is largely linked to the emergence of Big Data and its possibilities with the ability to process large and varied volumes of data [47]. Complex applications can be supported in real time. These data from connected objects make it possible, thanks to the power of algorithms, to design new information that is sometimes difficult to conceive on a human scale to predict early detection, but also to make decisions to improve the quality of life of patients. In our case and if we take the heart rate sensors already having a precise indication of the person such as age, normal pulse and knowing that the heart rate varies according to the age and the state of health of the patient, if an abnormal rhythm is observed, an alert is sent to the wearer to notify him of this anomaly, just like the doctor through a dashboard, linked to the patient's medical file, and which allows the doctor to recommend via digital communication to take specific measures in relation to this alert. Indeed, one of the characteristics of big data is the preponderant place of Big Data Analytics, which is the process of collecting, examining, managing, processing and exploiting massive sets of data from different and existing sources in various formats, structured, semi-structured or unstructured. It is characterized by the 6 V: volume, variety, velocity, veracity, value and visualization [48]. This alliance of connected objects and Bigdata analytics would give this practical approach with the extraction and processing of data to make them available to the various actors.

9.1 Connected Medical Objects for Health and the Case of Alzheimer's Disease

One of the main diseases linked to the deterioration of the quality of life in old age is Alzheimer's disease. This situation forces several actors in the care pathway to mobilize to preserve human dignity. In our approach we see from what has gone before that connected objects can anticipate the warning signs of the disease or its stages, as long as people equip themselves and participate in the prevention of the latter just as they can make it possible to follow its evolution but also to slow it down, if the observation of the protocol is respected. It seems simpler to us here, by combining telehealth and telemedicine, with connected objects. The management of the disease is useful for the whole chain, whether for the patient, for the caregiver but also for the health personnel in order to determine a course of care adapted to the person. The aim is thus to associate the data collected thanks to the IoT, with knowledge of the first symptoms of Alzheimer's to check whether or not the disease is declared in a person. This association could also extend to a person who has already had a diagnosis and to assess the evolution of the disease by analyzing their daily behavior. In conclusion, digital or digital medicine is like an approach that aims to support the use of reliable technologies in the field of neurocognitive diseases to improve therapeutic pathways, strengthen practices by involving several practitioners, anticipate the progression of the disease, model and predict clinical results from data collected to better respond to the quality of care and life of patients.

10 Practical Case of Follow-Up of Alzheimer's Disease

A study has been published by the University of Management of Singapore on the prediction of Alzheimer's disease through the use of IoT sensors on elderly people. This study is part of the SHINE Seniors program (Smart Homes and Intelligent Neighbors to Enable Seniors) and ICT (Information and Communications Technology) where researchers studied the behavior of individuals to predict health problems [49]. In this work, which serves as our starting model, the objective is to observe the symptoms of Alzheimer's through the behavior of patients and the analysis models provided by the exploitation of data from the IoT. Our approach would be to integrate more connected objects with the IoMTs but also the establishment of a weekly dashboard and a follow-up with an alert system thanks to the data processing models as we were able to show during our previous works [13]. In this context, three actions were measured at the level of activity, sleep cycles and repetitive actions.

Although these actions are not sufficient, they are useful since they appear in the panorama of Alzheimer's symptoms. The language structure of people with neurocognitive disorders is interesting to observe and it is in this respect that we wish to integrate the robotic solution into our approach, by integrating the notion of the GDPR also linked to ethical questions, by sending, not the recordings, but the treatment which will be done locally, thus only the dysfunctions would be transmitted by accompanying the other signs in order to consolidate the diagnosis. The ability to predict the disease very early, during stages 2 or 3 of Alzheimer's, validated by a medical diagnosis of course, allows rapid access to tools that slow down the progression of the disease. Indeed, it is still possible to stimulate brain activity with physical or mental activities that can slow the progression of the disease [50]. We describe here a few situations that could lead us to place a person in a neurocognitive disease approach. Indeed, people with Alzheimer's often do the same activities with the same gestures, say the same words or ask the same question repeatedly. They often have sleep disturbances and observe a change in their cycle, "for example a 20-min nap can turn into a nap of several hours". One of the common symptom is increased daytime sleep duration and restlessness, wandering at night.

Based on research on Alzheimer's the report defines three important models that can predict the appearance of the first signs of the disease:

- "Excessive activity within the place of residence", indeed "if there is too much activity over a short period of time" this could show a behavior of a person affected.
- "Unusual sleep cycles in the elderly" with "activity out of bed at night and sleep during the day" are also potential indicators of the disease.
- "Very high levels of repetition in the behavior" such as going back and forth between different places or doing an action several times, these repetitive actions can be perceived as abnormal if their frequency is high.

These connected objects allow, as we see here, to observe these behaviors and by integrating them with other factors related to IoMTs, we can thus help to establish a diagnosis but also to support caregivers on protocols validated by the medical profession to slow the progression of the disease, we are thinking of certain cognitive activities on applications, we are currently working on tools that allow us to work on language skills. The use of GPS sensor and video surveillance or motion detector as well as a connected bottle make it possible to monitor the patient on a daily basis but also to provide him with advice thanks to this robotic solution which could help and remind certain actions to be taken such as eating, … IoT must be operational solutions to assist the person on a daily basis and we see thanks to the TAM model, that it is possible to design a solution to be put into practice and which will be the subject of the following this work. For the detection of Alzheimer's, other studies use objects connected to everyday objects to measure the rate of forgetfulness and use (taps, gas, lights, doors, etc.). All this data then transformed into information is processed in order to build dashboards for the medical profession and we reproduce here an example of a dashboard with the main KPIs that seem relevant to us and the tools that we wish to put in place square (Fig. 3):

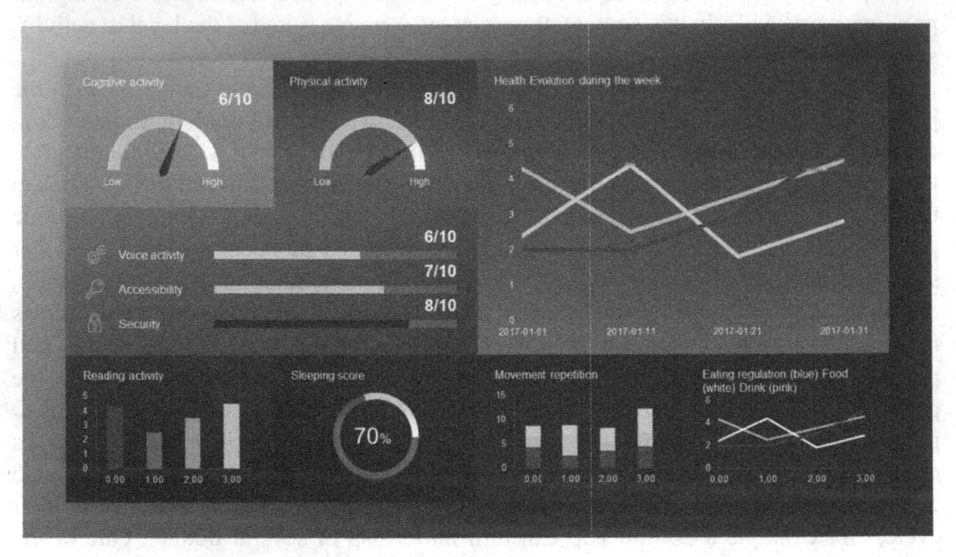

Fig. 3. Live patient activity visualization dashboard.

11 Conclusion

In this work, we show that the solution based on IoT or IoMT with the contribution of robotics would be relevant with an effective information system based on relevant data collection, and which would take into account the GDPR aspect. It seems useful or even necessary to us to create dedicated spaces themselves connected to the medical profession to promote interaction with patients and caregivers, to allow the establishment of this favorable environment and which could largely respond to problem of doctor shortage, to partly answer the question of medical deserts. This work is integrated into the vision of a medical approach based on the P5 medicine model. By installing dedicated centers, in which patients and their caregivers could have access to additional protocols, but also to measure the interest of technological solutions to sometimes respond to complex situations, which would result from the evolution of the disease, not having of medical skills, and which would promote their adoption by people, in order to answer the question also of the place of the device but also of its acceptance.

We also recommend, in order to support caregivers, the use of robotic solutions, which could assist patients in certain activities on a daily basis, to help them observe the protocols put in place to slow the progression of Alzheimer's disease but also on safety issues with a fall detector, and the presence of this robot could respond to the feeling of isolation of patients just like the fact of facilitating telephone communication through this robot, for example. This ecosystem will make it possible to see the signs of the onset of the disease, to validate the diagnosis by a doctor, but also by proposing at each stage technical solutions to support the health system, caregivers and patients in effective treatment. of this disease while waiting for the appearance of curative treatments.

References

1. https://www.insee.fr/fr/statistiques/2416631#tableau-figure1
2. Guyot, B.: Eléments pour une approche informationnelle dans les organisations. Sciences de la société (63) (2004)
3. https://www.health-data-hub.fr/
4. https://gdpr-info.eu/
5. André, A. (ed.): Digital Medicine. Springer, Cham (2018)
6. https://drees.solidarites-sante.gouv.fr/publications-documents-de-reference-communique-de-presse/panoramas-de-la-drees/CNS2022
7. Dwivedi, A., Dwivedi, S.S., Tariq, M.R., Qiu, X., Hong, S., Xin, Y.: Scope of artificial intelligence in medicine. J. Res. Med. Dent. Sci. **8**(3), 137–140 (2020)
8. Hamet, P., Tremblay, J.: Artificial intelligence in medicine. Metabolism **69**, S36–S40 (2017)
9. https://www.fondation-mederic-alzheimer.org/faits-et-chiffres-12-22
10. Kenigsberg, P.A., et al.: Impact socio-économique de la maladie d'Alzheimer et des maladies apparentées en Europe. Gérontologie et société **32128129**(1), 297–318 (2009)
11. https://www.has-sante.fr/upload/docs/application/pdf/2018-11/projet_strategique_2019-2024.pdf
12. Meliá, S., Nasabeh, S., Luján-Mora, S., Cachero, C.: MoSIoT: modeling and simulating IoT healthcare-monitoring systems for people with disabilities. Int. J. Environ. Res. Public Health **18**(12), 6357 (2021)
13. Fraoua, K.E., Bourret, C., Mouly, S.: Data for health, case of mental disorders and the use of machine learning for early detection. ISKO (2022)
14. Saleh, I.: Internet of Things (IoT): concepts, issues, challenges and perspectives (2018)
15. Chattu, V.K.: A review of artificial intelligence, big data, and blockchain technology applications in medicine and global health. Big Data Cognit. Comput. **5**(3), 41 (2021)
16. Simon, H.A.: The Sciences of the Artificial, Cambridge, MA (1969)
17. Forest, J., Micaëlli, J.P.: Artefact, les apports de l'approche simonienne. Revue du GRESEC (2007)
18. Matthewman, S.: Michel Foucault, technology, and actor-network theory. Techné Res. Philos. Technol. **17**(2), 274–292 (2013)
19. Carmagnat, F.: Une approche sociotechnique de l'histoire du telephone public. Réseaux **5**, 243–265 (2002)
20. Jézégou, A.: La présence à distance en e-Formation. Médiations et médiatisations-Revue internationale sur le numérique en éducation et communication **3**, 59–67 (2020)
21. Marangunić, N., Granić, A.: Technology acceptance model: a literature review from 1986 to 2013. Univ. Access Inf. Soc. **14**, 81–95 (2015)
22. Berx, N., Decré, W., Pintelon, L.: Examining the role of safety in the low adoption rate of collaborative robots. Procedia CIRP **106**, 51–57 (2022)
23. de Sant'Anna, M., Morat, B., Rigaud, A.S.: Adaptabilité du robot Paro dans la prise en charge de la maladie d'Alzheimer sévère de patients institutionnalisés. NPG Neurologie-Psychiatrie-Gériatrie **12**(67), 43–48 (2012)

24. Guiot, D., Sengès, E., Kerekes, M., Sancarlo, D.: Les solutions robotiques peuvent-elles favoriser le BienVieillir de la personne âgée en perte d'autonomie? In: 18th International Marketing Trends Conference (IMTC 2019), January 2019
25. Glende, S., Conrad, I., Krezdorn, L., Klemcke, S., Krätzel, C.: Increasing the acceptance of assistive robots for older people through marketing strategies based on stakeholder needs. Int. J. Soc. Robot. **8**(3), 355–369 (2016)
26. Vishnu, S., Ramson, S.J., Jegan, R.: Internet of medical things (IoMT)-an overview. In: 2020 5th International Conference on Devices, Circuits and Systems (ICDCS), pp. 101–104. IEEE, March 2020
27. https://www.fondation-mederic-alzheimer.org/le-projet-precos-bellan-laureat-2022-de-lappel-projets-inm-et-maladie-dalzheimer
28. Portz, J.D., et al.: Using the technology acceptance model to explore user experience, intent to use, and use behavior of a patient portal among older adults with multiple chronic conditions: descriptive qualitative study. J. Med. Internet Res. **21**(4), e11604 (2019)
29. Li, Y., Qi, J., Shu, H.: Review of relationships among variables in TAM. Tsinghua Sci. Technol. **13**(3), 273–278 (2008)
30. Alomary, A., Woollard, J.: How is technology accepted by users? A review of technology acceptance models and theories (2015)
31. Fishbein, M.: A theory of reasoned action: some applications and implications (1979)
32. Wingo, N.P., Ivankova, N.V., Moss, J.A.: Faculty perceptions about teaching online: exploring the literature using the technology acceptance model as an organizing framework. Online Learn. **21**(1), 15–35 (2017)
33. Venkatesh, V., Bala, H.: Technology acceptance model 3 and a research agenda on interventions. Decis. Sci. **39**(2), 273–315 (2008)
34. https://www.internetsociety.org/news/press-releases/2019/concerns-over-privacy-and-security-contribute-to-consumer-distrust-in-connected-devices/
35. Sagner, M., et al.: The P4 health spectrum–a predictive, preventive, personalized and participatory continuum for promoting healthspan. Prog. Cardiovasc. Dis. **59**(5), 506–521 (2017)
36. Pravettoni, G., Triberti, S.: A "P5" approach to healthcare and health technology. P5 eHealth: an agenda for the health technologies of the future, pp. 3–17 (2020)
37. Bellinger, G., Castro, D., Mills, A.: Data, information, knowledge, and wisdom (2004)
38. Hampel, H., et al.: Biomarkers for Alzheimer's disease: academic, industry and regulatory perspectives. Nat. Rev. Drug Discov. **9**(7), 560–574 (2010)
39. Roussel, C., et al.: Place of patient-reported outcomes & experiences measurements (PROMS/PREMS) in the assessment and pricing of health technologies in France. Therapies **77**(1), 103–115 (2022)
40. Graf, C.: The Lawton instrumental activities of daily living scale. AJN Am. J. Nurs. **108**(4), 52–62 (2008)
41. Croisile, B., Astier, J.L., Beaumont, C.: Standardization of the 5-word test in a group of 191 normal subjects aged 50 to 90 years. Revue Neurologique **163**(3), 323–333 (2007)
42. Solomon, P.R., Pendlebury, W.W.: Recognition of Alzheimer's disease: the 7 minute screen. Fam. Med. **30**(4), 265–271 (1998)
43. Solomon, P.R., et al.: A 7 minute neurocognitive screening battery highly sensitive to Alzheimer's disease. Arch. Neurol. **55**(3), 349–355 (1998)
44. Osborn, G.G., Saunders, A.V.: Current treatments for patients with Alzheimer disease. J. Am. Osteopath. Assoc. **110**(s98), 16–26 (2010)
45. Kaufer, D.I., et al.: Validation of the NPI-Q, a brief clinical form of the neuropsychiatric inventory. J. Neuropsychiatry Clin. Neurosci. **12**(2), 233–239 (2000)
46. Senanarong, V., et al.: Agitation in Alzheimer's disease is a manifestation of frontal lobe dysfunction. Dementia Geriatr. Cognit. Disord. **17**(1–2), 14–20 (2004)

47. Baker, S.B., Xiang, W., Atkinson, I.: Internet of things for smart healthcare: technologies, challenges, and opportunities. IEEE Access **5**, 26521–26544 (2017)
48. Sharma, M., Singh, G., Singh, R.: Accurate prediction of life style based disorders by smart healthcare using machine learning and prescriptive big data analytics. Data Intensive Comput. Appl. Big Data **29**, 428 (2018)
49. Chong, Z.H.K., et al.: Predicting potential Alzheimer medical condition in elderly using IOT sensors-case study (2017)
50. Cummings, J.L., Isaacson, R.S., Schmitt, F.A., Velting, D.M.: A practical algorithm for managing Alzheimer's disease: what, when, and why? Ann. Clin. Transl. Neurol. **2**(3), 307–323 (2015)

Message Recommendation Strategies for Tailoring Health Information to Promote Physical Activities

Longdan Hao[1], Stefan Goetze[2], and Mark Hawley[1](✉)

[1] Centre for Assistive Technology and Connected Healthcare (CATCH), The University of Sheffield, Sheffield, UK
{lhao4,mark.hawley}@sheffield.ac.uk

[2] Department of Computer Science, The University of Sheffield, Sheffield, UK
s.goetze@sheffield.ac.uk

https://catch.sites.sheffield.ac.uk/

Abstract. In many behaviour change interventions, computer-tailored health information has proven to be more effective than general health information. However, the majority of these studies have only achieved small effect sizes and the effectiveness of computer-tailored health communication (CTHC) remains inconsistent across different populations and behaviours. Since most CTHC studies measure a behaviour difference (e.g., steps per day) or biological difference (e.g., blood pressure), it is challenging to determine whether the intervention's success is due to the quality of message tailoring or other factors (e.g., user interface design). This paper presents a study that assesses the performance of various algorithms for tailoring health information. These algorithms include a rule-based approach, based on behaviour change theories and machine learning algorithms. Despite limited data, the evaluated algorithms significantly outperform random message selection, achieving a 1.7-fold increase in precision for predicting participants' preferred messages, and a 1.38-fold improvement in overall accuracy for anticipating participants' preferences.

Keywords: computer tailored health information · recommendation system · behaviour change

1 Introduction

Physical activity (PA) is beneficial for improving and maintaining people's health [1]. Regular PA is an important factor to increase people's quality of life (QoL) [2]. However, insufficient PA level is prevalent globally, increasing the risk of death [1]. As a form of health education, the communication of health information can promote people's health behaviour, such as increasing their PA level [3]. With computer technology, selecting and delivering health information to a large population based on their own situations is more practical and efficient [4–6].

Q. Gao et al. (Eds.): HCII 2023, LNCS 14055, pp. 536–555, 2023.
https://doi.org/10.1007/978-3-031-48041-6_36

1.1 Computer Tailored Health Communication (CTHC)

CTHC uses computer-based platforms for personal data collection and processing and to provide tailored information to its users [4–6]. CTHC is fostered by the development of two main fields: stage-based behaviour change theories[1] and computer technologies [4–6]. Another reason that highlights the critical need for further research in the field of CTHC is the suboptimal outcomes stemming from behaviour change interventions that rely on generic health information.

In CTHC systems, individuals' information can be collected via objective monitoring devices, self-reported data (e.g. by questionnaires), and third-party databases with individual's previous personal records (e.g., health apps, clinical records, web surfing data) [5,6]. The collected data is then processed for message selection. Two systems approaches for message selection are commonly used in CTHC: rule-based systems based on preset rules (more details are explained in Sect. 2.2), and recommendation systems (the popular algorithms used in RS are explained in Sect. 2.3) based on historical data. The selected message is then delivered via a message delivery channel, e.g. by print material, telephone, email, web or phone applications [6].

1.2 Behaviour Change Theories Applied in CTHC

Message selection rules in the majority of rule-based CTHC studies are supported by behaviour change theories [8]. Behaviour change theories are frameworks that aim to explain the underlying mechanisms and processes involved in human behaviour change and decision-making. These theories provide insights into the factors that shape an individual's behaviour, including cognitive, emotional, social, and environmental components. By identifying the key determinants of behaviour and the relationships between them, these theories help inform the development of effective strategies and interventions to promote positive behaviour change in various contexts, such as health promotion, education, and environmental conservation [9]. The most prominent behaviour change theories commonly applied in CTHC are transtheoretical model (TTM), Health Belief Model (HBM), Social cognitive theory (SCT) and theory of planned behaviour (TPB) [6,10].

The *stage of change* (SoC) as defined in the TTM [11,12], is the most prevalent behaviour change model[2] applied in the construction of personalised communication [6,10]. The Stage of change (SoC) theory assumes that behaviour changes in a cyclical process [11,12]. Each cycle contains *six stages of change*:

[1] Stage-based theories assume that psychological development and behaviour changes can be described by different continuous phases [7]. Further information is provided in Sect. 1.2.

[2] Behaviour change models are more specific and practical tools that are derived from behaviour change theories. These models provide a structured approach to designing and implementing behaviour change interventions. They offer step-by-step processes and techniques to initiate and sustain behaviour change.

1. *pre-contemplation* (no intention to change)
2. *contemplation* (being considerate to change in the foreseeable future)
3. *preparation* (starting to make plans for changes in the near future as well as measurable preparations)
4. *action* (changes happened within the past six months)
5. *maintenance* (keeping and preserving changes for more than six months)
6. *termination* (having no intentions to return to the unhealthy behaviour nor relapse)

The *SCT* assumes that behaviour change is influenced by an individual's characteristics, environment, and by the behaviour itself. Adoption of behaviour change is seen as an interactive and reciprocal process. *Self-efficacy* is considered the most critical influence of behaviour change in SCT. In addition, the likelihood of an individual engaging in a behaviour change is also influenced by outcome expectancy [12]; The *health belief model (HBM)* assumes that the perceived threats of the behavioural consequences influence the adoption or cessation of behaviour. Perceived threats consist of two components: susceptibility, such as e.g. the risk of an individual getting a disease, and severity, e.g. how severe a disease could develop [12];

In the *TPB*, positive attitudes, perceived normative pressure, and perceived behaviour control are positively associated with greater behaviour changes. Perceived behaviour control presents the extent of an individual's beliefs in the user's ability to control and manage a behaviour change [12,13]

In an effort to make behaviour studies more replicable and implementable, Michie et al. [14] consolidated the *active ingredients* used in behaviour change interventions into a unified reporting language. These behaviour change techniques (BCTs) are summarised in a respective BCT taxonomy [14] and are specific tactics or methods designed to facilitate individual behaviour modification. A total of 93 BCTs were identified and defined in [14]. Repeating all 93 BCTs identified in [14] is beyond the scope of this work but since the proposed algorithms described in Sect. 2 will be based on these BCTs, Table 1 summarises their main categories and how many sub-categories each main category has. The interested reader is referred to [14][3] for further details.

Table 1. Main BCT categories from [14] and number of respective sub-categories.

BCT main category (# sub.-cats.)	BCT main category (# sub.-cats.)	BCT main category (# sub.-cats.)
1 Goals and planning (9)	7 Associations (8)	13 Identity (5)
2 Feedback and monitoring (7)	8 Repetition and substitution (7)	14 Scheduled consequences (10)
3 Social support (3)	9 Comparison of outcomes (3)	15 Self-belief (4)
4 Shaping knowledge (4)	10 Reward and threat (11)	16 Covert learning (3)
5 Natural consequences (6)	11 Regulation (4)	
6 Comparison of behaviour (3)	12 Antecedents (6)	

[3] A list of the 93 BCTs [14] is also available only at https://digitalwellbeing.org/wp-content/uploads/2016/11/BCTTv1_PDF_version.pdf, Last access 23/06/2023.

1.3 Effectiveness and Challenges of CTHC

CTHC has been applied to promote different health behaviours to different populations, such as promoting disease screening behaviour [15], PA promotion [16], and nutrition promotion [17,18].

A meta-analysis [10] assesses the efficacy of computer-tailored *printed* materials on health behaviour changes and finds that CTHC is effective (but with an effective size less than *small*). Furthermore, the study finds that a larger effect size is seen in (i) studies using a combination of different behaviour change theories, (ii) studies targeting multiple behaviours, and (iii) tailoring on demographic features [10].

Another meta-analysis [19] assesses the efficacy of computer-tailored *web-delivered* health messages. Overall, tailored messages on behaviour changes show a greater effect compared to control conditions (with a small effect size). Seven health behaviours were targeted in the CTHC interventions: PA, nutrition/diet, smoking, drinking, medication adherence, stress management, and faecal soiling. Within the included studies, tailored interventions were more effective for the healthy population than for people with conditions [19].

The meta-analysis [20] assesses the efficacy of CTHC on promoting PA to people with or at risk of long-term conditions. Overall, tailored messages on PA promotion show a greater effect compared to no health information and general health information. The overall effect size was small to medium. The assessed conditions include cardiovascular diseases, cancer, diabetes, COPD, overweight and obesity.

Despite previous studies demonstrating the effectiveness of CTHC, the overall effect size has been found to be small [10,19,20]. The tailoring rule is a key component in CTHC that influences the effectiveness of behaviour change interventions. As a result, this study primarily focuses on evaluating the accuracy of tailoring rules using different algorithms.

This study has two primary aims. The first is to assess the feasibility of using a hybrid recommendation system, combining a predefined rule-based approach and machine learning (ML)-based algorithms, to deliver tailored health information related to PA via a web application. To evaluate the performance of the different tailoring algorithms, we will compare confusion metrics (cf. Table 2) between the system's predicted rating scores[4] Y_p and the actual rating scores Y. The second aim is to enhance the system's usability to be addressed in future development stages.

2 System Description

Most previous CTHC systems employ rule-based approaches, utilizing a set of predefined rules grounded in behaviour change theories [21]. These rules involve choosing suitable tailoring variables (e.g., individuals' stage of change), selecting

[4] rating scores are collected through a rating system to record participants' attitudes on messages. For details, see Sect. 3.2.

relevant behaviour change theories (e.g., the stage-of-change model), and establishing conditional "if-else" selection processes [21,22]. In CTHC, both individuals and messages are categorised into subgroups (also known as segmentation) based on the selected independent variables and predetermined rules [21]. If the message's subgroup aligns with the individual's subgroup, the message will be recommended [21]. Recently, research has shifted away from rule-based systems, with an increasing focus on exploring the application of recommendation systems (RSs) utilizing ML techniques to deliver tailored health communication [23].

The proposed CTHC system comprises, therefore, a rule-based algorithm (see Sect. 2.2) and machine learning algorithms (see Sect. 2.3). Their performance will be compared in Sect. 4.

2.1 System Framework

The CTHC system proposed in this study consists of three main modules: message delivery, message selection, and database. The *messages delivery module* is responsible for identifying users, presenting tailored messages to the user, and saving rating records from the user to the database. The *message selection module* employs two filters for message selection. The first filter consists of a rule-based algorithm informed by the TTM, the health action process approach (HAPA)[5] and SCT. The second filter comprises the RS algorithm as described in Sect. 2.3. This filter is trained using the dataset collected from participants, which is stored in the *database module* which stores all relevant data on users, messages and ratings.

2.2 Rule-Based Algorithm

The proposed rule-based algorithm is based on three aspects described in the following to produce a matching score $0 \leq M_{u,m} \leq 1$, evaluating the relationship between each user u and each message m. The matching score $M_{u,m}$ depends on:

(1) The difference between a user's stage of change regarding PA, defined as an integer value $S_{\mathrm{u}} \in \{1, ..., 6\}$, and the stage of change best suited for a given message, defined accordingly as $S_m \in \{1, ..., 6\}$, cf. (1)
(2) The required BCTs for the user at their stage of change, and the BCTs associated with a message, cf. (2.2)
(3) Whether the message contains information about the user's general preferences and barriers to perform PA, cf. (7)

(1) User and Message Stage of Change Difference: The SoC difference between user u and message m is denoted by $S_{u,m}$ and will be explained in the following, see. (1). The user's stage of change S_u is obtained by a baseline

[5] HAPA posits that health behaviour change occurs in two distinct phases: the motivation phase and the volition phase [24,25].

assessment detailed in Sects. 3.2 and 4.1. Messages can be categorized to fit users with different stages of change based on the message's topic and emphasis on BCT. For example:

- Messages aimed at raising consciousness for behaviour change are more effective for people in SoC 1 [11,12].
- Messages focused on problem solving (addressing barriers to physical activity) are more effective for people in SoC 2 (general barriers to performing PA) and SoC 3 (specific barriers to performing PA), so either a SoC of 2 or 3 is chosen for the SoC S_m best fitting for message m [12].
- Messages that convince people to create action plans are more effective for individuals in SoC 3 [24,25].
- Messages that encourage self-monitoring and goal-setting are more effective for people in SoC 4 [11,24,25].

Hence, each message is assigned a SoC label S_m by manual annotation. A (weighted) absolute difference between the SoC $S_u \in \{1, ..., 6\}$ of user u and the SoC $S_m \in \{1, ..., 6\}$ which is best suited for message m is calculated by

$$S_{u,m} = \beta_s \cdot |S_u - S_m|. \quad (1)$$

When user u has a higher SoC S_u compared to the message's labelled SoC S_m, the impact of the difference is less significant in (1) than when user u has a lower SoC compared to the message's labelled SoC. To represent this difference, the weighting factor

$$\beta_s = \begin{cases} 0.05 & \text{for } S_u \geq S_m \\ 0.1 & \text{for } S_u < S_m \end{cases} \quad (2)$$

is defined. Values 0.05 and 0.1 in (2) have been determined empirically since the value of the impact of the difference is unknown from previous studies.

(2) Matching Behaviour Change Techniques (BCTs) Between Users and Messages: BCTs are associated to each user depending on (i) the user's *SoCs*, (ii) their current *PA status* and a *psychological assessment* (self-efficacy on PA). The rules for labelling are supported by the TTM, the HAPA, and SCT.

The BCT taxonomy [14] (cf. Table 1) contains 16 main BCT categories ($1 \leq i \leq 16$) and a varying number $1 \leq j \leq J_i$ of techniques within each of these main categories, with J_i representing the number of BCTs within a main category i (cf. numbers in Table 1). Hence, a BCT vector

$$\mathbf{b} = \left[\underbrace{B_{1,0}}_{\text{cat. 1}}, \underbrace{B_{1,1}, ..., B_{1,J_1}}_{\text{BCTs in cat. 1}}, \underbrace{B_{2,0}}_{\text{cat. 2}}, \underbrace{B_{2,1}, ..., B_{2,J_2}}_{\text{BCTs in cat. 2}}, ..., \underbrace{B_{16,0}}_{\text{cat. 16}}, \underbrace{B_{16,1}, ..., B_{16,J_{16}}}_{\text{BCTs in cat. 16}} \right]^T \quad (3)$$

of length $93 + 16 = 109$ is defined, with all $B_{i,j} \in \mathbb{B}$, i.e. all entries of $\mathbf{b}$ are Boolean expressions $\mathbb{B} \in \{0, 1\}$. Operator $[]^T$ denoted the vector transpose.

In addition to identifying the required BCTs for each user, HAPA also suggested that some BCTs are more effective in particular SoCs than in others. For example, promoting perceived self-efficacy (BCT category 13, *Identity*, cf. Table 1) is considered more important in SoC $S_u = 3$ and $S_u = 4$ than in SoC $S_u = 1$ and $S_u = 2$. Risk perception is suggested to be more important in SoC $S_u = 1$ than other SoC statuses. Therefore, the vector $\mathbf{b}$ of Booleans is multiplied by a weighting vector $\boldsymbol{\beta}_{\mathrm{BCT},s}$ for each user for all SoCs S_u between 1 and 4. Since the quantitative effects of BCTs have not been reported in previous studies, three different weighting values for $\boldsymbol{\beta}_{\mathrm{BCT},s}$ are defined empirically, i.e. 0.05 (important BCTs), 0.02 (moderately important BCTs) or 0 (less important BCTs). Based on this, each user is assigned a user vector that represents the BCTs and their respective importance for that individual:

$$\mathbf{u}_s = \boldsymbol{\beta}_{\mathrm{BCT},s} \circ \mathbf{b} \tag{4}$$

The symbol $\circ$ denotes the Hadamard product, i.e. the element-by-element multiplication.

Similar to vector $\mathbf{b}$, a vector $\mathbf{m}$ of length 109 containing Boolean values $M_{i,j} \in \{0, 1\}$ is defined, By manual annotation of the messages, $M_{i,j}$ is set to 1 if the message content includes the corresponding BCT and to 0 otherwise. For example, if a message contains information for persuading individuals to make plans for walking 10,000 steps per day, we set $M_{1,4} = 1$ (action planning). If this message also provides reasons for why 10,000 steps per day are needed, we set $M_{5,1} = 1$, since the reason is related to information about health consequences. Similarly, $M_{5,3} = 1$ if the reason is related to making friends, i.e. if the message provides information about social and environmental consequences. $M_{5,6} = 1$ if the message discusses mental health, i.e. provides information about emotional consequences. This annotation leads to a vector

$$\mathbf{m}_m = [M_{1,0}, ..., M_{1,J_1}, M_{2,0}, ..., M_{2,J_2}, ..., M_{16,0}, ..., M_{16,J_{16}}]^T \tag{5}$$

matching the size of 109×1 of $\mathbf{b}$ in (3) and (4). The user BCT labels from (4) are then matched with the BCT features of each message as defined in (5) by calculating the product of the two vectors. This results in a value

$$B_{u,m} = \mathbf{u}_s^T \cdot \mathbf{m}_m, \tag{6}$$

representing the BCT matching level of SoC between each user u and each message m.

(3) Keyword Matching: In addition to matching BCTs and SoC, the rule-based algorithm also takes into account the user's general preferences and barriers to performing PA. The system generates a keyword list for each user's preferences and barriers (from the initial user assessment, see Sects. 3.2 and 4.1 for details), as well as a keyword list for each message's content (and subtitle, if the message contains a video). The message's keyword list is extracted using the rapid automatic keyword extraction algorithm (RAKE) algorithm[6]. Keywords from the two lists are combined into pairs. For each pair, a match between the user and the message is considered, if the *fuzzy string match score*[7], being a value between 0 to 100%, is greater than 50%. The number of matches is then weighted by the ratio score $\beta_{\mathrm{r}_i,u,m}$, and then summed up.

$$K_{u,m} = \begin{cases} \sum_{i=0}^{n} \lfloor \beta_{\mathrm{r}_i,u,m} \rfloor & \text{if } \beta_{\mathrm{r}_i,u,m} \geq 50\% \\ 0 & \text{if } \beta_{\mathrm{r}_i,u,m} < 50\% \end{cases} \tag{7}$$

In (7), n denotes the number of $\beta_{\mathrm{r}_i,u,m} \geq 50\%$.

Message-User Matching Score: The final score for the general *degree of matching* between a user u and a message m is then based on SoC matching in (1), BCT matching in (6), and keyword-matching in (7):

$$M_{u,m} = \frac{1}{1+e^{(S_{u,m}-B_{u,m}-K_{u,m})}} \tag{8}$$

The rationale behind the empirically determined sigmoid relation in (8) is that when there is a large difference, or number of matched BCTs and keywords between user u and message m, the change in the included features (SoC, BCTs, keyword matching) should have a smaller impact on $M_{u,m}$.

2.3 Machine Learning Algorithms for Message Selection

Since the rule-based approach described before relies on several empirically determined components, three different, relatively simple machine learning (ML) methods [26] are tested and applied for user-message matching in the following to predict users ratings, i.e. Naïve Bayes (NB), support vector machine (SVM), and k-nearest neighbors (KNN) classifiers.

Data Pre-processing: Due to the limited number of rating records, the 5-star rating scale ($1 \leq y \leq 5$) is converted to Boolean values *like* (i.e. 1, if $4 \leq y \leq 5$) and *dislike* (i.e. 0, if $1 \leq y \leq 3$). After conversion, y is the Boolean value of the rating $y \in \{0, 1\}$ (cf. Figs. 3 and 4 later in this document).

To reduce the variance of input features, individuals' PA levels are converted to Boolean values, with 1 representing the individual reaching the recommended PA level and 0 indicating otherwise. The individuals' self-efficacy (ranging from 5 to 40), delta stage of change, and the number of keyword matches generated by "TheFuzz" algorithm (see Sect. 2.2) were normalised using min-max normalisation (cf. (9)).

---

[6] Rapid automatic keyword extraction algorithm Python library: https://pypi.org/project/rake-nltk/, last access 23/06/2023.

[7] The fuzzy string match score is calculated using *TheFuzz* algorithm, https://pypi.org/project/fuzzywuzzy/, last access 23/06/2023.

Rating records were obtained from a trial run using the previously described rule-based approach. Those data were divided into a training dataset (70%) and a test dataset (30%).

All variants of input feature vectors $\mathbf{x}$ introduced in the following are normalised by min-max normalisation before being used as input for the classifiers, i.e.

$$\tilde{\mathbf{x}} = \frac{\mathbf{x} - x_{\min}}{x_{\max} - x_{\min}}, \tag{9}$$

with $x_{\min}$ and $x_{\max}$ denoting the minimum and maximum values of input feature vector $\mathbf{x}$, respectively.

Cosine Similarity of Text Embeddings: The cosine-similarity

$$\cos(\mathbf{a}, \mathbf{b}) = \frac{\mathbf{a} \cdot \mathbf{b}}{||\mathbf{a}|| \, ||\mathbf{a}||} \tag{10}$$

is widely used to evaluate pairwise distances of vectorised items (e.g., message representations) in the vector space model (VSM)[8] of documents. The cosine-similarity will be used in the following by the classifiers to compare two vectorised texts: $\mathbf{a}$ denotes the vectorised text of each user's preference in general and barriers to performing PA, and $\mathbf{b}$ is the respective vectorised message. In VSMs, information vectorisation is an important step before the information classification. Typical methods in the field of natural language processing (NLP) are bag-of-words with term frequency-inverse document frequency (Tf-Idf) representations. However, in recent years, approaches based on word embeddings, such as Word2Vec [27] or bidirectional encoder representations from transformers (BERT) [28], have been shown to be successful for various NLP-related tasks. In this work, BERT representations are therefore used to vectorise text from both users and messages, i.e. for vectors $\mathbf{a}$ and $\mathbf{b}$ in (10).

Input Feature Vectors: Different combinations of features are defined in the following as feature input vectors for the classifiers under test. First, a vector of dimension 3×1, composed of the user's stage of change S_u, the user's PA level P_u and the user's self-efficacy level on performing PA E_u is defined, all values are determined during baseline assessment as described in Sects. 3.2 and 4.1.

$$\mathbf{x}_u = [S_u, P_u, E_u]^T \tag{11}$$

A second input feature vector of size 4×1, capturing the user-message relationships is defined, comprising the number of BCT matches between the user and the message[9], $\mathbf{b}^T \cdot \mathbf{m}$, the similarity between the user's preferences and barriers and the message, $\cos(\mathbf{a}, \mathbf{b})$, as defined in (10), the absolute SoC difference

[8] a spatial representation of text [22].

[9] Please note that the weighting vector $\boldsymbol{\beta}_{\mathrm{BCT},s}$ from (4) is not applied here since no empirically determined factors are used for the ML-based algorithms. Therefore, vector $\mathbf{b}$ as defined in (3) is used directly instead of vectors $\mathbf{u}_s$.

between the user and the message $|S_u - S_m|$ as in (1), again without empirically determined weighting factor, and a keyword matching between the user's preference/barriers and the message $K_{\mathrm{u,m}}$ as defined in (7):

$$\mathbf{x}_{u,m} = \left[\mathbf{b}^T \cdot \mathbf{m}, \cos(\mathbf{a}, \mathbf{b}), |S_u - S_m|, K_{\mathrm{u,m}}\right]^T \tag{12}$$

A vector $\mathbf{x}'$ of length 7×1 is defined combining the user features $\mathbf{x}_u$ from (11), and user-message relationships $\mathbf{x}_{u,m}$ from (12).

$$\mathbf{x}' = \left[\mathbf{x}_u^T, \mathbf{x}_{u,m}^T\right]^T \tag{13}$$

Naïve Bayes (NB) Classifiers: A NB classifier is commonly in RS [22]. Naïve Bayes assumes that the probability that an event occurs (e.g., user i rated item j with 4 stars out of 5) is independently influenced by all the selected input variables X [22].

Support Vector Machines: SVMs are supervised ML models used for classification (support vector classification (SVC)) and regression (support vector regression (SVR)) [26]. For SVC, the goal is to find the decision boundary which can assign most of the samples to the correct class.

K-Nearest Neighbour Classifiers: The nearest neighbours method looks for the closest neighbours w.r.t. the (Eucledian) distance in the feature space between a new sample and the training samples [26]. The number of closest neighbours K is a parameter of the KNN approach [26].

2.4 Algorithm Assessment

The algorithms' performance will be assessed in terms of typical metrics *accuracy* A and *precision* P which can be derived from the confusion matrix (CM), shown in Table 2 for the case of binary classification.

Table 2. Confusion matrix for a binary classification task. TP: true positive, TN: true negative, FP: false positive, FN: false negative.

		Predicted		
		0 (negative)	1 (positive)	Total
True	0 (negative)	TN	FP	TN+FP
	1 (positive)	FN	TP	TP+FN
	Total	TN+FN	TP+FP	N

Each row in the CM in Table 2 corresponds to the instances in a predicted class, while each column represents the instances in an actual class. The *precision*

$$P = \frac{\mathrm{TP}}{\mathrm{TP} + \mathrm{FP}} \tag{14}$$

assesses the model's ability to correctly identify true positive instances out of all instances predicted as positive. The precision metric is particularly useful when the cost of false positives is high or when we want to ensure that positive predictions are highly reliable. *Accuracy*

$$A = \frac{\mathrm{TP} + \mathrm{TN}}{\mathrm{TP} + \mathrm{TN} + \mathrm{FP} + \mathrm{FN}} \tag{15}$$

is a measure of the overall correctness of the model predictions, regardless of the class.

3 Study Design

3.1 Enrollment

Flyers (in PDF format) were shared through the main researcher's WhatsApp and WeChat groups. Additionally, printed flyers were posted within the faculties of the University of Sheffield (UoS). The inclusion criteria were as follows:

1. Healthy individuals of age between 18 and 60 years
2. People studying or working at UoS who can read English
3. People with access to the internet through a computer, phone, or tablet

Participants were required to read the online information sheet and sign the electronic consent form before joining the study.

3.2 Experiments

Experiments were divided into two steps: a baseline assessment and daily message ratings for a duration of 7 days. After participants enroled, a baseline assessment was carried out to collect participants' geographic information and physical activity-related features for the RS. An account was created for each participant including a unique URL to collect their ratings. Participants were encouraged to rate at least three messages per day. On the rating start date, each participant received two messages through his preferred communicational channel (Email, WhatsApp, SMS or WeChat). The first one was a thank you letter, with a brief introduction to the study. The second was a reminder:

Dear "name",
Thanks for your great support!
This is the "x" day for this trial. Click url to check your new messages and provide your ratings.
If you want to set another time to receive this reminder, simply reply to this message.
NOTE: Sometimes the server might be slow, please refresh your web browser if it takes a longer time than expected.

The reminder was sent daily at 11:00 am for seven days; the name and URL were adapted according to each participant's chosen nickname in the baseline assessment, and the “x” was the countdown day of the study. Four-dimensional ratings were requested for each message (as shown in Fig. 1 in the 3rd panel): (perceived) *usefulness*[10], (perceived) *relevancy*[11], (perceived) *enjoyment*[12] and (perceived) *active trust*[13]. These four dimensions were drawn from the conceptual model [29] and adapted to the CTHC.

3.3 Web-Based Message Delivery

Figure 1 shows four interface pages of the designed web-based application for message delivery, which users could access using their personal URL provided in the daily reminder. It comprises:

1. a *homepage*, where users find information related to the project, an introduction and information on how to use this web application for rating messages;
2. a *list of new messages*, where users find all titles of unrated messages. The unrated messages were randomized and displayed as a list on this page for the user to view;
3. *message content* and *rating*, where users read the message and rate it;
4. a *list of rated messages*, where users can find the messages they have rated.

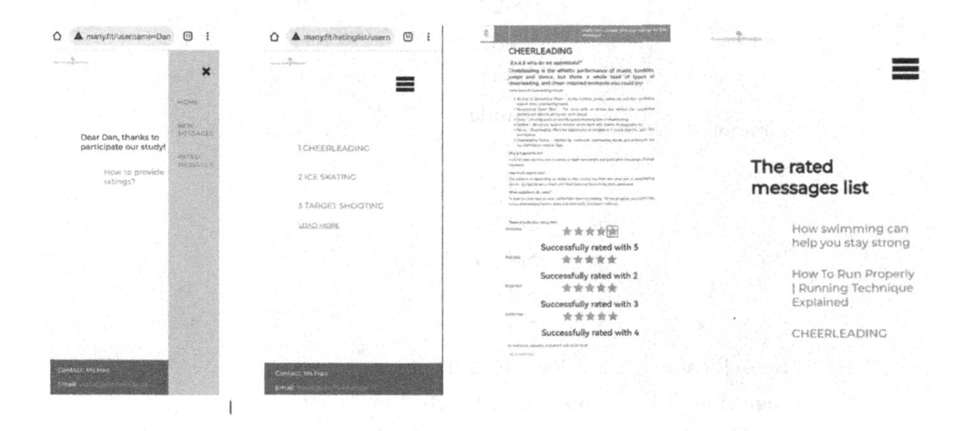

Fig. 1. Webpage layout, home page (leftmost), rating list, message content, and rated message list (rightmost)

[10] The degrees of the user’s belief that the information is beneficial. *Usefulness* is the cognitive perceptions of *Efficiency* and *Effectiveness*.
[11] The quality of the information to the users that can be effectively used by the user.
[12] Affective perceptions on reading the message.
[13] Believe and have the confidence to act on the information presented.

4 Results

4.1 Participant Disposition

In total, 25 participants signed the consent form and completed the baseline assessment. Out of these, 15 participants rated at least one message during the 7-day study period. Table 3 presents the participants' characteristics based on the results of the baseline assessment.

During the study, participants were asked to comment on the technical design shortcomings of the system. Regarding this, participants reported by webpage layout issues. For instance, the star rating system did not display correctly on some mobile phone models or a comment section under each message was requested. In some cases, the 'next message' button did not function properly, and the website occasionally reported errors during use. All reported design and technical issues were considered minor and resolved immediately during the study and therefore should not influence the results reported in the following.

Table 3. Summary of baseline assessment; participant characteristics (N=15).

Characteristics	Sub-category	No. of participants
Age	18-24	3
	25-34	11
	35-44	1
Gender	Female	8
	Male	7
SoC	SoC-1	0
	SoC-2	1
	SoC-3	1
	SoC-4	8
	SoC-5	5
Self-efficacy regarding PA (10-40)	low (10-20)	3
	medium (21-30)	6
	high (above 30)	6
Currently Smoking	Yes	0
	No	15
Reaching recommended PA level	Yes	3
	No	12
Message delivery channel	Email	13
	SMS	1
	Wechat	1

4.2 Technical Evaluation

In total, 1, 102 rating records were collected from the participants. Figure 2 shows the number of rating records collected from each participant.

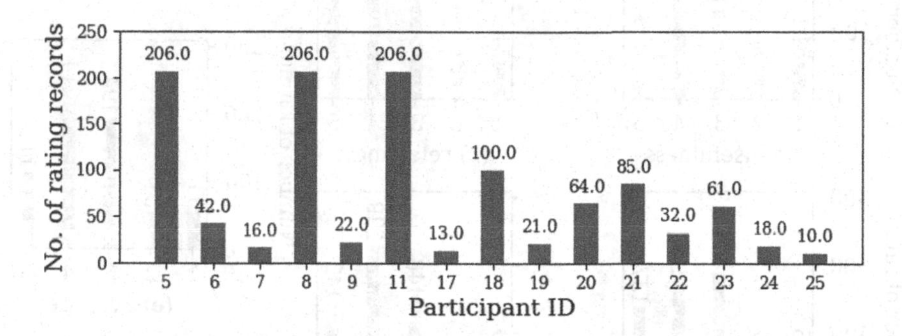

Fig. 2. Number of ratings per participant (participants without ratings are omitted).

Given the high correlations observed among the four-dimensional ratings (see Table 4), the "average" of these ratings, referred to as the *average* in the following, is calculated by aggregating the values across the four dimensions.

Table 4. Correlations between 4-dimensional ratings

	Usefulness	Relevancy	Enjoyment	Active trust
Usefulness	1	0.83	0.82	0.81
Relevancy	0.83	1	0.79	0.83
Enjoyment	0.82	0.79	1	0.79
Active trust	0.81	0.83	0.79	1

As the decision rules and persuasive messages in the system were designed for participants with SoC below 5 ($S_u \leq 4$), records collected from participants with their SoC level equal to or above 5 ($S_u > 4$) were excluded to avoid bias in evaluating the system performance. Therefore, 627 records remained for evaluating the RS system. The obtained rating scores, as shown in Fig. 3, with ratings between 1 and 5 To converte the dataset to Boolean values, the Boolean record was set to 1 if the participant's rating was equal to or above 4, otherwise, it was set to 0 (see. Fig. 4).

Rule-Based Algorithm: CMs were calculated to assess the performance of the RS as shown in Table 5. For the rule-based RS, precision on 1, as defined in (14), is 0.68 for *usefulness*, 0.65 for *relevancy*, 0.54 for *enjoyment*, 0.66 for *active trust*, and 0.60 for averaging all 4 dimensions. See also Table 6 for accuracy results.

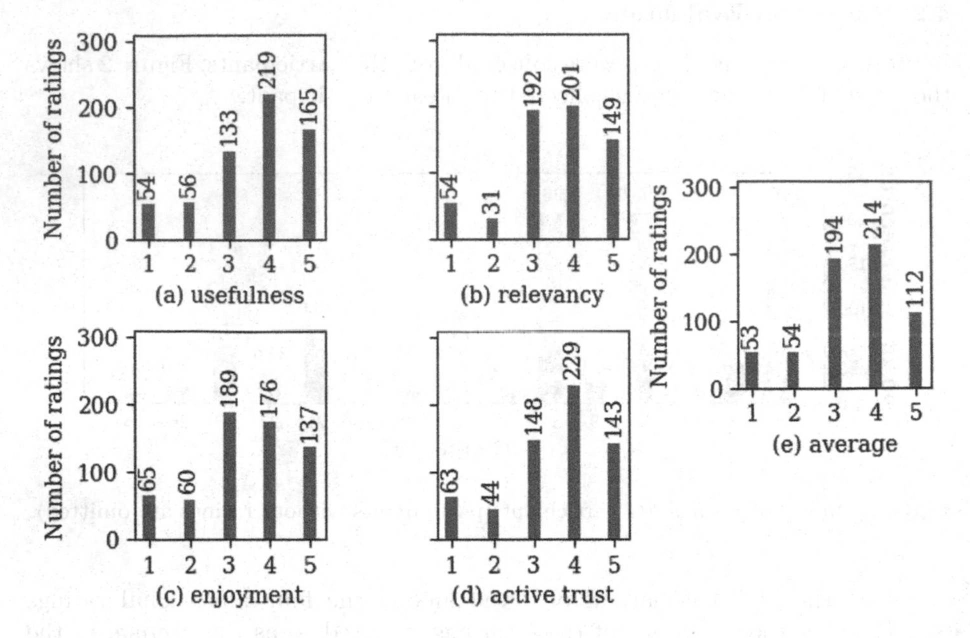

Fig. 3. Rating distribution for categories (top left to bottom middle) (a) *usefulness*, (b) *relevancy*, (c) *enjoyment*, and (d) *active trust*, as well as (e) averaged ratings.

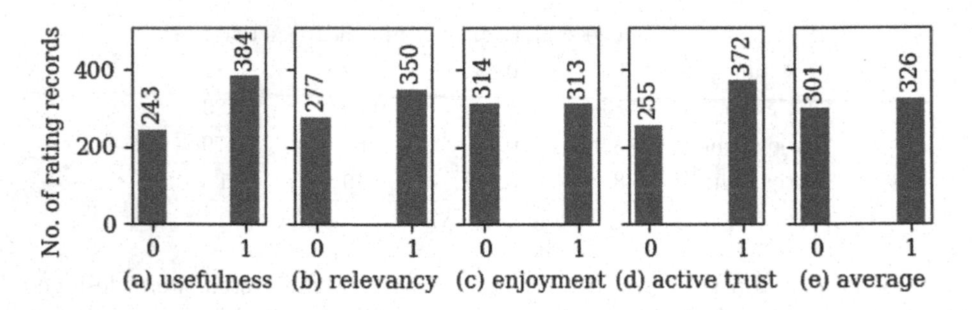

Fig. 4. Rating records distribution Boolean type 0 and 1.

Table 5. Confusion matrices of rule-based algorithm

(a) Usefulness

		predicted 0	predicted 1
true	0	81	40
	1	107	86

(b) Relevancy

		predicted 0	predicted 1
true	0	84	46
	1	104	80

(c) Enjoyment

		predicted 0	predicted 1
true	0	95	58
	1	93	68

(d) Active trust

		predicted 0	predicted 1
true	0	80	43
	1	108	83

(e) Average

		predicted 0	predicted 1
true	0	91	51
	1	97	75

ML-Based Algorithms: For the ML-based RSs, different combinations of the participants' attributions and messages' attributions were evaluated as the independent input features as listed in the 3rd column of Table 6, i.e. combinations from (11), (12), (13) and (10). ML algorithms include KNN KNeighbors classifier and a variant, i.e. NearestCentroid, Gaussian Naïve Bayes, linear and non-linear SVCs [26], as listed in the 1st and 2nd columns of Table 6.

Table 6. Algorithm performance in terms of accuracy A and precision P (precision on 1) depending on classifiers and input feature combinations; asterisk (*) indicates that the classifier decided on a single category for all data. Bold font indicates best performance.

Algorithm		Input feature $\mathbf{x}$	Usefulness		Relevancy		Enjoyment		Active trust		Average	
			A	P	A	P	A	P	A	P	A	P
Rule-based algorithm		$[S_{u,m}, B_{u,m}, K_{\mathrm{u,m}}]^T$	0.53	0.68	0.54	0.65	0.52	0.54	0.52	0.66	0.53	0.60
KNN	K-Nearest Neighbor Classifier	$\mathbf{x}_u$	0.66	0.68	0.55	**0.84**	**0.61**	**0.85**	**0.68**	0.70	**0.67**	**0.72**
		$[\mathbf{x}_u^T, \cos(\mathbf{a}, \mathbf{b})]^T$	**0.72**	**0.75**	**0.68**	**0.71**	0.62	0.66	**0.66**	**0.72**	**0.69**	**0.74**
		$\mathbf{x}_{u,m}$	0.65	0.68	0.59	0.65	0.51	0.52	0.60	0.67	0.59	0.62
		$\mathbf{x}'$	0.68	0.71	**0.67**	**0.74**	0.56	0.57	0.60	0.67	0.65	0.67
	K-Nearest centriod	$\mathbf{x}_u$	0.57	0.61	0.65	0.67	0.57	0.56	0.5	0.61	0.48	0.51
		$\mathbf{x}_{u,m}$	0.55	0.66	0.54	0.63	0.49	0.51	0.53	0.65	0.52	0.56
		x'	0.51	0.60	0.65	0.67	0.56	0.55	0.5	0.59	0.50	0.53
NB	Gaussian NB	$\mathbf{x}_u$	0.61*	0.62*	0.65	0.67	0.57	0.56	0.61*	0.61*	0.59	0.58
		$\mathbf{x}_{u,m}$	0.68	0.71	0.65	0.68	0.59	0.61	0.66	0.69	0.66	0.68
		$\mathbf{x}'$	0.61*	0.61*	0.68	0.76	0.58	0.57	0.52	**0.77**	0.65	0.72
SVM	SVC linear	$\mathbf{x}_u$	0.61*	0.61*	0.65	0.67	0.56	0.57	0.61*	0.61*	0.59	0.58
	SVM non-linear	$[\mathbf{x}_u^T, \cos(\mathbf{a}, \mathbf{b})]^T$	0.54	**0.75**	0.51	0.58	0.53	0.57	0.52	0.61	0.59	0.69
		$[\mathbf{x}_u^T, K_{\mathrm{u,m}}]^T$	0.59	**0.76**	0.56	0.61	0.57	0.57	0.53	0.64	0.40	0.41

For ML-based RS, the highest precision values for 1 were as follows: 0.76 (*Usefulness*, generated by SVM non-linear); 0.84 (*Relevancy*, generated by KNNeighbors Classifier); 0.85 (*Enjoyment*, generated by KNNeighbors Classifier); 0.77 (Active Trust, generated by Gaussian Naive Bayes); and 0.74 (Average, generated by KNeighbors Classifier). The highest value of accuracy were 0.72 (Usefulness, generated by KNNeighbors Classifier); 0.68 (Relevancy, generated by KNNeighbors Classifier ad Gaussian Naive Bayes); 0.62 (Enjoyment, generated by KNNeighbors Classifier); 0.68 (Active Trust, generated by KNNeighbors Classifier); and 0.69 (Average, generated by KNNeighbors Classifier). The results may vary slightly with different randomly split datasets; however, the KNNeighbors classifier demonstrated the best overall performance among all the RS.

Compared to randomised message delivery, the rule-based algorithm leads to a relative improvement of 20 % precision in average for positively rated messages over the four tested dimensions in comparison to random message selection. For the machine-learning-based algorithms, KNN leads to the best prediction of user ratings with a relative improvement of 48 % in average over the four tested dimensions, with 70 % relative improvement for dimension *enjoyment*.

5 Conclusion

5.1 System Performance on Recommending Tailored Health Messages

In conclusion, the obtained results show that the developed system is feasible for use as a recommendation system for tailoring messages related to PA promotion. The rule-based algorithm is superior to random message delivery, and it can be used in the initial stage of message selection when no historical data from users is available for training the ML-based algorithms. With limited data, the KNN method, using user features and text similarity scores, results in the best performance among the tested algorithms and combinations of independent variables (input features), markedly improving overall performance. Therefore, when dealing with a small amount of collected data, KNN can improve the performance of health message RS. The results of the correlation test reveal a significant correlation among the 4-dimensional ratings, which is in line with findings by Crutzen (2011) that active trust can act as a mediator for user perceptions. These perceptions encompass effectiveness (usefulness and relevancy) and enjoyment, ultimately leading to e-loyalty [29].

5.2 Effective Independent Variables

In this study, participants' characteristics were selected to generate user-message relationships. The participants' SoC, self-efficacy on PA, the current status of PA level, and text similarity between participants' preferences/barriers with messages were shown to be effective in increasing the precision rate in selecting the right messages for participants. It was shown that, using the rule-based system, a relationship between each participant and each message (matching score) can be established based on behaviour theories and BCT. The participants' SoC and current status of PA level can be linked to the messages' content by comparing with the messages' best-fitted SoC and PA level. BCTs necessary for behaviour change of participants can be linked to the messages' BCTs taxonomy [14]. Participants' preferences in general and barriers to performing PA can be used to link messages' content through keyword matching and text similarity matching. Due to current behaviour change theories providing more frameworks (i.e. what should be considered) than quantitative intervention doses (i.e. how much should be considered), the rule-based system still needs to identify the right coefficient (β's) for each independent variable to increase accuracy and precision. In the proposed RS based on ML algorithms, different classifiers achieved similar good performance with different combinations of independent variables (input features). Participants' features and text similarity between participants and messages worked better in the KNNeighbors Classifier and the non-linear SVM. The difference of SoC, number of BCTs matching, and text similarity between the participants and the messages worked better with the Gaussian Naïve Bayes classifier. In future studies, the rule-based system could be used as long as there are insufficient annotations (ratings). When the system obtains more than approx. 600 ratings from the participants, the KNNeighbors Classifier can be trained to generate new recommendations.

5.3 Limitations

The main limitation of this study is the limited size of the dataset. As a pre-pilot study, it aimed to assess the feasibility of the proposed approach. However, limited participants and a short study period resulted in a small dataset. The second limitation is the cohort of participants. The system used in this study is intended for people with COPD, but the participants did not have COPD, leading to the omission of some independent variables (e.g., COPD level, smoking status). This may contribute to low accuracy in message selection. Although the system achieved moderate precision in recommending participants' preferred messages, the accuracy was still relatively low, causing a significant loss of participants' preferred messages. To increase accuracy, future studies are needed to determine the coefficient of independent variables and to improve the algorithms.

5.4 Discussion

In addition to the advantages a RS for CTHC in obtaining more information related to physical health and psychological status, ML algorithms can further enhance its effectiveness. By integrating behaviour change theories and machine learning algorithms such as K-Nearest Neighbors (KNN), Support Vector Machines (SVM), and Gaussian Naive Bayes (Gaussian NB), a more personalized and effective health communication strategy can be created.

Unlike the industry field (content provide such as Youtube and Netflix, E-commerce company such as Amazon and Alibaba), one of the advantages of CTHC with a RS is the ability to obtain more information related to physical health and psychological status. This is particularly beneficial in addressing the challenge of the 'cold start' problem faced in the industry field, where it becomes difficult to recommend accurate information due to the presence of new users or limited data in the system. The obtained information can be integrated with behaviour change theories and models, along with ML algorithms, to create a more personalized and effective health communication strategy.

CTHC faces the challenge of categorising tailored information for users to increase adherence in the long term and maintain continuous inner motivation for behaviour change. Breaking down persuasive health information into smaller elements based on behaviour change theories and BCT holds promise, but the quantitative effectiveness of these elements remains unknown. This presents a significant challenge for current CTHC systems to consistently improve the effectiveness of behaviour change interventions when targeting different populations and behaviours.

To address this challenge, future studies should focus on investigating the correlations among user characteristics, health information features, user preferences on health information, and the effectiveness of behaviour changes. By exploring these correlations, researchers can optimise and refine CTHC strategies, leading to more successful and personalised behaviour change interventions.

These efforts to integrate machine learning algorithms and conduct further research would contribute to the continuous improvement of CTHC, ultimately enabling more successful behaviour change interventions tailored to individual needs.

References

1. World Health Organisation: Physical activity. https://www.who.int/news-room/fact-sheets/detail/physical-activity. Accessed 31 Mar 2023
2. Gill, D., et al.: Physical activity and quality of life. J. Prev. Med. Public Health **46**, S28–S34 (2013)
3. Op den Akker, H., Cabrita, M., Op den Akker, R., Jones, V.M., Hermens, H.J.: Tailored motivational message generation: a model and practical framework for real-time physical activity coaching. J. Biomed. Inf. **55**, 104–115 (2015)
4. Grant. Harrington, N., M. Noar, S.: Reporting standards for studies of tailored interventions. Health Educ. Res. **27**(2), 331–342 (2012)
5. Lustria, M.L.A., Cortese, J., Noar, S.M., Glueckauf, R.L.: Computer-tailored health interventions delivered over the web: review and analysis of key components. Patient Educ. Couns. **74**(2), 156–173 (2009)
6. Noar, S.M., Harrington, N.G.: Tailored communications for health-related decision-making and behavior change. In: Diefenbach, M.A., Miller-Halegoua, S., Bowen, D.J. (eds.) Handbook of Health Decision Science, pp. 251–263. Springer, New York (2016). https://doi.org/10.1007/978-1-4939-3486-7_18
7. American Psychological Association: Stage theory. https://dictionary.apa.org/stage-theory. Accessed 05 Apr 2023
8. Sadasivam, R.S., Borglund, E.M., Adams, R., Marlin, B.M., Houston, T.K.: Impact of a Collective Intelligence Tailored Messaging System on Smoking Cessation: the perspect randomized experiment. J. Med. Internet Res. **18**(11), e285 (2016)
9. Sutton, S.: Health behavior: psychosocial theories. In: International Encyclopedia of the Social & Behavioral Sciences, pp. 6499–6506 (2001)
10. Noar, S.M., Benac, C.N., Harris, M.S.: Does tailoring matter? Meta-analytic review of tailored print health behavior change interventions. Psychol. Bull. **133**(4), 673–693 (2007)
11. Prochaska, J.O., et al.: Stages of change and decisional balance for 12 problem behaviors. Health Psychol. **13**(1), 39–46 (1994)
12. Glanz, K., Rimer, B.K., Viswanath, K.: Health Behaviour and health education: theory, research, and practice. A Wiley Imprint (2008)
13. Ajzen, I.: The theory of planned behavior. Organ. Behav. Hum. Decis. Process. **50**(2), 179–211 (1991)
14. Michie, S., et al.: BCT taxonomy (v1) of 93 hierarchically clustered techniques: building an international consensus for the reporting of behavior change interventions. Ann. Behav. Med. **46**, 81–95 (2013)
15. Noar, S.M., et al.: Using computer technology for HIV prevention among African-Americans: development of a tailored information program for safer sex (TIPSS). Health Educ. Res. **26**(3), 393–406 (2011)
16. Zhou, M., et al.: Evaluating machine learning–based automated personalized daily step goals delivered through a mobile phone app: randomized controlled trial. JMIR Mhealth Uhealth **6**(1), e28 (2018)

17. Ryan, N.M., O'Donovan, C.B., Forster, H., Woolhead, C., Walsh, M.: New tools for personalised nutrition: the food4Me project. Nutr. Bull. **40**(2), 134–139 (2015)
18. Franco, R.Z., Fallaize, R., Hwang, F., Lovegrove, J.A.: Strategies for online personalised nutrition advice employed in the development of the eNutri web app. Proc. Nutr. Soc. **78**(3), 407–417 (2019)
19. Lustria, M.L.A., Noar, S.M., Cortese, J., Stee, S.K.V., Glueckauf, R.L., Lee, J.: A meta-analysis of web-delivered tailored health behavior change interventions. J. Health Commun. **18**(9), 1039–1069 (2013)
20. Hao, L., Goetze, S., Alessa, T., Hawley, M.: Effectiveness of computer tailored health communication in increasing physical activity in people with or at risk of long-term conditions: systematic review and meta-analysis. Subm. to J. of Medical Int. Res. (JMIR) **4**(25), e46622 (2023)
21. Sadasivam, R.S., et al.: Collective-intelligence recommender systems: advancing computer tailoring for health behavior change into the 21st century. J. Med. Internet Res. **18**(3), e42 (2016)
22. Ricci, F., Rokach, L., Shapira, B., Kantor, P.B. (eds.): Recommender Systems Handbook. Springer, Boston, MA (2011). https://doi.org/10.1007/978-0-387-85820-3
23. Cheung, K.L., Durusu, D., Sui, X., de Vries, H.: How recommender systems could support and enhance computer-tailored digital health programs: A scoping review. DIGITAL HEALTH 5
24. Schwarzer, R.: Self-Efficacy - Thought Control Of Action. Taylor & Francis (1992)
25. Schwarzer, R.: The Health Action Process Approach (HAPA). https://www.hapa-model.de/. Accessed 01 Dec 2022
26. Pedregosa, F., et al.: Scikit-learn: machine learning in python. J. Mach. Learn. Res. **12**, 2825–2830 (2011)
27. Mikolov, T., Chen, K., Corrado, G., Dean, J.: Efficient estimation of word representations in vector space. In: Conference on Learning Representations (2013)
28. Devlin, J., Chang, M., Lee, K., Toutanova, K.: BERT: pre-training of deep bidirectional transformers for language understanding. In: Proceedings of 2019 Conference of the North American Chapter of the Association for Computational Linguistics: Human Language Technologies, NAACL-HLT (2019)
29. Crutzen, R., Cyr, D., de Vries, N.K.: Bringing loyalty to e-health: theory validation using three internet-delivered interventions. J. Med. Internet Res. **13**(3), e73 (2011)

Causal Discovery of Health Features from Wearable Device and Traditional Chinese Medicine Diagnosis Data

Yuxi Li[1], Ou Deng[1], Atsushi Ogihara[2], Shoji Nishimura[2], and Qun Jin[2](✉)

[1] Graduate School of Human Sciences, Waseda University, Tokorozawa, Japan
liyuxi@akane.waseda.jp, dengou@toki.waseda.jp
[2] Faculty of Human Sciences, Waseda University, Tokorozawa, Japan
jin@waseda.jp

Abstract. This paper explores the cause-and-effect relationships among a set of health indices using causal discovery. The data we used to analyze was obtained from wearable devices, Traditional Chinese Medicine (TCM) diagnosis, and self-assessment of subjects in an experiment. Firstly, three machine learning algorithms were employed to address the issue of excessive missing values in the integrated dataset, and the coherence of this improved data was validated by statistical test. The NOTEARS algorithm was then employed to assess the causal relationships within the overall population as well as within subgroups based on gender, physical activity levels, and sleep duration. The results demonstrated that the NOTEARS algorithm yielded interesting and plausible outcomes, suggesting the presence of causal connections between variables of wearable devices and TCM diagnosis, as well as daily lifestyle habits.

Keywords: Causal discovery · Health data · Wearable devices · Traditional Chinese Medicine (TCM)

1 Introduction

For centuries, traditional Chinese medicine (TCM) has been an integral part of healthcare, particularly in China and East Asia [1]. Unlike Western medicine, which focuses on diagnosing and treating specific diseases based on pathological mechanisms, TCM emphasizes the concept of "prevention and treatment of disease in the absence of illness." It aims to maintain the overall health of the body by actively taking preventive measures before the onset of diseases [2]. In recent years, with the rapid development of sensing technologies, wearable devices have become common tools for capturing real-time health data. These health data can be used to detect early symptoms and adverse changes in an individual's health conditions, facilitating timely medical interventions [3].

Q. Gao et al. (Eds.): HCII 2023, LNCS 14055, pp. 556–569, 2023.
https://doi.org/10.1007/978-3-031-48041-6_37

However, the current system and philosophy of TCM are largely based on practice and experience, with few quantitative models based on health indicators. Moreover, due to the numerous factors influencing individual health, including physiological, psychological, social, and environmental factors, there may exist intricate causal relationships among various health indicators.

Health indicators are often interrelated, and traditional methods for health data analysis primarily focus on correlation analysis, which identifies the relationships between variables. However, correlation alone cannot establish causality and is often influenced by confounding factors [4]. Therefore, an increasing number of researchers have turned their attention to causal analysis to gain a more accurate understanding of the cause-effect relationships between variables, such as the use of randomized controlled trials (RCTs) and propensity score-based cohort studies [5]. Additionally, with the development of causal analysis methods, researchers have also begun to explore nonlinear and nonparametric causal relationships. These methods can better handle complex health data and identify nonlinear and non-monotonic relationships between variables [6].

Recently, the NOTEARS algorithm has emerged as a powerful method for causal discovery solely from statistical data [7]. Similar to the Linear Non-Gaussian Acyclic Model (LiNGAM), which identifies causal relationships between variables from observed data, NOTEARS is also applicable to variables with statistically distributed data [8]. Following LiNGAM, Shimizu and his colleagues proposed the Direct-LiNGAM algorithm, which directly estimates causal relationships between variables without the need for variable ordering. DirectLiNGAM offers improved robustness and computational efficiency compared to the regular LiNGAM model. However, it still faces challenges in handling nonlinear Gaussian distributed data, which is prevalent in most health-related datasets [9]. Unlike LiNGAM, NOTEARS has the advantage of handling both linear and nonlinear relationships [10]. Moreover, the NOTEARS algorithm can be viewed as an extension of structural equation modeling and Bayesian networks, two widely used approaches for causal inference. Notably, NOTEARS demonstrates effectiveness even with relatively small data samples, in contrast to LiNGAM, which typically requires a large dataset. Additionally, NOTEARS does not demand significant computing resources, making it a versatile and scalable tool for causal exploration [7,11,12].

In this study, we collect personal health data (electronic objective data) from wearable devices and simultaneously gather TCM diagnosis data as well as self-assessment data (subjective diagnostic data) from the same group of subjects [13]. Based on this experimental data, we employ causal discovery techniques to investigate the potential causal relationships between a set of health features and TCM diagnosis data, including the strength of causal relationships and influence thresholds. This further enhances the understanding of the causal relationships between wearable device health indicators and various TCM diagnostic indicators.

The rest of this paper is organized as follow. Section 2 provides a brief introduction to the NOTEARS algorithm and our research framework, and Sect. 3 introduces the TCM experimental dataset used for the NOTEARS algorithm analysis and its preprocessing methods. In Sect. 4, we present the experimental results and discuss on the results. Section 5 summarizes our work and the findings and highlights future work.

2 Causal Discovery of Health Features Based on NOTEARS

This section elucidates the NOTEARS algorithm and the primary steps involved in its implementation. Thereafter, we present the design of our research framework based on this algorithm.

2.1 The NOTEARS Algorithm

The NOTEARS algorithm is a principal method for learning Directed Acyclic Graphs (DAGs), which play a pivotal role in causal modeling. In such models, it is typically assumed that causal relationships do not form a closed loop, meaning that there is no sequence of variables where each variable is the cause of the next, adhering to the so-called "acyclic" assumption. Estimating the structure of DAGs, also known as Bayesian networks, is a challenging task due to the combinatorial nature of the search space for DAGs, which grows super-exponentially with the increase in the number of nodes.

The core idea of the NOTEARS algorithm is to transform the problem of structural learning of DAGs into a continuous optimization problem. It introduces a new graph feature, namely "acyclicity". This feature is defined in the form of a matrix trace and serves as a constraint during the optimization process to ensure that the learned graph is acyclic. The optimization is then solved using standard optimization algorithms. The objective of the optimization is to find a DAG that best explains the observed data while satisfying the acyclic constraint. The algorithm employs a gradient descent method to solve the optimization problem, thereby fully leveraging existing optimization tools.

Given the aforementioned complexity of the combinatorial space of DAGs, many causal relationships learning algorithms encounter computational difficulties when dealing with large-scale data. The NOTEARS algorithm, through its ingenious construction, alleviates this computational difficulty to a certain extent. Experimental results demonstrate that the NOTEARS algorithm outperforms most of other methods in causal discovery on large-scale datasets. Particularly when the in-degree of the graph (i.e., the number of parent nodes for each node) is large, the performance advantage of the NOTEARS algorithm is more pronounced, making it significantly applicable in the field of causal discovery.

Despite the NOTEARS algorithm's ability to avoid the difficulties of combinatorial optimization, it still faces the challenge of non-convex optimization. This implies that the algorithm may only find a local optimum of the problem, rather than the global optimum. In this study, to prevent the NOTEARS algorithm from falling into local optima, we employ data augmentation and introduce some medical knowledge for prior fine-tuning.

2.2 Research Framework

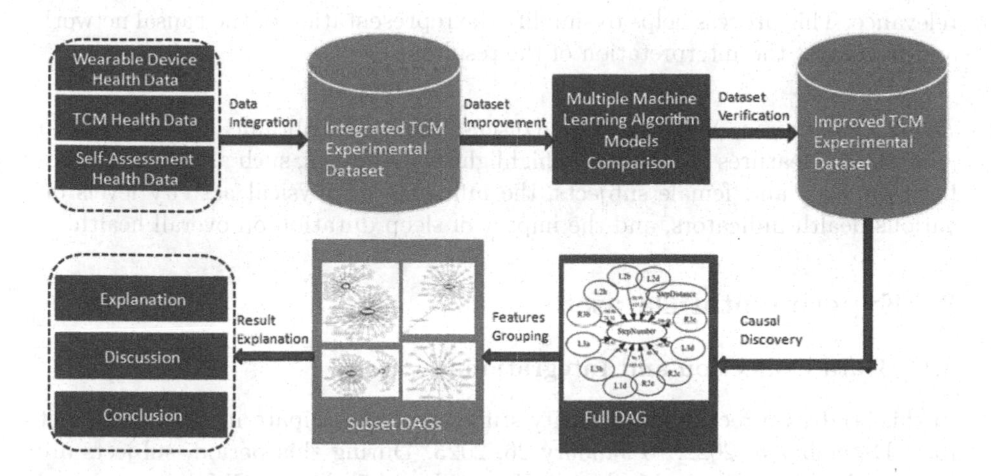

Fig. 1. Research framework

Figure 1 shows the framework for this research, which consists of six steps, including Data Integration, Dataset Improvement, Dataset Verification, Causal Discovery, Features Grouping, and Result Explanation. We provide a detailed description of each step, outlining the specific actions taken and the underlying objectives as follows.

Data Integration: We collect various health-related data and indicators, including sleep patterns, physical activity levels, pulse characteristics, and lifestyle habits through automatic records from wearable devices, weekly TCM diagnoses, as well as weekly submissions of self-health assessments. These three-dimension source datasets are combined into a single integrated dataset, enabling a more comprehensive analysis of health-related variables.

Dataset Improvement: Our integrated dataset contains missing values, we employ machine learning algorithms and statistical techniques for data imputation. This process enhances the completeness of the dataset and ensures a more accurate representation of the health data.

Dataset Verification: To ensure the quality of the dataset, we verify the integrity and consistency of the improved dataset. We apply paired t-test to validate the relationships between variables and ensure the reliability of the data.

Causal Discovery: This step involves utilizing DAGs to explore and establish causal relationships between health factors. By analyzing the overall causal structure, we identify key variables that significantly influence or are influenced by other health indicators.

Features Grouping: To manage the complexity of the causal relationships, we categorize health factors into several groups based on their causal strength and relevance. This process helps to simplify the representation of the causal network and facilitates the interpretation of the results.

Result Explanation: We compare and discuss the results obtained from the causal analysis and features grouping. We highlight key findings, such as the differences between male and female subjects, the influence of physical activity levels on various health indicators, and the impact of sleep duration on overall health.

3 Experimental Dataset

3.1 Data Collection and Integration

In this study, we recruited university students to participate in our experiment from December 5, 2022, to January 26, 2023. During this period, subjects are requested to wear a wearable device (Huawei Band 7), have TCM diagnoses, and submit their health-assessment forms.

We categorized the data into three groups: Wearable Device Health Data (WDHD), Traditional Chinese Medicine Health Data (TCMHD), and Self-Assess-ment Health Data (SAHD). At the end, an integrated dataset of 16 subjects (7 males and 9 females) were used for analysis, which contained their health information in 53 days, a total of 848 records.

3.2 Dataset Improvement and Verification

Our dataset was a composite of time-series data from three sources, namely, wearable device data, TCM diagnoses, and self-assessments. Among these, the wearable device data was relatively the most complete, while the TCM diagnoses and self-assessment data had missing values due to the objective inability of the respondents to participate in all diagnoses. We employed time-series analysis techniques to impute these missing values. The enhancement of data representation in causal relationships, post imputation, was validated by assessing the consistency of the comprehensive health score indicators.

Model Comparison by Three Machine Learning Algorithms: Considering that both the wearable device data and TCM diagnoses provided comprehensive evaluations of the health status on the same day, we utilized these two relatively objective indicators as label variables to assess the imputation of missing values. The evaluation employed three commonly used regression methods: Support Vector Regression (SVR), Random Forest (RF), and Gradient Boost (GB).

The outcome was shown in Table 1. Table 1 illustrates the evaluation outcomes of various machine learning models using two performance metrics: R-Squared and RMSE (Root Mean Squared Error). R-Squared, also known as the

Table 1. Machine Learning Model Comparison Table

Model	R-squared	RMSE
SVR on WDHD	0.315	0.932
SVR on TCMHD	0.597	0.715
RF on WDHD	0.342	0.914
RF on TCMHD	0.622	0.693
GB on WDHD	0.364	0.898
GB on TCMHD	0.614	0.700

coefficient of determination, measured the proportion of the variance in the target variable that could be explained by the input variables. Its values ranged from 0 to 1, with higher values indicating a better fit to the data. On the other hand, RMSE represents the average difference between the predicted values and the actual values. It served as a measure of the model's prediction accuracy, with lower values indicating better performance. The R-squared and RMSE values in the table indicated that the GB on WDHD and RF on TCMHD were the two top-performing methods, which we selected to predict the wearable device and TCM data separately.

Result Verification by Paired t-Test: Furthermore, a paired t-test was conducted to examine if there were any significant differences between the two sets of predicted data. The result showed that the p-value, 0.169, was far greater than the chosen significance level (0.05). Therefore, we fail to reject the null hypothesis, indicating no statistical difference between the two sets of predicted values, which means that the missing values can be filled using TCM experimental data that have similar WD variable values and the same GHI (General Health Index), a composite health score obtained by averaging health scores from three-dimensions data sources, which serves as an indicative measure of overall health status for regression prediction. This procedure verified that our data improvement methods ensured the data consistency.

4 Experiment Results and Discussions

4.1 Estimation of Causal Order

Correlation alone does not establish causation, but a strong correlation between variables may suggest the possibility of a causal relationship. Causality often leads to observable patterns of correlation, as changes in one variable may result in systematic changes in another. Thus, high correlation can indicate a potential causal relationship. Therefore, a pair plot is created to show the correlations between numerical variables, as shown in Fig. 2.

Figure 2 reveals a strong linear correlation between sleep-related and activity-related data, confirming the expected link between deep sleep duration and sleep

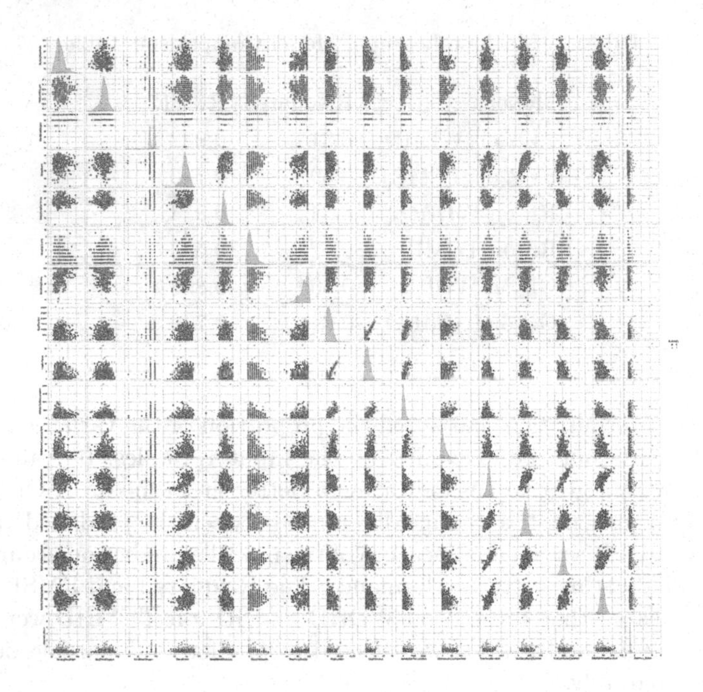

Fig. 2. Pair Plot of Numerical Variables

quality. We also found a negative linear relationship, indicating that those who sleep more consume fewer calories. Moreover, the association between resting heart rate and breathing quality warrants further investigation through DAG analysis for potential causal factors.

4.2 DAG as Causal Diagram

Different from correlation, causation requires additional evidence and rigorous experimental designs, such as controlled experiments or randomized controlled trials, to establish a cause-and-effect relationship definitively. These methods allow for the manipulation of variables and the isolation of potential confounding factors. In causal inference, DAG is used to represent the causal relationships between variables. A complete DAG represents the causal relationship among all variables, where the nodes in the DAG represent variables, and the directed edges represent the causal relationships between variables. Figure 3 shows the DAG that captures the causal relationships among all variables, trained using all the records.

From Fig. 3, we can see that "StepNumber" and "A8," representing daily step count and level of concern for health, respectively, exhibit strong causal relationships with various health factors and serve as influential factors. The causal relationships between the pulse characteristics in the left and right hands exhibit noticeable differences, aligning with the traditional Chinese medicine

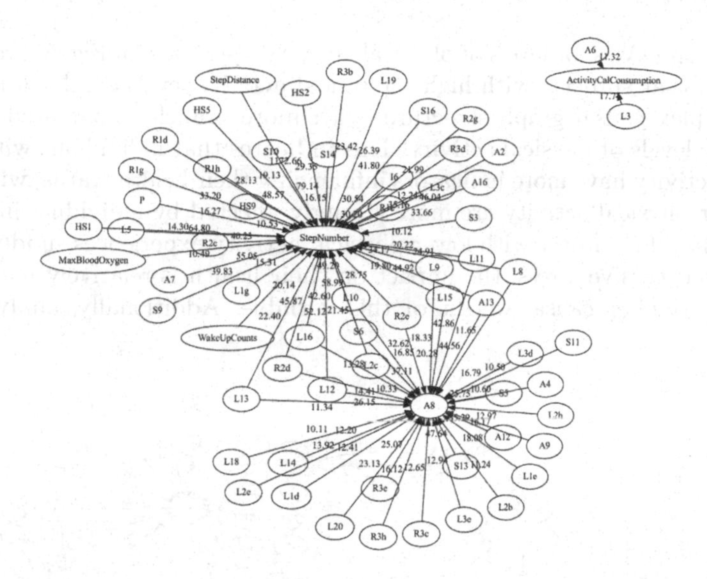

Fig. 3. Overall DAG

principle that emphasizes the distinct meridians corresponding to the left and right sides of the body. Moreover, variables R2c, R2e, and R3b, aside from their inherent relationship with step distance (StepDistance), show significant positive causal weights with daily step count, indicating close associations between pulse characteristics and physical activity.

4.3 Subgroups Causal Diagrams

Subsequently, we shifted our focus from the overall analysis to a more targeted perspective by segmenting the dataset based on specific criteria. Our goal was to explore significant differences among subject groups derived from this segmentation. We horizontally divided the dataset using three criteria: gender (male and female), daily step count (higher and lower activity levels), and total daily sleep duration (sufficient and insufficient sleep). By constructing and comparing separate causal graphs for each subgroup, we sought to identify distinct patterns and relationships within these groups.

Subgroup DAGs for subject genders are shown in Fig. 4. Based on the comparison of male and female subjects, we can see that the causal graph structure is simpler for males, exhibiting fewer branches than females. The female graph contains additional causal relationships directed towards variable A8, indicating greater health concern among females when various health indicators change. Additionally, variables starting with A and L constitute a higher proportion in the female causal graph. This suggests that the responses of female subjects more accurately reflected their actual health status compared to the male subjects, demonstrating a balanced and objective perspective on their health.

Subgroup DAGs for levels of physical activity are shown in Fig. 5. From Fig. 5 we can see that subjects with higher physical activity levels exhibit a relatively more complex causal graph structure, with more branches compared to those with lower levels of physical activity. This indicates that individuals with higher physical activity have more indicators influencing their health status, while those with lower physical activity are more strongly affected by individual indicators. For instance, if a subject with lower physical activity experiences sudden insomnia due to excessive stress, the impact on their health is relatively more severe due to the higher causal weight of this variable. Additionally, analyzing the

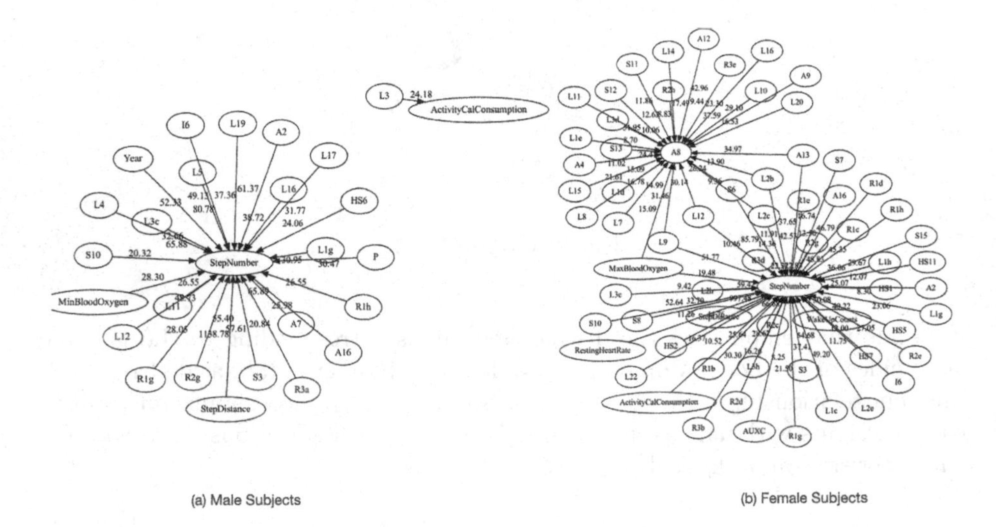

Fig. 4. DAGs for subject genders.

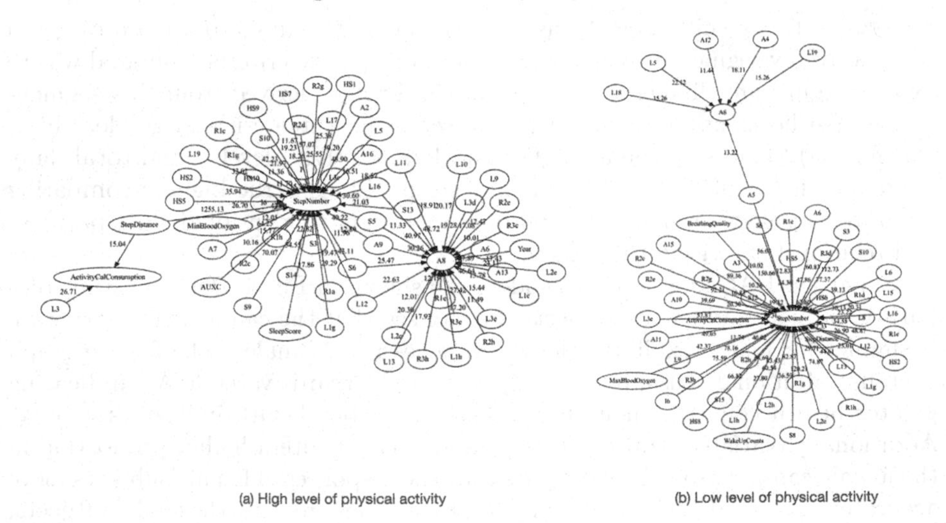

(a) High level of physical activity
(b) Low level of physical activity

Fig. 5. DAGs for levels of physical activity

number of causal factors pointing towards variable A8 indicates that the level of physical activity reflects the subjects' concern for their health. In other words, individuals prioritizing their health engage in higher levels of physical activity, while those with lower health concern engage in lower levels.

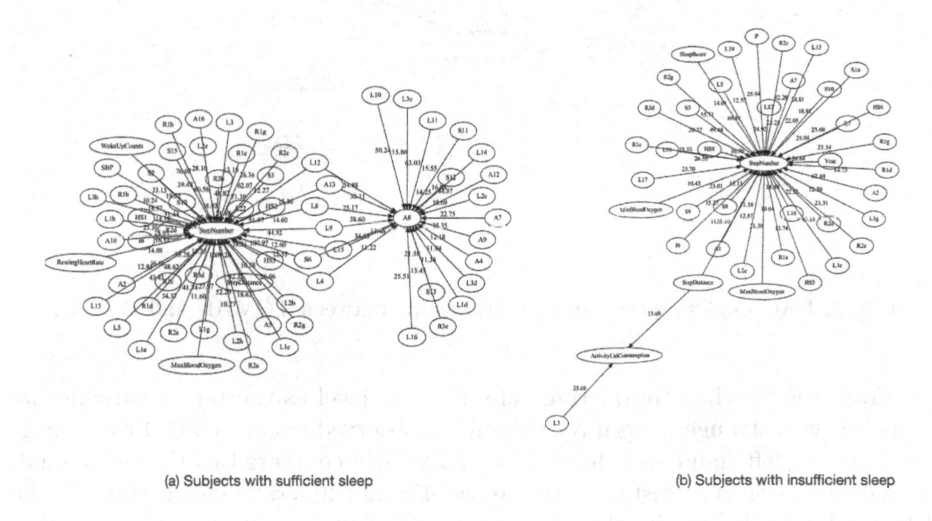

(a) Subjects with sufficient sleep (b) Subjects with insufficient sleep

Fig. 6. DAGs for sleep duration

Finally, subgroup DAGs for sleep duration are shown in Fig. 6. The comparison between subjects with sufficient and insufficient sleep in Fig. 6 reveals that the group with sufficient sleep exhibits a more complex causal graph structure, with twice as many branches compared to the group with insufficient sleep. This implies the critical role of adequate sleep in influencing an individual's health. Similar to the observations regarding physical activity levels, individuals prioritizing their health are likely to be mindful of their sleep sufficiency. Moreover, due to the variations in causal weights, individuals with insufficient sleep are more vulnerable to changes in other indicators, further impacting their health.

4.4 Centralized DAG for the Causal Relationships Between TCMHD and WDHD

In the aforementioned approach, we conducted horizontal segmentation of the dataset and performed comparisons. Next, we try vertical segmentation of the dataset, focusing only on the causal relationships between specific fixed variables, to examine a smaller portion of the overall causal graph in a more localized manner. Figure 7 shows DAG for the causal relationships between TCMHD and WDHD.

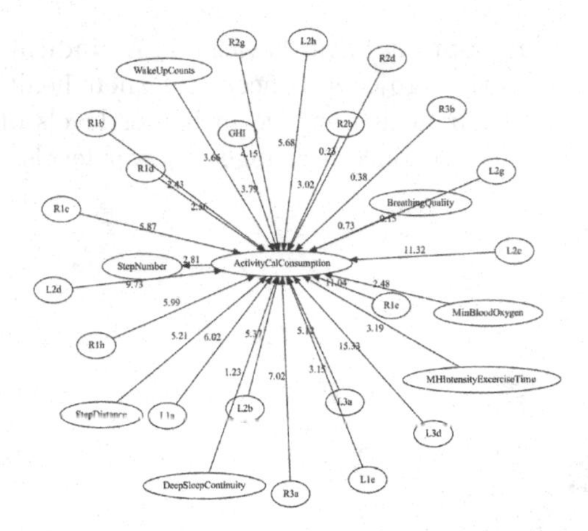

Fig. 7. DAG depicting the causal relationships between TCMHD and WDHD.

From Fig. 7, when considering daily activity level as the target variable, we can observe a stronger causal relationship is observed between TCM pulse diagnosis on the left hand and the daily activity level compared to the right hand. This observation is consistent with the traditional Chinese medicine theory, "the left-hand pulse is associated with the heart and spleen, reflecting the condition of Qi, blood, and nutrition in the body, while the right-hand pulse is related to the liver and stomach, reflecting the balance of Yin and Yang and the digestive function of the body." Furthermore, variables related to the strength or weakness of the pulse, denoted by lowercase letters ending with "e" demonstrate discernible and varying degrees of causal connections with the central variables. This indicates a close causal relationship between pulse strength or weakness and health, which is aligning with the diagnostic principles of TCM that consider pulse strength or weakness in assessing one's health.

4.5 Discussions

Overall, our study contributes to the understanding of complex causal relationships in health and provides valuable insights into the influence of lifestyle habits, gender, and TCM pulse diagnosis on individuals' health. The results highlight the need for a holistic approach to health management, considering multiple factors that influence well-being. This research may facilitate the development of personalized health interventions and inform the design of AI-based diagnostic devices, advancing the wider application of TCM healthcare practices. However, there are a few limitations in this study. First of all, the small size of the dataset limits the generalizability of the findings. With a limited number of observations, the results may not accurately represent the broader population or provide robust evidence for the causal relationship at hand. At the same time, the presence of a substantial number of missing values introduces uncertainty and potential bias into the analysis. Missing values can lead to incomplete or biased estimates of the variables of interest, affecting the validity and reliability of the findings. Secondly, the current conclusions reached so far are based on a holistic approach. However, the exploration and visualization based solely on the data itself are not sufficiently comprehensive, and further comparisons and investigations are required. Conducting targeted causal explorations on this foundation will provide more persuasive findings. Thirdly, the relationships between variables appear to be redundant and complex. It is necessary to test for multicollinearity or consolidate similar or correlated variables in order to establish more concise causal relationships. Additionally, the performance of the NOTEARS algorithm heavily relies on the selection of the tuning parameter, which controls the trade-off between sparsity and goodness-of-fit in the causal graph estimation.

5 Conclusion

In this study, we have explored causal relationships and patterns within an integrated, three-dimension dataset, encompassing data from wearable devices, TCM diagnoses, and self-assessments. By employing correlation-based cause order estimation, NOTEARS-based Directed Acyclic Graph (DAG) modeling, and subgroup and centralized DAG analysis, we investigated the interplay of health factors and provide valuable insights into health assessment.

The outcomes of the causal discovery attempts have revealed several robust causal relationships among health indicators. We observed that individuals' level of attention to their health significantly influences other health factors, indicating the importance of self-awareness and health consciousness. Our analysis indicated that multiple health factors have simultaneous effects on daily physical activity, suggesting the intricate interconnections within an individual's health profile. Moreover, individuals with healthier lifestyle habits exhibited a more complex and diverse causal structure, underscoring the significance of maintaining a healthy lifestyle in promoting overall well-being. We also found that individuals with unhealthy lifestyle habits tend to have fewer, yet more influential, health-influencing factors, emphasizing the need for targeted interventions in such cases. Our study demonstrated that changes in a single health variable can have cascading effects on overall health status, underlining the interconnectedness of health factors, and our findings revealed that females tend to have a higher accuracy in self-estimating their health status compared to males, indicating potential gender-specific differences in health awareness. In addition, we identified noticeable variations in the causal relationships between sleep duration and health status among different individuals, highlighting the complex nature of sleep-related health factors.

This study contributes to a deeper understanding of health assessment by elucidating causal relationships among various health factors. The insights gained from our study can inform the development of more accurate and comprehensive methods for data analysis and health assessment study. However, this study has limitations, including a relatively limited sample size and insufficient consideration of psychological health factors among adolescents. Future research endeavors to address these limitations by focusing on variable selection, accuracy enhancement, and the incorporation of additional health dimensions. Additionally, exploring the relevance of TCM in providing theoretical support for our results will pave the way for defining a new composite health measure that accounts for multidimensional evidence from wearable devices, individual self-assessments, and medical diagnoses, ultimately providing a comprehensive understanding of individual health.

Acknowledgement. The work was supported in part by 2022–2024 Masaru Ibuka Foundation Research Project on Oriental Medicine, 2020–2025 JSPS A3 Foresight Program (Grant No. JPJSA3F20200001), 2022–2025 Japan National Initiative Promotion Grant for Digital Rural City, 2023 Waseda University Grants for Special Research Projects (No. 2023C-216), and 2023 Waseda University Advanced Research Center for Human Sciences Research Project (C) for Promoting Regional Cooperation.

References

1. Tago, K., Nishimura, S., Ogihara, A., Jin, Q.: Improving diagnosis estimation by considering the periodic span of the life cycle based on personal health data. Big Data Res. **23**, 139–148 (2020)
2. Wang, W., Zhou, H., Yang, Y.F., Sang, B.S., Liu, L.: Current policies and measures on the development of traditional Chinese medicine in china. Pharmacol. Res. **163**, 105187 (2020)
3. Tago, K., Takagi, K., Jin, Q.: Detection of health abnormality considering latent factors inducing a disease. IEEE Access **8**, 139433–139443 (2020)
4. Glymour, C., et al.: Review of causal discovery methods based on graphical models. Front. Genet. **10**, 94 (2019)
5. Nakao, Y.M., et al.: Effectiveness of nationwide screening and lifestyle intervention for abdominal obesity and cardiometabolic risks in Japan: the metabolic syndrome and comprehensive lifestyle intervention study on nationwide database in Japan (MetS ACTION-J study). PLoS ONE **13**(1), e0190862 (2018)
6. Cheng, L., et al.: Exposing the causal effect of body mass index on the risk of type 2 diabetes mellitus: a mendelian randomization study. Front. Genet. **10**, 94 (2019)
7. Zhang, K., Zhang, J., Lu, W., Ye, J.: Causal discovery with complementary search. In: Proceedings of the 24th ACM SIGKDD International Conference on Knowledge Discovery and Data Mining, pp. 295–304. ACM (2018)
8. Zhang, K., Peters, J., Janzing, D., Schölkopf, B.: Learning nonlinear causal models by independent nonlinear ICA. J. Mach. Learn. Res. **19**(1), 1705–1741 (2018)
9. Shimizu, S., Hoyer, P.O., Hyvärinen, A., Kerminen, A.: A linear non-Gaussian acyclic model for causal discovery. J. Mach. Learn. Res. **7**, 2003–2030 (2006)
10. Kotoku, J., et al.: Causal relations of health indices inferred statistically using the DirectLiNGAM algorithm from big data of Osaka prefecture health checkups. PLoS ONE **15**(12), e0243229 (2020)
11. Zheng, X., Aragam, B., Ravikumar, P., Xing, E.P.: Dags with NO TEARS: continuous optimization for structure learning. J. Mach. Learn. Res. **19**(1), 2745–2790 (2018)

12. Lu, W., Zhang, K., Ye, J.: Identifiability and algorithms for non-gaussian causal discovery. J. Mach. Learn. Res. **20**(29), 1–61 (2019)
13. Wu, J., et al.: Multidimensional data integration and analysis for youth health care during the Covid-19 pandemic. In: Proceedings of the 25th International Conference on Human-Computer Interaction (HCII), Denmark (2023)

Measuring User Engagement in Virtual, Augmented, and Mixed Reality Interventions for Stress Reduction

Nishu Nath(✉), Apostolos Kalatzis, and Laura Stanley

Montana State University, Bozeman, MT 59717, USA
nishunath@montana.edu

Abstract. Stress affects individuals across the world, posing significant challenges on the mental and physical states and overall quality of life. These detrimental consequences may include increased risk of mental disorders, such as anxiety, depression, and higher risk to physical ailments. Therefore, there is an urgent need for effective interventions which can reduce stress. Cognitive Behavioral Therapy (CBT) videos and Biofeedback techniques offer supportive approaches in alleviating stress. CBT provides cognitive restructuring and behavioral strategies to modify negative patterns, while Biofeedback utilizes physiological measurements to provide real-time feedback for stress symptom regulation. Integrating CBT, Biofeedback, and immersive technology, such as immersive technologies, including virtual reality (VR), augmented reality (AR), and mixed reality (MR), enhances the effectiveness of stress reduction interventions through immersive and engaging experiences. This paper proposes a solution that combines the principles of CBT videos and Biofeedback techniques within immersive environments. CBT videos within immersive environments provide engaging and immersive therapeutic content, while Biofeedback interventions enable users to regulate their physiological responses in an immersive environment but in real-time, empowering the users to regulate stress levels effectively. Building upon this premise, the study aims to comprehensively assess user engagement and evaluate the effectiveness of immersive interventions in stress reduction across VR, AR, and MR platforms. In addition to measuring user engagement, the study also aims to investigate factors such as user presence, immersion, emotion, and perceived usability to identify the most conducive immersive environment for stress reduction interventions. The research seeks to contribute to the development of personalized and effective stress reduction interventions, providing valuable insights into the potential of immersive technologies for stress minimization. The expected outcome of this study is to demonstrate the effectiveness of immersive interventions in minimizing stress and promoting wellness.

Keywords: Stress reduction · Immersive technology · Virtual Reality · Augmented Reality · Mixed Reality · Cognitive Behavioral Therapy · Biofeedback · User engagement

Q. Gao et al. (Eds.): HCII 2023, LNCS 14055, pp. 570–583, 2023.
https://doi.org/10.1007/978-3-031-48041-6_38

1 Introduction

Stress prevails in every aspect of human experience. However, continual exposure to stress can be detrimental to an individual's emotional and physical state [1, 2]. Stress is commonly classified as acute or chronic. Acute stress is characterized by a relatively brief duration and elicits by recent or future demanding events. Whereas, chronic stress is caused by persistent demands and prolonged exposure to stressors [3]. Both acute and chronic stress can lead to insomnia, anxiety, mild depression, and cardiovascular diseases [4, 5]. Traditional stress reduction methods, such as traditional therapy, self-care techniques, and relaxation techniques, have limitations in terms of cost, accessibility, and availability. Despite the existence of these techniques, there is a need for a comprehensive understanding of how immersive technology can be useful for stress reduction.

Recent advancements in immersive technology, including remote accessibility along with the interactivity of Virtual Reality (VR), Augmented Reality (AR), and Mixed Reality (MR), have shown promise to be effective tools for reducing stress [6]. These technologies have the potential to create realistic and engaging experiences that can effectively mitigate stress and promote relaxation. By immersing individuals in virtual environments, immersive technology allows for user-centric interventions that can address individual needs and preferences, ultimately enhancing user engagement and treatment outcomes.

Despite the growing interest in immersive technology, including VR, AR, and MR, the research on the impact of these technologies for stress reduction remains limited [7]. This study aims to address this gap in the literature by investigating the effectiveness of Cognitive Behavioral Therapy (CBT) and Biofeedback breathing exercises for stress reduction in immersive environments (i.e., VR, AR, and MR). The immersive nature of these technologies offers a unique opportunity to engage individuals in a virtual world and potentially reduce acute stress. In order to promote user engagement, more studies are required to clarify how technological, content, psychological, cognitive, and behavioral factors relate to user adoption and successful implementation of immersive technologies [7]. To achieve this, the study will investigate the factors that contribute to user engagement within the immersive environment and how these factors are associated with presence, immersion, emotion, and usability. By examining these key elements, we aim to identify the most effective means of reducing stress symptoms. The hypothesis is that increased engagement in the immersive world will result in greater stress reduction. The findings of this study will contribute to the understanding of the role of immersive technology in stress reduction using CBT and Biofeedback methods and may inform the design of effective interventions for stress management.

This paper is structured into four distinct Sections. Section 1 presents a comprehensive literature review on various topics that are relevant to this study, including user engagement, presence, immersion, cognitive-behavioral therapy (CBT), and biofeedback in the context of VR, AR, MR technologies. This section serves to establish the theoretical foundation and provide a comprehensive understanding of the concepts and theories that underpin this research. Section 2 of the paper focuses on the proposed interventions and the immersive devices that will be utilized in the study. This section provides detailed descriptions and explanations of the interventions and the technological tools that will be employed to create immersive experiences for stress reduction.

In Sect. 3, the proposed research methodology is discussed. This section outlines the methodological approach that will be implemented to investigate the efficacy of the previously discussed interventions in different immersive devices. In Sect. 4, we provide the future works, expected results, and limitations. Finally, the conclusion section provides a comprehensive summary of the entire paper. It offers a holistic perspective on the research of stress reduction using immersive technology and suggests potential future exploration and development in the field of immersive technology and stress reduction.

2 Background

2.1 User Engagement in AR/VR/MR Technology

User engagement is a crucial factor in determining the effectiveness of immersive technologies like VR, AR, and MR applications. Extensive research in fields such as information systems, media and communication, education, marketing, and computer science has explored user engagement [8]. O'Brien [9] defines user engagement as the depth of cognitive, temporal, affective, and behavioral investment during interactions with digital systems. Immersive environments have been found to elicit emotions that enhance user engagement, leading to positive therapeutic outcomes, including stress reduction [10]. However, the relationship between user engagement and stress reduction in VR, AR, and MR environments remains relatively unexplored. User engagement can be understood across various contexts, encompassing psychological states, intrinsic motivation, behavioral experiences, affective experiences, user involvement, and the quality of user experience [8, 10, 11]. In this study, we aim to investigate user engagement from emotional, behavioral, and psychological perspectives. Specifically, we will examine how user engagement influences negative affect (stress) and positive affect (relaxation) during the performance of interventions in immersive environments.

2.2 Presence in AR/VR/MR Technology

Within the VR/AR/MR presence community, it is commonly accepted that greater presence leads to greater engagement [12]. Immersive technology aims to engage users and foster a heightened sense of presence within a virtual environment [13]. The concept of presence relates to the illusion of "being there" and experiencing the virtual environment as if it were real [11, 14]. Through presence, users become less aware of the technology, and they can experience the virtual space directly. This results in greater user engagement and interaction with the environment. Tele-presence, as proposed by [15], is composed of three key determinants: 1) the ability to control the relationship of one's senses to the stimulus (control), 2) the ability to modify the stimulus to increase its realism, interactivity, and excitement (color and graphics vividness or interactivity), and 3) the extent to which online sensory information approximates real-world stimulus (3D authenticity). Other researchers also suggest that control and interactivity are the main influencers of user engagement [16, 17]. Building upon these determinants, our project adopts a stimulus-organism-response (SOR) framework to investigate the emotional and behavioral sources of user engagement, as measured by physiological and self-reported data.

2.3 Immersion in AR/VR/MR Technology

In the field of immersive research, immersion is often conceptualized in two contexts: subjective [18] and objective [14]. Scholars suggest that immersion refers to the quality that engages the user's senses and enhances their involvement with the virtual environment. In the objective context, immersion is defined based on "immersion factors" such as frame rate, aural effects, system responsiveness, interface allowances for body movement [12], field of view, and display resolution [14]. However, subjective immersion is determined by the user's perception and experience of the virtual environment. This study focuses on objective immersion. It is worth noting that some researchers use the terms presence and immersion interchangeably in their studies. Scholars have posited a correlation between immersion, presence, and engagement [12]. Studies argue that as the quality of the technology improves, users experience greater presence, which leads to increased engagement. In the current study, simulated user experience functions as an intermediate variable among presence, immersion, emotion, usability, and user engagement. Thus, it is expected that with the improvement of technology quality, users will have the potential to experience heightened levels of presence, immersion, and interactivity, ultimately leading to increased levels of user engagement.

2.4 CBT and AR/VR/MR Technology

Cognitive Behavioral Therapy (CBT) is a psychosocial intervention aimed at enhancing mental health by focusing on an individual's coping strategies and helping to change their cognition, behavior, and emotions. Traditional CBT has demonstrated success in treating various psychiatric conditions, such as reducing stress levels for opiate-dependent patients in Opioid Replacement Therapy (ORT) [19] and reducing anxiety symptoms [20]. In a recent study, traditional CBT was found to be slightly more effective than integrated multimodal VR-CBT in reducing worries among participants, while both were equally effective in reducing anxiety levels [20]. Additionally, the effectiveness of computerized CBT as an adjunct therapy shows that virtual CBT could be effective for stress reduction as well [21, 22]. In this study, CBT videos will be integrated within the immersive environments. To achieve this, volumetric video of a therapist will be captured and integrated into VR, AR, and MR environments. The study proposes that integrated CBT will be effective for reducing acute stress in humans.

2.5 Biofeedback Breathing Exercise and AR/VR/MR Technology

Biofeedback breathing exercise is considered an effective method for reducing stress [23]. Research has shown that five to six respirations per minute leads to the engagement of the parasympathetic system, which activates calm states [24, 25]. This controlled breathing frequency slows down the respiratory rate and reduces the activity of the sympathetic nervous system (the "fight or flight" response), while increasing the activity of the parasympathetic nervous system (the "rest and digest" response). These two nervous systems are components of the autonomic nervous system (ANS), which is responsible for various physiological functions and is linked to the emotional system [26, 27]. The breathing exercise training aims to modify the breathing cycle pattern and reduce stress by decreasing heart rate and inducing relaxation. This is achieved by enhancing the regulation of Respiratory Sinus Arrhythmia, which is reflected in high-frequency Heart Rate Variability (HRV) oscillations. The potential restorative benefits of HRV, which facilitate the transition from stress to calm, suggest the potential benefits of combining the breathing exercise with CBT. HRV will be measured using ECG signals, which assess the common stress indicator, HRV, along with other physiological markers, such as cortisol and blood levels [28]. By aiding participants in controlling their heart rate patterns, the VR, AR, and MR technology can promote a state of calmness, thus reducing stress levels. In 2008, Amon & Campbell [29] conducted a research on the efficacy of breathing exercises with biofeedback video games involving children diagnosed with Attention Deficit Hyperactivity Disorder (ADHD) which demonstrates that biofeedback video games have the potentiality to reduce their disruptive behavior. Moreover, the profound applications of HRV via biofeedback may mitigate the real-time effects of emotional dysregulation, including anxiety [6] and improving daily life, such as academic performance [30]. These research findings suggest that using biofeedback video games for breathing exercises could be beneficial for improving behavioral and emotional changes. This study employs a respiratory breathing exercise, facilitated by VR, AR, and MR which prompts participants to breathe at a rate of five to six respirations per minute. Overall, the integration of VR, AR, and MR technology in our study's breathing exercise aims to reduce acute stress levels and promote relaxation among participants.

3 Development of Intervention for the Proposed Study

The VR, AR, and MR interventions, CBT videos and Biofeedback breathing exercises are integrated in VR headset (Oculus Quest 2), AR glasses (Vuzix Blade Upgrade) and MR headset (Microsoft HoloLens 2). Figure 1 illustrates a virtual beach scenario in Oculus Quest 2.

Fig. 1. Virtual beach environment designed in Unity for Oculus Quest 2

The VR, AR, and MR intervention consists of a natural scene and an expanding-shrinking breathing circle. The approach of this proposal is informed by a comprehensive literature review on related fields. A central point of the proposal is to simulate a user's cognitive behavior and reduce their parasympathetic system, by creating immersive scenarios and activities that users can carry out when they feel stressed.

3.1 Immersive Devices

Oculus Quest 2 Device (Virtual Reality): The Oculus Quest 2, developed by Meta, is a Virtual Reality (VR) device designed to showcase the capabilities of immersive virtual environments. It employs projected and magnified screens within an enclosed headset to create fully virtual views for users. The device incorporates tracking technology to monitor the user's physical surroundings and accurately capture the movements of the handheld controllers, enabling seamless interaction within the virtual environment. By utilizing the Oculus Quest 2, this study aims to leverage the advanced features and functionality of the device to create an immersive and engaging VR experience for participants.

Oculus Quest 2 is a rectilinear 3D Virtual Reality (VR) system with a wide field of view (FOV) of 97° horizontally and 93° vertically. The per-eye resolution of the system is 1832 × 1920, providing a high-quality visual experience. The immersive environment created by this VR system offers a full virtual display, enabling users to engage with virtual content in a highly immersive and realistic manner. The system used for this study is the Meta Quest, which is known for its advanced features and capabilities in delivering immersive experiences. By utilizing this full immersion VR system, the study aims to provide participants with a highly engaging and realistic virtual environment that can enhance the effectiveness of stress reduction interventions.

Vuzix Blade Upgraded Device (Augmented Reality): The Vuzix Blade Upgraded device serves as a demonstrator for the capabilities of an Augmented Reality (AR) environment. It achieves this by projecting an overlay onto the lenses of specialized glasses, enabling the display of basic user-interface prompts. The device does not incorporate external object tracking but operates on a processing mechanism similar to a phone, facilitating the presentation of fundamental overlays that allow users to interact with a virtual phone platform in a hands-free manner.

The Vuzix device, utilizing Stereoscopic Augmented Reality (AR), offers a form of light immersion where users can experience a blended virtual and real environment. With a 19-degree diagonal field of view (FOV) and a per-eye resolution of 480 × 853, the device presents a 2D display that overlays virtual content onto the user's view of the real world. This technology enables users to perceive digital information in their field of vision while maintaining awareness of their physical surroundings.

HoloLens 2 Device (Mixed Reality): The HoloLens 2 is a Microsoft Device that is meant to demonstrate the capabilities of a Mixed Reality environment, which is done with a visor style device that projects 3D objects in real spaces and areas. The device tracks 3D space and allows for interaction with hologram-styled projections that are persistent on the platform when integrated properly.

The Microsoft HoloLens 2 device offers a medium level of immersion through its Stereoscopic 3D-Holographic Mixed Reality technology. With a 43° horizontal field of view (FOV) and a 29° vertical FOV, the device provides users with an immersive experience that combines virtual and real-world elements. The HoloLens 2 boasts a resolution of 1280 × 960, enabling the presentation of high-quality holographic content. This advanced technology allows users to perceive and interact with virtual objects that appear as if they are integrated into their physical environment. By leveraging the capabilities of the HoloLens 2, users can engage in a mixed reality experience where digital holograms are seamlessly blended with their real-world surroundings, providing opportunities for interactive and immersive applications in various fields such as education, design, and healthcare.

3.2 Immersive Intervention Applications Proposed for the Stress Reduction

CBT Videos: The CBT intervention includes videos for reducing stress. A licensed psychologist will develop the video scripts. We will record CBT videos in volumetric video capture that allows us to play holographic CBT videos on HoloLens2. Figure 2 illustrate a holographic 3-dimensional view of a model for our CBT videos therapist session. The script would help the participant to resolve the stressful situation. For instance, the video would tell them to imagine a balloon, rope, and green leaf. Based on these imaginary objects, the video might propose some activity to the user, which will help them reduce the stressful situation.

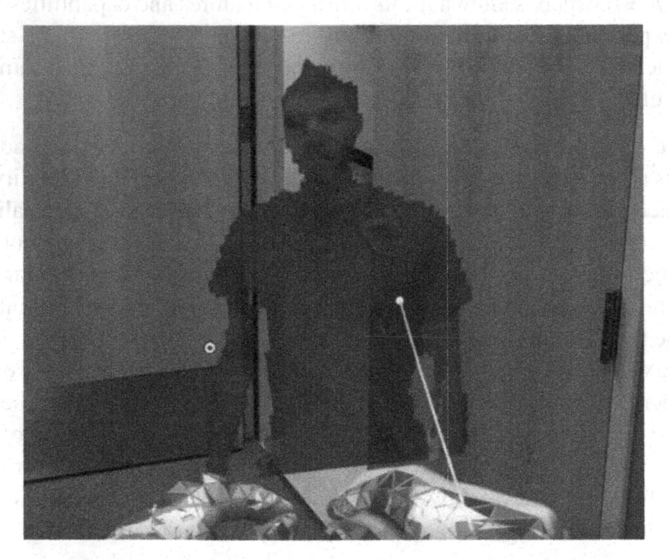

Fig. 2. Working prototype for CBT videos in HoloLen2

Biofeedback Breathing Exercise: Biofeedback breathing exercise would be composed of a virtual ring object which will expand and collapse in every five to six minutes. The breathing circle would be resided in a beach scenario where participants can see the ocean view and sound of the surrounding beach environment. In this article, Fig. 3 and Fig. 4 provides a visual representation of the experimental setup for biofeedback breathing exercise in VR and MR. In the VR, the circle is fully immersed in the developed virtual world, while in the MR, the breathing circle is blend in with the surrounding real world. The text instruction provided under the circle would help participants to do their breath-in and breathe-out activity easily. We would also implement an interactive user interface so that users can open and exit the application as they demand.

Fig. 3. Biofeedback breathing exercise circle designed in Unity for Oculus Quest 2

Fig. 4. Biofeedback breathing exercise holographic circle designed in Unity for HoloLens2

4 Proposed Method

4.1 Participants

Thirty college students will be recruited to participate in the study. The order of the interventions will be counterbalanced. A counterbalanced Latin square design was used to assign each participant to one of the three groups (VR, AR, and MR). Advertisements will be distributed to recruit college student age ranging from 18–40 around the campus. Exclusion criteria include participants with acute or chronic disease (e.g., photosensitive epilepsy) and simulation sickness.

4.2 Protocol

Participants will undergo two different sessions: the stress and the post-stress session. In the stress session, acute stress will be induced to the participants using a valid stressor, the Trier Social Stress Test (TSST) [31]. In this experiment, the participants will be exposed to five minutes of public speech and five minutes of mental arithmetic tasks to induce stress. In the post-stress session, participants will perform biofeedback breathing exercise or a CBT intervention. Figure 5 serves as a protocol diagram, illustrating the step-by-step procedures followed in the experimental protocol. This study is designed as a between-subjects. Interventions (i.e., Biofeedback, CBT) will be assigned to participants in a counterbalanced Latin square design randomized order. During these sessions, continuous physiological data (Heart Rate Variability (HRV), respiration rate, and skin conductance) will be collected. Additionally, subjective responses will be collected after each session and intervention. The Perceived Stress Scale (PSS-10) [32] and Positive or Negative Affect Schedule (PANAS) [33] questionnaires will be utilized to assess in-the-moment state stress and negative emotions after the stressor. Furthermore, after the interventions, participants will report to PANAS, iGroup Presence Questionnaire [34], Self-Assessment manikin (SAM) [35], System Usability Scale (SUS) [36], and user engagement scale (UES) questionnaire [9]. Comparing these collected immersive groups' participant data with a control group participant where CBT delivered through a computer screen, the study will investigate the efficacy of the immersive technology in stress reduction and the optimal effective technology.

4.3 Dependent Measurements

In this study, physiological measurements (HRV, respiration rate, and skin conductance) will be utilized as indicators for the participants' stress levels during different stages of the experiment. Respiration rate were collected using respiratory belt transducer manufactured by BIOPAC (BIOPAC Systems Inc., CA, USA), HRV will be collected using electrocardiogram (ECG) signals via BIOPAC MP160 System and skin conductance (Electrodermal activity (EDA)) will be collected via BIOPAC Skin Conductance Response (SCR) Analysis. We will also determine the immersion based on the immersive technology's classification such as, (low, medium and high) based on the technical factors (resolution, Field of View (FOV), dimensions).

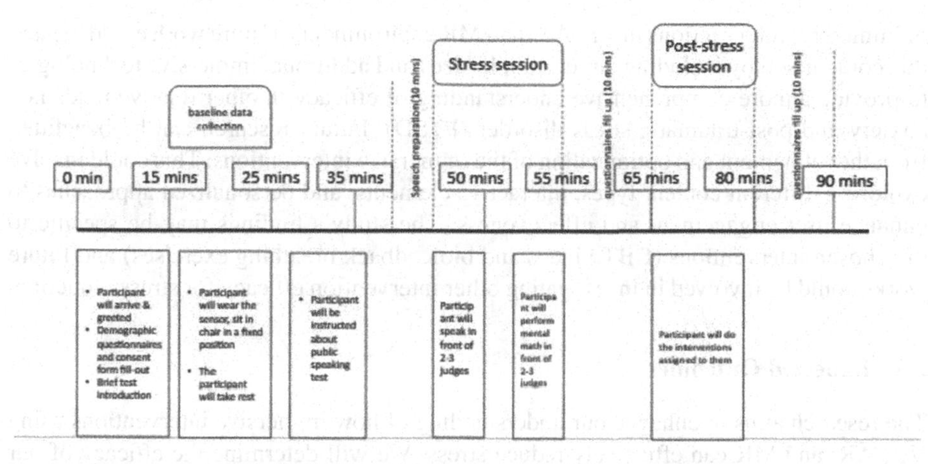

Fig. 5. Proposed designed protocol for the study

4.4 Subjective Response

The previously mentioned valid matrixes will be utilized to measure different key factors in immersive technology. UES measures user engagement on four factors, such as, aesthetic appeal, focused attention, perceived usability, and reward. To capture users' presence in the different modalities, we will use the iGroup Presence Questionnaire. By PSS-10, we will measure users' perceived stress during the TSST. To measure a human's emotional state, we will use several questionnaires (PANAS, SAM). PANAS consists of two-10 mental state scales, one measuring positive affect and other measuring Negative affect. SAM is a visual scale that records a participant's level of dominance, arousal, and enjoyment. SUS provides Likert scale from Strongly agree to Strongly disagree to report the system usability.

4.5 Analysis

The data will be analyzed using descriptive statistics (mean, median, std. deviation, sample distribution) to describe the sample and the distribution of the variables. Repeated measures ANOVA can be used to examine changes in data over time since we will collect between-groups and within-groups data over the period.

5 Future Works, Expected Outcomes and Limitations

5.1 Future Works

The proposed study serves as a foundation for further exploration and research in the field of immersive technology for stress reduction. Several implications for future work can be considered. Future research could investigate the long-term impact of these interventions, examining whether the benefits persist over time and exploring potential mechanisms underlying sustained stress reduction. This study will compare the effectiveness of immersive interventions in VR, AR, and MR environments. Future work could expand this comparison by including larger sample sizes and additional immersive technologies to provide a more comprehensive understanding of efficacy in other relative fields i.e., anxiety and post-traumatic stress disorder (PTSD). Future research can be benefitted from the refinement and optimization of the immersive interventions. This could involve exploring different content types, interactive elements, and personalized approaches to enhance user engagement and effectiveness. The study's findings may be specific to the chosen interventions (CBT videos and biofeedback breathing exercises) and future works could be involved in investigating other intervention efficacy for stress reduction.

5.2 Expected Outcomes

The research aims to enhance our understanding of how immersive interventions using VR, AR, and MR can effectively reduce stress. We will determine the efficacy of our proposed work after conducting a lab study. The stress level induced by TSST will be investigated to reduce stress effect using immersive interventions on those induced stress levels. The results of our analysis will provide insights into the factors that contribute to user engagement, including presence, immersion, emotion, and usability within these immersive environments.

The findings will investigate the potential of immersive technology as a viable approach for stress reduction. Demonstrating the effectiveness of immersive interventions could lead to greater acceptance and adoption of these technologies in clinical and therapeutic settings. Additionally, Comparing the effectiveness of immersive interventions across VR, AR, and MR environments will provide valuable insights into the strengths and limitations of each technology. This information can guide decision-making regarding the most suitable immersive technology for specific stress reduction interventions. Furthermore, the study results will contribute to the development of guidelines and best practices for designing immersive stress reduction interventions. By identifying the key elements that enhance user engagement and effectiveness, these guidelines can inform future intervention design and implementation.

5.3 Limitations

There are certain limitations that should be acknowledged. The study's findings may be limited by the characteristics of the sample used. Since only college students are used as sample size, the study may not fully represent the diverse population experiencing stress. Also, the study's outcomes may be influenced by the technological limitations of the immersive systems used. The current study primarily focuses on measuring the immediate effects of immersive interventions on stress reduction. Long-term effects and sustained benefits are not a part of the experiment and beyond the lab's capacity. Moreover, there might still be limitations in replicating the complexity and nuances of real-life stressors.

6 Conclusions

By leveraging the immersive capabilities of VR, AR, and MR, individuals can engage in realistic and interactive experiences that offer tailored stress management strategies. The findings from this research will inform researchers, practitioners, and designers on the optimal utilization of immersive technologies for stress reduction, ultimately contributing to the improvement of human healthcare and well-being. The study is expected to inspire further research and exploration in the field of immersive technology for healthcare. The outcomes will serve as a foundation for future studies, allowing researchers and practitioners to build upon the findings and refine immersive interventions to better address the complex and multifaceted nature of stress.

Acknowledgement. This project is sponsored by the National Institutes of Health and The National Science Foundation. The award no is 2013651.

References

1. Bolger, N., DeLongis, A., Kessler, R.C., Schilling, E.A.: Effects of daily stress on negative mood. J. Pers. Soc. Psychol. **57**, 808–818 (1989). https://doi.org/10.1037/0022-3514.57.5.808
2. Khansari, D.N., Murgo, A.J., Faith, R.E.: Effects of stress on the immune system. Immunol. Today **11**, 170–175 (1990). https://doi.org/10.1016/0167-5699(90)90069-l
3. Elzeiny, S., Qaraqe, M.: Stress classification using photoplethysmogram-based spatial and frequency domain images. Sensors **20**, 5312 (2020). https://doi.org/10.3390/s20185312
4. Zhu, Q., Zheng, F., Xie, Y.: Respiratory training biofeedback system (2011). https://doi.org/10.1109/icecc.2011.6067578
5. Crosswell, A.D., Lockwood, K.G.: Best practices for stress measurement: how to measure psychological stress in health research. Health Psychol. Open **7**, 205510292093307 (2020). https://doi.org/10.1177/2055102920933072
6. Prabhu, V.G., Stanley, L.M., Linder, C., Morgan, R.: Analyzing the efficacy of a restorative virtual reality environment using HRV biofeedback for pain and anxiety management (2020). https://doi.org/10.1109/ichms49158.2020.9209432
7. Suh, A., Prophet, J.: The state of immersive technology research: a literature analysis. Comput. Hum. Behav. **86**, 77–90 (2018). https://doi.org/10.1016/j.chb.2018.04.019
8. Suh, A., Cheung, C.M., Lin, Y.Q.: Revisiting user engagement: concepts, themes, and opportunities. Presented at the Pacific Asia Conference on Information System (PACIS), p. 150 (2019)
9. O'Brien, H.L., Cairns, P., Hall, M.: A practical approach to measuring user engagement with the refined user engagement scale (UES) and new UES short form. Int. J. Hum. Comput. Stud. **112**, 28–39 (2018). https://doi.org/10.1016/j.ijhcs.2018.01.004
10. Flavián, C., Ibáñez-Sánchez, S., Orús, C.: Impacts of technological embodiment through virtual reality on potential guests' emotions and engagement. J. Hosp. Mark. Manag. **30**, 1–20 (2021). https://doi.org/10.1080/19368623.2020.1770146
11. Kukkakorpi, M., Pantti, M.: A sense of place: VR journalism and emotional engagement. J. Pract. **15**, 785–802 (2021). https://doi.org/10.1080/17512786.2020.1799237
12. Dow, S., Mehta, M., Harmon, E., MacIntyre, B., Mateas, M.: Presence and engagement in an interactive drama. In: Proceedings of the SIGCHI Conference on Human Factors in Computing Systems (2007). https://doi.org/10.1145/1240624.1240847

13. Jenkins, H.: Game design as narrative architecture. Computer **44**(3), 118–130 (2014)
14. Schuemie, M.J., van der Straaten, P., Krijn, M., van der Mast, C.A.P.G.: Research on presence in virtual reality: a survey. Cyberpsychol. Behav. **4**, 183–201 (2001). https://doi.org/10.1089/109493101300117884
15. Sheridan, T.B.: Musings on telepresence and virtual presence. Presence Teleoper. Virtual Environ **1**, 120–126 (1992). https://doi.org/10.1162/pres.1992.1.1.120
16. Sukoco, B.M., Wu, W.-Y.: The effects of advergames on consumer telepresence and attitudes: a comparison of products with search and experience attributes. Expert Syst. Appl. **38**, 7396–7406 (2011). https://doi.org/10.1016/j.eswa.2010.12.085
17. Fiore, A.M., Kim, J., Lee, H.-H.: Effect of image interactivity technology on consumer responses toward the online retailer. J. Interact. Mark. **19**, 38–53 (2005). https://doi.org/10.1002/dir.20042
18. Wu, H., Cai, T., Luo, D., Liu, Y., Zhang, Z.: Immersive virtual reality news: a study of user experience and media effects. Int. J. Hum. Comput. Stud. **147**, 102576 (2021). https://doi.org/10.1016/j.ijhcs.2020.102576
19. Pan, S., et al.: Efficacy of cognitive behavioral therapy on opiate use and retention in methadone maintenance treatment in China: a randomised trial. PLoS ONE **10**, e0127598 (2015). https://doi.org/10.1371/journal.pone.0127598
20. Popa, C.O., et al.: Standard CBT versus integrative and multimodal CBT assisted by virtual-reality for generalized anxiety disorder. Front. Psychol. **13** (2022). https://doi.org/10.3389/fpsyg.2022.1008981
21. Kiluk, B.D., Nich, C., Babuscio, T., Carroll, K.M.: Quality versus quantity: acquisition of coping skills following computerized cognitive-behavioral therapy for substance use disorders **105**, 2120–2127 (2010). https://doi.org/10.1111/j.1360-0443.2010.03076.x
22. Carroll, K.M., et al.: Computer-assisted delivery of cognitive-behavioral therapy: efficacy and durability of CBT4CBT among cocaine-dependent individuals maintained on methadone. AJP **171**, 436–444 (2014). https://doi.org/10.1176/appi.ajp.2013.13070987
23. Perciavalle, V., et al.: The role of deep breathing on stress. Neurol. Sci. **38**, 451–458 (2017). https://doi.org/10.1007/s10072-016-2790-8
24. Prabhu, V.G., Linder, C., Stanley, L.M., Morgan, R.: An affective computing in virtual reality environments for managing surgical pain and anxiety (2019). https://doi.org/10.1109/aivr46125.2019.00049
25. Steffen, P.R., et al.: Integrating breathing techniques into psychotherapy to improve HRV: which approach is best? Front. Psychol. **12** (2021). https://doi.org/10.3389/fpsyg.2021.624254
26. Jänig, W.: The autonomic nervous system and its coordination by the brain. In: Davidson, R.J. (ed.) Handbook of Affective Sciences. Oxford University Press, New York (2009)
27. Waxenbaum, J.A., Reddy, V., Varacallo, M.: Anatomy, autonomic nervous system (2019)
28. Narvaez Linares, N.F., Charron, V., Ouimet, A.J., Labelle, P.R., Plamondon, H.: A systematic review of the trier social stress test methodology: issues in promoting study comparison and replicable research. Neurobiol. Stress **13**, 100235 (2020). https://doi.org/10.1016/j.ynstr.2020.100235
29. Amon, K.L., Campbell, A.: Can children with AD/HD learn relaxation and breathing techniques through biofeedback video games? Aust. J. Educ. Dev. Psychol. **8**, 72–84 (2008)
30. Aritzeta, A., Soroa, G., Balluerka, N., Muela, A., Gorostiaga, A., Aliri, J.: Reducing anxiety and improving academic performance through a biofeedback relaxation training program. Appl. Psychophysiol. Biofeedback **42**, 193–202 (2017). https://doi.org/10.1007/s10484-017-9367-z
31. Kirschbaum, C., Pirke, K.-M., Hellhammer, D.H.: The 'trier social stress test' – a tool for investigating psychobiological stress responses in a laboratory setting. Neuropsychobiology **28**, 76–81 (1993). https://doi.org/10.1159/000119004

32. Cohen, S., Williamson, G.: Perceived stress in a probability sample of the united states. In: Spacapan, S., Oskamp, S. (eds.) The Social Psychology of Health: Claremont Symposium on Applied Social Psychology, pp. 31–67 (1988). Sage, Newbury Park, CA
33. Watson, D., Clark, L.A., Tellegen, A.: Development and validation of brief measures of positive and negative affect: the PANAS scales. J. Pers. Soc. Psychol. **54**, 1063–1070 (1988). https://doi.org/10.1037/0022-3514.54.6.1063
34. Schubert, T., Friedmann, F., Regenbrecht, H.: The experience of presence: factor analytic insights. Presence Teleoper. Virtual Environ. **10**, 266–281 (2001). https://doi.org/10.1162/105474601300343603
35. Bradley, M.M., Lang, P.J.: Measuring emotion: the self-assessment manikin and the semantic differential. J. Behav. Ther. Exp. Psychiatry **25**, 49–59 (1994). https://doi.org/10.1016/0005-7916(94)90063-9
36. SUS: A 'quick and dirty' usability scale, 207–212 (1996). https://doi.org/10.1201/9781498710411-35

Rehabilitation of Executive Functions: Systematic Review of Technological Stimulation Devices

Carlos Ramos-Galarza[1](✉) and Patricia García-Cruz[2]

[1] Facultad de Psicología, Pontificia Universidad Católica del Ecuador, Quito, Ecuador
caramos@puce.edu.ec

[2] Centro de Investigación en Mecatrónica y Sistemas Interactivos - MIST, Facultad de Psicología , Universidad Tecnológica Indoamérica, Quito, Ecuador

Abstract. Executive functions are high-level mental abilities that are located in the frontal lobe and allow humans to regulate their behavior. These cognitive skills are initiative, working memory, problem solving ability, inhibition, monitoring, verification, planning, among others. In the processes of stimulation or rehabilitation of executive functions, we work with material based on pencil and paper, therefore, it is essential to generate technological proposals that can help in the processes of rehabilitation of executive functions. In this context, we present a research that conducted a quantitative systematic review of technological devices used for neuropsychological stimulation and rehabilitation of executive functions. The research concludes by analyzing the contribution of having technological resources to rehabilitate executive functions and the need for future research to develop new technological tools in the neuropsychological rehabilitation process.

Keywords: Neuropsychological Rehabilitation · Technological Devices · Executive Functions · Systematic review

1 Introduction

The conscious activity of the human being is product of the work of several brain structures, being the frontal lobe one of the most important parts for human beings to regulate our impulses, behavior, desires and everything we are able to produce [1, 2].

Several researches have described that human beings who have an adequate development of the central nervous system can act with awareness of the consequences of their actions, while people who have some kind of frontal damage (Fig. 1), act irresponsibly, without having objectives or a clear planning of what they want to achieve in life [3, 4].

The mental functions that allow this conscious work in the human being are the executive functions [5, 6]. These cognitive abilities are defined as high-level mental skills that allow human beings to have a creative and effective behavior within the respect of social parameters [7].

Q. Gao et al. (Eds.): HCII 2023, LNCS 14055, pp. 584–599, 2023.
https://doi.org/10.1007/978-3-031-48041-6_39

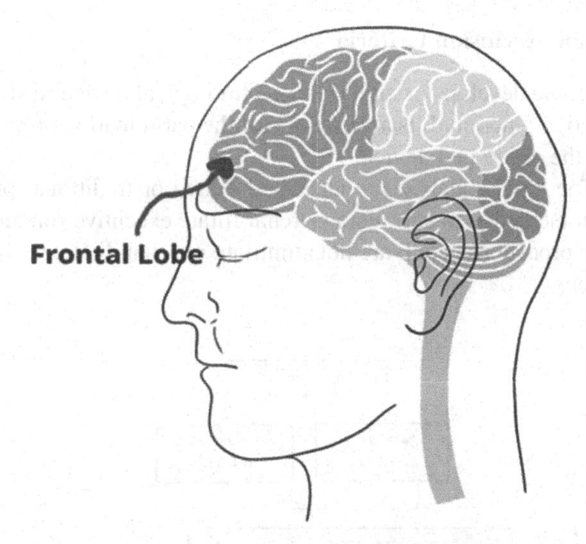

Fig. 1. Graphic location of the frontal lobe in the human brain.

There are several proposals of executive functions, for example, inhibition, working memory, planning, monitoring, emotional regulation, organization of materials, initiative, verification, internal language regulating behavior, metacognition, behavioral regulation, and cognitive flexibility; among others [8]. At present there is no absolute consensus on the number of executive functions that should exist, but there is agreement that we are referring to mental abilities that allow the conscious regulation of behavior [9].

Regarding the rehabilitation processes of executive functions, there is currently no complete development of this process, since the rehabilitation proposals are from recent years and are based on traditional pencil and paper processes [10, 11]. In this sense, it is of great importance to identify what technological developments have been proposed to rehabilitate executive functions for human beings suffering frontal damage [12].

Therefore, a contribution to the current state of the art of neuropsychology research is to identify the new proposals that are being developed for the rehabilitation of executive functions. In this sense, a systematic review of recent technological developments for the rehabilitation of executive functions is presented below.

2 Method

The present investigation was carried out by means of a systematic review methodology of the collection of 13 academic articles [13–25]. The present study was carried out through two processes: (a) first, the inclusion and exclusion criteria of the articles to be included in this review were determined; (b) then, a protocol was elaborated to analyze the information of the selected articles to achieve the objective of identifying the devices developed to stimulate and rehabilitate executive functions.

2.1 Inclusion and Exclusion Criteria

Inclusion: The article develops or analyzes a technological device to stimulate or rehabilitate the executive function. It is an article with the participation of human beings and measurement of the developed device.

Exclusion: The article analyzes a paper and pencil or traditional procedure, without technological elements, to stimulate or rehabilitate executive functions. The article develops another procedure which are not stimulate or rehabilitate, such as, assessment executive functions.

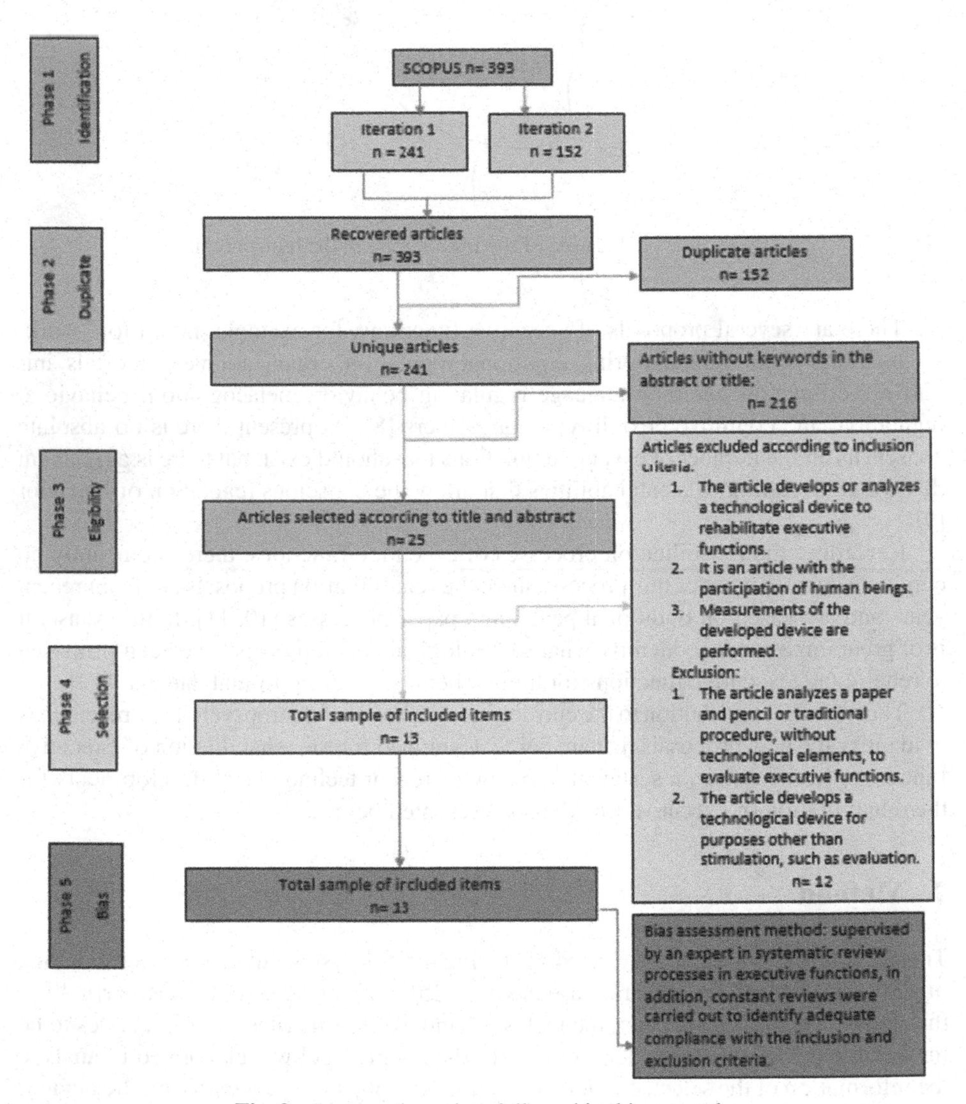

Fig. 2. Systematic review followed in this research.

In order to carry out this systematic review, it was necessary to complete 5 stages (see Fig. 2):

A. Identification stage: a search for academic articles was carried out in the Scopus metabase and main journals in the context of psychology. Scopus was used, due to its importance in the Latin American context, in addition to the fact that it is a meta-base that offers greater precision when considering time ranges and provides a large number of articles of great scientific prestige. The temporal range was papers published between 2015 and 2023, using keywords in the English and Spanish languages "executive functions, technology, rehabilitation, stimulation, psychology, frontal lobe".
B. Duplicate stage: duplicate articles were deleted.
C. Eligibility stage: inclusion and exclusion criteria were determined to obtain relevant data that contribute to the research objective.
D. Selection stage: the articles were downloaded to be read completely and by applying the inclusion and exclusion criteria, the articles linked to the study were selected.
E. Bias stage: the whole process was supervised by an expert in systematic review processes in executive functions, and constant revisions were made to identify the adequate fulfillment of the inclusion and exclusion criteria in the analysis of the articles worked on in the research.

3 Results

Statistical analyses were performed with the 13 studies that met the criteria for inclusion in the study [13–25]. All the data analyzed for the 13 scientific articles statistically analyzed are shown in appendix 1. In reference to the average number of participants found in the studies, a mean sample size M = 65.77 (SD = 61.95) was identified. In most of the studies a frequency between 0 and 50 participants was found. The data can be seen in Fig. 3.

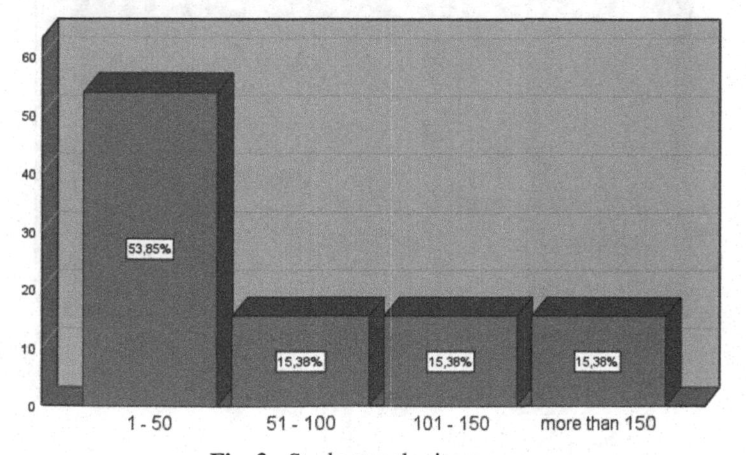

Fig. 3. Study sample size ranges.

In relation to the countries that have developed technological developments that help stimulate and rehabilitate executive functions, it was found that Italy is the country with the most developments in this regard. Figure 4 shows the results.

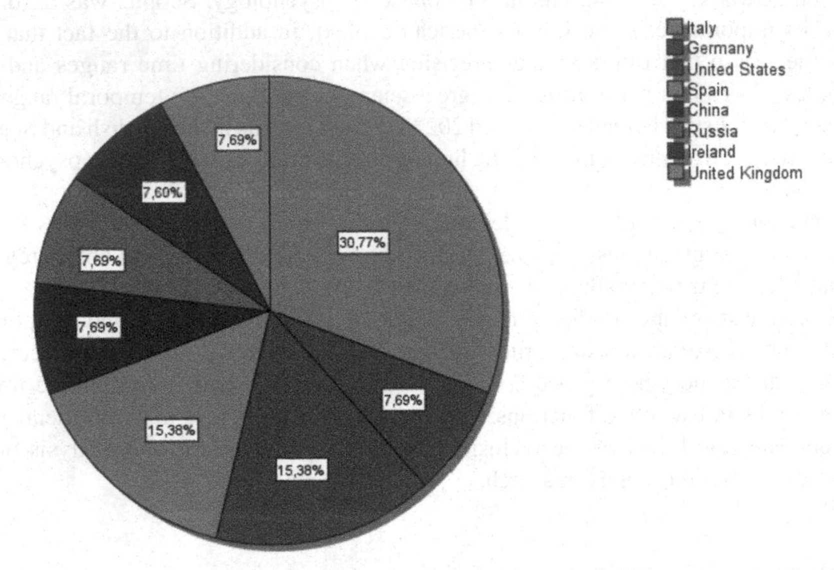

Fig. 4. Countries that have generated technology to stimulate or rehabilitate executive functions.

When observing the educational level of the participants, it was found that most of the studies did not specify this criterion in their articles. Figure 5 shows the different educational levels of the participants in the different studies.

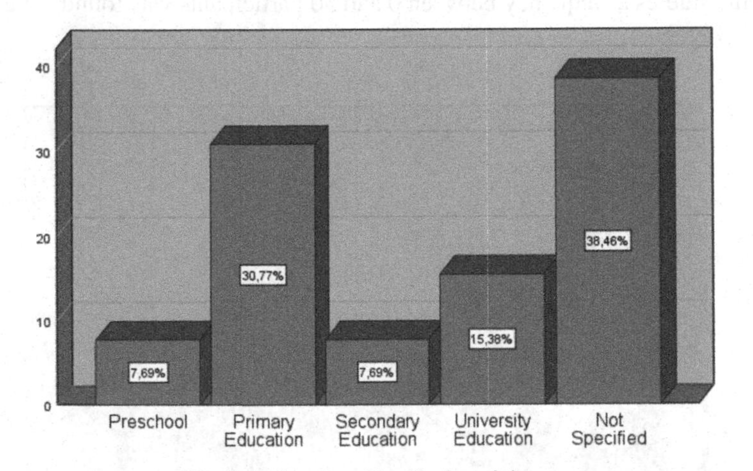

Fig. 5. Educational level of participants.

In relation to the type of population that participated in the studies with technological developments for the stimulation and rehabilitation of executive functions, it indicates that in most of the investigations adults with some disorder were chosen. Figure 6 shows the different types of populations with which the studies worked.

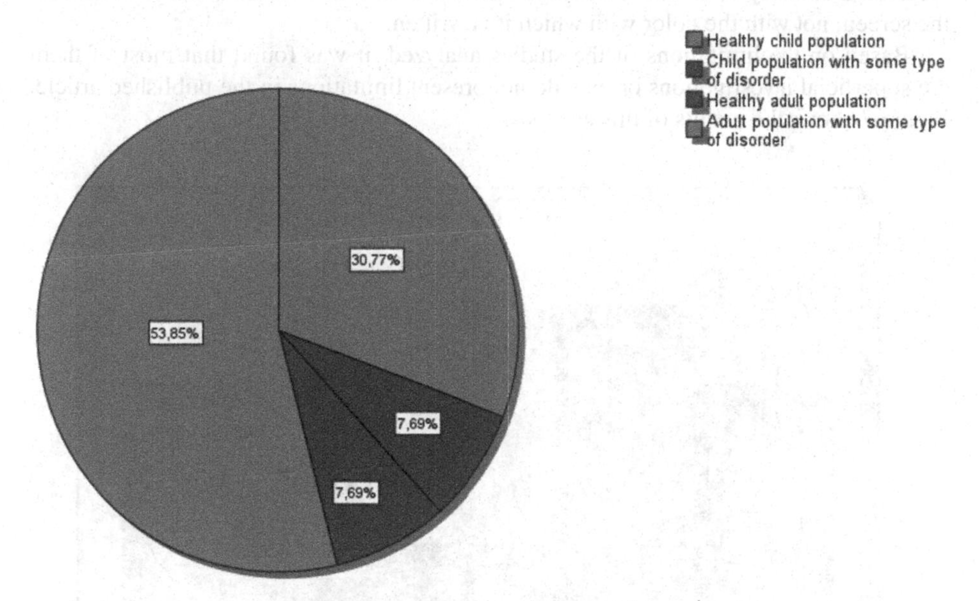

Fig. 6. Characteristics of the participants.

The following technological developments were found in the 13 studies [13–25]: (a) Bee-Bot Robot, which is a bee-shaped device that is used in an ER-Lab, where children must complete goals programmed by the Bee- Bot Robot [13]; (b) CortexVR, is an application with different virtual reality games to stimulate executive functions that must be complemented with the CoachApp for training [14]; (c) Computer-based training, composed of working memory and mathematical tasks, for this training 3 stages need to be fulfilled in order to measure the stimulation performed [15]; (d) Computer Aided Technology (CAT), which is a specialized training program for each patient performed by doctors specialized in rehabilitation [16]; (e) Smartwatch Executive Function Supports, is an application for the Smartwatch that allows patients with ID and ASD to schedule appointments and stimulate or rehabilitate their planning [17]; (f) Brain-Computer Interface + Exoskeleton Technology in Complex Multimodal Stimulation (BCNI), 3 mental commands are given on the computer screen and with the help of exoskeleton technology the patient is rehabilitated; (g) LEGO Mindstorms EV3, is a programmable robotic kit in which children must assemble and program the robot to do certain activities that increase in difficulty [19]; (h) Ozobot, is a small educational robot, which is coded to follow colors on a linear surface, then children must use the colors to solve what they are asked [20]; (i) CityQuest, is a virtual reality game of a city, where patients must navigate avoiding obstacles [21]; (j) The use of a wearable camera to record significant events over 6 weeks to help Alzheimer's patients [22]; (k) Eye-tracking technology, is a computerized version of the Tower of Hanoi, where they have a limited number of movements to solve the instructions [23]; (l) A set of 3 robots and a sensor-based device, which focused on interactive games with force support assisted by the 3 robots [24]; (m) Bimodal VR-Stroop, which is a virtual reality game that has two scenarios that has visual and auditory distractors, where the person must read the color that is written on the screen, not with the color with which it is written.

Based on the limitations of the studies analyzed, it was found that most of them are superficial investigations or they do not present limitations in the published article. Figure 7 shows the results of this analysis.

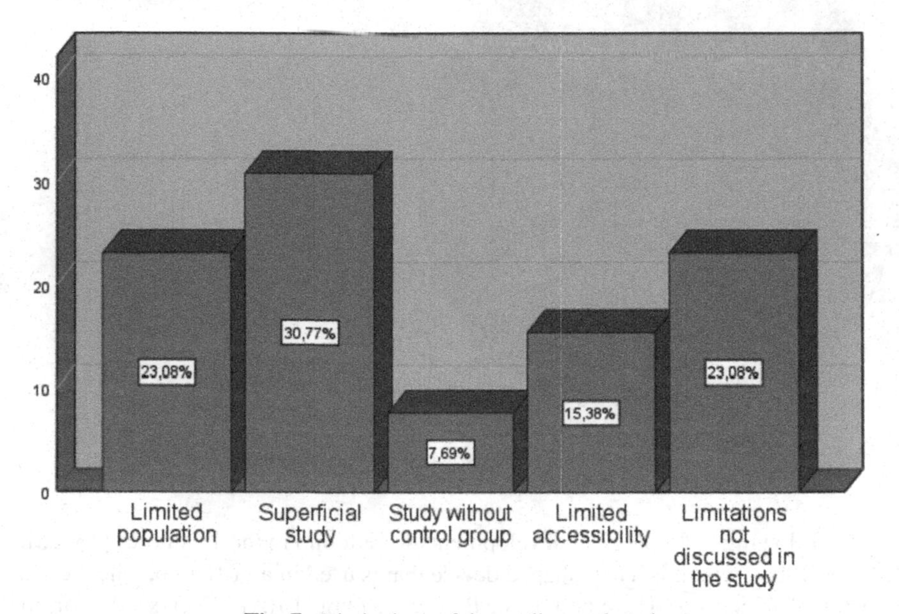

Fig. 7. Limitations of the studies analyzed

In the research analyzed, it was found that they focus on rehabilitating various executive functions, among which working memory and problem-solving skills stand out. Figure 8 shows the executive functions worked on in each study.

In relation to the time required for rehabilitation with the different technological devices, it was found that the most predominant time to stimulate or rehabilitate the patients was from 1 to 5 weeks. Figure 9 shows the ranges of time required to rehabilitate patients.

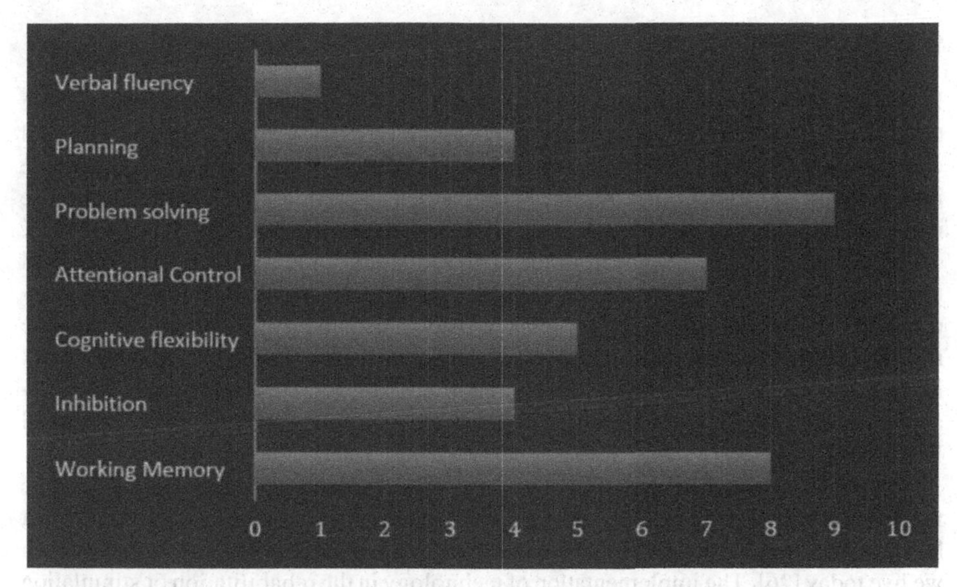

Fig. 8. Executive functions stimulated in the technological developments reviewed

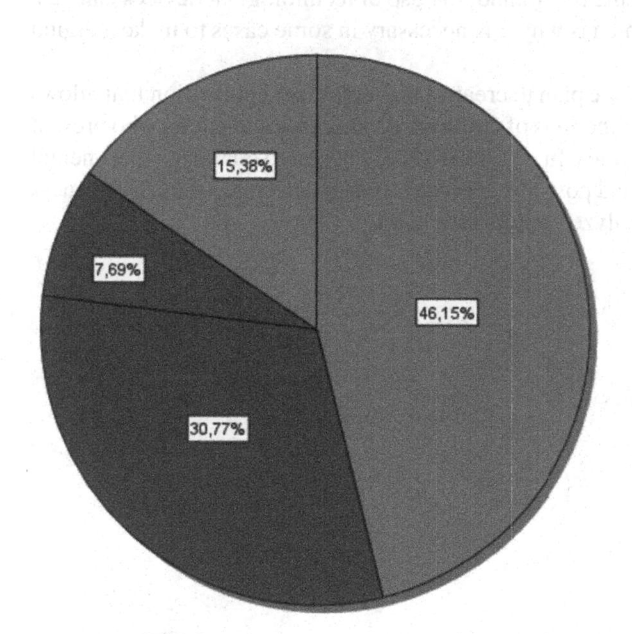

Fig. 9. The ranges of time required to rehabilitate or stimulate patients.

4 Conclusions

In this article we have reported an investigation that conducted a systematic review of the technological developments that exist to rehabilitate executive functions. The essential contribution of this study to the line of research on executive functions has to do with the identification of technological resources for the neuropsychological treatment of these mental abilities, which is a topic that is still under construction.

In the extraction of results from the analyzed studies, the following technological tools were found to stimulate and rehabilitate executive functions: Bee-Bot Robot, CortexVR, Computer Based Training, Computer Aided Technology, Smartwatch Executive Function Supports, Brain-Computer Interface + Exoskeleton Technology in Complex Multimodal Stimulation, LEGO Mindstorms EV3, Ozobot, CityQuest, use of a wearable camera to record more significant events, Eye Tracking Technology and Bimodal VR-Stroop.

The main benefit of having technological tools to stimulate and rehabilitate executive functions is based on the fact that the patient who needs this type of attention can feel that he/she is carrying out activities that are consistent with the technological world in which we live today [26]. The implementation of technology in the rehabilitation or stimulation of executive functions can be very useful for patients, because nowadays technology is part of everyday life and in the case of children or younger patients this alternative optimizes the intervention. On the other hand, the use of technological devices can be a challenge with older adults, which is why it is necessary in some cases to make a digital literacy and pre-training [27].

In a future research project, we plan to create a technological application that allows us to rehabilitate the executive functions of children, adolescents and adults who present deficiencies in these mental abilities. In addition, it is of interest to conduct experimental studies in which, through pre- and post-test analysis, we can determine the effectiveness of the technological devices analyzed in this article.

Appendix 1

Title	Sample	Research countries	Ed. Level	Population type	Technological development	How is it used?	Limitations	Executive functions stimulation	Intervention time
Empowering Executive Functions in 5- and 6-Year-Old Typically Developing Children Through Educational Robotics: An RCT Study	187	Italy	Preschool students	Children between 5 and 6 years of age, who are studying in a school	Bee-Bot robot, bee-shaped device with boards or complementary material	It is used in an ER-lab, where children must complete goals programmed by the BEE-Bot robot. As this robot has buttons to move forward, stop, delete the memory, etc., the children must use these buttons according to the goals to be accomplished	It is important that you are in a school or classroom environment	Mamory of visuospatial work, inhibition, self-control, cognitive flexibility, sustained attention, problem solving	20 training sessions of 60 min each
CortexVR: Immersive analysis and training of cognitive executive functions of soccer players using virtual reality and machine learning	37	Germany	Don't specify	Men and women from 21 to 35 years old	CortexVR, is an application with different virtual reality games	By means of virtual reality glasses, the CortexVR application is used, which has some game modes (player tracking, counting players, finding the ball), then, while people play, they stimulate some executive functions. Similarly, it should be complemented with the CachApp for training and analysis	The full benefits of this adaptation are not yet fully known	Inhibition, working memory, cognitive flexibility, reasoning and problem solving	It does not show an exact time, but you must play the 3 game modes in a specific order and repeat it 4 times

(*continued*)

(continued)

Title	Sample	Research countries	Ed. Level	Population type	Technological development	How is it used?	Limitations	Executive functions stimulation	Intervention time
Smartwatch Executive Function Supports for Students With ID and ASD	3	United States	University	Patients with a diagnosis of intellectual disability and autism spectrum disorder	A smartwatch app to help support executive functions	It is an application that requires students to be digitally literate, so that they can enter the alarms of their appointments through an appointment formula and through the Smartwatch access the information. With the purpose of helping the student to have more independence	The application does not allow selecting the date of the appointment, only the day of the week. In addition, as the study sample was very limited, it is not possible to ensure that it works for other age groups	Planning, organization and independence	3 sessions per week of 50 min. Each one
Educational robotics to develop executive functions visual spatial abilities, planning and problem solving	30	Italy	5th grade of primary education	Healthy children attending school	LEGO Mindstorms EV3. It is a programmable robotic kit, created by Lego	The children have to assemble the robot, then they are given programs, which they have to program and they increase in difficulty. In addition, the children can observe the movements of the toy and what it does according to the environment in which it is	Don't specify	Visuospatial attention, planning, problem solving, working memory, control of complex tasks	10 meetings, 2 h each and one meeting per week

(continued)

(*continued*)

Title	Sample	Research countries	Ed. Level	Population type	Technological development	How is it used?	Limitations	Executive functions stimulation	Intervention time
Computer-based training in math and working memory improves cognitive skills and academic achievement in primary school children: Behavioral results	104	Spain	Primary Education	Children from 7 to 12 years old in rural schools in Murcia (Spain)	Computer-based training, consisting of: working memory and mathematical tasks	This training consists of 3 phases: pre-training, training and post-training. Through tasks of mathematical ability, reading, and verbal skills. In order to measure the stimulation, a test is performed before and after the training	Therefore, it is not possible to measure long-term effects because the post-training measurement is a short-term measurement	Working memory, adaptability, inhibition	17 weeks
Computer aided technology-based cognitive rehabilitation efficacy against patients' cerebral stroke	128	China	10 a 11 years of basic education	Cardiovascular accident patients, 18 to 80 years old	Computer Aided Technology (CAT)	Doctors specialized in rehabilitation have designed a specialized training program for each patient, so in addition to the one-on-one training with the patient, CAT is applied and the respective medication for each patient	Because MOCA is used for rehabilitation assessment, there may be certain limitations and misdiagnoses	Memory, visual and spatial executive function, abstract ability, orientation and language	4 weeks, 30 min per day, 6 days per week
Use of a Brain–Computer Interface + Exoskeleton Technology in Complex Multimodal Stimulation in the Rehabilitation of Stroke Patients	44	Russia	Don't specify	Patients with cardiovascular stroke, 61 years of age	Brain–Computer Interface + Exoskeleton Technology in Complex Multimodal Stimulation (BCNI)	The patient is seated in a chair in front of a computer with both wrists attached to an exoskeleton. Then on the screen comes out 3 mental commands: relax, imagine the state of the muscles when opening the right or left hand. The hand opens after the system recognized the correct classification of execution	Patients only have an average capacity and tolerance of 20 to 30 min	Problem solving, visuospatial thinking, attention, working memory (practice)	8 to 10 procedures, 10 min per session, with a 3 to 5 min break

(*continued*)

(*continued*)

Title	Sample	Research countries	Ed. Level	Population type	Technological development	How is it used?	Limitations	Executive functions stimulation	Intervention time
Enhancing the potential of creative thinking in children with educational robots	171	Italy	4th and 5th year elementary school students	Children	Ozobot, a small educational robot	It is a robot that is coded to follow colors on a linear surface, so the children use the colors to determine the robot's movements according to the instructions they receive	Don't specify	Problem-solving, visuospatial thinking, attention, working memory	There is no time limit, it depends on how long the children take
"CityQuest," A Custom-Designed Serious Game, Enhances Spatial Memory Performance in Older Adults	56	Ireland	Don't specify	Healthy older adults 65 years of age and older	CityQuest, a virtual city game	A virtual game that through navigation of unfamiliar and crowded locations that require participants to control navigation through city spaces and avoid obstacles	Don't specify	Spatial memory, working memory, problem-solving, sustained attention, cognitive flexibility	2 sessions per week of 60 min, for 5 weeks
Using a wearable camera to support everyday memory following brain injury: A single-case study	1	United Kingdom	Don't specify	A 48-year-old man with Alzheimer's disease	Handheld Camera	The use of a wearable camera to record significant events over a 6-week period to aid memory recall	It was only a case study, so we need to deepen the effectiveness with a larger sample	Working memory	6 weeks
Reading Goals and Executive Function in Autism: An Eye-Tracking Study	22	Spain	School and high school	Middle-class children and adolescents with a diagnosis of autism	Eye-tracking technology	Using a computerized and modified version of The Tower of Hanoi, they must read the instructions on the screen and solve the problem with a maximum of 15 moves per problem, moving the computer mouse to do so. While the eye tracker evaluates it	Its application cannot be generalized to the entire population with autism	Problem solving, inhibition, planning	40 min

(*continued*)

(*continued*)

Title	Sample	Research countries	Ed. Level	Population type	Technological development	How is it used?	Limitations	Executive functions stimulation	Intervention time
Robotic Rehabilitation: An Opportunity to Improve Cognitive Functions in Subjects With Stroke. An Explorative Study	51	Italy	Less than 26 years of education	Persons between 35 and 85 years of age, who have had a cardiovascular accident in the last 6 months	A set of three robots and a sensor-based device for upper limb rehabilitation	The rehabilitation program focused on interactive games, carried out with the support of the assistance forces provided by the 3 robots (Amadeo, Pablo and Diego)	Lack of a control group in the application of robots	Planning, problem-solving, selective attention, cognitive flexibility	30 rehabilitation sessions, 45 min each, 5 days a week
Application of virtual environments in a multi-disciplinary day neurorehabilitation program to improve executive functioning using the Stroop task	21	United States	Don't specify	Brain-injured patients with executive dysfunction	Bimodal VR-Stroop	It consists of two scenarios (a classroom and an apartment), then in both there are visual and auditory distractions that appear for 5 s, in intervals of 10, 15 and 25 s. The task is to say the color that comes up, not the color it is written in	Excludes patients who lack the cognitive sufficiency to participate in tasks	Sustained attention, attention to visual details, cognitive flexibility	Sessions 1 and 8 of 60 min; Sessions 2 to 7 of 30 min

References

1. Ramos-Galarza, C., Benavides-Endara, P., Bolaños-Pasquel, M., Fonseca-Bautista, S., Ramos, D.: Scale of clinical observation to evaluate the third functional unit of the Luria theory: EOCL-1. Revista Ecuatoriana de Neurología **28**(2), 83–91 (2019)
2. Ramos-Galarza, C., Acosta-Rodas, P., Bolaños-Pasquel, M., Lepe-Martínez, N.: The role of executive functions in academic performance and behaviour of university students. J. Appl. Res. High. Educ. **12**(3), 444–445 (2020)
3. Silva-Barragán, M., Ramos-Galarza, C.: Etiology of brain damage: a neuropsychological contribution in its theoretical construction (First part). Revista Ecuatoriana de Neurología **30**(1), 154–165 (2021)
4. Silva-Barragán, M., Ramos-Galarza, C.: Modelos de Organización Cerebral: Un recorrido neuropsicológico. Revista Ecuatoriana de Neurología **29**(3), 74–83 (2020)
5. Ramos-Galarza, C.: Adaptation of Victoria stroop test in ecuadorians students. Revista Iberoamericana de Diagnostico y Evaluacion Psicologica **2**(44), 57–64 (2017)
6. Ramos-Galarza, C., Bolaños-Pasquel, M., García-Gómez, A., Suárez, P., Jadán-Guerrero, J.: Efeco scale for assessing executive functions in self-report format. Revista Iberoamericana de Diagnostico y Evaluacion Psicologica **51**(1), 83–93 (2019)
7. Lezak, M.: Neuropsychological Assessment, 3rd edn. University Press, Oxford (1995)
8. Ramos-Galarza, C., Cruz-Cárdenas, J., Bolaños-Pasquel, M., Acosta-Rodas, P.: Factorial structure of the EOCL-1 scale to assess executive functions. Front. Psychol. **12**(585145), 1–14 (2021)
9. Ramos-Galarza, C., et al.: Evaluación de las Habilidades de la Corteza Prefrontal: La Escala Efeco II-VC y II VR. Revista Ecuatoriana de Neurología **27**(3), 36–43 (2018)
10. Ramos-Galarza, C., et al.: Fundamental concepts in the neuropsychological theory [Conceptos fundamentales en la teoría neuropsicológica]. Revista Ecuatoriana de Neurología **26**(1), 53–60 (2017)
11. Arruda, M., Arruda, R., Anunciação, L.: Psychometric properties and clinical utility of the executive function inventory for children and adolescents: a large multistage populational study including children with ADHD. Appl. Neuropsychol. Child **11**(1), 1–17 (2022)
12. Ramos-Galarza, C., Acosta-Rodas, M., Sanchez-Gordon, S., Calle-Jimenez, T.: Mobile technological apps to improve frontal lobe functioning. In: Ayaz, H., Asgher, U. (eds.) AHFE 2020. AISC, vol. 1201, pp. 89–93. Springer, Cham (2021). https://doi.org/10.1007/978-3-030-51041-1_13
13. Lieto, M.C.D., et al.: Empowering executive functions in 5- and 6-year-old typically developing children through educational robotics: an RCT study. Frontiers **10**(3084), 1–10 (2020)
14. Krupitzer, C., et al.: CortexVR: immersive analysis and training of cognitive executive functions of soccer players using virtual reality and machine learning. Frontiers **13**(754732), 1–13 (2022)
15. Pérez, N.S., et al.: Computer-based training in math and working memory improves cognitive skills and academic achievement in primary school children: behavioral results. Frontiers **8**(2327), 1–12 (2018)
16. Liu, X., Huang, X., Lin, J., Zhang, R., Ding, R.: Computer aided technology-based cognitive rehabilitation efficacy against patients' cerebral stroke. NeuroQuantology **16**(4), 86–92 (2018)
17. Wright, R.E., McMahon, D.D., Cihak, D.F., Hirschfelder, K.: Smartwatch executive function supports for students with ID and ASD. J. Spec. Educ. Technol. **37**(1), 1–11 (2020)
18. Slyun'kova, E., Isakova, E., Kotov, S.: Use of a brain–computer interface + exoskeleton technology in complex multimodal stimulation in the rehabilitation of stroke patients. Neurosci. Behav. Physiol. **50**(8), 987–991 (2020)

19. Paglia, F.L., Francomano, M.M., Riva, G., Barbera, D.L.: Educational robotics to develop executive functions visual spatial abilities, planning and problem solving. Annu. Rev. Cyber Ther. Telemed. **2018**(16), 80–86 (2018)
20. Mazzoni, E., Benvenuti, M., Tartarini, A., Giovagnoli, S.: Enhancing the potential of creative thinking in children with educational robots. Annu. Rev. Cyber Ther. Telemed. **18**, 37–40 (2020)
21. Merriman, N.A., et al.: "CityQuest," a custom-designed serious game, enhances spatial memory performance in older adults. Frontiers **14**(806418) (2022)
22. Mair, A., Shackleton, R.: Using a wearable camera to support everyday memory following brain injury: a single-case study. Brain Inpairment **22**(3), 312–328 (2021)
23. Micai, M., Vulchanova, M., Saldaña, D.: Reading goals and executive function in autism: an eye-tracking study. Autism Res. **14**(5), 1007–1024 (2021)
24. Aprile, I., et al.: Robotic rehabilitation: an opportunity to improve cognitive functions in subjects with stroke. An explorative study. Frontiers **11**(588285), 1–12 (2020)
25. Dahdah, M.N., Bennet, M., Prajapati, P., Parsons, T., Sullivan, E., Driver, S.: Application of virtual environments in a multi-disciplinary day neurorehabilitation program to improve executive functioning using the Stroop task. NeuroRehabilitation **41**(4), 721–734 (2017)
26. Ramos-Galarza, C., Cóndor-Herrera, O., Cruz-Cárdenas, J.: Evaluation of online learning platforms in Latin America. Emerg. Sci. J. **6**(1), 253–263 (2022)
27. Cóndor-Herrera, O., Ramos-Galarza, C.: The impact of a technological intervention program on learning mathematical skills. Educ. Inf. Technol. **26**(2), 1423–1433 (2021)

Change Management Model for the Quality of the Telehealth Service in a Regional Hospital in Northern Peru

Miriam Isabel Ruiz-Llontop[1], Moises David Reyes-Perez[2](✉), Carmen Graciela Arbulú Pérez Vargas[3], Jhoselit Lisset Facho-Cornejo[4], Dina Marisol Calonge De la Piedra[5], and Jesús Emilio Agustín Padilla Caballero[5]

[1] Universidad Tecnológica del Perú, Chiclayo, Peru
[2] Mayor de San Marcos National University, Chiclayo, Peru
moisesreyesperez@gmail.edu.pe
[3] Cesar Vallejo University, Pimentel, Peru
[4] San Martin de Porres University, Pimentel, Peru
[5] Cesar Vallejo University, Lima, Peru

Abstract. The objective of this research was to propose a theoretical Change Management Model for the quality of the Telehealth service in a Regional Hospital in Northern Peru. In addition, the quantitative methodology was applied, since, with the help of valid instruments, the information gathered from health professionals and patients attended by this service was analyzed and discussed. This research is based on the theory of the application of cybernetics in public administration and the theory of change management. The instruments that measured the variables Quality of Service and Telehealth obtained valid Cronbach's alpha values. The conclusions were as follows: internal users reported a low level of 46.6% for the "Tele-education" dimension; in addition, the "Tele-assistance" dimension obtained a high level of 47.9%. External users, on the other hand, determined that the "Responsiveness" dimension scored 43.3% at a low level. Regarding the last dimension "Security", 39.3% reached a low level. The theoretical model of change management for the quality of Telehealth services was developed based on Kurt Lewin's model of organizational change. Finally, the model was validated by professional experts.

Keywords: Telehealth · quality of service · change management model

1 Introduction

1.1 Problematic Reality

Telehealth has been widely studied in our last decade, especially since the appearance of Information and Communication Technologies (ICT) in the social environment. According to the World Health Organization (WHO), telehealth is distinguished by the organization of service administrations by experts who use the improvements in information,

Q. Gao et al. (Eds.): HCII 2023, LNCS 14055, pp. 600–609, 2023.
https://doi.org/10.1007/978-3-031-48041-6_40

either through virtual scenarios, calls, texts, sounds, images or different types of technological means, determined to exchange meaningful information to provide certified diagnoses, effective medical tests, drugs and disease prevention (WHO 2015).

In December 2019, a record of a pneumonia outbreak of unknown origin in Wuhan, China, alerted the international community. The virus that caused it was identified as SARS-coV-2, of the coronavirus genus. In the course of approximately 30 days, after international authorities took note of this phenomenon and due to its high level of contagion, it had already spread around the entire world (Ciotti et al. 2020).

In Peru, due to the health emergency caused by the appearance of COVID-19, the mortality rate rose to more than 50% without control, day by day. Faced with this, the priority work of front-line care in hospitals in our country was provided quasi-preferentially to COVID-19 patients, in addition to this, the number of patients with other types of diseases also increased by 30% and other clinical pictures of recent onset that required medical assistance and to which the health service was unable to reach. This concomitant lack of access to medical care and other health specialties is based on the lack of access to remote areas of our national territory, as well as the limited time availability of health personnel and specialist doctors for primary health care (Bautista 2017).

In the department of Lambayeque, the authors Sosa and Sosa in 2018 carried out an investigation in two health centers, on the expectations and perceptions of external users, treated in general medicine, nursing, obstetric, psychology and dental offices, about the care in two health establishments of the first level of care, where it was obtained that of the total number of respondents, 63.3% and 71.7% were dissatisfied with the quality of the service received in the health establishments, that is, say an unsatisfactory SERVQUAL quality was obtained.

Given the critical situation evaluated, the research problem posed is the following: How would the change management model guarantee the quality of the Telehealth service in a Regional Hospital in Northern Peru? In addition, other research questions are presented, such as: What perception would external and internal users have about the quality of Telehealth service in a Regional Hospital in Northern Peru during the COVID-19 pandemic; Do we have instruments that would measure the perception of external and internal users about the quality of the Telehealth service in a Regional Hospital in Northern Peru during the COVID-19 pandemic that are valid and reliable? Will the change management model that would guarantee the quality of the Telehealth service in a Regional Hospital in Northern Peru be valid? And finally, what are the fundamental pillars that would support the Change Management Model to guarantee the quality of the Telehealth service in a Regional Hospital in Northern Peru.

1.2 Literature Review

Theory of the Application of Cybernetics in Public Administration

In relation to the first component, we have the theory of the application of cybernetics in public administration. This theory considers that, in the context of public administration, cybernetics and/or information technologies (ICTs) study how organizations use these innovative tools to essentially guarantee their resistance. Nobert Wiener, its promoter, points out that the ability to gather and process data decides the capacity of a country's public administration.

The social isolation experienced during the COVID-19 pandemic forced the entire world to change their usual lifestyle, from the way a person interacts in their work environment, to the way they communicate with their family or friends. In this sense, cybernetics and information technologies in general, allowed rapprochement through the use of digital platforms, and these new remote ways of accessing various vital services in our country were even implemented, especially the health care service.

Telehealth Health Model

The Telehealth Health Model considers that Telehealth is characterized by the organization of the administration of health services -with distance being a fundamental angle- by experts who use information technologies, with the aim of collecting data that allow diagnoses, treatments, prescribe medicines and prevent diseases, in addition, under this modality, carry out distance education and develop research work (Arroyo 2015).

The last component comprises contains the model of necessary medical services, which incorporates the State, society, associations, individuals and their families, whose general utility is to ensure the right to well-being, accepting jobs and obligations to ensure, shield and safeguard this right (Bautista 2017).

Currently, data innovation and the advanced world have impacted the improvement of medication. Today we have equipment that offers detailed images of a space in the body, the assistance of robots to carry out an activity, prostheses that allow us to recover lost development and many other mechanical advances that fully introduce us to the 21st century (Bautista 2017).

Organizational Change Management Model

For García and Sánchez (2021), the most accurate definition of "organizational change" goes back to a vision with a tendency to transform the way an organization thinks and acts and to the respective alignment of human and physical resources, in such a way that so that the structure of this existing institution can be reorganized. Likewise, it can be pointed out that organizational change is a cluster of variations that easily translate into a new organizational behavior and greatly adds the level of quality to the service provided. This has the purpose of generating a positive impact on the organizational culture inside and outside the company (Reyes et al. 2021).

In various stages of our history, new scientific methods have been associated that seek to make business work more efficient, producing changes in the philosophy of the workforce. The adoption of new work technologies by employees is, on several occasions, difficult to achieve, generating in most cases great resistance to the changes proposed by those in charge of the areas of large, small and medium-sized organizations. Given this problem, a series of models have been generated that allow to face change management, and, thus, one of the most outstanding and that has obtained the best results, corresponds to the classic change management model called Model of the Three Lewin's steps (Martínez Bustos et al. 2018).

Kurt Lewin's Organizational Change Model

For Murillo and Bonilla (2020) this model of change can be seen as a modification of the forces that safeguard the behavior of a constant system. For this reason, said behavior most of the time is the consequence of the struggle between two types of forces, those that help to achieve the change and those that make it difficult for the change to be carried out. Lewin's model is composed of three stages: thawing, displacement and refreezing.

The first stage is one in which workers show uncertainty and resistance to change to maintain their status quo. The thawing of the current level of behavior serves to reduce prejudices and the creation of dispositions for change, in which individuals understand the need for it. It is essential to work with one of the two opposing forces, either by reducing the restraining forces or by increasing the driving forces to achieve basic transformations. In this stage, they work with a series of activities that range from a characterization of the problem to the typification and socialization of the agents of change (Martínez Bustos et al. 2018).

The second stage warns that such dangerous movement implies the process of moving from the comfort zone to the desired goal. The techniques used in this stage involve the review, readjustment and implementation of strategies within the institution. And in the final stage, the vision is harbored that the collaborators have internalized the change in a habitual way. The techniques within this stage consist of monitoring the change process (Murillo and Bonilla 2020) (Table 1).

Table 1. Advantages of Telehealth

Increases the admission of all degrees of care	Offers logical and mechanical help to experts
Move medical care to isolated regions	Work with the uninterrupted preparation of the experts
He works with the exhaustive consideration of the patient	Promote innovative work
Improves organizational measures by expanding the productivity of care	Increases the well-being of the population and encourages self-care

Note: National Telehealth Plan (2009). Ministry of Health of Peru (MINSA).

According to another perspective, in view of an exhaustive investigation of its Telehealth framework, carried out by the Undersecretariat of the Government of Chile, it has been feasible to affirm the various benefits of the uses of Telemedicine, both for health establishments and for patients in general (Table 2):

Objectives

Propose a theoretical Change Management Model for the quality of the Telehealth service in a Regional Hospital in Northern Peru. Likewise, within the specific objectives are considered i) to identify the perception of external and internal users about the quality of Telehealth service in a Regional Hospital in Northern Peru during the COVID-19 pandemic; ii) Build and validate the theoretical model of change management for the quality of the Telehealth service in a Regional Hospital in Northern Peru, based on Kurt Lewin's Organizational Change Model.

Table 2. Benefits of Telehealth for users and primary care physicians

Population	Benefits
Users	• Diagnosis and treatments done quickly • Decrease in the number of complementary exams • Comprehensive and quality care from the beginning • Avoid the inconvenience of transferring patients and relatives • Abbreviate monetary expenses
Primary care physicians	• Access to requests for consultations with specialists • Avoid displacement inconveniences • Improves the quality of examination images in order to diagnose • Improves the information transmission circuits between professionals • Transfer of knowledge and experiences

Note: Chilean Ministry of Health (2020). Telehealth. Ministry of Health - Undersecretariat of Assistance Networks - Assistance Network Management Division.

2 Method

The research entitled "Management model for the quality of the Telehealth service in a Regional Hospital of Northern Peru", was framed in the quantitative method (Sánchez 2015), which uses numerical data to analyze in a systematic, organized and structured way a particular problem. Likewise, it is a non-experimental and descriptive type of research, because it is in charge of knowing the characteristics of a study population, through its evaluation through valid and reliable instruments (Hernández 2018).

The sample size is defined as obtaining a figure from the universe of the population and allowed the study to be carried out, in direct relation to the objective of the research (Otzen and Manterola 2017). The sample of patients attended by the Telehealth service between the period 2020–2022 is 193. In addition, the sample of health professionals who attended through the Telehealth service between the period 2020–2022 is 109. In conclusion, 150 patients and 73 health professionals were evaluated, having in compliance with the inclusion and exclusion criteria.

3 Results

The results obtained regarding the variable "Telesalud" at the Hospital Regional de Lambayeque in internal users, indicate that, regarding the first dimension "Teleducation", 46.6% showed a low level, that is, that a little less than half of the professionals highlighted the learning process managed with the help of ICTs as deficient and which favors accessibility to professional training. These results do not correspond to the application of the Telehealth strategy that the Ministry of Health of Peru (MINSA) has been carrying out. Since this same institution points out in 2018 that, in order to potentiate medical care in health establishments in our country, access to a flexible and interactive education of professionals is needed, which includes the correct application of computer tools, whose purpose lies in contributing to the improvement of learning related to public health and

Table 3. Dimension levels Internal user

Dimension	Level	Internal user	
		N°	%
Tele-education	High	23	31.5
	Half	16	21.9
	Low	34	46.6
Telemedicine	High	25	34.2
	Half	32	43.8
	Low	16	21.9
Telecare	High	35	47.9
	Half	24	32.9
	Low	14	19.2

Table 4. Dimension levels External user

Dimension	Level	External user	
		N°	%
human interaction	High	35	47.9
	Half	24	32.9
	Low	14	19.2
Answer's capacity	High	19	12.7
	Half	74	49.3
	Low	57	38.0
Answer's capacity	High	16	10.7
	Half	69	46.0
	Low	65	43.3
Security	High	13	8.7
	Half	78	52.0
	Low	59	39.3

health administration. Therefore, many of these theoretical approaches have apparently not had a realistic impact on health establishments in our country (Tables 3 and 4).

Change Management Model

This model has been developed with the objective of increasing the quality of the Telehealth service provided to patients and implemented in the different clinical services, depending on their needs, offered by the Lambayeque Regional Hospital (HRL).

This is an instrument that will be available to the health authorities, responsible for the administration of Peruvian State resources, who can develop plans within a framework of cooperation and strengthening under the public management approach.

Importance

Quispe et al. (2019) point out that telehealth is the use of medical data that is shared from one place to another through electronic communication, thanks to ICTs, in order to raise the quality of health care. Likewise, telehealth is considered an excellent strategy to increase access to health services for the population living in remote places, improve the quality of care through the training of professionals who work in rural areas, and increase the efficiency of health services. Health services.

It is a latent reality that in Europe, America, Asia and Africa telehealth is part of an existing public policy, however, in all these territories there are still differences and obstacles to its implementation and development.

The purpose of this proposal is to design a theoretical model that, in the hospitals of our country, can be established and put an end to the deficiencies that have arisen during the development of the Telehealth service, such as a feeling of decreased social interaction between patients. And health personnel, risks of confidentiality of patient information, increased demand for specialists, loss of data and images due to the increase in the speed of the Internet signal and technological infrastructure not implemented to be able to develop Telehealth within a health system.

In Lewin's Three Steps model. Murillo and Bonilla (2020) refer that the change model can be seen as a modification of the forces that safeguard the behavior of a constant system. For this reason, said behavior most of the time is the consequence of the struggle between two types of forces, those that help to achieve the change and those that make it difficult for the change to be carried out.

Lewin's model is composed of three stages: thawing, displacement and refreezing. The first stage is one in which workers show uncertainty and resistance to change to maintain their status quo. The second stage warns that such dangerous movement implies the process of moving from the comfort zone to the desired goal. And in the final stage, the vision is harbored that the collaborators have internalized the change in a habitual way. The techniques within this stage consist of monitoring the change process (Martínez Bustos et al. 2018) (Fig. 1).

This research proposal is based on Kurt Lewin's three-step model, which includes a modification of the forces that safeguard the behavior of a constant system. Said behavior most of the time is the consequence of the struggle between two types of forces, those that help to achieve the change and those that make it difficult for the change to take place. Lewin's model is composed of three stages: thawing, displacement and refreezing (Murillo and Bonilla 2020).

The first stage is one in which workers show uncertainty and resistance to change to maintain their status quo. The thawing of the current level of behavior serves to reduce prejudices and the creation of dispositions for change, in which individuals understand the need for it. It is essential to work with one of the two opposing forces, either reducing the restraining forces or increasing the driving forces to achieve transformations. In this stage, they work with activities that range from a characterization of the problem to the typification and socialization of the agents of change (Martínez Bustos et al. 2018).

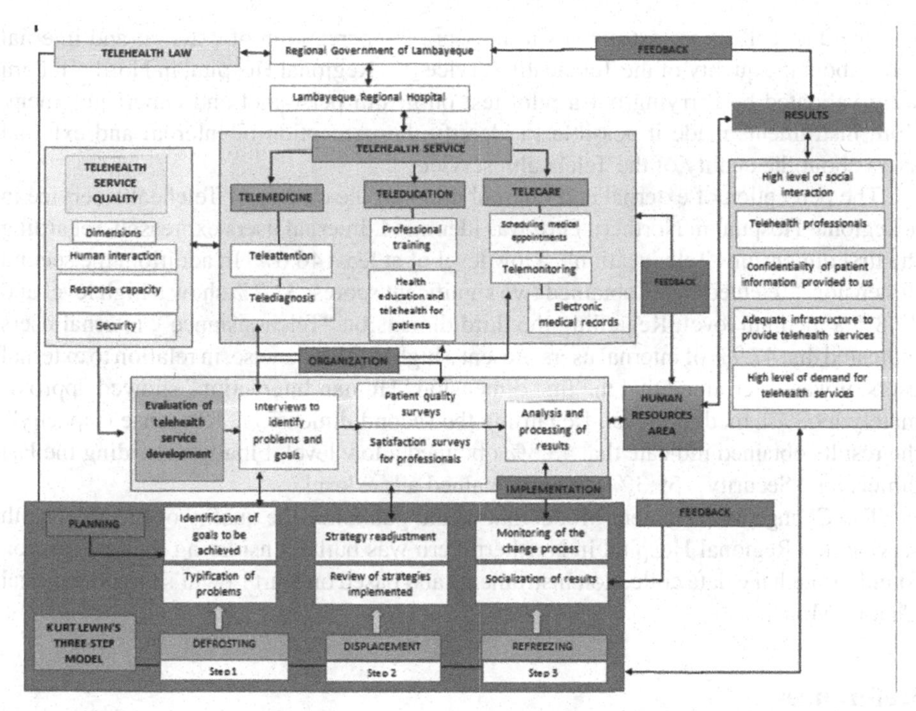

Fig. 1. Change Management Model for the quality of the Telehealth service in a Regional Hospital in Northern Peru

The second stage warns that such dangerous movement implies the process of moving from the comfort zone to the desired goal. The techniques used in this stage involve the review, readjustment and implementation of strategies. And in the final stage, the vision of the internalization of the change in the collaborators is housed. The techniques within this stage consist of monitoring the change process (Murillo and Bonilla 2020).

Within this proposal, the variables Telehealth and quality of service and their respective dimensions are contemplated. Both variables come together to improve the service. As a procedure for evaluating the development of the Telehealth service, at least 3 evaluations are contemplated in the year, taking into account the interviews with health professionals, specialists in Telehealth, the quality surveys addressed to the patients treated and the professionals of the health that carry out this service in a Regional Hospital of the North of Peru, with the objective of implementing continuous improvements in said institution.

4 Conclusions

The theoretical Model of Change Management that guarantees the quality of the Telehealth service in a Regional Hospital in Northern Peru, based on Kurt Lewin's model of organizational change, was validated. Likewise, the proposal was validated through expert judgment and it was considered appropriate and applicable to solve the problem proposed in this scientific investigation.

The data collection instruments to measure the perception of external and internal users about the quality of the Telehealth service in a Regional Hospital in Northern Peru were validated by carrying out a pilot test on health personnel and expert judgment. Both instruments made it possible to identify the perception of internal and external users about the quality of the Telehealth service.

The perception of external and internal users on the quality of Telehealth service in a Regional Hospital in Northern Peru was identified. Internal users expressed, regarding the first dimension "Teleducation", a low level of at least 46.6%; In addition, the second dimension "Telemedicine" obtained two significant scores: 34.2% show a high level and 43.8% a medium level; Regarding the third dimension "Teleassistance", internal users indicated that 47.9% of internal users present a high level. Likewise, in relation to external users, it was determined that the first dimension "Human Interaction" showed approximately 49.3% a medium level. Regarding the second dimension "Response Capacity", the results obtained indicate that 43.3% obtained a low level. Finally, regarding the last dimension "Security", 39.3% of them obtained a low level.

The Change Management Model that would guarantee the quality of the Telehealth service in a Regional Hospital in Northern Peru was built, considering the information found through the data collection instruments and based on Kurt Lewin's Organizational Change Model.

References

Arroyo, J.: Health today: problems and solutions. CENTRUM Pontifical Catholic University of Peru (PUCP) (2015). National Library of Peru

Baptist, C.: Telehealth in Peru. Diagnosis and Improvement Proposals. San Martin de Porres University (USMP). Government and Public Management Magazine (2017). http://www.revistagobiernoydegestionpublica.com/index.php/RGGP/article/view/10/18

Ciotti, M., et al.: COVID-19 outbreak: an overview. chemotherapy (2020). https://doi.org/10.1159/000507423

García-Magariño, S., Sánchez-Bayón, A.: Change and knowledge management in cooperative and social transformation organizations: comparative case studies. Int. J. Organ. **27**, 137–171 (2021). https://doi.org/10.17345/rio27.137-171

Hernández, R., Mendoza, C.: Investigation Methodology. Quantitative, Qualitative and Mixed Routes. Editorial Mc Graw Hill Education, Mexico (2018)

Martínez Bustos, E., Carrasco Sagredo, C., Bull, M.T.: Methodological proposal to implement the first phase of Lewin's organizational change management model. Manag. Stud., 88–98 (2018). https://doi.org/10.18046/j.estger.2018.146.2813

Ministry of Health: Ministerial Resolution 146, which approves the HIS registration of teleguidance and telemonitoring. Lima Peru (2020). http://www.saludarequipa.gob.pe/redislay/manuales_HIS/Registro_HIS_Telemonitoreo_Teleorientacion.pdf

Murillo, B., Marcela, C., Bonilla Morán, L.: Faculty of philosophy, letters and sciences of education career of organizational psychology topic: strategic planning through Kurt Lewin's model of change in the organizational structure of Viña San Joaquín SA Author, 223.180 (nd). http://201.159.223.180/bitstream/3317/15205/1/T-UCSG-PRE-FIL-CPO-277.pdf. Accessed 24 July 2022

Otzen, T., Manterola, C.: Sampling techniques on a population study. Int. J. Morphol., 227–232 (2017)

Quispe, C., Moquillaza, V., Arapa, K.: Telehealth in Latin America: a look at the studies registered in clinicaltrials.gov. J. Cuban Health Sci. Inf. (ACIMED) **30**(4), 1–12 (2019)
Reyes, M., Gomez, A., Ramos, E.: Desafíos de la gestión del talento humano en tiempos de pandemia covid 19. **13**(6), 232–236 (2021)
Sánchez Gómez, M.C.: The qualitative-quantitative dichotomy: integration possibilities and mixed designs. Open Field **1**(1), 11–30 (2015)
World Health Organization (WHO - OMS): Global Observatory for eHealth series Telemedicine – Opportunities and developments in Member States. WHO (2015). http://www.who.int/goe/publications/ehealth_series_vol2

A Systematic Review of Workplace Stress and Its Impact on Mental Health and Safety

Gabriella Maria Schr Torres(✉), Jessica Backstrom(✉), and Vincent G. Duffy

Purdue University, West Lafayette, IN 47906, USA
{gmtorres,jbackst,duffy}@purdue.edu

Abstract. Workplace stress and health are important subsets of the safety engineering field. Engineers need to maintain physical, emotional, and mental health to be productive and safe employees, which is beneficial to their employers through the reduction of accidents. Besides the human element, which may involve injury, death, or other lasting physical or mental consequences, accidents cost companies time, money, and valuable resources spent on extensive litigation. This paper focuses on mental health within the context of workplace stress since the globally felt adverse effects of the COVID-19 pandemic have brought high priority to research on identifying and combating mental health problems. While most mental health research focuses on healthcare professionals, our contribution is the extrapolation of this research to engineering. A systemic literature review was performed, which consisted of gathering data, using multiple bibliometric software, and providing discussion and conclusions drawn from the metadata. The software utilized for analysis included Vicinitas, Scopus, Google n-gram and Google Scholar, VOSviewer, Scite.ai, CiteSpace, BibExcel, Harzing, and MaxQDA. The original keywords included "workplace stress", "mental health", and "engineering," but our analysis revealed additional trending terms of mindfulness, nursing, and COVID-19. Our findings showed that workplace stress is experienced throughout multiple industries and causes significant harm to employees and their organizations. There are practical solutions to workplace stress studied in nursing and construction that can be applied to other fields that need intervention.

Keywords: Workplace stress · employee health · mental health · engineering · COVID-19 · healthcare

1 Introduction and Background

1.1 Workplace Stress and Safety

Workplace stress is the "human reaction to threatening situations at work or related to the workplace" (Goetsch 2019, 701). There is an important caveat; the perceived threats do not have to be real to cause stress, only believed to be potentially harmful. The presence of stress has many harmful effects on employees, including mental, physical, and emotional dimensions. Brauer (2016, 907-908) provided a table of identified stressors in the workplace, including tasks, equipment, and personal factors. The data highlights

Q. Gao et al. (Eds.): HCII 2023, LNCS 14055, pp. 610–627, 2023.
https://doi.org/10.1007/978-3-031-48041-6_41

the complex nature of workplace stress and health; one employee may experience a high degree of stress in a situation due to their unique set of home, work, and personal characteristics, while the same situation may not stress another employee. Moreover, these factors may influence each other in varying ways depending on the total simultaneous number of factors at a single point in time.

Regardless of the source, employee stress reduces work productivity and quality and increases the risk of accidents or near misses (Goetsch 2019). For example, shift work has been shown to cause disrupted circadian rhythms, which lead to poor sleep and exhaustion (Sallinen 2010, Goetsch 2019). Fatigue impairs alertness and decision-making abilities, which can cost lives, property, and capital when working with heavy machinery or dangerous materials. Thus, proactively addressing workplace stress is in companies' best interests (Goetsch 2019). While engineers, technicians, and manufacturing plant operators all undergo shift work, it is also a tenant of the medical industry (Goetsch 2019). This commonality serves as a bridge between medical workers and engineers, and we will examine research that can potentially transcend employment fields. By providing recommendations for improving engineers' and technicians' mental health, we hope to contribute to reduced workplace stress and improved safety culture.

1.2 Mental Health and COVID-19

Employees must be healthy to function in society and the economy. One category of workplace stress and health is mental health. Multiple work- and home-related factors can negatively impact workers' mental health, leading to increased risk during work (Brauer 2016). Individuals are prone to health problems and safety accidents, and companies risk losing money and resources through accidents. Since healthcare professionals estimate that 1 in every 20 employees is clinically depressed (Goetsch 2019), it is a significant problem in the American workforce. While some efforts to address mental health have occurred in past years, the COVID-19 pandemic has arguably had the worst effect on this field in the past decade (Moustafa 2021). Although it began to spread worldwide in 2020, COVID-19 is still impacting mental health three years later. Numerous studies have demonstrated a negative impact on workers' mental health. COVID-related stressors include physical isolation, job loss, and an unstable global economy (Moustafa 2021). Extensive research has been done on COVID- 19-induced stress in the healthcare industry since it was the front-line witness to the pandemic. However, thousands of other occupations were negatively affected by COVID-19, including engineering. Approaches to addressing mental health include yoga programs for teachers (Latino et al. 2021), mental health programs for nurses and healthcare professionals (Darling et al. 2013), and efforts to reduce stress for construction workers (Ayalp et al. 2023). However, there appears to be a gap in literature and research explicitly addressing mental health for engineers and other roles in technical industries, including the aftermath of the COVID-19 pandemic.

1.3 Justification and Purpose Statement

Justification. The workplace stress directly experienced by engineers, technicians, and operators is a significant safety risk (Goetsch 2019, Brauer 2016). While workplace stress and mental health struggles exist in many industries, it has historically been studied within the context of healthcare (NIOSH 2022). Thus, there is a need to extrapolate existing research into the engineering fields to promote physical, mental, and emotional safety in the workplace.

Purpose Statement. This systematic literature review will examine previous efforts to study workplace stress and present opportunities to translate the findings into safety and engineering. It will also link the research to current events by examining COVID- 19's effect. The methodology for the review will be addressed in the next section.

2 Procedure

2.1 Systematic Review Steps

The University of Maryland (2023) provided detailed steps to complete a systematic review:

(1) create a research question
(2) define the requirements for inclusion and exclusion
(3) search, select, and extract data from relevant studies
(4) evaluate and present results

This framework will guide our methodology in collecting, analyzing, and synthesizing the research surrounding workplace stress and mental health. A systematic review is "a high-level overview of primary research on a focused question, utilizing high-quality research evidence" (University of Maryland 2023).

Additionally, one can utilize the "10 research questions" presented in class. The questions relevant to this analysis that we used when reviewing potential papers were the following:

(1) What is the applicability and practical contribution of this study?
(2) What were the results of this study?
(3) What conclusions were drawn from this study?

We can pull relevant, valuable information through these questions in our systematic review process.

2.2 Topic Choice and Key Terms

Since mental health within the context of workplace stress and health was identified as the paper's focus, a brainstorming session was held to identify key terms to use when searching for relevant data. The key terms included workplace stress, mental health, and engineer. These words were used in multiple databases to yield consistent and relevant data. Workplace stress is the "human reaction to threatening situations at work or related to the workplace" (Goetsch 2019). Mental health is a state of mental well-being that enables people to cope with the stresses of life, realize their abilities, learn well and work well, and contribute to their community (WHO 2022). An engineer is a person who designs and builds complex products, machines, systems, or structures, using scientific knowledge for practical applications (Wasser 2022).

2.3 Research Questions

Following the University of Maryland's systematic review process, the first step is to create a list of research questions. These were formulated after initial reviews of the papers generated from the "workplace stress" keywords:

1. What are the causes and other contributing factors to workplace stress, and how do they differ across industries?
2. What are the results of workplace stress on productivity, employee well-being, and job satisfaction?
3. What methods have been studied and proven to reduce workplace stress?
4. What other considerations related to workplace stress may not be as well known?

2.4 Data Inclusion and Exclusion

Before we began data collection, we defined inclusion as (1) found through keyword search "workplace stress" and possibly "mental health," (2) must be studying a place of work anywhere in the world, (3) should include studies of effects as well as potential solutions, and (4) must contain clearly expressed data collection and analyses methodologies. The exclusions were papers that had narrowed their scope further than overall workplace stress as the issue and existing systematic reviews since we wanted to collect original research.

2.5 Data Collection

Multiple Purdue University Library system databases were searched for relevant articles and information. Table 1 summarizes the databases searched, the terms used, and the number of papers yielded.

Table 1. Data Collection for Workplace Stress and Mental Health Research.

Databases	Keywords	# of Papers
SCOPUS (1/3)	Workplace stress, mental health	280
SCOPUS (2/3)	Occupational stress, engineer	38
SCOPUS (3/3)	Job stress, engineer	53
Web of Science	Workplace stress, mental health	500
Harzing	Workplace stress, mental health	1000
Scite.ai	Workplace stress	4798

Once the articles were gathered from the three SCOPUS searches, the duplicates were removed. Next, each article's abstract was reviewed to determine the degree of relevancy to the topic of mental health or workplace stress and the rigor of the research. A final list of 120 SCOPUS articles was compiled for analysis. Web of Science was also used to collect data. The top 500 most relevant articles were used after a search for workplace stress and mental health yielded 3,300 results. Similarly, searches from Harzing produced downloadable lists of pertinent articles for use in bibliometric analysis software, and Scite.ai provided insight into research trends.

2.6 Data Analysis

The data collected in the previous step was analyzed using multiple software, including Vicinitas and Twitter, SCOPUS, Google N-Gram and Scholar, Scite.ai, VOSviewer, CiteSpace, BibExcel, Harzing, and MaxQDA. Each tool generated unique insights into the research by producing different metadata. The initial results of the literature searches and associated trends and diagrams are presented in Sect. 3. An in-depth discussion of the implications of the results, future work, and overall conclusions are presented in Sects. 4, 5, and 6.

3 Results

3.1 Vicinitas Search

Vicinitas was used to identify trending posts on Twitter, a social media platform. One of the authors logged in with their Twitter account to use it. Next, they searched for the hashtag #workplacestress and generated data showing a word cloud of related tweets, related trending tweets, and the timeline of the posts and engagement.

The Vicinitas.io images in Figs. 1 and 2 were created in April 2023. The results showed 59 posts with the hashtag #workplacestress, with an overall influence of 262.4k people. Engagement seemed to be steadily increasing since the beginning of the month. Other related hashtags included #stressawarenessmonth, #stressatwork, #mentalhealth, and #workplaceculture.

Fig. 1. Hashtag cloud and trending hashtags in relation to "Workplace Stress" from Vincinitas.io search.

The word cloud generated from these tweets mentions other terms past the keywords, such as burnout, employees, and tips. This indicates that those engaging in the discussion asked and provided helpful advice from their experiences.

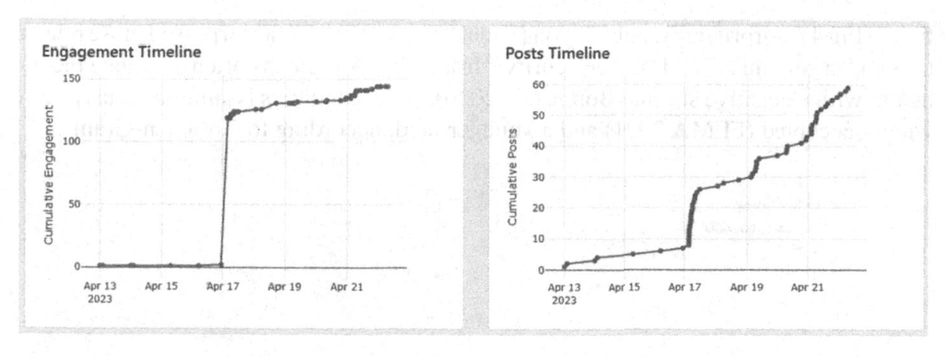

Fig. 2. Engagement and Posts Timeline from Vincinitas.io search.

3.2 SCOPUS Trends

SCOPUS was used to determine the age of the trending research about workplace stress and mental health. Using the most recent publications from 2020 and onwards, a word cloud was created using the wordcloud.com website to reveal critical terms. The trend from our SCOPUS database search for "workplace stress" and "mental health" is displayed in Fig 3. The number of published articles increased significantly in the early 2000s, and the rate surged around 2017. The trend peaked from 2020-2022, corresponding with the spread of COVID-19 in America and worldwide. Since this paper was written in 2023, the number of articles published could exceed the past few years' works if the high publication rate is maintained for the remainder of the year.

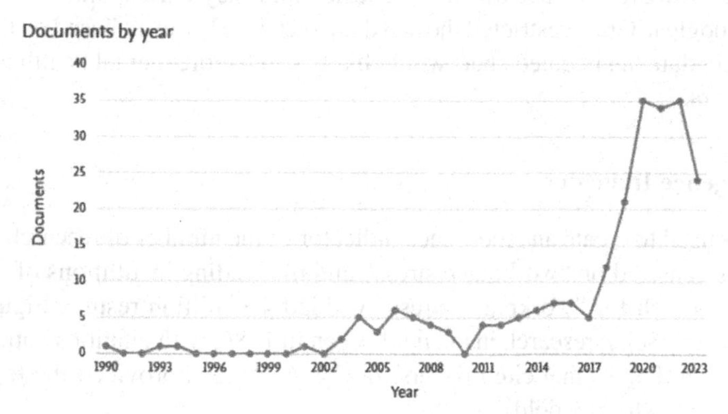

Fig. 3. The image of the graph shows the number of publications pulled from a SCOPUS search of "workplace stress".

3.3 Google n-Gram

This tool compared the research on workplace stress and mental health to other fields. A diagram was generated to identify the research published from 1900 to 2019 in three fields (Fig 4). Surprisingly, publications about "mental health" far surpassed those related to both "ergonomics" and "cybersecurity." Ironically, Americans often associate mental health with a negative stigma (Borenstein 2020), yet ergonomics is simultaneously more widely accepted (FEMA 2021) and a younger field, according to Google n-Gram.

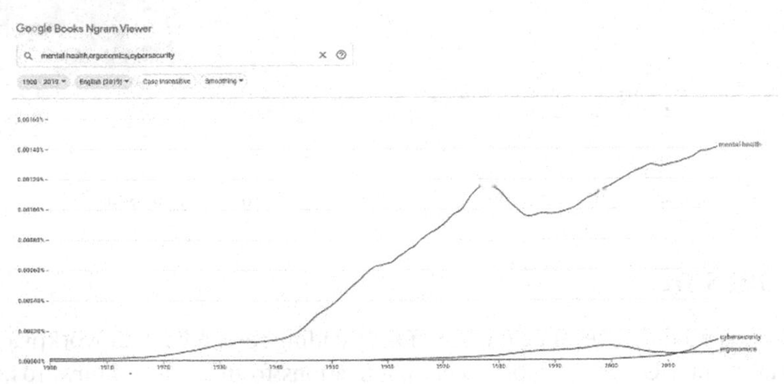

Fig. 4. A graph from Google n-Gram compares the keywords "mental health," "ergonomics," and "cybersecurity".

The mental health peak of 1978 may be closely related to President John F. Kennedy's push for mental health studies in 1963 through the Community Mental Health Act (CMHA) (Bell 2022). The legislation encouraged community-based mental health facilities and even led to the 1980 Mental Health Systems Act by President Jimmy Carter (Bell 2022). However, the act was later repealed and may correspond to the decline in research. Google n-Gram restricted the end date to 2019. However, based on the Vicinitas and SCOPUS data, an updated chart would likely show more mental health publications in recent years.

3.4 Emergence Indicator

Scite.ai was used to create an emergence indicator of the number of research citations of publications centered on "workplace stress" and the leading institutions of publication. The Scite.ai search for "workplace stress" yielded 4.3 million results. Figure 5 shows that according to Scite, research in the field began in 1986, with citations both supporting and contrasting the original cited papers. In Fig. 6, Scite.ai provided the top identified research locations for the field.

While most locations in Fig. 8 were in the United States, a center in France and an institution in the United Kingdom were also listed, showing that workplace stress is a topic of global importance.

Web of Science generated a TreeMap chart of the top 15 funding agencies within search results for workplace stress and mental health. As shown in Fig. 7, the USA led the research funding.

According to our data, research in this space started in the year 1896 and has continued until 2021.

Below, you can see the distribution of citation statements from these publications, with a breakdown of what percent of them support, mention, or contrast claims made by papers they reference.

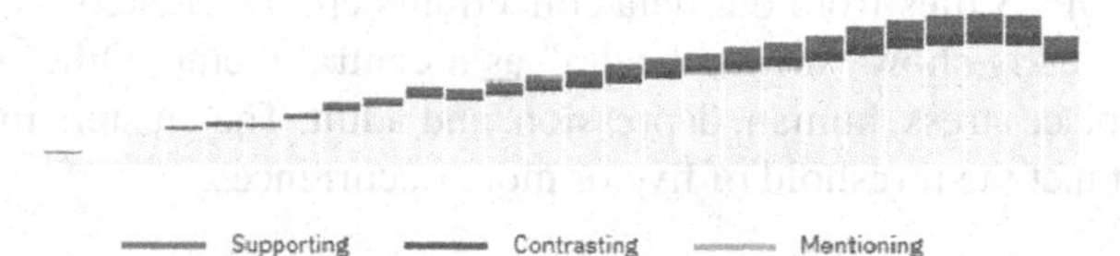

Fig. 5. Scite.ai search analysis of papers pertaining to keywords "workplace stress".

The institutions with the most supported papers in this area.

Institution	Publication Count
Harvard University	10,247
Max Planck Society	6,478
National Institutes Of Health	6,167
French National Centre For Scientific	5,868
University Of Michigan Ann Arbor	4,939
Stanford University	4,451
University Of Washington	4,389
University Of California Los Angeles	4,258
University Of Cambridge	4,232
University Of Pennsylvania	3,925

Fig. 6. Scite.ai top "Workplace Stress" research institutions with the most supported papers.

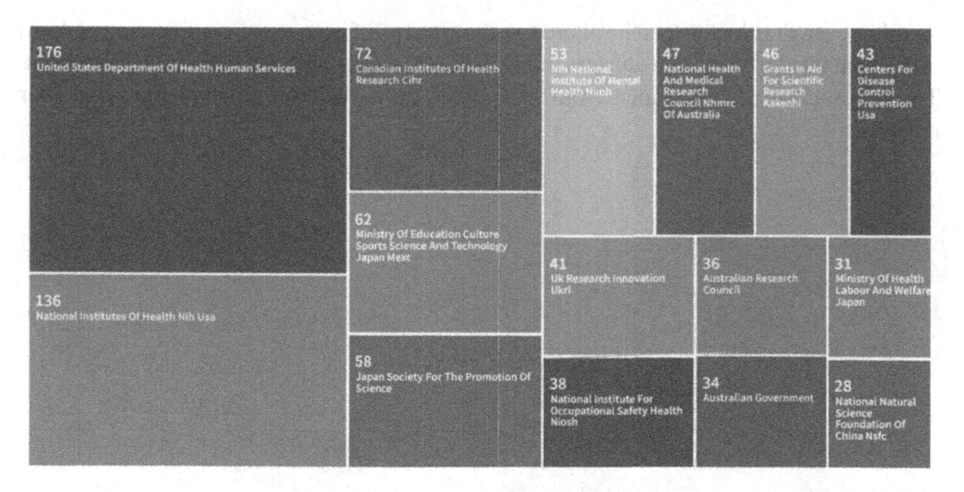

Fig. 7. Web of Science TreeMap Chart of Top 15 Funding Agencies. Search terms: work-place stress, mental health.

3.5 VOSviewer Cluster and Co-Citation

Google Scholar was used in conjunction with VOSviewer to collect research related to workplace stress and analyze the main themes within the text. Co-citation was also performed to show the network of citations among the primary authors and papers. VOSviewer is a powerful tool because it creates clusters of themes in a given dataset. Using the SCOPUS files from our data collection step, the clusters in Fig. 8 were generated. They clearly show "mental health" as a central theme. Other significant terms include workplace stress, human, depression, and adult. The clusters in Fig. 9 consist of 70 words that met the threshold of five or more occurrences.

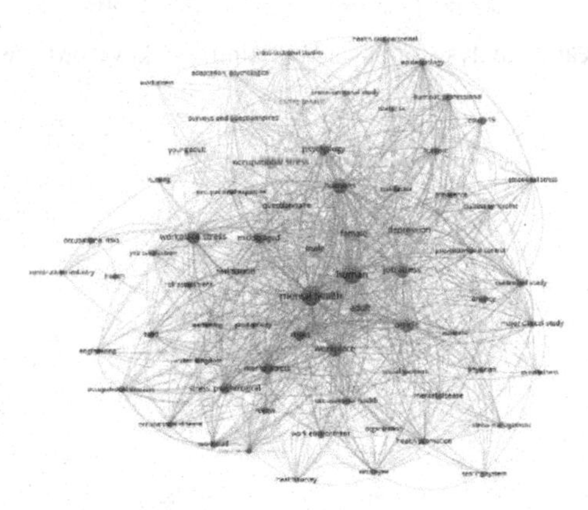

Fig. 8. VOSviewer Cluster showing 70 words that met the threshold of 5 or more occurrences from the SCOPUS database.

However, the clusters can be altered to show terms of even more significance and add additional information. The clusters in Fig. 9 are 30 words with ten or more occurrences. The yellow clusters show papers from 2020-2023; the darker blue clusters represent older research.

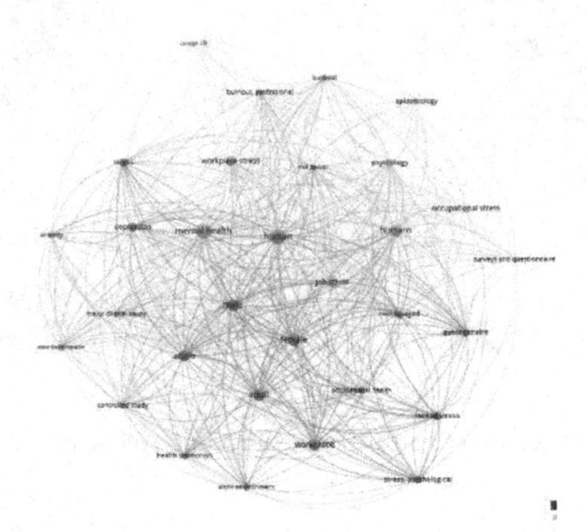

Fig. 9. Refined VOSviewer Clusters showing edited 30 words had 10+ occurrences. Yellow shows 2020+, and the darker blue signifies older papers. (Color figure oniline)

Another helpful feature of VOSviewer is the ability to generate co-citation networks, which show how papers and research relate to each other regarding citation and age. The image in Fig. 10 shows the top authors of the SCOPUS data and how their work relates to each other.

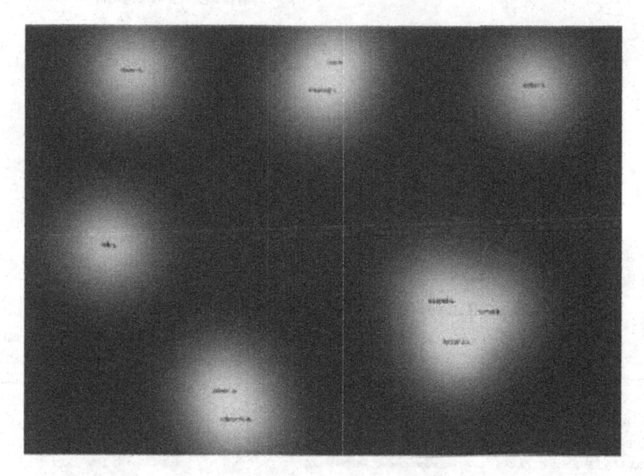

Fig. 10. Vosviewer Co-citation Clusters with the most influential authors.

Six primary clusters were identified, with 1-3 main research articles within each cluster. This tool helps narrow the research articles of interest from the more extensive SCOPUS data set (124 articles).

3.6 CiteSpace Clusters and Citation Burst

CiteSpace is a tool similar to VOSviewer but advantageous in naming clusters after forming them. After creating a dataset using Web of Science and "workplace stress" as a search term, the top 500 relevant articles were downloaded. Citespace then created the clusters illustrated in Fig. 11.

The Citation Burst function highlighted the top seven articles in the dataset with the most robust citations and visually showed when the research was the most cited. This information makes it possible to determine when the articles were considered relevant (Fig. 12).

While the first article's burst was eight years old, the remaining articles were especially cited in the past four years or less. The study of workplace stress is crucial in both academic and practical contexts because it offers insights into its causes, effects, and valuable solutions. Additionally, research on workplace stress is a dynamic and developing field with new difficulties and trends arising in response to shifts in the nature of work, such as the expansion of remote work and the COVID-19 pandemic's effects. The CiteSpace Clusters clearly show that COVID-19, technostress, workplace intervention and violence, and professional development are trending topics among recently published research.

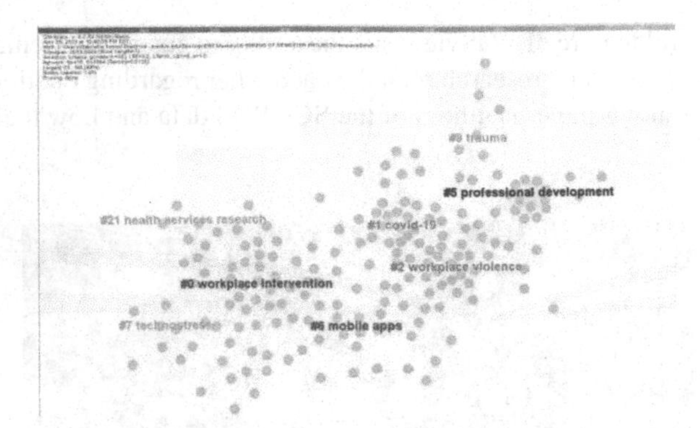

Fig. 11. CiteSpace Clusters for Web of Science dataset.

Top 7 References with the Strongest Citation Bursts

References	Year	Strength	Begin	End	2013 - 2023
Nielsen MB, 2012, WORK STRESS, V26, P309, DOI 10.1080/02678373.2012.734709, DOI	2012	3.18	**2014**	2015	
LaMontagne AD, 2014, BMC PSYCHIATRY, V14, P0, DOI 10.1186/1471-244X-14-131, DOI	2014	3.54	**2016**	2019	
Joyce S, 2016, PSYCHOL MED, V46, P683, DOI 10.1017/S0033291715002408, DOI	2016	4.32	**2018**	2019	
Theorell T, 2015, BMC PUBLIC HEALTH, V15, P0, DOI 10.1186/s12889-015-1954-4, DOI	2015	3.24	**2018**	2020	
Itzhaki M, 2015, INT J MENT HEALTH NU, V24, P403, DOI 10.1111/inm.12151, DOI	2015	2.83	**2018**	2020	
Lai JB, 2020, JAMA NETW OPEN, V3, P0, DOI 10.1001/jamanetworkopen.2020.3976, DOI	2020	3.02	**2020**	2023	
Pappa S, 2020, BRAIN BEHAV IMMUN, V88, P901, DOI 10.1016/j.bbi.2020.05.026, 10.1016/j.bbi.2020.11.023, DOI	2020	2.69	**2021**	2023	

Fig. 12. CiteSpace citation burst.

3.7 BibExcel, Harzing, Pivot Charts of Leading Authors and Sources

The Harzing software was used to collect data, which was then analyzed with the BibExcel tool to search leading authors and sources in research related to workplace stress and mental health. The output of BibExcel was imported into Excel to generate pivot charts and graphs representing the leading authors in the space (Fig. 13) and the leading sources (Fig. 14). The top 4 sources of the leading sources graph are only medical or nursing field journals. This supports the idea that the nursing and medical industry have had much support in workplace stress, but other industries that may need an intervention just as much do not have the support in terms of research.

3.8 MaxQDA Word Cloud, Lexical Search, and Word Table

A selection of articles was chosen from the SCOPUS database and imported into MaxQDA in order to create a detailed word cloud with higher editing capabilities than the previous software. MaxQDA also offers a lexical search option and a table of the top reoccurring phrases in the group of articles. Using a database of 16 articles gleaned from the final SCOPUS list, the word cloud in Fig. 9 was generated with MaxQDA. The top terms were "stress," "work," and "covid," emphasizing the impact of the pandemic on workplace stress. "Physicians" and "medical" were also leading terms, supporting the conclusion that much of the research on workplace stress and mental health has been performed in the context of the healthcare industry (Fig. 15).

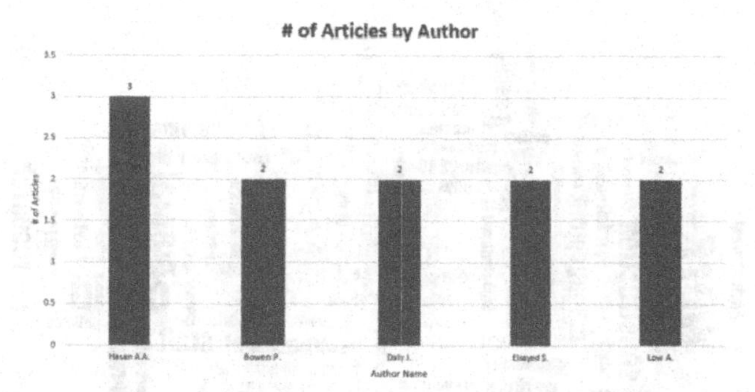

Fig. 13. Leading authors from Harzing database of keyword search "workplace stress". Hasan A.A. has the most papers at three, while four other authors have two papers each.

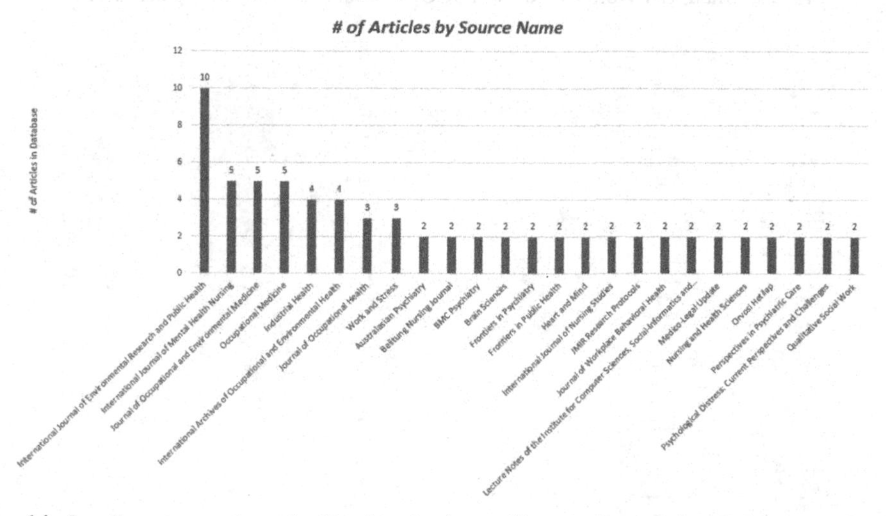

Fig. 14. Leading sources from the Harzing database of keyword search "workplace stress". The top 4 sources representing 25 papers are all from medical or nursing journals.

Since COVID-19 was identified as a key term within recent mental health research, it was entered into the MaxQDA word cloud. Figure 16 shows the search and the complete word table corresponding to the word cloud.

4 Discussion

4.1 Mindfulness Programs

One of the practices shown to reduce workplace stress and provide other employees with mental health support was through mindfulness programs. Mindfulness is described as thoughtful awareness, observation, and typically meditative-like state (Bartlett et al. 2017). Through these studies quantifying the effect of Mindfulness, the programs tested lasted from 5 to 8 weeks long and included body scans, meditation exercises, and group

Fig. 15. MaxQDA Word Cloud from SCOPUS database for "workplace stress".

Word	Word length	Frequency	%	Rank	Documents	Documents %
stress	6	[illegible]	1.68	1	16	100.00
work	4	743	1.41	2	16	100.00
covid	5	[illegible]	1.07	3	9	56.25
mental	6	[illegible]	0.74	4	15	93.75
job	3	310	0.59	5	13	81.25
construction	12	296	0.56	6	5	31.25
research	8	268	0.51	7	15	93.75
staff	5	264	0.50	8	9	56.25
support	7	261	0.50	9	15	93.75
workplace	9	241	0.46	10	16	100.00
management	10	232	0.44	11	13	81.25
pandemic	8	207	0.39	12	9	56.25
occupational	12	194	0.37	13	13	81.25
care	4	190	0.36	14	12	75.00
stressors	9	189	0.36	14	11	68.75
turnover	8	186	0.36	16	6	37.50
resilience	10	187	0.36	17	9	56.25
social	6	172	0.33	18	14	87.50
university	10	165	0.31	19	15	93.75
healthcare	10	162	0.31	20	8	50.00
policy	6	162	0.31	20	9	56.25
burnout	7	161	0.31	22	10	62.50
symptoms	8	157	0.30	23	10	62.50
significant	11	153	0.29	24	13	81.25
working	7	152	0.29	25	15	93.75
personal	8	151	0.29	26	14	87.50
psychological	13	147	0.28	27	13	81.25
students	8	146	0.28	28	6	37.50
employees	9	142	0.27	29	12	75.00
interventions	13	138	0.26	30	10	62.50
model	5	133	0.25	31	14	87.50
professionals	13	[illegible]	[illegible]	32	10	62.50
life	4	127	0.24	33	12	75.00
group	5	125	0.24	34	11	68.75
balance	7	124	0.24	35	6	37.50
satisfaction	12	124	0.24	35	7	43.75
workforce	9	122	0.23	37	9	56.25
[illegible]	[illegible]	[illegible]	[illegible]	[illegible]	[illegible]	[illegible]

Fig. 16. MaxQDA lexical search and word table

counseling or general group work. Most studies of mindfulness programs are in person through coaching with some homework. However, online mindfulness programs were analyzed as well. This program (WSM) functions like a traditional program with online interactive activities with auditory prompts, email reminders, and meditation walk-throughs (Allexandre et al. 2016). Overall, the mindfulness programs studied from 2016 – 2018 were effective in reducing perceived stress, psychological distress, and burnout and increasing general employee well-being.

Beyond those standard measured effects, in some cases, these programs could effectively improve other essential elements of worker health, such as attention, productivity, stress, emotional regulation, and relationship improvement (Bartlett et al. 2017). These sorts of programs require a high level of participation and dedication to the tasks. Some struggles that companies wanting to implement something like this could be finding enough interest (through management and employees) as well as physical limitations such as quiet spots to meditate (Bartlett et al. 2017). However, the study of the online mindfulness program proved to be just as effective as other similar programs. In-person programs may be costly and time-consuming to productivity for most employers, but an online format may be just as effective as well as meet other company wide objectives (Allexandre et al. 2016). Sustaining these mindfulness practices was greater than 50%, and improvements were witnessed even beyond the timeline of the study. A study of workers compensation for stress shows strategies such as employee education, early intervention meditation services and more work to reduce the risk of individual dysfunction and workplace stress (Larsen 1995).

Overall, mindfulness programs are shown to be effective in reducing perceived employee workplace stress as well as providing other benefits. Companies can consider implementing similar in-person or at-home-based programs to improve their employees' mental well-being.

4.2 COVID and Its Effects on Workplace Stress

COVID, over the past five years, has played a significant role in workplace stress through many examples. In Hong Kong, nurses reported various wellness ailments such as chronic past-year illness, poor self-perceived mental health, anxiety and stress, depression and divorce, widowhood and separation, job dissatisfaction, disturbance with colleagues, low physical activity levels and sleep problems (Cheung, Yip 2015). In one study, COVID brought unprecedented challenges to nurses in Hong Kong. The study conducted via telephone with these nurses revealed four main themes: intense fear, worry, and anxiety; feeling worn out and psychologically distressed; impact on psychosocial and physical health; and limited options to cope with psychological distress during difficult times (Cheung, Ho, et al. 2022). Another study conducted in three non-acute-care facilities in St. Louis, Missouri, between April and May 2021 found that many healthcare professionals reported increased job stress due to COVID. Specifically, these challenges were communication through wearing a mask or face shield and additional responsibilities due to staff shortages, all leading to a significant proportion of participants considering quitting their job (Mansoor, McDonald, et al. 2023).

It is well-documented that large-scale natural disasters and pandemics are associated with significant increases in mental health disorders among healthcare providers. In one study, however, early interventions, both individual and system-based, were able to potentially mitigate the mental health impact on providers (Restauri 2020). The weight of the COVID pandemic was felt across the world through more than just the healthcare industry as well. This is an important factor to take into consideration on this topic of workplace stress over the past few years.

4.3 The Link Between Healthcare and Engineering Industries

Within the engineering industry setting, workplace stress and mental health often fall under the responsibility of multiple company organizations. While Goetsch (2019, p.250-251) suggests some measures to reduce workplace stress, such as including Mental Health and Employee Assistance Program (EAP) benefits in employees' health insurance, creating formal employee-manager communication programs, and encouraging open communication about workplace stress, such efforts are often dispersed throughout companies' Human Resource and Safety departments. In addition, workplace stress is highly dependent on individual managers' leadership and communication styles (Goetsch 2019). A need still exists for a centralized, prioritized effort to address workplace stress and mental health.

Other industries beyond the medical field were also studied and proved to have sources of workplace stressors. One study shows the negative impact of workplace stress on safety performances in the construction industry. Organizational stressors were found to be the main contributor to physical stress, behavioral stress, and job burnout among these construction professionals. It continues to emphasize the need for effective stress management strategies to improve construction personnel's overall well-being and safety (Enshassi, El-Rayyes, et al. 2015).

Engineering fields across different industries also experience workplace stress and are shown to require intervention. A study in Taiwan found that high demands, low work social support, high effort/reward ratio, and low frequency of physical exercise were consistent risk factors for depressive disorders in microelectronics engineers and that depressive disorders were associated with impaired work performance (Chen, Wang, et al. 2011). Another study of 249 male engineers found that higher levels of internal personal control and job involvement were associated with lower stress levels and higher job satisfaction, while Type A behavior was associated with higher stress levels but also with higher job satisfaction (Saleh, Desai, et al. 1990).

Lastly, this study highlights the importance of understanding the factors that impact the mid-career satisfaction of professional women. The results suggest that stress and job-related factors are the most powerful determinants. Organizations can address these issues by providing more transparency, exciting work, flexible schedules, and support for stress management (Auster, Ekstein 2005).

5 Future Work

The National Science Foundation (NSF) website reports over 2,600 active awards related to the search term "workplace stress." This section will present two awards of particular interest and relevance to the systematic literature review.

5.1 Workplace Stress and Multimodal Models

The first award described is an August 2022 award of $1.1MM to research new patterns and pathways of workplace stress using multimodal models under the NSF's Smart and Connected Health category. The work originates from the University of Southern California and ends in 2026. The principal investigator for the research is Dr. Shawn Roll, who is the Director of the Ph.D. in Occupational Science Program and an Associate Professor. Although "stress" often carries a negative connotation, Dr. Roll and his colleagues seek to reduce *distress* and maximize *eustress*, which has positive, energetic benefits (NSF 2022). The project will create new multimodal models to track the patterns of workplace stress in order to understand the major contributing factors. It will also serve as a base for new sensing systems in "smart workplaces" that can automate environmental changes or provide behavioral responses (NSF 2022). The work is multidisciplinary and will contribute to awareness of workplace stress and the reduction of worker health and wellness problems.

As of April 2023, one publication has already been released: "Ten Questions concerning the impact of environmental stress on office workers", which was authored by Mohamad Awanda, Burcin Becerik-Gerber, Ruying Liu, Mirmahdi Seyedrezaei, Zheng Lu, Matheos Xenakis, Gale Lucas, and Shawn Roll. The article was published in a 2023 issue of *Building and Environment*. The project appears to be successful and fast-paced, and future research will greatly contribute to the field.

5.2 Workplace Stress Reduction

This $400,000 award is from June 2017 (amended in June 2022) to review and research reliable methods for reducing workplace stress and is expected to end in July 2023. The principal investigator is Dr. Ricardo Gutierrez-Osuna, a professor of Computer Science and Engineering associated with the Texas A&M Engineering Experiment Station (TEES). The work is vital for the future and longevity of our workforce and overall human experience. Most industries do not have reliable programs specific to stress and mental health or societies focusing on productivity and hard work over these underlying health issues (NSF 2017). Through investigation of effective methods, this award could give good movement into the space of program implementations across industries. The main focus of the research involves using experimental, human-computer methods to detect stress cues while workers perform routine cognitive tasks such as emailing. A novel framework was also developed to administer stress-reduction exercises using mobile apps that incorporate biofeedback, games, and music (NSF 2017).

As of April 2023, six publications were released under the NSF award. The articles date back to 2019 and include conferences and journals such as the 2019 CHI Conference on Human Factors in Computing Systems, the IEEE Transactions of Affective Computing, and Frontiers in Digital Health. While the award is ending shortly, the impacts of the research and publications will likely continue to spread throughout the scientific community.

6 Conclusion

Workplace stress and mental health are important to industrial engineering because they are related to productivity and the overall improvement of human processes. By considering critical factors in workplace success and providing potential areas of improvement, there are tangible benefits that many companies and individuals can gain. The systematic literature review on workplace stress and mental health led to several significant conclusions. The first was that workplace stress has been extensively researched in the medical field, but it is also a prevalent issue in engineering. Promoting mental health is crucial to reducing workplace stress in all fields, and by studying mental health research in other fields, we can translate the findings to improve mental health in engineering. Reducing workplace stress in engineering can improve safety and decrease risks, making it a priority for the well-being of workers and the industry's success.

To better respond to workplace stress, employers must embrace programs that have proven effective in other industries like healthcare. While engineers have historically focused primarily on the technical aspects of their work, there is a need for change. Engineering education and professional development rarely include curricula related to health and wellness and its intersections with professional work. Implementing these programs takes time, money, and culture shifts from all levels of management to be effective, so solutions should be recommended by the workforce and embraced by higher management. A chain reaction will take place by first addressing mental health, thus reducing workplace stress and increasing engineering safety and productivity.

References

Goetsch, D.: Chapter 11: stress and safety. In: Occupational Safety and Health for Technologists, Engineers, and Managers, Ninth, pp. 243–55. New York, Pearson (2019)

Brauer, R.: Section 31–6: job stress and other stresses in chapter 31: human behavior and performance in safety. In: Safety and Health for Engineers, Third, pp. 921–24. Hoboken, NJ: Wiley (2016)

Sallinen, M., Kecklund, G.: Shift work, sleep, and sleepiness differences betwen shift schedules and systems. Scandanavian J. Work, Environ. Health **36**(2), 121–133 (2010)

Moustafa, A.: Mental Health Effects of COVID-19. Elsevier, London (2021)

Latino, F., Cataldi, S., Fischetti, F.: Effects of an 8-week yoga-based physical exercise intervention on teachers' burnout. Sustain. (Switzerland) **13**(4), 1–16 (2021). https://doi.org/10.3390/su13042104

Darling, E.L., et al.: A mixed-method study exploring barriers and facilitators to midwives' mental health in ontario. BMC Women's Health **23** (155) (2013). https://doi.org/10.1186/s12905-023-02309-z

Ayalp, G.G., Serter, M., Metinal, Y.B., Tel, M.Z.: Well-being of construction professionals: modelling the root factors of job-related burnout among civil engineers at contracting organisations. In: Advances in Sociology Research, vol. 40, pp. 1–38 (2023)

National Institute for Occupational Safety and Health (NIOSH). 2022. Healthcare Workers: Work Stress & Mental Health. Centers for Disease Control and Prevention. 1 Dec 2022. https://www.cdc.gov/niosh/topics/healthcare/workstress.html

University of Maryland. 2023. Systematic Review. University Libraries. 12 April 2023. https://lib.guides.umd.edu/SR/welcome

World Health Organization (WHO). 2022. "Mental Health." WHO Newsroom. 17 June 2022. https://www.who.int/news-room/fact-sheets/detail/mental-health-strengthening-ourresponse

Wasser, J.: NASA for Kids: Intro to Engineering. National Geographic. 27 Sept 2022. https://education.nationalgeographic.org/resource/nasa-kids-intro-engineering/

Borenstein, J.: 2020. Stigma, Prejudice, and Discrimination Against People with Mental Illnesses. American Psychiatric Association. Aug 2020. https://www.psychiatry.org/patients-families/stigma-and-discrimination

Federal Emergency Management Agency (FEMA). 2021. A Brief History of the Origin of Ergonomics and Human Factors. Emergency Services Ergonomics and Wellness. 8 Feb 2021. https://www.usfa.fema.gov/a-z/health-safety-wellness/ergonomics/ch1-origin-ergonomics-human-factors.html

Bell, K.: "The Mental Health Systems Act of 1980." Documents to the People. 2022. https://journals.ala.org/index.php/dttp/article/view/7933/11034

Bartlett, L., Lovell, P., Otahal, P., Sanderson, K.: Acceptability, feasibility, and efficacy of a workplace mindfulness program for public sector employees: a pilot randomized controlled trial with informant reports. Mindfulness **8**(3), 639–654 (2017). https://doi.org/10.1007/s12671-016-0643-4

Allexandre, D., Bernstein, A.M., Walker, E., Hunter, J., Roizen, M.F., Morledge, T.J.: A webbased mindfulness stress management program in a corporate call center. J. Occup. Environ. Med.up. Environ. Med. **58**(3), 254–264 (2016). https://doi.org/10.1097/JOM.0000000000000680

Larsen, R.C.: Workers' compensation stress claims: Workplace causes and prevention. Psychiatr. Ann. **25**, 234–237 (1995). https://doi.org/10.3928/0048-5713-19950401-10

Cheung, T., Yip, P.S.F.: Depression, anxiety and symptoms of stress among Hong Kong nurses: a cross-sectional study. Int. J. Environ. Res. Public Health (2015). https://doi.org/10.3390/ijerph120911072

Cheung A.T., Ho, L.L.K., Li, W.H.C., Chung, J.O.K., Smith G.D.: Psychological distress experienced by nurses amid the fifth wave of the COVID-19 pandemic in Hong Kong: a qualitative study, Front. Public Health **10**, 1023302 (2023). https://doi.org/10.3389/fpubh.2022.1023302

Mansoor, A.E.R., O'Neil, C.A., McDonald, D., Fraser, V.J., Babcock, H.M., Kwon, J.H.: Knowledge, beliefs, and practices related to coronavirus disease 2019 (COVID-19) infection and vaccination in healthcare personnel working at nonacute care facilities. Infect. Control Hosp. Epidemiol. **44**(10), 1657–1662 (2023). https://doi.org/10.1017/ice.2023.45

Restauri, N., Sheridan, A.D.: Burnout and posttraumatic stress disorder in the Coronavirus disease 2019 (COVID-19) pandemic: intersection, impact, and interventions. J. Am. Coll. Radiol. **17**(7), 921–926 (2020). https://doi.org/10.1016/j.jacr.2020.05.021

Enshassi, A., El-Rayyes, Y., Alkilani, S.: Job stress, job burnout and safety performance in the palestinian construction industry. J. Financ. Manag. Prop. Constr. **20**(2), 170–187 (2015). https://doi.org/10.1108/JFMPC-01-2015-0004

Chen, S.W., Wang, P.C., Hsin, P.L., Oates, A., Sun, I.W., Liu, S.I.: Job stress models, depressive disorders and work performance of engineers in microelectronics industry. Int. Arch. Occup. Environ. Healthnt. Arch. Occup. Environ. Health **84**(1), 91–103 (2011). https://doi.org/10.1007/s00420-010-0538-y

Saleh, S.D., Desai, K.: An empirical analysis of job stress and job satisfaction of engineers. J. Eng. Tech. Manage. **7**(1), 37–48 (1990). https://doi.org/10.1016/0923-4748(90)90024-2

Auster, E.R., Ekstein, K.L.: Professional women's mid-career satisfaction: An empirical exploration of female engineers. Women Manag. Rev. **20**(1), 4–23 (2005). https://doi.org/10.1108/09649420510579540

National Science Foundation. SCH: Detecting and mapping stress patterns across space and time: Multimodal modeling of individuals in real-world physical and social work environments. Award Number 2204942, 22 Aug 2022

National Science Foundation. CHS: Medium: collaborative research: managing stress in the workplace: Unobtrusive Monitoring and Adaptive Interventions. Award Number 1704636, 21 June 2017

A Review on the Effects of Chanting and Solfeggio Frequencies on Well-Being

Xuyu Yang, Fiona Fui-Hoon Nah(✉), and Fen Lin

City University of Hong Kong, Kowloon, Hong Kong SAR, China
xuyuyang2-c@my.cityu.edu.hk, {fiona.nah,fenlin}@cityu.edu.hk

Abstract. This paper presents our literature review on how chanting and solfeggio frequencies affect brain activity, enhance well-being, and inform the design of sound therapy. We call for more scientific research to investigate and better understand the effects of chanting and solfeggio frequencies on well-being.

Keywords: Chanting · Solfeggio Frequencies · Brain Science · Well-being · Sound Therapy

1 Introduction

Chanting is a well-known and popular method of meditation. Chanting improves well-being and helps to reduce blood pressure and negative emotions [35]. Chanting can also 'awaken' people to increase their attention and consciousness [12, 26, 30]. Solfeggio frequencies, which comprise nine electromagnetic tones (i.e., 174 Hz, 285 Hz, 396 Hz, 417 Hz, 432 Hz, 528 Hz, 639 Hz, 741 Hz, and 852 Hz), have similar effects as chanting [5]. Ancient religions utilize certain solfeggio frequencies for chanting and meditation to heal or to spiritually connect to the Universe.

Mindfulness-based interventions, such as meditation, can enhance well-being [44]. In modern society, brief mindfulness meditation is becoming increasingly popular [44]. Chanting, one of the most widespread forms of meditation, has a long history in the tradition of meditation and religion [34]. Consequently, in the contemporary post-pandemic society, chanting is used for emotion adjustment and mindfulness training. The effects of solfeggio frequencies, the tones frequently used in chanting, warrant further investigation and understanding.

To more fully understand the effects of chanting and solfeggio frequencies, we reviewed the literature to find answers to the following questions:

1. How do chanting and solfeggio frequencies benefit people's physical and mental well-being?
2. What are the effects of chanting and solfeggio frequencies on brain activity?
3. What applications of chanting and solfeggio frequencies have been used in the medical field?

Q. Gao et al. (Eds.): HCII 2023, LNCS 14055, pp. 628–639, 2023.
https://doi.org/10.1007/978-3-031-48041-6_42

From a review of the literature, we found that chanting helps to increase attention and decrease mind wandering; solfeggio frequencies can heal the human body by relieving pains physically and mentally; and sound therapy can be designed based on the effects of chanting and solfeggio frequencies.

2 Literature Review

2.1 Chanting

A chant can take many forms (e.g., speech or music) and uses repetitive phrases. According to Gregorian Chant Academy [17], a chant can range from a simple melody that uses a small number of notes to highly complex musical structures of repeated sub-phrases. Besides, chanting is a mode of meditation, and it involves an oral expression of a prolonged and reduplicative sound, word, and phrase that can serve as a point of focus to help increase one's attention [12, 26, 30].

Chanting & Well-being. Chanting is regarded as a mantra [26]. In Sanskrit, a mantra refers to a combination of "man" and "tra" where "man" refers to 'mind' and "tra" refers to 'instrument.' Thus, a mantra, also a chant, is considered an instrument of the mind (or a powerful sound or resonance) which can play a significant role in personal mind management. Practicing mantras is helpful for increasing mental satisfaction and reducing negative emotions [26, 43].

It is common for people to experience stress frequently, to the extent that it can be experienced daily [36]. Stress and anxiety can lead to physical and mental health issues, including depression. These issues are vivid in the post-pandemic era, where many people have encountered various types of stress, pressure, and failures, including losing precious or meaningful relationships (e.g., family, friendship, or marriage), jobs, businesses, or possessions [41]. In a cross-sectional study by Taylor et al. [42], it was found that many 18- to 65-year-old adults in most countries in Asia have a high degree of severe negative emotions, where 49% experienced extremely severe anxiety, 47% experienced depression, and 36% experienced stress frequently. In the U.S., about 40% of adults suffered depression or anxiety in February 2021, which means four in ten people reported these negative emotions. In February 2023, approximately 32% of adults experienced emotional disorders such as depression or anxiety [32].

Thus, it is important to address mental health problems by improving well-being and quality of life, such as by using chant music [26]. Chanting can enhance a person's cognitive functions, altered states, and quality of life [36]. We discuss each of them next.

Cognitive Functions. Chanting is beneficial for increasing concentration and mindfulness, strengthening cognitive functions, and minimizing mind wandering through self-regulation and an attitude of acceptance [35]. There exists a two-attribution model related to mindfulness. The first attribution is related to three abilities: attention sustainability, shift from mind wandering back to concentration, and restraint for overly sophisticated pondering on irrelevant things. Hence, chanting increases mindfulness and helps to maintain one's focus. The second attribution relates to acceptance and curiosity [6, 35]. The chanting practice helps to increase one's faith and outlook on life, resulting in higher acceptance and a sense of curiosity [35]. Hence, chanting benefits growth mindfulness and the reduction of mind wandering [35]. Figure 1 shows the association between mindfulness and chanting.

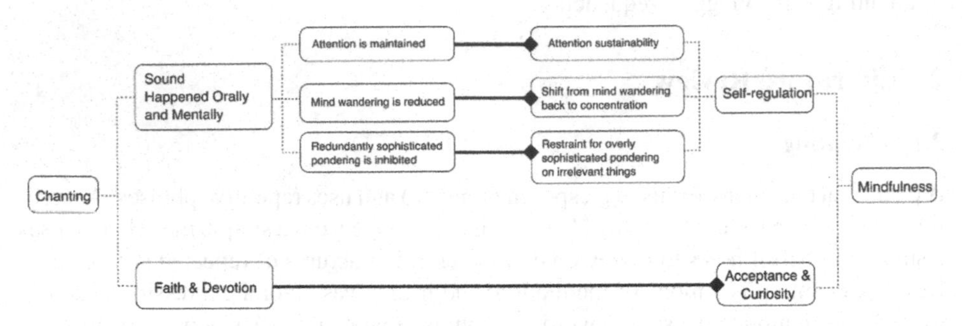

Fig. 1. Associations between mindfulness and chanting

Altered States. With regard to chanting, the occurrence of altered states usually relates to longer durations and practices. Individuals could experience a state of flow (i.e., deep cognitive absorption) if they frequently practice chanting for long durations [35]. Flow is a state in which one gets highly involved in a self-rewarding activity to the point where nothing else seems to matter [9]. Hence, people's inner states could be altered when they experience a state of flow and are deeply engaged in the chanting practice [35]. An altered state of effortless concentration emerges with frequent chanting practices of longer durations over time [35].

Quality of Life. Chanting plays a positive role in people's quality of life. Chanting benefits individuals' cognitive functions, increases their focused concentration, and helps them ignore or minimize distractions. Additionally, sustained chanting practices can alter people's inner states, leading to a devotion to attention.

Chanting can also enhance social interaction with individuals. Chanting believers are encouraged to share their synchronized faith, contributing to an ultimate spiritual unity [35]. Therefore, chanting is beneficial for enhancing the quality of life.

Chanting & Brain Science. Gao et al. [14] found that religious chanting has neurophysiological correlates with the posterior cingulate cortex (PCC) by decreasing eigenvector centrality. Religious chanting also has the effect of increasing endogenous neural oscillations in the low-frequency delta band. Delta waves are the slowest recorded brain waves (i.e., 1–3 Hz) in human beings. They are primarily discovered in infants and young children and are linked to the deepest levels of relaxation and restorative, healing sleep. Delta waves are also notably found in brain injuries, learning difficulties, inability to think, and severe ADHD [2]. Religious chanting has different neurophysiological correlates from other mindfulness meditations [14].

Compared to the resting state, during mindfulness-based stress reduction meditation, the alpha band (8–12 Hz) power increases while the delta band (1–3 Hz) power decreases. Alpha band oscillations play a remarkable role in the human brain, as the alpha band performs an inhibitory function during relaxation [23]. Different religious or meditative practices may be more effective for relieving particular neuropsychiatric symptoms, as different forms of meditation are associated with different brain activity patterns, despite overlaps between mindfulness and spiritual prayer [14].

Variations in delta activity result from afferent inputs from all sensory systems that communicate with the PCC by ascending (efferent connectivity) through the thalamus [14]. Prior research has independently demonstrated that default mode network (DMN) activity is related to self-monitoring functions and that delta band power accounts for 53% of the variance in DMN functional connectivity [14]. Religious chanting is a streamlined procedure for modulating biological processes, while positive emotions and calmness nurse relaxation [14]. The findings are consistent with earlier research indicating that prayers facilitate relaxation, which is associated with low metabolism, low breath rate, and distinctive slow brain waves.

Resting-state connectivity shows strongly correlated signals between functionally related brain regions [7]. When compared to the resting state, religious chanting increases the stability of the cardiac function [16]. Specifically, this phenomenon explains the enhanced stability in regulating the cardiovascular tone and the parasympathetic modulation of the cardiac function. Such physiological alterations highlight the mechanisms by which calming meditation techniques (such as chanting) can reduce stress [14].

2.2 Solfeggio Frequencies

Solfeggio frequencies refer to precise tones that consist of six basic electromagnetic tones extended to nine tones [5]. These frequencies have been documented to originate from ancient history, as far as the 8th century [5]. They serve as the fundamental sounds in both Western Christianity and Eastern Indian religions. Additionally, solfeggio frequencies are the foundation of many ancient sacred music traditions [5].

Frequency. In sound science, the number of vibrations per second is known as "frequency" that is measured in Hertz (Hz for short). The human ear can only hear a certain range of vibrations per second, ranging from 20 Hz to 20,000 Hz (20 kHz) [5].

Range of Solfeggio Frequencies. The fundamental idea behind solfeggio frequencies is that the vibrational signature of specific sounds, ranging from 174 Hz to 963 Hz, can positively affect physical, mental, and spiritual well-being [5].

Musical Scale & Frequency. The modern musical scale, Do-Re-Mi-Fa-So-La-Si/Ti, can be retrospected from the first stanza of The Hymn to St John the Baptist [5]:

Ut *queant laxis.*
Re*sonare fibris.*
Mi*ra gestorum.*
Fa*muli tuorum.*
So*lve polluti.*
La*bii reatum.*
Sancte Iohannes.

The first syllable (or its variation) was used as the basis of the modern musical scale. Every scale contains a unique frequency that can be expressed in Hz. UT = 396 Hz, Re = 417 Hz, Mi = 528 Hz, Fa = 639 Hz, So = 741 Hz, La = 852 Hz.

Effects on Physical & Mental Wellness. Apart from the above six frequencies, three frequencies were added afterward, resulting in nine tones [5]. It is believed that solfeggio frequencies are related to a concept called "chakra" which means "wheel" in Sanskrit [22], or more specifically, it refers to a wheel-like energy center in people's inner heart, with seven chakras in total reflecting seven aspects of consciousness that form the mind of human beings [28]. These nine tones are described next.

174 Hz is used as the healing frequency. This solfeggio frequency plays the most significant role in the physical body. For example, it can relieve physical pain in the body, such as in the back, legs, feet, and head; it also has the ability to loosen muscles and reduce tension. Distinctly, it can release stress and strain [5]. It is also considered a natural aesthetic that has the power to reduce misery energetically. In addition, it conveys a sense of safety and love for organs in the body [13].

285 Hz is a tone linked to the healing of the root chakra [5]. "Chakra" indicates the energy centers (or the spinning disks or wheels) in the body where each of them is in accordance with certain nerve bundles and major organs [27]. The physical framework of the body is built on the root chakra [20]. Due to the link with the root chakra, 285 Hz provides a sense of security, has the ability to heal and restore tissues, affects energy fields, increases the immune system, and sends instructions to repair damaged organs [5, 13].

396 Hz is similar to 285 Hz in that it is also associated with the root chakra. It is one of the lower tones on the solfeggio scale and is one of the fundamental tones used in sound healing [5]. It can heal the emotion of guilt and doubt and help eliminate fear (because fear is a type of emotion with a very low vibration that induces negative circumstances and outcomes). If the low vibration in fear or guilt is increased by 396 Hz, it can aid in generating cures to enhance the emotional body. It is also believed that this tone enables the transition from grief to joy and helps to wake the emotional body when it is trapped in a spiral of negative thinking by raising it to a higher vibrational state of positivity [5]. In other words, this tone can improve the body by relieving the sense of guilt that blocks the body. It decreases the defense mechanisms and alleviates subconscious negative beliefs to achieve peace [13].

417 Hz is close to the sacral chakra that can be impeded by traumatic life events [5]. This tone mainly relieves the pain of trauma by clearing destructive influences of past awful experiences, broadening vision and insight, and improving self-transformation [13].

432 Hz is believed to be "the heartbeat of the Earth" or the frequency at which the Universe vibrates. Hence, it can offer a very intimate experience with the energy and vibration of the Universe. It is also believed to lower blood pressure [5].

528 Hz is a popular tone named "the love frequency" or "the miracle tone." Solar plexus chakra, which is related to the energy of the sun and fire, is believed to enhance self-esteem and confidence [4]. It is suggested that this tone has the ability to facilitate creativity, concentration, positivity, and inner peace. It can also decrease stress and hormone levels and restore damaged DNA to its original state [5].

639 Hz is associated with the heart chakra [5] that manages people's love and supports empathy, compassion, and forgiveness. It could bring peace and balance to broken relationships due to the facilitation of connections between opposites. It helps clarify thoughts so emotions can be better expressed [5]. This tone promotes the communication

of cells with the environment and enhances harmonious interaction, tolerance, and love between partners, family, and friends [13].

741 Hz is connected to the throat chakra and is responsible for speaking up and expressing oneself [40]. This tone boosts the expression and open mind of the highest self [5]. It could effectively eliminate toxins from one's mental and physical health. Mentally, it dispels various negative emotions, such as anger, jealousy, and deceit; it also detoxes the physical body from contamination containing viruses, fungi, bacteria, and electromagnetic toxins [5].

852 Hz works with the third eye chakra [5]. The third eye chakra is a window into the "internal screen" which displays intuition, fantasy, images, and archetypes [19]. Therefore, it is able to awaken intuition and strengthen a constructive connection with the higher self [5]. It also encourages the exploration of spiritual order and protects the reality of situations from being contaminated by illusions [5].

Consequently, the nine solfeggio frequencies have been argued to have different benefits in physical and mental wellness (see Table 1).

Solfeggio Frequencies & Brain Science. Five frequency bands have been defined and studied in the literature: delta (1–3 Hz), theta (4–8 Hz), alpha (8–12 Hz), beta (12–30 Hz), and gamma (>30 Hz) [8]. Delta and theta are *low-frequency* wave bands. The "delta" state corresponds to the sleep state and is associated with brain injuries and cognitive dysfunction. The "theta" state relates to the subconscious mind and reflects the transitional state between wakefulness and sleep. The low-frequency wave bands are powerful when internal focus, meditation, and spiritual awareness are high [31], as they boost relaxation and improve sleep [8]. *Mid-range frequencies* are associated with attention. When the focus is inward (as in meditation), the brain enters the "alpha" state, indicating relaxed wakefulness [45]. When the focus is on the outside world, the brain enters the "beta" state [8], which refers to normal waking consciousness [37]. *Higher frequencies* stimulate brain waves into the "gamma" state, which may produce a sense of attention and alerts to the brain and is related to the ability to recall memories [8].

Because of the relationship between sound, vibration, and the human brain and body, solfeggio frequencies can impact physical and spiritual well-being [18]. When solfeggio frequencies are presented to and detected by the body via sound, those frequencies will resonate with various body parts that aid in healing and relaxation, increasing spiritual well-being [3, 18]. For example, sound therapy, a popular form of treatment, can successfully reduce pain through sound and vibrations [10].

Solfeggio Frequencies & Chanting. The nine solfeggio frequencies are often used in different chanting forms. Specifically, ancient Egyptians usually played at 528 Hz, one of the most popular tones in solfeggio frequencies, when chanting for curing and healing. The frequency of 528 Hz is also used to strengthen consciousness in spacious sound chambers, resulting in the tone propagating throughout the chambers and generating a positive effect on humans. Correlatively, 528 Hz is mostly used in mantras and syllables [33]. Apart from 528 Hz, 432 Hz is used by Hinduism when doing OM, which refers to a form of ancient mantra believed by saints to be a sound of creation connected to the Universe [39].

Table 1. Benefits of 9 types of solfeggio frequencies

Solfeggio Frequency	Reference & Benefits - Physical	Reference & Benefits - Mental	Role in Body/Mind
174 Hz	Bevan et al. [5] • Relieve pain • Relieve muscle and tension	Ford [13] • Reduce misery • Convey a sense of safety and love for organs	Healing
285 Hz	Bevan et al. [5] • Cure cuts, burns, and lacerations • Facilitate the immune system	Ford [13] • Send instructions to repair damaged organs	Restoring
396 Hz		Bevan et al. [5] • Heal guilt and doubt • Eliminate fear • Transit grief to joy • Wake body in a negative-thinking trap	Relieving, alleviating
417 Hz		Ford [13] • Clear pain of past trauma • Improve self-transformation	Broadening
432 Hz	Bevan et al. [5] • Lower blood pressure		Connecting with the Universe
528 Hz	Bevan et al. [5] • Decrease stress and hormone levels • Restore damaged DNA to its original state	Bevan et al. [5] • Facilitate creativity, concentration, positivity, and inner peace	Energizing
639 Hz	Ford [13] • Promote communication of cells with their environments	Bevan et al. [5], Ford [13] • Bring a balance to broken relationships • Boost harmonious interaction, tolerance, and love between partners, family, and friends	Balancing

(continued)

Table 1. (*continued*)

Solfeggio Frequency	Reference & Benefits - Physical	Reference & Benefits - Mental	Role in Body/Mind
741 Hz	Bevan et al. [5] • Detox the physical body from contamination containing viruses, fungi, bacteria, and electromagnetic toxins	Bevan et al. [5] • Boost the expression and open mind of the highest self • Dispel negative emotions	Detoxing
852 Hz		Bevan et al. [5] • Awaken intuition • Construct a higher self • Protect spiritual order and reality from illusions	Awakening

2.3 Sound Therapy

Sound therapy is a synthetic and therapeutic vibration technique applied to medicine [16]. Sound therapy generally uses bell-like vibrational instruments called singing bowls; however, gongs and other vibrational musical instruments have also been used. Sound therapy, specifically in the context of meditation, is capable of decreasing tense, anxiety, and depressed moods and invoking spiritual wellness [15].

Sound therapy can be considered vibroacoustic therapy. It usually employs audible sound vibrations to lighten symptoms, trigger relaxation, and relieve stress and strain [38]. Evidence of the therapy is attributed to the awareness that outer oscillations can stimulate body functions [29]. Sound therapy can also be viewed as an aesthetic interaction through sound, where the technology triggers internal motivation and underlines the fluent process of working from the "inside-out" [11].

Application & Development. Sound therapy is generally utilized to eliminate negative emotion variables but could boost positive mind variables that are responsible for enhanced internal peace [16]. Sound therapy has been applied to treat certain issues, such as tinnitus (i.e., ringing or other noises in the ear) and autism.

Tinnitus. According to a case study by Kutyba et al. [24], sound therapy can satisfy patients' needs for treatment and is an option for doctors and patients. Compared to basic sound therapy, adding white noise to the basic sound used in tinnitus rehabilitation therapy increases tinnitus treatment effectiveness [25]. Furthermore, sound therapy is highly effective when the therapy is carried out over a time period of three hours a day over at least six months [21].

Autism. Sound therapy that uses music with low acoustic energy has a positive effect on children with autism [1]. The essence of this phenomenon is that the brain processes a comprehensive framework in sounds and sensory data such that the outcomes of external stimuli reduce autistic symptoms. Sound therapy increases lexical entry and verbal communication. The therapy also increases social interaction for autistic children, increasing their self-confidence.

3 Conclusion

Chanting is a popular form of meditation that enhances people's spiritual well-being because the presentation of chanting, which is usually the reduplication of certain sounds, words, or phrases, can induce high concentration and inner enjoyment. Furthermore, chanting enhances people's cognitive functions and altered states to induce flow, increasing quality of life and wellness. From the brain science perspective, chanting can enhance endogenous neural oscillations in the low-frequency delta band and alleviate physiological and psychological stress and pain.

The solfeggio frequencies are nine tones associated with healing, restoring, relieving and alleviating, broadening, connecting to the Universe, energizing, balancing, detoxing, and awakening. Low frequencies boost relaxation and improve sleep via the delta state in the brain; higher mid-range frequencies awake relaxation via the beta state in the brain; and high frequencies stimulate attention and insight via the gamma state in the brain.

In ancient society, people conducted activities to heal themselves or others, especially in religious contexts. They carried out meditation by means of chanting. They could heal devotees or connect with the Universe. In modern society, where more research has been conducted, there is a better understanding of the effects of chanting and solfeggio frequencies. Hence, medical techniques and treatments have been created based on the science behind chanting and solfeggio frequencies, especially in sound therapy. Chanting and solfeggio frequencies have been applied in sound therapy to facilitate curing illnesses. Sound therapy can play an important role in medical treatments of specific diseases. More research is needed to identify these illnesses as well as understand the effects of chanting and solfeggio frequencies on well-being.

In summary, chanting and solfeggio frequencies are tightly bonded and related, and the scientific theories behind them are similar in that both can treat physical and mental pains. Evidence of the positive effects of chanting and solfeggio frequencies has led to the development of the modern medical technique – sound therapy, which is meaningful to people with illnesses who are seeking relief or treatments. Unfortunately, the current research is limited in depth and breadth (quantity) on how chanting and solfeggio frequencies affect brain activity and mental health. Hence, we call for more scientific research to investigate and better understand the effects of chanting and solfeggio frequencies on well-being and their application in the design of sound therapy.

References

1. AbediKoupaei, M., Poushaneh, K., Mohammadi, A., Siampour, N.: Sound therapy: an experimental study with autistic children. Procedia Soc. Behav. Sci. **84**, 626–630 (2013). https://doi.org/10.1016/j.sbspro.2013.06.615

2. Abhang, P.A., Gawali, B.W., Mehrotra, S.C.: Introduction to EEG- and speech-based emotion recognition. Academic Press (2016). https://doi.org/10.1016/c2015-0-01959-1
3. Bettersleep.com, The science behind solfeggio frequencies. https://www.bettersleep.com/blog/science-behind-solfeggio-frequencies/. (2019)
4. Bevan, K.: Solar plexus chakra affirmations. https://dailydish.co.uk/solar-plexus-chakra-affirmations. (2022)
5. Bevan, K.: The 9 solfeggio frequencies and their benefits. https://dailydish.co.uk/the-9-solfeggio-frequencies-and-their-benefits. (2023)
6. Bishop, S.R., et al.: Mindfulness: a proposed operational definition. Clin. Psychol. Sci. Pract. **11**, 230–241 (2004). https://doi.org/10.1093/clipsy.bph077
7. Biswal, B.B.: Resting-state functional connectivity. . Brain Mapp. **1**, 581–585 (2015). https://doi.org/10.1016/b978-0-12-397025-1.00335-3
8. Booth, S.: This is your brain on binaural beats. https://www.healthline.com/health-news/your-brain-on-binaural-beats. (2019)
9. Csikszentmihalyi, M.: Toward a psychology of optimal experience. In: Csikszentmihalyi, M. (ed.) Flow and the Foundations of Positive Psychology, pp. 209–226. Springer, Dordrecht (2014). https://doi.org/10.1007/978-94-017-9088-8_14
10. Deng, G.: Integrative medicine therapies for pain management in cancer patients. Cancer J. **25**, 343–348 (2019). https://doi.org/10.1097/ppo.0000000000000399
11. Ellis, P.: Improving quality of life and well-being for children and the elderly through vibroacoustic sound therapy. In: Miesenberger, K., Klaus, J., Zagler, W.L., Burger, D. (eds.) ICCHP 2004. LNCS, vol. 3118, pp. 416–422. Springer, Heidelberg (2004). https://doi.org/10.1007/978-3-540-27817-7_61
12. Engström, M., Pihlsgård, J., Lundberg, P., Söderfeldt, B.: Functional magnetic resonance imaging of hippocampal activation during silent mantra meditation. J. Altern. Complement. Med. **16**, 1253–1258 (2010). https://doi.org/10.1089/acm.2009.0706
13. Ford, L.J.: Stress management certification - solfeggio frequencies, study guide 2. https://www.talkaboutlight.com/wp-content/uploads/securepdfs/2022/03/Solfeggio-Frequencies_SG2.pdf
14. Gao, J., Leung, W., Wu, B.W.Y., Skouras, S., Sik, H.: The neurophysiological correlates of religious chanting. Sci. Rep. **9**(1), 4262 (2019). https://doi.org/10.1038/s41598-019-40200-w
15. Goldsby, T.L., Goldsby, M.G., McWalters, M., Mills, P.J.: Effects of singing bowl sound meditation on mood, tension, and well-being: An observational study. J. Evidence-Based Complement. Altern. Med. **22**, 401–406 (2016). https://doi.org/10.1177/2156587216668109
16. Goldsby, T.L., Goldsby, M.G., McWalters, M., Mills, P.J.: Sound healing: mood, emotional, and spiritual well-being interrelationships. Religions. **13**, 123 (2022). https://doi.org/10.3390/rel13020123
17. Gregorian chant academy gregorian chant academy: chant tutorial: single note forms. https://www.youtube.com/watch?v=cdqXuaCAivU. (2021)
18. Williams, G.: Solfeggio frequency science: what you need to know. https://mindeasy.com/solfeggio-frequency-science/. (2023)
19. Groff. R.: Exploring your intuition: the third eye chakra. https://midtownyogastudios.com/blog/third-eye-chakra. (2021)
20. Jain, R.: Root chakra: complete guide to the muladhara chakra. https://www.arhantayoga.org/blog/all-you-need-to-know-about-muladhara-chakra-root-chakra/. (2020)
21. Jin, I.K., Choi, S.J., Yoo, J., Jeong, S., Heo, S., Oh, H.: Effects of tinnitus sound therapy determined using subjective measurements. Am. Acad. Audiol. **32**, 212–218 (2021). https://doi.org/10.1055/s-0041-1722984
22. Judith, A.: Wheels of life: A user's guide to the chakra system. Llewellyn Worldwide, Saint Paul (2012)

23. Klimesch, W.: Alpha-band oscillations, attention, and controlled access to stored information. Trends Cogn. Sci. **16**, 606–617 (2012). https://doi.org/10.1016/j.tics.2012.10.007
24. Kutyba, J., Jedrzejczak, W.W., Raj-Koziak, D., Gos, E., Skarżyński, H.: Tinnitus sound therapy with a mobile application: case study. J. Hear. Sci. **9**(4), 51–56 (2019). https://doi.org/10.17430/1003717
25. Lee, E.K., Ko, H.Y., Kim, M.H.: A literature review on sound therapy for tinnitus. J. Korean Med. Ophthalmol. Otolaryngol. Dermatol. (한방안이비인후피부과학회지). **36**, 45–59 (2023). https://doi.org/10.6114/jkood.2023.36.2.045
26. Lee, L.A.: The impact of chanting on wellness, well-being, and stress: a qualitative study, doctoral dissertation, Alliant International University (2021). https://www.proquest.com/openview/a89e3da9756098c11c7cac9a9940e410
27. Lindberg, S.: What are the 7 chakras and how can you unblock them. https://www.healthline.com/health/what-are-chakras#about-chakras. (2020)
28. Mageau, M.: Our chakra system. https://www.trans4mind.com/download-pdfs/transformational/ourchakrasystem.pdf
29. Lynn, C.E., McCaffrey, R.: Vibroacoustic sound therapy improves pain management and more. Holist. Nurs. Pract. **18**, 111–118 (2004)
30. Naranjo, C., Ornstein, R.E: On the Psychology of Meditation. Allen & Unwin, New South Wales (1973)
31. NeuroHealth associates: the science of brainwaves - the language of the brain neurohealth associates. https://nhahealth.com/brainwaves-the-language/
32. Panchal, N., Saunders, H., Rudowitz, R., Cox, C.: The implications of COVID-19 for mental health and substance use. https://www.kff.org/coronavirus-covid-19/issue-brief/the-implications-of-covid-19-for-mental-health-and-substance-use/. (2023)
33. Pereira, C.: A comparative study of frequencies of a Buddhist mantra – Om Mani Padme Hum and a Hindu mantra - Om Namah Shivaya. Inte. J. Innov. Sci, Eng. Technol. **3**(4), 32–329 (2016)
34. Perry, G., Polito, V., Thompson, W.F.: Chanting meditation improves mood and social cohesion. In: The Society for Music Perception and Cognition (SMPC) (2016)
35. Perry, G., Polito, V., Sankaran, N., Thompson, W.R.: How chanting relates to cognitive function, altered states and quality of life. Brain Sci. **12**, 1456 (2022). https://doi.org/10.3390/brainsci12111456
36. Pollock, K.: On the nature of social stress: Production of a modern mythology. Soc Sci Med **26**, 381–392 (1988). https://doi.org/10.1016/0277-9536(88)90404-2
37. Rangaswamy, M., et al.: Beta power in the EEG of alcoholics. Biol. Psychiat. **52**, 831–842 (2002). https://doi.org/10.1016/s0006-3223(02)01362-8
38. Salamon, E., Kim, M., Beaulieu, J., Stefano, G.B: Sound therapy induced relaxation: down regulating stress processes and pathologies. https://pubmed.ncbi.nlm.nih.gov/12761468/
39. Sarkar, D.: Can chanting OM reduce stress and anxiety. https://www.discovermagazine.com/health/can-chanting-om-reduce-stress-and-anxiety. (2021)
40. Snyder, S.: Everything you need to know about the throat chakra. https://www.yogajournal.com/yoga-101/chakras-yoga-for-beginners/chakratuneup2015-intro-visuddha/. (2021)
41. Tay, W.W., Jesuthasan, J., Wan, K.Y., Ong, T., Mustapha, F.I.: Eighteen months into the COVID-19 pandemic: The prevalence of depression, anxiety, and stress symptoms in Southeast Asia and the associated demographic factors. Front. Pub. Health. **10**, 863323 (2022). https://doi.org/10.3389/fpubh.2022.863323
42. Taylor, S., Asmundson, G.J.G.: Life in a post-pandemic world: What to expect of anxiety-related conditions and their treatment. J. Anxiety Disord. **72**, 102231 (2020). https://doi.org/10.1016/j.janxdis.2020.102231

43. Tomasino, B., Fregona, S., Skrap, M., Fabbro, F.: Meditation-related activations are modulated by the practices needed to obtain it and by the expertise: An ALE meta-analysis study. Front. Hum. Neurosci. **6**, 346 (2013). https://doi.org/10.3389/fnhum.2012.00346
44. Wu, R. et al.: Brief mindfulness meditation improves emotion processing. Front. Neurosci. **13**, 1074 (2019). https://doi.org/10.3389/fnins.2019.01074
45. APA Dictionary of Psychology. https://dictionary.apa.org/alpha-state. Accessed 20 June 2023

Estimation of Stress Resilience from Eye-Gaze Data Collected by a Tablet Terminal When Performing a Dot-Probe Task: Application to Junior High School Students

Tomoki Yokota(✉), Kentaro Kotani, Takafumi Asao, and Satoshi Suzuki

Department of Mechanical Engineering, Kansai University, Osaka, Japan
k371100@kansai-u.ac.jp

Abstract. In recent years, the number of patients with mental disorders due to mental health problems has been increasing. In a previous study of this researchO, we created an application that collects eye gaze data using tablet terminals and investigated the possibility of obtaining a higher correlation with resilience scores by analyzing the gaze data. As a result, we reported that it was possible to predict resilience tendencies to some extent from eye gaze information in the experiment with university students. However, it has been reported in previous studies that the average resilience score decreases significantly from elementary school to adolescence, and then increases again among college students, showing a U-shaped curvilinear change, so it is unclear whether the estimation of resilience by eye gaze measurement can be applied to middle and high school students as well as to college students. The purpose of this study was to investigate the relationship between attentional bias and resilience using eye gaze information and to investigate the effectiveness of these methods for children. Using multiple regression analysis with the gaze indicator as the explanatory variable and the resilience questionnaire as the objective variable, we found that the degree-of-freedom-adjusted coefficient of determination R^{*2} of the regression equation predicting ARS was 0.67, and the degree-of-freedom-adjusted coefficient of determination R^{*2} of the regression equation predicting BRS was 0.41.

Keywords: Eye Gaze · Resilience · Attentional Bias

1 Introduction

The effect of Mental health has become a major social problem in Japan. According to an international survey on mental health conducted by the OECD (Organization for Economic Cooperation and Development) [1], the percentage of people in Japan suffering from depression and other conditions has doubled from 7.9% in the 2013 survey to 17.3% in 2020 after the outbreak of the new coronavirus. In addition, according to the Ministry of Health, Labour and Welfare's overview of patient surveys in 2020 [2], the number of patients with mood disorders is estimated to be as high as 1.2 million.

Q. Gao et al. (Eds.): HCII 2023, LNCS 14055, pp. 640–653, 2023.
https://doi.org/10.1007/978-3-031-48041-6_43

The issue of student's mental health is no exception. According to the "Corona × Children Questionnaire" [3] conducted by the National Center for Child Health and Development in 2020, 24% of junior high school students and 30% of high school students had moderate or severe depressive symptoms in the survey on the severity of depressive symptoms.

In our previous study [4], an experiment to estimate psychological resilience using eye-tracking data was conducted on college students, and it was found that a certain degree of psychological resilience tendency can be predicted from eye-tracking information. However, a previous study [5] reported that one of the psychological resilience factors showed a U-shaped curvilinear change in which the average value decreased significantly from elementary school to adolescence (junior and senior high school students) and increased again among college students. In other words, the characteristics of psychological resilience may differ between college students and junior and senior high school students, and it is unclear whether the estimation of psychological resilience by eye tracking can be applied to junior and senior high school students in the same way as to college students.

Therefore, this study aims to investigate the relationship between attentional bias and psychological resilience using eye-tracking information and to investigate the effectiveness of these methods for children.

2 Experiment

2.1 Participants

Fifteen junior high school students (ages 12 to 15) participated in the experiment. The experiment was conducted by two persons, the experimental participant and an assistant. The assistant gave the same explanation to all participants. Horizontal gaze data for both eyes of all participants were obtained.

2.2 Apparatus

An Apple MacBook Pro and an iPad Pro 12.9-inch were used in the experiment. The distance between the participant's eyes and the tablet terminals was fixed at 35 cm, and a chin rest was used to fix the participants' faces to ensure that eye gaze was measured. The eye measurement system used in the experiment and the management of the image presentation was developed using Xcode, and the development language Swift was used.

2.3 Stimuli

The emotional stimulus images used in the experiment are selected from the Karolinska Directed Emotional Faces database (KDEF) [6] and The Geneva affective picture database (GAPED) [7]. From KDEF, we used Neutral, Happy, Angry, and Sad images of emotional faces. We selected 20 images of males and 20 images of females and used 10 Neutral images, 4 Happy images, and 3 Angry and Sad images for males and females, respectively. When using the emotional stimulus images, two images, one with a neutral expression and the other with an emotional expression, were presented in pairs, and the images that matched the person in the pair were used. Ten pairs of emotional images were created for both male and female images.

2.4 Experimental Procedure

The experiment is started by the assistant pressing the start button at the bottom of the tablet terminal screen. Immediately after the start of the experiment, the fixed viewpoint is displayed in the center of the screen. The fixed viewpoint is displayed for 1.5 s and then disappears. After the disappearance of the fixation viewpoint, the emotional stimulus images are presented on the left and right sides of the screen, respectively, with the position of the fixation viewpoint in between. Two images are presented on the screen for 3.0 s before they disappear. The size of the fixed viewpoint is $2.6° \times 2.6°$. Recording of the gaze measurement by the tablet terminal starts the moment the start button is pressed and stops automatically after all images have been presented. The first two trials were conducted to obtain the gaze information for the left and right calibration so that 64 images were used in 32 trials in total.

The experimental procedure is described below.

Explain the procedure to the participants. The participants were instructed not to move their eyes except to the fixed viewpoint and the images presented to the left and right of the fixed viewpoint, not to move their head or body position, and to always look at the images presented to the left and right at least once.

The participant placed his/her face on the chinrest and confirmed that the distance between the tablet and his/her face was 35 cm.

The experiment assistant presses the start button on the terminal to begin the experiment.

The participant gazes at the fixation viewpoint while the fixation viewpoint is presented. After the solid viewpoint disappears, a black dot is presented on the right side for the first time and on the left side for the second time, respectively, for calibration. The participant gazes at the black dots similarly to at the fixed viewpoint.

After the black spot disappears, the fixed viewpoint is presented again. Similarly, after the fixed viewpoint disappears, images are presented on the left and right. The participant observes the images presented to the left and right while shifting his or her gaze arbitrarily. The images are presented for 3.0 s and then disappear. The trial is repeated.

The experiment is conducted for 32 trials. The message "End of experiment" is displayed on the screen when the experiment is completed.

After all the trials are completed, the participants answer the resilience questionnaire.

2.5 Data Analysis

Explanatory Variables

In this experiment, five gaze indices [8, 9], which evaluate attentional bias, were extracted from the horizontal gaze information obtained from the experiment and are used as explanatory variables.

The five gaze indices are First Fixation, Latencies, Dwell Time, Frequency, and Viewing Time. The details of these variables are described in the previous paper [4].

Response Variables

Two resilience questionnaires developed in previous studies [10, 11] are used as the response variables in this experiment. The Adolescent Resilience Scale (ARS) [10] is a scale that measures mental resilience, a psychological characteristic that promotes recovery from mental depression. The Bidimensional Resilience Scale (BRS) [11] focuses on the fact that an individual's psychological resilience is guided by various factors that the individual possesses. The scale was created based on the assumption that there are factors strongly related to one's natural disposition and acquired factors that are easily acquired. These scales consist of 21 questions, answered on a 5-point scale from 1 to 5. The score, therefore, ranges from 21 to 105 points.

3 Results

3.1 Confirmation of Multicollinearity

When conducting multiple regression analysis, it is necessary to consider multicollinearity. Multicollinearity is a phenomenon in multiple regression analysis in which, when a linear relationship is observed among explanatory variables, some regression equations become unreliable due to the increase in the variance of the regression equations [12]. The VIF (Variance Inflation Factor) is often used to describe the occurrence of multicollinearity. It is said that multicollinearity occurs when VIF < 10 [12].

Table 1 shows the correlation matrix of the explanatory variables, and Table 2 shows the VIF calculated from the correlation coefficients obtained in Table 1.

Table 1. Correlation coefficients for each explanatory variable (correlation matrix table)

	First Fixation	Latencies	Dwell Time	Frequency	Viewing Time
First Fixation	1	-	-	-	-
Latencies	0.041	1	-	-	-
Dwell Time	0.52	0.16	1	-	-
Frequency	−0.067	0.24	−0.089	1	-
Viewing Time	0.30	0.27	0.15	0.42	1

Table 2 shows that VIF < 10 for all the explanatory variables, and therefore, multicollinearity is not observed. Therefore, in this multiple regression analysis, all variables can be used.

3.2 Result of Multiple Regression Analysis

Table 3 shows the results of multiple regression analysis with ARS as the response variable, and Table 4 shows the results of multiple regression analysis with BRS as

Table 2. Variance Augmentation Factor (VIF)

	First Fixation	Latencies	Dwell Time	Frequency	Viewing Time
First Fixation	-	-	-	-	-
Latencies	1.00	-	-	-	-
Dwell Time	1.37	1.02	-	-	-
Frequency	1.00	1.06	1.00	-	-
Viewing Time	1.10	1.08	1.00	1.00	-

the response variable. Each table shows the coefficient of determination R^2, the adjusted coefficient of determination R^{*2}, and the p-value of the regression equation. In the present analysis, all combinations of explanatory variables were analyzed by the random effects method.

Determination of Multiple Regression Equations From the combinations of explanatory variables shown in Table 3 and Table 4, the best combination is selected by considering R^{*2} and p-value.

· When the response variable is ARS.

From Table 3, the maximum value of R^{*2} is 0.67, and the minimum value of the p-value is 0.013. Both results are obtained when the explanatory variables are First Fixation (*x1*), Latencies (*x2*), and Viewing Time (*x5*). The standard error is 4.4, and the regression equation is shown in Eq. (1). The analysis of the variance table is shown in Table 5, and the statistics of each variable are shown in Table 6. Figure 1 shows a correlation chart between the ARS values measured by the questionnaire and the estimated values using Eq. (1).

$$\hat{y}_{ARS} = 83x_1 - 164x_2 + 50x_5 + 86 \quad (1)$$

· When the response variable is the BRS.

Table 4 shows that the maximum value of R^{*2} is 0.41, and the minimum value of p-value is 0.032. When R^{*2} is the maximum value, the explanatory variables are Dwell Time (*x3*) and Viewing Time (*x5*), and when the p-value is the minimum value, the result is only for Viewing Time (*x5*).

In this case, the regression equation is determined by giving priority to R^{*2}. The standard error is 7.8, and the regression equation is shown in Eq. (2). The analysis of the variance table is shown in Table 7, and the statistics of each variable are shown in Table 8. Figure 2 shows a correlation chart between the BRS values measured by the questionnaire and the values estimated by Eq. (2).

$$\hat{y}_{BRS} = -64x_3 + 121x_5 + 40 \quad (2)$$

Table 3. Results of multiple regression analysis with ARS as the response variable

response variable	R^2	R^{*2}	*p*-value
(First Fixation, Latencies, Dwell Time, Frequency, Viewing Time)	0.79	0.58	0.088
(First Fixation, Latencies, Dwell Time, Frequency)	0.69	0.49	0.090
(First Fixation, Latencies, Dwell Time, Viewing Time)	0.78	0.64	0.035
(First Fixation, Latencies, Frequency, Viewing Time)	0.77	0.62	0.039
(First Fixation, Dwell Time, Frequency, Viewing Time)	0.70	0.51	0.081
(Latencies, Dwell Time, Frequency, Viewing Time)	0.60	0.33	0.18
(First Fixation, Latencies, Dwell Time)	0.67	0.53	0.040
(First Fixation, Latencies, Frequency)	0.68	0.54	0.039
(First Fixation, Latencies, Viewing Time)	0.77	0.67	0.013
(First Fixation, Dwell Time, Frequency)	0.59	0.41	0.086
(First Fixation, Dwell Time, Viewing Time)	0.71	0.57	0.030
(First Fixation, Frequency, Viewing Time)	0.62	0.46	0.063
(Latencies, Dwell Time, Frequency)	0.24	–0.085	0.56
(Latencies, Dwell Time, Viewing Time)	0.60	0.43	0.079
(Latencies, Frequency, Viewing Time)	0.60	0.43	0.078
(Dwell Time, Frequency, Viewing Time)	0.47	0.25	0.19
(First Fixation, Latencies)	0.66	0.58	0.013
(First Fixation, Dwell Time)	0.58	0.47	0.031
(First Fixation, Frequency)	0.50	0.37	0.063
(First Fixation, Viewing Time)	0.62	0.53	0.020
(Latencies, Dwell Time)	0.22	0.029	0.36
(Latencies, Frequency)	0.23	0.033	0.36
(Latencies, Viewing Time)	0.60	0.50	0.026
(Dwell Time, Frequency)	0.0069	–0.24	0.97
(Dwell Time, Viewing Time)	0.47	0.34	0.078
(Frequency, Viewing Time)	0.45	0.31	0.092
(First Fixation)	0.50	0.44	0.015
(Latencies)	0.20	0.11	0.17

(continued)

Table 3. *(continued)*

response variable	R^2	$R*^2$	*p*-value
(Dwell Time)	0.0030	–0.11	0.87
(Frequency)	0.0021	–0.11	0.89
(Viewing Time)	0.45	0.38	0.025

4 Discussion

4.1 Possibility of Estimating Psychological Resilience of Junior High School Students Using Eye Gaze Information

This study aims to estimate the psychological resilience of junior high school students by assessing their attentional bias based on their eye gaze information. The coefficient of determination (contribution ratio) is an indicator of the goodness of fit of the regression equation. In the case of the present ARS results, for example, it can be interpreted as "this regression equation can explain 67% of the relationship between eye gaze data and psychological resilience of junior high school students". As a result of the experiment, the adjusted coefficient of determination R^{*2} of the regression equation estimating ARS was 0.67, and the adjusted coefficient of determination R^{*2} of the regression equation estimating BRS was 0.41. In addition, the p-values of the regression equations for both ARS and BRS were below 5% probability of significance in the results of this experiment.

The coefficient of determination of regression equations used in medical statistics and other fields is considered to be somewhat accurate if it is 0.5 or higher [13]. Considering this criterion, $R^{*2} = 0.67$ satisfied the criterion for the ARS in this study, but $R^{*2} = 0.41$ was obtained for the BRS, which did not reach 0.5. However, the results of a previous study were $R^{*2} = 0.47$ for ARS and $R^{*2} = 0.45$ for BRS, so the results for ARS were higher than those of the previous study. The multiple correlation coefficients were $R = 0.88$ for ARS and $R = 0.73$ for BRS, showing high values. In other words, since each variable has a certain degree of correlation, it is possible to estimate approximate resilience scores and psychological resilience using eye gaze data.

4.2 Discussion of the Relationship Between Each Explanatory Variable and the Response Variable

In this experiment, we attempted to estimate resilience scores using five gaze indices. Table 9 shows the correlation coefficients between each explanatory variable and psychological resilience.

The correlation coefficients between ARS and psychological resilience for First Fixation($x1$) were 0.71 for ARS and 0.34 for BRS. The correlation coefficient between ARS and psychological resilience was the highest among the correlation coefficients between each explanatory variable and psychological resilience. In other words, it can be considered that First Fixation affects psychological resilience scores and that those who look at positive images first are more psychologically resilient.

Table 4. Results of multiple regression analysis with BRS as the response variable

response variable	R^2	R^{*2}	p-value
(First Fixation, Latencies, Dwell Time, Frequency, Viewing Time)	0.58	0.16	0.37
(First Fixation, Latencies, Dwell Time, Frequency)	0.35	–0.091	0.57
(First Fixation, Latencies, Dwell Time, Viewing Time)	0.55	0.25	0.24
(First Fixation, Latencies, Frequency, Viewing Time)	0.47	0.12	0.35
(First Fixation, Dwell Time, Frequency, Viewing Time)	0.57	0.29	0.21
(Latencies, Dwell Time, Frequency, Viewing Time)	0.56	0.27	0.23
(First Fixation, Latencies, Dwell Time)	0.28	–0.033	0.49
(First Fixation, Latencies, Frequency)	0.24	–0.088	0.57
(First Fixation, Latencies, Viewing Time)	0.46	0.23	0.20
(First Fixation, Dwell Time, Frequency)	0.33	0.044	0.39
(First Fixation, Dwell Time, Viewing Time)	0.55	0.35	0.12
(First Fixation, Frequency, Viewing Time)	0.42	0.17	0.26
(Latencies, Dwell Time, Frequency)	0.16	–0.21	0.74
(Latencies, Dwell Time, Viewing Time)	0.53	0.33	0.13
(Latencies, Frequency, Viewing Time)	0.47	0.25	0.19
(Dwell Time, Frequency, Viewing Time)	0.55	0.36	0.11
(First Fixation, Latencies)	0.20	–0.0050	0.42
(First Fixation, Dwell Time)	0.27	0.087	0.28
(First Fixation, Frequency)	0.15	–0.055	0.51
(First Fixation, Viewing Time)	0.42	0.27	0.16
(Latencies, Dwell Time)	0.090	–0.14	0.68
(Latencies, Frequency)	0.12	–0.010	0.59
(Latencies, Viewing Time)	0.46	0.32	0.085
(Dwell Time, Frequency)	0.11	–0.12	0.63
(Dwell Time, Viewing Time)	0.53	0.41	0.049
(Frequency, Viewing Time)	0.42	0.27	0.11
(First Fixation)	0.14	0.040	0.26
(Latencies)	0.072	–0.030	0.42

(*continued*)

Table 4. (*continued*)

response variable	R^2	R^{*2}	*p*-value
(Dwell Time)	0.056	–0.050	0.49
(Frequency)	0.025	–0.084	0.65
(Viewing Time)	0.41	0.35	0.032

Table 5. The analysis of the variance table

Regression	3	445.7	148.6	7.7	0.013
Residual	7	134.5	19.2	-	-
Total	10	580.2	-	-	-

Table 6. The statistics of each variable

	Coefficient	Standard Error	*t*-value	*p*-value
x_1(First Fixation)	83	36.7	2.26	0.058
x_2(Latencies)	–164	78.3	–2.09	0.075
x_5(Viewing Time)	50	27.8	1.80	0.12
Intercept	86	44.0	1.95	0.093

The correlation coefficients between Latencies($x2$) and psychological resilience were -0.41 for ARS and 0.052 for BRS. This can be interpreted as follows: People who glance at positive images have high psychological resilience, while people who glance at negative images have low psychological resilience.

The correlation coefficients of Dwell Time ($x3$) with each psychological resilience were ARS: 0.13 and BRS: 0.64. ARS was uncorrelated, while BRS was positively correlated. Therefore, it can be considered that the psychological resilience of the BRS is higher for those whose gaze remains on the first positive image they saw for a more extended period.

The correlation coefficients of frequency ($x4$) with each psychological resilience were ARS: 0.10 and BRS: -0.32, and both ARS and BRS were uncorrelated. These results suggest that the frequency of paying attention to positive images is not related to the level of psychological resilience in this experiment.

Finally, the correlation coefficients of Viewing Time ($x5$) with psychological resilience were 0.67 for ARS and -0.19 for BRS. In other words, it can be interpreted that the longer people viewed positive images in the ARS, the higher their psychological resilience was.

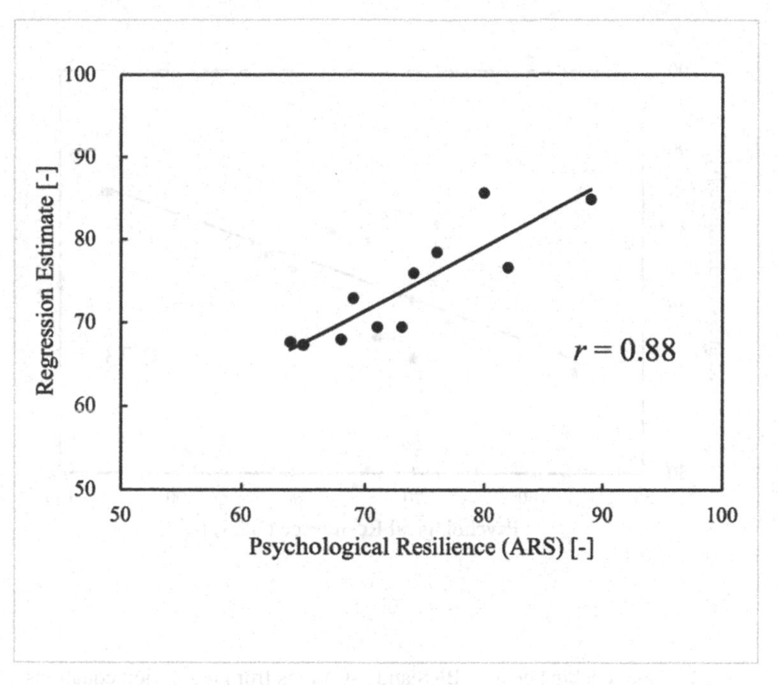

Fig. 1. Relationship between ARS and estimates from regression equations

Table 7. The analysis of the variance table

Regression	2	547.7	273.9	4.5	0.049
Residual	8	487.2	60.9	-	-
Total	10	1034.9	-	-	-

Table 8. The statistics of each variable

	Coefficient	Standard Error	*t*-value	*p*-value
x_3(Dwell Time)	-64	46.1	-1.39	0.20
x_5(Viewing Time)	121	42.7	2.84	0.022
Intercept	40	28.7	1.40	0.20

4.3 Comparison with the Results of University Students

In this experiment, we experimented with junior high school students as participants. Table 10 compares the regression equation for estimating the resilience of university students with the regression equation for estimating the psychological resilience of junior high school students and the coefficient of determination adjusted for degrees of freedom.

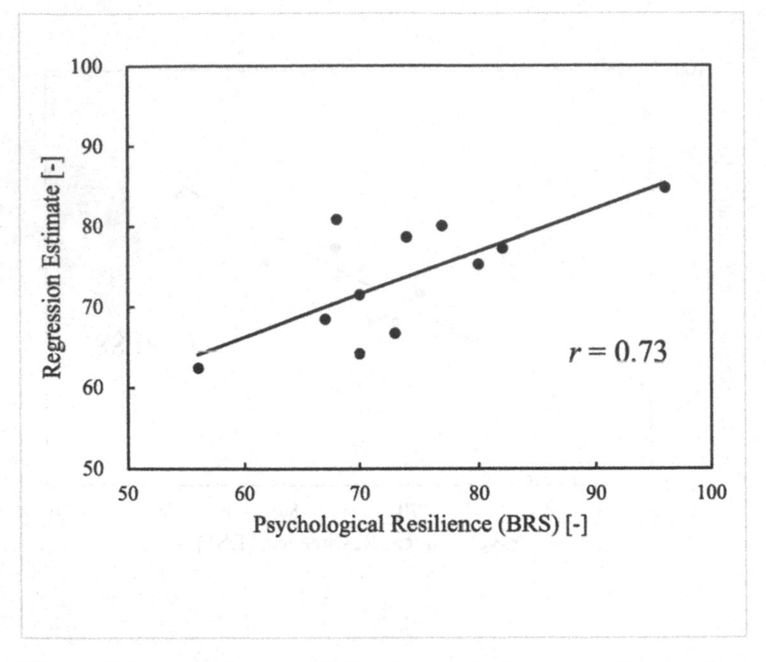

Fig. 2. Relationship between BRS and estimates from regression equations

Table 9. Correlation coefficients between each explanatory variable and psychological resilience

Correlation Coefficient	ARS	BRS
First Fixation	0.71	0.34
Latencies	–0.46	0.052
Dwell Time	0.13	0.64
Frequency	0.10	–0.32
Viewing Time	0.67	–0.19

The regression equation for estimating ARS for college students was a simple regression equation with Latencies as the explanatory variable, while the explanatory variables for the regression equation estimating ARS for junior high school students obtained from the present experiment were First Fixation, Latencies, and Viewing Time. The adjusted coefficients of determination were $R^{*2} = 0.47$ for the experiment with college students and $R^{*2} = 0.67$ for the experiment with junior high school students. From these results, the present psychological resilience estimation equation for junior high school students is more accurate than the one for university students. In addition, it can be seen that the latency taken to look at a positive image affects the psychological resilience scores of college students. In contrast, for junior high school students, in addition to the latency, the percentage of first looking at a positive image and thc total time spent looking at positive images are also related to the psychological resilience scores.

Latencies, Dwell Time, Frequency, and Viewing Time were the four explanatory variables for the regression equation estimating BRS for college students. At the same time, Dwell Time and Viewing Time were the explanatory variables for the regression equation estimating BRS for junior high school students. The adjusted coefficient of determination was $R^{*2} = 0.45$ for the experiment with college students and $R^{*2} = 0.41$ for the experiment with junior high school students, showing no significant difference. As in the ARS, the explanatory variables that make up the regression equation for estimating psychological resilience differed between college and junior high school students.

Table 10. Comparison of psychological resilience estimating equations for college students and junior high school students

college students	ARS	$y_{ARS} = 234x_2 - 39$	$R^{*2} = 0.47$
	BRS	$y_{BRS} = 168x_2 + 30x_3 + 124x_4 + 113x_5 - 138$	$R^{*2} = 0.45$
junior high school students	ARS	$y_{ARS} = 83x_1 - 164x_2 + 50x_5 + 86$	$R^{*2} = 0.67$
	BRS	$y_{BRS} = - 64 x_3 + 121x_5 + 40$	$R^{*2} = 0.41$

A previous study [5] reported that the characteristics of psychological resilience might differ between college students and junior and senior high school students since the psychological resilience factor showed a U-shaped curvilinear change in which the mean value decreased significantly from elementary school to adolescence (junior and senior high school students) and then increased again among college students. The present results are consistent with this previous study.

5 Conclusion

With the recent increase in mental health problems, psychological resilience, which is the ability to maintain and overcome psychological health conditions even after experiencing stress, has been attracting attention. Currently, self-administered questionnaires are used to measure resilience, but more objective indices are needed to measure psychological resilience daily and to verify the effects of interventions in programs to improve resilience. In this study, we aimed to verify whether it is possible to estimate the psychological resilience of middle and high school students by measuring their attentional bias to emotional images using eye gaze data based on a previous study that estimated the psychological resilience of college students by eye gaze measurement.

Five gaze indices were used in the experiment: First Fixation, Latencies, Dwell Time, Frequency, and Viewing Time. The resilience questionnaires used to estimate resilience were the Alliance Resilience Scale (ARS) and the Bidimensional Resilience Factors Scale (BRS). Multiple regression analysis was used to analyze the resilience questionnaires with the gaze index as the explanatory variable and the resilience questionnaire as the objective variable.

The regression equation predicting the ARS had an adjusted coefficient of determination of 0.67, and the BRS was 0.41. Compared to the previous study, the contribution rate of ARS is higher than that of the previous study, while that of BRS does not differ much from that of the previous study. In conclusion, it is possible to estimate resilience scores and psychological resilience of middle and high school students using the regression equations derived in this study.

The adjusted coefficient of determination of the regression equations obtained in this study was 0.67 for ARS and 0.41 for BRS. The coefficient of determination for ARS exceeded 0.5, which is considered somewhat accurate, but the coefficient of determination for BRS was slightly lower than that in the previous study.

As a future perspective, although the experiment was conducted only once with junior high school students, we may investigate changes in psychological resilience over time by conducting the experiment multiple times with the same participants and comparing the results. In common with previous studies and the present study, the contribution rate of the regression equation was higher for the ARS than for the BRS, which is also an area for further consideration. Another issue is verifying the reproducibility of the regression equation. In order to confirm the generality of the regression equation derived in this experiment, it was necessary to increase the number of participants in the experiment and compare the resilience scores obtained in the experiment with the estimated values by the regression equation.

References

1. OECD, a new benchmark for mental health systems, international survey on mental health. https://www.oecd.org/health/a-new-benchmark-for-mental-health-systems-4ed890f6-en.htm. Accessed 20 Jan 2023
2. Ministry of health, labour and welfare, 2020 patient survey overview. https://www.mhlw.go.jp/toukei/saikin/hw/kanja/20/index.html. Accessed 20 Jan 2023
3. National center for child health and development, Corona×Children questionnaire fourth survey report. https://www.ncchd.go.jp/center/activity/covid19_kodomo/report/CxC4_finalrepo_20210210.pdf. Accessed 20 Jan 2023
4. Maeshiba, N., Kotani, K., Suzuki, S., Asao, T.: Development for tablet-based perimeter using temporal characteristics of saccadic durations. In: Stephanidis, C., Kurosu, M., Degen, H., Reinerman-Jones, L. (eds.) HCII 2020. LNCS, vol. 12424, pp. 194–208. Springer, Cham (2020). https://doi.org/10.1007/978-3-030-60117-1_14
5. Satoko, T.: Developmental changes in resilience from childhood to young adulthood, gender differences, and facilitating factors -a meta-analytic perspective-, Taisho Univ. Graduate Sch. Res. Rev. **46**(007), 110–128
6. Karolinska Directed Emotional Faces (KDEF) documents. https://www.ugent.be/pp/ekgp/en/research/research-groups/panlab/kdef. Accessed 20 Jan 2023
7. Dan-Glauser, E.S., Scherer, K.R.: The Geneva affective picture database (GAPED): a new 730-picture database focusing on valence and normative significance. Behav. Res. Methods **43**(2), 468–477 (2011)
8. Waechter, S., Nelson, A.L., Wright, C., Hyatt, A., Oakman, J.: Measuring attentional bias to threat: reliability of dot probe and eye movement indices. Cogn. Ther. Res. **38**(3), 313–333 (2014)
9. Skinner, I.W.: The reliability of eyetracking to assess attentional bias to threatening words in healthy individuals. Behav. Res. Methods, **50**(5), 1778–1792 (2018)

10. Shinji, K., Motoyuki, N., Hitoshi, K., Shinji, N.: Psychological characteristics leading to recovery from negative events.-Creating the Adolescent Resilience Scale-. Couns. Res. **35**, 57–65 (2002)
11. Mari, H.: An Attempt to Classify Resilience Qualities and Acquired Factors -Creation of the Bidimensional Resilience Scale (BRS)-, Pers. Res. **19**, 94–106 (2010)
12. Checking for multicollinearity in Excel. https://corvus-window.com/all_multi-collinearity/. accessed 20 1 2023
13. Statistics web. -Coefficient of Determination and Multiple Correlation Coefficient-. https://bellcurve.jp/statistics/course/9706.html, last accessed 2023/01/20

Improving Motivation to Support Physical Activity Through Fitness App in China: A Co-design Approach

Jing Zhou[1,2](✉), Jo Jung[2], and Christopher Kueh[2]

[1] College of Communication and Art Design, University of Shanghai for Science and Technology (USST), Shanghai 200093, China
jzhou@usst.edu.cn, jzhou9@our.ecu.edu.au

[2] School of Arts and Humanities, Edith Cowan University (ECU), Perth, WA 6050, Australia

Abstract. Unhealthy lifestyles and habits are negatively affecting people across the globe. The fitness and wellbeing industry has been evolving rapidly since the COVID-19 outbreak in China. While health and fitness applications (apps) serve as platforms to support people in becoming more physically active, these apps are primarily instructional and may lack personalized features that motivate users to achieve and maintain their fitness goals. Persuasive design strategies, such as social influence, personalization, and entertainment, have clearly shown benefits in promoting engagement. However, the consideration of intrinsic motivation, which drives individuals in self-improvement, is not commonly featured in fitness app design. This proposed research aims to explore the design of fitness app features from User Experience (UX) perspectives, which focuses on motivating people and maintaining a healthy exercise routine. By utilizing a co-design process, the research outcome includes a prototype fitness app that emphasizes cultivating long-term motivation for users to engage in physical activities.

Keywords: User Experience · Fitness Apps · Motivation · User Engagement · Co-design · Prototype · mHealth

1 Introduction

1.1 mHealth and Fitness Apps

People are witnessing an accelerated pattern of digitalization in many areas of life especially in the field of health. Various scholars and practitioners have focused on mobile health (mHealth), supported by mobile technologies and communication advances like the 4G, LITE network [1]. From 2020, the COVID-19 virus brought even more home-exercise technology challenges. The COVID-19 outbreak in China forced Chinese people to stay at home, promoting the use of more online fitness apps. As mHealth technologies advance, the desired lifestyle of 'feeling good' (highest quality of 'being healthy') has increased interest in preventive healthcare. In particular, the world is facing an unprecedented mental health crisis as people feel the effects on their emotional health. Young

Q. Gao et al. (Eds.): HCII 2023, LNCS 14055, pp. 654–673, 2023.
https://doi.org/10.1007/978-3-031-48041-6_44

adults must deal with the additional stress and anxiety of today's public healthcare challenges of a modern lifestyle. mHealth is becoming an increasingly popular method for delivering public health programs and is particularly appropriate for engaging young digital natives [2].

Diet and fitness apps are examples of health apps that are frequently downloaded [3]. Research indicated that in 2012, 19% of smartphone users were using health apps. of some type. 38-percent used them for exercise services, 31% used the apps to control their diet, while 12% used the apps for weight management [4]. The year 2014 was named the year of health and fitness due to increased downloads of apps related to that field. By 2015, the number of smartphone users utilizing the mHealth apps in diet and fitness rose to 58%. The global fitness market is estimated to reach 13 billion dollars by 2025 [5]. According to a survey conducted by QuestMobile, 64.2 million of the total population in China now uses mobile fitness apps. At the same time there is also stiff competition with many people attending gyms (just 4 million fewer than those using an app). So this all suggests an increase in the growth of the fitness application market across the globe.

1.2 Young Adults in China

College students, younger adults and office workers tend to be those who aspire to be fit and healthy [4] and to use fitness apps [3]. According to the Chinese National Sports Life report [6], it is the young adult age group who exhibit preferences concerning health and fitness apps.

In China, it is young adults who most suffer from the stress and anxiety of modern city life. Mental health claims have increased over 100% during the past decade in China, this is particularly pronounced when looking at issues relating to work and study [7]. Most Chinese fitness apps focus on young adults in cities. Convenient time and affordable cost are the two main reasons for Chinese young adults downloading fitness apps [8]. Young adults have a strong willingness to work out because of their stressful daily work and irregular lifestyle [7].

In China, another significant consideration as a fitness goal is social competition and approbation, which they may achieve through showing off their outcomes and receiving praise from peers [9]. However, Tao, Liu [7] and Chen, Yang [8] argue that social media aspects of fitness apps may cause potentially less positive effects; 1) pictures and videos are photoshopped; 2) influences to make inappropriate lifestyle choices and 3) persuasion in product purchasing. Tao, Liu [7] illustrates that fitness community apps deserve more attention; these negative features may affect motivation and cause young adults to abandon the apps.

It is a fact that many fitness app users give up prematurely [9]; Chen, Yang [8] showed a statistic revealing only 13% of Chinese who have fitness plans achieve their goals. More data is required to effectively analyse user requirements and desired outcomes.

1.3 Research Aim and Question

As people' attitudes in the world have changed with respect to the importance of everyday healthcare in their lives so this has brought about a positive impact and developments within fitness apps technology. There are different types of fitness apps available for a range of needs including, diet, nutrition, activity tracking apps, and workout routines. Each fitness app has a different function and offers unique features to motivate users. There is, for example, the fitness tracker (step counter) which supports people by tracking, monitoring, and analysing their physical movements [10–12]. Other features focus on personalisation (fitness plans, calorie counter etc.), social influence (e.g. online communities, goal-supporting, coaching videos), and entertainment use (giving rewards, gamification of competitions) in order to try to ensure users stay motivated and reach their health goals.

In spite of all the technological advances used within current health products, a study conducted by Byambasuren, Hoffmann [13] found that few health and fitness apps have proven to be effective. 80% of users stopped engaging with their fitness apps after just one month from downloading [6, 14, 15]. Why most health and fitness apps fail to have long-term engagement with their users is a vital question. People have different body types, habits and fitness goals which are often not identified. Functionalities and features within most current health and fitness apps seem to rarely cater to users' individual needs and provide supportive solutions [13]. This results in lost motivation after a certain period of use. On the other hand, apps in other categories which are able to identify user needs and provide timely solutions such as traveling apps (i.e., people can pick a destination, book a flight, and reserve a hotel room) are viewed as more effective. User Experience (UX) design can be improved by health and fitness apps to encourage longer user engagement with the app by looking more closely at user motivation.

Encouraging and motivating users to be more self-aware and experience self-improvement presents an opportunity for the future of health technology [16]. Generally, the user wants more 'want to' but not 'have to' motivation. Besides, people do not want to rely fully on tangible rewards to motivate them to train [16]. Deci and Ryan [17] argue that products that fail to employ intrinsic motivation may ultimately lead to discontinued use of the technology. The Self-Determination Theory (SDT) also stresses human motivation that highlights the user's inner resources is beneficial for personality development and behavioural self-regulation [18, 19]. Nonetheless there are still gaps in our understanding in human-computer interaction (HCI) when it comes to fitness apps when speaking of user engagement and long-term user motivation. So, currently there is no adequate evidence for which design factors contribute to intrinsic motivation in fitness apps. Understanding these factors can help fitness app users build self-improvement for themselves and enhance motivation.

This study aims to explore motivation and user engagement improving the longevity of health and fitness apps. The research question is: *How might UX-design improve the engagement of fitness apps to motivate and support the fitness goals of young adults in China?*

2 Related Work

2.1 Two Types of Motivation

There are two types of motivation; intrinsic and extrinsic motivation (Ryan & Deci 2008). In fitness apps, extrinsic motivation is stimulated for external reasons such as competitions, social pressures, rewards, and gamification [20]. Extrinsic motivation has been judged not to be as sustainable as shown in the Deci, Koestner [21]'s studies. From Self-determination Theory (SDT) psychological perspective, intrinsic motivation comes from within a person to focus on self-determination to engage in exercise. Intrinsic motivation is stronger than extrinsic motivation as it is determined by an individual's character [21]. As shown in Fig. 1, Deci and Ryan [17] argue that technology, such as fitness apps, that fail to form intrinsic motivation can finally lead to disconnection with such technology. The strategy of goal-process-mastery is the key for enhancing users' engagement, and ultimately maintaining users' fitness goals.

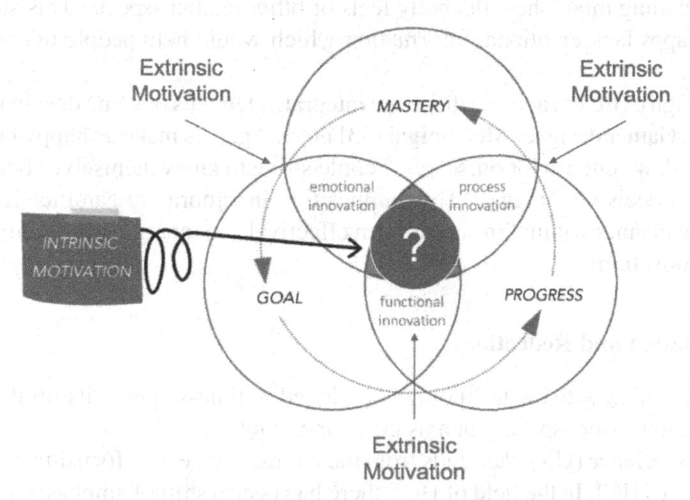

Fig. 1. This figure shows how two types of motivations build in fitness apps. Extrinsic motivation relies on external rewards and incentives to encourage individuals to engage in fitness activities. On the other hand, intrinsic motivation focuses on fostering a sense of personal fulfillment and mastery in users' fitness journeys.

2.2 Goals, Motivation and Positive Experience

Setting clear goals and fostering positive experiences are crucial for enhancing motivation in fitness apps [22–25]. Motivation serves as the starting point for embarking on a fitness journey, while goals play a vital role in keeping users engaged throughout their fitness endeavours. Positive experiences act as the driving force that empowers users to persist and continue moving forward in their journey towards better fitness.

Most of the existing research on user motivation has used the Technology Adoption Model (TAM) [14]. TAM implies three types of goal-setting context: 1) setting specific and not generic goals 2) setting challenging goals 3) setting short-term and long-term goals [26, 27]. Unless the fitness habits have been established, setting goals for oneself has been proven to contribute toward various aims such as fun, fulfilment, skill development, a challenge competition. However, TAM research finds that users do not understand how to set an appropriate goal and ultimately abandon the fitness apps. For example, one prominent issue in fitness features is the perpetuation of the 'calories in and out' myth, which can be considered a significant dark pattern [28].

The Theory of Reasoned Action (TRA) [29], which assesses people's beliefs and attitudes, and the Uses & Gratifications approach [30–32] both suggest that positive and constructive feedback in fitness apps is insufficient to support people in their fitness journeys. Angosto, García-Fernández [31] argue that the information such as step counts, heart rate and energy expenditure lack features that enable better analysis of relationship between data/information and activities. People are easily susceptible to getting hurt without proper guidance. Additionally, individuals may feel bored when engaging with data-driven activities. The format should potentially be used in a more holistic way, thereby including mood, how the body feels or other related aspects. This suggests that the fitness apps lack emotional information which would help people understand their behaviours.

The design of fitness app can therefore integrate elements of game design and gaming experience. Gamer designer McGonigal [33] notes, "games make us happy because they are hard work we choose for ourselves. People strive to know themselves better through the action of decision-making." This implies that incorporating gamification elements in a suitable manner within fitness apps can effectively encourage individuals to develop intrinsic motivation.

2.3 UX Design and Reflection

An issue identified with the technology employed in fitness apps is its limited ability to consider various user aspects, such as goals and emotions.

User-Experience (UX), descends from the interaction design, focusing on the experiential aspect of HCI. In the field of HCI, there has been a shift of emphasis along several dimensions over the last twenty years: from cognition to emotion, from pragmatic to hedonic, from productivity to experiential quality, from quantitative to qualitative methods [18, 25, 34–36]. Products that provide great UX (such as the iPhone) can draw people's motivation from satisfaction with the app to behaviour change [37]. UX-design is helping users understand, become motivated, and act on their personal goals and these are the key areas where UX aids app development [38]. UX-design including improving motivation such as Norman [25]'s emotional design, Fogg [39]'s persuasive design, and Hassenzahl and Tractinsky [40], Bucher [41]'s behaviour patterns will be discussed.

Emotional Design. Norman [25] discusses how emotions influence our behaviour such as motivation should give their users a positive experience. In fitness apps, a more positive and engaging experience for users, leading to better outcomes and increased adherence to a fitness routine. A well UX-design should address the needs of users on multiple levels: visceral, behavioral, and reflective. Designing the user interface (UI) of fitness apps, specifically the visceral aspect, is not the main focus of our research. However, fitness UX research conducted by Zhang and Xu [6], Angosto, García-Fernández [31], Ahola, Pyky [42], Ajana [43] to identify "why fitness apps do not work" about negative emotions. From their findings, it is essential for most fitness apps to delve deeper into two levels of design: behavioral and reflective. The following Table gives critical thinking of emotional design in fitness apps (Table 1).

Table 1. Behavioral, and reflective level in emotional design in fitness apps. Some points can be questionable to consider; 1) offer immediate feedback with credibility; 2) create a sense of control with fulfilment; and 3) encourage goal-setting with enjoyment.

Functions	Behavioral	Reflective thinking
Progress visualisation	A full illustration of user's progress	However, whether they are actually effective in achieving the desired outcomes?
Personalisation	Providing users easy access to exercise plans on the landing page and guiding them through correct execution of each exercise	Will the app's emotional design remain effective and engaging over time, or will it lose its novelty and appeal?
Social features	Enabling users to connect with friends or a community of like-minded individuals can provide social support and accountability; chat gives users the ability to share experiences as well as share tips with others who use the app	However, social features may not appeal to users who prefer exercising alone or have social anxiety
Feedback and progress tracking	Regular feedback on progress and achievements motivates users to continue their fitness journey	Does the app's emotional design enhance the user experience and engagement, or does it feel gimmicky and distracting?

Persuasive Design. Persuasive design is often used in the development of fitness apps to encourage users to adopt and maintain healthy behaviours [44–47]. It delves into human behaviour, including how people think, react, and make decisions. Previous research on PT helps designers gain a better understanding of what motivates users and nudges them to take action.

In the context of using computers as persuasive technologies *captology*, Fogg [44] defined persuasion as an attempt to change attitudes or behaviours, or both, without using coercion or deception. Many scholars such as Gram-Hansen [48], Ham and Spahn [49], Toxboe [50] have concerned the "Intention-Outcome" of designing PT. They critically assesse the goals, values, and actions of a persuasive system within fitness app. Most PT design by research explore three approaches: an enforced PT (i.e., recognition, playing on authority), an encouraged PT (i.e., completing a goal, challenges), and a remediation-based PT (i.e., tools for users to tunnelling or utilizing their status quo bias). (as shown in Table 2.)

Table 2. Three PT approaches in fitness apps. Prior research on PT design mainly reveals that users are reluctant or demotivated to use fitness apps due to ethical, credibility, practicality, and pressure-related issues.

Approaches	Design intention	Outcome
Enforced PT	Using recognition instead of recall to get more valuable data from users;	It raises concerns about how the fitness app handles user data and privacy
	Establishing credibility by playing on authority	
Encouraged PT	Rewarding users upon completing a goal to give them a sense of closure;	By gradually increasing the challenging level, it cannot provide users with a sense of continuous achievement; The lack of challenge hinders users from improving their skills in a supportive environment; Competition, as a trigger, may not be appealing or motivating for every user
	Providing appropriate challenges to accommodate for experience over time	
Remediation-based PT	Making decision processes easier for users by utilizing their status quo bias;	Users may not be interested in a new experience; Users may not like the default option; Users may need make desirable behaviour as easy as possible
	Directing user attention by closing off detours through tunnelling	

Design Patterns and Changing Behaviour. Alexander [51] introduced the concept of design patterns as proven and reusable solutions for architectural design problems. While the raised questions mainly pertain to practical, research on design patterns can be used when critically evaluating the products such as fitness apps. Design patterns have been applied in various fields, such as interaction design, software engineering, and game design, serving as reusable solutions to address specific problems within their respective contexts [28, 52]. On the other side, dark patterns were introduced by Brignull [28] when he catalogued different types of interfaces that trick users into doing things that are not in their best interest. One interesting finding is that dark patterns do not necessarily begin with bad intentions [53]. It implies that there could be chances where dark patterns are used craftly.

Research found that fitness apps incorporate dark patterns [54–56]. Dark patterns in fitness apps include deceptive pricing, aggressive upselling, hidden cancellation processes, or misleading claims about progress or results. For example, Finkelstein, Krishnan [56]'s research revealed that the dark pattern of the "calories in and out" pervasive myth does not make people healthier. "Exercise causes many people to overeat by giving them permission to indulge."

Apart from the harms caused by dark patterns, game design patterns have two sides to the coin. Within the realm of "Games for Health" (GFH) research, numerous studies [24, 57, 58] have explored how gamification and game elements can enhance engagement and provide an immersive and enjoyable experience in health contexts. The three areas of game design patterns (i.e. Temporal, Monetary, and Social) have been deliberately implemented in many fitness apps [52]. They potentially deceive users into immersive enjoyment of physical activity through game design patterns. However, despite collecting user feedback from the most downloaded fitness apps (i.e., App Store, Google Store), the research [6, 15, 31, 59] still identifies some negative outcomes. Some case studies' outcomes from fitness apps have been shown in Table 3.

Table 3. Analysis of game design and how to keep users motivated using three dark design patterns in fitness apps.

Dark Patterns	Game design patterns	Dark outcomes
Temporal dark patterns:	*Playing by appointment:* This design pattern creates a sense of obligation for users to create a sense of obligation for users to attend classes at specific times. This issue becomes more prominent in livestreaming fitness apps (i.e., Instagram, TikTok) *Daily rewards:* The daily reward system in fitness apps motivates users to visit regularly. This feature encourages consistent engagement with the app's collecting badges such as fitness trackers (i.e., AppleWatch, Xiaomi)	1) Users have their own daily routines and cannot always align them with live fitness training schedules; 2) When the user loses their reward due to missing a day, forcing them to restart the reward system from the beginning. This design tactic compels the user to return daily, even against their preferences or intentions; 3) Perpetuating the problems are fitness trackers that fail to differentiate between different types of calories consumed and neglect to assist users in cultivating a positive relationship with exercise
Monetary dark patterns	*Try for free:* The design pattern aims to attract and encourage users to experience the app's features and benefits before committing to a paid subscription (i.e., Keep, Fitbod, Nike Training Club, 7 min Workout, MyFitnessPal)	1) User disappointment upon subscription, limited access to features, unwanted subscription charges; 2) Some users may view the free trial as sufficient for their needs and not find enough value in the paid subscription; 3) Expensive limited-class or special-themed in-app purchases may create a sense of fear of missing out (FOMO) in users, compelling them to hastily purchase a class; 4) Trainer encourages users to purchase too much can result in users feeling rejected and experiencing long-term negative effects

(*continued*)

Table 3. (*continued*)

Dark Patterns	Game design patterns	Dark outcomes
	Scarcity: The design pattern utilizes limited availability or time-bound offers to create a sense of urgency and encourage users to subscribe to a training program or membership (i.e., gym membership, influencer class)	
Social dark patterns	*Social pyramid schemes:* The design pattern relies on increasing the user base by motivating existing users to invite their friends through incentives. The game offers rewards or bonuses to users for bringing in new users, thereby encouraging them to engage in this activity (i.e., Stridekick, StepBet, Strava, Squaddy);	1) This can lead the user to play fitness app due to the pressure of not disappointing their friends; 2) This causes social obligation to participate; 3) The users feel competitive pressure from other players or influencers in various aspects, including body shape, diet, and goal achievement 4) Some users prioritize social connection over physical activity
	Goal-setting progress: The design pattern discourages users from abandoning it midway by setting group goals that need to be completed. Additionally, it instils a sense of accomplishment in high-ability players. This motivates users in a group setting to continue playing, engage in repetitive tasks, consider options like paying to skip, or spend more time than originally intended	

In summary, design patterns within fitness apps can turn dark when they deliberately shift the balance away from the well-being aspects and the interests of their users. In line with previous research on designing for behaviour change [41, 60] in health, there are certain considerations to critical thinking; a. control health-related data to improve users' autonomy; b. allow users to set fitness goals for making more informed decisions; and c. tailor users' needs to provide them with continuous progress support. Those three considerations attempt to form habits for behaviours people feel they "have to do" instead of "want to do" does not work over the long-term. This is the core motivation behind the majority of fitness apps.

Based on the literature review, individual needs for trust/credibility, fun/enjoyment, and purpose/fulfillment emerge as most factors in motivating users within a fitness app. In our research, we aimed to validate those motivations through a UX approach.

3 Methodology

3.1 Co-design Approach

A practice-led approach (PLR) encourages participants to share their insights, perspectives, and lived experiences related to a specific design challenge. It is the most commonly applied approach when working with studies that require practical research or user-centric approach.

Our research conducted the co-design workshop (which belongs to PLR) because it includes both collaborative and individual sessions. A co-design workshop refers to a collaborative session where different stakeholders, such as designers, users, and other relevant parties, come together to actively participate in the design process [61]. As Norman [25] states that involving stakeholders contributes to the overall idea that UX is necessary. A co-design workshop also recognizes that the individuals involved have valuable design thinking skills and can contribute to the design process through their active involvement [62–64]. Therefore, we used the co-design workshop as our main research method because it enabled participation, observation and collaboration.

The Challenge. The primary objective of the initial co-design workshop was to discover effective strategies for keeping users motivated and sustaining a healthy exercise routine.

The Solution. The main purpose of this first co-design workshop was to gain valuable insights into the factors that influence users' desire to exercise and what motivates or hinders their commitment to continue with it. Using these insights as a foundation, we developed an initial design for a fitness prototype. Every participant was granted a period of three months to individually access the prototype and document their experiences through diary writing. The objective of the second co-design workshop was to enhance the solutions based on the valuable feedback received from the users.

The Process. The process of research involved getting participants to integrate their ideas on the factors affecting the user experience (UX) of fitness apps, agreeing on the importance of these insights, and creating prototypes for evaluating those insights. Adhering to the principles of design thinking, the design processes typically did not adhere to a linear path. Nevertheless, in order to maintain a semblance of structure, we divided the process into the following distinct steps: Empathize, Define, Ideate, Prototype, Test and Implement. As shown in Fig. 2, this co-design workshop was adapted from the Nielsen & Norman's (world leaders in research-based UX) design process.

Fig. 2. This figure demonstrates the three phases of the co-design workshop, which include collaborative and individual practices.

The Participants. The research methods comprised three phases and two co-design workshops. The recruited 12 participants were aged between 18 and 35 years, representing Chinese young adults. The two co-design workshops included fitness product stakeholders and fitness trainers. The study's demographic was based in Shanghai, China.

4 Results

4.1 Phase One: Understanding the Motivational Factors

Empathize. The 12 participants were divided in G1 (mid-motivation, mid-ability), G2 (low-motivation, mid-ability), G3 (high-motivation, high-ability) and G4 (low-motivation, low-ability) (see in Fig. 3). The researcher explained Fogg [44]'s behavioural model and let participants to determine which group of them.

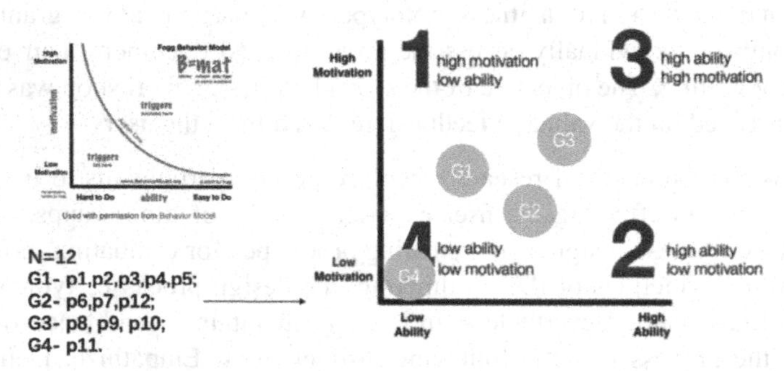

Fig. 3. This figure demonstrates the four user groups, from G1 to G4, based on their abilities and motivations. This step helped us define the pain points experienced by users at different levels. Subsequently, we asked the four groups to sketch ideas and create user personas.

Define. During the initial phase of the co-design workshop process, the interviews and context mappings regarding the needs of four user groups could be summarized as follows in Table 4.

Table 4. Define the statements from four groups of user needs and insights.

Groups	Problem Statements	Some User Insights
G1 (mid-motivation, mid-ability)	The need for tracking fitness activities with more familiar interest or fun;	1) A good balance between work and interest so that users can find time for exercise; 2) The lack of a suitable exercise environment and smart equipment, AI poses a challenge; 3) A lack of adequate instructions for beginners with fun or keep interested elements; 4) Expecting the super idols who can be the presence of idealized images and promote goals for users; 5) Expecting a personalised music or video playlist during activities
G2 (low-motivation, mid-ability)	The need for patience and attaining desired results;	1) The inclination to establish a fixed exercise schedule within a professional trainer; 2) Despite making an effort to invest time and money into high-intensive exercises, users were unable to maintain it; 3) Developed unhealthy eating habits due to hectic and stressful work routine
G3 (high-motivation, high-ability)	The need for improving overall health conditions and compliments;	1) Having no proper guidance has led to injury in the past; 2) Wanting to look physically fit from before and after; 3) Always like the praise from friends
G4 (low-motivation, low-ability)	The need for engaging in group exercise and gamification	1) Desiring a physically fit appearance without being willing to put in the necessary effort; 2) The preference for engaging in group exercise; 3) The inclination to play game or watch video with exercise

Ideate. Once the users' needs were clearly defined, we generated Point of Views (POVs) to identify the most critical needs that needed to be addressed. This allowed us to create a POV ideate model, which is basically inserting our POV information into a template: [User] *needs* [Need] *because* [Insight].

1. A group of new beginners *needs* to balance their interests and personal life in order to find time to exercise *because* they desire to maintain overall fitness while enjoying the process.
2. A group of impatient or anxious users *needs* to be guided regarding their overall consciousness of fitness goals and exercise habits *because* they want to strike a balance between working out and eating healthier.
3. A group of experienced users *needs* to exercise properly *because* they seek better results and want to avoid injuries.
4. A group of demotivated users *needs* to feel relaxed and confident *because* they want to find the motivation to exercise consistently.

Based on the users' needs, insights, and ideation sketches, we identified four groups of users with distinct requirements. The primary exploratory requirements were summarized as follows:

- Ensuring a fun and enjoyable process within fitness.
- Reducing stress data (weight, calories..) and fostering a sense of purpose related to health condition.
- Relying on technology that should provide concreate analysis and credible knowledge instead of numerical data.
- Incorporating gamification or accountable supports.

The some of four motivating factors (i.e., enjoyment, fulfillment, fun, credibility) were aligned with the literature review mentioned above.

4.2 Phase Two: Prototyping the Motivational Factors

During this phase, we focused on creating the visual design of a fitness product and developing a design system for the users of the final product. We conducted tests and observations to understand how these design elements were received by users and to identify patterns that could enhance engagement and assist them in reaching their goals. Based on insights gathered from four user groups, we collaborated with them to design and produce a fitness prototype called "FIRE," which incorporated four features: Fun, Interest, Relax, and Education. Table 5 presents the completed design of the prototype along with the tasks users need to accomplish.

Table 5. FIRE fitness prototype.

Groups	Motivational Feature	Design Description
G1 (mid-motivation, mid-ability) Pain point: Cannot enjoy the process Strategy: The need for more fun process	Fitness + Interest: Music	-Switch the experience from music to exercise: Music combined with fitness; -Tailor users' exercise lists to their favorited songs or allow them to select their idols as trainers; -Users can unlock a wide range of exclusive songs during their daily workout as part of an activity called "Rcpair Songs"; -Users have the option to compose their own melodies using videos and songs; -Users can choose their difficulty levels, ranging from two songs to three songs.
G2 (low-motivation, mid-ability) Pain point: Lack of confidence; more stressful Strategy: The need for patience and purposed goals	Fitness + Relax: No more distracting 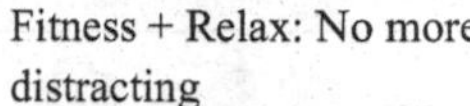  	-The feature ensures that no stressful data is collected while it is being used; -Users are forbidden to use any numerical data that could cause them to feel anxious about their weight; -Before starting a workout, the feature will switch to silent mode, disabling notifications and social media distractions. This provides users with a calm and uninterrupted moment, where they can engage in mindful physical movement guided by meditation music.

(*continued*)

Table 5. (*continued*)

G3 (high-motivation, high-ability) Pain point: No professional guidance Strategy: The need for progressing results	Fitness + Education: Endowed progress effect	-This feature enhances personalization by offering precise search and modification options; -Users have the ability to customize their timetables based on specific schedules, such as busy days, periods, or after-dinner time; -Users can select their preferred trainer voice, whether it is the language or local accent, virtual idols, or vocal bullet comments; -By utilizing integrated smart technology, users can create before+after images and videos according to their preferences.
G4 (low-motivation, low-ability) Pain point: Lack of group support and enjoyment. Strategy: The need for joyful rewards and accountable supports	Fitness + Fun: Movement collection 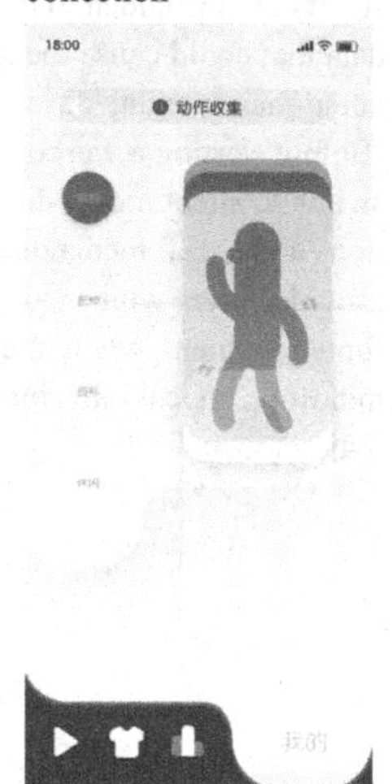	-The movement collection feature introduces gamification to the exercise experience; -Users can perform specific movements as a result of collecting randomly assigned cards; -Adorable cartoon characters use their cute voices to encourage users to exercise together; -Users can share and exchange movement cards to invite approved friends to participate in the same fitness activities; -Users have the option to create their own cartoon videos by collecting a required number of movement cards.

4.3 Phase Three: Evaluating the Motivational Factors

After a three-month trial, 12 participants evaluated the design features during the second co-design workshop. Based on their feedback, as table 6 shown, resulting in the ranking of the four new features.

Table 6. Shows the user evaluating results. Most participants gave high rankings to two features: "Music" and "Movement collection". Participants with high ability particularly liked the feature of 'No-more-distracting.' However, there are still some areas for improvement with the 'Endowed-progress-effect' feature. Participants provided many suggestions, indicating that AI should be integrated into the fitness app.

Features	Ranking	Further Improvements
Music	G1 ★★★ G2 ★★ G3 ★★ G4 ★★★	-The most engaging and satisfied feature of all groups; -Could make it competitive by allowing users to challenge each other.
No more distracting	G2 ★★★ G3 ★★★	-Some users needed to check the current weight data; -Could have chances to watch movies with fitness; -Some users needed focusing a sleeping level.
Endowed progress effect	G3 ★★★	-Users felt that reminders do not motivate them to exercise; -Users felt annoyed receiving tips every time before they began an exercise; -Users felt bored with pre-workout and post-workout; -User want to have harder exercises; -Before exercises, showing a brief of performance was necessary.
Movement collection	G1★★★ G2 ★★ G3 ★★★	-Users needed skip if they collected the same card; -Some users needed longer exercise (more than 3 songs); -Some of the exercise movements could be more accurate; -If the design card can show user tips on what to eat, it will be more fun.

5 Conclusion

5.1 Six Hidden Motivational Factors and Reflection

Based on our findings, we have identified new motivations that can help users sustain engagement with fitness apps. These six hidden motivational insights have been concluded and are presented in Table 7.

Table 7. Shows the six hidden motivations and reflection on design patterns.

Motivation	User patterns	Reflection
Truth	Users who are strong in the truth factor or passionate about truth	Learn the right answers
Results	Users who are passionate about results focus on things like the bottom line	Want return authority
Power	Users who are very focused on their own role	Need influence others
Assistance	Users who are focused on helping or challenging others	Find out others' needs
Form	Users who are attentive to their subjective experience	Need a harmonious environment around them
Structure	Users who are motivated to find a consistent, straightforward, repeatable way of doing things	Produce gamified or familiar patterns repeatedly

References

1. Free, C., et al.: The effectiveness of M-health technologies for improving health and health services: a systematic review protocol. BMC. Res. Notes **3**, 250 (2010)
2. Tanaka, K., et al.: Professional dietary coaching within a group chat using a smartphone application for weight loss: a randomized controlled trial. J. Multidiscip. Healthc. **11**, 339–347 (2018)
3. Krebs, P., Duncan, D.: Health app use among US mobile phone owners: a national survey. JMIR Mhealth Uhealth **3**, e101 (2015)
4. Fox, S., Duggan, M.: Health online 2013. Health **2013**, 1–55 (2013)
5. Organization, W.H.: Obesity: preventing and managing the global epidemic (2000)
6. Zhang, X., Xu, X.: Continuous use of fitness apps and shaping factors among college students: a mixed-method investigation. Int. J. Nurs. Sci. **7**(Suppl. 1), S80–S87 (2020)
7. Tao, K., et al.: Associations between self-determined motivation, accelerometer-determined physical activity, and quality of life in Chinese college students. Int. J. Environ. Res. Public Health **16**(16), 2941 (2019)
8. Chen, S., et al.: COVID-19 control in China during mass population movements at New Year. Lancet **395**(10226), 764–766 (2020)
9. Foster, N.F., Gibbons, S.L.: Studying students: the undergraduate research project at the University of Rochester. Association of College & Research Libraries (2007)
10. Davidson, J., Jensen, C.: Participatory design with older adults: an analysis of creativity in the design of mobile healthcare applications, pp. 114–123 (2013)
11. Torning, K., Oinas-Kukkonen, H.: Persuasive system design: state of the art and future directions. In: Proceedings of the 4th International Conference on Persuasive Technology (2009)
12. Lupton, D.: Self-tracking cultures: towards a sociology of personal informatics, pp. 77–86 (2014)
13. Byambasuren, O., et al.: mHealth app prescription in Australian general practice: pre-post study (2020)

14. Cho, H., Chi, C., Chiu, W.: Understanding sustained usage of health and fitness apps: incorporating the technology acceptance model with the investment model. Technol. Soc. **63**, 101429 (2020)
15. Cai, J., Zhao, Y., Sun, J.: Factors influencing fitness app users' behavior in China. Int. J. Hum. Comput. Interact. **38**(1), 53–63 (2022)
16. Berrouiguet, S., et al.: Fundamentals for future mobile-health (mHealth): a systematic review of mobile phone and web-based text messaging in mental health. J. Med. Internet Res. **18**(6), e135 (2016)
17. Deci, E.L., Ryan, R.M.: Optimizing students' motivation in the era of testing and pressure: a self-determination theory perspective. In: Liu, W., Wang, J., Ryan, R. (eds.) Building Autonomous Learners, pp. 9–29. Springer, Singapore (2016). https://doi.org/10.1007/978-981-287-630-0_2
18. Molina, M., Myrick, J.: The 'how' and 'why' of fitness app use: investigating user motivations to gain insights into the nexus of technology and fitness the 'how' and 'why' of fitness app use: investigating user motivations to gain insights into the nexus of technology and fitness. Sport Soc. (2020)
19. Saksono, H., et al.: Storywell: designing for family fitness app motivation by using social rewards and reflection. In: Proceedings of the 2020 CHI Conference on Human Factors in Computing Systems, pp. 1–13 (2020)
20. Yalanska, M.: Two types of user motivation: design to satisfy (2017)
21. Deci, E.L., Koestner, R., Ryan, R.M.: A meta-analytic review of experiments examining the effects of extrinsic rewards on intrinsic motivation. Psychol. Bull. **125**(6), 627 (1999)
22. Demirbilek, O., Sener, B.: Product design, semantics and emotional response. Ergonomics **46**(13–14), 1346–1360 (2003)
23. Duvnjak, N., Bašić, J., Pehar, F.: Emotional design in mobile fitness applications. In: Information and Technology Transforming Lives: Connection, Interaction, Innovation (2019)
24. Esmaeilzadeh, P.: The Influence of gamification and information technology identity on postadoption behaviors of health and fitness app users: empirical study in the united states. JMIR Serious Games **9**(3), e28282 (2021)
25. Norman, D.: Emotional Design: Why We Love (or Hate) Everyday Things (2004)
26. Zhou, M., et al.: Personalizing mobile fitness apps using reinforcement learning. In: CEUR Workshop Proceedings, vol. 2068 (2018)
27. Herrmann, L.K., Kim, J.: The fitness of apps: a theory-based examination of mobile fitness app usage over 5 months. Mhealth **3**, 2 (2017)
28. Brignull, H.: Dark patterns: deception vs. honesty in UI design. Interact. Des. Usability **338**, 2–4 (2011)
29. Oyibo, K., Vassileva, J.: Relationship between perceived UX design attributes and persuasive features: a case study of fitness app. Information **12**(9), 365 (2021)
30. Middelweerd, A., et al.: Apps to promote physical activity among adults: a review and content analysis. Int. J. Behav. Nutr. Phys. Act. **11**(1), 97 (2014)
31. Angosto, S., et al.: The intention to use fitness and physical activity apps: a systematic review. Sustainability **12**(16), 6641 (2020)
32. Lee, H.E., Cho, J.: What motivates users to continue using diet and fitness apps? Application of the uses and gratifications approach. Health Commun. **32**(12), 1445–1453 (2017)
33. McGonigal, J.: Gaming can make a better world (2010)
34. Nielsen, J.: Ten usability heuristics (2005). http://www.nngroup.com/articles/ten-usability-heuristics/
35. Law, E., et al.: Towards a shared definition of user experience. In: CHI 2008 Extended Abstracts on Human Factors in Computing Systems, pp. 2395–2398 (2008)
36. Csikszentmihalyi, M., Larson, R.: Flow and the Foundations of Positive Psychology, vol. 10. Springer, Dordrecht (2014)

37. Taylor, A.: Get Fit with Apple Watch: Using the Apple Watch for Health and Fitness. Apress (2015)
38. Dix, A.J., et al.: Human-Computer Interaction, 2nd edn. (1998)
39. Fogg, B.J.: Captology: the study of computers as persuasive technologies. In: CHI 98 Conference Summary on Human Factors in Computing Systems (1998)
40. Hassenzahl, M., Tractinsky, N.: User experience - a research agenda. Behav. Inf. Technol. **25**(2), 91–97 (2006)
41. Bucher, A.: Engaged: Designing for Behavior Change. Rosenfeld Media (2020)
42. Ahola, R., et al.: Gamified physical activation of young men–a multidisciplinary population-based randomized controlled trial (MOPO study). BMC Public Health **13**, 32 (2013)
43. Ajana, B.: Digital health and the biopolitics of the quantified self. Digit Health **3**, 2055207616689509 (2017)
44. Fogg, B.: Fogg behavior model (2019). https://behaviormodel.org. Accessed 2020 Dec 12
45. Hoy, M.B.: Personal activity trackers and the quantified self. Med. Ref. Serv. Q. **35**(1), 94–100 (2016)
46. Kanter, R.M.: The Happiest People Pursue the Most Difficult Problems (2013). https://hbr.org/2013/04/to-find-happiness-at-work-tap.html
47. Orji, R., Moffatt, K.: Persuasive technology for health and wellness: state-of-the-art and emerging trends. Health Inform. J. **24**(1), 66–91 (2018)
48. Gram-Hansen, S.B.: Persuasive everyware-possibilities and limitations. WMSCI. IIIS, Orlando (2010)
49. Ham, J., Spahn, A.: Shall i show you some other shirts too? The psychology and ethics of persuasive robots. In: Trappl, R. (eds.) A Construction Manual for Robots' Ethical Systems. Cognitive Technologies, pp. 63–81. Springer, Cham (2015). https://doi.org/10.1007/978-3-319-21548-8_4
50. Toxboe, A.: The Power and Danger of Persuasive Design (2018). https://www.uxbooth.com/articles/the-power-and-danger-of-persuasive-design/
51. Alexander, C.: A Pattern Language: Towns, Buildings, Construction. Oxford University Press, Oxford (1977)
52. Zagal, J.P., Björk, S., Lewis, C.: Dark patterns in the design of games. In: Foundations of Digital Games 2013 (2013)
53. Stock, O., Guerini, M., Pianesi, F.: Ethical dilemmas for adaptive persuasion systems. In: Proceedings of the AAAI Conference on Artificial Intelligence (2016)
54. Oyibo, K., Morita, P.P.: Designing better exposure notification apps: the role of persuasive design. JMIR Public Health Surveill. **7**(11), e28956 (2021)
55. Eyal, N.: Why Most Fitness Apps Don't Work (2017).https://nireyal.medium.com/why-most-fitness-apps-dont-work-736feda86507
56. Finkelstein, E.A., Krishnan, A., Doble, B.: Beyond cost-effectiveness: a five-step framework for appraising the value of health technologies in Asia-Pacific. Int. J. Health Plann. Manag. **35**(1), 397–408 (2020)
57. Arif, Z., Kiron, N., Vassileva, J.: Comparing the student engagement with two versions of a game-based learning tool, pp. 55–64 (2022)
58. Linehan, C., et al.: Games against health: a player-centered design philosophy. In: Proceedings of the 33rd Annual ACM Conference Extended Abstracts on Human Factors in Computing Systems (2015)
59. Care, N.P.: How Fitness Apps Are Impacting Our Exercise Habits (2023). https://www.nwpc.com/fitness-apps-impacting-exercise-habits/
60. Zhuang, D.: Designing for Behavioral Change in Health (2013). https://www.uxbooth.com/articles/designing-for-behavioral-change-in-health/
61. Noorbergen, T.J., et al.: Co-design in mHealth systems development: insights from a systematic literature review. AIS Trans. Hum. Comput. Interact. **13**(2), 175–205 (2021)

62. Dorst, K.: The core of 'design thinking' and its application. Des. Stud. **32**(6), 521–532 (2011)
63. Howard, Z., Senova, M., Melles, G.: Exploring the role of mindset in design thinking: implications for capability development and practice. J. Des. Bus. Soc. **1**(2), 183–202 (2015)
64. Kimbell, L.: Rethinking design thinking: Part I. Des. Cult. **3**(3), 285–306 (2011)

Author Index

Q. Gao et al. (Eds.): HCII 2023, LNCS 14055, pp. 675–677, 2023.
https://doi.org/10.1007/978-3-031-48041-6

Printed in the United States
by Baker & Taylor Publisher Services